Doing Race

Recent Sociology Titles from W. W. Norton

Norton Critical Editions

For more information on our publications in sociology,
please visit *wwnorton.com/college/soc*

Doing Race

21 essays for the 21st century

Edited with an introduction by

Hazel Rose Markus *and*

Paula M. L. Moya

W. W. Norton & Company, Inc.

New York • *London*

W. W. Norton & Company has been independent since its founding in 1923, when William Warder Norton and Mary D. Herter Norton first published lectures delivered at the People's Institute, the adult education division of New York City's Cooper Union. The firm soon expanded its program beyond the Institute, publishing books by celebrated academics from America and abroad. By mid-century, the two major pillars of Norton's publishing program—trade books and college texts—were firmly established. In the 1950s, the Norton family transferred control of the company to its employees, and today—with a staff of four hundred and a comparable number of trade, college, and professional titles published each year—W. W. Norton & Company stands as the largest and oldest publishing house owned wholly by its employees.

First Edition

Editor: Karl Bakeman
Managing Editor, College: Marian Johnson
Project Editor: Sarah Mann
Editorial Assistants: Sarah Johnson and Becky Charney
Copyeditor: Patterson Lamb
Production Manager: Christine D'Antonio
Design Director: Rubina Yeh
Book Designer: Guenet Abraham
Photo Researcher: Stephanie Romeo
Composition and Illustrations by TexTech Inc.
Manufacturing by Sheridan Books, Inc.

Library of Congress Cataloging-in-Publication Data

Doing race : 21 essays for the 21st century / edited by Hazel Rose Markus and Paula M. L. Moya.
    p. cm.

Includes bibliographical references and index.

ISBN: 978-0-393-93070-2 (pbk.)

1. Race. 2. Ethnicity. 3. Racism. 4. Race awareness. I. Markus, Hazel. II. Moya, Paula M. L.
  HT1521.D64 2010
  305.8—dc22

                                                                2010002487

W. W. Norton & Company, Inc., 500 Fifth Avenue, New York,
NY 10110

www.wwnorton.com

W. W. Norton & Company Ltd., Castle House, 75/76 Wells Street, London W1T3QT

1 2 3 4 5 6 7 8 9 0

CONTENTS

PART FIVE: Re-presenting Reality

The singular and powerful role of the arts in challenging racial inequality by imagining alternate worlds

PREFACE

Doing Race reflects our conviction that knowledge about race and ethnicity should be part of a twenty-first-century liberal arts education for *all* students. Our resolve grows from team-teaching a multidisciplinary course at Stanford University called Introduction to Comparative Studies in Race and Ethnicity. Over time, we discovered that as our knowledge of our subject increased, so did our comfort with approaching these sensitive topics. The more we understood about race and ethnicity as systems of social distinction, the less we worried about saying the wrong thing at the wrong time, or even about marginalizing ourselves by teaching and researching in a "special interest" field. Such concerns paled in the light of our growing understanding that race and ethnicity are central to all individuals' experiences and to the workings of society.

Many of our students were equally energized about what they were learning but reported having trouble talking about race and ethnicity to their friends, their dormmates, and their parents. They were persistently challenged by claims that the study of race and ethnicity divides people, that it is unnecessary in a "post-race" world, that it isn't relevant to people who are white, and that it doesn't produce knowledge in the way that studying the human genome or the laws of economics does. This book is our effort to help students meet such challenges, as well as to broaden the reach and the relevance of research on race and ethnicity. Drawing on the latest science and scholarship, this volume focuses on race and ethnicity in everyday life: what they are, how they work, and why they matter.

The essays reveal that race and ethnicity are central to understanding individual and collective behavior in the United States and throughout the world; they are important resources in answering the universal questions "who am I?" and "who are we?" They shape the ways people identify with some peoples and groups, and how they derive or are denied power and privilege from those affiliations. They also shape the ways people discriminate against, distance themselves from, and wield influence over other peoples and groups. Going to school and work, renting an apartment or buying a house, watching television, voting, listening to music, reading books and newspapers, attending religious services, and going to the doctor are all everyday activities that are influenced—explicitly or implicitly—by widespread assumptions about race and ethnicity, including who counts, whom to trust, whom to care about, whom to include, and why. Race and ethnicity are powerful precisely because they organize modern society and play a large role in fueling violence around the globe. For all these reasons, race and ethnicity must be taken into account when formulating public policy.

This volume collects essays by scholars from across the disciplines, including sociology, history, biology, psychology, anthropology, literature, education, drama, and communication. Together, their essays present a framework for understanding the general dynamics that underlay processes of racial and ethnic identification and exclusion. Although these dynamics are historically, culturally, and contextually variable, some common elements emerge across time and space, and many key aspects are systematic. This volume's comparative and interdisciplinary approach is thus a complement to an historically specific, single ethnic or racial group approach. It should be useful for students new to the study of race and ethnicity and also to scholars with a more advanced understanding of these dynamic social processes. The book is organized into six parts for which brief synopses are given below.

Why did we call the book *Doing Race?* We chose this unusual formulation to emphasize that race is not something that people or groups *have* or *are*, but rather a set of actions that people do. More specifically, race is a dynamic system of historically derived and institutionalized ideas and practices. Certainly, the process involved in doing race takes different forms in various times and places. But doing race always involves creating groups based on perceived physical and behavioral characteristics, associating differential power and privilege with these characteristics, and then justifying the resulting inequalities.

We have decided to call this process "doing race" rather than the more familiar "racism" because calling it "racism" leaves the concept of "race" intact and unquestioned. One of the central goals of this book is challenging the "thing-ness" of race by drawing attention to race as an ongoing social process. A second reason is that people are now more afraid than ever of being suspected of racism; as a result, some avoid studying or talking about race altogether. With the phrase "doing race," we hope to emphasize that race is a widespread system of social interactions involving everyone. It is true that individuals, groups, and societies often use race-relevant ideas and practices to reinforce and justify enduring social inequality. Yet, doing race doesn't require racism. Even people without "racist" thoughts or feelings will participate in the process of doing race just by being part of a society that is organized according to race. Understanding race as a system of everyday practices in which we are all implicated allows insight into how our own actions might inadvertently support practices or institutions that perpetuate racial inequality. Further, it allows for the realization that individuals and society together construct and give meaning to human differences. Since difference-constructing and meaning-making are human projects, we should be able to do them differently. Certainly, we ought to be able to approach human difference such that racial and ethnic identity can be positive sources of belongingness, motivation, and meaning.

DOING RACE: AN INTRODUCTION

This three-part essay directly addresses the central theme of the volume, which is that race and ethnicity are everyday doings involving our routine social interactions as well as society's institutional policies and practices. The first part describes eight conversations people commonly have about race and ethnicity and concludes by providing new and comprehensive definitions of race and ethnicity. The second part highlights the centrality of race and ethnicity to the U.S. American story. It shows that our current confusions about race and ethnicity are rooted in two fundamental but problematic philosophical assumptions and one powerful defining ideal. These two assumptions are that race is a biological thing and that the individual is the source of all thought, feeling, and actions. These assumptions are intertwined with a defining ideal of the United States—that all people are created equal. The third section explains why achieving a just society requires attending to, rather than ignoring, race and ethnicity. The essay concludes with suggestions for alternative ways to approach race and ethnicity.

PART ONE: INVENTING RACE AND ETHNICITY

This section reveals how race is made real through governmental policies, scientific research, and medical marketing. Matthew Snipp (Sociology) examines the role that the Supreme Court and the U.S. Census have played in shaping and defining the way race and ethnicity are understood in the United States. George Fredrickson (History) examines the four forms that American ethnic relations have taken throughout American history. They include *ethnic hierarchy, one-way assimilation, cultural pluralism,* and *group separatism*. Barbara Koenig (Medical Anthropology) considers how new findings in molecular genetics are being used in the domain of biomedicine. She suggests that these findings may inadvertently reinstate a *biological* understanding of human racial categorization, replacing the hard fought scientific compromise that differences among human groups are primarily cultural in nature. Marcus Feldman (Biology) discusses the implications of recent technological advances on researchers' ability to detect human genomic variation at minute levels, and suggests that the social category of "race" is less useful to scientists than what might be more accurately called "ancestry groups."

PART TWO: RACING DIFFERENCE

Part Two demonstrates the historically specific but universal processes by which difference, via race, becomes understood as inferiority. Aron Rodrigue (History) reviews the construction of the Jew as Christianity's original other. He argues that many issues associated with race in modern times reproduce elements of the construction of difference that can be traced to older anti-Jewish tropes. Joel Beinin (History) shows that throughout history, Islam and the Muslim world have been misunderstood and misrepresented as inferior in ways that have served the West's own political and economic purposes. He observes that the way the West understands Islam tells us more about the West than it tells us about Arabs or Muslims. Gordon Chang (History) focuses on three episodes from the history of Asians in the United States to illustrate the ways that Asian Americans have been viewed as perpetually foreign. His examples reveal the importance of the international context to any discussion about race in American life. Norman Naimark (History) cites cases from East Central Europe, Bosnia, Germany, and Armenia to define and then develop a taxonomy of ethnic cleansing.

He concludes by noting that traces of ethnic cleansing can be seen in every society, and thus that its potentiality is part of all of us.

PART THREE: INSTITUTIONALIZING DIFFERENCE

This section discusses how race organizes what we know, where we live, how we are educated, and whom we punish. Shanto Iyengar (Communication and Political Science) provides data showing that local news programs systematically over-emphasize the issue of violent crime and frame it in ways that encourage viewers to associate crime with racial minorities. Albert Camarillo's (History) auto-ethnographic essay chronicles the tremendous demographic shifts that took place in Los Angeles in the second half of the twentieth century. He argues that new dynamics between people of color are reshaping race and ethnic relations in the twenty-first century. Linda Darling-Hammond (Education) demonstrates that many students under-perform, fail, and drop out from large urban high schools because they do not have access to well-prepared teachers or to quality curricula. She argues that addressing the achievement gap requires new policies designed to equalize access to school resources, to develop thoughtful methods of assessment and to support well-prepared teachers. Lawrence Bobo and Victor Thompson (Sociology) maintain the United States has recently developed a law and order regime that features racialized mass incarceration. This incarceration binge, they argue, has created a serious problem of legitimacy for the criminal justice system in the eyes of many Americans, especially African Americans.

PART FOUR: RACING IDENTITY

Part Four addresses how race and ethnicity shape the way we see, the way we act, and who we are. Hazel Markus (Psychology) suggests that if race and ethnicity are organizing dimensions of a nation, neighborhood or classroom, they will necessarily be important for everyone who participates in these settings. The influences of race and ethnicity on behavior will vary, however; they can be sources of prejudice, discrimination, and inequality, but also sources of meaning, motivation, and belongingness. Claude Steele (Psychology) explores the phenomenon of "stereotype threat" to examine the subtle but powerful ways in which the devaluing views of others can influence individual performance and achievement. He suggests ways for educators to remedy the detrimental effects of stereotype threat by creating conditions of "identity safety." Monica McDermott (Sociology) focuses on white identity. She shows that white identity is not monolithic; it can be experienced as a privilege to defend, a perceived stigma, or an identity to be transcended. She concludes by identifying four crucial social and economic factors that determine which form white identity will take in a given context. Jennifer Eberhardt (Psychology) examines two common representations of blacks in contemporary society: blacks as criminals and blacks as apes. She presents social psychological studies to document the pervasiveness of these representations and to demonstrate their power to influence basic psychological functions of perception, attention, memory, and judgment. Stephanie Fryberg and Alisha Watts (Psychology) examine the psychological impact that social representations of American Indian mascots can have on Native American people. They demonstrate that seemingly positive stereotypical social representations, such as the Cleveland Indians team mascot, can have negative psychological consequences, even for those who support the use of these mascots.

PART FIVE: RE-PRESENTING REALITY

Finally, Part Five illustrates the singular and powerful role of the arts to challenge racial inequality by imagining alternate worlds. Paula Moya (English) considers the role that literature can play in shaping, confirming, and challenging the pervasive sociocultural ideas of society. Through a close examination of a short story by Chicana writer Helena María Viramontes, she highlights the way literature can re-vision an unjust social world. Marcyliena Morgan and Dawn-Elissa Fischer (African and African American Studies) discuss hip-hop's role in criticizing mainstream American practices of exclusion, indifference, and white supremacy. They show how hip-hop uses African American language to confront racism and injustice. Michele Elam (English) examines how the comic strip *The Boondocks* intervenes in conversations about race and "mixed race." She demonstrates popular culture's potent role in generating and shaping racial identities and experiences. Finally, Harry Elam (Drama) analyzes race as a type of performance. Using examples drawn from slavery, the plays of Lorraine Hansberry, the O. J. Simpson trial, and the film *Bamboozled*, he suggests that viewing race as performance can inform our understanding of its constitution, operation, and significance.

Acknowledgments

A project such as this one involves the labor of many people, and we are grateful to all of them. Our first acknowledgment must go to our students in the Spring 2003, Spring 2005, and Winter 2007 classes of "CSRE 196: Introduction to Comparative Studies in Race and Ethnicity" who, by questioning and challenging us, presided over the conception of this project. Our teaching assistants for these same three classes helped us think through several of the more difficult puzzles we encountered in the process of thinking and teaching about race and ethnicity; for their numerous contributions we thank Sarosh Anwar, Manishita Dass, MarYam Hamedani, Valerie Jones, Rachael Miyung Joo, Shantal Marshall, Julie Avril Minich, Aneeta Rattan, Elda Maria Román, Frank Lao Samson, Krishna Savani, and Nicole Stephens. We also owe a debt of gratitude to our faculty colleagues from the Center for Comparative Studies in Race and Ethnicity at Stanford University (CCSRE), without whose work this volume would not have been possible, and also to the Raikes Foundation for their support of the Center. In addition to those colleagues whose essays appear in this volume and whose names are listed in the table of contents, we would like to recognize the contributions of the past and present faculty directors and staff of CCSRE including Clayborne Carson, Arnold Eisen, Charlotte Fonrobert, Margarita Ibarra, Teresa LaFromboise, Tania Mitchell, David Palumbo-Liu, Renato Rosaldo, Chris Queen, Gary Segura, Vered Shemtov, Jeanne Tsai, Guadalupe Valdes, Gina Wein and Yvonne Yarbro-Bejarano.

Over the duration of this multi-year project, we have been privileged to work with an exceptionally talented and helpful group of research assistants, in particular Guadalupe Carrillo, Liyam Eloul, Alyssa Fu, Sara Hackenberg, and Nora Soledad Martín. For their comments on the penultimate version of the introductory essay, we thank our teaching assistants as well as Jennifer Harford Vargas, Vicky Plaut, Alana Conner, and Cynthia Levine. For their material and artistic contributions to CSRE 196, we thank Carol Porter and the Office of the Vice Provost for Undergraduate Education (VPUE) at Stanford University, and David Goldman of the National Center for New Plays at Stanford.

Several scholarly networks, both inside and outside Stanford University, have provided important inspiration and critical feedback. We thank Hazel's psychology colleagues, Toni Antonucci, Carol Dweck, Patricia Gurin, James Jackson, Mark Lepper, Dale Miller, Daphna Oyserman, Lee

Ross, and Phil Zimbardo; Paula's colleagues from the Future of Minority Studies (FMS) national research project, Linda Martín Alcoff, Johnnella Butler, Leslie Feinberg, Beverly Guy-Sheftall, Michael Hames-García, Joseph Jordan, Amie Macdonald, Ken McClane, Satya Mohanty, Chandra Talpade Mohanty, Tobin Siebers, Ernesto Martinez, Minnie Bruce Pratt, Susan Sanchez-Casal, Sean Teuton, and John Su; our coauthors on related projects Barbara Buchenau and Shinobu Kitayama; Paula's students in the 2006 FMS Summer Seminar, "Theory From the Periphery: Minority Struggles for Social Justice"; Hazel's colleagues in the 2008–09 Center for Advanced Studies in the Behavioral Sciences (CASBS) working group, "How Culture and Race Shape Experience," Glenn Adams, Jean-Claude Croizet, Kimberle Crenshaw, Lani Guinier, Luke Harris, George Lipsitz, Justine Cassell, and Alfredo Artiles; the coordinators and participants of the 2003–07 Stanford Humanities Center (SHC)/Research Institute of Comparative Studies in Race and Ethnicity (RICSRE)/FMS faculty and graduate student workshop, "How Do Identities Matter?"; the members of the CCSRE National Advisory Board, especially board president Margaret Andersen; the organizers of the Latina/o Academy, especially Nelson Maldonado-Torres, Eduardo Mendieta, and Walter Mignolo; David Kyuman Kim, Jim Campbell, and the other participants of the 2008 Center for the Comparative Study of Race and Ethnicity Faculty Development Workshop at Connecticut College; the Stanford student group Students Promoting Ethnic and Cultural Knowledge (SPEACK); and the many scholars (too numerous to list) who have presented in the CCSRE Faculty Seminar Lecture Series, the RICSRE Fellows Forum, and other CCSRE-sponsored events since the Center's founding in 1996. Thanks also to Karl Bakeman, the outstanding editor at Norton who encouraged us to develop this volume and made great suggestions throughout the process, and to the team who guided the book through the production stages—Christine D'Antonio, Sarah Mann, Stephanie Romeo, and Becky Charney. They could not have been more competent or more helpful.

Lastly, we want to express our deep appreciation and love for those close friends and family members who provided crucial inspiration, motivation and support throughout important stages in the realization of this project: Nancy Cantor, Patricia Black Esterly, Eva Martínez, Halina Martínez, R. F. Moya, Alice Rose, Ramón Saldívar, Claude Steele, Dorothy Steele, Timothy Young, Robert Zajonc and Krysia Zajonc. Thank you.

DOING RACE

An Introduction

Doing Race
An Introduction

Paula M. L. Moya and Hazel Rose Markus

I

WE DO RACE AND ETHNICITY — ALL OF US, EVERY DAY.

Consider the following events, which stirred emotions and kept people talking for months. In each of these national or international events, race or ethnicity was in some way central to how the event unfolded, how it was reported, and how it was understood. Yet what these concepts meant in each case and why they mattered to the situation was both confusing and controversial.

Mexifornia. In May 2005, billboards advertising a Spanish-language television news show were prominently displayed along the freeways of Los Angeles. The billboards showed newscasters posed in front of the L.A. skyline, with a well-known Mexico City landmark, the Angel of Independence, inserted into it. Over the newscasters' heads were the words "LOS ANGELES, CA." The "CA" was crossed out and replaced with the word "MEXICO" in large red letters so that the sign read "LOS ANGELES, MEXICO." The only other words on the billboard, which were in Spanish, read "News 62" and "Your City, Your Team." Following a huge outcry by some commuters offended by the idea of a Mexican takeover of Los Angeles, the billboards were hastily removed (Gorman and Enriquez 2005).

Model Minority. In April 2007, an undergraduate student at Virginia Tech University, Seung-hui Cho, shot and killed thirty-two students and faculty members and wounded many others. He then turned the gun on himself. Cho, a South Korean national, had lived in the United States since he was eight years old. Many South Koreans in the United States responded by expressing shame, embarrassment, and collective responsibility. Several community leaders—even those who did not know Cho or his family personally and lived on the other side of the country—rushed to apologize to the families of the victims, fearing that the killings would reflect poorly on Korean Americans as a whole. Many Americans outside the Korean community were puzzled by this reaction; they could not imagine feeling responsible for the actions of an obviously troubled stranger, even one who was a member of their own ethnic or racial group (Steinhauer 2007).

You Can't Say That! Also in April 2007, CBS radio and television talk show host Don Imus sparked a national uproar. After the Rutgers women's basketball team lost the NCAA championship to Tennessee, he described the Rutgers women as "nappy-headed hos." Following vehement protests by prominent African American leaders, CBS employees, and corporate sponsors—all of whom were outraged by the racism and sexism of the remarks directed at blameless student athletes—CBS suspended Imus's show for two weeks. When that did not quell the firestorm, the network finally canceled his show (Faber 2007).

Change Has Come? In November 2008, Barack Obama, the son of a Kenyan immigrant father and a white Kansas-born mother, was elected president of the United States. Around the globe, headlines heralded the dawning of a new age: "Change Has Come," "A New Dawn," "A Changed Nation," "A New Hope," "America Chooses Change," "A Dream Realized," and "Race Is History." Within weeks of Obama's inauguration, a series of events suggested that some of these headlines were overly optimistic. The *New York Post* printed a cartoon depicting President Obama as a dead monkey, while the mayor of a small town in California sent around an e-mail with a cartoon portraying the front lawn of the White House as a watermelon patch. The response to these and similar cartoons was rapid and mixed. Some people were outraged; others defended the *New York Post*'s journalistic freedom and responsibility to stir debate by playing with stereotypes. Meanwhile, a black journalist chided her white colleagues for worrying about appearing racist even as they avoided talking about substantive issues involving racial representations. "Why can't we debate," she asked, "why a mug shot of a black defendant is four times more likely to appear in a local television news report than one of a white defendant?" (Kelley 2009). Change is surely on its way, but race is far from a relic of history.

Its Not Our Fault! Prior to the G20 Summit that took place in London in March 2009, the president of Brazil, Luiz Inácio Lula da Silva, met with British Prime Minister Gordon Brown. At that meeting, da Silva vented his frustration about the effect of the global financial crisis on his country. Suggesting that poorer countries like Brazil should not have to pay for the mistakes made by richer countries, he laid the blame for the financial meltdown squarely at the feet of Western bankers: "This crisis was fostered and boosted by irrational behavior of some people that are white and blue-eyed. Before the crisis they looked like they knew everything about economics, and they have demonstrated they know nothing about economics." Subsequently, defending himself against charges of racism, Lula responded: "I only record what I see in the press. I am not acquainted with a single black banker" (Watt 2009).

Events like these occur frequently, provoking strong emotions and heated reactions. And while the events narrated here may have largely receded from collective memory, similar ones are no doubt happening as you read these words. Such newsworthy incidents involving race and ethnicity are simultaneously engrossing and disturbing. They result in charged private and public conversations that reveal a mix of feelings and states—anxiety, fear, hostility, suspicion, ignorance, hope, and trust. Besides underscoring the continuing importance of race and ethnicity, these sorts of events point to huge differences among people in their understanding of how these phenomena shape our lives. Moreover, such events raise basic questions that challenge us as individuals and as a society. How important are race and ethnicity? Does your opinion about their importance depend on your own race or ethnicity? Is noticing or referring to them the same as being racist? If these things matter, *why* do they matter? How much do race and ethnicity influence our life chances? Are we responsible for the actions of people— some of whom were dead long before we were born—who share our race or ethnicity? How much responsibility do we bear for those who do not share them? Do we get to choose what race or ethnicity we are? If not, who gets to choose for us? And finally, who is allowed to say what about race?

These questions are not new, nor are they easily answered. They are as old as our republic and as current as the reality that a majority of voters have elected a man with visible African ancestry as the forty-fourth president of the United States of America. But even though race and ethnicity pervade every aspect of our daily lives, many of us become deeply uncomfortable whenever the conversation turns to those topics. The discomfort takes a variety of forms and affects people differently. Some people believe that the United States has successfully moved beyond what were painful racially conflicted chapters in its national history; others think that race and ethnicity are unrelated to their own lives and should be the concern of those in barrios, ghettos, and ethnic studies programs. Some worry about race and ethnicity but avoid talking about them for fear of being thought racist. Yet others think that even noticing race and ethnicity is wrong and that these concepts should not be taken into account when someone is deciding how to interact with another person. Still others believe that U.S. Americans have not begun to talk seriously about these topics and that no one can understand society without analyzing how race and ethnicity are linked and deeply intertwined with wealth, status, life chances, and well-being in general.

Given the wide range of possible reactions, we might ask, Why are race and ethnicity so central to our lives and at the same time so difficult and taboo?

In this essay, the authors propose an understanding of race and ethnicity that, at first, may be hard to accept. Contrary to what most people believe, race and ethnicity are not *things* that people *have* or *are*. Rather, they are *actions* that people *do*.[1] Race and ethnicity are social, historical, and philosophical *processes* that people have done for hundreds of years and are still doing. They emerge through the social transactions that take place among different kinds of people, in a variety of institutional structures (e.g., schools, workplaces, government offices, courts, media), over time, across space, and in all kinds of situations.

Our framework for understanding them draws on the work of scholars of race and ethnicity around the world, including professors associated with the Center for Comparative Studies in Race and Ethnicity (CCSRE) at Stanford University. Over the past several decades, the topics of race and ethnicity have become increasingly central to the research and theorizing of sociologists, psychologists, and historians as well as scholars in the humanities, the law, and education. Psychologists most often focus on why people stereotype others and on the multiple negative outcomes for those who are the target of these stereotypes (e.g., Baron and Banaji 2006; Dovidio, Glick, and Rudman 2005; Eberhardt and Fiske 1998; Jones 1997; Steele 1992), while sociologists often concentrate on racism as a system of beliefs that justifies the privilege of the dominant

---

1 Although the term *doing race* has yet to gain wide currency either within or outside the academy, several race scholars have previously used the phrase to mean something very close to what we use it to mean. See, for example, John Jackson's *Harlemworld* and Amy Best's "Doing Race in the Context of Feminist Interviewing."

group (e.g., Bonilla-Silva 2003; Brown et al. 2005; Feagin 2006; Omi and Winant 1994; Massey and Denton 1998; Wilson 1990). For their part, historians reveal the sources of various notions of race and how these notions are perpetuated in both informal and formal practices over time (e.g., Fredrickson 1971, 2002; Roediger 1991). Philosophers focus on the philosophical foundations of racist schemas (e.g., Alcoff 2005; Goldberg 2009, 1993; Mills 1998; West 1993; Fanon 1952), while literary critics focus on meanings conveyed by the motifs, images, and narratives that recur in the representations of racialized people and characters (Gates 1988; Lott 1993; Morrison 1992; Said 1978; Sundquist 1993, 2005). While scholars from different disciplines take a variety of approaches to the topics, they share the view that race and ethnicity are central to understanding both individual and societal experience in the twenty-first century.

To illustrate the central point of this essay—that race and ethnicity are everyday doings involving routine social interactions as well as the institutional policies and practices of our society—we begin by describing eight conversations people commonly have about these topics. We conclude Section I by providing new and comprehensive definitions of these terms. In Section II, we reveal the centrality of race and ethnicity to the U.S. American story (Omi and Winant 1994; Higginbotham and Andersen 2005) and show why current popular understandings of them create widespread confusion and discord. We further show that *all of us*—regardless of the races or ethnicities we claim or to which we are assigned—are involved in doing race and ethnicity, often in unseen and subtle ways. The workings of race and ethnicity, we contend, are the result of universal human endeavors and concerns. In Section III, we explain why achieving a just society requires attending to, rather than ignoring, race and ethnicity. We then return to a discussion of strategies for forging new, more productive conversations about them. Finally, we conclude with some alternative and positive ways people can appreciate ethnic and racial differences, and propose six suggestions for how we can all learn to do race and ethnicity differently.

EIGHT CONVERSATIONS ABOUT RACE AND ETHNICITY

In the process of teaching a course called Introduction to Comparative Studies in Race and Ethnicity, the authors of this essay have identified eight types of conversations that people have with one another as they make sense of events in which race and ethnicity figure prominently (see Table i.1). By "conversations" we mean interpretive frameworks, or

TABLE I.1 | **EIGHT CONVERSATIONS ABOUT RACE AND ETHNICITY**

1. We're beyond race.
2. Racial diversity is killing us.
3. Everyone's a little bit racist.
4. That's just identity politics.
5. It's a black thing—you wouldn't understand.
6. I'm _____ and I'm proud.
7. Variety is the spice of life.
8. Race is in our DNA.

what other scholars—depending on their disciplinary training—might call models, schemas, discourses, or scripts. As a literary scholar (Moya) and a social psychologist (Markus), we have chosen the term "conversation" as a disciplinary compromise. We also hope it might appeal to students who are not yet committed to a particular disciplinary way of describing the world we live in.

Each of the eight conversations identified with a characteristic phrase in Table i.1 uses a set of assumptions, words, images, and narratives to interpret the confusion and uncertainty generated by events involving race and ethnicity. No one of these conversations is, by itself, either accurate or complete; rather, each is a partial way of understanding the racial and ethnic dynamics that gave rise to the conversation in the first place. Even so, the conversations as a whole are crucially important. People from across the political spectrum rely on some version of one or more of these readily available and malleable conversations to help them manage the pervasive tensions surrounding race and ethnicity. Which conversation someone uses to help make sense of an event will depend on that person's social circle, identity, and past experiences. For that reason, analyzing the conversations is an important step in understanding and changing the way our society creates and reacts to human difference.

Importantly, all eight conversations contain powerful hidden assumptions about the importance, nature, and meaning of race and ethnicity in the United States. However, they do not all have the same status in U.S. society. Some cross the color line, while others are more common among certain ethnic or racial groups. Some conversations are relatively new, while others have been around for as long as the concept of race has existed. Some conversations overlap, while others flatly contradict each other. The more common conversations tend to be especially robust and to come in different versions.

1. We're beyond race.

This conversation is pervasive among middle-class Americans and it often comes up in discussions of affirmative action for college admission or employment. It is the conversation that says, "Sure, there are lots of differences, but racial and ethnic differences are merely superficial. At the end of the day, wherever you go, people are just people." Like some of the others, this conversation comes in several versions, the first of which might be called "I'm color-blind." This version shows up in the way a teacher in a multi-ethnic high school talks about her students. She explains, "We have a lot of different kinds, but I don't see color. None of us really do, we just see all our students as the same. That's what is so wonderful about [this school]" (Olsen 1997, 180).

A second version of the *We're beyond race* conversation says, effectively, "race doesn't matter any more." This version first surfaced in the mid-1990s with the claim that the twenty-first century will be "post-race" or "post-ethnic" (Hollinger 1995). It reappeared among the supporters of Barack Obama during his presidential campaign: after Obama's win in the South Carolina democratic primary—a win that came in the wake of racially charged accusations between him and his primary rival, Hillary Clinton—supporters at his victory party began chanting, "Race doesn't matter" (*USA Today* 2008). The idea that race no longer matters has proved popular in both academic and corporate circles and has prompted a spate of conferences and books proclaiming the dawn of a "post-race America."

Finally, a third version of the *We're beyond race* conversation shows up in discussions and political activity around mixed-race identity, especially activity involving the U.S. census. Advocates of mixed-race identity imagine a world in which more and more "brown" and "beige" people are born of parents who claim different races. They envision that race as we currently know it will gradually disappear and something else, something post-racial, will take its place. In an ironic response to this notion, novelist Denzy Senna—herself the daughter of an African American father and a white mother—has suggested that we are entering a new "Mulatto Millennium" (Senna 1998).

2. Racial diversity is killing us.

This multidimensional conversation comes in several versions, some of which are less mean-spirited than others. The mildest version says, "If you want to come here, fine, but you have to check your ethnic coat at the border." This perspective accepts cultural or linguistic difference but only as long as that difference is quickly abandoned in favor of what adherents of this position understand to be the "American way."

A harsher articulation of the *Racial diversity is killing us* conversation is the "Seal the border now!" version. It is common among people who imagine themselves as the racial or ethnic "gold standard" of the United States and who would like to prevent people who differ from that standard from immigrating into the country—or, in the unfortunate event that they are already here, would send them home. A historical example can be found in the American Colonization Society, a U.S.-led movement that began in 1816 and advocated the "colonization," or repatriation back to Africa, of freed black slaves. That effort, which resulted in thousands of freed black Americans going to Africa, was responsible for the 1847 founding of the country of Liberia in Africa.

Contemporary examples of the "Seal the border now!" version of this conversation are common. One example can be found in the Minuteman Civil Defense Corps, a self-appointed (and predominantly white) vigilante militia that currently patrols the U.S.–Mexican border with the intention of ending undocumented immigration from Mexico and Central America. Another can be found in the work of Samuel Huntington, professor of government at Harvard University. Huntington advocates the maintenance of the white Anglo-Saxon Protestant values and traditions that he believes are the bedrock of this country. Expressing worry that the large wave of immigrants from Mexico and Central America is changing the country in fundamental and negative ways, Huntington contends that "Mexican immigration poses challenges to our policies and to our identity in a way nothing else has in the past" (2005).

Finally, some politicians use the "Seal the border now!" version of the *Racial diversity is killing us* conversation to stir up racial distrust and create political divisions. Such an effort was evident in an August 16, 2006, appearance by Congressman Ted Poe of Texas on the program *Your World* on Fox News. In his interview with the show's host, Neil Cavuto, Congressman Poe worked to forge a connection between Mexican and Central American immigration and Islamic terrorism:

> CAVUTO: Could I ask you this, Congressman, do you believe that if there is another terror attack here it will somehow have originated from those who came into this country illegally?
>
> CONGRESSMAN POE: Yes, that is a, a tremendous possibility because we know the southern border, of Texas especially, is open, and in-

dividuals, we have heard that individuals of Al-Qaeda persuasion have gone to Mexico, have assimilated into the population, have learned the language, have learned the culture, and then they have moved across into the United States pretending and posing to be immigrant Mexican workers, which they're not. (Cavuto 2006)

3. Everyone's a little bit racist.

The strongest version of this third conversation is very familiar and might be called "You're a racist." In part because many people believe that we are now "post-race," calling someone a racist usually involves a serious assault on his or her character. Indeed, being the target of such a remark can undermine a person's claim to being a decent and moral human being and can seriously damage his or her reputation. For that reason, the "You're a racist" version is one of the most charged and feared discussions about race that anyone can engage in.

Because there is no shared understanding of what race is, and therefore what it means to be a racist, people use the "You're a racist" version of this conversation across a wide range of situations. Sometimes a person is accused of being racist when he or she denies another person fair and equal treatment because that person is from a different racial or ethnic group. At other times, a person who merely refers to his or her race or ethnicity, or to another person's, is charged with being a racist. For example, after President Obama nominated Judge Sonia Sotomayor for the Supreme Court, several conservative commentators were quick to condemn what they labeled as Sotomayor's racism. The source of their ire was that Sotomayor, in public speeches and especially when talking to law students, had often spoken about growing up as a Puerto Rican Latina in the United States. Because she mentioned race and ethnicity as factors that contributed to her ability to make good judgments, people—including former Republican House Speaker Newt Gringrich and the conservative talk show host Rush Limbaugh—called Sotomayor a racist and demanded that she withdraw her name from consideration. The stakes regarding whether Sotomayor was, in fact, a racist were very high, even though there was not (and is not) one agreed-upon standard regarding what counts as racism. The controversy was quelled only after Sotomayor testified at her Senate confirmation hearings that she did "not believe that any ethnic, racial or gender group has an advantage in sound judgment."

A second version of the *Everyone's a little bit racist* conversation provides a way of sidestepping or calming the heated exchanges that follow most explicit accusations of racism. Like the "You're a racist" version of the conversation, this one recognizes the existence of racial and ethnic differences. However, it differs in that it spreads around the blame for racism by claiming that we just have to acknowledge that people will pay attention to race and that they will make judgments based on it. Moreover, since judging people according to racial and ethnic stereotypes is just an inconvenient truth of life, we should not be so worked up about it—whether we are the target or the perpetrator of the racist action or word. In the movie *Crash* (2005), for example, a mix of people in contemporary Los Angeles—the white cop, the Arab storeowner, the black cop, and the Asian human trafficker—all make unfair and seemingly unavoidable racist judgments about each other. The title refers both to the automobile crash in the movie's opening scene and also to the movie's guiding motif—the idea that urban America is so racially and ethnically diverse that people cannot help bumping up against and "crashing" into each other.

Most of us have participated in the *Everyone's a little bit racist* conversation if, after a racially insensitive remark, we have ever said to someone "Don't be so sensitive!" or had someone say that to us. This attitude shows up in the signature song of the award-winning *Avenue Q* (Lopez and Marx 2003), a Broadway production inspired by the muppets of the popular and long-running children's television show *Sesame Street*. At a key moment in the plot, three lead characters (all of whom are twenty-somethings trying to make their way in a diverse New York City) cheerfully admit that since "everyone's a little bit racist," telling ethnic jokes and stereotyping are perfectly acceptable. The chorus sings:

> *Everyone's a little bit racist today.*
> *So, everyone's a little bit racist. Okay!*
> *Ethnic jokes might be uncouth,*
> *But you laugh because they're based on truth.*
> *Don't take them as personal attacks.*
> *Everyone enjoys them — so relax!*

4. That's just identity politics.

The *That's just identity politics* conversation is common among people who think that race and ethnicity are irrelevant to, or a distraction from, the more important universal human concerns we all should be paying attention to. According to this view, race and ethnicity are superficial and do not mark important and consequential differences in people's history, contexts, or perspectives. The *That's just identity politics* conversation is a favorite of those who think that drawing attention to one's race or ethnicity is a strategy used by weak people to gain unfair sympathy or advantage. They attach the word "identity" to the term "politics" to convey the idea that someone who advocates something on the basis of racial or ethnic identity is acting illegitimately. Sometimes this conversation says "I'm tired of all this emphasis on race and ethnicity." At other times it surfaces as an accusation that an opponent is "playing the race card," or through sarcastic comments like "When is *white* history month?" The *That's just identity politics* conversation expresses a frustration that those who "have" race or ethnicity are getting some special privilege that will be unfairly denied to those who "don't have" race or ethnicity and who must therefore play by standard race-neutral rules. People who use this conversation often complain that if they object to the pervasiveness of race talk in the United States, they will be branded as "politically incorrect" and even as racist.

A second version of this conversation common among white Americans is the one that says, "Race isn't relevant to me." Many whites are quite comfortable with the idea that race (especially) and ethnicity are things that Asians, Latina/os, and blacks have to contend with, but that white people do not. They regard themselves as a neutral or standard, without race or ethnicity, or as a member of the "human race." This line of thinking is apparent in the comment made by a student who, when asked by one of the authors of this essay to fill out a questionnaire about racial attitudes, left the questions blank and wrote across it, "I'm white." Moreover, when experimental social psychologists ask people to describe themselves on open-ended questionnaires, white people tend not to mention the racial or ethnic aspects of their identity (Tatum 2002). They are likely to describe themselves in terms of personality traits (i.e., "I am friendly; I am optimistic; I tend to be shy"). Nonwhite people, by contrast, will generally include their race or ethnicity in their self-descriptions.

While the *That's just identity politics* conversation is common among whites, people of color sometimes participate in it as well. African American commentator Michel Martin invoked the "race isn't relevant" sentiment after Barack Obama's early win in the Iowa primary. She wrote: "Even if the Obama steamroller ends tomorrow, his success so far has proven that race is no longer the determinant of human potential in this country. A passion for excellence is—or can be" (Martin 2008).

Similarly, the African American comedian Bill Cosby's exhortation to African Americans to stop whining about racial disadvantage and discrimination and instead to work hard, show individual fortitude, and take personal responsibility for their own success or failure, is also a variant of this conversation. His statements can be seen as a way of expressing the core idea that an undue concern with racial identity is a distraction from the more important issues at hand.

5. Variety is the spice of life.

People who participate in this conversation appear to be more comfortable than some others with talking about the positive importance of race and ethnicity. They mark an appreciation for other people and cultures by saying, "I love ethnic diversity—it's what makes the world interesting." In the course of this conversation, people usually talk about their favorite ethnic foods, the world music festivals they have gone to, or the good times they have had while traveling around the world.

A version of this conversation can be seen in the "It's a Small World after All" ride popular with people of all ages at the Disney theme parks. In this attraction, passengers embark on a small boat and take a voyage around the world. As they float past the seven continents, passengers encounter groups of dancing, singing dolls. Some dolls are dark-skinned, others light, and while the Hawaiian dolls wear grass skirts, the Eskimo dolls wear hooded, fur-lined parkas. Despite their surface differences, all dolls are basically the same, smiling and belting out these lyrics: "It's a world of hopes/It's a world of fear/There's so much that we share/That it's time we're aware/It's a small world after all."

This conversation is also central to the clothing retailer Benetton's advertising campaigns, which consist of striking color photographs accompanied by the tag line "The United Colors of Benetton." A typical Benetton image shows a group of young, highly attractive, smiling people in casual Benetton clothing arrayed in a line or other close formation as if they were members of a sports team. Because they are all similar in age, attractiveness, attitude, and dress, the only obvious visual differences among them are skin and eye color, and hair color and texture. Both the Disney attraction and the Benetton ads convey the same basic message: we may look different, and those differences are intriguing, but they are only skin deep. By embracing each other and sharing similar human feelings, we can easily transcend the superficial (and appealing) differences between us.

The last version of the *Variety is the spice of life* conversation also understands differences as basically positive. However, it sees differences as consequential rather than merely superficial. Many school and workplace settings emphasize the value of what is often called "multiculturalism." This often translates into having meatballs, pierogis, tacos, samosas, and sushi at the end-of-the-year picnic, and saying "Happy Holidays" rather than "Merry Christmas" in December. An example comes from the General Telephone and Electronics (GTE) Corporation. GTE ran a recruitment advertisement featuring a beautiful quilt with patches of different colors and textures accompanied by the following message: "A community is made up of dreams, ideas and hard work. It is a blend of the ideals of men and women from diverse backgrounds, like woven threads in a colorful tapestry. . . . Each new idea inspires us to work and grow within this diverse fabric called community."

6. It's a black thing—you wouldn't understand.

Just as some conversations might be more common among whites, this conversation is more frequent among people of color. Those who have this conversation are proclaiming a certain pride in their racial or ethnic identity while also claiming an exclusive relationship to a wide range of experiences and cultural products typically associated with their racial group. Although sometimes these experiences or cultural products are seen as hip and valuable—such as a sensibility for jazz or hip-hop improvisation—they are just as often meant to refer to more painful experiences such as what it is like to be a victim of racist stereotyping. The main idea behind this conversation is that, as a result of one's racial identity, one's life is different in significant ways—ways that cannot be adequately understood by outsiders whose experiences have been very different from one's own. It follows from this idea that outsiders have no authority to interpret the meaning of one's racialized life, even if they mean well. Rather, they should sit back, listen, and learn instead of trying to contribute what could only be false knowledge to the conversation about what it means to be a person of color.

The slogan *It's a black thing—you wouldn't understand* is a sound bite for a whole set of attitudes and beliefs about how race works in U.S. American society. This particular saying was popularized in the late twentieth century on T-shirts worn by young black people, often but not exclusively, on college campuses. It was intended as a rebuke to those people who might assume, too quickly, that they could understand what it was like to be black or that they could be easily accepted into a black community. On one level, this slogan and the conversation behind it might be viewed as an attempt by some blacks to discourage poseurs (i.e., nonblacks who dress hip-hop style or use African American English). On another level, it might be understood as an aggressive insistence on the significance of race for shaping experience and knowledge. It is a refusal to entertain and accept the sentiment expressed by the "It's a small world after all" conversation and is a pointed rejection of the liberal assumption that all human experience is universal and thus can be shared, via reasonable discussion, with others (LaVaque-Manty 2002).

7. I'm _____ and I'm proud.

Like the previous one, this conversation is common among racial minorities, and comes in many ethnic variants: I'm black and I'm proud, Asian pride, yo soy Chicana/o, and so on. Although this conversation persists into the present, it first came into full flower in the United States during the 1960s and 1970s. Ethnic civil rights activists—primarily young people involved in the Black Power movement, the American Indian movement, the Asian American movement, and the Chicano movement—strongly rejected the idea that being nonwhite meant that they were less intelligent, less moral, or less worthy than those with exclusively European ancestry (Louie and Omatsu 2001; Muñoz 1989; Smith and Warrior 1997; Ture and Hamilton [1967] 1992). These activists further turned their backs on the assimilationist and accommodationist behaviors of their forebears by demanding recognition of and respect for their particular racial identities. They took denigrated racial identities that had been imposed upon them by others and then *claimed* them as positive sources of belongingness, pride, and motivation.

When those who are associated with the dominant racial group participate in this conversation, it often has a different set of meanings and consequences from the ones it has when racial minorities employ the conversation to counter marginalization and denigration. For example, white supremacists, including those who belong to fringe groups such as the Aryan Nations, White Nationalists, Skinheads, Ku Klux Klan, or the American Nazi Party, use it to make an explicit claim for European racial superiority. People who belong to White Pride groups bemoan what they see as the possible disappearance of the white race due to miscegenation and a low white birthrate and call alternately for kicking all nonwhites out of the United States or for returning to Europe where they can create a homogenous white nation.

8. Race is in our DNA.

The final conversation on our list is both one of the oldest and one of the most current. It is the conversation that says race cannot be ignored because it is an essential part of a person and that race can be found in a person's blood, genome, or culture. The idea that race is in the blood has been the basis of many different discriminatory policies, ranging from laws in the United States to prevent people associated with different races from marrying each other, to the genocidal murder of millions of European Jews during World War II. Following German Chancellor Adolf Hitler's defeat in World War II, this conversation appeared to go into decline as people tried to avoid the topic of race or had the *We're beyond race* conversation. It turns out, however, that the *Race is in our DNA* conversation had only gone into hiding.

Recent developments in biology and medicine have sparked this conversation anew. For example, DNA testing that gives people information about their genetic heritage has become increasingly available to the average consumer. Internet ads claim that with a simple cheek swab and $199, you can learn about your past and "who you really are." These new DNA testing techniques are exciting and have the potential to reveal very significant information about people's individual ancestry and the history of human migrations across the globe. However, these techniques also reinforce the centuries-old notion that race is a biological entity inside people's blood or bodies and that it marks something significant about their characters or behaviors (Koenig, Lee, and Richardson 2008).

One important variant of the *Race is in our DNA* conversation says, "It's their culture; it can't be helped." Although this version focuses on culture rather than biology, it similarly regards people as essentially unchanging and determined by the circumstances of their birth or early upbringing. This version of the *Race is in our DNA* conversation draws on a narrow and outdated understanding of culture as being so deeply rooted in a person, and so stable and predictable in its effects, that even important changes in a person's social environment are unlikely to make a difference in his or her values and behavior.

Nobel Prize winner James Watson, who helped discover the double helix structure of DNA, is one of the latest and best-known contributors to the *Race is in our DNA* conversation. Watson noted in a 2007 speech that he was "inherently gloomy about the prospect of Africa" because "all our social policies are based on the fact that their intelligence is the same as ours—whereas all the testing says not really." He added that while many of us have a natural desire to believe that all human beings should be equal, "people who have to deal with black employees find this not true." Watson was strongly criticized and he apologized for his remarks. Nevertheless, the fact that a highly respected and accomplished scientist would make this kind of statement shows that confusion about what race is and what it means is still frighteningly widespread (Dean 2007).

Taken together, these eight conversations show some of the most common ways of thinking and feeling about race and ethnicity in the United States today. Clearly, U.S. Americans both appreciate and fear our racial and ethnic difference. On the one hand, we are proud of our diversity: as a nation of immigrants, we want to incorporate racial and ethnic differences into our lives. We celebrate our differences (*Variety is the spice of life*), proclaim them (*I'm ____ and I'm proud*), argue for their reality (*Race is in our DNA*), and believe that they matter in our lives (*It's a black thing—you wouldn't understand*). On the other hand, we are worried about the changes to the country and to our lives that racial and ethnic differences bring with them: we are panicked by differences (*Racial diversity is killing us*), try to minimize their significance (*Everyone's a little bit racist*), ignore their relevance to our own lives (*That's just identity politics*), and proudly claim that differences no longer matter (*We're beyond race*). However we feel about race and ethnicity, they are clearly central to who "we" are as U.S. Americans.

At the heart of all the conversations are questions about ethnically and racially associated human differences: what they are, where they come from, and what we should do with them. An even thornier question involves who the "we" is who gets to decide which differences count. When people are deemed to be racially or ethnically different, who are they different from? Which group gets to represent the "norm," and which groups are forced to represent the "difference?" Answering these questions in a way that does not involve racial or ethnic discrimination, ethnic cleansing, or even genocide requires us to have a better understanding of race and ethnicity than any of the eight conversations discussed above can provide. In the service of moving toward a better understanding, we offer new and comprehensive definitions of race and ethnicity as *doings*, that is, as systems of social relations involving everyday interactions, as well as the institutional policies and practices of society.

RACE AND ETHNICITY AS DOINGS

Consider the graphic representations in Figures i.1 and i.2. In Figure i.1, race and ethnicity are shown as essential characteristics that reside within people and that distinguish them from other people who have different essential characteristics. In the case of race, especially, these characteristics are understood to be negative, and often biological and/or genetic. The individual people shown are designated as "dots," "squares," "triangles," or "stars" because they have "dot," "square," "triangle," "star," or "triangle/star" (i.e., mixed-race) qualities inside of them. They are grouped with others who apparently share these innate characteristics (e.g., skin color, hair texture, intelligence, athletic ability, mathematical propensity). So "white" people are grouped with other people who have "white" characteristics, while "Asian" people are grouped with other people who have "Asian" characteristics, and "mixed race" people have a mix of racial and ethnic characteristics. This is the way almost all of us are used to thinking about race and ethnicity; we imagine that people fit

FIGURE I.1 | **RACE AND ETHNICITY AS ESSENTIAL CHARACTERISTICS**

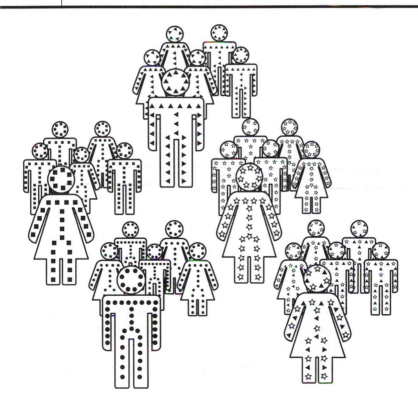

FIGURE I.2 | **RACE AND ETHNICITY AS SOCIAL PROCESSES**

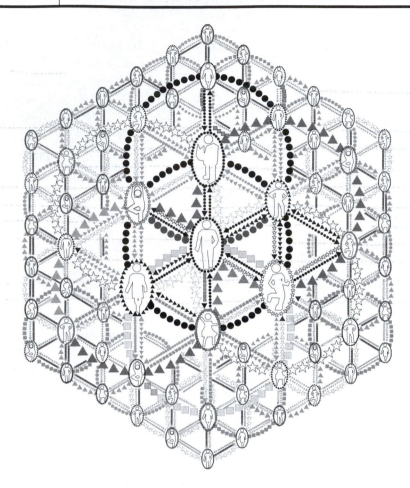

easily within one or another category because they have the same internal or "racial" characteristics as other members of the group.

In Figure i.2, by contrast, race and ethnicity are shown as social processes rather than as essential characteristics. The people are shown not as the same with different essential characteristics, but as different from each other because they are both doing and having different actions done to them. The categories of "dots," "squares," "triangles," or "stars" emerge as people try to make sense of themselves and their social worlds. The designations arise as answers to universal questions like "Who am I?" "Who are we?" and "Who are they?" So, for example, small dots outline the person in the very center of the Figure i.2; unlike in Figure i.1, this person does not have the dots inside him or her. This visual representation conveys the idea that the person is not inherently a "dot" but becomes one in *relationship* with the surrounding others. The reason he or she is a "dot" is because the people surrounding that person see him or her as a "dot," assume he or she is a "dot," explain what it means to be a "dot," and treat that person as if her or she is a "dot"—in other words, they *make him or her into* a "dot." The arrows made up of smaller dots pointing toward her indicate this process.

The people surrounding the "dot" person in the middle of Figure i.2 represent the person's immediate social context. They include parents, teachers, peers, employers, bankers, judges, religious leaders, and medical workers. They also include powerful and influential people such as government officials and media personalities with whom the "dot" person might not have any direct contact. All these people can play a powerful role in how the person in the middle thinks about being a "dot." Everyone with whom this person comes into some kind of contact makes use of widely accepted meanings and representations of "dotness."

The larger dots making up the outer ring around the "dot" person in the middle represent formalized laws, institutions, media, and shared societal ideas of what it means to be a "dot." If "dots" in a particular society are privileged and have a lot of social power, then the widely accepted meanings and representations in that society will be largely positive, and "dot" people will experience themselves as being in charge of how they are seen and treated by others. If, however, "dots" have less power or are regarded as inferior, then the meanings and representations are likely to be largely negative, and "dot" people will experience themselves as having much less control over how they are seen and treated.

Of course, each person who is made into a "dot" will respond somewhat differently. Some will resist and try to counter the ideas, actions, and practices that come their way. Others will try to ignore, or will fail to notice, how race and ethnicity are done. Still others will accept or incorporate these ideas and practices into their sense of what it means to be a "dot." Regardless, no one lives outside the web of relationships that create and maintain race and ethnicity. Even when someone resists having "dotness" imposed on himself or herself, his or her identity will be formed in relation to that process.

Each person in the matrix participates as both giver and receiver of the different ideas of what it means to be a "dot," although each person does not do so equally. Some will have more power to shape the meanings and consequences of what it means to be a "dot" than will others. Finally, the gray periphery denotes these social processes as they occur across time and throughout history. It demonstrates that people do not make each other and themselves into "squares," "dots," "triangles," and "stars" from scratch. Rather, they do so through the images, narratives, metaphors, conversations, policies, and everyday social routines that are already part of their worlds. Figure i.2 illustrates some of the important elements common to what we call here doing race or doing ethnicity.

As will become ever more evident over the course of this essay, much of the confusion around race and ethnicity stems from a misunderstanding of them as essential characteristics that people either *have* or *are,* as depicted in Figure i.1. The preceding illustrations are graphic representations of how race and ethnicity are commonly understood (Figure i.1) and how they could be accurately understood (Figure i.2). As depicted in Figure i.2, race and ethnicity are social, relational processes that take place over time and across space. Moreover, they cannot be the work of an individual alone but are the product of society as a whole.

DEFINING RACE AND ETHNICITY

Before we go any further, we need to say that the human differences marked by race and ethnicity can be a source of either pride or prejudice. So, for example, when people have the *It's a black thing—you wouldn't understand*, or *I'm _____ and I'm proud* conversations, they often intend to claim positive commonalities with others in their group as a way of conveying a sense of belonging, pride, and motivation. People who have the *Variety is the spice of life* conversation sometimes do this and even more. In addition to claiming positive commonalities with others in their group, they usually want to express admiration for the ethnic particularities of one or more other groups. These all point to positive ways of understanding the differences commonly marked by race and ethnicity. By contrast, when people have the *Racial diversity is killing us, Everyone's a little bit racist, That's just identity politics,* and *Race is in our DNA* conversations, the purpose and/or outcome is frequently to target, and impose negative characteristics on, those people who do not share the conversation participants' own racial or ethnic associations. Finally, the *We're beyond race* conversation appears, on the surface, to be neither positive nor negative. As we will see, however, this increasingly popular conversation fails to recognize, or else knowingly ignores, the claiming and imposing of ethnic and racial differences involved in the social transactions that make up everyday life in the twenty-first century.

In what follows, we outline two different social processes—one negative and the other positive—commonly associated with the terms "race" and "ethnicity." For the sake of analytical clarity, we will call the negative process "doing race" (see Table i.2) and the positive process "doing ethnicity" (see Table i.3). In actual practice, however, the distinction between the two processes, and between the two terms, is much muddier. Under certain conditions, the reverse can be true: the term "ethnicity" can be associated with negative consequences, while the term "race" can be associated with positive ones. In other situations, the two processes overlap to such a degree that they are impossible to distinguish from each other.

As the definitions show, both race and ethnicity are much more than simple terms or concepts. Rather, they are complex systems of ideas and practices that do important personal and societal work. Specifically, they help people to answer the basic identity questions of "Who am I?" and "Who are we?" Asking and answering the questions of who one is and where one belongs are universal human activities—although the possible answers to these questions necessarily depend on the context in which they are asked. In the present historical moment, at least, race and ethnicity are undeniably significant bases for organizing human communities and societies. For that reason, everyone is associated with one or more racial and/or ethnic groups. Of course, race and ethnicity as organizing systems are not inevitable, nor are they the only ones that matter to twenty-first-century global society. Other important organizing systems, while not the focus of this book, receive similar

TABLE I.2 | **DEFINITION OF RACE**

Race is a doing—a dynamic set of historically derived and institutionalized ideas and practices that

- sorts people into ethnic groups according to perceived physical and behavioral human characteristics that are often imagined to be negative, innate, and shared.
- associates differential value, power, and privilege with these characteristics; establishes a hierarchy among the different groups; and confers opportunity accordingly.
- emerges
  ▸ when groups are perceived to pose a threat (political, economic, or cultural) to each other's worldview or way of life; and/or
  ▸ to justify the denigration and exploitation (past, current, or future) of other groups while exalting one's own group to claim an innate privilege.

TABLE 1.3 | **DEFINITION OF ETHNICITY**

Ethnicity is a doing—a dynamic set of historically derived and institutionalized ideas and practices that

- allows people to identify, or be identified, with groupings of people on the basis of presumed, and usually claimed, commonalities, including several of the following: language, history, nation or region of origin, customs, religion, names, physical appearance and/or ancestry group.
- when claimed, confers a sense of belonging, pride and motivation.
- can be a source of collective and individual identity.

attention and analysis from scholars working in related fields: gender, religion, age, able-bodiedness, social class or caste, and sexuality.

As is clear from the definitions of race and ethnicity, the processes involved in doing them overlap in important ways. In addition, the terms "race" and "ethnicity" are sometimes used interchangeably. In the United States, for example, a person's race and a person's ethnicity can both be claimed as sources of pride and identity. This is not the case, however, in Europe, where the word "race" is almost never used. Nevertheless, we define "race" negatively because the term has historically been tied to asymmetries in power and privilege—to inequality. In the same spirit, we define the term "ethnicity" positively because it is more often used, in the United States, to refer to endorsed or claimed differences. Again, this is not the case in Europe and some other parts of the world. In Europe and elsewhere, ethnicity is commonly used to refer to cultural, linguistic, religious, and/or geographical "others." As a result, ethnicity often functions in Europe the way race usually works in the United States.

Race, then, is a complex system of ideas and practices regarding how some visible characteristics of human bodies such as skin color, facial features, and hair texture relate to people's character, intellectual capacity, and patterns of behavior. According to this definition, race is a doing that involves several, often simultaneous, actions: (1) noticing particular physical characteristics like skin color, hair color, or eye or nose shape; (2) assuming that those characteristics tell us something general and important, such as how intelligent or how hard-working or conscientious a person is or has the capacity to be; (3) participating in the maintenance and creation of social and economic structures that preserve a hierarchy in which people associated with one race are assumed to be superior to people who are associated with another; and (4) justifying or rationalizing the resulting inequalities. Although people can do some of these actions to themselves, doing race is very often a one-sided process in which people associated with one group impose a set of negative characteristics on people associated with another group (usually, but not always, one with less power) and relegate them to an inferior status. For the most part, people do race *to* others; they do not do race to themselves.

Because the negative, inequality-producing process associated with the concept of race has developed across time in response to changing, locally specific economic, political, cultural, and technological conditions, race has referred to different configurations of human difference in diverse environments over the course of history. Even so, the concept has at its core the idea that people can be classified into distinct and readily identifiable races based on inherited and unalterable biological characteristics that indicate who is worthy of having access to respect and resources. Importantly, race is given tangible and visible form in the structures and institutions of a society, as well as in people's everyday beliefs and attitudes. The ideas and practices of race do the work of explaining, justifying, and promoting emergent (as well as long-standing) conditions of racial inequality among different groups of people. This is why changing individual people's prejudicial attitudes is only one part of addressing the inequalities promoted by race. Another crucial part will involve reforming the existing societal institutions that reflect, and further enable and constrain, individuals' attitudes and actions.

Ethnicity is also a complex system of ideas and practices. We distinguish it from race as being a more mutual, power-neutral, and positive process (see Table i.3). But, as we have taken pains to emphasize, any group, even one considered an ethnicity, can be the target of the negative, inequality-producing process we call race. The conflict between Hutus and Tutsis in Rwanda in 1994, for example, was widely reported and understood as an ethnic conflict. Yet, at the heart of that conflict (as with most ethnic conflict) was a long history of Rwandans doing to each other what we call here doing race. That is, in the course of reproducing a social order imposed on them by their Belgian colonizers, Rwandans were sorting people into ethnic groups according to perceived physical and behavioral human characteristics; associating differential value, power, and privilege with these characteristics; establishing a hierarchy among the different groups; and conferring opportunity accordingly (Gourevitch 1999).

Just as ethnicity can be associated with the negative inequality-producing process we call doing race, so can race be associated with the positive identity-generating process we call doing ethnicity. We see this when people who have had a stigmatized racial identity imposed on them by others turn around and claim, for example, "black" or "American Indian" as a source of belonging, pride, and motivation. During the ethnic civil rights movements of 1960s and 1970s, young people of African descent in the United States collectively declared that "black is beautiful," while people from many different Native American tribal communities came together under the rubric of "American Indian." To understand why we might see these as examples of a positive use of race (or an ethnicizing of race), we need keep in mind that people of African descent who currently live in the United States are a very diverse bunch. The African people who survived the grueling voyage across the Atlantic to be enslaved in the United States came from several different geographic regions, spoke a variety of languages, and had different religious and cultural practices. Even so, the laws of the early American republic treated these people as if they were all the same, with the same set of interests, desires, and capacities. They were, in effect, created as a single, minoritized racial group without ever having been a single ethnic group. And yet, when their descendents joined together in the black civil rights movement to assert a feeling of pride and solidarity *as* black people, they were participating in the creation of a (politicized) black ethnic identity.

For similar political purposes, young radicals whose people were indigenous to what is now North America looked past their real differences of language, culture, tribal affinity, and geographic origin to claim an identity (American Indian) that had been originally imposed upon them by the U.S. government. In both cases, individual people were identifying with a group on the basis of presumed and claimed commonalities of history (in both cases a history of racialized oppression in the United States), nation or region of origin (Africa in the case of blacks, North America in the case of American Indians), values and ideals, and physical appearance. Also in both cases, the politicized ethnic identities that came into being in these ethnic civil rights movements conferred a sense of belonging, pride, and motivation on those who simultaneously created and claimed them. It is for this reason that the term "black," for example, can be used to refer to both a racial identity and an ethnic identity. What the term "black" means in a given situation depends, as with all language, on the context in which it is used.

Because there is a delicate balance between the positive and negative aspects of noting human ethnic or racial difference, the negative and positive processes we detail above occasionally overlap or even work together. For example, a person who is doing ethnicity (by claiming positive commonalities with others in his or her group to convey a sense of belonging, pride, and motivation) can easily slide over into doing race. This happens when someone who is claiming positive commonalities with others in a given group construes his or her own group's way of being as normative or superior while also imposing negative characteristics onto people in other groups. Such a slide is evident, for example, in the beliefs and practices of the neo-Nazi White Pride groups discussed above in the *I'm _____ and I'm proud* conversation. It is similarly evident in the Samuel Huntington example presented in the *Racial diversity is killing us* conversation. Most dramatically, the overlap between the processes of doing ethnicity and of doing race was manifest in World War II. Under Hitler, Europeans experienced firsthand the way German ethnic nationalism, paired with European racial superiority, justified the genocide of over six million Jews and people in other minority groups. Indeed, Europeans, and especially Germans, are so well acquainted with the negative consequences of doing race that they are understandably reluctant to use the word "race" at all. It is for that reason that the German word for race is almost never used in polite company or scholarly work. German scholars who study the kinds of processes we identify in this introductory essay use the terms "ethnic groups" or "immigrants" to refer to the communities of people who, in the United States, we might refer to as racial minorities.

As fundamentally social beings, humans want and even need to identify with and feel connected to others who are like (in one way or another) themselves. There is nothing wrong with recognizing someone else's ethnicity or with claiming one's own, because there is nothing negative or pernicious, per se, about ethnic groupings. Group differences in history, language, religion, name, ancestry group, physical appearance, nation or region of origin, and/or customary ways of being are and will continue to be evident in diverse societies like our own. Moreover, because these groupings reflect alternative perspectives and practices, they can be important resources for creativity, innovation, and societal well-being. In a society where race and ethnicity have been and still are so central, paying attention to them is not only important, it is necessary.

DOING RACE AND ETHNICITY: EXAMPLES

In the course of our everyday social interactions, people in the United States collectively perpetuate sets of ideas and practices about what it means to be white, Latina/o, black, Asian American, or American

Indian. Sometimes people actively and intentionally devalue and treat people associated with groups other than their own as if they are lesser or unequal. Very often, however, people do race unknowingly and unintentionally just by participating in a world that comes prearranged according to certain racial categories (Adams et al. 2008a). We can see the consequences of the fact that people have done (and continue to do) race everywhere we look. We can observe, for example, that even in states where there are substantial Latina/o or Asian populations, there are very few Latina/o or Asian newscasters and pundits. We can see the effects of race when committees in charge of awarding construction contracts, educational fellowships, prizes for essays or art works, or engineering competitions are entirely made up of white people or have only one committee member who is associated with a minority racial group. Most crucially, we can see that the chances of being in poor health, having no insurance, and dying young are much greater for people associated with a minority racial group. These are institutionalized patterns that reflect and perpetuate the inequality resulting from centuries of doing race.

The following examples illustrate race and ethnicity as actions done by *all of us*, regardless of our own ethnic or racial associations. Race and ethnicity are actions we do individually and institutionally, sometimes with awareness of the consequences and sometimes without. The examples show, moreover, that simply noting an ethnically or racially associated difference is not—as many of the common conversations about race and ethnicity assume—the same as doing race. Whether one is doing race depends on *what* is noted, *how* it is noted, *why* it is noted, and *what one does* with the information gathered as a result of that noting.

Take the hypothetical case of Leticia, a Latina in tenth grade in the Houston Independent School District. Leticia has been absent from school for the last month and nobody at school knows why. The African American assistant principal, who does not know Leticia personally, told her first-period teacher, who is South Asian, "not to worry," that Leticia's absence from school was not at all surprising. He explained, "Well, you know those Hispanics. They don't value education that much. Her mother probably just wants her to stay home." For at least two reasons, this is an example of doing race. The first is that the African American assistant principal has not made an effort to know or take into account the circumstances of Leticia's individual case but instead judges her in light of a negative and false generalization about the essential interests, desires, and capacities of all Latina/os. In other words, he stereotypes her in the manner represented graphically in Figure i.1. Second, his directive "not to worry" implies that the source of the problem is Leticia and her ethnic group rather than the kinds of interactions her school and mainstream society are having (and have had in the past) with her and others in her ethnic group (as indicated by Figure i.2). The South Asian teacher, who has an overenrolled first-period class, is relieved to let the matter rest. The responses of the assistant principal and the teacher to Leticia's absence thus fail to account for the social, political, and historical context supporting Leticia's behavior within the educational system, even as they fail Leticia as an individual student. By imagining that there is little that either they or the educational system can do to create a better learning environment for Leticia, and by failing to pay attention to the specifics of Leticia's situation, the African American assistant principal and the South Asian teacher together explain away the problem by using the cultural version of the *Race is in our DNA* conversation. They see the problem in terms of the essential characteristics of Leticia and her group and thus divest themselves, the school, and the educational system of any responsibility for her well-being.

Now, consider another example of doing race that is less personal but that is in some ways more powerful because it appears, on the surface, to be race-neutral. Public officials sitting on city councils and county commissions all over the country make decisions about where to locate chemical plants and toxic and solid waste dumps, or through which communities to run rail lines or freeways. More often than not, these facilities are located in or near minority communities. Far from being a coincidence, the decisions about where to locate a plant, dump, or freeway are made in ways that, expressly or inadvertently, do race. Officials often believe that putting a plant or a dump in a minority community is a rational thing to do because the land is relatively cheap or because industrial operations already exist nearby. Additionally, the officials may assume that the people in these areas are less likely to vote or mount a successful protest, and sometimes they are right about this. Occasionally, they argue that the minority community wants the facility as a source of jobs or income. However, a decision about where to locate a chemical plant or toxic waste dump has huge ramifications. It increases incidences of environmental illness, depresses the values of homes, decreases the likelihood that businesses will invest in the area, lowers the tax base, and isolates communities from mainstream commerce and society. And yet, were a community member to object to the locating of a dump on the grounds that the officials are doing race, the officials involved would likely point out that they have been asked to solve a legitimate problem and that race really has nothing to do with it. They would likely, in other words, answer with the *That's just identity politics* or the *We're beyond race* conversations. Moreover, some might sincerely believe that they are color-blind, that race had nothing to do with the outcome, and that the decision-making processes were rooted in practical and economic considerations for the larger community as a whole.

Together, these two examples show that race is done in multiple ways. While doing race sometimes involves people making stereotypical and hostile judgments about others, the process of doing race does not require "racists" (Bonilla-Silva 2003). As illustrated in Figure i.2, race is simultaneously individual and institutional because individual people are institutional actors. Just as individuals do not live outside social systems, social systems operate only with the involvement of individuals. It is in this sense that race is done personally and impersonally, individually and institutionally, with awareness and without.

Now consider another set of examples showing that the mere act of noting a racially or ethnically associated difference is not, by itself, the problem. The problem arises with the validity of the evidence people use to make an observation, how they explain the origins of the noted differences, and what actions they take as a result. For this set of examples, we refer to another group of people frequently stereotyped in the United States—the diverse populations of people often grouped together and labeled "Asian Americans."

The first notable difference is that East Asian American university students often do very well in math and science classes and outperform their student peers. This observation is supported by data on the grade point averages of East Asian American math and sciences students in universities across the country and has held true over a period of time (Tseng, Chao, and Padmawidjaja 2006). This is a difference that is valued positively by others and would be proudly claimed by many East Asian American students. Now, bear in mind a noting of difference that is similarly directed at people of Asian descent but that involves negative valuation and would not be claimed by most Asian people. According to a popular stereotype of the nineteenth and twentieth centuries, Asian people are inscrutable—it is impossible to tell what they are thinking and feeling, and whatever they are thinking or feeling is probably something crafty and sly.

The second example, the one involving the "Asians are inscrutable" stereotype, is a clear instance of doing race. To begin with, unlike the example involving math and science grades of East Asian American university students, the origin of the observation involved in the "Asians are inscrutable" stereotype is anecdotal as opposed to evidentiary. Second, the "Asians are inscrutable" stereotype is tied to a long history of racist portrayal of Asians in the United States (Chang, this volume). And finally, the consequence of describing as inscrutable a very diverse group of people is to make the group of people identified by others (and sometimes by themselves) as "Asian" seem different and lesser.

Even if we take seriously the source of the stereotype of "Asian as inscrutable," we need to remember that people associated with one race or ethnicity often have difficulty interpreting the behavior and communicative codes of people associated with a different race or ethnicity. A behavioral characteristic that appears to someone from an out-group as inscrutability, for example, might be understood by someone from the in-group as appropriate and decorous behavior. Understanding that "inscrutability" is not an essential characteristic of a group of people but rather a judgment that rests on the particular perspective of the person making the observation requires an acknowledgment that there are other viable ways of being in the world. It also requires the recognition of multiple legitimate perspectives on what is considered culturally "normal" or "neutral."

It should be clear, as well, that the problem with noting racial or ethnic difference does not result solely from bad evidence; it results also from how the differences are explained and what actions are taken as a result. In the case of the high-performing East Asian students, for example, the evidence for the difference is fairly reliable. However, we would still be doing race if we were to assume that the group difference in scores or GPA meant that *every* East Asian student is superior in math and science to *every other* student of another racial or ethnic group. We would also be doing race if we were to assume that the difference results from some essential (fixed and unchanging) aspect of East Asian biology or culture. In fact, any simple explanation would be equally suspect; the only way we might be able to give an adequate explanation would be by attending to the particular social and historical contexts within which the difference occurs. So, while it is not wrong or "racist" to look out on the world and notice difference, explaining those differences in terms of attributes inside people rather than in terms of social relations and economic conditions over time can, in fact, be racist.

Think about this next example and about the diverse ways the noting of a difference can be explained and acted upon. Currently, Latina/os have a disproportionately high school dropout rate. Moreover, the dropout rate is increasing dramatically in California, especially among girls. We might explain this trend in at least two ways, only one of which involves doing race. The first is by following the example of the assistant principal at Leticia's high school—by implying that Latina/os are not smart, that they are not interested in education, that they refuse to learn to speak English, and so forth. In this scenario, we would be assuming that the poor performance of Latina/os in school is a result of an essential characteristic of their biology or culture about which nothing can be done.

Alternatively, we might begin our explanation by looking at the social processes (see Figure i.2) that contribute to the high Latina/o dropout rate. We might consider the often negative interactions Latina/os have now and have had in the past with mainstream society, the quality of the underfunded schools Latina/os are likely to attend, the training of the teachers they usually have, and the relative lack of role models and support systems they encounter (Darling-Hammond, this volume). We might further consider the radical instability many Latina/os face because they may well have family members who are directly threatened by the immigration rhetoric and policies of the United States—policies that stigmatize all Latina/os and construct them as "not-American." How might this instability affect these students' sense of well-being? Also, we can look to research done by social psychologists and educational researchers that shows that Latina/os, like people from all ethnic groups, are products of their historical circumstances and sociocultural environments, and that their performance in school is related to their socioeconomic status as well as to the educational opportunities they encounter (e.g., Suárez-Orozco, Suárez-Orozco, and Todorova 2008; Fryberg and Markus 2003; Perry, Steele, and Hilliard 2003).

Again, the problem is not simply noting racial or ethnic difference but what follows from this noting. Regardless of how we explain the high dropout rate among Latina/os, in both cases we are noting a correlation between the race or ethnicity of a particular group of people and a pattern of behavior. But only in the first case—the scenario in which we explain Latina/os' high dropout rate by attributing it to some essential biological or cultural characteristic that cannot be remedied—would we be doing race. Not surprisingly, the two different ways of explaining the phenomenon lead to radically different policy directives. If, on the one hand, we do race to Latina/os, excusing our history, our institutions, and ourselves from any responsibility, then we might try to exclude as many Latina/os as possible from the United States—seal the border, lower the birthrate, and deport all illegal aliens now! Additionally, as has been done in the past, we might subject Latina/os to a program of intense "Americanization" (Deutsch 1987; Gutiérrez 1995). If, on the other hand, we believe that any given student's behavior—her intellectual capacity, her athletic ability, her moral judgment—is not a fixed entity but instead emerges as a transaction between her and her environment, we might instead decide to make changes to the educational practices and institutions responsible for training our future workforce (Cohen et al. 2006; Dweck 2006; Fryberg and Markus 2003; Steele 2010). For instance, we might work to communicate to students that they are valued and belong to the school community, equalize school funding, put more time and resources into teacher education, increase the percentage of Latina/o teachers, make the curriculum more inclusive to accurately represent the participation of Latina/os in the development and defense of the United States, and find a workable solution to the problem of undocumented immigration. Explaining the situation in this way is a good example of how we might *do difference differently*, an idea to which we return in Section III of this essay.

Racial and ethnic differences are everywhere. We cannot sweep them under the rug or assume it is possible to judge people only as individuals, on the "content of their character." Everyone has racial and ethnic associations, and those associations affect their lives in consequential ways, both positive and negative. On the one hand, our current ethnic diversity is an impressive record of past human creativity and learning, besides being a great future resource. As a species, we humans have been successful precisely because we have adapted to whole new sets of circumstances, contexts, and environments. On the other hand, ethnic and racial differences serve as crucial indicators of persistent racial and ethnic inequality; they point to the work that has yet to be done to realize social justice in the United States.

The question, then, is not whether we should deal with difference, but rather how we address the differences we encounter. Which differences are noted? Which differences are valued? Why are some differences valued while others are put down? Who decides which differences are worth noticing or valuing? How do the decisions made on the basis of noticing and valuing differences affect the way status and resources are distributed? What actions should we take in light of the information we have gathered?

The primary way people have approached ethnically associated human differences in the past has been to do race. But, as we have shown, doing race leads to misunderstanding, discord, and pervasive societal inequality.

To the extent that we accept the unequal arrangements of the world as natural or neutral and do not challenge or work to change them, we are responsible for perpetuating inequality. While we may not be actively attributing negative characteristics to individuals, consigning them to an inferior status and discriminating against them, we are, nonetheless, part of a system that fosters racial injustice. While we may not be racists in the sense that we believe in our own inherent superiority or in the essential inferiority of any other group, we are all still doing race.

In Section II of this essay, we review the history of racial formation in the United States, examine the philosophical assumptions underlying our country's everyday racial realities, and propose some reasons that U.S. Americans are so uncomfortable talking about race. In Section III, we show that while differences are a feature of human life, we need not be imprisoned by our current ways of handling them. After providing a few examples of the many we could give showing how race has become institutionalized in the basic structures of our society, we return to our claims that race is a doing, and that it is pervasive in our society. We conclude by returning in Section III to the conversations and making some suggestions for how we can *do difference differently*.

II

RACE IN THE UNITED STATES—
TWO ASSUMPTIONS AND ONE IDEAL

Race is central to the U.S. American story; it has been here from the beginning and it continues to be a powerful force shaping our attitudes and institutions (Omi and Winant 1994). Yet, as we have seen, U.S. Americans have many different and contradictory ideas about what race is as well as what it means for our lives. To understand why, consider that what is commonly said about race addresses only the tip of what we might call, for the sake of illustration, a "racial iceberg."

An iceberg typically has only about one-ninth of its mass above the surface, so that what an observer on the surface of the ocean sees makes up only a small part of the whole. Imagine that the sorts of events discussed at the beginning of Section I are like the collisions that occur when a ship hits an iceberg before sinking. The point of visualizing the process in this way is to emphasize that much of what affects our thinking about race lies below the surface of our awareness. Extending the metaphor further, we can think of the eight conversations as in the air around us. Whenever an event occurs, people use one or more of the

FIGURE I.3 | **THE RACIAL ICEBERG**

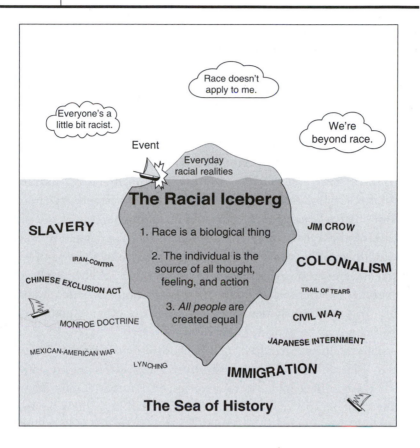

At the core of the racial iceberg are two fundamental but problematic philosophical assumptions and one powerful defining ideal (see Figure i.3). An assumption, by definition, is implicit—taken for granted, not questioned, fundamental. Until it is made explicit, it cannot be examined in detail, put into context, compared with other possible beliefs, and either affirmed or rejected. The assumptions concerning us here are that race is a biological thing and the individual is the source of all thought, feeling, and action. They are intertwined with a defining ideal of the United States—the ideal that all people are created equal. Together, the two assumptions and the ideal of equality shape our characteristically U.S. American reactions to, and ways of thinking about, everyday realities involving race and ethnicity.

conversations to make sense of it—often with little thought about why we have these particular conversations and not others.

Of course, *all* of our everyday realities—not just the ones involving race and ethnicity—make use of concepts, terms, assumptions, and ideals that have come down to us through history. Such concepts, terms, assumptions, and ideals are human inventions, products of our own or our ancestors' activities over the course of time and, as such, could have been invented differently. Making up the everyday realities of U.S. American lives are barely remembered (but world-making) historical events like the Trail of Tears and the Spanish-American War, significant (but often misre-membered) social movements such as abolitionism and the United Farm Workers' boycotts, established (and evolving) institutions like slavery or the prison system, and foundational (but continually retold) narratives such as the "City on the Hill" story invoked by many people to character-ize America as a beacon for freedom and liberty for all.

Many of the events, movements, institutions, and narratives that make up the realities of life in our country seem to us to be completely natural and universal, as just the way the world should be. And yet, as the existence of other societies with other institutional systems and other cultural practices clearly demonstrates, there are other, equally viable ways of being in the world. Even so, we frequently have a hard time imagining that history could have taken a different path; that our fore-bears could have built different institutions using different assumptions; that they might have told different stories; or that there might be other equally valuable and viable ways of thinking, talking, and behaving in the world. Despite our habit of thinking that our ways of being in the world are the right and normal ways, they are *not* universal; they are particular. Consequently, understanding how race and ethnicity have evolved in the United States requires analyzing the historical events, political movements, social and economic institutions, foundational narratives, social practices, defining ideals, and underlying assumptions that have made us who we are. In what follows, we illuminate in turn each of the assumptions, and the defining ideal, to show how they have shaped our understandings of race in the United States.

Race Is a Biological Thing

Racial Classifications across Time

The dominant understanding of race today, which began to emerge in the fifteenth century, holds that all people can be classified into distinct races based on inherited biological characteristics. During the Age of Explo-ration (fifteenth through seventeenth centuries), Europeans' encounters with other civilizations—the resources and inhabitants of which they exploited as part of their imperial projects—created the need to place these civilizational "others" in some sort of relationship to themselves. The conundrum created in the European mind—who are these people and how do we relate to them?—was not easily or immediately resolved. As late as 1550, some sixty years after the first European encounter with Native Americans, the Bishop of Chiapas, Fray Bartolomé de las Casas, engaged in a debate with fellow cleric Juan Ginés de Sepúlveda regarding whether the natives of Mesoamerica should be considered free peoples or natural slaves. The question at stake in the debate was whether the Spanish Crown was justified in its enslavement of the people they had succeeded in bringing under their dominion (Todorov 1999; Mignolo 1995; Quijano 2000).

The seventeenth century saw various efforts to settle upon the number and the characteristics of different "races," with various taxonomies proposed. However, it was not until the eighteenth and nineteenth centuries, with the publication of works by Swedish naturalist Carolus Linnaeus (*Systema Naturae* 1767), German anatomist Johann Friedrich Blumenbach (*On the Natural Varieties of Mankind* 1776), and American anatomist Samuel George Morton (*Crania Americana* 1839) that the modern notion of race crystallized. Although noticing phenotypical and cultural differences between groups of humans has a much longer history, the modern concept of race is rooted in three claims: (1) that race is a *universal* scheme that can accommodate all observed human differences; (2) that it is a *scientifically based* system of classification; and (3) that it is *predictive* of humans' differing capacities and characters. The emergence of the concept of race was thus fueled by the more general Western scientific project of trying to make sense of the world by classifying and ordering its subject matter—plants, animals, and humans—according to observable physical traits (see Facing History 2002).

By the early nineteenth century, a scientific consensus had emerged regarding the existence of either four or five distinct races corresponding roughly to the different continents. Perhaps not surprisingly, the scientists doing the classifying found their own race to have the superior characteristics. Linneaus, for example, divided humankind into four racial categories corresponding to the four largest continents and determined that each race had certain characteristics common to the individuals in it: Native Americans were reddish in color, obstinate, easily angered, and governed by custom; Africans were black, relaxed, negligent, and governed by caprice; Asians were sallow, avaricious, haughty, and governed by opinions; Europeans were white, acute, inventive, and governed by laws (Linnaeus 1767; Smedley 2007, 164). To bolster their conclusions, several of these scientists developed procedures to test their arguments—procedures that have not survived subsequent scientific scrutiny. Morton, for example, believed there was a link between brain size and intelligence. He set out to measure the skulls of people of different races to determine their brain size. On the basis of his measurements, he concluded that Caucasians had larger brains than people of other races and thus possessed superior intelligence. However, in the 1970s, evolutionary biologist and historian of science Stephen Jay Gould examined Morton's data and measurements and found that Morton's results were drawn from an unrepresentative sample of skulls and that his measurements and conclusions were faulty. Furthermore, the real and crucial question—whether the size of someone's skull predicts his or her intelligence—was never tested by Morton but simply assumed by him (Gould 1996).

The Swiss-American naturalist and Harvard professor Louis Agassiz thought that people who were assigned to different racial categories were biologically very different from one another and even had different biological origins (Agassiz 1850). His view, polygenesis, was subsequently discredited. Current scientific knowledge holds that all humans derive from a common ancestor and that much of human evolution occurred while early humans were living on the continent of Africa. Scientists such as Morton and Agassiz were most likely not trying to mislead the public with their science. Rather, the commonsense ideas and conversations of their day shaped their scientific practice and predisposed them to look for, and then find, evidence in support of what they already believed.

Evolution and Heredity: Biologizing Race

After Charles Darwin published *On the Origin of Species* in 1859, his ideas about the way nature selects those traits and forms of life most likely to survive and thrive were taken up by "social Darwinists" who concluded that Morton's and Linnaeus's racial group rankings must be a reflection of human evolutionary development. Gregor Mendel's laws of heredity, developed in the mid-1800s, were similarly enlisted to support the belief that Europeans (and especially Northern Europeans) represented the epitome of human development. Some fifty years after Mendel published his findings on the inheritance of traits in pea plants, Francis Galton used Mendel's research to bolster his conviction that human intelligence was inherited. Galton's "eugenics" program advocated restricting sexual relations and marriages between what he deemed to be "superior" and "inferior" races (Facing History 2002). The eugenics movement eventually spread to the United States, where its popularity was strengthened by nativist fears that the American gene pool was being polluted by undesirable immigrants from Southern and Eastern Europe. Eugenicist assumptions were so much a part of the everyday thinking of the time that even some very distinguished scholars subscribed to them. For example, David Starr Jordan, an ichthyologist, peace activist, and the first president of Stanford University, was an early and unapologetic leader of the American eugenics movement (Jordan 1911).

Further historical developments in the United States contributed to the promotion of eugenicist thinking in the United States. The biggest wave of immigration to this country, from 1880 to 1920; the buildup to World War I; and the establishment of compulsory education for all children were key in this regard. American policy makers, perceiving a need to classify immigrants, recruits, and students according to mental capacity, readily adopted the idea of "mental tests" that could identify those people who were "feeble minded" and therefore "unfit" for citizenship, service, or schooling. The implementation of mental testing fueled the assumption that intelligence was a fixed attribute of a person, and that some persons, by virtue of their racial group association, were more or less intelligent than others. For example, Stanford professor Lewis Terman believed that non–Northern European people were less intelligent than Northern European people. He adapted a test that had been developed in France to measure students' *performance* on specific academic tasks, and claimed that his test measured people's *innate intelligence*. Terman's Stanford-Binet test—which is a test that measures culturally specific knowledge—purported to be an efficient way of measuring the fixed mental capacities of large groups of people. Applying his test to non–Northern European immigrant children, Terman had this to say: "The tests have told the truth. These boys are ineducable beyond the merest rudiments of training. No amount of school instruction will ever make them intelligent voters or capable citizens" (Terman 1916, 91).

The establishment of the I.Q. or Intelligence Quotient test developed by Terman is an example of how a questionable idea that accords with popular opinion can too easily be taken as truth. When a scientist's conclusions support the status quo—when they tell us what we already believe—they often do not receive appropriate scientific scrutiny. Moreover, alternative hypotheses—for example, that good performance on an I.Q. test measures familiarity and comfort with culturally specific objects and activities rather than the innate capacity of a person—are often not examined. This is the way that unwarranted scientific conclusions can be enshrined as the "truth," at least for a time, even when they later turn out to be entirely wrong.

Race and Culture

Not until the early part of the twentieth century did some scientists begin to question the belief that cultural, linguistic, and behavioral differences among people were the result of inherent and fixed physical characteristics. An important figure in promoting a new understanding of race was Franz Boas, generally considered to be the founder of American anthropology. In 1911, Boas published *The Mind of Primitive Man*, which included his studies of Native Americans along the northwest coast of the United States. Boas's research demonstrated that many of the most significant features of people's behavior (their language, values, ways of cooking, kinship ties, child rearing, and so on) are not related to inherited biological difference. His research showed that all these cultural features overlap and vary independently of each other. So, for example, two populations who looked very similar might speak different languages and behave very differently from each other. Conversely, groups who spoke the same language and had similar cultural practices might differ greatly in terms of physical features (Boas 1911).

Boas's research allowed scientists to understand in new ways the differences they noted among humans. Boas and his students, including scholars such Ruth Benedict, Margaret Mead, and Zora Neale Hurston, understood culture as fluid and dynamic. They held that cultural differences among people's prevalent ideas and practices could account for important variations in individual behavior. They further understood these cultural patterns and processes as not fixed, but rather evolving, and regarded them as worthy objects of scientific inquiry. As a result of his and his students' findings, Boas rejected the existence of a racial or ethnic hierarchy in which some groups are more evolved than others; he became a forceful proponent of cultural pluralism, which held that there are many equally evolved and viable human cultures.

After World War II, conversations about race in the United States continued to change in the direction of rejecting the idea of innate racial differences. Americans' awareness of the horrors of Nazi genocide— a program of institutionalized murder that targeted Jews, Gypsies, homosexuals, and the mentally ill and that was justified on eugenicist grounds—further contributed to this shift. It was at this point that many scholars switched from talking about "race," a term that became associated with the Nazis and their "final solution," to talking about "ethnicity" (Snipp, this volume; Sollors 1996). Many scholars began to avoid using the term "race," even as racial thinking and heated debates about the role of nature versus nurture as determinants of human behavior persisted in the scientific community and in the public sphere.

The switch from talking about race to talking about ethnicity and culture did not signal an end to the thinking about ethnic and racial others in negative and essentialist terms. While considering the importance of culture in shaping people's behavior bolstered arguments in favor of integrating the schools and the military, it also created the space for analyses like the one included in the infamous 1965 Moynihan Report, titled "The Negro Family: The Case for National Action." That report, published a year after the passage of the Civil Rights Act, was prompted by what Senator Daniel Patrick Moynihan saw as a "new crisis in race relations." The report located the source of African American poverty not in race per se but in the African American family structure. Moynihan argued that without a father in the house, black families became disorganized and isolated from mainstream values. This caused them to fall into poverty, delinquency, and crime (Moynihan 1965). The narrow analysis provided in the report failed to highlight the powerful and ongoing gaps in educational employment and housing opportunities that gave rise to and perpetuated this cycle. As a result, the report made it seem as if there were some fixed "thing" that could be isolated and identified as "black culture," and that black culture (as an entity residing within people and their families) was to blame for the failure of African Americans to advance quickly to economic and social equality with whites. The effect of the report was to stigmatize the African American family as a "tangle of pathologies" in need of therapy. The Moynihan report had a negative impact on attitudes about African Americans. Even though the term *culture* was intended to refer to distributions of ideas and practices, following the Moynihan report, it came to be used in the same way race had been used, i.e., to indicate an unchanging essence or set of traits. As a result, many social scientists concerned with race avoided any discussion of culture.

Genomic Research and the Re-biologization of Race

Given the remarkable history of the concept of race and its impressive capacity to adapt to changing social circumstances, we should not be surprised that ideas and conversations about race continue to evolve in the present day. The recent discovery of ways to understand DNA sequencing over the last thirty years has had at least one unfortunate consequence: the re-biologization of the concept of race. As the claims of nineteenth-century scientific racism were disproved in the second half of the twentieth century by scholars like Stephen Jay Gould (1981) and Richard Lewontin (1984), the idea that the concept of race had no biological basis was gradually acknowledged in many sectors of American society, if not in the minds of the American public at large. With the mapping of the human genome, however, the direction of thinking about race has reversed.

In part because the racial classification systems developed in the eighteenth and nineteenth centuries were tied to continental origin, recent developments in population genetics that allow scientists to determine, with a high degree of accuracy, an individual's continental origin(s) have reinvigorated old ideas about the biological significance of racial difference. It can be difficult, at first, to separate the fact that scientists can now determine the continental origins of an individual's ancestors, from the fiction that they are able to say—even to the extent of breaking it down into percentages—what someone's biological race is. To make the situation even more confusing, several Web-based businesses, genealogical societies, and even a few television specials have capitalized on the powerful desire of many of us to find out "who we are" by discovering our ancestral roots (Bolnick et al. 2007). Biogeographical ancestry groups (or populations) and race are not the same thing. Understanding the difference requires a close examination of the relationship between these two concepts.

As Marcus Feldman's essay in this volume makes clear, current research on the human genome indicates several important facts about biological diversity. First, all humans can trace their beginnings to a common ancestor who lived in the part of the world that we now know as the continent of Africa. Second, approximately 100,000 years ago, one or more groups of people migrated out of Africa, with the great majority of humans who were then alive remaining in Africa. Third, all the populations of humans that eventually came to reside in continents other than Africa are descended serially from these first groups of migrants. As some of the migrants settled along the way, some of their descendents pushed across Europe and the Middle East and settled in those regions. Eventually, smaller subsets of these people's descendents migrated into China and Russia, until even smaller subsets crossed the Bering land bridge into what is now America (Feldman, this volume).

We come now to the fourth fact indicated by current genomic research: about 89 percent of human genomic variation occurs *within* populations of people, with at most 9 percent occurring *between* populations (Li 2008). What this means is that any given human being is much more genetically similar to any other human being than he is different and what genomic variation does occur between himself and another human being is more likely to be found within his own population than outside it. Moreover, most people who were alive when the migrations started stayed in Africa. This means that the greatest amount of human genomic variation in the world today exists *within* the different populations of people descended from those ancestors who stayed in Africa. By contrast, the least amount of within-population genomic variation occurs among the descendents of the ancestors who migrated the farthest from Africa: into South America.

A fifth important fact about biological diversity is that it is not patterned in such a way that we can cleanly divide people into completely separate and unconnected populations according to either genetics or observable physical features. As previously noted, most genomic variation occurs within populations. Additionally, observable physical features such as skin color, hair texture, and limb shape actually vary continuously across geographic space; there are no obvious sets of features that anyone can definitively identify as characteristic of only this or that particular population. So, for example, if a person were to hike around the world observing different populations of people, she would see that the physical features we often use to assign racial group membership blend into one other in a way that is consistent with the migratory path of ancient humans out of Africa and across the globe.

Even though humans cannot be divided up into completely separate populations, very recent advances in human genomic research have enabled scientists to identify genomic variations at the level of the single nucleotide (of which there are about three billion in the human genome). This ability to detect incredibly minute differences at a level even smaller than the human gene means that scientists can now sort most people into nondiscrete and overlapping, but nevertheless identifiable, population clusters. In his essay, Feldman refers to these biogeographically based clusters as populations or *ancestry groups*. When considering how the biogeographical concept of ancestry groups relates to the practice of human racial categorization, it helps to remember that—depending on how finely scientists draw the distinctions and which specific criteria they use to divide the human species into smaller groups—researchers can identify anywhere from 5 different human populations to 6,000. This is why even the concept of a biogeographical ancestry group, though firmly based in biology, can also be said to be a socially constructed conceptual category. How finely to draw the distinctions and what criteria should be used are finally *social* decisions, made by people who participate in the larger societies of which they are part and who are subject to all the social pressures and common sense that are part of those societies.

What, then, do biogeographical ancestry groups have to do with the sociohistorical concept of race? In answering this question, we first have to remember that the concept of race continues to be persistently associated with biological difference. As our brief history of the modern and Western concept of race has demonstrated, race has long been tied—in the way it has been understood and represented—to inherited biological difference. As noted above, there was a period in the twentieth century during which cultural critics, anthropologists, and other behavioral scientists interrupted that persistent association in order to highlight the role that ideas and practices play in creating different populations of people. But perhaps because human genetics and race are both so poorly understood by most people, the advances in population genetics discussed above have tended to reinforce the association between race and biology. The resulting confusion poses a serious challenge for scholars of race and ethnicity interested in understanding the workings of race as a significant social identity category.

So is race biological? On a scale of 1 to 10, with 10 being "yes" and 1 being "no," the answer would be about a 2. It is true that humans are biological beings. Moreover, it is clear that some aspects of physical appearance that traditionally have been used to assign racial group membership (including skin color, hair texture, and limb shape) are biologically inherited. These aspects of a person's physical appearance are part of what make up her *phenotype* (the measurable or observable features of her organism). However, a person's phenotype does not derive in a clear or obvious way from her *genotype* (all of the genes present in her organism). Other environmental factors (e.g., the availability and the quality of food, cultural ideas and practices, and the presence or absence of stress, trauma, disease, or environmental pollution) all interact with her genotype to make up what other people might observe or measure as her phenotype. Furthermore, nonvisible biological traits (e.g., blood factors, enzymes) that vary independently of visible physical features also contribute significantly to an individual's phenotype (Feldman, this volume). What this means is that phenotypic features that are sometimes assumed to be racial characteristics (e.g., a person's height, sickle cell anemia) may have *something* to do with biogeographical ancestry—but they also may be greatly affected—even caused—by diet, social behaviors, or some other environmental factor that is independent of the continental origin(s) of a person's ancestors. Scholars of race and ethnicity need to grapple seriously with the way race comes into being in connection with visible human biological difference.

Finally, *race* differs from *biogeographical ancestry groups* in that the concept of race comes loaded with a great deal of ideological baggage. Consider this: if a man has blue eyes and blond hair, and if he is successful according to some standard measure of our society, then many people will probably assume that the same genes that produced his blue eyes and his blond hair are also responsible for producing the specific behavioral and intellectual characteristics that made him successful. This is the fallacy of biological thinking in general, and an example of doing race in particular: we see the man's pale skin and blue eyes and know that they are biologically caused; then we observe his material success and assume that it is similarly biologically caused; we conclude, mistakenly, that everything a person is or becomes is a direct result of his racial identity. The logical fallacy of biological thinking causes people to err when they look exclusively to a person's genotype for answers to their questions about differences in people's behaviors or capacities. The human genotype simply does not have all the answers to the kinds of questions about individuals and societies that people want to ask.

Examining the origins, associations, and uses of the concept of race helps us to understand why the recent ability of scientists to pinpoint the continent(s) of origin of individuals' recent ancestors has contributed to the general, if mistaken, impression that race is a biological thing located inside people's bodies. It is crucial to remember, then, that even though race is realized in connection with visible human difference, it is not something that can be located in our genes or examined in isolation from the environmental factors around it. As an organizing feature of our society, the concept of race has much more powerful effects on people's lives than any set of genetic markers will ever have.

The Individual Is the Source of All Thought, Feeling, and Action

Independence and the Importance of the Individual

The second assumption that underlies all our conversations about and reactions to events involving race and ethnicity is the assumption that the individual is the source of all thought, feeling, and action. Indeed, understanding the role of and the challenges posed by race in the United States depends on the recognition that our society is fundamentally individualist in character (Bellah et al. 1985). In core values and beliefs—in legal and political systems, in educational and care-taking practices, and even in interpersonal relationships—U.S. Americans have a certain idea of what it means to be a person. People are independent individuals who are free from the constraints of history, other people, and society. According to this way of thinking, each individual has her own preferences, motives, attitudes, abilities, and goals—all of which guide and motivate her thoughts, feelings, and actions. As an autonomous being, she holds the reins, captains the ship, or is behind the wheel of the Prius that is her life. Ideally, she is minimally beholden to those around her; other people can influence her, but she should not allow them too much control over her behavior. She is the main beneficiary of her actions, and she alone is responsible for them.

In fact, the independent model of the self is so thoroughly inscribed in American society that we often do not realize that there are other models of what it means to be a person. Research shows that outside middle-class North American contexts, there are other ways of being a self; being a person with agency does not require an independent model. In some societies, for example, people are not viewed as independent entities separate from others. Rather, they are viewed as fundamentally *inter*dependent and responsive to the expectations and requirements of others. From the perspective of an interdependent model of the self, the individual is not alone responsible for his or her behavior; instead, people bear some responsibility both for themselves and for the others with whom they are related or connected. (Markus and Kitayama 1991, 2003).

Importantly, the independent model of the self is more than just a set of values that Americans hold. It is deeply ingrained in our daily lives: it shapes how we raise and educate our children, the way we interact with each other at work, and what we do on the weekends or when we retire. A good way to imagine its significance is to think of it as a "to do" list that organizes the flow of everyday American life. For example, American parents love and care for their dependent newborn babies, but they do so with the anticipation that their babies will grow up, leave home, and be responsible for themselves. To encourage and foster independence, parents (especially in middle-class European American contexts) put infants in their own cribs and sometimes in their own rooms. Very often, the events recorded in their child's baby book are milestones on the child's path toward self-determination: rolling over, sitting and standing up, and walking. Even everyday admonishments reinforce an American child's sense that she should march to the beat of her own drum: "If everyone jumped off the cliff, would you?" "Just be yourself, don't worry about other people." Parents urge their children to "stand up for themselves" on the playground, and to fight back when a classmate bothers them. Beyond home and school, many other institutions of society also stress the values of independence and uniqueness. For example, advertisers use these themes to sell every type of product. Gerber touts its baby foods as "A good source of iron, zinc, and independence." Tommy Girl calls its cologne "A declaration of independence," while Gap markets its widely appealing yet wholly unremarkable clothing basics with the command, "Individualize." Perpetuating the lone hero model of history, Apple paired famous artists, scientists, and activists—for example Einstein, Picasso, César Chávez, the Dalai Lama—with the American mantra "Think Different" (Fiske et al. 1998; Shweder et al. 2006).

People who live within a society organized according to the independent model of the self do tend to experience themselves as autonomous. They see themselves as in control of their actions and imagine that they should be relatively free from other people or institutions. Although being an independent self is a learned way of being, the socialization process is often invisible. As a result, those who learn the independent way of being a person often believe that it is the good, the natural, and the only way to be a person.

The idea of the independent and self-determining individual is central not just to U.S. Americans' daily lives but also to our systems of government, law, finance, and health care. Many of our most treasured ideals—freedom, equality, self-governance, the pursuit of happiness—are based on the idea of free individuals who have the right to govern themselves and to pursue the achievement of their full potential. The idea of the autonomous individual is an idea that underlies the "reasonable man" of the law, the "rational self-interested actor" of economics, and the "authentic self" of counseling and clinical psychology (Schwartz 1986).

Origins of the Independent Model of the Self

What is the origin of the independent view of the person? The idea of the self-determining individual can be found in various philosophical systems throughout the world at different points in history, but its rise to prominence in the West emerged from a confluence of historical, philosophical, religious, political, and sociological forces that began in the

late fifteenth century and continues until the present day. This confluence is referred to in some scholarly circles as "modernity/coloniality"
to account for the link between European modernization, imperialism,
and the founding of a hierarchical system of racial dominance (Mignolo
2005; Quijano 2000). Although modernity/coloniality is a notoriously
difficult concept to define, a useful way to think of it is as a widespread
socioeconomic and cultural changeover in ideas and practices that profoundly challenged traditional sources of authority and upset conventional understandings of how humans are able to know the natural
world. So, for example, when in 1492 Europeans encountered the continent of what is now known as America, they literally had to remap
their known world. When in 1514 Copernicus introduced the idea that
the earth revolved around the sun, his observations radically upset the
common wisdom (not to mention the Church doctrine) that the earth
was the center of the universe (Copernicus and Wallis 1995). When
in 1517, Martin Luther claimed that man could have a personal relationship with God without the priest as an intermediary, he spawned
a movement that eventually posed a radical challenge to the dominance
of the Catholic Church and its rigidly hierarchical structure (Luther
[1517] 2004). Descartes famously declared in 1637 that "I think, therefore
I am," thus asserting his own thought as authoritative for proving his
existence (Descartes [1637] 2006). John Locke, the seventeenth-century
British philosopher, encouraged individuals to use reason rather than
accept the dictates of authority or hold beliefs unsupported by empirical
evidence. In Locke's view, individuals existed prior to society; he saw
societies as made up of autonomous individuals who enter into a social
contract with other individuals to protect their right to self-determination (Locke [1689] 2005).

The idea of the self-determining and self-knowing individual was thus
enabled by the gradual shift in authority from God (or the King as God's
representative on Earth) to Man that occurred during the Age of Reason
and the Enlightenment. What gradually emerged in Western thought
was a picture of the independent individual who could know the world
through his own observation, imagine a kind of social mobility that was
previously impossible, and read and interpret the scriptures according to
his own conscience. This idea of the individual has had a profound impact
on Europeans' and Americans' imagination of themselves and their place
in the universe; it is still very powerful today. It is so broadly and deeply
ingrained in our way of life that it is often hard for us to imagine how it
could be otherwise (Fiske et al. 1998; Markus and Kitayama 1991).

One Cannot Be an Individual by Oneself

There is a problem, however, with the admittedly powerful (world-shaping, civilization-crafting) idea of the autonomous individual. The liberal individualism that abstracts and separates the individual from society makes sense of the practices of a capitalist society (D'Agostino 1998; Plaut 2002), but it can also obscure the reality that all people—including middle-class Americans—exist within, and as members of, various communities. Yes, people are individuals; but they are not *only* individuals. People everywhere live out their lives in families, neighborhoods, schools, teams, clubs, workplaces, and places of worship. Their thoughts, feelings, and actions are influenced by the thoughts, feelings, and actions of others (Asch 1952). In fact, a significant evolutionary advantage of humans is that they enter a world filled with the ideas, goods, and institutions of those who have gone before them; they do not have to build the world anew. From a baby's very first moment of awareness, she is saturated with the sounds, touch, sight, and rhythms of those around her. She is dependent on others for food, care, and company—if she is left alone, she will either die or fail to develop into a mature adult person. As a result, all people form bonds with other people; they love, help, depend on, learn from, teach, and compare themselves to those around them. They experience the world through other people's images, ideas, and words. Becoming a person is a social project; in a very real way, people make each other up.

Because the idea of the autonomous individual is both powerful and appealing, accepting the notion that people are fundamentally *interdependent* can be difficult for many people who have grown up in the United States to accept. Nevertheless, no matter how tough or strong or self-reliant a person is, no one is completely autonomous. Consider this: when a person is first learning to speak, she does not invent the language. She does not make up the words or create the grammatical logic. Rather, she learns the words and acquires the logic of the language(s) she is exposed to; she uses them in conventional ways so that others will understand her. (Even if she becomes an avant-garde writer and experiments or plays games with the languages in which she is writing, she will still have to learn the linguistic conventions in order to bend them.) So, whether she is aware of it or not (and typically she is not), she is eating, dressing, walking, as well as thinking and feeling and acting not in neutral or basic or universal human ways but in culturally particular ways. Virtually all of her behavior is dependent on and requires others. It is not possible to be a neutral, ahistorical, or asocial individual or to achieve an identity of any type without the contribution of others. People's thoughts, feelings, language, and actions are always influenced by (and also influence) the thoughts, feelings, language, and actions of others—even when their philosophy or ideology tells them they should not be so influenced. To say that other people constitute the self is not, however, to say that other people wholly determine the self. People are indeed individuals; they are intentional agents who can—within the constraints allowed by the social context—resist and contest the views of others.

In many other parts of the world (and outside a middle-class European American context), the reality of relatedness is more obvious. An interdependent model of self has long been prevalent in many of the cultures of East and South Asia, as well as in some minority communities within the United States (Doi 1973; Geertz 1973; Markus and Kitayama 1991; Marsella, Do Vos, and Hsu, 1985; Triandis 1995). From the perspective of an interdependent model of the self, people are understood to be inherently and fundamentally connected to others. It is not the individual alone but her relationship to family, clan, tribe, or work group that is the primary focus. It is a model of the self that stresses empathy, reciprocity, belongingness, kinship, hierarchy, loyalty, respect, politeness, and social obligations. People are expected to adjust to meet others' expectations and to work for the good of the relationship. Indeed, well-being comes not from being able to choose for oneself (as in a middle-class European American context) but rather from being part of relationships that are defined as good within the value-system of that society. For example, a Japanese mother does not typically ask for a child's preference but instead tries to determine what is best and then to arrange it. Punishing or reprimanding Japanese children often involves a threat to the relationship rather than a withholding of rights and privileges. Mothers might say, "I don't like children like you." Similarly, Chinese parents often use an explicitly evaluative, self-critical framework with their children. Parents in societies that put a premium on interdependence do not ignore their children's shortcomings or transgressions because the goal is to keep the children from losing their all-important relationships to others (Fiske et al. 1998).

Just as idea of the independent and self-determining individual is central to the basic practices and systems of U.S. Americans' daily lives, the idea of the interdependent and accommodating individual is central to the daily practices and systems of cultures in which interdependence is highly valued. In most East Asian preschools, for example, it is group achievement rather than individual achievement that is celebrated, and children are not tracked according to ability or singled out for special instruction (Stevenson and Stigler 1992). Schooling practices often place a great emphasis on learning to live in society, and teachers emphasize the importance of discerning how others are feeling. Similarly, advertisements in Japan use the deep cultural themes of relating to others and meeting expectations to connect products to desirable people—usually a Hollywood celebrity. For example, Brad Pitt swoons over coffee, while Cameron Diaz reveals that the secret to her success is an English school. In the United States, movie stars often avoid associating themselves with ordinary objects because doing so might seriously undermine their essential coolness and uniqueness. But these same movie stars routinely partner with Japanese corporations to promote ordinary Japanese products. In Japan, where the focus is more on relationships and less on attributes, the advertised products gain in popularity because they provide a tangible link to admired and desirable others.

In societies organized around the value of interdependence, being a human individual means understanding and accepting that people are fundamentally social beings (Fiske et al. 1998). Individual behavior—one's thoughts, feelings, and actions—is experienced and understood as the result of a person's actively attending and adjusting to others. In such contexts, autonomous individuals who insists on expressing their preferences are considered immature. If flexible adaptation to the demands of the situation is the goal, then cultivating the expectation and habit of choice is counterproductive. People who live in societies that emphasize interdependence are as unaware of how their thoughts, feelings, evaluations, plans, and actions are organized by interdependence as most U.S. Americans are unaware of how our lives are organized by independence. Organizing values like independence and interdependence are difficult for us to perceive; they are like the air that we breathe, noticeable only in its absence.

In a society like the United States—where individuality and independence are valued above almost all else—the key to understanding how and why race and ethnicity work the way they do is recognizing that people are not just individuals. Individuals are also always associated with other people and with groups; they are known to themselves and to others through significant social categories such as race, ethnicity, gender, or religion. As a result, their identities will necessarily be shaped by how others regard the social groups with which they are associated. So, people *are* individuals, but they *are* also Americans, women, Texans,

Muslims, African Americans, Stanford alumni, Europeans, Demo-crats, lawyers, artists, Ford factory workers, baby boomers, Christian Evangelists, and Blue State dwellers. Such social identities are highly mutable (some more than others) and can be shuffled by context and circumstance.

Though malleable and constantly changing in terms of their mean-ings and personal significance, however, identities are much more than just labels. Identities provide sets of interpretive frameworks for mak-ing sense of the world, for understanding the past and present, and for predicting the future. Which of a person's many identities will be most salient in any given situation—which will organize his or her experience in that case—will depend on the nature of the situation and the other people involved in it. In any given circumstance, being seen by others in terms of one's social identities (and in particular one's racial or ethnic identities) will have real and powerful consequences (e.g., Mohanty 1997; Moya 2002; Steele, Spencer, and Aronson 2002; Thomas 1923). In Section III of this essay, we return to what some of those consequences can be.

All Men Are Created Equal

Individuality and Equality and Doing Race

Intimately linked to the growing significance of the individual in the modern era was the new and radical idea of equality—that is, the idea that individuals are not only self-determining but they are also in some important ways equal to each other. This link—the one between indi-viduality and equality—requires particular attention in any attempt to understand why race is such an important part of American society. Like the two assumptions discussed above, the ideal that all men are cre-ated equal (and that they should have equal rights) is at the foundation of the American republic.

The idea of equality among individuals has roots in both ancient Greek and Hebrew traditions, but it became a more central and formative idea in the West with the advent of modernity/coloniality. Martin Luther's stand against the Church as the sole source of spiritual authority not only set the Protestant Reformation in motion but it also helped foster the modern liberal notion that free individuals are equal in their capacity to reason for themselves with no need of an intermediary. As Protestant notions of equal moral worth before God spread and were blended with Enlightenment ideals about secular authority, many Europeans began to envision a world of free and equal individuals who could govern themselves and determine their own futures (Taylor 1989). In the Declaration of the Rights of Man and Citizen, French revolutionaries declared, "Men are born, and always continue, free and equal in respect of their rights." Thomas Jefferson reflected the same Enlightenment thought when he wrote the Declaration of Independence: "We hold these truths to be self-evident, that all men are created equal, that they are endowed by their Creator with certain unalienable Rights, that among these are Life, Liberty and the pursuit of Happiness." Jefferson's forceful declaration, enshrined in what was to become a sacred American text, was antimonarchial and antihereditary. From this perspective, an individual did not just inherit his status. Rather, the individual was endowed, by a power higher than any king, with the essence of equality. The individual was then responsible for making himself; he was to be the author of his own earthly existence.

The inspirational and powerful Enlightenment ideals about individuality and equality that were reflected in the political revolutionary documents of the day and diffused throughout the West were also, however, deeply at odds with the reality of social and political life. Different groups of people lived in radically unequal circumstances and were treated unequally by a range of institutions. The existence of massive economic and political inequality, including slavery, in the midst of the rhetoric of equality required an explanation, and one ready tool was the concept of biological race. Perhaps, the reasoning went, some people were not equal to others because they were somehow inherently (that is, biologically) different.

History shows that as the heady ideas of individuality and equality developed and spread, so did the practice of using race as a system to rank humans. In fact, at the time of the signing of the Declaration of Independence, equality among individuals was meant to apply only to people of a certain race (white), class (property owners), and gender (male). At the founding of the U.S. republic, those people who had been brought by force from West Africa—who made up one-fifth of the U.S. population— were held as slaves. The U.S. Constitution counted slaves, for the purpose of political representation, as three-fifths of a person, even as it completely excluded Indians who lived outside the jurisdiction of the new republic from the imagined community.

Given the disconnect between the rhetoric of equality in documents like the Declaration of Independence and the reality of slavery and unequal conditions of life in countries like the United States, the Enlightenment appeal to the equality of mankind set in motion a fervent debate about what was meant by the claim that "all men are created equal." Does the term "men" refer to all humans? Is any one man equal to any other? If we grant that all men are equal before God, do we have to grant that they are all equal before the State? Even assuming that all men are equal in moral worth—does that mean they are all equal in talents? If not, then which talents are most important? What about women? Are they created equal? Equal to other women, or equal to men? How do we even measure equality? Should the measure of equality be one of opportunity, capacity, or outcome? Who will make these decisions, and how will they be made? These are not idle questions; they preoccupied the minds of our country's architects and founders and they continue to occupy us to this very day.

Our country's founders came up with a set of temporary answers and working solutions to the kinds of questions articulated above. Their temporary answers served the needs of the day, yet their solutions have had profound consequences for the history of race relations in this country. For example, Thomas Jefferson—the man who penned the phrase "all men are created equal"—was a slave owner who struggled to reconcile the ideals of equality and difference in his own personal life and for the country. In his *Notes on the State of Virginia* (1781), for instance, Jefferson showed that he admired Native Americans:

> I may challenge the whole orations of Demosthenes and Cicero, and of any more eminent orator, if Europe has furnished more eminent, to produce a single passage, superior to the speech of Logan, a Mingo chief, to Lord Dunmore, when governor of this state. ([1781]1995, 62)

By comparing Native Americans to the icons of Western civilization and arguing that they were brave, kind, and affectionate, in addition to being superior orators, Jefferson represents them in this passage as being equal in capacity to white men.

As Jefferson's later actions revealed, however, he did not consider superior speech-making sufficient to qualify Indians as ideal citizen-subjects of the new nation. When the U.S. colonies were expanding into Indian territory some two decades later, Jefferson was unsympathetic to Native Americans' situation. In his Second Inaugural Address, on March 4, 1805, Jefferson showed his frustration with what he saw as Native Americans' stubborn refusal to move from a "primitive" and collectivist way of life to an "enlightened" and individualist way of life:

These persons inculcate a sanctimonious reverence for the customs of their ancestors; that whatsoever they did must be done through all time; that reason is a false guide, and to advance under its counsel in their physical, moral, or political condition is perilous innovation; that their duty is to remain as their Creator made them, ignorance being safety and knowledge full of danger; in short, my friends, among them also is seen the action and counteraction of good sense and of bigotry. ([1805] 2001)

Along with Jefferson's frustration came a willingness to remove those Indians who would not assimilate to European American norms and values. Moreover, his attack on the "customs" of the Native Americans in this passage reveals that he is unaware of how his own "customs" shaped his own particular way of interpreting the situation. He used the concept of race—what he defined as an "inculcated" difference in mentality and way of life—to justify Native Americans' removal and mistreatment. Many others, like Jefferson, also found reasons to explain why some people could not or should not receive equal treatment. Scientific systems of ranking groups of people according to race were useful for this purpose and gained in popularity as the need to rationalize inequality and perpetuate exploitative socioeconomic systems became more pressing.

Doing Inequality While Claiming Equality: An Example

Many of the significant events of the next two centuries of American history are a direct result of the attitudes, norms, and organizational structures of a society that was struggling with the question of whom to include within the imagined community of U.S. American society. For example, in 1857, an enslaved man by the name of Dred Scott sued for his freedom. Scott was taken by his owner to a newly acquired territory of the United States—what is now Missouri—where slavery was illegal. In the Supreme Court decision of *Scott v. Sandford*, Chief Justice Roger B. Taney argued that slaves were "so far inferior that they had no rights which the white man was bound to respect" (1857, 407). We can clearly perceive, here, that the American legal system was doing race by justifying the continuing inequality between blacks and other Americans. The *Scott v. Sandford* case reflected a growing conflict between the slaving-owning, plantation-rich southern states and the northern states where many opposed slavery and its expansion into the new territories. This conflict culminated in the U.S. Civil War.

The eventual defeat of the South and the freeing of the slaves with the passage of the Thirteenth Amendment in 1865 did little to remedy the United States' problems with slavery and inequality. For a combination of economic, political, and social reasons, many Southerners continued to resist the idea of blacks as free and equal people. Such resistance was significant because at the end of the war, 95 percent of blacks lived in the South and made up one-third of the population of the South; by comparison, only 1 percent of the black population lived in the North (McPherson 1996). Many state and local laws in the South included a set of so-called "Black Codes" that prohibited blacks from voting, serving on juries, traveling freely, or working in many occupations. The Black Codes so clearly violated the ideal of equality enshrined in the U.S. Constitution that many Americans fought to overturn them. Finally, in 1868 with the passage of the Fourteenth Amendment, the U.S. Constitution was amended to overrule the decision of *Scott v. Sandford*. The Fourteenth Amendment guarantees due process and equal protection under the law for all citizens. It broadened the definition of citizenship so that constitutional rights were finally accorded to former enslaved people and their descendents.

While the Fourteenth Amendment would eventually have far-reaching societal consequences, nearly a century passed before federal law guaranteed these rights. The initial reaction to the fourteenth Amendment by many whites who were opposed to black equality was the creation of a vast new set of practices, policies, and laws. These laws, referred to as Jim Crow laws, were rooted in a presumption of inherent white moral and intellectual superiority.[2] Between 1876 and 1965 in many southern and border states, Jim Crow laws mandated "separate but equal status" for whites and nonwhite racial groups (principally black, but also Mexican American in states like Texas). Jim Crow laws supported the segregation of neighborhoods, public schools, public transportation, restrooms, drinking fountains, swimming pools, and libraries.

In 1896, Jim Crow laws were challenged in the Supreme Court case of *Plessy v. Ferguson*. At that point, the Court held that the idea of separate but equal facilities for whites and blacks did not violate the Fourteenth Amendment (*Plessy v. Ferguson* 1896). Despite the legal justification for these laws, enforced segregation between whites and nonwhites did not result in equal facilities but instead served to maintain and extend

---

2 The name Jim Crow marks the deceptive nature of these laws and refers to a minstrel show character from the early nineteenth century that was typically performed by a white actor wearing black makeup.

inequality. For example, schools built for blacks and Mexicans during Reconstruction and the first half of the twentieth century were massively underfunded, poorly constructed, and inadequately maintained. These practices had the effect of further cementing the inequality between whites and nonwhite racial groups.

Thus, for almost a century, the Black Codes and Jim Crow laws structured social life and ensured a strict separation between whites and blacks. Even in the North, where such laws were not instituted, there was virtually no racial integration; separation between the races was maintained by a set of informal codes and practices of exclusion. Given the strict separation between races, as well as the developing debate during the 1920s and on through the 1960s on the biological basis of race and intelligence, it is hardly surprising that many whites continued to believe what their forebears had believed since the founding of the Republic—that whites were essentially superior to all other races. It was not until 1954, with the *Brown v. Board of Education* Supreme Court ruling, that school segregation was declared unconstitutional (1954). Invoking the Fourteenth Amendment, the Supreme Court declared that separate schools were inherently unequal and that they denied black children equal educational opportunities. Some ten years later, the Civil Rights Act of 1964 and the Voting Rights Act of 1965 overturned the remaining Jim Crow laws (United States Congress House Committee on the Judiciary 1981).

All of American history has been similarly shaped by efforts to resolve the contradiction between an ideology that emphasized equality, and the reality of a hierarchy in which some individuals were not counted among those deserving of equality and so not worthy to control their own fates. In the example above, we have detailed the case at some length for African Americans to show how the ideal of equality has been paired with structures and practices that generated inequality. We could tell a somewhat similar story with respect to Mexican Americans, Puerto Ricans, Japanese Americans, Chinese Americans, Filipina/os, American Indians, and other minority groups (Takaki 1993).

Color-blindness: An Inadequate Solution to Inequality

With the passage of the Civil Rights Act and the Voting Rights Act in 1964 and 1965, respectively, legal barriers to formal racial equality were overturned. The civil rights legislation marked a milestone in the history of American race relations at the same time that it ushered in a tumultuous era in U.S. society—one that has been instrumental in shaping our current race relations. Once those two bills were signed into law, U.S. citizens of all races across the country could, for the first time, claim equal rights and equal protection before the law. In the wake of these events, many in the United States believed that our country had turned a corner and could finally live up to its founding ideal of individual equality.

There were, however, a few remaining difficulties. Extending formal legal equality to blacks, Mexican Americans, Puerto Ricans, Japanese Americans, Chinese Americans, Filipina/os, and American Indians could not, by itself, reduce the massive social and economic inequality that had been created and maintained between these groups and the majority European-origin population over approximately two hundred years. In the mid-twentieth-century United States, people associated with U.S. racial minority groups were mostly poor, undereducated, and underemployed. They held either no or relatively little property; they had long been excluded from networks of power and privilege; and they were often devalued, disrespected, and despised by many of those European Americans who held the keys to societal inclusion. While Irish, Italian, and German Americans had all similarly struggled as immigrants (or as the children of immigrants) to be accepted as full Americans following their arrival in the United States, they had the significant advantage of having European biogeographical ancestry (Ignatiev 1995). While they were certainly not immediately regarded as equal to the descendents of the early British, French, and Dutch settlers, they nevertheless held a higher rank in the racial hierarchy than did those people who were associated with non-European racial and ethnic groups. So, while the extension of formal legal equality to non-European-origin Americans represented a significant step in the path toward racial equality in the United States, there remains a long way to go on the road to real social and economic equality for racial minorities.

In the wake of the civil rights legislation, a debate soon erupted about the best way to resolve the newly reapparent contradiction between the ideal of equality and existing inequality. Throughout the twentieth century, the dominant American narrative regarding the treatment of cultural and racial difference was the metaphor of the "melting pot." Native-born European Americans and European immigrants alike shared a strong expectation that full and equal participation required immigrants to "melt" into U.S. society by taking on the customs and linguistic traditions of the European American middle and upper classes.

The melting pot story resolved the equality/difference paradox by presuming that only those who successfully melted into the United States mainstream and became indistinguishable from the people in power merited equality. In this view, those who did not conform to white middle-class American values and ways of life were responsible for their unequal plight. It did not consider that many people *could not* conform—either because they were actively excluded on the basis of race or because they lacked the economic or cultural capital to do so.

Most of the activists who were involved in the various civil rights movements of the mid-twentieth century (e.g., Black Power movement, Chicano movement, United Farm Workers, Young Lords, American Indian movement, Asian American movement) were highly critical of the melting pot metaphor. They pointed out that the story behind it had been told with European-origin groups in mind. They argued that the narrative did not work for the groups with which they were associated, either because they had been involuntary immigrants (e.g., blacks) or they were several-generation U.S. citizens (e.g., Mexican Americans and Asian Americans). Most minority activists were not, in other words, immigrants; they were citizens of the United States, even though they had not always been recognized as such. Moreover, people who were perceived to have non-European racial origins and thus were racially nonwhite—that is blacks, Mexican Americans, Puerto Ricans, Japanese Americans, Chinese Americans, Filipina/os, and American Indians—did not so easily melt into European American middle-class anonymity. In response to what they saw as the failure of the melting pot metaphor and as a marking and rejection of the unequal treatment to which their ancestors had been subjected for generations, the civil rights activists forwarded what was then considered a new and radical idea. They refused the expectation that to be full participants in the social and political order they needed to assimilate culturally and linguistically to a white middle-class American way of being in the world. Instead, they demanded respect for and recognition of their particular racial and ethnic identities and declared that the new era of race relations meant that nonwhite peoples in the United States would no longer have to occupy the place of second-class citizens (Ture and Hamilton [1967] 1992; Muñoz 1989; Smith and Warrior 1997; Louie and Omatsu 2001). It was at this point that the *I'm ___ and I'm proud* conversation came forcefully into being among U.S. American racial minority groups.

Adherents of the older melting pot narrative responded to minority claims for recognition by arguing that we should be color-blind—that the best way to foster the development of a newly integrated society would be to ignore racial and ethnic differences. They argued that identity movements such as the Black Power movement, American Indian movement, or the Chicana/o movement were divisive and declared that the strength of the United States comes from the forging of one uniquely American identity out of many different types of people. Once legal barriers to equality had been removed, they contended, the best strategy would be to ignore the differences that had previously served to mark some people as full citizens and others not. Advocates of color-blindness claimed that to pay attention to group-based differences, whether in negative *or* positive ways, would be to stereotype or pigeonhole people as well as to deny people their uniqueness and curtail their freedom to be individuals. They figured that being "blind" to race was a recommitment to the founding principle of individual equality, as well as a morally good way to be.

The motivation behind color-blindness has been in many cases a worthy one. For many people, color-blindness describes the idea of trying to treat all individuals the same regardless of their racial or ethnic associations. Nevertheless, as a strategy of race relations, color-blindness could not begin to undo the inequalities that had, for so long, been built into the institutions, policies, representations and everyday social interactions of U.S. American life. A serious flaw in the ideology of color-blindness is its assumption that race and ethnicity are merely superficial characteristics of a person and that they should not matter to how individual people are seen or treated. A color-blind stance is reflected in comments like "I treat everyone the same," or "Race doesn't matter to me," or "People are basically all the same." In conversation, a claim of color-blindness often takes the form of suggesting that while there was some unfairness in the system in the past, legal equality is now a reality, so racial and ethnic differences ought to be ignored. Thus, the ideology of color-blindness ignores interdependence and participates in the classic confusion between the "ought" and the "is."

The impulse to treat everyone the same is laudable and has the merit of rejecting the faulty assumption that race is a biological thing. Yet, in doing so, it relies too much on the problematic assumption that the individual is the source of all thought, feeling, and action. A color-blind ideology does not consider that people's thoughts, feelings, and actions—not to mention their opportunities and resources—are often greatly shaped by their racial or ethnic group associations and by others' views of these associations. Because color-blindness does nothing to counteract the effects of ongoing group-based advantages and disadvantages, it can (and has) become a way to avoid or stall the racial transformation of U.S. society (Markus, Steele, and Steele 2000). As our further discussion of how race is done in the United States in Section III shows, simply avoiding the topics of race or ethnicity does nothing to counteract the real effects they have on people's everyday lives.

Why Americans Are So Uncomfortable Talking about Race

At the beginning of this essay, we noted that although race is a pervasive presence in our everyday lives, talking about it makes many of us anxious and uncomfortable. Now that we have reviewed the history of racial formation in the United States and examined the philosophical assumptions underlying our country's everyday racial realities, we can propose some answers for why Americans are so uncomfortable talking about race.

First, race is disturbing to many of us because we view it as a biological thing; we believe that race is predictive of people's differing capacities and characters and that a person's race can be determined according to a scientifically based system of classification. This faulty but very common view of race is what undergirds the belief (or in some cases, the fear) that the disadvantages that come with being nonwhite in U.S. society— whether those disadvantages be physiological, cognitive, or cultural— might be, in fact, insurmountable by individual effort.

Second, race makes us uncomfortable because many assume that the individual is the source of all thought, feeling, and action. Given our strong faith in the power of the individual, the idea that a person might be unavoidably associated with other people who share that individual's gender, religion, race, or ethnicity is not always a welcome idea. Historically, such associations have been the foundation upon which group-based structures of oppression and inequality have been built. Because we value so highly the ideal of individual equality, we understandably want to reject anything that interferes with the achievement of the individualist ideal.

Both possibilities—that individuals might not be able to surmount the disadvantages of being nonwhite in U.S. society and that they might not be able to free themselves from their group-based associations—can be upsetting. The idea that a person might be inescapably associated with groups of people or histories of oppression with which she does not personally identify seems to undermine one of this country's most cherished narratives, the one known as the American Dream. This story says that no matter who people are or where they come from, if they work hard enough, they can achieve whatever they want to in the United States. The legend of the United States as the land of opportunity has been repeated in countless variations in our literature, movies, theater, music, and government documents and proclamations. It is such a powerful narrative that it gives hope to people from all over the world; it has been, and it continues to be, the motivating story for millions of global migrants who set out for our shores or our borders every year.

The American Dream was powerfully invigorated with the election of Barack Obama to the presidency of the United States. As the son of a Kenyan father and raised by his working-class white grandmother and single white mother in both Indonesia and Hawaii, Obama's meteoric rise to the leadership of the free world could not have been easily foretold. Apart from being a person with visible African ancestry, Obama was a hard-working scholarship student whose birthright did not include access to a ready-made political dynasty and whose childhood and adolescence did not place him in proximity to a ready-made political machine. For all these reasons, the prospect of his election to the presidency seemed, initially, to be unlikely at best and perhaps impossible.

With Obama's electoral victory and his inauguration to the presidency, this country's everyday racial realities appear primed to undergo some sort of change. The fact that he won may indicate either that many U.S. Americans no longer have entrenched racial prejudices or that they now see race and ethnicity as *one* aspect of an individual's identity—one that might be considered but that no longer trumps every other consideration (e.g., wisdom, ability to lead, moral character). The 2008 U.S. presidential election made one thing very clear: the people of the United States desired some sort of change. What is less obvious is the nature of the desired change and to what extent it reflects or prefigures a major shift in U.S. race relations.

Barack Obama's election to the presidency provides the people of the United States with the opportunity to re-commit to our founding ideal of equal opportunity and to change the meanings associated with having non-European ancestry in the United States. We need to be careful, though, to understand the pace as well as the process of real racial transformation; it is unrealistic to imagine that we can change the racial landscape of this country all at once. As tempting as it might be, it would be irresponsible to allow the Barack Obama story to conceal the reality that the activities involved in doing race—noticing that people in other groups are different from people in one's own group, devaluing the other groups relative to one's own, creating and maintaining institutional structures and practices that advantage one's own group at the expense of the other groups, and then promoting ideas and narratives that justify the resulting inequality in a way that makes it seem natural— were present at the founding of our country and remain with us today. This country has more than two hundred years' worth of inequality-generating and inequality-reinforcing institutions, ideas, and practices that support a European racial hierarchy. Complicating the task, the concept of race no longer belongs solely to the West. The globalization of the world that began in earnest with the making of the modern world system facilitated the movement of ideas and practices along with the movement of material goods and financial capital. The concept of race has traveled well and has taken on geographically and culturally specific manifestations as it has combined with preexisting local traditions of social hierarchy.

Just as the playing field was not leveled with the passage of the civil rights legislation, so it is not leveled with the election of President Obama. The two problematic assumptions—that race is a biological thing, and that the individual is the source of all thought, feeling, and action—remain at the heart of this country's numerous inequality-producing institutions, ideas, and practices. Consequently, to really level the playing field, we need to reshape almost all of our existing institutions. And we need to do so while taking into account that race and ethnicity are not biological facts about people, and that all individuals are always known to themselves and to others through significant social categories including race, ethnicity, gender, or religion. In addition, we need to change the character of everyday social relations, both formal and informal, between people of different ancestry groups before real change can occur. In the words of Justice Harry Blackmun: "In order to get beyond racism, we must first take account of race. There is no other way. And in order to treat some persons equally, we must treat them differently" (*Regents of the University of California v. Bakke* 1978, 407).

The task facing us now is to fully take account of race. This involves identifying the wide range of inequality-producing institutions and practices that contribute to the way people in this country do race—often in unintended ways. We need to study how race emerges over time and across space in the most minute, and even banal, interactions that people who are phenotypically or culturally different have with each other.

Understanding race as a doing means acknowledging that, yes, we are biological beings, and that biology accounts for some differences in how we look (hair texture, skin color, facial features). But it also means recognizing that biology cannot account for more significant phenotypic differences involving health, temperaments, and capacities. More important to who we become—how we think, feel, and act—are the environments we create and by which we are shaped. In the next section, we sketch out some of the most important new research about race and ethnicity. This research is crucial to identifying the inequality-producing institutions and practices that contribute to the way we all do race.

III
DOING RACE—ALL OF US, EVERY DAY

Most people do not get up in the morning and make a conscious decision to discriminate against someone else on the basis of race. Although some people are intentionally discriminatory, very often we do race without a clear awareness of the negative consequences for ourselves or for others. As illustrated by the racial iceberg in Section II (Figure i.3), there is a lot underneath the surface when it comes to the way race works in our country. At least some of those unseen historical events, political movements, institutions, narratives, and social practices will have to be understood, and many will have to be transformed, before all people's life chances are free from the negative constraints of race.

Race, as defined in Section I, is a complex system of ideas and practices regarding how some visible characteristics of human bodies such as skin color, facial features, and hair texture relate to people's character, intellectual capacity, and patterns of behavior. It is a relational system that comes into being through the interactions between individual people, and through individuals' interactions with institutions that are set up in ways that—purposely or inadvertently—do race. As suggested in Sections I and II, our environments are crucially arranged by institutions—schools, courts, news sources, banks, legislatures, prisons, city councils, hospitals—that have been created over time through the assumptions and actions of others. Such institutions both inherit and produce ideas and practices involving race and thus have a lot to do with keeping racial inequality alive (Eberhardt and Fiske 1998; Sidanius, Levin, and Pratto 1998).

Among the most pervasive ideas that animate our institutions are stereotypes about various racial and ethnic groups. These stereotypes are often so entrenched in everyday life that they form the very lenses through which we see the world. For example, while most U.S. Americans endorse the ideals of integration and racial equality, well over 50 percent of whites still rate blacks and Latina/os as less intelligent and more prone to violence than whites. Well over two-thirds rated blacks and Latina/os as actually preferring to be supported by welfare (Bobo 2004). A recent study of five- to seven-year-old white children from a diverse community in Texas revealed that these stereotypes are picked up early in life. When asked, "How many white people are mean?" the children responded, "almost none." When asked, "How many black people are mean?" they answered, "some" or "a lot" (Bronson and Merryman 2009).

People who are not subject to such stereotypes are often unaware of how powerful and pervasive they are, while those who are subject to the stereotypes are much more aware of how their lives are affected by them. Part of the experience of racialized minority individuals in the United States is living with the threat that negative stereotypes will be applied to them in any situation (Steele 1992, also this volume). Nevertheless—and however much we might want to—none of us can live outside the ideas, practices, and institutions that make up our society (Hames-García 2004; Fiske et al. 1998). As we go to school, rent an apartment, read the newspaper, use the Internet, pay our bills, and so on, the ideas and practices promoted by these various institutions strongly shape our behavior. People often do race unknowingly and unintentionally just by participating in a world that comes prearranged according to certain racial categories.

The imprint of the ideas and practices promoted by the institutions we live among can be tracked by noting some habits of thought (what social psychologists call "implicit associations") that are common to people who live in the United States. For example, many people in this country associate "American" with "white." Similarly, people with all types of racial and ethnic associations connect "white" with "good," and "black" with "bad" (Nosek et al. 2007; Devos and Banaji 2005). These associations are the basis for thoughts, feelings, and judgments that lead to actions with real consequences for people's lives. This can be the case even when we have no conscious desire or intention to discriminate on the basis of race.

Having a better understanding of how race works helps us to see why doing race in the twenty-first century can be so difficult to combat. To illustrate its pervasiveness, we provide below a variety of examples across many domains of life showing the ways that people—individually and institutionally, intentionally and unintentionally—do race to each other (and sometimes, even to themselves).

Employment

People's jobs or career are fundamental to their well-being. A job or career often determines how much money people make, how their time is spent, what kinds of other people they meet, where they live, whether they have health insurance, the quality of their health care, and where their children go to school. Employment is also fundamental to societal well-being. An effective democracy depends on the inclusion and participation of all types of people from many different groups in a healthy economic system. People who are not part of the economic system are unable to pay taxes or to spend money to stimulate the economy. They lack the resources, and sometimes the motivation, to participate in the democratic process.

Even though people associated with various racial and ethnic groups are no longer legally barred from particular occupations as they were under Jim Crow Laws, many occupations remain largely segregated by race, ethnicity, and gender. One major question facing policy makers concerns the cause of this segregation. Recent studies by economists and sociologists reveal a variety of subtle mechanisms at work. One study sent 5,000 similar résumés to 1,300 actual job postings in Chicago and Boston (Bertrand and Mullainathan 2004). Sometimes the résumés carried typically white-sounding names such as Emily Walsh or Greg Baker; sometimes they had more typically black-sounding names like Lakisha Washington and Jamal Jones. The names were drawn from a list indicating the frequency with which various ethnic groups used each name. Each job posting received four résumés, of which two were from highly qualified applicants, one black, one white, and two were from less qualified applicants, one black, one white. The résumés with the white names were 50 percent more likely to receive a callback response than those with black names. This was the case even when the résumés indicated comparable educational and occupational experience.

In a second study, focusing on low-wage workers in New York City, researchers posed as prospective job applicants in interview situations (Pager 2007; Pager and Western 2005). The results were striking. White interviewees received many more callbacks than black and Latina/o interviewees, even though all of them had been trained to present themselves in similar ways with equivalent credentials. Notably, a second phase of this study revealed that white applicants *with a felony conviction* were as likely to be called back as were black and Hispanic applicants *without* a criminal record. Moreover, while white applicants were

sometimes channeled toward jobs that offered supervisory or manage-
rial opportunities, black and Hispanic applicants tended to be offered
positions that required more manual labor, less customer contact, and
less authority than the job for which they had applied.

Bias in the workplace is not a problem solely for low- or middle-wage
workers. Surveys reveal that although blacks have gained access to many
professions from which they had been largely excluded—law, academia,
medicine, and business—the highest echelons of leadership, as well as
full-scale professional respect, remain elusive (Cose 1993). For example,
prestigious law firms are increasingly hiring black lawyers, but those
whom they hire rarely attain the rank of partner. The reasons this occurs
are not clear—sometimes the lawyers feel unsupported or undermined
and leave the law firm before coming up for partner; in other cases they
are passed over because they are perceived to be less effective at bringing
in new clients. President Obama's spectacular piercing of the political
glass ceiling is notable, but much has to be done before it can result in
the incorporation of blacks and other minority groups into leadership
positions across the board.

Housing

Almost half a century after passage of the Civil Rights Act, American
cities remain largely segregated along racial lines. Although disagreement exists about the exact causes of racial segregation, scholars and
journalists have recently amassed a great deal of evidence to suggest that
various people interacting in different ways with the U.S. housing system (e.g., as rental agents, loan officers, or prospective home buyers) may
all do race in a manner that maintains the segregation.

For example, a recent study reveals ongoing racial discrimination by
landlords and rental agents toward black prospective renters (Fischer
and Massey 2004). Building on previous studies suggesting that the
degree of racial discrimination varied according to a range of factors
including gender, class, and type of accent, researchers wanted to find
out if the location of the rental unit (i.e., geographic proximity to a predominantly black neighborhood) and the type of rental agent (i.e., private landlord or professional agent) made a difference to rental housing
access for blacks. The researchers conducted a series of phone-based
audit studies in Philadelphia in which they had six different callers—
one each male and female speaking white middle-class English, black-
accented English, or black English vernacular—call about the same

advertised rental unit. They examined what type of caller was more likely to gain access to rental housing. What they found was that *all* the factors (i.e., race, class, gender, location of the rental unit, and type of rental agent) made a difference regarding what type of renter was likely to get a positive response to an inquiry. Apparently, rental agents were making decisions about whether to call back, admit to the availability of the unit, and show the rental unit both on the basis of what the agent assumed about the prospective renter's gender, race, and class status from the sound of the renter's voice, and depending on where the unit was located. The study provides conclusive evidence that blacks—especially those who were perceived by private landlords to be lower class and female—have less access to rental units than whites. It also shows that rental agents are actively involved in doing race, whether or not they *intend* to act in prejudicial ways. Through the decisions they make, they end up determining where different kinds of people will live.

Rental housing is not the only realm in which racial housing discrimination occurs. In 2005, a watchdog report using federal data found that Latina/os who took out home loans in Santa Clara County, California, in the previous year ended up with high interest rates two to three times more often than whites or Asians (Lohse and Palmer 2005). Although Latina/os received only 14 percent of the total loans made in the county that year, they received fully 47 percent of the high-rate subprime loans. Because the type of loan and the rate of interest a homeowner is able to secure can affect the long-term cost of the loan by hundreds of thousands of dollars, the financial stakes of getting a fair loan can be high. Kevin Stein, associate director of the California Reinvestment Coalition, noted in the article: "If someone is paying even 1 percent more than they deserve, that's potentially tens of thousands of dollars of stripped equity that the homeowner no longer has available to finance a child's education, start a business, or prepare for retirement" (Lohse and Palmer 2005). According to the report, the racial disparities remained even for Latina/os with high incomes and solid credit. These same Latina/o borrowers were then disproportionately negatively affected when the nation's housing market began its downslide in 2006, as they found themselves with skyrocketing home payments and declining home values.

Race is not only done *to* homebuyers. In the process of choosing where they want to live, homebuyers can also do race to others. For example, a study designed to measure the effect of race on people's judgment of neighborhood quality found that white people rate neighborhoods with black or mixed-race residents more negatively than they do neighborhoods that have exclusively white residents (Krysan, Farley, and Couper 2008). Researchers conducted the random sample study by having each respondent privately view a brief video of several different neighborhoods, each of which showed several "residents" (actually actors) doing normal everyday things (getting the mail, talking to a neighbor, walking down the street). The interviewers instructed each respondent to rate the quality of the neighborhoods according to a range of factors including cost of housing, property upkeep, safety, future property value, and quality of schools. What researchers found was that whites consistently rated neighborhoods with black residents more negatively than those with white residents—quite apart from the actual characteristics of the homes located in the neighborhood and the number of amenities the neighborhood contained. The study showed that many whites hold a bias, of which many may be unaware, against neighborhoods with black residents, and so they are likely to make home-buying choices that contribute to ongoing racial segregation. Whether or not buying a home in a primarily white neighborhood might be justified as a wise economic decision because of the greater resale value of the house later on, it is still an example of how people do race in ways that maintain a segregated society.

Schooling

Public schools are the main vehicle for equal opportunity in America. Nearly all students and their parents believe education is linked to achievement and upward mobility in American society. Despite these widely shared beliefs in the transforming effects of education, and the good intentions of many people throughout the educational system, American schools are more racially segregated than ever before. Nationwide, only half of Latina/o, African American, and American Indian students graduate from high school, let alone begin college (Orfield 2004). Segregation in schools is linked, of course, to segregation in housing, but racial disparities in educational attainment can be traced to a variety of practices and strategies through which educators inadvertently do race even if they are committed to equality.

The ideas and practices that systematically divide students based on race and ethnicity are so woven into everyday practices that they are difficult to see. Take, for example, teachers' expectations and assessments. A recent study shows that teachers give higher grades to children of their own race (Ouazad 2008). In particular, white teachers give significantly lower assessments to black and Latina/o children. While this is unlikely to be a malicious bias, its consequences are enormous given the fact that more than 70 percent of teachers in American classrooms are white, middle class, and female (American Association of Colleges for Teacher Education 1999). The link between similarity to oneself and expectations of success serves as a pervasive and subtle mechanism of doing race.

Another example of doing race that does not require explicit awareness can be found in the explanations that are commonly given for student underachievement. Public and private conversations about the performance gap in schools are now part of daily life. When students do poorly in school, the typical question policy makers ask is whether students lack the capacity to do well, or whether they are unwilling to work. Given the pervasive notions of minority group intellectual inferiority that are still very prevalent in America, these seem to many people to be the right questions to ask (Tormala and Deaux 2006; Perry 2003). Yet the most obvious and empirically well-supported explanation for the performance gap is not a "capacity gap" or a "motivational gap," but rather an "opportunity gap" (Krysan and Lewis 2005). Study after study show that underperforming students are taught by teachers who have not received the highest quality training and who do not have access to the best curricular materials. Furthermore, the schools they attend are underfunded and in poor repair (Darling-Hammond, this volume). Given the demonstrated link between underperformance and lack of opportunity, the policy maker who asks the "capacity" question (Are these students less able, lazy, or uncaring?) without asking the "opportunity" question (Do these students have the resources they need?) is ignoring the root of the problem and doing race. The story about a grandmother from the rural South who is perplexed by the school's discussion of why students were underperforming helps illustrate this way of doing race. The grandmother noted that in her experience from years of farming, when the corn did not grow, no one asked what was the matter with the corn. Instead, they concerned themselves with the quality of the soil and the amount of rain (Ladson-Billings 1994)—the agricultural ecology.

Differences in the educational ecology—in how school environments are set up and resourced—are not always immediately obvious. For example, the proportion of black, Latina/o, and Native American high school graduates who go on to college is less than the proportion of white students. Why? What is the source of this inequality in educational attainment? Are black, Latina/o, and Native American students less motivated or interested in college? A recent California report reveals nonobvious differences in opportunity and in the educational environment. Students who take Advanced Placement (AP) or college-prep courses have the opportunity to be intellectually challenged, are better prepared for college-level courses, can earn college credits while in high school, and are looked on more favorably by college admissions officers. The problem is that schools with a higher percentage of students of color offer fewer college preparatory or AP courses than schools with mainly white students (Tomás Rivera Policy Institute 2004). Consequently, students who attend schools that have a majority of students from racial minority groups have less opportunity to take college-prep classes. This suggests a powerful but overlooked answer to why some students may not gain admission to colleges of their choice or may perform less well when they do enroll.

Another institutional mechanism that creates a different educational ecology for some students is the common practice of "tracking," a practice that creates unequal educational ecologies even in well-resourced schools. Throughout much of the country, students are tracked according to their level of achievement from their kindergarten days; almost everywhere, a clear racial divide is evident. Even in schools that do offer AP courses, students of color often do not have the opportunity to take them. This is because, given the current correlation between race and ethnicity and the likelihood of going on to college, teachers often rely on race and ethnicity to make decisions about course assignments. Students in the high-performing groups—the students called "smart" and "motivated"—are likely to be white or Asian, and/or to have parents who went to college. Students in low-performing groups—the students "who don't care about school or about their futures"—are more likely to be working-class black, Latina/o, or Native American students. In fact, researchers find that black and Latino students who have similar grades and test scores as white students are less likely to be tracked into the AP courses (Oakes and Guiton 1995). In this way, tracking creates and reinforces the link between minority status and underachievement. It is an effective and highly institutionalized mechanism of doing race.

If there were no barriers to upward mobility linked to race and ethnicity, then students from all races and ethnicities would be represented proportionally in all categories of achievement from lowest to highest. The practice of tracking continues, however, and is commonly justified as necessary for motivating students, even though studies indicate that de-tracking does not harm students who are doing well and helps those who are doing less well (Darling-Hammond 2004; Gorski and

EdChange 1995–2008; Oakes 1990). As noted by one educational researcher, it takes amazing denial not to see that "the skin color and language background of the student is closely correlated with the chances of being among those who do cross the stage [to graduate]" (Olsen 1997, 187). Educators, parents, students, and other community members who are not surprised by this correlation and who do nothing to combat it are doing race—passively, if not actively. The assumption that race is a biological thing within individual students underpins the idea that group differences in capacity or effort or values are the reason for the variable rates of graduation. This idea fuels the practice of tracking, which then fosters the observed differences in the educational performance of various ethnic groups.

Medicine

Yet another domain in which racial disparities are evident is health care. One of the biggest selling points for the project of mapping the human genome has been the argument that better knowledge of the genome would lead to better health care. The media has trumpeted the idea that knowledge of the human genome would lead to "gene therapy" and "personalized medicine." In fact, one major pharmaceutical company has already begun production of a heart drug they claim is especially effective for African Americans. The promises of gene therapy have yet to be realized, however, and at least some scientists are beginning to doubt that genes have much to tell researchers about diseases at all (Wade 2008). Emphasizing the relationship between genes and disease obscures the way health care outcomes are closely related to available resources (food, water, medicine), properly trained medical personnel, and everyday ideas and practices—in health care facilities as well as in patients' homes and communities. Indeed, over the past decade, public health researchers have documented a powerful association between good health and social status (Marmot 2004). Because racial minorities in the United States have, on average, lower social status and less wealth, they also have less access to resources such as health care, home ownership, sick leave, vacation, clean air and water, and fresh and abundant food. This translates into greater stress, shorter life spans, and higher rates of disease for racial minorities as compared to whites.

Even when people have access to health care, the race with which they are associated affects the quality of health care they get. In one study, researchers asked emergency room and internal medicine residents (trainee doctors) at four medical centers in Atlanta and Boston to complete an Internet-based survey (Green et al. 2007). The doctors were asked to evaluate the symptoms of, and recommend treatment for, a hypothetical patient who had come into the emergency room complaining of chest pain. All the patients were identical with respect to age and symptoms, but they were either black males or white males. After deciding whether and how to treat the patient, the doctors responded to a questionnaire, called the Implicit Awareness Test (IAT) designed to measure their unconscious (implicit) racial biases. Although none of the doctors admitted to holding negative attitudes about blacks, their answers revealed that most of them had an unconscious *preference for* whites. Those who showed the unconscious preference for whites were *twice* as likely to recommend life-saving medical treatment such as clotbusting drugs for the white patients as for the black patients. Given the importance of aggressive early treatment for heart attacks, the willingness of the doctors to recommend life-saving treatment for whites twice as often as for blacks is hugely significant. Put plainly, the study suggests that blacks who go to the emergency room with symptoms of a heart attack are twice as likely as whites to die as a result of their doctor's failure to treat them adequately. This is a perfect example of how even well-meaning people who explicitly reject racist attitudes can still be involved in doing race.

Justice

Large differences among racial and ethnic groups on any important societal outcome raise the possibility that race is being done (Guinier and Torres 2002). Nowhere are racial disparities greater than in the criminal justice system. Because of the kinds of stereotypes and implicit associations most of us hold, people associated with nondominant racial and ethnic groups are much more likely to be under suspicion for breaking the law. As a result, they are more likely to be stopped, interrogated for possible violations, arrested, prosecuted, and given harsh sentences, including the death penalty. In the United States, racial disparities in surveillance and punishment have become particularly evident in recent decades. For example, the number of people in prison has increased fivefold since 1980, and most of those incarcerated are black and Latino men.

Combining data from a variety of sources, Pettit and Western (2004) estimate that among men born between 1965 and 1969, 3 percent of whites and 20 percent of blacks had spent time in prison by their early thirties. Those without formal education are particularly likely to be incarcerated. Among black men born during this period, 30 percent of those without a college education and almost 60 percent of those who had not finished high school were in prison by 1999. These facts are so stark and the racial disparities so great and so clearly associated with poverty and the lack of education and access to opportunity that come with it that they have drawn the attention of researchers and policy workers in many fields (see Bobo, this volume).

Why are those associated with minority racial groups overrepresented among the prison population? The answer is a consequence of doing race at many levels and across time. It involves a powerful confluence of factors, including persistent poverty and its legacy, a persistent and society-wide anti-black bias, intensified policing and enforcement in minority communities (e.g., the three-strikes law in California), and the fact that there is money to be made from building prisons. Some states such as California now spend more money on prisons than on schools. Between 1985 and 2000, the increase in state spending on corrections was nearly double the increase for higher education ($20 billion versus $10.7 billion), and the total increase in spending on higher education by states was 24 percent compared with 166 percent for corrections (Schiraldi and Ziedenberg 2002).

The steep increase in minority involvement with the criminal justice system that characterizes the United States today coincided with the war on drugs that began in the 1970s. At this time, police were trained and authorized to look at all aspects of a target's behavior and to stop those who met the profile of a potential criminal. The goal of the program was to stop drug trafficking and transport, but the immediate consequence was a campaign of racial profiling that had an impact on all racial and ethnic minorities; it was not confined to those with relatively little education. Many observers of this intensification in surveillance and enforcement believe that race was unfairly emphasized in these profiling efforts and that police and security were targeting people based on their belief that certain ethnic groups were more likely to commit certain crimes (Webb 1999).

Traffic stops of minority men became especially common and led to the expressions "Driving while black" or "Driving while brown." One study of this effort in California found that since 1991, 80 to 90 percent of the arrests involved minorities and 66 percent of those stopped were Latina/os. A similar study of a ten-year period showed that 70 percent of the people pulled over on New Jersey's highways were black or Latina/o drivers (Harris 1999). Black and Latina/o students on college campuses frequently report being the target of such stops on campus roads or in campus bars. Accurate data on the extent of racial profiling is difficult to collect, but firsthand accounts from people who have endured the humiliating ritual of being singled out and searched are abundant. Since the protest over racial profiling began, more than twenty states have made the practice illegal. Notably, racial profiling is not confined to blacks or Latina/os. Since the attacks on the World Trade Center in New York and the Pentagon in Washington on September 11, 2001, people who look like they are of Middle Eastern descent have also been the target of racial profiling; they are more likely to be stopped and thoroughly searched at airports than are people of European descent.

Sports

Sports was one of the first domains of American life to become racially and ethnically integrated. Fans, players, and scholars generally agree that in most sports there is a lot of respect for athletes' training and talent, and relatively little overt or old-school racism. They also agree that bad calls are part of the game. They sometimes disagree, however, about whether race is a factor in the likelihood that some players are more often the target of bad calls than others. A recent study of the National Basketball Association by business researchers revealed a consistent racial bias in calling fouls (Price and Wolfers 2007). The study analyzed more than 600,000 foul calls made in regular season games for the thirteen seasons between 1991 and 2004. The researchers concluded that a basketball referee is more likely to blow the whistle and call a foul against a player of a different race than one of his own race. White referees called fouls against black players more frequently than they did against white players, and black officials called fouls on white players more frequently than they did against black players—although the disparity was less marked. Upon hearing the report, several black basketball players, including Kobe Bryant and LeBron James, sharply rejected its findings. Lakers star Bryant, for example, retorted that he had gotten "more techs from black than white refs." Disturbed by the report, the NBA carried out its own study of 148,000 calls made during three seasons and also found support for this racial bias in refereeing. The initial report suggests that, as in many other domains of society, the racial preference in foul-calling is a result of unconscious or implicit bias and is not a matter of the referees disliking certain players or trying to undermine their performance. In the split second the referee has to call a block or a charge, the negative association that is often attached to blacks in American society can influence how white referees see a particular pattern of activity on the court.

Something similar happens on the baseball diamond. Carrying out a study of 2.1 million calls, an economist found that 1 percent of the calls was affected by race (Parsons et al. 2007). He found that umpires are more likely to call strikes when the pitcher is of their own race. Asian pitchers in the major leagues are especially likely to be affected by this bias because there are no Asian umpires in the major leagues—in fact, 71 percent of pitchers and 87 percent of umpires are white. Although the racial bias is relatively small—in the course of a particular game, two calls are likely to be influenced by race—it is consistent. Some suggest this bias would be larger except that eleven of the thirty major league ballparks use a series of cameras and a computer network to review calls, a practice that enhances umpire accuracy.

Media

The examples given above show that real estate agents, bank officers, doctors, referees, and teachers—sometimes unknowingly and without hostile intent—all draw on associations and stereotypes about various racial groups. It seems that no one, no matter the person's education level or goodness of heart, is immune. So where do these stereotypes come from, and how might we track their influence? Clearly, one powerful source of racial stereotypes is the media.

Recent studies suggest that as we go about our daily business—reading the newspaper, shopping online, going to the movies, watching television, riding the bus, amusing ourselves with YouTube, updating our Facebook pages, or scanning the kiosks at work—we are exposed to as many as 3,000 images each day (Kukutani 1997, 32). These images are not a representative set of all that can be found in our various worlds. Instead, they present images and ideas that reflect what viewers are already likely to believe. Advertisers or movie directors eager to convey a particular message or feeling typically draw on the common stock of images and associations with which people are comfortable to quickly and effectively transmit a message. They typically avoid images and ideas that are unfamiliar, that might make a viewer uncomfortable, or that might disrupt a sales pitch.

Take, for example, Hollywood movies. A recent documentary asked why most U.S. Americans held negative and prejudicial attitudes about Arabs even before the tragic events of 9/11 (*Reel Bad Arabs* 2006; Shaheen 2001). A survey of more than 900 films with Arab characters or images, from the earliest silent films to more recent more box office hits, reveals that Hollywood portrays only a very narrow range of ways to be Arab—they can be bandits, submissive women, ruthless sheikhs, or evil, gun-toting terrorists. They are almost universally portrayed as outsiders and as different and threatening. Across all the 900 portrayals of Arab characters, only twelve depictions were positive and fifty were balanced; the rest were negative. Among the most notable for their narrow and negative views of Arabs are the movies *Back to the Future* (1985), *Bonfire of the Vanities* (1990), and *Rules of Engagement* (2000).

Cartoons and films targeted at children are often particularly rife with negative sentiments. For example, in the original version of the Disney film *Aladdin*, an Arab character introduced himself with a catchy tune and with the following lyrics: "I come from a land . . . where they cut off your ears if they don't like your face. It's barbaric, but hey, it's home." Although protests convinced the filmmakers to modify these particular lyrics, older Disney films with equally negative images of other ethnic and racial groups remain part of the standard "safe" fare in many children's media diet. One of the earliest Disney movies, *Dumbo*, shows a number of black men (whose faces are obscured) working and singing in unison as they set up the circus tents. As they swing their mallets, they sing the following lyrics: "We work all day, we work all night / We never learned to read or write / We work all night, we work all day / Can't wait to spend our pay away." Other groups fare no better in other classic movies. For example, *Lady and the Tramp* includes Siamese cats that have features and attributes that are often used to stereotype Asians. Aside from being the villains, the cats are depicted as being cunning and as having slanted eyes, buckteeth, and heavy accents. What the impact of Disney's new black princess might be on ideas about race remains to be seen.

The advertising industry is also centrally involved in doing race. Gone are the most overtly stereotypic images: Aunt Jemima of pancake fame is no longer a Mammy figure but instead a modern black woman. For his part, Uncle Ben of rice fame has moved from the kitchen to the boardroom—no longer the cook, he is now portrayed as the CEO of the company. But like movie directors, advertisers still often perpetuate stereotypes in the service of selling their products. Although advertisers are using more nonwhite models in their ads, people of color are shown in only a limited number of roles—as entertainers and as models—and not as lawyers, doctors, or other business professionals (Wilson, Gutiérrez, and Chao 2003).

If we all lived in racially diverse environments, the images and stereotypes presented by movies, cartoons, and advertisers would not be consequential. But because many of us live in racially and ethnically homogenous contexts where we do not encounter people and behavior that disavow these stereotypes, the media can do race and be a powerful force in perpetuating racial inequality.

The foregoing examples give just a hint of how varied the processes are that are involved in doing race. Of course, the specifics vary widely by culture, context, and historical period. In fact, the social processes involved in arranging the world and living life *as if* people associated with some racial or ethnic groups were inherently more valuable than others appear across history, and not just in the United States but throughout the world. Moreover, as we have seen, these processes sometimes operate quite independently of the term "race" in other parts of the world. These processes are not always easy to see or to analyze, probably because doing so disturbs many of our taken-for-granted assumptions about our worlds and ourselves. Yet thinking about race and ethnicity as doings— as sets of ideas and practices developed and perpetuated by many people over time—is an important step toward more knowledgeable, enlightened, and trusting conversations.

Changing the Conversations

The tendency to create distinctions and organize societies based on assumed commonalities in history, language, region, religion, customs, physical appearance, and ancestry group appears to be a human universal. For this reason, framing new and better conversations about race and ethnicity will be central to any attempt to change their meanings in our society. An important first step is reviewing the eight conversations we identified in Section I in light of what we have learned so far. This will allow us to steer the conversations and the actions they guide in more productive and accurate directions. Informed and useful conversations will have to confront the best ways to recognize, include, and incorporate our differences without using them to do race—that is, using them as a basis for unequally distributing opportunity and life chances.

The *Race is in our DNA* conversation is one of the oldest and, not surprisingly, the most resistant to change. The concept of race has assumed from the beginning that a person's race can be found in his or her body. The contemporary form of this conversation focuses on the human genome, but it borrows its logic from many old, troublesome, and hard-to-shake discourses and schemas. For example, in Spain the label *sangre pura* ("pure blood") was used to distinguish those born into the Catholic religion from the Jewish and Muslim *conversos*, and in Spanish American countries like Mexico to distinguish the *criollo* (a person born in Spanish America of Spanish parents) from the *mestizo* (a person born in Spanish America who has one Indian parent and one Spanish parent). One of the reasons for the lasting appeal of the idea of race as biological is that it promises clear and simple answers to deep-seated questions we all have about who are we and where our place in the world might be. The possibility that we might be able to look inside our bodies (to our DNA, in the current version) to discover precisely who we *really* are is very attractive to many people.

It is not surprising, then, that trying to discover one's ancestral histories—finding one's "roots in a test tube"—is an increasingly popular activity (Gates 2007). And this may be an especially popular activity for people whose histories and identities have been interrupted and denied. Yet the results of DNA tests need to be interpreted carefully. People with a wide variety of racial and ethnic associations can be shown through current DNA testing to have ancestors who came from the continent of Africa, for example. Yet not all of them would identify, nor would others identify them, as black or African American. Speaking practically, finding out the geographic origins of some of your direct forebears may have little effect on where you might be placed in terms of today's racial categories—white, African American, Native American, Asian American, or Latina/o. DNA testing, even as it becomes more comprehensive and complex, cannot tell us "who one really is." This is because while humans are biological beings, *being a person* is simultaneously a human social achievement (Bruner 1990). A person's identity is more than his or her geographical origin; it is an ongoing synthesis of personal, political, historical, and social factors.

The version of the *Race is in our DNA* conversation that says, "It's their culture, it can't be helped," is also deeply flawed. First, culture is not something located *inside* people as one of their internal attributes. Instead culture is located *outside* the person in the ideas, practices, and institutions that people use to make sense of their lives and to guide their actions (Adams and Markus 2004). Culture conveys what is and is not good, valuable, and worth doing. Second, culture is dynamic. Cultural ideas and practices are attached to all the important social distinctions in our lives—race and ethnicity, but also social class, gender, religion, birth cohort, region of the country, and so on. These cultural ideas and practices shape behavior, but they are constantly changing—and as they do, so will people and their actions. Ideas and practices about race (who is valued and who is not) are important elements of culture, and changing them will change behavior.

In the end, the problem with the *Race is in our DNA* conversation, in both its biological and cultural versions, is that it is wrong. Race is not in our DNA; in fact, it is not a thing located inside people at all. Rather, race is a doing; it is a dynamic system of historically derived ideas and practices involving the whole of society and every individual in it. We do race every day in every domain of our lives, sometimes knowingly and intentionally, and sometimes not. A large body of multidisciplinary research on race and ethnicity (much of which is either discussed or referenced in this essay and in this volume) provides compelling evidence that race and ethnicity are central to how people in the United States and throughout the world think and behave. And although the election of an American president who is black is a powerful event that has begun to change some understandings and practices of race in the twenty-first century, it will not by itself dismantle the historically rooted and pervasive system of interactions and institutions that have produced and still maintain racial inequalities.

For this reason, however optimistic and well-meaning the *We're beyond race* conversation may be, it is also wrong. It is wrong not because we cannot approach the post-race ideal, but because we are not there yet. At best, this conversation reflects a lack of experience and exposure; at worst, it shows an effort—most often by those whose race accords them the advantaged position in the racial hierarchy—to deny racial disparities (Crenshaw et al. 1996). Fueled by a very American desire for change and self-improvement, and by re-committing to the ideal of individual equality, this conversation could be made more productive. We can do this by changing it from a declarative into a question: "What remains to be done to move beyond race?"

Another unproductive and inaccurate, but common, conversation is the one that says *That's just identity politics*. This is the conversation that allows students to sidestep courses on race and ethnicity and encourages employees to use their time more effectively by avoiding seminars on diversity and inclusion. Because virtually all of our societal institutions are structured by the ideas and practices of race, we must remember that none of us can escape its reach. Anyone who goes to school, gets a loan, applies for a job, watches television news, engages in sports, or visits the doctor (just to name a few mundane activities) is participating actively in a society that has been organized according to race. It is inescapable, then, that we will be affected either positively or negatively by the meanings and representations associated with our own and others' racial groups. People associated with a stigmatized racial group, not surprisingly, are likely to be negatively affected by those meanings. They may have a hard time getting into a college preparatory class in high school or finding a good job—even if they have good grades and a promising résumé—because of the stereotypes about intelligence and work ethic that are associated with their group (Steele 2010).

People associated with the dominant racial group, on the other hand, are likely to be positively affected or privileged by the meanings and representations associated with their group (Johnson 2005). Middle-class whites, at least, are more likely to be tracked into college preparatory classes, hired for highly sought-after positions in favor of other equally or more-qualified applicants, given more aggressive treatment for common medical conditions, passed over during racial profiling for criminal or terrorist activity, and untroubled by the ever-present prospect of being seen through the lens of a stereotype. Anyone who says that race is not a factor in his or her life is either dishonest or clueless. Like many of the conversations, this one talks about race without acknowledging that in a society and in a world organized by race, everyone is necessarily associated with a racial group. Whether or not they claim the race as relevant to them, many others, particularly those who do not share it, will perceive them as having a race and will respond to them accordingly. Moreover, this conversation does not take account of the many research findings that clearly reveal that those with the most power and authority in the racial hierarchy with are the ones mostly likely to claim they are unaffected by race (Plaut 2002).

Several of the other conversations are not wholly wrong as much as they are incomplete. *The Racial diversity is killing us* conversation is a case in point. Rather than being wholly wrong, it is credible in at least one important way. Because the doing of race over centuries has created great enmity between people associated with different ethnic groups, the consequences of interethnic conflict are often deadly. The Armenian genocide in Turkey, the Jewish Holocaust in Germany, and the ongoing warfare against tribal peoples by the Janjaweed in Darfur are all painful examples discussed in essays in this volume that underscore how inter-ethnic conflict can indeed kill individuals and societies (Naimark, this volume; Rodrigue, this volume). The problem with the *Racial diversity is killing us* conversation is that it locates both the blame and the solution in the wrong place. It sees the problem in the difference itself rather than in why and how we create, maintain, and respond to socially created differences. In other words, this conversation conceives of race as a thing—a thing that resides inside "other" people and makes them evil, unfit, or problematic. The logical end point of this conversation is to get rid of the people whose values, beliefs, and practices are different from one's own through assimilation, exclusion, or genocide.

If the *Racial diversity is killing us* conversation were to change in a direction that understood race as a systematic social process, it might serve as the beginning of a discussion about how to meaningfully take account of difference—especially the way difference is used to devalue and construct others as inferior or less than human. So, yes, racial diversity *is* killing us and it will continue to do so until we (1) stop doing race and (2) come to terms with the often difficult notion that within the one world, there are multiple viable understandings of what is good, true, beautiful, and efficient (Moya 2002; Shweder 2003). Our global society is not "just a small world after all." It is true that we all have hopes and fears, but the hopes and fears one person has are often quite different from, or even at odds with, those that another person has. We live in a vast, unruly, and complicated matrix of a world, replete with conflict and disagreement.

The *Everyone's a little bit racist* conversation is related to the *Racial diversity is killing us* conversation, although it incorporates the important realization that doing race is a common process and that no one is exempt. We are born into a racist world, so the conversation goes, and are greatly influenced by the images, values, and narratives in our environments, the majority of which are racially biased to the core. Beyond this understanding, however, the conversation does not take the discussion very far and in fact allows people to let themselves off the hook. Acknowledging the fact that *Everyone's a little bit racist* is a revelation appropriate to the beginning of a conversation focused on how to raise awareness of individual and societal biases and how to transform the practices that perpetuate racial inequality. This conversation might include asking *why* we are a little bit racist, what the effect of that racism might be, and what we might be able to do about it. The song discussed in Section I that gives this conversation its name suggests that people just "relax" and not get upset about how others view difference. Whether people can relax, however, depends on what is at stake and what consequences follow from the observation of racial and ethnic differences. Unless this conversation is expanded beyond its first observation, it is a cop-out that ignores how social, economic, and political power, along with the privilege and peace of mind such power confers, work to advantage some people unfairly at the expense of others.

Another partially correct conversation that might be productively expanded is *It's a black thing—you wouldn't understand*. People of color do have different experiences—experiences that give them a different perspective on the world. One of these experiences, for example, includes spending a lot of time and effort explaining to people associated with the dominant group why race matters. It is often really difficult for people who do not share one's racialized minority identity to understand this (Moya and Hames-García 2000). But it is probably defensiveness or hubris (not to mention an interethnic conversation killer) to say that someone who is not black can never understand. It may not be easy, and it may not be total, but humans *are* able to communicate across difference. It is, moreover, our only hope. Instead of turning off potential allies, we might try to make the point that simply listening to music, wearing clothes, and reading books by writers with an ethnicity other than one's own does not necessarily lead to understanding. We might also try to convey the truth that understanding others takes a lot of interaction, study, empathy, and a well-developed capacity to listen, appreciate, and accept others unlike oneself.

The *I'm _____ and I'm proud* conversation can be similarly positive or negative depending on who is participating in it and what they mean to imply by it. If the participants in this conversation are countering centuries of stigmatization, marginalization, and downward constitution by the larger society by revealing why the ideas and practices associated with their particular ethnic group are valuable, then this conversation can foster group solidarity and pride. To the extent that this conversation appreciates difference without doing race—without denigrating or isolating others—it can be a useful opening out to other people.

Finally, the *Variety is the spice of life* conversation is also partially right and has considerable positive potential. However, in its present form, it resembles the *Everyone's a little bit racist* conversation by ignoring the role of power in structuring how different groups of people interact with each other. Just as the word "spice" conveys a sense of something that is added to or overlaid on the basic ingredients, this conversation often skirts the fact that the differences associated with our various ethnic and racial identities can be quite substantial. They are usually much more than just spice to the main dish or a minor variation in flavor or style; instead, they are consequential for the kinds of lives that people are able to lead. Beyond differences in regions of origin, languages, and food, our various ethnic and racial associations can indicate very different histories and very different ideas of the right way to be.

Take, for example, the very basic question "Who am I?" Recall from Section II that in mainstream America, the most popular cultural model for a self says that people should be *independent*—that is, unique, separate from others, and in control of their environments. In other contexts, by contrast, a popular model for the self among people with East Asian, South Asian, or Latino heritage says that people should be *interdependent*—that is, similar to others, connected to others, and adjusting to others (Markus 2008). Yet American classrooms are set up for people with an independent model of the self. Being a good student according to this model means asserting oneself, questioning authority, thinking for oneself, and communicating one's own attitudes and beliefs. Being a good student from an interdependent perspective means respecting one's place in the hierarchy and honoring the teacher, who likely knows more than the students. Reflecting an interdependent model of self, students often will not answer a question with information that they assume the professor must already know or will wait for a more senior student to ask an important question (Kim 2002; Rothstein-Fisch, Greenfield, and Turnbull 1999). A teacher with an independent mindset who is unaware that there are different models for how to be a good student is likely to think less well of those students who are not raising their hands and making their own ideas known. Moreover, even a teacher who is aware of these differences cannot know which model a student is likely to hold without getting to know their students and their individual histories.

Clearly, there is more than one good way to be a student or employee or person. When only one way of being a good student, employee, or person is valued and accommodated within a given society, though, people who have other ways of being can end up at a substantial disadvantage. They might be unfairly judged as being unintelligent, unmotivated, undeserving, and without merit. Creating a diverse democratic society that recognizes and legitimizes different ways of being resulting from different life opportunities and experiences will require imagination, and flexibility, as well as changes in policies, practices, and institutions.

SIX SUGGESTIONS FOR DOING DIFFERENCE DIFFERENTLY

The disparities among racial groups that can be found in every domain of life are a sign that, as a society, we have not yet lived up to our country's founders' vision of a free society that included the ideal of human equality. As discussed above, however, this vision was severely limited by their ideas and practices regarding race. As twenty-first-century U.S. Americans, we must now accept responsibility for the future of our country. Can we build on the best part of the founders' vision to create a better society—one that rejects their mistaken assumptions about the nature of the individual and the individual's relationship to race? Answering this question will involve serious thinking about the kind of society we want. Building a freer and more equal society will not be easy. Change will not happen by appealing to ideals alone; it will require the effortful participation of all people to create and maintain it.

By recognizing that race and ethnicity are human-made and reinforced processes, we are better situated to figure out what actions we can take both individually and institutionally to *undo* the most pernicious aspects of making sense of human difference. Moreover, we can begin to create practices and institutions that take advantage of the differences in perspective and understanding that our various racial and ethnic associations make possible. In Table i.4 we offer a few brief suggestions that may be useful for changing our behavior regarding race. What follows is an elaboration of each suggestion.

1. *Recognize that people are not just autonomous individuals; rather, their thoughts, feelings, language, and actions are always made up of (and also make up) the thoughts, feelings, language, and actions of others.* The idea of the self-determining individual is a powerful one that emerged in the West over the centuries and now structures everyday life. In the United States, we grow up wanting to be unique, self-sufficient, and responsible for ourselves. We work hard to become independent of other people's influence and control. This view of the individual as autonomous and self-determining, however, is an incomplete way of describing human behavior. Moreover, it is increasingly at odds with the scientific understanding of how people and societies function. People *are* individuals; but they are not *only* individuals. As shown in Figure i.2, people live in a matrix of

TABLE I.4 | **SIX SUGGESTIONS FOR DOING DIFFERENCE DIFFERENTLY**

1. Recognize that people are not autonomous individuals; rather, their thoughts, feelings, language, and actions are always made up of (and also make up) the thoughts, feelings, language, and actions of others.

2. Study history to understand the emergence and development, as well as the contemporary significance, of race and racism.

3. Learn the science to understand how the sociohistorical concept of race and the biogeographical concept of ancestry groups differ from each other.

4. Be aware that in a world organized according to race and ethnicity, the races or ethnicities with which people are associated will always matter for their life experiences and perspectives.

5. Change the usual way of explaining racial and ethnic inequalities by recognizing the role that power and the unequal distribution of resources have played in their creation and maintenance.

6. Help reform the ideas and practices—both as they are part of individuals, and as they have become institutionalized in the structures of society—that lead to unequal outcomes associated with race.

relationships with others; they make their lives as members of families, neighborhoods, schools, teams, clubs, workplaces, and places of worship. They experience the world through the images, ideas, and words of other people.

This is why understanding race and ethnicity requires us to acknowledge that being a person is a relational as well as an individual project. Although we have a lot of control over our actions, thoughts, and feelings, we are not the sole authors of our existence. Just as we are constrained by and interdependent with our physical worlds, so are we constrained by and interdependent with our social worlds. Race and ethnicity are powerful examples of this fundamental interdependence. They are sets of human-made ideas and practices for grouping and ranking people that are created and held together by people and systems in interaction. Recognizing that race and ethnicity are not fixed attributes of people but instead emerge through social relations shifts our understanding of these two complex social processes. We come to understand that rather than trying to rid ourselves of race, as if it were an essential aspect of our beings, we must change the way we all collectively do race.

2. *Study history to understand the emergence and development, as well as the contemporary significance, of race and ethnicity.* As we have shown in this essay, the ideas and practices of race and ethnicity have powerfully shaped U.S. society and its people. U.S. history and society have, in turn, shaped our understanding of race and ethnicity. As a consequence, understanding history requires understanding race and ethnicity, and understanding race and ethnicity requires understanding history. (Adams et al. 2008c). Consider, for example, how race has typically affected (and continues to affect) a person's economic position and sense of well-being. Anybody who does not own a home, some land, or a business will have a very hard time saving enough extra money to do more than just pay the bills. For the most part, simple wage earners do not have very much (if any) money to leave to their children. They will not, in other words, accumulate the kind of wealth that their children could build on to advance in the world. Consider that for much of our country's history, most people with non-European ancestry were able to approach the market only as slaves (blacks), as wards of the state (some indigenous peoples), or as very low-wage laborers (Latina/os, Asian Americans, Native Americans, and blacks after the abolition of slavery). In some cases, they were denied access to property ownership by law or custom; in other cases, they lacked the personal relationships or social status necessary to raise the money (either from a family member or a bank) to go to school or start a business. As a result, a large and persistent wealth gap has grown up between whites and nonwhites in the United States (Oliver and Shapiro 1997; Darrity 2005). These circumstances have conspired to create a link between monetary success and people with European ancestry. This link is strengthened by the enduring remnants of the eighteenth- and nineteenth-century systems of racial classification and ranking, and although it is thoroughly man-made, it seems natural in the minds of many Americans.

The fact that Oprah Winfrey is now one of the richest women in the world is a clear and welcome sign that some people with non-European ancestry can fully participate in the American economic system. The success of people like Oprah Winfrey and Barack Obama will be important for helping to undo the link in the minds of many Americans between European ancestry and success. It will, however, take more than a few spectacular exceptions to the general rule to reverse the lasting effects of centuries of ideas and practices that systematically produced economic inequality. This is why understanding any contemporary racial disparity—as with the example of the wealth gap—will always require a historical understanding of how and why social systems and practices that advantage some groups over others have been created and maintained.

3. *Learn the science to understand how the sociohistorical concept of race and the biogeographical concept of ancestry groups differ from each other.* One of the most powerful, persistent, and mistaken ideas about humankind is the idea that race is a biological thing. As we have emphasized repeatedly throughout this essay, the sociohistorical concept of race is not a thing at all. Rather, it is a multifaceted and relational process that has had important effects on our experiences and on how the social world is organized. This system, what we call doing race, refers to a set of ideas and practices that involve several, often simultaneous, actions: (1) noticing particular physical characteristics like skin color, hair color, or eye shape; (2) assuming that those characteristics tell us something general and important such as how intelligent, hard-working, moral, or conscientious a person is or has the capacity to be; (3) participating in the creation and maintenance of social and economic structures that preserve a hierarchy in which people associated with one race are assumed to be superior to people who are associated with another; and (4) justifying or rationalizing the inequalities that result. By contrast, the biogeographical concept of *ancestry groups* refers to identifiable, but nondiscrete and overlapping, biologically and geographically based clusters of people.

There is a clear and practical distinction between race and ancestry group that affects how each of the terms can be legitimately used. When historians and other social scientists refer to a "black" race, they are referring to a dynamic set of historically derived and institutionalized ideas and practices involving people with visible African ancestry. Population geneticists, by contrast, would not be able to find a corresponding "black" ancestry group. In fact, most people who identify themselves (or who would be identified by others) as black or African American actually belong to multiple ancestry groups. This is a result both of the rape and sexual coercion of black women by white men during slavery and Reconstruction, as well as of the (increasingly common) consensual relationships between men and women associated with different races throughout the course of U.S. history. Most people in the United States belong to many different biogeographical ancestry groups. In whatever way the mixing occurred, our forebears usually come from many different geographic locales.

Understanding the difference between race and ancestry groups makes it easier to use each concept in its proper context. It makes sense to talk about race when talking about the way certain groups have been favored or disadvantaged by societal structures or about the lingering effects of disparate structures of opportunity on the current organization of U.S. society. By contrast, it makes sense to use the concept of biogeographical ancestry groups when talking about the genetic transmission of diseases. Race is not a useful proxy for biogeographical ancestry groups in this case and could actually result in the unnecessary or inadequate medical treatment of an individual. Understanding the difference between these two concepts can help us to use each in its proper context; it is also fundamental to our efforts to stop doing race.

4. *Be aware that in a world organized according to race and ethnicity, the races or ethnicities with which people are associated will always matter for their life experiences and perspectives.* Although race and ethnicity do not determine experience, they shape it in multiple ways. Those at the top of the racial hierarchy are likely to have more access to opportunities for wealth, status, and respect than those at the bottom. As a result, people associated with different races are likely to have divergent perspectives on a wide variety of issues. Working successfully across racial or ethnic groups requires recognizing these differences as significant and worth attending to. Remembering that there is no uniquely "natural" or "right" way of being in the world—that *all* people are products, as well as producers, of their environments—might help us to consider the validity of someone else's perspectives even in those cases where they contradict our own. Taking difference seriously requires us to consider the possibility that people associated with other races and ethnicities may have a different, and possibly better, understanding of a given event or situation (Mohanty 1997; Moya 2002; Moya and Hames-García 2000).

Race matters for how one is treated by others. Because individuals are always part of numerous relationships and institutions, they can influence, but never create by themselves, the environments they live in. Even if a person chooses to ignore the concept of race, the very fact of being seen by others as associated with a particular racial group will matter—sometimes very much. As an extreme example, consider the situation of Jews living in early twentieth-century Germany. Some German Jews of the time felt little experiential connection to their ethnic associations. Many were nonobservant, secular individuals whose primary identification was as German citizens. However, because Hitler and his Nazi party insisted on viewing these people as racially Jewish, they were disenfranchised, stripped of their property, and eventually subjected to genocide. These individuals' apparent disregard of their association with Jewishness mattered less to their lives, in this case, than the larger German society's belief in their racial otherness.

Finally, race matters for how one acts in the world. As demonstrated by the study of emergency room doctors described earlier, the racial biases of white doctors play a central role in the health care that they give to their white, as opposed to their black, patients. In that study, the racially disparate health outcomes that put whites at an advantage had nothing to do with blacks' genetic predisposition to heart disease but everything to do with the doctors' ideas and practices involving race. The doctors were *unaware* of their preference for whites—they thought they were treating all patients equally. The doctors in the study are not unusual. Like everyone else, they live in a society organized by race—one in which whiteness is consistently associated with privilege and represented by positive images while blackness is associated with disadvantage and represented by negative images. This has predictable and consistent consequences: white is seen as good and virtuous while black is seen as less good and less virtuous. These racial associations shape behavior regardless of what someone might intend. Race is a pernicious aspect of our contemporary society, especially when it is dismissed too quickly as a thing of the past. Just because our environments shape us, however, does not mean that we have no power over what values we finally hold or practices we engage in. According to the psychologist who helped design the test used to discover the doctors' unconscious biases, the "great advantage of being human, of having the privilege of awareness, of being able to recognize the stuff that is hidden, is that we can beat the bias" (Smith 2007). So, while an awareness of our unconscious biases cannot solve all the problems related to racially disparate outcomes, it can help us to rethink our opinions in a way that might lead us to make more informed judgments and act in less prejudicial ways.

5. *Change the usual way of explaining racial and ethnic inequalities by recognizing the role that power and the unequal distribution of resources have played in their creation and maintenance.* To the extent that we want a fair and democratic society that does not distribute opportunity according to race and ethnicity, we need to understand how our society became what it is and what keeps it that way. Such an understanding requires noting racial and ethnic disparities wherever they occur and critically examining the answers justifying them. When, for example, we see white students doing well while Latina/o or Filipina/o students are not, we should ask why. The usual answer is that those who are doing well

have more ability, intelligence, motivation, and merit than those who are doing poorly. This familiar way of explaining disparate outcomes among racial and ethnic groups thus locates the problem *inside* the students. Yet because individual behavior is always interdependent with others' behavior and with their situations, locating the problem inside the student will provide at best an incomplete answer and many times a flawed one. Assuming that the problem lies inside the student hides the fact that race is not a thing but a dynamic set of ideas and practices. What might appear as a single situation for everyone (i.e., a classroom) can in fact be very different depending on a student's race. For example, teachers have different expectations, give different levels of encouragement, and reward different students differently—often without awareness of their biases. In other words, white students typically have the advantage of being expected to do well. Unlike black, Latina/o, or Native American students, they do not have to deal with a whole set of cues, associations, and daily reminders that people in their racial group are rarely academically successful (Steele 2010).

Another explanation that needs to be examined is the one that says minority students do not perform well in school because of negative peer pressure. According to this explanation, doing well in school is associated with being white. To avoid "acting white," so the story goes, minority students underperform in school. This explanation locates the source of the problem inside the underachieving racial group and is at best only part of the story. Careful analyses of school settings reveal another possibility—many principals, teachers, and parents have never associated being black or Latina/o or American Indian with being a good student (Carter 2005). This negative association held by the adults in power sets up a cascade of subtle but powerful effects. For example, because they do not expect racial minority students to do well, they do not count them among the good or successful students even when the students do perform well. Consequently, they do not offer to minority students the same opportunities they offer to the majority students and are not surprised or perturbed when minority students underperform. Because the outcomes match their expectations, some educators do not feel responsible for the result and fail to take any action that might change the situation.

Some situations and social systems offer people many more resources, opportunities, and supportive relationships than do others. People's environments shape what they can do as well as what they and others believe is important and possible to do. The representations, social practices, and institutional policies that make up our social worlds are not in addition to, or separate from, an individual's ability, effort, motivation, or interest. Instead, they constitute these qualities. They create, stimulate, scaffold, and foster an individual's ability, effort, motivation, and interest.

Ending the way we do race will require a move away from individual, simple, and scientifically inaccurate explanations of behavior (e.g., she did well because she is smart) and toward more informed, scientifically accurate, and comprehensive understandings and explanations of socially motivated behavior (e.g., she did well because she was expected to do so by scores of family members, neighbors, and friends, and because she attended well-funded, well-resourced schools with well-prepared teachers who understood ability not as fixed but as growing and changing, who countered negative and marginalizing representations while creating positive selves, and who helped her develop an identity as a successful student).

6. *Help reform the ideas and practices—both as they are part of individuals, and as they have become institutionalized in the structures of society— that lead to unequal outcomes correlated with race and ethnicity.* Changing the usual explanations for racial and ethnic disparities is an important step toward doing difference differently. Completing the journey requires that we also change the ideas and practices that promote and maintain these disparities. As we have noted throughout this essay, there are many obvious candidates for reform, and one does not have to travel far to find them. Consider, for example, the images in the local school or in most workplaces—on bulletin boards, kiosks, Web sites, and official materials. If the racial identities of the people in power—the teachers and the supervisors—are not diverse, then not all students and employees will have an equal opportunity to see people who are associated with their ethnic or racial groups in positions of power and influence. This will affect their opportunities to find role models and to imagine a wide range of possibilities for themselves (see Steele, this volume; Fryberg and Watts, this volume). Another way that people typically move into positions of power and influence is by participating in a range of activities, both official and unofficial, where they make the personal connections that will create later opportunities for success and advancement. Noticing and working to change the structure of schools and workplaces so that all students and workers can participate equally in those kinds of activities can be a significant action.

Other candidates for reform are less obvious because they masquerade as neutral or unbiased instruments for sorting people into apparently non-racial achievement or ability groups. Consider, for example, the SAT, the test widely used to select and sort students into colleges and universities in the United States. Research shows that the test is very modestly related to how students will do in their freshman year of college and hardly related at all to how students will do by the time they are seniors (Zwick and Sklar 2005). The test is, however, strongly related to a student's parental socioeconomic status. In what is dubbed the "Volvo effect," some researchers argue that the best predictor of students' scores on the SAT is the car their parents' drive. If it is an expensive new Volvo, for example, the students are likely to do well on the test; if it is an old Ford, the students are likely to do less well (Croizet 2008). Of course, it is not the car itself that matters. Rather, the Volvo effect captures the fact that students in richer communities have access to the best schools and the most prepared teachers, as well as to an array of other educational opportunities and resources that are common in these communities. Because of the correlation between income and race and ethnicity in the United States, reliance on the SAT to select students for college admissions systematically fosters and maintains racial and ethnic inequality. Doing difference differently will require asking why we are using this test to distribute educational opportunity. And indeed, some colleges and universities are now asking themselves this very question.

Our point here is not that we have to stop making decisions about whom to select for different positions or opportunities. Rather, we need to find selection practices that are relatively more fair and do not systematically advantage people from some ethnic and racial groups over others. Doing difference differently will require asking who designed the criteria, what racially biased assumptions about intelligence and ability might be built into them, and whether different criteria might produce a less racially biased result. Consider that management positions in the American corporate sector are highly correlated with race and ethnicity; even though the number of Asian American employees has been growing steadily, there are still relatively few Asian American managers in the corporate sector. The criteria for becoming a manager in American organizations include being extroverted, highly verbal, and able to present oneself and one's ideas positively and enthusiastically. Yet studies of Asian Americans reveal that being able to positively promote oneself and one's ideas is not the most important signature of talent (Kim 2002; Xin 2004; Tsai 2007). Instead, calmness, balance, and an ability to focus on a task are more highly valued ways of being. The selection criteria, then, are not neutral, and they do not provide for equal opportunity. Rather, the criteria are committed to a particular set of ideas about what is a good or desirable way to be that systematically advantages some ethnic and racial groups over others.

Finally, one of the most important ways we can transform the system is by striving to change our behaviors that support the racial hierarchy. Ending the doing of race by doing difference differently will require recognizing that our social worlds are human constructions, and they contain and foster particular assumptions about different kinds of people. Doing difference differently requires each of us to recognize and remedy our personal contributions to maintaining an unjust racial hierarchy. They have been and could be otherwise. We can begin building a more equal world by recognizing the ways in which we each may have done race in the past and may be doing it currently. This is not an exercise in inducing guilt; instead, it is the beginning of thinking differently about race. We might want to ask ourselves these questions: In what ways have I failed to question or just accepted—in school, in my workplace, on the basketball court—the superiority of people in one racial group over another? How have I explained this difference? In what ways are the organizations or institutions I participate in set up to create advantages for people in some groups relative to others? What role have I played in maintaining those unequal situations? What can I do to change them?

We return to our opening claim: we do race, all of us, every day. The challenge we face now is to learn how to stop doing race.

Our goal has been to show that race is a system of ideas and practices involving the whole of society and everyone in it. Race is not a quality of people—it does not inhere in individuals or in groups. Rather, it is a product of the interactions all of us have with the people and institutions that make up the worlds in which we live. Race, then, is a system of marking and dealing with ethnically associated human differences; it identifies various racial groups (e.g., whites, blacks, Latina/os), ranks them by according more value and worth to some and less to others and finally, justifies and maintains the resulting inequalities. As with most highly significant activities, doing race takes a village—in fact, a world of villages. This is why we cannot ignore race any more than we can do (or undo) race as individuals.

The racial system in the United States, for example, has developed over hundreds of years and has explained and organized our social world for so long that we often take it for granted; we often see race as part of the natural world, as something that just *is*. Marking differences arising from history, language, region, religion, customs, physical appearance, or ancestry group will likely always be part of our world. Certainly ethnicity will always be with us. The point is that marking difference need not lead to creating and maintaining some groups as less equal than others. Our claim that as a society we can and must live without doing race is not to deny or underestimate the huge challenge of engaging an already vast and growing array of significant ethnic differences. It is to say that we can find a more productive way of approaching those differences, one that does not involve creating racial groups, ranking them, and justifying the resulting racial inequalities. We humans created and maintain the racial system; working together, we have the power to dismantle and undo it. We can, as the saying goes, be the change we would like to see in the world.

We can reshape the conversations through which we make sense of events highlighting race and ethnicity. We can also reform the ideas and practices—both as they are part of individuals and as they have become institutionalized in the structures of society—that lead to racial disparities. Finally, we can re-commit to our nation's founding ideal—the equality of individuals—even as we appreciate the fact that ensuring equality of opportunity for individuals (even independent, self-sufficient individuals) is necessarily a group project. We are, after all, in it together.

Works Cited

•

Adams, G., Monica Biernat, Nyla R. Branscombe, Christian S. Crandall, and Lawrence W. Wrightsman. 2008a. Beyond Prejudice: Toward a Sociocultural Psychology of Racism and Oppression. In *Commemorating Brown: The Social Psychology of Racism and Discrimination*, edited by Glenn Adams, et al. Washington, DC: American Psychological Association, 215–246.

Adams, Glenn, Monica Biernat, Nyla R. Branscombe, Christian S. Crandall, and Lawrence S. Wrightsman. 2008b. *Commemorating Brown: The Social Psychology of Racism and Discrimination*. Washington, DC: American Psychological Association.

Adams, Glenn, Vanessa Edkins, Dominika Lacka, Kate M. Pickett, and Sapna Cheryan. 2008c. Teaching About Racism: Pernicious Implications of the Standard Portrayal. *Basic and Applied Social Psychology* 30 (4):349–361.

Adams, Glenn, and Hazel R. Markus. 2004. Toward a Conception of Culture Suitable for a Social Psychology of Culture. In *The Psychological Foundations of Culture*, edited by M. Schaller and C. S. Crandall. Hillsdale, NJ: Lawrence Erlbaum.

Agassiz, Louis. 1850. Diversity of Origin of the Human Races. *Christian Examiner* 49:110–145.

Alcoff, Linda Martín. 2005. *Visible Identities: Race, Gender, and the Self*. New York: Oxford University Press.

Alcoff, Linda Martín, Michael Hames-García, Satya P. Mohanty, and Paula M. L. Moya, eds. 2006. *Identity Politics Reconsidered*. New York: Palgrave Macmillan.

American Association of Colleges for Teacher Education. 1999. *Teacher Education Pipeline IV: Schools, Colleges, and Departments of Education*. Washington, DC: AACTE.

Asch, Solomon. 1952. *Social Psychology*. New York: Prentice Hall.

Baron, A. S., and M. R. Banaji. 2006. The Development of Implicit Attitudes: Evidence of Race Evaluations from Ages 6, 10 and Adulthood. *Psychological Science* 17:53–58.

Bellah, Robert N., Richard Madsen, William M. Sullivan, Ann Swidler, and Steven M. Tipton. 1985. *Habits of the Heart: Individualism and Commitment in American Life*. Berkeley: University of California Press.

Bertrand, Marianne, and Sendhil Mullainathan. 2004. Are Emily and Greg More Employable than Lakisha and Jamal? A Field Experiment on Labor Market Discrimination. *American Economic Review* 94 (4):991–1013.

Best, Amy L. 2003. Doing Race in the Context of Feminist Interviewing: Constructing Whiteness through Talk. *Qualitative Inquiry* 9 (6):895–914.

Boas, Franz. 1911. *The Mind of Primitive Man, a Course of Lectures Delivered before the Lowell Institute, Boston, Mass., and the National University of Mexico, 1910–1911*. New York: Macmillan.

Bobo, Lawrence D. 2004. Inequalities that Endure? Racial Ideology, American Politics, and the Peculiar Role of Social Science. In *The Changing Terrain of Race and Ethnicity*, edited by M. Krysan, A. Lewis, and T. Forman. New York: Russell Sage Foundation, 13–42.

Bolnick, Deborah A., Duana Fullwiley, Troy Duster, Richard S. Cooper, Joan H. Fujimura, Jonathan Kahn, Jay S. Kaufman, et al. 2007. The Science and Business of Genetic Ancestry Testing. *Science* 318:399–400.

Bonilla-Silva, Eduardo. 2003. *Racism without Racists: Color-blind Racism and the Persistence of Racial Inequality in the United States*. Lanham, MD: Rowman and Littlefield.

Bronson, Po, and Ashley Merryman. 2009. See Baby Discriminate. *Newsweek*, September 14, 53–60.

Brown v. Board of Education. 1954. 347 U.S. 483.

Brown, Michael K., Martin Carnoy, Elliott Currie, Troy Duster, David B. Oppenheimer, Marjorie M. Schultz, and David Wellman. 2005. *Whitewashing Race: The Myth of a Colorblind Society*. Berkeley: University of California Press.

Bruner, Jerome. 1990. *Acts of Meaning*. Cambridge, MA: Harvard University Press.

Carter, Prudence L. 2005. *Keepin' It Real: School Success beyond Black and White*. Oxford, UK: Oxford University Press.

Cavuto, Neil. 2006. Interview with Congressman Ted Poe. *Your World*, Fox News, August 16.

Cohen, Geoffrey, Julio Garcia, Nancy Apfel, and Allison Master. 2006. Reducing the Racial Achievement Gap: A Social-Psychological Intervention. *Science* 313 (5791): 1307–1310.

Copernicus, Nicolaus, and Charles G. Wallis. 1995. *On the Revolution of Heavenly Spheres*. Amherst: Prometheus Books.

Cose, Ellis. 1993. *The Rage of a Privileged Class*. New York: HarperCollins.

Crash. 2005. Written and directed by Paul Haggis. DVD. Santa Monica, CA: Lions Gate Entertainment.

Crenshaw, Kimberlé, Neil Gotanda, Garry Peller, Kendall Thomas, and Cornel West, eds. 1996. *Critical Race Theory: The Key Writings that Formed the Movement*. New York: New Press.

Croizet, J. C. 2008. The Pernicious Relationship between Merit Assessment and Discrimination in Education. In *Commemorating Brown: The Social Psychology of Racism and Discrimination*, edited by Glenn Adams, et al. Washington, DC: American Psychological Association, 153–172.

D'Agostino, F. 1998. Two Conceptions of Autonomy. *Economy and Society* 27 (1):28–49.

Darity, William A., Jr. 2005. Stratification Economics. *Journal of Economics and Finance* 29 (2):144–153.

Darling-Hammond, Linda. 2004. What Happens to a Dream Deferred? The Continuing Quest for Equal Educational Opportunity. In *Handbook of Research on Multicultural Education*, 2nd edition, edited by James A. Banks. San Francisco: Jossey-Bass, 607–630.

Dean, Cornelia. 2007. James Watson Quits Post After Remarks on Races. *New York Times*, October 26.

Descartes, René. [1637] 2006. *A Discourse on the Method of Correctly Conducting One's Reason and Seeking Truth in the Sciences*. Translated by I. Maclean. New York: Oxford University Press.

Deutsch, Sarah. 1987. *No Separate Refuge: Culture, Class, and Gender on an Anglo-Hispanic Frontier in the American Southwest, 1880–1940*. New York: Oxford University Press.

Devine, Patricia G., E. Ashby Plant, David M. Amodio, Eddie Harmon-Jones, and Stephanie L. Vance. 2002. The Regulation of Explicit and Implicit Race Bias: The Role of Motivations to Respond Without Prejudice. *Journal of Personality and Social Psychology* 82 (5):835–848.

Devos, Thierry, and Mahzarin R. Banaji. 2005. American = White? *Journal of Personality and Social Psychology* 88 (3):447–466.

Doi, Takeo. 1973. *The Anatomy of Dependence*. New York: Kodansha America.

Dovidio, John, Peter Glick, and Laurie Rudman, eds. 2005. *Reflecting on the Nature of Prejudice: Fifty Years after Allport*. Malden, MA: Blackwell.

Dweck, Carol S. 2006. *Mindset: The New Psychology of Success*. New York: Random House.

Eberhardt, Jennifer. 2005. Imaging Race. *American Psychologist* 60 (2):181–190.

Eberhardt, Jennifer L., and Susan T. Fiske, eds. 1998. *Confronting Racism: The Problem and the Response*. Thousand Oaks, CA: Sage.

Faber, Judy. 2007. CBS Fires Don Imus over Racial Slur: Dismissal Caps Week of Uproar over Radio Host's Comments about Rutgers Women's Basketball Team. CBS/AP News. April 12. www.cbsnews.com/stories/2007/04/12/national/main2675273_page2.shtml.

Facing History and Ourselves. 2002. *Race and Membership in American History: The Eugenics Movement*. Brookline, MA: Facing History and Ourselves National Foundation, Inc.

Fanon, Frantz. 1952. *Black Skin, White Masks*. Translated by Richard Philcox. New York: Grove Press.

Feagin, Joe R. 2006. *Systemic Racism: A Theory of Oppression*. New York: Routledge.

Feldman, Marcus W. 2010. The Biology of Ancestry: DNA, Genomic Variation, and Race. In *Doing Race: 21 Essays for the 21st Century*, edited by H. R. Markus and P. M. L. Moya. New York: W. W. Norton.

Fischer, Mary J., and Douglas S. Massey. 2004. The Ecology of Racial Discrimination. *City and Community* 3 (3):221–241.

Fiske, Alan Page, Shinobu Kitayama, Hazel Rose Markus, and Richard E. Nisbett. 1998. The Cultural Matrix of Social Psychology. In *The Handbook of Social Psychology*, edited by D. T. Gilbert, S. T. Fiske and G. Lindzey. San Francisco: McGraw-Hill, 915–981.

Fredrickson, George M. 1971. *The Black Image in the White Mind: The Debate on Afro-American Character and Destiny, 1817–1914*. New York: Harper & Row.

Fredrickson, George M. 2002. *Racism: A Short History*. Princeton, NJ: Princeton University Press.

Fryberg, Stephanie A., and Hazel Rose Markus. 2003. Cultural Models of Education in American Indian, Asian American and European American Contexts. *Social Psychology of Education* 10 (2):214–246.

Galilei, Galileo. 2008. *The Essential Galileo*. Translated by M. A. Finocchiaro. Indianapolis: Hackett.

Gates, Henry Louis, Jr. 1988. *The Signifying Monkey: A Theory of Afro-American Literary Criticism*. New York: Oxford University Press.

Gates, Henry Louis, Jr. 2007. *Finding Oprah's Roots: Finding Your Own*. New York: Crown.

Geertz, Clifford. 1973. *The Interpretation of Cultures*. New York: Basic Books.

Geiser, S., and M. V. Santelices. 2007. Validity of High-School Grades in Predicting Student Success Beyond the Freshman Year: High-School Record vs. Standardized Tests as Indicators of Four-Year College Outcomes. *Research and Occasional Paper Series: CSHE*, cshe. berkeley.edu/publications/publications.php?s=1.

Goldberg, David Theo. 1993. *Racist Culture: Philosophy and the Politics of Meaning*. Cambridge, MA: Blackwell.

Goldberg, David Theo. 2009. *The Threat of Race: Reflections on Racial Neoliberalism*. Malden, MA: Wiley-Blackwell.

Gorman, Anna and Susana Enriquez. 2005. Ad Putting L.A. in Mexico Called Slap in Face. *Los Angeles Times*, April 27, B-3.

Gorski, Paul, and EdChange. 1995–2008. Teacher's Corner of EdChange's Multicultural Pavilion. www.edchange.org/multicultural/teachers.html (accessed Febrary 27, 2009).

Gould, Stephen Jay. 1981. *The Mismeasure of Man*. New York: W. W. Norton.

Gould, Stephen Jay. 1996. *The Mismeasure of Man*. Rev. and expanded ed. New York: W. W. Norton.

Gourevitch, Philip. 1999. *We Wish to Inform You That Tomorrow We Will Be Killed with Our Families: Stories from Rwanda*. New York: Picador.

Green, Alexander R., Dana R. Carney, Daniel J. Pallin, Long H. Ngo, Kristal L. Raymond, Lisa I. Iezzoni, and Mahzarin R. Banaji. 2007. Implicit Bias among Physicians and Its Prediction of Thrombolysis Decisions for Black and White Patients. *Journal of General Internal Medicine* 22 (9):1231–1238.

Guinier, Lani, and Gerald Torres. 2002. *The Miner's Canary: Enlisting Race, Resisting Power, Transforming Democracy*. Cambridge, MA: Harvard University Press.

Gutiérrez, David. 1995. *Walls and Mirrors: Mexican Americans, Mexican Immigrants, and the Politics of Ethnicity*. Berkeley: University of California Press.

Gutierrez, K. D., and B. Rogoff. 2003. Cultural Ways of Learning: Individual Traits or Repertories of Practice. *Educational Researcher* 32:19–25.

Hames-García, Michael R. 2004. *Fugitive Thought: Prison Movements, Race, and the Meaning of Justice*. Minneapolis: University of Minnesota Press.

Harris, David. 1999, Dec. The Stories, the Statistics, and the Law: Why "Driving While Black" Matters. *Minnesota Law Review*, 277–288.

Higginbotham, Elizabeth, and Margaret L. Andersen. 2005. *Race and Ethnicity in Society: The Changing Landscape*. New York: Cengage Learning.

Hollinger, David A. May, 1995. *Postethnic America: Beyond Multiculturalism*. New York: Basic Books.

Huntington, Samuel P. 2005. *Who Are We? The Challenges to America's National Identity*. New York: Simon & Schuster.

Ignatiev, Noel. 1995. *How the Irish Became White*. New York: Routledge.

Jackson, John L., Jr. 2001. *Harlemworld: Doing Race and Class in Contemporary Black America*. Chicago: University of Chicago Press.

Jefferson, Thomas. [1781] 1995. *Notes on the State of Virginia*. Edited by William Harwood Peden. Chapel Hill: University of North Carolina Press.

Jefferson, Thomas. 2001. *The Inaugural Addresses of President Thomas Jefferson, 1801 and 1805*. Edited by N. E. Cunningham. Columbia: University of Missouri Press.

Johnson, Allan. 2005. *Privilege, Power, and Difference*. 2nd ed. New York: McGraw-Hill.

Jonas, Michael. 2007. The Downside of Diversity. *Boston Globe*, August 5, D1.

Jones, James M. 1996. *Prejudice and Racism*. New York: McGraw-Hill.

Jordan, David Starr. 1911. *The Heredity of Richard Roe; a Discussion of the Principles of Eugenics*. Boston: American Unitarian Association.

Kakutani, M. 1997. Bananas for Rent. *New York Times Magazine*, November 9.

Kelley, Raina. 2009. No Apologies. *Newsweek*, March 9.

Kim, Heejung S. 2002. We Talk, Therefore We Think? A Cultural Analysis of the Effect of Talking on Thinking. *Journal of Personality and Social Psychology* 83:828–842.

Koenig, Barbara A., Sandra Soo-Jin Lee, and Sarah Richardson. 2008. *Revisiting Race in a Genomic Age*. Piscataway, NJ: Rutgers University Press.

Krysan, Maria, Reynolds Farley, and Mick P. Couper. 2008. In the Eye of the Beholder. *Du Bois Review: Social Science Research on Race* 5 (1):5–26.

Krysan, Maria, and Amanda Lewis. 2005. The United States Today: Racial Discrimination Is Alive and Well. *Challenge* 48:34–49.

Ladson-Billings, Gloria. 1994. *The Dreamkeepers: Successful Teachers of African-American Children*. San Francisco: Jossey-Bass.

LaVaque-Manty, Mika. 2002. *Arguments and Fists: Political Agency and Justification in Liberal Theory*. New York: Routledge.

Le Bon, Gustave. 1879. Recherches Anatomiques et Mathématiques sur les Lois des Variations du Volume du Cerveau et sur Leurs Relations avec l'Intelligence. *Revue d'Anthropologie* 2: 27–104.

Lewontin, Richard C., Steven P. R. Rose, and Leon J. Kamin. 1984. *Not in Our Genes: Biology, Ideology, and Human Nature*. New York: Pantheon.

Li, Jun Z., et al. 2008. Worldwide Human Relationships Inferred from Genome-Wide Patterns of Variation. *Science* 319: 1100–1104.

Linnaeus, Carolus. 1767. *Systema Naturae*, 13th ed. Vienna: Typis Ioannis Thomae nob. de Trattnern.

Lipsitz, George. 1998. *The Possessive Investment in Whiteness: How White People Profit from Identity Politics*. Philadelphia: Temple University Press.

Locke, John. [1689] 2005. Two Treatises on Government. In *The Selected Political Writings of John Locke*. Edited by P. E. Sigmund. New York: W. W. Norton, 4–167.

Lohse, Deborah, and Griff Palmer. 2005. Not All Home Loans Are Equal— Analysis: Latinos May Pay Thousands More in Higher Mortgage Rates. *San Jose Mercury News*, 1A.

Lopez, Robert, and Jeff Marx. 2003. *Avenue Q the Musical: Original Broadway Cast Recording*. New York: RCA Victor: BMG Distribution. Sound recording.

Lott, Eric. 1993. *Love and Theft: Blackface Minstrelsy and the American Working Class*. New York: Oxford University Press.

Louie, Steven G., and Glenn K. Omatsu. 2001. *Asian Americans: The Movement and the Moment*. Los Angeles: University of California, Asian American Studies Center.

Luther, Martin. [1517] 2004. *Martin Luther's 95 Theses: With the Pertinent Documents from the History of the Reformation*. Translated by K. Aland. St. Louis: Concordia.

Markus, Hazel R. 2008. Identity Matters: Ethnicity, Race, and the American Dream. In *Just Schools: Pursuing Equal Education in Societies of Difference*. New York: Russel Sage Foundation.

Markus, Hazel Rose, and MarYam G. Hamedani. 2007. Sociocultural Psychology: The Dynamic Interdependence among Self-Systems and Social Systems. In *Handbook of Cultural Psychology*, edited by S. Kitayama and D. Cohen. New York: Guilford, 3–39.

Markus, Hazel Rose, and Shinobu Kitayama. 1991. Culture and the Self: Implications for Cognition, Emotion, Motivation. *Psychological Review* 98:224–253.

Markus, Hazel Rose, and Shinobu Kitayama. 2003. Models of Agency: Sociocultural Diversity in the Construction of Action. In *The 49th Annual Nebraska Symposium on Motivation: Cross-Cultural Differences in Perspectives on Self*, edited by V. Murphy-Berman and J. Berman. Lincoln: University of Nebraska Press.

Markus, Hazel Rose, Claude M. Steele, and Dorothy M. Steele. 2000. Colorblindness as a Barrier to Inclusion: Assimilation and Nonimmigrant Minorities. *Daedalus* 129 (4):233–259.

Marmot, M. G. 2004. *The Status Syndrome: How Social Standing Affects Our Health and Longevity*. 1st American ed. New York: Times Books/Henry Holt.

Marsella, Anthony, George DeVos, and Francis Hsu. 1985. *Culture and Self*. New York: Tavistock.

Martin, Michel. 2008. Obama's Climb Says a Mouthful. *Tell Me More!*: NPR, January 7.

Massey, Douglas S., and Nancy Denton. 1998. *American Apartheid: Segregation and the Making of the Underclass*. Cambridge, MA: Harvard University Press.

Massey, Douglas S. and Mary J. Fischer. 2004. The Social Ecology of Racial Discrimination. *City and Community* 3:221–243.

McPherson, James M. 1996. *Drawn with the Sword: Reflections on the American Civil War*. New York: Oxford University Press.

Mignolo, Walter. 1995. *The Darker Side of the Renaissance: Literacy, Territoriality, and Colonization*. Ann Arbor: University of Michigan Press.

Mignolo, Walter. 2005. *The Idea of Latin America, Blackwell Manifestos*. Malden, MA: Blackwell.

Mills, Charles W. 1998. *Blackness Visible: Essays on Philosophy and Race*. Ithaca, NY: Cornell University Press.

Mohanty, Satya P. 1997. *Literary Theory and the Claims of History: Postmodernism, Objectivity, Multicultural Politics*. Ithaca, NY: Cornell University Press.

Morrison, Toni. 1992. *Playing in the Dark: Whiteness and the Literary Imagination*. Cambridge, MA: Harvard University Press.

Morton, Samuel George. 1839. *Crania Americana; Or, A Comparative View of the Skulls of Various Aboriginal Nations of North and South America*. Philadelphia: Dobson.

Moya, Paula M. L. 2002. *Learning from Experience: Minority Identities, Multicultural Struggles*. Berkeley: University of California Press.

Moya, Paula M. L., and Michael R. Hames-García, eds. 2000. *Reclaiming Identity: Realist Theory and the Predicament of Postmodernism*. Berkeley: University of California Press.

Moynihan, Patrick. 1965. *The Negro Family: The Case For National Action*. Washington, DC: United States Department of Labor, Office of Policy Planning and Research.

Muñoz, Carlos. 1989. *Youth, Identity, Power: The Chicano Movement*. London: Verso.

Nosek, Brian A., Frederick L. Smyth, Jeffrey J. Hansen, Thierry Devos, Nicole M. Lindner, Kate A. Ranganath, Colin Tucker Smith, Kristina R. Olson, Dolly Chugh, Anthony G. Greenwald, and Mahzarin R. Banaji. 2007. Pervasiveness and Correlates of Implicit Attitudes and Stereotypes. *European Review of Social Psychology* 18: 36–88.

Oakes, Jeannie. 1990. Multiplying Inequalities: The Effects of Race, Social Class, and Tracking on Opportunities to Learn Mathematics and Science. Santa Monica, CA: The RAND Corporation.

Oakes, Jeannie, and Gretchen Guiton. 1995. Matchmaking: The Dynamics of High School Tracking Decisions. *American Educational Research Journal* 32:3–33.

Oliver, M. L., and T. M. Shapiro. 1997. *Black Wealth, White Wealth: A New Perspective on Racial Inequality*. New York: Routledge.

Olsen, Laurie. 1997. *Made in America: Immigrant Students in Our Public Schools*. New York: New Press.

Omi, Michael, and Howard Winant. 1994. *Racial Formation in the United States: From the 1960s to the 1990s*. New York: Routledge.

Orfield, Gary. 2004. *Dropouts in America: Confronting the Graduation Rate Crisis*. Cambridge, MA: Harvard Education Press.

Ouazad, Amine. 2008. *Assessed by a Teacher Like Me: Race, Gender, and Subjective Evaluations*. London: Centre for the Economics of Education.

Pager, Devah. 2007. *Marked: Race, Crime, and Finding Work in an Era of Mass Incarceration*. Chicago: University of Chicago Press.

Pager, Devah. and Bruce Western. 2005. Discrimination in Low-Wage Labor Markets: Results from an Experimental Audit Study in New York City. In *Annual Meeting of the American Sociological Association*. Marriott Hotel, Loews Philadelphia Hotel, Philadelphia, PA.

Parsons, Christopher A., Johan Sulaeman, Michael C. Yates, and Daniel S. Hamermesh. 2007. Strike Three: Umpires' Demand for Discrimination. NBER Working Paper Series, National Bureau of Economic Research, Cambridge, MA.

Perry, Theresa. 2003. Up from the Parched Earth: Toward a Theory of African American Achievement. In *Young, Gifted, and Black: Promoting High Achievement* *among African American Students*, edited by C. S. Theresa Perry and Asa Hilliard III. Boston: Beacon Press, 1–10.

Perry, Theresa, Claude Steele, and Asa G. Hilliard. 2003. *Young, Gifted, and Black: Promoting High Achievement Among African-American students*. Boston: Beacon Press.

Pettit, Becky, and Bruce Western. 2004. Mass Imprisonment and the Life Course: Race and Class Inequality in U.S. Incarceration. *American Sociological Review* 69:151–69.

Plaut, Victoria C. 2002. Cultural Models of Diversity: The Psychology of Difference and Inclusion. In *Engaging Cultural Differences: The Multicultural Challenge in Liberal Democracies*, edited by R. Shweder, M. Minow, and H. R. Markus. New York: Russell Sage Foundation Press.

Plessy v. Ferguson. 1896. 163 U.S. 537.

Price, Joseph, and Justin Wolfers. 2007. Racial Discrimination among NBA Referees. Cambridge, MA: National Bureau of Economic Research.

Quijano, Aníbal. 2000. Coloniality of Power, Eurocentrism, and Latin America. *Nepantla: Views from the South* 1 (3):533–580.

Reel Bad Arabs: How Hollywood Vilifies a People. 2006. DVD. Directed by Sut Jhally. Northampton, MA: Media Education Foundation.

Regents of the University of California v. Bakke. 1978. 438 U.S. 265.

Roediger, David R. 1991. *The Wages of Whiteness: Race and the Making of the American Working Class*. New York: Verso.

Rothstein-Fisch, Carrie, Patricia Greenfield, and Elise Turnbull. 1999. Bridging Cultures with Classroom Strategies: Understanding Individualism-Collectivism. *Educational Leadership* 56 (7):64–67.

Said, Edward W. 1978. *Orientalism*. New York: Pantheon.

Sanneh, Kelefa. 2008. Chris Rock Is Back. Give Him a Cookie. *New York Times*, January 2.

Schiraldi, Vincent, and Jason Ziedenberg. 2002, Aug. Cellblocks or Classrooms? The Funding of Higher Eduation and Corrections and Its Impact on African American Men. Washington, DC: Justice Policy Institute. Available at www .justicepolicy.org.

Schwarz, Alan. 2007. Study of N.B.A. Sees Racial Bias in Calling Fouls. *New York Times*, May 2, 1.

Schwartz, Barry. 1986. *The Battle for Human Nature: Science, Morality, and Modern Life*. New York: W. W. Norton.

Scott v. Sandford. 1857. 60 U.S. 393.

Senna, Danzy. 1998. The Mulatto Millennium. In *Half and Half: Writers Growing Up Biracial and Bicultural*, edited by Claudine Chiawei O'Hearn. New York: Pantheon Books, 12–27.

Shaheen, Jack G. 2001. *Reel Bad Arabs: How Hollywood Vilifies a People*. New York: Olive Branch Press.

Shweder, Richard A. 2003. *Why Do Men Barbecue? Recipes for Cultural Psychology*. Cambridge, MA: Harvard University Press.

Shweder, Richard A., Jacqueline J. Goodnow, Giyoo Hatano, Robert A. LeVine, Hazel Rose Markus, and Peggy J. Miller. 2006. The Cultural Psychology of Development: One Mind, Many Mentalities. In *Handbook of Child Psychology, Vol. 1: Theoretical Models of Human Development*, edited by R. Lerner and W. Damon. Hoboken, NJ: John Wiley and Sons.

Shweder, Richard, M. Minow, and Hazel R. Markus, eds. 2002. *Engaging Cultural Differences: The Multicultural Challenge in Liberal Democracies*. New York: Russell Sage Foundation.

Sidanius, Jim, Shana Levin, and Felicia Pratto. 1998. Hierarchical Group Relations, Institutional Terror, and the Dynamics of the Criminal Justice System. In *Confronting Racism: The Problem and the Response*, edited by J. Eberhardt and S. Fiske. Thousand Oaks, CA: Sage.

Smedley, Audrey. 2007. *Race in North America: Origin and Evolution of a Worldview*, 3rd ed. Boulder, CO: Westview Press.

Smith, Paul Chaat, and Robert Allen Warrior. 1997. *Like a Hurricane: The Indian Movement from Alcatraz to Wounded Knee*. New York: New Press.

Smith, Stephen. 2007. Tests of ER Trainees Find Signs of Race Bias in Care: Study Seeks Root of Known Disparity. *Boston Globe*, July 20, A1.

Sollors, Werner. 1996. *Theories of Ethnicity: A Classical Reader*. New York: New York University Press.

Steele, Claude M. 1992. Race and the Schooling of Black Americans. *Atlantic Monthly*, 68–78.

Steele, Claude M. 2010. *Whistling Vivaldi: And Other Clues to How Stereotypes Affect Us*. New York: W. W. Norton.

Steele, Claude M., S. J. Spencer, and J. Aronson. 2002. Contending with Group Image: The Psychology of Stereotype and Social Identity Threat. In *Advances in Experimental Social Psychology*, edited by M. P. Zanna. San Diego, CA: Academic Press.

Steinhauer, Jennifer. 2007. Korean-Americans Brace for Problems in Wake of Killings. *New York Times*, April 19. Accessed at nytimes.com

Stevenson, Harold, and James Stigler. 1992. *The Learning Gap: Why Our Schools Are Failing and What We Can Learn from Japanese and Chinese Education*. New York: Summit Books.

Suárez-Orozco, Carola, Marcelo M. Suárez-Orozco, and Irina Todorova. 2008. In *Learning a New Land: Immigrant Students in American Society*. Cambridge, MA: Belknap Press of Harvard University Press.

Sundquist, Eric J. 1993. *To Wake the Nations: Race in the Making of American Literature*. Cambridge, MA: Belknap Press of Harvard University Press.

Sundquist, Eric J. 2005. *Strangers in the Land: Blacks, Jews, Post-Holocaust America*. Cambridge, MA: Belknap Press of Harvard University Press.

Takaki, Ronald T. 1993. *A Different Mirror: A History of Multicultural America*. Boston: Little, Brown.

Tatum, Beverly. 2002. The Complexity of Identity: "Who Am I?" In *Why Are All the Black Kids Sitting Together in the Cafeteria? Rev. ed.* New York: Basic Books.

Taylor, Charles. 1989. *Sources of the Self: The Making of the Modern Identity*. Cambridge, MA: Harvard University Press.

Terman, Lewis Madison. 1916. *The Measurement of Intelligence; An Explanation of and a Complete Guide for the Use of the Stanford Revision and Extension of the Binet-Simon Intelligence Scale*. Boston: Houghton Mifflin.

Thomas, William Isaac. 1923. *The Unadjusted Girl*. Boston: Little, Brown.

Thompson, Ginger. 2008. Seeking Unity, Obama Feels Pull of Racial Divide. *New York Times*, February 12.

Todorov, Tzvetan. 1999. *The Conquest of America: The Question of the Other*. Norman: University of Oklahoma Press.

Tormala, Teceta Thomas, and Kay Deaux. 2006. Black Immigrants to the United States: Confronting and Constructing Ethnicity and Race. In *Cultural Psychology of Immigrants*, edited by R. Mahalingam. Mahwah, NJ: Lawrence Erlbaum.

Triandis, Harry. 1995. *Individualism and Collectivism*. Boulder, CO: Westview Press.

Tsai, Jeanne L. 2007. Ideal Affect: Cultural Causes and Behavioral Consequences. *Perspectives on Psychological Science* 2 (3):242–259.

Tseng, Vivian, Ruth K. Chao, and Inna Artati Padmawidjaja. 2006. Asian Americans' Educational Experiences In *Handbook of Asian American Psychology*, edited by F. Leong, A. Inman, A. Ebreo, L. Yang, L. M. Kinoshita and M. Fu. Thousand Oaks, CA: Sage.

Ture, Kwame, and Charles Hamilton. [1967] 1992. *Black Power: The Politics of Liberation*. New York: Vintage.

United Colors of Benetton. 1989–2008. Photo gallery. www.benettongroup.com/en/whatwesay/sottosezioni/campaigns_photo_gallery.htm (accessed April 22, 2009).

United States Congress, House Committee on the Judiciary. 1981. *Civil Rights Acts of 1957, 1960, 1964, 1968 (as amended through the end of the 96th Congress): Voting Rights Act of 1965 (as amended through the end of the 96th Congress)*. Washington, DC: U.S. Government Printing Office.

USA Today. 2008. Race Mattered in South Carolina Democratic Primary. January 27.

Wade, Nicholas. 2008. A Dissenting Voice as the Genome Is Sifted to Fight Disease. *New York Times*, September 16, 3.

Watt, Nicholas. 2009. "Blue-eyed Bankers" to Blame for Crash, Lula Tells Brown. *Guardian*, March 26. www.guardian.co.uk/world /2009/mar/26/lula-attacks-white-bankers-crash.

Webb, Gary. 1999. DWB: Police Stops Motorists to Check for Drugs. *Esquire*, April 1, 118–127.

West, Cornel. 1993. *Race Matters*. Boston: Beacon Press.

Wilson, Clint C., Félix Gutiérrez, and Lena M. Chao. 2003. *Racism, Sexism, and the Media: The Rise of Class Communication in Multicultural America*. 3rd ed. Thousand Oaks, CA: Sage.

Wilson, William Julius. 1990. *The Truly Disadvantaged: The Inner City, the Underclass, and Public Policy*. Chicago: University of Chicago Press.

Witt, Howard. 2007. School Discipline Tougher on African Americans. *Chicago Tribune*, September 25.

Xin, Katherine R. 2004. Asian American Managers: An Impression Gap?: An Investigation of Impression Management and Supervisor-Subordinate Relationships. *The Journal of Applied Behavioral Science* 40 (2):160–181.

Zarate, Maria Estela, and Harry P. Pachon. 2006. Gaining or Losing Ground?: Equity in Offering Advanced Placement Courses in California High Schools, 1997–2003. Los Angeles: Tomás Rivera Policy Institute. www.trpi.org/update/education.html.

Zuberi, T., and E. Bonilla-Silva, eds. 2008. *White Logic, White Methods*. Lanham, MD: Rowman and Littlefield.

Zwick, Rebecca, and Jeffery Sklar. 2005. Predicting College Grades and Degree Completion Using High School Grades and SAT Scores: The Role of Student Ethnicity and First Language. *American Educational Research Journal* 42(3): 439–464.

PART ONE

Inventing Race and Ethnicity

1

Defining Race and Ethnicity

The Constitution, the Supreme Court, and the Census

C. Matthew Snipp

•

This essay examines different definitions and understandings of race and ethnicity in American society. Given the commonplace reality of these phenomena within our world, we might assume that some consensus exists about the meaning of these terms. Such an assumption, however, would be deeply flawed. Definitions of race and ethnicity abound, and what each term means varies dramatically over historical time and from one nation to another. The French, for example, are dismissive of the idea of race and prefer to exclude it from polite conversation and government statistics. Given the limitations of space, this essay, which is written from the perspective of a sociologist, is specific to the United States and focuses on demographic practices and governmental policies. After presenting a brief history of the origins of the terms "race" and "ethnicity," the essay examines the impact of several Supreme Court cases on our notions of race before turning to the racial cosmologies articulated over time by the U.S. Census. In general, the analysis presented in this essay highlights the role that institutions, government agents, and political agendas play in shaping and defining the way race and ethnicity are understood in the United States.

THERE ARE FEW TERMS THAT ARE MORE DEEPLY EMBEDDED WITHIN the conversations of everyday life than the descriptors of "race and ethnicity." Applications for jobs, scholarships, drivers' licenses, and other modern privileges routinely request this information. As we encounter others in our everyday world, we instantly and unconsciously assess their age, sex and race, or ethnicity. Race and ethnicity are relevant considerations when choosing our friends, future mates, and clandestinely, when we choose our neighbors and co-workers. To settle any doubt about the pervasive presence of race and ethnicity in modern society, a Google search is one powerful measure of popular discourse. Using the phrase "race and ethnicity" yields a list consisting of 47,500,000 entries—a considerable number. This number is even more imposing when, and for the sake of comparison, searches for personalities in popular culture such as "Britney Spears" produce lists that are impressive in number yet are still significantly smaller than the number of entries for race and ethnicity.

HISTORICAL ORIGINS

It is impossible to discuss the meaning of race and ethnicity in American society, or in any society, without taking note of the intellectual roots of the ideas we hold about them.[1] Most scholars agree that race and ethnicity exist mainly as a means for accentuating or highlighting differences that may exist between groups (Omi and Winant 1994; Fredrickson 2002). The terms serve as shorthand for designating people belonging to some groups as "others" or "not one of us." The practice of identifying some people as "like us" and others as "not like us" is one that predates written history and quite possibly was present in the earliest forms of human societies.

In its modern usage, race often has been used to reflect some set of biological properties, and the Spanish Inquisition is credited with being the first to connect biological qualities with social and cultural habits. The Inquisition linked "blood" and "blood purity" with the Jewish faith by presenting the question of whether it was possible to cleanse the Jewish blood from Jews who converted to Christianity (Fredrickson 2002). This connection has provided a vocabulary for racial discourse framed in terms of blood and blood purity that persists into the twenty-first century.[2]

---

1 A lengthier and very accessible discussion of the intellectual history of race and racism can be found in George Fredrickson's *Racism: A Brief History* (2002).

2 For example, an agency of the U.S. government, the Bureau of Indian Affairs, issues a document known as a "Certificate Degree of Indian Blood" that is evidence of American Indian ancestry.

The concept of race, and its association with blood and other biological traits, remained an ill-formed idea for at least three centuries. However, the Enlightenment embedded the concept of race within modern secular thought in several ways. The Swedish naturalist and one of the founders of modern biology, Carl Linnaeus, introduced in 1735 a classification to describe the several varieties of *Homo sapiens*. Linnaeus differentiated Europeans, American Indians, Asians and Africans, and a residual category of "monstrous" races that later proved to be nonexistent (Fredrickson 2002). Forty years later, Johann Friedrich Blumenbach, a founder of physical anthropology, published *On the Natural Varieties of Mankind* (1776). This work proved to be an authoritative classification of the known races and introduced the terms "Caucasian," "Mongolian," "Ethiopian," "American," and "Malay" to describe them.

Although many of the founding fathers of the United States, especially Thomas Jefferson, were deeply influenced by Enlightenment thinking, it is not clear how much they were influenced by the work of Linnaeus and Blumenbach. Nonetheless, the crafting of the U.S. Constitution took special notice of race and incorporated it into the political framework of the United States as a category of civil status. The necessity of recognizing race stemmed from the controversies surrounding slavery and a tacit acknowledgment that American Indian tribes were sovereigns beyond the jurisdiction of the U.S. government. Specifically, Article I, Section 2, of the Constitution stipulates that

> Representatives and direct Taxes . . . shall be determined by adding to the whole Number of free Persons, including those bound to Service for a Term of Years, and excluding Indians not taxed, three fifths of all other Persons. . . . The actual Enumeration shall be made . . . within every subsequent Term of ten Years, in such Manner as they shall by Law direct.

Thus, for purposes of determining political representation and taxes—the two issues most critical in the American Revolution—African slaves were counted as 60 percent (3/5) of a whole person and American Indians were excluded. In this manner, race was used to determine civil status in the most fundamental legal document of the nation.

In the nineteenth century, race and racial differences were the pre-eminent concerns of the racial sciences, eugenics and ethnology, better known today as scientific racism. Scholars such as Lewis Henry Morgan, Francis Galton, and Arthur de Gobineau labored to identify and catalog racial differences and to establish a biological basis for why some races were superior or inferior to others. By the late nineteenth century, others scholars such as Franz Boaz and his students began to challenge key tenets in scientific racism, such as the presumption of cultural inferiority or superiority. This challenge also led scholars critical of scientific racism to embrace the concept of ethnicity as an alternative to the concept of race (McKee 1993).

The term "ethnicity" is derived from the Greek word "ethnikos" or "ethnos," meaning people or nation (Peterson 1980). As an alternative to the concept of race, ethnicity is rooted in national identity or in behavior sets connected with subgroups within nations. An ethnic group may share a common language, religion, family structure, diet, and lifestyle—to name only a few traits associated with ethnic differences. Most significantly, ethnicity connotes a group's differences that are wholly disconnected from biology, and further, does not imply invidious judgments about these differences.

In the twentieth century, the popularity of the term "ethnicity" grew slowly and coincided with the growing presence and influence of the social sciences within the academy. After World War II, the social sciences vigorously undertook the task of debunking ideas that for many years served as the conventional wisdom of scientific racism. In 1942, Ashley Montagu published his groundbreaking work *Race: Man's Most Dangerous Myth*. Montagu's work laid the foundation for understanding race as purely a social construction that can change over time and from one social environment to another. In the years after World War II, a consensus has grown behind the idea that race is nothing more than a social construct and that ethnicity is tied to social, as opposed to biological distinctions. By the late twentieth century, the terms "race" and "ethnicity" had come to be used interchangeably. Clearly, however, the two terms have very different intellectual pedigrees and as the discussion to follow will show, these ideas involve considerably different social and political implications.

ALTERNATIVE APPROACHES TO DEFINING RACE AND ETHNICITY

In the early years of the twentieth century, social scientists seemed content to agree that ethnic differences represented cultural and behavioral differences that were uniquely social in nature; however, debates about the content and quality of racial characteristics continued to rage (McKee 1993). A recurring issue within these debates was how best to define and understand the fundamental content of the concept of race. Was race fundamentally a biological characteristic, a product of the social environment, or both? How did the biology of race connect with the sociology of race and how did biological characteristics come to have social consequences?

For much of the twentieth century, social scientists, especially those in sociology and anthropology, struggled to define the meaning of race. But after decades of debate, dozens if not hundreds of different definitions for the concept of race could be found in the social scientific literature. By 1953 it was clear to at least two sociologists, George Simpson and Milton Yinger, that efforts to define race were at an intellectual dead end; countless inquiries had yielded countless variations on themes about which little or no consensus existed. However, they noted that while an absence of consensus existed about the true meaning of race, certain themes seemed to emerge from these disparate accounts. Simpson and Yinger argued that while it might not be possible to obtain a single conceptual definition of race that would be widely accepted, it was possible to classify racial definitions into several different types of concepts. Specifically, they suggested that there are at least three types of racial definitions: *mystical definitions, biological definitions, and administrative definitions* (Simpson and Yinger 1953). Understanding these definitional types provides some useful insights about the way that race is defined in the United States.

Mystical definitions of race are rooted in folklore, religious beliefs and other traditions such as origin stories that are largely outside of empirical experience. They represent attempts to explain variations in the human race by ascribing them to the actions of gods, spirits, and other mythological beings that transcend everyday human experience. One noteworthy example from the 1930s is the creation of the mythological race of Aryans by Nazi propagandists to justify the extermination of "lesser" races, especially European Jews. Needless to say, while mystical definitions may be interesting, they are of little value for most purposes in scientific inquiry.

Biological definitions of race are perhaps best known owing to more than a century of publications on the subjects of eugenics and ethnology. Following Linnaeus and Blumenbach, biologists, geneticists, physical anthropologists, and others debated intensely the exact number of races into which human beings could be classified. Advances in modern genetics in the late nineteenth and early twentieth centuries allowed the argument to progress to the point that a race could be defined as a "homogeneous gene pool." The discovery of various genetic markers enabled scientists to develop tests that could be used to assign individuals to a particular race. For example, earwax texture and fingerprint patterns could be used to identify certain "races" (Snipp 1989). However, as the numbers of these markers proliferated, they often yielded contradictory results that could only be reconciled by increasing the numbers of possible races. That is, as more markers became available, the more difficult it was to identify gene pools that could be considered truly homogeneous.

By the late twentieth century, scientists were beginning to seriously question whether race was a meaningful scientific construct, and many were skeptical about its utility (Gould 1996; Cavalli-Sforza 2001). However, recent discoveries connected to the mapping of the human genome have allowed geneticists to reliably assay the continental origins of genetic material. This has paved the way for a resurrection of biological interpretations of race associated with continental origins insofar as unique patterns of genes can be identified with Europe, Asia, Africa, and the Americas. This research and its nascent implications for a revitalized biology of race has been the object of intense controversy since its discovery (Erlich and Feldman 2003). The social and political implications of this work remain highly ambiguous.

Administrative definitions of race are constructions promulgated by government agencies and other bureaucratic institutions for the purpose of realizing a political agenda or completing an administrative task. This type of definition is the most commonplace insofar as administrative definitions of race are encountered in applications for employment, scholarships, and a variety of other situations for which government agencies require information about race or ethnicity to be collected from a particular constituency. Administrative definitions of race can vary a great deal over time and from one nation-state to another.

The reason for the variability in administrative definitions of race over time and across nation-states should be obvious. As governments and the agendas they pursue change, so do the racial classifications that they use. Classifications change in response to evolving conditions in the social and political environment. For example, as new ethnic groups immigrate en masse from nation-state to another, national governments often seek to monitor their movement and deploy various kinds of surveillance to estimate their numbers, locations, movements, and other details. Obtaining this information requires some sort of method for determining membership within the ethnic group of interest. This entails, of course, devising a new ethnic classification system that may replace or modify any existing systems already in place.

There are many examples of administrative definitions of race. In the eighteenth century, the authorities responsible for the Spanish colonies in what is now Mexico promulgated an elaborate system of *castas* to describe the various combinations of racial and ethnic mixing taking place among Europeans, Native Americans, and Africans. This classification included the term "mestizo" to describe the offspring of Spanish and Indian parents, and labeled the children of Spanish and African parents as "mulattos." The *castas* included fourteen other possible combinations and they were preserved for posterity in a series of paintings depicting the physical features of each racial/ethnic admixture.

Besides the *castas*, another noteworthy administrative definition of race was devised by South Africa during the era of racial apartheid. Unlike the *castas*, the South African system was relatively simple. It consisted of three categories: black, white, and colored. However, the South African system illustrates the arbitrary and sometimes nonsensical nature of administrative definitions. Specifically, the South African system classified as "Colored" persons who were neither black nor white. This included most persons from Asia, except for the Japanese, who were considered white. This was a concession to Japanese business representatives, with whom the South African government was trying to curry favor during the years when South Africa was boycotted by the international community.

DEFINING RACE AND ETHNICITY IN AMERICA

As indicated above, counting people by race is a tradition deeply embedded within the governing framework of the United States. Indeed, some notation of race has been taken since the first census in 1790.[3] As mandated by the Constitution, the first administrative definition of race used by the United States took note of African slaves and American Indians subject to taxation who were living under the jurisdiction of the United States. The implementation of this classification in the decennial census is significant because for most of this nation's history—at least throughout the nineteenth century and into the first half of the

---

3 A lengthy discussion of census practices can be found in Snipp (2003).

twentieth century—the census was the only reliable source of information about race and ethnicity in the United States.

In the nineteenth century, the official racial and ethnic classification used by the federal government evolved in response to the changing composition of the population and in response to political concerns of the era. In 1820, for example, the census began collecting information about the foreign-born population as concerns mounted about the national "stock" of new immigrants. The 1820 census also was noteworthy because for the first time enumerators were instructed to take note of each person's "color" and record whether they were white, black, or American Indian.

In the second half of the nineteenth century, scientific racism was virtually unassailable as a scientific doctrine, and hostility to foreigners—especially from Asia—was an established norm. These attitudes and beliefs were reflected in the approach of the United States to counting its inhabitants in each decennial census and in its efforts to articulate a racial cosmology more complex than one that distinguished only between whites, blacks and American Indians. The 1850 census acknowledged for the first time the existence of black-white and black–American Indian sexual relations by adding a category for mulatto to the census questionnaire. In the 1860 census, categories were added to include Chinese and Asian Indians, reflecting concerns about immigrant railroad workers. Ten years later, a category for Japanese was added to the 1870 census (Snipp 2003).

The 1890 census followed the Chinese Exclusion Act (1882), the cessation of the Indian Wars in the West, and a growing concern among politicians over racial purity. To address these concerns, the census counted Chinese and Japanese, and American Indians (both taxed and not taxed), and it subdivided the mulatto population into "Quadroons" and "Octoroons." It responded to nativist concerns about the impact of immigration on the nation by showing that a substantial amount of the growth in the U.S. population was due to immigration from Europe, particularly southern and eastern Europe. This finding provided potent fuel to the anti-immigration movement and others concerned with the "degradation" of American stock (Anderson 1988).

The official classification of race in the early decades of the twentieth century continued to evolve with changes in immigration and changing ideas about the nature of race. For example, in 1922 the Supreme Court was challenged to define the meaning of "White" in *Takao Ozawa v. U S*, a case involving a man of Japanese descent who claimed a right to become a naturalized citizen. The Court concluded that only persons of the white race were eligible for membership. In trying to establish the meaning of white, the Court said:

> Manifestly the test afforded by the mere color of the skin of each individual is impracticable, as that differs greatly among persons of the same race, even among Anglo-Saxons, ranging by imperceptible gradations from the fair blond to the swarthy brunette, the latter being darker than many of the lighter hued persons of the brown or yellow races. Hence to adopt the color test alone would result in a confused overlapping of races and a gradual merging of one into the other, without any practical line of separation. Beginning with the decision of Circuit Judge Sawyer, . . . the federal and state courts, in an almost unbroken line, have held that the words "white person" were meant to indicate only a person of what is popularly known as the Caucasian race. . . . With the conclusion reached in these several decisions we see no reason to differ. . . . The determination that the words "white person" are synonymous with the words "a person of the Caucasian race" simplifies the problem, although it does not entirely dispose of it. Controversies have arisen and will no doubt arise again in respect of the proper classification of individuals in border line cases. The effect of the conclusion that the words "white person" means a Caucasian is not to establish a sharp line of demarcation between those who are entitled and those who are not entitled to naturalization, but rather a zone of more or less debatable ground outside of which, upon the one hand, are those clearly eligible, and outside of which, upon the other hand, are those clearly ineligible for citizenship. (*Ozawa v. U.S.* 1922)

As it happened, the Court was called upon to clarify its tortured logic in *U.S. v. Bhagat Singh Thind*. This 1923 case involved an Asian Indian man, Bhagat Singh Thind, who claimed the right to naturalization. Thind argued that because he was born in a northwestern region of India that many ethnologists considered part of the Caucasus, he was eligible for citizenship as a Caucasian. Trying to clarify its use of the term "Caucasian" in the Ozawa case, Justice Sutherland delivered the opinion:

> The word "Caucasian," not means [*sic*] clear, and the use of it in its scientific [*sic*] probably wholly unfamiliar to the original framers of the statute in 1790. When we employ it, we do so as an aid to the ascertainment of the legislative intent and not as an invariable

substitute for the statutory words. Indeed, as used in the science of ethnology, the connotation of the word is by no means clear, and the use of it in its scientific sense as an equivalent. . . . But in this country, during the last half century especially, the word by common usage has acquired a popular meaning, not clearly defined to be sure, but sufficiently so to enable us to say that its popular as distinguished from its scientific application is of appreciably narrower scope. It is in the popular sense of the word, therefore, that we employ is as an aid to the construction of the statute, for it would be obviously illogical to convert words of common speech used in a statute into words of scientific terminology when neither the latter nor the science for whose purposes they were coined was within the contemplation of the framers of the statute or of the people for whom it was framed. . . . They imply, as we have said, a racial test; but the term "race" is one which, for the practical purposes of the statute, must be applied to a group of living persons now possessing in common the requisite characteristics, not to groups of persons who are supposed to be or really are descended from some remote, common ancestor, but who, whether they both resemble him to a greater or less extent, have, at any rate, ceased altogether to resemble one another. It may be true that the blond Scandinavian and the brown Hindu have a common ancestor in the dim reaches of antiquity, but the average man knows perfectly well that there are unmistakable and profound differences between them to-day; and it is not impossible, if that common ancestor could be materialized in the flesh, we should discover that he was himself sufficiently differentiated from both of his descendants to preclude his racial classification with either. (*U.S. v. Thind* 1923)

For African Americans, the ascendancy of Jim Crow legislation in the late nineteenth century and early twentieth century institutionalized the so-called one-drop rule. The one-drop rule held that even the smallest amount of black heritage was sufficient to warrant the designation of "black." In the 1930 census, enumerators received the instruction that

a person of mixed White and Negro blood was to be returned as Negro, no matter how small the percentage of Negro blood; someone part Indian and part Negro also was to be listed as Negro, unless the Indian blood predominated. (Snipp 2003)

This instruction, of course, relies on terminology (blood) rooted in medieval beliefs about race.

In addition to institutionalizing the one-drop rule, the 1930 census also added categories for Mexicans, Hindus, Koreans, and Filipinos. These groups were beginning to immigrate to the West Coast, mostly as agricultural labor, in sufficient numbers to attract the attention of politicians and their constituencies. In California, for example, there was considerable public concern about the numbers of Filipinos entering the state.

DEFINING RACE AND ETHNICITY IN POSTWAR AMERICA

From 1940 to 1960, the federal government published relatively little information about racial and ethnic minorities. The information that was available was produced once a decade in reports from the decennial census usually titled *Nonwhite Population by Race*. The racial and ethnic landscape of early postwar America consisted of whites, blacks, American Indians, and a polyglot category of Asians and other races. Latinos were absent from consideration insofar as Mexican American advocacy groups, including the Mexican government, had lobbied to have Mexicans counted as white for statistical purposes (Snipp 2003).

In the 1950 census, as in previous censuses, enumerators ascribed race on the basis of physical appearances. Because census enumerators received no instructions from their supervisors about how to code race on their questionnaires, we can presume that the ascription of race was regarded as a self-evident exercise. However, in 1960, in an effort to reduce the cost of the census, the Census Bureau drastically reduced the number of enumerators it used and replaced them with a form that was delivered through the mail and was to be completed returned to the Census Bureau by the nominal head of the household. This meant that race was no longer ascribed by enumerators on the basis of physical appearance. Instead, race became a matter of personal identification, based on self-reports provided by the person completing the census form. Race in the 1960 census was now based instead on subjective judgments about the self-identification of racial and ethnic ancestry. Wittingly or unwittingly, Census Bureau planners devised a statistical measure of race that was wholly consistent with constructionist theories. That is, race is purely a matter of subjective experience in the everyday social environment—race meant whatever an individual understood it to mean. One by-product of this change was a dramatic increase in the American Indian population, especially in urban

TABLE 1.1 | **FEDERAL AGENCIES THAT COLLECT AND REPORT INFORMATION ABOUT RACE AND ETHNICITY**

- Commerce
- Education
- Equal Employment Opportunity Commission (EEOC)
- Federal Reserve
- Health and Human Services (HHS)
- Housing and Urban Development (HUD)
- Justice
- Labor
- Agriculture
- Veterans Affairs

areas where they had been misidentified in earlier censuses as white, black, or possibly Asian (Snipp 1989).

After the 1960 census, federal efforts involving the collection of information about race proliferated. This development was largely in response to the passage of civil rights and other race-based legislation and the desires of Congress to ensure that the laws, policies, and programs it was creating were having the intended effect. Throughout the executive branch of the federal government, agencies began to collect and monitor information about the racial composition of the constituencies and to widely disseminate this information (Table 1.1).

As the volume of race-based data increased exponentially, problems connected with the comparability and coverage of this information soon became apparent. For example, some agencies produced reports showing information about "Whites" and "Nonwhites." These reports could not be compared to the reports of other agencies showing information about "Whites," "Blacks,"[4] and "Others" without sacrificing the detailed information about blacks in the latter report. Of course, neither of these approaches was satisfactory for persons seeking information about Latinos, American Indians, Asians, or any other group subsumed under the "Other" category.

By 1974, the Office of Management and Budget (OMB) set about the task of creating a standard classification for the production of statistical information about race. The Federal Interagency Committee on Education (FICE) was assigned the task of devising a standard taxonomy and set

---

4 In the 1960s, these reports most often used the term "Negro" instead of "Black."

of definitions for racial and ethnic groups of particular interest to the federal government. After months of deliberation, the committee adopted a recommendation late in 1976 that the federal government should collect information about five more or less distinct groups: (1) American Indians and Alaska Natives; (2) Asians and Pacific Islanders; (3) Non-Hispanic Blacks; (4) Non-Hispanic Whites; and (5) Hispanics, of any race. This recommendation became official policy when OMB adopted it and designated it as *OMB Directive No. 15*. Although this document stipulated the groups for whom information should be collected, it did not try to define the meaning of these designations beyond to state simply, "These classifications should not be interpreted as being scientific or anthropological in nature" (OMB 1977).

The importance of the adoption of *OMB Directive No. 15* should not be underestimated. Because this document became the standard for all agencies of the federal government, including its grantees and contractors, its five mandated categories became, in effect, a racial cosmology for the United States. *Directive No. 15* stipulated the categories by which most Americans would identify themselves on job applications, college scholarship applications, census forms, and virtually every other form and application that requested information about race. This directive also constrained social scientific inquiry insofar as it made government data available about some groups but not others. For example, as a result of *Directive No. 15*, information about births and deaths is readily available for blacks but not for Arab Americans because the latter are not included in the directive. In short, OMB *Directive No. 15* defined the known racial and ethnic landscape in the late twentieth century.

Conveniently, the categories mandated by *Directive No. 15* closely coincided with those used by the census. The 1980 census was administered under the mandate of this directive and it included categories for race and a new question designed to obtain information about persons of Hispanic origins. The Census Bureau also introduced a new open-ended question requesting information about ethnic ancestry. Although these new questions posed a number of difficulties, they were used again in the 1990 census (Snipp 2003).

The 1990 census proved to be a pivotal event in the way that public perception focused on the meaning of race. Two sets of controversies surfaced from the 1990 census questionnaire and the way that it solicited information about race. One set of complaints was lodged by groups who were omitted from the race question. For example, advocacy groups representing Taiwanese and Arab American interests argued that each

FIGURE 1.1 | **FACSIMILE OF THE RACE QUESTION FROM THE 1990 DECENNIAL CENSUS**

4. Race
Fill ONE circle for the race that the person
considers himself/herself to be.

   If Indian (Amer.), print the name of
   the enrolled or principal tribe. ____ ➤

   If Other Asian or Pacific Islander (API),
   print one group, for example: Hmong,
   Fijian, Laotian, Thai, Tongan, Pakistani,
   Cambodian, and so on. _____ ➤

   If Other race, print race. _____ ➤

- ○ White
- ○ Black or Negro
- ○ Indian (Amer.) (Print the name of the
      enrolled or principal tribe.) _____

- ○ Eskimo
- ○ Aleut
      Asian or Pacific Islander (API)
- ○ Chinese   ○ Japanese
- ○ Fillipino   ○ Asian Indian
- ○ Hawaiian   ○ Samoan
- ○ Korean   ○ Guamanian
- ○ Vietnamese   ○ Other API _____

- ○ Other race (Print race) ___

7. Is this person of Spanish/Hispanic origin?
Fill ONE circle for each person.

   If Yes, other Spanish/Hispanic,
   print one group. _____ ➤

- ○ No (not Spanish/Hispanic)
- ○ Yes, Mexican, Mexican-Am., Chicano
- ○ Yes, Puerto Rican
- ○ Yes, Cuban
- ○ Yes, other Spanish/Hispanic
      (Print one group, for example: Argentinean,
      Colombian, Dominican, Nicaraguan,
      Salvadoran, Spaniard, and so on.) _____

SOURCE | U.S. Census Bureau

of these groups should be included as an option on the race question. Native Hawaiians also complained that they should not be grouped with Asians and other pacific islanders (see Figure 1.1). Another set of complaints stemmed from the instruction that respondents should mark only one race for each person in the household. Representatives of multiracial family organizations argued that by forcing parents to choose only one race for their children, they were causing multiracial couples to privilege the race of one parent over another when identifying the racial heritage of their children. They claimed that this was a source of marital stress and that it did not adequately capture the true multiracial heritage of children who have parents of different races.

DEFINING RACE AND ETHNICITY IN
TWENTY-FIRST-CENTURY AMERICA

These complaints caused the Office of Management and Budget to begin a thorough review of *Directive No. 15* in 1993. This review included consultation with expert social scientists, hearings held around the country, numerous meetings of a large interagency committee, and a program of testing by the Census Bureau to find alternative approaches to measuring the racial and ethnic composition of the United States. In October 1997, OMB issued a revised standard for *Directive No. 15* that attempted to address the concerns raised by the various groups who objected to this rule.

Specifically, the revised standard for the collection of data about race and ethnicity mandated a new set of categories and a new set of instructions. The new categories included whites, blacks, American Indians and Alaska Natives, Asians, and Native Hawaiians and Other Pacific Islanders. It also stipulated that Hispanics should be regarded as an ethnic group to be identified separately from the categories of race, suggesting that the Hispanic ethnic group included people of different races and that the identification of groups such as non-Hispanic whites and Hispanic blacks should be retained.

The new categories were a modest departure from past practices and at most represent a significant gain by Native Hawaiians insofar as they were able to obtain recognition as a group distinct from Asians and other Pacific islanders. A more far-reaching modification was the new language instructing agencies to allow multiple entries for the identification of racial heritage. Specifically, questions soliciting information about racial heritage should include an instruction permitting respondents to "mark one or more" or to "select one or more." This change allowed individuals to identify themselves with multiple races, and it was first implemented in the 2000 census. A facsimile of the question used in the 2000 census to obtain information about race is shown in Figure 1.2.

Although the vast majority of Americans (274.6 million persons) reported only one race in the 2000 census, 6.8 million persons reported two or more races. The modified race question created a number of complex problems, including some that still remain unsolved. One of the first dilemmas to arise in connection with the new question was how to report the information that was generated from the 2000 census. There are sixty-three unique racial combinations that can be constructed from the choices offered in the 2000 census form. When these sixty-three racial designations are combined with the Hispanic/non-Hispanic

FIGURE 1.2 | **FACSIMILE OF THE RACE QUESTION FROM THE 2000 DECENNIAL CENSUS**

➔ **NOTE: Please answer BOTH Questions 5 and 6.**

5. Is this person Spanish/Hispanic/Latino? *Mark ☒ the*
*"No" box if **not** Spanish/Hispanic/Latino.*
  ☐ **No,** not Spanish/Hispanic/Latino   ☐ Yes, Puerto Rican
  ☐ Yes, Mexican, Mexican Am., Chicano   ☐ Yes, Cuban
  ☐ Yes, other Spanish/Hispanic/Latino—*Print group.* ⤿

| | | | | | | | | | | | | | | | | | | |

6. What is this person's race? *Mark ☒* **one or more races** *to*
indicate what this person considers himself/herself to be.
  ☐ White
  ☐ Black, African Am., or Negro
  ☐ American Indian or Alaska Native—*Print name of enrolled or principal tribe.* ⤿

| | | | | | | | | | | | | | | | | | | |

  ☐ Asian Indian   ☐ Japanese   ☐ Native Hawaiian
  ☐ Chinese   ☐ Korean   ☐ Guamanian or Chamorro
  ☐ Filipino   ☐ Vietnamese   ☐ Samoan
  ☐ Other Asian—*Print race.* ⤿   ☐ Other Pacific Islander—*Print race.* ⤿

| | | | | | | | | | | | | | | | | | | |

  ☐ Some other race—*Print race.* ⤿

| | | | | | | | | | | | | | | | | | | |

SOURCE | U.S. Census Bureau

---

distinction, the census yields 126 possible categories. This number of categories produces unwieldy tabulations. In response to this problem, the Census Bureau publishes subsets of the data for persons who identify with one race only and for persons who report two or more races. The OMB also has offered guidance for possible aggregations of these categories for the purposes of civil rights enforcement (Snipp 2003).

Several vexing and still unresolved problems involve how to compare these numbers with statistics collected earlier in time given the fact that some multiracial persons may change the way they report their race from one time to another. Comparisons over time are particularly problematic since only one race was reported in the past; consequently, persons who report more than one race today must be reallocated to a single racial category as in previous reports. There is no agreed-upon way regarding how this should be done or whether such a reallocation is even possible. Another problem is that when persons have two more races that they can report, they do not always report this information consistently. Sometimes they may report two or more races and other times they may selectively report only one race. Statistics from the American Community Survey, a precise, nationally representative sample collected in conjunction with the decennial census, show about two million fewer multiracial persons than were enumerated in the census. Ostensibly, these two numbers should have been approximately the same. Finally, how to obtain accurate third party reports from employers or school administrators about the complex multiracial heritages of employees or students also has been a significant and unresolved problem.

CONCLUSION: DEFINING RACE AND ETHNICITY IN THE UNITED STATES AND BEYOND

As this essay has attempted to show, the business of defining race and ethnicity is a tricky one. In some respects, pinpointing the meaning of ethnicity is an easier task than trying to define race. This is only because the concept of ethnicity is a relatively new idea that was developed with a specific reference in mind and for many years remained within the confines of scholarly discourse.

In contrast, the notion of race is an old idea that dates back to medieval Europe and possibly earlier. At different times, it has referred to differences in blood, differences in a variety of biological characteristics, differences in character, and lately, to a set of social categories constructed to achieve some set of legal and political objectives. These different meanings are rooted in mythology, pseudo-science, and the intentions of governments and other institutions with particular agendas in mind. Under these circumstances, the muddle and confusion attached to the idea of race and what it means is hardly surprising. What is perhaps more surprising is that we often act as if none of this confusion exists. Laws are written, policies are enacted, and judges render opinions as if the meaning of race is both well understood and the subject of great agreement.

Assuming that the meaning of race is fixed and unchanging is a convenient fiction that anchors a great deal of our everyday thinking and an even larger amount of public policy. But despite the convenience of this sort of thinking, the conceptual content of the term "race" has evolved tremendously over the centuries. It continues to be a shorthand expression for describing "otherness," but how we understand and deal with others has shifted over time. We understand that enslaving and mistreating others simply because they are different is no longer acceptable in civilized society. We are beginning to understand that because people are different, they are not inherently superior or inferior to one another.

Works Cited

•

Anderson, Margo J. 1988. *The American Census: A Social History*. New Haven: Yale University Press.

Blumenbach, Johann Friedrich. 1776. *On the Natural Varieties of Mankind*. New York: Bergman, 1969.

Cavalli-Sforza, Luigi Luca. 2001. *Genes, Peoples, and Languages*. Berkeley: University of California Press.

Erlich, Paul, and Marcus Feldman. 2003. Genes and Cultures: What Creates Our Behavioral Phenome? *Current Anthropology* 44:87–107.

Fredrickson, George M. 2002. *Racism: A Short History*. Princeton, NJ: Princeton University Press.

Gould, Stephen Jay. 1996. *The Mismeasure of Man*. New York: W. W. Norton.

McKee, James B. 1993. *Sociology and the Race Problem: The Failure of a Perspective*. Urbana: University of Illinois Press.

Office of Management and Budget (OMB). 1977. *Directive No. 15, Race and Ethnic Standards for Federal Statistics and Administrative Reporting*. Washington, DC: United States Office of Management and Budget.

Omi, Michael, and Howard Winant. 1994. *Racial Formation in the United States: From the 1960s to the 1990s*. New York: Routledge Press.

Peterson, William. 1980. Concepts of Ethnicity. In *Harvard Encyclopedia of American Ethnic Groups*, edited by Stephan Thernstrom. Cambridge, MA: Harvard University Press.

Simpson, George Eaton, and J. Milton Yinger. 1953. *Racial and Cultural Minorities: An Analysis of Prejudice and Discrimination*. New York: Harper & Bros.

Snipp, C. Matthew. 1989. *American Indians: The First of This Land*. New York: Russell Sage Foundation.

———. 2003. Racial Measurement in the American Census: Past Practices and Implications for the Future. *Annual Review of Sociology* 29: 563–588.

2

Models of American Ethnic Relations
Hierarchy, Assimilation, and Pluralism[†]

George M. Fredrickson

•

This essay describes four models that provide different answers to the question: how should members of different ethnic groups relate to one another? They include (1) the ethnic hierarchy model in which a dominant group claims rights and privileges that are not shared with minority groups considered unfit or unready for equal rights or citizenship, (2) the ethnic assimilation model in which minority groups are expected to conform to the mainstream as the price of admission to full citizenship, (3) the cultural pluralism model in which groups maintain their distinctive ideas and practices while adhering to a set of rules and understandings that enable them to coexist peacefully with other ethnic groups in the society, and (4) the group separatism model in which groups withdraw from the mainstream and form autonomous communities. These models are important for thinking about how to do difference differently. The essay argues that given the shrinking Euro-American majority, it is essential that American society move quickly away from the ethnic hierarchy model (the doing race model) that has prevailed in the past and toward the cultural pluralism model. Such a move is essential if America is to remain a stable and democratic society.

---

† This essay originally appeared as "Models of American Ethnic Relations: A Historical Perspective." In *Cultural Divides: Understanding and Overcoming Group Conflict*, edited by Deborah A. Prentice and Dale T. Miller. New York: Russell Sage Foundation, 1999. Permission to reprint was granted by the Russell Sage Foundation.

THROUGHOUT ITS HISTORY, THE UNITED STATES HAS BEEN INHABITED
by a variety of interacting racial or ethnic groups. In addition to the obvious "color line" structuring relationships between dominant whites and
lower-status blacks, Indians, and Asians, there have at times been important social distinctions among those of white or European ancestry.
Today we think of the differences between white Anglo-Saxon Protestants and Irish, Italian, Polish, and Jewish Americans as purely cultural
or religious, but in earlier times these groups were sometimes thought
of as "races" or "subraces"—people possessing innate or inborn characteristics and capabilities that affected their fitness for American citizenship.
Moreover, differences apparently defined as cultural have sometimes
been so reified as to serve as the functional equivalent of physical distinctions. Indians, for example, were viewed by most nineteenth-century
missionaries and humanitarians as potentially equal and similar to
whites. Their status as noncitizens was not attributed to skin color or
physical appearance; it was only their obdurate adherence to "savage
ways" that allegedly stood in the way of their possessing equal rights
and being fully assimilated. Analogously, conservative opponents of
affirmative action and other antiracist policies in the 1990s may provide
a "rational" basis for prejudice and discrimination by attributing the disadvantages and alleged shortcomings of African Americans to persistent
cultural "pathology" rather than to genetic deficiencies (D'Souza 1995).

It can therefore be misleading to make a sharp distinction between
race and ethnicity when considering intergroup relations in American
history. As I have argued extensively elsewhere, ethnicity is "racialized" whenever distinctive group characteristics, however defined or
explained, are used as the basis for a status hierarchy of groups who are
thought to differ in ancestry or descent (Fredrickson 1997, ch. 5).

Four basic conceptions of how ethnic or racial groups should relate to
each other have been predominant in the history of American thought
about group relations—ethnic hierarchy, one-way assimilation, cultural
pluralism, and group separatism. This chapter provides a broad outline
of the historical career of each of these models of intergroup relations,
noting some of the changes in how various groups have defined themselves or been defined by others.

ETHNIC HIERARCHY

Looking at the entire span of American history, we find that the most influential and durable conception of the relations among those American

racial or ethnic groups viewed as significantly dissimilar has been hierarchical. A dominant group—conceiving of itself as society's charter membership—has claimed rights and privileges not to be fully shared with outsiders or "others," who have been characterized as unfit or unready for equal rights and full citizenship. The hierarchical model has its deepest roots and most enduring consequences in the conquest of Indians and the enslavement of blacks during the colonial period (Axtell 1981; Jordan 1968). But it was also applied in the nineteenth century to Asian immigrants and in a less severe and more open-ended way to European immigrants who differed in culture and religion from old-stock Americans of British origin (Higham 1968; Miller 1969). The sharpest and most consequential distinction was always between "white" and "nonwhite." The first immigration law passed by Congress in 1790 specified that only white immigrants were eligible for naturalization. This provision would create a crucial difference in the mid-nineteenth century between Chinese "sojourners," who could not become citizens and voters, and Irish immigrants, who could.

Nevertheless, the Irish who fled the potato famine of the 1840s by emigrating to the United States also encountered discrimination. Besides being Catholic and poor, the refugees from the Emerald Isle were Celts rather than Anglo-Saxons, and a racialized discourse, drawing on British precedents, developed as an explanation for Irish inferiority to Americans of English ancestry (Knobel 1986). The dominant group during the nineteenth and early twentieth centuries was not simply white but also Protestant and Anglo-Saxon. Nevertheless, the Irish were able to use their right to vote and the patronage they received from the Democratic Party to improve their status, an option not open to the Chinese. Hence, they gradually gained the leverage and respectability necessary to win admission to the dominant caste, a process that culminated in Al Smith's nomination for the presidency in 1928 and John F. Kennedy's election in 1960.

The mass immigration of Europeans from eastern and southern Europe in the late nineteenth and early twentieth centuries inspired new concerns about the quality of the American stock. In an age of eugenics, scientific racism, and social Darwinism, the notion that northwestern Europeans were innately superior to those from the southern and eastern parts of the continent—to say nothing of those light-skinned people of actual or presumed west Asian origin (such as Jews, Syrians, and Armenians)—gained wide currency. A determined group of nativists, encouraged by the latest racial "science," fought for restrictive immigration policies that discriminated against those who were not of "Nordic" or "Aryan" descent (Higham 1968). In the 1920s the immigration laws were changed to reflect these prejudices. Low quotas were established for white people from nations or areas outside of those that had supplied the bulk of the American population before 1890. In the minds of many, true Americans were not merely white but also northern European. In fact, some harbored doubts about the full claim to "whiteness" of swarthy immigrants from southern Italy.

After immigration restriction had relieved ethnic and racial anxieties, the status of the new immigrants gradually improved as a result of their political involvement, their economic and professional achievement, and a decline in the respectability of the kind of scientific racism that had ranked some European groups below others. World War II brought revulsion against the genocidal anti-Semitism and eugenic experiments of the Nazis, dealing a coup de grâce to the de facto hierarchy that had placed Anglo-Saxons, Nordics, or Aryans at the apex of American society. All Americans of European origin were now unambiguously white and, for most purposes, ethnically equal to old-stock Americans of Anglo-Saxon, Celtic, and Germanic ancestry. Hierarchy was now based exclusively on color. Paradoxically, it might be argued, the removal of the burden of "otherness" from virtually all whites made more striking and salient than ever the otherness of people of color, especially African Americans.

The civil rights movement of the 1960s was directed primarily at the legalized racial hierarchy of the southern states. The Civil Rights Acts of 1964 and 1965 brought an end to government-enforced racial segregation and the denial of voting rights to blacks in that region. But the legacy of four centuries of white supremacy survives in the disadvantaged social and economic position of blacks and other people of color in the United States. The impoverished, socially deprived, and physically unsafe ghettos, barrios, and Indian reservations of this nation are evidence that ethnic hierarchy in a clearly racialized form persists in practice if not in law.

ONE-WAY ASSIMILATION

Policies aimed at the assimilation of ethnic groups have usually assumed that there is a single and stable American culture of European, and especially English, origin to which minorities are expected to conform as the price of admission to full and equal participation in the society and polity of the United States (Gordon 1964, ch. 4). Assimilationist thinking is not racist in the classic sense: it does not deem the outgroups in question to be innately or biologically inferior to the ingroup. The professed goal is equality—but on terms that presume the superiority, purity, and unchanging character of the dominant culture. Little or nothing in the cultures of the groups being invited to join the America mainstream is presumed worthy of preserving. When carried to its logical conclusion, the assimilationist project demands what its critics have described—especially in reference to the coercive efforts to "civilize" Native Americans—as "cultural genocide."

Estimates of group potential and the resulting decisions as to which groups are eligible for assimilation have varied in response to changing definitions of race. If an ethnic group is definitely racialized, the door is closed because its members are thought to possess ineradicable traits (biologically or culturally determined) that make them unfit for inclusion. At times there have been serious disagreements within the dominant group about the eligibility of particular minorities for initiation into the American club.

Although one-way assimilationism was mainly a twentieth-century ideology, it was anticipated in strains of nineteenth-century thinking about Irish immigrants, Native Americans, and even blacks. Radical white abolitionists and even some black antislavery activists argued that prejudice against African Americans was purely and simply a result of their peculiarly degraded and disadvantaged circumstances and that emancipation from slavery would make skin color irrelevant and open the way to their full equality and social acceptability (Fredrickson 1987, ch. 1). These abolitionists had little or no conception that there was a rich and distinctive black culture that could become the source of a positive group identity, and that African modes of thought and behavior had been adapted to the challenge of surviving under slavery.

If the hope of fully assimilating blacks into a color-blind society was held by only a small minority of whites, a majority probably supposed that the Irish immigrants of the 1840s and 1850s could become full-fledged Americans, if they chose to do so, simply by changing their behavior and beliefs. The doctrine of the innate inferiority of Celts to Anglo-Saxons was not even shared by all of the nativists who sought to slow down the process of Irish naturalization (Knobel 1986). A more serious problem for many of them was the fervent Catholicism of the Irish; Anglo-Protestant missionaries hoped to convert them en masse. The defenders of unrestricted Irish immigration came mostly from the ranks of the Democratic Party, which relied heavily on Irish votes. Among them were strong believers in religious toleration and a high wall of separation between church and state. They saw religious diversity as no obstacle to the full and rapid Americanization of all white-skinned immigrants.

The most sustained and serious nineteenth-century effort to assimilate people who differed both culturally and phenotypically from the majority was aimed at American Indians. Frontier settlers, military men who fought Indians, and many other whites had no doubts that Indians were members of an inherently inferior race that was probably doomed to total extinction as a result of the conquest of the West. Their views were graphically expressed by General Philip Sheridan when he opined that "the only good Indian is a dead Indian." But an influential group of eastern philanthropists, humanitarian reformers, and government officials thought of the Indians as having been "noble savages" whose innate capacities were not inferior to those of whites. Thomas Jefferson, who had a much dimmer view of black potentialities, was one of the first to voice this opinion (Koch and Peden 1944, 210–11). For these ethnocentric humanitarians, the "Indian problem" was primarily cultural rather than racial, and its solution lay in civilizing the "savages" rather than exterminating them. Late in the century, the assimilationists adopted policies designed to force Indians to conform to Euro-American cultural norms; these included breaking up communally held reservations into privately owned family farms and sending Indian children to boarding schools where they were forbidden to speak their own languages and made to dress, cut their hair, and in every possible way act and look like white people. The policy was a colossal failure; most Native Americans refused to abandon key aspects of their traditional cultures, and venal whites took advantage of the land reforms to strip Indians of much of their remaining patrimony (Berkhofer 1978; Hoxie 1984; Mardock 1971).

In the early twentieth century, the one-way assimilation model was applied to the southern and eastern European immigrants who had arrived in massive numbers before the discriminatory quota system of the 1920s was implemented. While some nativists called for their exclusion on the grounds of their innate deficiencies, other champions of Anglo-American cultural homogeneity hoped to assimilate those who had already arrived through education and indoctrination. The massive "Americanization" campaigns of the period just prior to World War I produced the concept of America as a "melting pot" in which cultural differences would be obliterated. The metaphor might have suggested that a new mixture would result—and occasionally it did have this meaning—but a more prevalent interpretation was that non-Anglo-American cultural traits and inclinations would simply disappear, making the final brew identical to the original one (Gordon 1964, ch. 5).

Before the 1940s, people of color, and especially African Americans, were generally deemed ineligible for assimilation because of their innate inferiority to white ethnics, who were now thought capable of being culturally reborn as Anglo-Americans. Such factors as the war-inspired reaction against scientific racism and the gain in black political power resulting from mass migration from the South (where blacks could not vote) to the urban North (where the franchise was again open to them) led to a significant reconsideration of the social position of African Americans and threw a spotlight on the flagrant denial in the southern states of the basic constitutional rights of African Americans. The struggle for black civil rights that emerged in the 1950s and came to fruition in the early 1960s was premised on a conviction that white supremacist laws and policies violated an egalitarian "American Creed"—as Gunnar Myrdal had argued in his influential wartime study *An American Dilemma* (1944). The war against Jim Crow was fought under the banner of "integration," which, in the minds of white liberals at least, generally meant one-way assimilation. Blacks, deemed by Myrdal and others as having no culture worth saving, would achieve equal status by becoming just like white Americans in every respect except pigmentation.

When it became clear that the civil rights legislation of the 1960s had failed to improve significantly the social and economic position of blacks in the urban ghettos of the North, large numbers of African Americans rejected the integrationist ideal on the grounds that it had been not only a false promise but an insult to the culture of African Americans for ignoring or devaluing their distinctive experience as a people. The new emphasis on "black power" and "black consciousness" conveyed to those whites who were listening that integration had to mean something other than one-way assimilation to white middle-class norms if it was to be a solution to the problem of racial inequality in America (Marable 1991; Van Deburg 1992).

It should be obvious by now that the one-way assimilation model has not proved to be a viable or generally acceptable way of adjusting group differences in American society. It is based on an ethnocentric ideal of cultural homogeneity that has been rejected by Indians, blacks, Asians, Mexican Americans, and even many white ethnics. It reifies and privileges one cultural strain in what is in fact a multicultural society. It should be possible to advocate the incorporation of all ethnic or racial groups into a common civic society without requiring the sacrifice of cultural distinctiveness and diversity.

CULTURAL PLURALISM

Unlike assimilationists, cultural pluralists celebrate differences among groups rather than seek to obliterate them. They argue that cultural diversity is a healthy and normal condition that does not preclude equal rights and the mutual understandings about civic responsibilities needed to sustain a democratic nation-state. This model for American ethnic relations is a twentieth-century invention that would have been virtually inconceivable at an earlier time. The eighteenth and nineteenth centuries lacked the essential concept of the relativity of cultures. The model of cultural development during this period was evolutionary, progressive, and universalistic. People were either civilized or they were not. Mankind was seen as evolving from a state of "savagery" to "barbarism" to "civilization," and all cultures at a particular level were similar in every way that mattered. What differentiated nations and ethnic groups was their ranking on the scale of social evolution. Modern Western civilization stood at the apex of this universal historical process. Even nineteenth-century black nationalists accepted the notion that there were universal standards of civilization to which people of African descent should aspire. They differed from white supremacists in believing that blacks had the natural capability to reach the same heights as Caucasians if they were given a chance (Moses 1978).

The concept of cultural pluralism drew on the new cultural anthropology of the early twentieth century, as pioneered by Franz Boas. Boas and his disciples attempted to look at each culture they studied on its own terms and as an integrated whole. They rejected theories of social evolution that ranked cultures in relation to a universalist conception of "civilization." But relativistic cultural anthropologists were not necessarily cultural pluralists in their attitude toward group relations within American society. Since they generally believed that a given society or community functioned best with a single, integrated culture, they could favor greater autonomy for Indians on reservations but also call for the full assimilation of new immigrants or even African Americans. Boas himself was an early supporter of the National Association for the Advancement of Colored People (NAACP) and a pioneering advocate of what would later be called racial integration.

An effort to use the new concept of culture to validate ethnic diversity within the United States arose from the negative reaction of some intellectuals to the campaign to "Americanize" the new immigrants from eastern and southern Europe in the period just before and after World

War I. The inventors of cultural pluralism were cosmopolitan critics of American provincialism or representatives of immigrant communities, especially Jews, who valued their cultural distinctiveness and did not want to be melted down in an Americanizing crucible. The Greenwich Village intellectual Randolph Bourne described his ideal as a "transnational America" in which various ethnic cultures would interact in a tolerant atmosphere to create an enriching variety of ideas, values, and lifestyles (Bourne 1964, ch. 8). The Jewish philosopher Horace Kallen, who coined the phrase "cultural pluralism," compared the result to a symphony, with each immigrant group represented as a section of the orchestra (Higham 1984, ch. 9; Kallen 1924). From a different perspective, W. E. B. DuBois celebrated a distinctive black culture rooted in the African and slave experiences and heralded its unacknowledged contributions to American culture in general (Lewis 1993). But the dominant version advocated by Kallen and Bourne stopped, for all practical purposes, at the color line. Its focus was on making America safe for a variety of European cultures. As a Zionist, Kallen was especially concerned with the preservation of Jewish distinctiveness and identity.

Since it was mainly the viewpoint of ethnic intellectuals who resisted the assimilationism of the melting pot, cultural pluralism was a minority persuasion in the twenties, thirties, and forties. A modified version reemerged in the 1950s in Will Herberg's (1960) conception of a "triple melting pot" of Protestants, Catholics, and Jews. The revulsion against Nazi anti-Semitism and the upward mobility of American Jews and Catholics inspired a synthesis of cultural pluralism and assimilationism that made religious persuasion the only significant source of diversity among white Americans. Herberg conceded, however, that black Protestants constituted a separate group that was not likely to be included in the Protestant melting point. He therefore sharpened the distinction between race or color and ethnicity that was central to postwar thinking about group differences. Nevertheless, Herberg's view that significant differences between, say, Irish and Italian Catholics were disappearing was challenged in the 1960s and later, especially in the "ethnic revival" of the 1970s, which proclaimed that differing national origins among Euro-Americans remained significant and a valuable source of cultural variations.

The "multiculturalism" of the 1980s operated on assumptions that were similar to those of the cultural pluralist tradition, except that the color line was breached and the focus was shifted from the cultures and contributions of diverse European ethnic groups to those of African

Americans, Mexican Americans, Asian Americans, and Native Americans. Abandonment of the earlier term "multiracialism" signified a desire to escape from the legacy of biological or genetic determinism and to affirm that the differences among people who happened to differ in skin color or phenotype were the result of their varying cultural and historical experiences. Under attack was the doctrine, shared by assimilationists and most earlier proponents of cultural pluralism, that the cultural norm in the United States was inevitably European in origin and character. Parity was now sought for groups of Asian, African, and American Indian ancestry. This ideal of cultural diversity and democracy was viewed by some of its critics as an invitation to national disunity and ethnic conflict (Schlesinger 1992). But its most thoughtful proponents argued that it was simply a consistent application of American democratic values and did not preclude the interaction and cooperation of groups within a common civic society (Hollinger 1995). Nevertheless, the mutual understandings upon which national unity and cohesion could be based needed to be negotiated rather than simply imposed by a Euro-American majority.

GROUP SEPARATISM

Sometimes confused with the broadened cultural pluralism described here is the advocacy of group separatism. It originates in the desire of a culturally distinctive or racialized group to withdraw as much as possible from American society and interaction with other groups. Its logical outcome, autonomy in a separate, self-governing community, might conceivably be achieved either in an ethnic confederation like Switzerland or in the dissolution of the United States into several ethnic nations. But such a general theory is a logical construction rather than a program that has been explicitly advocated. Group separatism emanates from ethnocentric concerns about the status and destiny of particular groups, and its advocates rarely if ever theorize about what is going to happen to other groups. Precedents for group separatism based on cultural differences can be found in American history in the toleration of virtually autonomous religious communities like the Amish and the Hutterites and in the modicum of self-government and immunity from general laws accorded to Indian tribes and reservations since the 1930s.

The most significant and persistent assertion of group separatism in American history has come from African Americans disillusioned with the prospects for equality within American society. In the nineteenth century, several black leaders and intellectuals called on African Americans to emigrate from the United States in order to establish an independent black republic elsewhere; Africa was the most favored destination. In the 1920s, Marcus Garvey created a mass movement based on the presumption that blacks had no future in the United States and should identify with the independence and future greatness of Africa, ultimately by emigrating there. More recently, the Nation of Islam has proposed that several American states be set aside for an autonomous black nation [Fredrickson 1995, chs. 2, 4, 7]. At the height of the black power movement of the 1960s and early 1970s, a few black nationalists even called for the establishment of a noncontiguous federation of black urban ghettos—a nation of islands like Indonesia or the Philippines, but surrounded by white populations rather than the Pacific Ocean.

The current version of black separatism—"Afrocentrism"—has not as yet produced a plan for political separation. Its aim is a cultural and spiritual secession from American society rather than the literal establishment of a black nation. Advocates of total separation could be found among other disadvantaged groups. In the late 1960s and 1970s: Mexican American militants called for the establishment of the independent Chicano nation of Atzlan in the American Southwest (Gutierrez 1995, 184–85) and some Native American radicals sought the reestablishment of truly independent tribal nations.

Group separatism might be viewed as a utopian vision or rhetorical device expressing the depths of alienation felt by the most disadvantaged racial or ethnic groups in American society. The extreme unlikelihood of realizing such visions has made their promulgation more cathartic than politically efficacious. Most members of groups exposed to such separatist appeals have recognized their impracticality, and the clash between the fixed and essentialist view of identity that such projects entail and the fluid and hybrid quality of group cultures in the United States has become increasingly evident to many people of color, as shown most dramatically by the recent movement among those of mixed parentage to affirm a biracial identity. Few African Americans want to celebrate the greater or lesser degree of white ancestry most of them possess, but many have acknowledged not only their ancestral ties to Africa but their debt to Euro-American culture (and its debt to them). Most Mexican Americans value their cultural heritage but do not have the expectation or even the desire to establish an independent Chicano nation in the Southwest. Native Americans have authentic historical and legal claims to a high degree of autonomy but generally recognize that total independence on their current land base is impossible and would worsen rather than improve their circumstances. Asian Americans are proud of their various cultures and seek to preserve some of their traditions but have shown little or no inclination to separate themselves from other Americans in the civic, professional, and economic life of the nation. Afrocentrism raises troubling issues for American educational and cultural life but hardly represents a serious threat to national unity.

Ethnic separatism, in conclusion, is a symptom of racial injustice and a call to action against it, but there is little reason to believe that it portends "the disuniting of America." It is currently a source of great anxiety to many Euro-Americans primarily because covert defenders of ethnic hierarchy or one-way assimilation have tried to confuse the broad-based ideal of democratic multiculturalism with the demands of a relatively few militant ethnocentrists for thoroughgoing self-segregation and isolation from the rest of American society.

Of the four models of American ethnic relations, the one that I believe offers the best hope for a just and cohesive society is a cultural pluralism that is fully inclusive and based on the free choices of individuals to construct or reconstruct their own ethnic identities. We are still far from achieving the degree of racial and ethnic tolerance that realization of such an ideal requires. But with the demographic shift that is transforming the overwhelmingly Euro-American population of thirty or forty years ago into one that is much more culturally and phenotypically heterogeneous, a more democratic form of intergroup relations is a likely prospect, unless there is a desperate reversion to overt ethnic hierarchicalism by the shrinking Euro-American majority. If that were to happen, national unity and cohesion would indeed be hard to maintain. If current trends continue, minorities of non-European ancestry will constitute a new majority sometime in the next century. Well before that point is reached, they will have the numbers and the provocation to make the country virtually ungovernable if a resurgent racism brings serious efforts to revive the blatantly hierarchical policies that have prevailed in the past.

Works Cited

•

Axtell, James. (1981). *The European and the Indian: Essays in the ethnohistory of colonial North America*. New York: Oxford University Press.

Berkhofer, Robert F., Jr. (1978). *The white man's Indian: Image of the American Indian from Columbus to the present*. New York: Alfred A. Knopf.

Bourne, Randolph S. (1964). *War and the intellectuals: Collected essays, 1915–1919.* New York: Harper Torch.

D'Souza, Dinesh. (1995). *The end of racism: Principles for a multiracial society.* New York: Free Press.

Fredrickson, George M. (1987). *The black image in the white mind: The debate on Afro-American character and destiny, 1817–1914.* Middletown, Conn.: Wesleyan University Press.

———. (1995). *Black liberation: A comparative history of black ideologies in the United States and South Africa.* New York: Oxford University Press.

———. (1997). *The comparative imagination: On the history of racism, nationalism, and social movements.* Berkeley: University of California Press.

Gordon, Milton M. (1964). *Assimilation in American life: The role of race, religion, and national origins.* New York: Oxford University Press.

Gutierrez, David. (1995). *Walls and mirrors: Mexican Americans, Mexican immigrants, and the politics of ethnicity.* Berkeley: University of California Press.

Herberg, Will. (1960). *Protestant-Catholic-Jew: An essay in American religious sociology.* Garden City, N.Y.: Anchor Books.

Higham, John. (1968). *Strangers in the land: Patterns of American nativism, 1860–1925.* New York: Atheneum.

———. (1984). *Send these to me: Jews and other immigrants in urban America.* Baltimore: Johns Hopkins University Press.

Hollinger, David. (1995). *Postethnic America: Beyond multiculturalism.* New York: Basic Books.

Hoxie, Frederick E. (1984). *A final promise: The campaign to assimilate the Indians, 1880–1920.* Lincoln: University of Nebraska Press.

Jordan, Winthrop D. (1968). *White over black: American attitudes toward the Negro, 1550–1812.* New York: University of North Carolina Press.

Kallen, Horace. (1924). *Culture and democracy in the United States: Studies in the group psychology of American peoples.* New York: Boni & Liveright.

Koch, Adrienne, and Peden, William. (Eds.). (1944). *The life and selected writings of Thomas Jefferson.* New York: Modern Library.

Knobel, Dale T. (1986). *Paddy and the republic: Ethnicity and nationality in antebellum America.* Middletown, Conn.: Wesleyan University Press.

Lewis, David Levering. (1993). *W. E. B. DuBois: Biography of a race, 1868–1919.* New York: Henry Holt.

Marable, Manning. (1991). *Race, reform, and rebellion: The second reconstruction in black America.* Jackson: University of Mississippi Press.

Mardock, Robert W. (1971). *The reformers and the American Indian.* Columbia, Mo.: University of Missouri Press.

Miller, Stuart Creighton. (1969). *The unwelcome immigrant: The American image of the Chinese, 1785–1882.* Berkeley: University of California Press.

Moses, Wilson Jeremiah. (1978). *The golden age of black nationalism, 1850–1925.* Hamden, Conn.: Archon Books.

Myrdal, Gunnar. (1944). *An American dilemma.* New York: Harper and Row.

Schlesinger, Arthur M., Jr. (1992). *The disuniting of America.* New York: Norton.

Van Deburg, William L. (1992). *New day in Babylon: The black power movement and American culture, 1965–1975.* Chicago: University of Chicago Press.

3

The Biology of Ancestry
DNA, Genomic Variation, and Race

Marcus W. Feldman

•

Emerging knowledge about genomic variation within and across different human populations suggests the ways genes affect human phenotypes (e.g., skin color, hair texture, and disease), how natural selection works, and what has been the history of human migrations out of Africa and onto other continents. After noting the role biology has played in the historical classification of human beings, this essay discusses the implications of recent technological advances on researchers' ability to detect human genomic variation at minute levels. Following a review of the methods used to determine different populations' continental ancestries, the essay turns to the relationship between natural selection, phenotypes, and genotypes, especially as they are associated with continental origin. The essay concludes by noting that only a small fraction of human DNA is responsible for the visible physical differences that are used to assign people to different "races," and moreover, that phenotypes are never attributable to genes alone. While further research into humans' genetic ancestries should increase knowledge of the role of genes in the manifestation of diseases, the social category of "race" is less useful to scientists than what we might more accurately call "ancestry groups."

WHO WERE THE ETRUSCANS? FOR A PERIOD FROM ABOUT THE NINTH century BCE to the first century BCE, a region of Italy that includes Tuscany and parts of Umbria was the center of an advanced and distinctive culture that we now recognize as Etruscan. Etruscan culture then disappeared. Although no Etruscan community remains today, by examining the genetic constitution of people living in a part of Tuscany thought to have been a center of Etruscan culture more than two thousand years ago, the origin of the Etruscans can be inferred. One part of this genetic constitution—which is contained in mitochondria (maternally inherited bodies found inside all human cells) taken from today's residents of the town of Murlo in Tuscany—shows great similarity to the corresponding genetic material from people in the Near East (Achilli et al. 2007). Modern population and molecular genetics have, in this way, helped to solve a long-standing conundrum; it is most likely that the Etruscans were part of or the result of a post-neolithic migration from the Near East, possibly Anatolia (Renfrew 1987).

This story of the Etruscans is introduced as an example of how our understanding of relationships among humans—both historical and contemporary—can be informed by modern genetic and statistical technologies. Population geneticists are able to analyze genetic material from humans sampled around the world, from different populations on different continents, and to ask how and why these individuals, and the populations from which they derive, are related. Understanding the patterns of human diversity around the world and how these patterns came about is essential if we are to understand patterns of human migration and cultural contact.

The same molecular and statistical techniques can be helpful to scientific efforts to understand the relationship between genetics and observable human phenotypes. Phenotypes are the measurable or observable features of an organism. For a fruit fly, we might be interested in the number of bristles on its abdomen; for a mouse, how it reacts to threatening situations, and for humans, phenotypes might include diseases (versus non-disease states) or height or hair color or intelligence. So, for example, when people with a disease are compared to healthy people who have been selected to match them on criteria such as age, socioeconomic status (SES), and ethnicity (these are called matched controls), then scientists can more easily isolate which parts of humans' genetic material contribute to producing that disease. If families are available with some members having the disease and others healthy, even greater reliability can be achieved for an inference that some gene is involved as a cause or origin of that disease. An important part of current genetic research—the search for genetic factors related to diseases, especially complex diseases such as hypertension or coronary heart disease—continues apace.

As helpful as new genetic research is in finding biological contributors to diseases or how populations came to have their current genetic relationships, this research can be confusing and even pernicious if it is misinterpreted by those without a sophisticated understanding of the possible relationships between genes, phenotypes, and environments. This is especially dangerous in the context of contentious issues such as race and ethnicity and phenotypic differences between presumed races or ethnic groups. Accordingly, this essay reviews the data pertaining to human genetic diversity and asks how these data relate to the definition and meaning of racial classification. At stake is the question of whether there is any connection between recent discoveries about human genomic variation and the social science concept of "race." The essay concludes with the finding that only a small fraction of all genomic variation is responsible for the differences such as skin color, facial features, or hair form that are commonly used to assign people to different races. More important, the small fraction of genomic variation that does exist between people of different continental ancestry has nothing to do with supposed racial differences related to intelligence, moral character, or tendency to criminality.

VARIATION IN HUMAN DNA

The problem of classification has always played a central role in the biological sciences. Indeed, Darwin's great contribution to science was to show how the well-studied level of biological classification, namely, the subdivision of life forms into species, could arise by natural selection within accepted classes. Although the variation within species had been observed and recorded, it was not until Darwin's groundbreaking work that its relevance to between-species variation was recognized.

In his travels, Darwin observed and was intrigued by the great deal of variation among humans and by attempts to classify them into groups commonly identified at the time as races. In his review of attempts at classification in his 1871 book, *The Descent of Man*, Darwin expressed doubt about the usefulness of phenotypic variation for the purpose of racial classification, stating that "it may be doubted whether any character can be named which is distinctive of race" (225). He added, moreover, that the "variability of all the characteristic differences between the races . . . indicates that these differences cannot be of much importance" (249). Nevertheless, scholars that Darwin saw as "capable judges" had attempted to divide humans into subgroups; Darwin cites claims that there were from two to sixty-three "races" (226). The most famous of these "judges" was Johann Friedrich Blumenbach, whose partition of human phenotypes into five major racial groups became widely accepted.

Since *The Descent of Man* was published, a vast amount of biological knowledge has accumulated about the relationships between species and the genetic material—DNA, or deoxyribonucleic acid—that is passed from a parent to its offspring. In the past fifteen years, billions of dollars have been spent to produce a picture of the human DNA, which is referred to as the human genome, and now billions more are being devoted to an assessment of how this genome varies between people from the same and different parts of the world.

DNA is the genetic material in the cells of all kinds of organisms from bacteria to humans that contains the information needed to produce things like the red cell antigens that make human blood groups such as A, B, and O, or the pigment molecules that determine the color patterns on butterfly wings. We now know that the part of the DNA that is responsible for these molecules, called the coding regions, comprises only about 5 percent of the three billion units of DNA that make up the human genome. These units are called nucleotides, and the coding strings of nucleotides are the genes. The function of the rest of the human genome is not yet fully understood, although some of it acts to control how much product a gene makes or when and in what tissue the gene product is produced.

Before the 1990s, biologists predominantly studied human diseases whose patterns of occurrence among relatives exhibited the same rules as the blood groups referred to above, namely, Mendel's rules. But since the human genome was sequenced, techniques have become available to detect many kinds of DNA sequence variation, including variation at single nucleotides (single nucleotide polymorphisms, or SNPs), variation in the number of times a short arrangement of nucleotides is repeated (short tandem repeats, STRs), or variation in the presence, absence, or duplication of a segment of DNA (copy number variants, CNVs). These classes of variation, most often in nongenic regions that make up 95 percent of the human genome, have emerged as the foci of study. To date, large amounts of money have been spent on documenting these new kinds of genomic variation in four samples of the human population: European Americans (from Utah), Africans (members of the Yoruba people from Nigeria), Japanese, and Chinese. Millions of SNPs have been discovered in these samples, and there have been hundreds of studies devoted to interpreting this variation (e.g., Barreiro et al. 2008). These data and much of their analysis are referred to as the HapMap project. We now know that the world's human population exhibits thousands of CNVs, thousands of STR polymorphisms, and millions of SNPs—levels of DNA variation not suspected a mere fifteen years ago.

These new types of genomic variation have begun to dominate the study of human genetics for three reasons. The first is the search for genetic contributions to complex phenotypes such as height, weight, schizophrenia, coronary artery disease, or intelligence. No single gene is responsible for these phenotypes, and any genetic contributions to their variation are likely to be small, to involve many parts of the genome, and to interact with environments in complex ways. However, if variation in a part of the genome is found to contribute to variation in the risk of having some disease, it might provide clues as to the biochemical nature of the causes of the disease and perhaps suggest biochemical interventions, namely, drugs. On the other hand, knowledge that you have a variant that adds slightly to your risk of eventually having a specific disease might make you particularly conscientious about elements of your behavior or your diet that also are known to affect your risk of getting that disease.

The second reason the study of human genetics has begun to focus on the new types of genomic variation comes from the hope that the patterns of variation across the genome will enable scientists to understand more about natural selection. Investigators are interested, for example, in knowing which parts of the genome exhibit signals of the action of natural selection due to the different environments that different human populations have occupied. These patterns of variation are much more cryptic than the well-known hemoglobin A–hemoglobin S polymorphism that gives some people a genetic advantage against malaria in the parts of the world where this parasitic disease is common.

Finally, the third reason for the new focus in the study of human genetics is that if we know the pattern of genomic variation around the world—say, which populations seem to be genetically close to one another, and which are far apart—we can say how these relationships came about. For example, we can develop quantitative models of human migration and see which models give the closest fit to the observed pattern of genomic relationships. In this third endeavor, geneticists incorporate knowledge from paleobiology and linguistics as aids in confirming inferences about how today's patterns of variation arose. It is this pattern of worldwide genomic variation that will be our main focus in this piece, although we shall allude to the issues of associations between DNA and phenotypes and signals of natural selection at the end of this essay.

PHENOTYPES AND GENOTYPES, CONTINENTS AND POPULATIONS

It has been known for centuries that certain physical features of humans are concentrated within families: hair, eye, and skin color; height; inability to digest milk; curliness of hair; and so on. These phenotypes also show obvious variation among people from different continents. Indeed, skin color, facial shape, and hair form are examples of phenotypes whose variation among populations from different geographical regions is noticeable. No one has any difficulty seeing visible physical differences between a random person chosen from West Africa, from China, from Norway, or from the tropical rainforest of the Orinoco basin. Some classic blood group polymorphisms are also geographically differentiated, although most are not (Cavalli-Sforza et al. 1994). All of the above-mentioned phenotypic variation is largely due to variation in genes, although the specific parts of the DNA responsible for this variation are just beginning to be discovered and the genes responsible are only now beginning to be located in the genome.

Over the course of history, the typological and geographic notions of race have become merged because of the observation that continental regions are characterized by some phenotypic differences of color, facial features, or hair form. Of course, variation in these traits also occurs among individuals whose ancestors come from the same continent—and who thus might be considered to be of the same "race"—which means that categorization according to these phenotypes can be problematic (Brown and Armelagos 2001). Nevertheless, many people are interested in knowing what fraction of all of the variation in the DNA is of the kind that produces the typological distinctions most commonly used to assign racial categories.

The technology for genotyping DNA at the individual human level—and thus our ability to answer some of our questions about human genetic differentiation and continental origin—has advanced rapidly over the past ten years, and the cost has also begun to decline. This progress has been driven by the search for statistical association between one or a few SNPs and disease phenotypes; such studies are now called "whole genome association studies" (WGAS), although they do not involve the whole (three billion nucleotides) genome but up to a million

SNPs. An important by-product of the improved technology and lower price of genotyping is an explosion of knowledge about variation in the DNAs of individuals sampled from different populations around the world.

The above-mentioned HapMap project has represented one approach to producing a picture of the world's genomic variation, but since it involves samples from only four of the world's populations, HapMap cannot claim to be very comprehensive. There is, however, another approach whose aim has been to produce a much broader picture of the world's genomic variation. This is the human genome diversity project (HGDP). HGDP was begun in the early 1990s, at the impetus of the population geneticist L. L. Cavalli-Sforza, with the ambitious objective of sampling about twenty-five people from each spoken language on Earth— perhaps five thousand to six thousand populations. The idea was to ask each population to donate blood samples and convert these samples into cell lines, each of which could, in principle, provide a near inexhaustible source of DNA for current and future research. A combination of political and financial limitations led to the restriction of HGDP to a collection of 1,064 cell lines representing fifty-two sampled populations. These cell lines were provided by researchers who had them in their laboratories as a result of previous collections of blood from donors who had participated in earlier projects. An organization in Paris, France, the Centre Etude Polymorphism Humaine (CEPH), became the repository for these 1,064 cell lines, and the provider of DNA from them to qualified investigators (Cann et al. 2002; Cavalli-Sforza 2005). The collection is now called the CEPH-HGDP panel, and although it is seriously deficient in representation of indigenous (and other) populations from many parts of the world, it represents the broadest and best-documented sampling of human populations available today. An important component of the process that culminated in the CEPH-HGDP panel was an investigation of the ethical protocols that should characterize any such collection, taking account of different tribal authority systems and avoiding exploitation of indigenous blood donors. This document, by Hank Greely, a Stanford law professor, was published in the *Houston Law Review* and can be accessed online at www.stanford.edu/group/morrinst/hgdp/protocol.html.

It should be noted that there is an important difference between "populations" as used in this chapter and what are generally referred to as "races." "Population" is a term used by biologists to refer to a circumscribed group of people identified by geographical and/or linguistic characters that differentiate them from another population. Depending on how fine we draw the distinctions, one could say that there are as many as 6,000 populations as identified by distinct languages. "Races," on the other hand, is an imprecise term generally used to refer to groups of people who differ in some way (physically or culturally) from one's own group. Only a small fraction of all of the variation in the DNA is of the kind that produces the typological distinctions most commonly used to assign racial categories. What this means is that while "race" can be a useful term in the study of societal dynamics, it is not, as the studies below suggest, helpful in a discussion of human genomic variation. This is addressed in more detail below.

BETWEEN- AND WITHIN-POPULATION VARIATION

Ever since the human blood groups were discovered, geneticists have accumulated data on how the frequencies of the genes determining these blood groups varied within and among different human populations. This interest arose partly from issues at the individual level, such as paternity testing and avoiding incompatible transfusions, but also from issues at the population level, such as the necessity of maintaining correct inventories at blood banks. The application of biochemical techniques to detect variation in enzymes, first used in 1966, led to research on patterns of variation in the genes coding for such proteins in many species, including humans.

The first attempt to statistically partition variation in human blood group genes and enzymes into between- and within-group components suggested that about 85 percent of the variation occurred *within* populations and at most 11 percent was *between* what we usually refer to as "races" (Lewontin 1972). It took twenty-five years until DNA-level variation, in STRs, was able to augment the earlier blood group and enzyme data to a total of 109 variable sites in the DNA. The statistical result hardly changed; about 85 percent of the variation in these genes resided within the fourteen populations studied (Barbujani et al. 1997). The availability of the CEPH-HGDP panel with its fifty-two populations has massively expanded these initial geographically-limited sets of data.

The first statistical study of the CEPH-HGDP panel of fifty-two populations used 377 STRs and estimated that about 94 percent of the variation in frequencies of the STR alleles was within populations and only 3 percent to 4 percent between populations whose origins lie on different continents (Rosenberg et al. 2002). A recent assessment of variation at 650,000 single nucleotides within and between the CEPH-HGDP populations gave an estimate that 89 percent of the variation was within populations and about 9 percent between populations from different continents (Li et al. 2008). It follows that the genomic variation among people from the same population is about ten times that between people from different continents. Thus, the modern data confirm Lewontin's original conclusion that the overwhelming majority of genomic variation among humans occurs within populations.

People who have identified themselves as belonging to the same population are often indigenous to the same continent and might, therefore, be considered to be of the same "race." It is in the many cases of people whose ancestry derives from more than one continent that the arbitrariness of race and its social construction emerge. Thus, in the United States, a person with an African father and a European mother would probably be assigned by most people to a black race. This is a matter of historical precedent and social identification by the majority white population. It would be correct to say that such a person has ancestry on two continents (or more in many cases) and remove any racial designation which, as just mentioned, is equally European and African. In the same way, a racial designation of African American can be regarded as arbitrary because such a person can have ancestry of 1 percent or 90 percent in either Europe or Africa. It is in such cases that the social designation of race today usually trumps the much more complicated but more exact notion of genetic ancestry.

Some of the DNA differences that produce the 9 percent of between-continent variance can be assumed to be associated with genes whose functions produce the differences in skin color, hair texture, facial shape, and height of people from different geographical regions and whose detection does not require sophisticated biochemical tools. We can conclude from this that only a small fraction of all genomic variation is responsible for the differences that are commonly used to assign people to different races.

GEOGRAPHY AND LEVEL OF HETEROZYGOSITY

Although the fraction of genomic variation that is attributable to between-continent differences is very small, we can still ask whether this fraction contains enough information to tell us something about human evolution or even about the historical relationships between different populations of humans. In fact, it is possible to make a number of such inferences. The principle is one that is well known and widely exploited in the social and behavioral sciences: namely, that if each of the variables to be studied contributes a tiny fraction to the overall variation in some measure (or measures), then with a sufficient number of such variables a pattern in the variation of the measure may be detectable. In the genetic case, if most of the 650,000 positions on the DNA show small differences between continents, correlation between and accumulation of these differences combine to allow important inferences to be made.

A natural first step in the analysis of such large sets of STR (Ramachandran et al. 2005) or SNP data is to compare the amount of genomic variation among all fifty-two populations in the HGDP-CEPH panel. One measure of this variation is the level of the heterozygosity. At a particular position in the DNA, if the contribution that an individual received from his or her mother differs from that given by the father, then that individual is a heterozygote and the average over all tested positions in the DNA of the fraction of heterozygotes in all individuals in the population is that population's heterozygosity. For both STRs and SNPs, African populations have the highest heterozygosity while indigenous American populations have the lowest. Moreover, the plot of the heterozygosity of each population against geographical distance from Addis Ababa, in Ethiopia, shows a steady decline all the way to the Americas (Ramachandran et al. 2005). In other words, populations are less genetically variable the farther they are from Africa.

Population genetic theory provides the explanation for this steady loss of within-population variation with distance from Africa: Africa has the most genomic variation, and the first small group of humans that ventured out of Africa and colonized either Asia or Europe represented a small sample of the original variation. Then the next group of migrants going south or east was a sample of that first sample and had even less within-population variation. This continued loss of heterozygosity as a function of the continued sampling of earlier samples is called the serial founder effect. The observed pattern of decline in heterozygosity provides strong genetic evidence that all modern humans originated in Africa. Figure 3.1 illustrates the consensus view among population geneticists of the migration of modern humans over the past 100,000 years. Undoubtedly the dates in Figure 3.1 will be made more precise as more research is carried out on the CEPH-HGPD panel and more population samples from around the world become available.

FIGURE 3.1 | **THE MIGRATION OF MODERN HUMANS.**

This map shows the likely routes and approximate dates of the major migrations of modern humans that began from East Africa, with the most recent arrivals in the Americas.

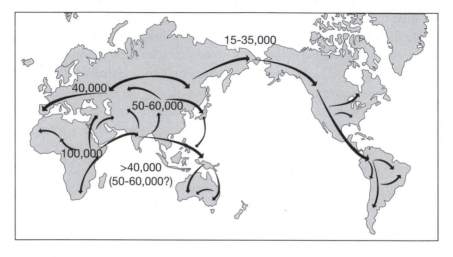

SOURCE | Cavalli-Sforza and Feldman 2003.

CONTINENTAL ANCESTRY

The explosion of data concerning human genomic variation has produced new statistical and computational methods that help us understand these data. Two methods have been particularly useful in addressing questions concerning the continental ancestry of different ancestral groups and of the individuals who form those groups. These are STRUCTURE, a statistical algorithm devised by Pritchard et al. (2000), and FRAPPÉ, which was developed by Tang and colleagues (Tang et al. 2005a, 2006). This is not the appropriate place to present the statistical details that underpin these methods. Suffice it to say that both methods produce for each individual in the study an estimate of the probability that a randomly chosen STR or SNP from that individual originates from one of a set of ancestral groups. The number of such ancestral groups, K, is chosen to produce the (statistically) best estimate of these probabilities, which are averaged over all STRs or SNPs to assign a membership coefficient, namely, a fraction of each individual's ancestry, to one of the ancestral groups. In principle, each person in the study could have part of his or her ancestry in many groups of populations, and the membership coefficient represents the fraction of his or her genome that has ancestry in each of these groups.

It is important to emphasize that when researchers do this analysis, the ancestral groups are not specified in advance and the population memberships of all individuals are removed prior to the analysis. Only the genetic information enters this analysis. Graphical representation of the pattern of membership coefficients in each group makes use of a program, DISTRUCT (Rosenberg 2004), that uses colors to represent the fractions of membership in each group. The population from which each individual actually comes is noted after the statistical analysis has been carried out. This method of analysis allows us to graphically represent, using bars of various shades of gray, genomic variation as it relates to the ancestral origin of populations from differing geographic regions of the world.

The results of two recent studies on the genomic variation among populations who have been sampled by the CEPH-HGDP panel are illustrated in Figure 3.2. The membership coefficients shown in Figure 3.2a are inferred using STRUCTURE on 783 STR polymorphisms (Rosenberg et al. 2005), while Figure 3.2b is based on the 642,690 autosomal SNPs from the study by Li et al. (2008), analyzed using the program FRAPPÉ. The similarities between the two sets of results are important. With $K = 5$ groups in Figure 3.2a, the populations from Africa, Eurasia, East Asia, Oceania, and the Americas form statistically separable continental clusters. With $K = 6$ groups, the Surui, a small indigenous Brazilian population, forms its own cluster, as do the Kalash. With the vastly increased number of polymorphisms in Figure 3.2b, the huge Eurasian "supercontinent" west of the Himalayas separates into three statistically recognizable subgroups: Middle Eastern populations, European populations, and Central-South Asian populations (Note: all sampled populations in this last group are in Pakistan; there are no populations from India in the HGDP panel). Because of the long history of migration and colonization across Eurasia, resolution of the CEPH-HGDP population samples from this part of the world required much more data than was provided by just the STRs.

Thus, although only 9 percent of the genomic variation in the SNP study is attributable to differences between large geographic regions (i.e., continents), the huge amount of data allows multivariate statistical analysis to produce from this 9 percent the regional clusters represented by the colored bars in Figure 3.2. The clusters contain within them individuals who are genetically more similar than they are to members of other clusters; the large amount of data makes this clustering statistically detectable.

Geographic clustering and spatial gradients are features of these large data sets of human genomic variation. Between pairs of populations

FIGURE 3.2a | **REPRESENTATION OF ANCESTRY IN THE CEPH-HGDP SAMPLE OF 1,056 INDIVIDUALS FROM 52 POPULATIONS AROUND THE WORLD.**

Each individual is represented by a vertical line, and the location of each person's ancestry is shown with different levels of shading. The K values 2 through 6 refer to the number of regions assumed to encompass the possible range of ancestries. The figure is based on genetic variation at 783 STR (short tandem repeats) in the DNAs of the sampled people. Many people have more than one level of shading, indicating ancestry in more than one place.

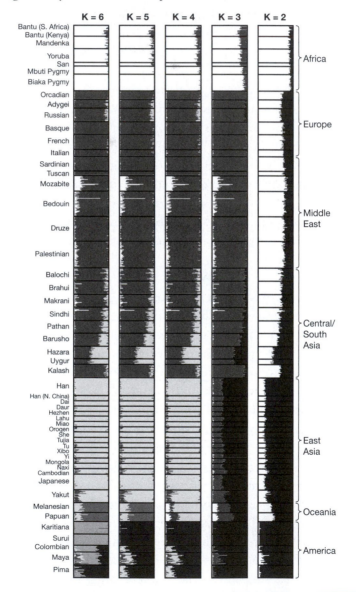

SOURCE | Rosenberg et al. 2005.

FIGURE 3.2b | **REPRESENTATION OF ANCESTRY IN 938 PEOPLE FROM THE CEPH-HGDP PANEL GENOTYPED AT 642,690 POSITIONS ON 22 CHROMOSOMES.**

With this large number of polymorphisms, seven regions are identified as sources of ancestry for these 938 people. Note that many have ancestry in three regions, which indicates the geographic origins of the ancestors of the people sampled.

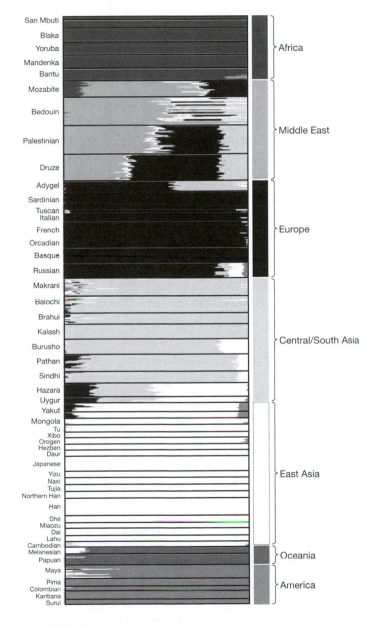

SOURCE | Li et al. 2008.

from the same cluster, genetic distance increases as geographic distance increases. But for pairs of populations from different clusters, genetic distance is generally larger than that between pairs of populations from the same clusters that are separated by the same geographic distance. This suggests that major geographic barriers, such as oceans, deserts, or mountain ranges, result in genetic discontinuities because they prevent migration from being geographically uniform. It is conceivable that some details of Figures 3.2a and 3.2b will have to be modified as more population samples expand the CEPH-HGDP panel. But it is unlikely that our general picture of the migration out of Africa to the rest of the world will change.

ADMIXTURE, MIGRATION, AND ASSIGNMENT

In Figures 3.2a and 3.2b, we see that members of many populations have ancestry in two or more continental regions. This is particularly true of the Middle Eastern populations whose ancestry includes components from Europe and Pakistan; the Mozabite population who have ancestry in Europe, Africa, and the Middle East; and populations from Pakistan and North West China. The Hazara are an ethnic group from the Hazarajat region of Afghanistan, many of whom now live in Pakistan, which is where this sample was taken. Three regions—Europe, East Asia, and Pakistan—are represented in the genomic ancestry of the Hazara. The same is true of the Uygur from Xinjiang province in China. They descend from groups who speak Turkic, Indo-European, and Mongol languages and show the same pattern of ancestry in three regions as the Hazara, although the historical events that have produced this pattern are different for these two ethnic groups.

The multiple ancestries of the Middle East on populations that we see in Figure 3.2b undoubtedly reflect that region's importance as a migration corridor between Europe and Asia. Also, the Siberian group, the Yakuts, shares common ancestry with the indigenous American populations even though the latter were sampled south of the United States, and this shared ancestry most likely reflects the migration across the Bering bridge by the Siberian founders of the indigenous American peoples.

Most people today would not refer to a "Middle Eastern race," even though the pattern of Middle Eastern ancestries in Figure 3.2b differs from all others. This phenomenon of multiple ancestry is referred to as "admixture," and its extent in any population reflects that population's history of subjugation, colonization, invasion, and even trade. The fact that a population is admixed does not preclude its assignment to a cluster, even a cluster of which it is the sole member, provided enough data are available.

Indeed, even in the population of the United States, with the use of sufficient DNA polymorphisms, clusters of African Americans, Hispanic Americans, Asian Americans, and European Americans are clearly identifiable (Tang et al. 2005a, 2006). The first three of these obviously have ancestry in two or more of the colored blocks representing continental origin in Figure 3.2, but within the U.S. population they form their own statistically identifiable clusters. This suggests that the term "race," with its negative baggage, could be replaced by a less pejorative and more accurate term "ancestry group." This term would apply equally well to any of the clusters in Figure 3.2, including those which, like the Middle Eastern bar, comprise individuals with ancestry from three continental regions. And without any pejorative connotation, it could be applied to a sample of individuals from the United States, who if studied in a worldwide context, would have ancestries in multiple clusters of Figure 3.2, or if studied only in the context of the United States, would form separate statistically detectable ancestry groups.

The statistical analyses that produced Figures 3.2a and 3.2b show that given an individual's genotype and enough worldwide genomic data, he or she can be assigned to specific genetic clusters with a high degree of certainty. So we can pinpoint a person's geographical origin (or origins, in the case of admixture) by knowing his or her genotype. However, it is very important to note that the reverse is not the case. Merely knowing a person's geographical origin does not give us enough information to predict his or her genotype. This is so because, as in the example discussed above with people from Africa, the majority of genomic variation occurs within, rather than between, populations.

GEOGRAPHIC PATTERNS OF NATURAL SELECTION

Natural selection occurs when some individuals in a population have a higher likelihood of surviving to adulthood, or reproducing, or finding mates with whom to reproduce because they carry some phenotype that others in their population do not. We then say that this phenotype is under natural selection, and because of its greater chance of being represented in future generations, the phenotype will increase in frequency over time. In the same way, a phenotype that has a disadvantage will decrease in frequency and would be expected to eventually be rare in the population. Thus the frequency of a phenotype on a population is expected to change under evolution by natural selection.

Human phenotypes emerge from a complex interaction between genotypes and environments, the latter including gestational, early developmental, educational and other environments that might be expected to affect a phenotype. To the extent that human phenotypic differences have a genotypic contribution, natural selection on phenotypes will be reflected in changes in genotype frequencies. The observation that individuals vary in both phenotypes and genotypes raises the question of whether it is possible to infer whether natural selection has produced the current pattern of variation, and if so, what was the environmental agent (or agents) that caused the natural selection. The availability of large genomic data sets and rapid computational methods for their analysis has opened new avenues in the search for evidence of selection.

The classical case of natural selection on a single human gene concerns variation in the hemoglobin gene. The most common hemoglobin allele has undergone a number of small changes that result in an altered hemoglobin molecule. The best known of these mutations of the normal hemoglobin A is called hemoglobin S. In the malarial environments of West Africa, southern Europe, the Middle East, and India, individuals of genotype AS have a selective advantage over those with the normal genotype AA (as well as those who are severely anemic and have genotype SS) due to the superior ability of blood cells in AS individuals to resist invasion by the malarial parasite. The result is that in areas where malaria is endemic, A and S types are both prevalent. Without malaria, S would be very rare. This is a case of natural selection that favors the AS genotype, thereby maintaining both A and S forms in malarial environments. More on the biology and population genetics of this system can be found in any human genetics text.

Now that we have the millions of SNPs from the four HapMap populations and the 650,000 SNPs from the fifty-two CEPH-HGDP populations, can we detect signals that part of the genome has responded to selection in one or more populations or continental regions? And if a statistical signal is detectable in the genome, can we identify the phenotypes that have been subject to this natural selection and the environmental agent(s) that are likely to be responsible for the selection?

A number of methods have been used to detect a signal of selection that favors a particular part of the genome, that is, positive selection, or that keeps parts of the genome related to deleterious phenotypes at low frequencies. One method, suggested originally by Cavalli-Sforza (1966), examines the degree of differentiation among the different populations for each genetic variant—for example, all the microsatellites or SNPs in a study. The idea is that all parts of the genome should be equally affected by any demographic forces, such as migration or changes in population size. Hence, if one DNA segment gives a statistical signal of differentiation that is either too high or too low relative to the distribution of that signal across all DNA segments, this extreme value may be due to selection.

Barreiro et al. (2008) examined 2.8 million SNPs assayed in the four HapMap project samples using a standard measure of population differentiation for individual SNPs. They found many signals of selection against SNPs located in genes known to be related to diseases. They also found evidence of strong positive selection for SNPs associated with genes for skin color, olfaction, immune response to pathogens, as well as other phenotypes. An earlier study by Voight et al. (2006) of HapMap data had also detected positive selection on these classes of genes as well as others related to spermatogenesis and fertilization. Over the past few years, genomic analyses have repeatedly confirmed that genes involved in skin pigmentation show strong signs of positive selection in Europeans for the lighter colored pigmentation alleles. The suggestion is that in the European environment with reduced solar radiation, lighter skin probably had a selective advantage.

A fascinating example of natural selection in both Europeans and Africans has emerged from analyses of SNPs associated with the enzyme lactase, which controls the ability of adults to digest milk. Lactase persistence, which enables milk to be digested into adulthood, had previously been thought to be a European trait. Indeed, there is a SNP associated with lactase persistence that shows strong signs of selection in Europeans (Enattah et al. 2002, 2007). However, a recent study by Tishkoff et al. (2007) identified a different SNP that is associated with tolerance of milk in some Kenyan and Tanzanian populations. In Europeans and these African populations, the selected allele apparently spread rapidly along with the culturally transmitted practice of pastoralism and drinking milk. These examples of recent analyses of selection at the genomic level illustrate that at least a small part of the variation in the human genome can be attributed to environmental effects and/or cultural practices.

SELF-IDENTIFICATION AND GENETIC ANCESTRY

Admixture (mixed ancestry) in a population is known to produce spurious associations between a phenotype and genes. This can be important in epidemiological studies where cases of a disease are matched with healthy controls, and large numbers of DNA variants, usually SNPs, are tested to see if they differ in frequencies between the two phenotypic samples. Especially in admixed populations, such as ethnic minorities in the United States, it is important to assess the extent of genetic substructure that may affect estimates of association of genes with chronic complex diseases. Such substructure may occur if the population from which the cases and/or controls are taken is stratified in any way—for example, by socioeconomic status, routine use of different diets or exercise regimes, or ancestry from different parts of the world. For this reason it is important to ask whether self-reported population ancestry is concordant with that determined by genetic studies.

From their analysis of the CEPH-HGDP panel, Rosenberg et al. (2002) pointed out that "self-reported ancestry likely provides a suitable proxy for genetic ancestry." These authors worried, however, that in recently admixed populations variation in genetic ancestry might correlate with risk of disease as a consequence of genetic or cultural factors. Thus, in such recently admixed groups as the ethnic minorities in the United States, it is important to ascertain how well self-identified race or ethnicity matches the genetic structure of these populations when the latter is estimated from a larger number of markers.

An important attempt to answer this question was made by Tang et al. (2005b), who genotyped 326 STRs on 3,636 people of varying race or ethnicity sampled from fifteen locations in the United States and Taiwan. Subjects identified themselves as being white non-Hispanic, black non-Hispanic, Hispanic, Chinese, and Japanese. As in the study by Rosenberg et al. (2002), the statistical determination of genetic clusters was done by researchers who had knowledge of how the people being studied self-identified. Using STRUCTURE (Pritchard et al. 2000), four genetic clusters were identified, and these corresponded almost perfectly to the self-identified categories with one cluster containing the Chinese and Japanese subjects; only five of the people sampled were differentially classified. The results, taken from Tang et al. (2005b), are presented in Table 3.1.

Two of the conclusions reached by Tang et al. should be emphasized. The first is that the genetic clustering in Table 3.1 reflects ancient geographic ancestry rather than the geography of current residence. Second, in the absence of self-identified ethnic labels, it is dangerous to attribute phenotypic differences—for example, in disease incidence

TABLE 3.1 | **GENETIC CLUSTER ANALYSIS VERSUS SELF-IDENTIFIED ETHNICITY OF 3,636 PEOPLE**

Self-Identified Ethnicity	Number of Subjects in Genetic Cluster			
	A	**B**	**C**	**D**
White non-Hispanic	1,348	0	0	1
Black non-Hispanic	3	0	1,305	0
Hispanic	1	0	0	411
Chinese	0	407	0	0
Japanese	0	160	0	0

SOURCE | After Tang et al. 2005b.

or life expectancy—between genetically defined clusters as being due to genes because these differences may actually be due to environmental, cultural, or behavioral factors.

GENES, DISEASE, AND ANCESTRY

Since the sequencing of the human genome and the subsequent development of technologies that allow detection of hundreds of thousands or millions of SNPs, hundreds of studies have attempted to find associations between SNPs and disease phenotypes. From the position of a SNP found to be associated with a disease, the genes in the neighborhood of that SNP can be located from one of the public databases. To the extent that the nature and amount of the products of these genes are known, the biochemical causes of the disease might then be revealed. Such studies have focused on complex diseases, that is, those for which no single gene is known to cause the disease. Important examples include hypertension, coronary artery disease, rheumatoid arthritis, type 2 diabetes, and behavioral disorders such as bipolar disease, autism, and schizophrenia.

The largest study of this kind was carried out in the United Kingdom and involved 2,000 cases of each of seven major diseases and a shared set of 3,000 controls. All subjects were of European ancestry (Wellcome Trust Case Control Consortium 2007). One example of the many interesting associations found was the SNP on chromosome 9 that showed the highest signal of association with coronary artery disease.

We can ask whether a SNP found to be associated with coronary artery disease in Europeans (i.e., British) is also a risk factor for people of other ancestries. In other words, can we extrapolate from a genome-wide association study of people with ancestry on one continent to those with ancestry on another continent? An elegant study by McPherson et al. (2007) shows that the answer is no. These investigators in a very carefully replicated study found an association between two SNPs and chronic artery disease in people of European ancestry. These were located very close to the part of the genome identified in the British study. When these same SNPs were assessed in the HapMap sample of Yoruba people (the Yoruba are a large ethnic group from Nigeria), the alleles strongly associated with chronic artery disease in Europeans were either absent or very rare. Further, the two SNPs which were significant risk factors in European Americans were not associated with the disease in African Americans from two different samples. The conclusion is inescapable: alleles associated with risk factors for this disease have widely different frequencies in different ancestry groups.

The amount of RNA produced by a gene can be measured and treated as a continuously varying phenotype for each gene and is called the "expression level" for that gene. Variation in the expression level of a gene can be due to difference in other parts of the genome called "regulators." Spielman et al. (2007) examined expression levels in 4,197 genes in people of European and East Asian (Chinese and Japanese) ancestry and found significant differences between the expression levels in the two groups for 1,097 genes. This raises the possibility that other phenotypic differences between populations of different ancestries could also be due to variation in the regulatory parts of the genome. It is unlikely that such phenotypic differences will be large. Indeed it is worth quoting a major conclusion of the British study referred to above:

> The novel variants we have uncovered are characterized by modest effect size . . . and even these estimates are likely to be inflated. . . . The observed distribution of effect sizes is consistent with models based on theoretical considerations, and empirical data from animal models that suggest that, for any given trait there will be few (if any) large effects, a handful of modest effects, and a substantial number of genes generating small or very small increases in disease risk. (674–675)

It seems reasonable, then, to assume that the differences between people who belong to different ancestry groups in the added risk of disease from such genes is also likely to be modest, small, or very small.

CONCLUSION

After reviewing the available data pertaining to human genetic diversity and asking how these data relate to the definition and meaning of racial classification, we have shown that people can be assigned to ancestry clusters that usually agree with their self-identified ethnicity. We have also shown that only a small fraction of all genomic variation is responsible for the visible morphological differences such as skin color, facial features, or hair form that are commonly used to assign people to different races. Moreover, that small fraction of genomic variation has nothing to do with supposed racial differences related to intelligence, moral character, or tendency to criminality. For that reason, we suggest that a more accurate name for such genetically defined clusters—rather than race or ethnicity—might be "ancestry groups."

While most genomic variation occurs within ancestry groups, an examination of the pattern of differences within and between ancestry groups can reveal those parts of the genome that have been subject to selection in different parts of the world. Admixture and mixed ancestry can generate spurious correlations between genes and disease, so proper development of control groups for epidemiological studies should take continental ancestry into account. However, as pointed out by Epstein (2006), "genetic risk assessment will attain sufficient predictive power to be of use if—and only if— analyses of many loci are combined with evaluations of non-genetic lifestyle and environmental factors" (436). There is potential for lines of ancestry to provide medically useful information. But because phenotypes are never attributable to genes alone, for diagnosis and treatment, individual properties—both genetic and environmental—are likely to provide the most useful information.

Works Cited

•

Achilli, A., A. Olivieri, M. Pala, E. Metspalu, Simona Fornarino, V. Battaglia, M. Accetturo, I. Kutuev, E. Khusnutdinova, E. Pennarun, N. Cerutti, C. Di Gaetano, F. Crobu, D. Palli, G. Matullo, A.S. Santachiara-Benerecetti, L.L. Cavalli-Sforza, O. Semino, R. Villems, H.-J. Bandelt, A. Piazza, and A. Torroni. 2007. Mitochondrial DNA variation of modern Tuscans supports the Near Eastern origin of Etruscans. *Am. J. Hum. Genet.* **80**: 759–768.

Barbujani, G., A. Magagni, E. Minch, and L. L. Cavalli-Sforza. 1997. An apportionment of human DNA diversity. *Proc. Natl. Acad. Sci. USA* **94**: 4516–4519.

Barreiro, L. B., G. Laval, H. Quach, E. Patin, and L. Quintana-Murci. 2008. Natural selection has driven population differentiation in modern humans. *Nat. Genet.* **40**: 340–345.

Brown, R. A., and G. J. Armelagos. 2001. Apportionment of racial diversity: A review. *Evol. Anthro.* **10**: 34–40.

Cann, H. M., C. de Toma, L. Cazes, M.-F. Legrand, V. Morel, L. Piouffre, J. Bodmer, W. F. Bodmer, B. Bonne-Tamir, A. Cambon-Thomsen, Z. Chen, J. Chu, L. Contu, C. Carcassi, R. Du, L. Excoffier, G. B. Ferrara, J. S. Friedlaender, E. Groot, D. Guwitz, T. Jenkins, R. J. Herrera, X. Huang, J. Kidd, K. K. Kidd, A. Langaney, A. A. Lin, S. Q. Mehdi, P. Parham, A. Piazza, Q. Yaping, Q. Shu, J Xu, S. Zhu, J. L. Weber, H. T. Greely, M. W. Feldman, G. Thomas, J. Dausset, L. L. Cavalli-Sforza. 2002. A human diversity cell-line panel. *Science* **296**: 261–262.

Cavalli-Sforza, L. 1966. Population structure and human evolution. *Proc. Roy. Soc. London Ser. B* **164**: 362–379

Cavalli-Sforza, L. L. 2005. The Human Genome Diversity Project: Past, present and future. *Nat. Rev. Genet.* **6**: 333–340.

Cavali-Sforza, L. L., and Feldman, M. W. 2003. The application of molecular genetic approaches to the study of human evolution. *Nature Genetics Supplement* **33**: 266–275.

Cavalli-Sforza, L. L., P. Menozzi, and A. Piazza. 1994. *The History and Geography of Human Genes*. Princeton, NJ: Princeton University Press.

Darwin, C. 1871. *The Descent of Man*. London: John Murray.

Enattah, N. S., T. Sahi, E. Savilahti, J. D. Terwilliger, L. Peltonen, and I. Järvelä. 2002. Identification of a variant associated with adult-type hypolactasia. *Nat. Genet.* **30**: 233–237.

Enattah, N. S., A. Trudeau, V. Pimenoff, L. Maiuri, S. Auricchio, L. Greco, M. Rossi, M. Lentze, J. K. Seo, S. Rahgozar, I. Khalil, M. Alifrangis, S. Natah, L. Groop, N. Shaat, A. Kozlov, G. Verschubskaya, D. Comas, K. Bulayeva, S. Q. Mehdi, J. D. Terwilliger, T. Sahi, E. Savilahti, M. Perola, A. Sajantila, I. Järvelä, and L. Peltonen. 2007. Evidence of still-ongoing convergence evolution of the lactase persistence T_{-13910} alleles in humans. *Am. J. Hum. Genet.* **81**: 615–625.

Epstein, C. J. 2006. Medical genetics in the genomic medicine of the 21st century. *Am. J. Hum. Genet.* **79**: 434–438.

Greely, Henry T. 1997. Proposed model ethical protocol for collecting DNA samples. *Houston Law Rev.* **33**: 1431–1473.

Lewontin, R.C. 1972. The apportionment of human diversity. *Evol. Biol.* **6**: 381–398.

Li, J. Z., D. M. Absher, H. Tang, A. M. Southwick, Cann, H., A. M. Casto, S. Ramachandran, H. M. Cann, G. S. Barsh, M. Feldman, L. L. Cavalli-Sforza, and R. M. Myers. 2008. Genome-wide characterization of genetic diversity in human populations. *Science* **319**: 1100–1104.

McPherson, R., A. Pertsemlidis, N. Kavaslar, A. Stewart, R. Roberts, D. R. Cox, D. A. Hinds, L. A. Pennacchio, A. Tybjaerg-Hansen, A. R. Folsom, E. Boerwinkle, H. H. Hobbs, and J. C. Cohen. 2007. A common allele on chromosome 9 associated with coronary heart disease. *Science* **316**: 1488–1491.

Pritchard, J. K., M. Stephens, and P. Donnelly. 2000. Inference of population structure using multilocus genotype data. *Genetics* **155**: 945–959.

Ramachandran, S., O. Deshpande, C. C. Roseman, N. A. Rosenberg, M. W. Feldman, and L. L. Cavalli-Sforza. 2005. Support from the relationship of genetic and geographic distance in human populations for a serial founder effect originating in Africa. *Proc. Natl. Acad. Sci. USA* **102**: 15942–15947.

Renfrew, A. C. 1987 *Archaeology and Language: The Puzzle of Indo-European Origins*. London: Pimlico.

Rosenberg, N. A. 2004. DISTRUCT: A program for the graphical display of population structure. *Molec. Ecol. Notes* **4**: 137–138.

Rosenberg, N. A., J. K. Pritchard, H. Cann, J. Weber, K. K. Kidd, L. A. Zhivotovsky, and M. W. Feldman. 2002. Genetic structure of human populations. *Science* **298**: 2381–2385.

Rosenberg, N. A., S. Mahajan, S. Ramachandran, C. Zhao, J. K. Pritchard, and M. W. Feldman. 2005. Clines, clusters, and the effect of study design on the inference of human population structure. *PLoS Genet.* **1**: 660–671.

Spielman, R. S., L. A. Bastone, J. T. Burdick, M. Morley, W. J. Ewens, and V. G. Cheung. 2007. Common genetic variants account for differences in gene expression among ethnic groups. *Nat. Genet.* **39**: 226–231.

Tang, H., J. Peng, P. Wang, and N. J. Risch. 2005a. Estimation of individual admixture: analytical and study design considerations. *Genet. Epidemiol.* **28**: 289–301.

Tang, H., T. Quertermous, B. Rodriguez, S. L. R. Kardia, X. Zhu, A. Brown, J. S. Pankow, M. A. Province, S. C. Hunt, E. Boerwinkle, N. J. Schork, and N. J. Risch. 2005b. Genetic structure, self-identified race/ethnicity, and confounding in case-control association studies. *Am. J. Hum. Genet.* **76**: 268–275.

Tang, H., M. Coram, P. Want, X. Zhu, and N. Risch. 2006. Reconstructing genetic ancestry blocks in admixed individuals. *Am. J. Hum. Genet.* **79**: 1–12.

Tishkoff, S. A., F. A. Reed, A. Ranciaro, B. F. Voight, C. C. Babbitt, J. S. Silverman, K. Powell, H. M. Mortensen, J. B. Hirbo, M. Osman, M. Ibrahim, S. A. Omar, G. Lema, T. B. Nyambo, J. Ghori, S. Bumpstead, J. K. Pritchard, G. A. Wray, and P. Deloukas. 2007. Convergent adaptation of human lactase persistence in Africa and Europe. *Nat. Genet.* **39**: 31–40.

Voight, B.F., S. Kudaravalli, X. Wen, and J.K. Pritchard. 2006. A map of recent positive selection in the human genome. *PLoS Biol.* **4**: 446–458.

Wellcome Trust Case Control Consortium. 2007. Genome-wide association of 14,000 cases of seven common diseases and 3,000 shared controls. *Nature* **447**: 661–678.

4

Which Differences Make a Difference?

Race, DNA, and Health

Barbara A. Koenig

•

This essay considers the implications of new findings in molecular genetics for our understanding of the meaning of race, particularly within the domain of biomedicine. New methods of studying the full complexity of genetic ancestry in human populations—scientific practices that pinpoint millions of points of variation in the DNA—are employed in the study of disease etiology, in treatment, and in explaining persistent health inequalities between minority and majority groups in the United States. Although it is well-known that illnesses cluster, the exact reasons are often unclear: Is it genetics, shared social environment, or some combination? Less well-examined are the consequences of searching for the roots of health disparities utilizing new genomic tools. This essay argues that genomics may inadvertently reinstate a biological understanding of human racial categorization, replacing the hard-won scientific compromise that differences among human groups are primarily cultural in nature. Ironically, well-intentioned scientific practices for "doing race" through genetic studies may obscure the health implications of how race is "lived."

New York, perhaps more than any other big city, harbors all the ingredients for a continued epidemic. It has large numbers of the poor and obese who are at higher risk. It has a growing population of Latinos, who get the disease in disproportionate numbers, and of Asians, who can develop it at much lower weights than people of other races.

NEW YORK TIMES, JANUARY 9, 2006 (EMPHASIS ADDED)

THE STATEMENT ABOVE APPEARED UNDER THE HEADLINE "DIABETES and Its Awful Toll," in a series of articles alerting readers to an emerging public health threat. This quote includes several clues about which differences "matter" in health care and biomedicine. There are hints that disease is somehow associated with certain populations, and that rates of ill health may vary by race. Asians and Latinos are described as separate "races," yet without much explanation. Poverty is implicated as another factor, yet its relationship to race is not mentioned. We might ask: Why are such categories of difference used? What logic, what practices of classification undergird this method of engaging in health research? Will new genetic research tools affect health research, and as a consequence, change the ways race is talked about and understood? And what are the policy consequences?

WHAT'S AT STAKE: GENETICS AND HEALTH DISPARITIES

The United States' persistent health disparities are widely recognized. In 2003 the Institute of Medicine (IOM 2003) published a major report examining the state of minority health in the United States. The report documented differences in rates of common diseases like cancer or heart disease, as well as significant variations in mortality rates and overall life expectancy. Black–white differences are especially troubling; U.S. whites consistently outlive blacks. And these differences persist even among those with equal access to health insurance, such as those older than 65 who are covered by Medicare. The experts convened by the IOM cited a large body of empirical research that underscores the existence of these and other health disparities among U.S. groups.

For example, minorities are *less likely* than whites to be given appropriate heart medications or to undergo cardiac bypass surgery and are less likely than whites to receive kidney dialysis or transplants. By contrast, they are *more likely* to undergo certain less desirable procedures, such as lower limb amputations for diabetes. Eliminating the root cause of such persistent inequalities has become a shared national goal—and it is a laudable objective, though hard to realize.

Although lack of access to health services, and unequal treatment when care is sought, account for a significant portion of racial and ethnic health disparities, the completion of the Human Genome Project has focused attention on *biological* (hence genetic) variation across human populations. The tools of the new genetics are increasingly aimed at targets like soaring rates of diabetes and obesity. Even complex behaviors like smoking are being investigated using genetic hypotheses (NCI 2009). Even without meaning to, this genetic research deflects attention away from well-documented social determinants of ill health.

For decades, research investigating the causes of addiction has used difference across human populations as a starting point for analysis. Addiction—a trait that inevitably combines biology and behavior—provides a useful example when considering the implications of genetics research targeted by race. The use of some illicit substances is more common in U.S. "racialized" population groups, and addiction is associated with differential health outcomes among these groups. For example, certain Native American communities have high rates of alcoholism and alcohol-related disease, and U.S. minority populations are addicted to nicotine at higher rates than middle-class whites. It is appealing to cite genetic explanations for these differences (Caron et al. 2005), since locating the cause in the body, at the level of the gene, emphasizes personal responsibility for health. In turn, genetic causes tend to privilege pharmaceutical solutions, rather than social strategies for harm reduction, such as smoking bans or tax increases (Dingel and Koenig 2008). Viewing addiction through a genomic lens can direct attention away from interventions designed to change the underlying social conditions that support higher rates of addiction in racialized minorities.

NIH CENTER FOR GENOMICS AND HEALTH DISPARITIES

In 2008, the U.S. National Institutes of Health (NIH) announced the formation of a special center to study the intersection of genomics and health disparities. Note that *genetic* research examines specific genes and their health consequences; in contrast, *genomic* approaches target an organism's full complement of genes acting together, which is called the genome. The center initially was to be named the NIH Intramural Center for Genomics and Health Disparities. Said its director, Charles Rotimi, "The priority of our center will be to understand how we can use the tools of genomics to address some of the issues we see with health disparities" (NIH 2008). In the United States, health disparities are measured, tracked, and compared using categories of race. Perhaps because of the political sensitivity of linking genes and racial disparities in health, within months both the name and the mission of the new agency had changed. Now called the Center for Research on Genomics and Global Health (CRGGH), its research goal is:

> to facilitate a global understanding of the relationship between human genetic variation and population differences in disease distribution, with the ultimate goal of informing health dispari- ties. Investigators in the CRGGH will develop genetic epidemi- ology models that will explore the patterns and determinants of common complex diseases in populations in the United States and other human populations around the world. (CRGGH 2009)

This framing avoids granting scientific privilege to U.S. racial catego- ries or to a priori assumptions that health disparities are predominantly caused by biological differences, rather than by lack of access to health services or structural social inequalities (Sankar et al. 2004). Within NIH, the intersection of race and genetics is clearly understood to be politically sensitive territory.

LINKING GENES, DISEASE, AND POPULATION

NIH's decision to create a new center, and the initial choice to link health disparities firmly to genetics, is hardly novel. The idea that cer- tain diseases occur in specific human groups appears self-evident and noncontroversial. Indeed, it has long been established that some dis- eases occur at greater frequency in populations that share what I will call in this essay "biogeographical ancestry": descent from a particular region of the world. Note that biogeographical ancestry does not map perfectly onto common understandings of race. The two concepts are not synonymous.

We often speak casually about the link between illness and race. The classic cases in which disease is linked to race stem from the study of Mendelian (single-gene) disorders by population geneticists. Rare dis- eases caused by a mutation in a single gene often cluster in certain human populations. Two kinds of *chance* events lead to clustering: (1) population "bottlenecks" happen when only a small number of ancestors form the basis of a larger population, for example, after an environmental disaster significantly reduces the population size; and (2) "random genetic drift" occurs over time when groups are isolated from each other because of geographic barriers like oceans or mountain ranges. Clusters may also occur when a genetic variant confers a selective advantage. It is often difficult to ascertain whether random events or selective advantages have caused the differences in gene frequencies between different populations. For example, sickle cell anemia, an autosomal recessive genetic condition, is widely understood as a "black" disease in the United States, even though in reality it is distributed throughout the world (Wailoo 2001). Variations in the sickle cell gene are found throughout Africa, the Mediterranean, the Middle East, and South Asia—areas where falciparum malaria is common. Those with sickle cell often die young. But because of a selective advantage among those who carry one (but not two) copies of a single-gene mutation that affects the blood's oxygen carrying ability, the variant persists. Having one copy of the gene variant protects against malaria; having two copies leads to lethal sickle cell disease. Sickle cell anemia was the first disease to be fully understood at the molecular level: It is caused by a mutation in a single gene that codes for hemoglobin.

Likewise, Tay-Sachs disease is widely understood as a condition affecting those of Ashkenazi Jewish background (even though it also occurs in other groups, such as French Canadians), and cystic fibrosis is considered a disease of northern Europeans (even though it is actually found throughout the world). Thus the idea of what might be called racialized diseases is commonplace, even though it is scientifically inaccurate. The problem, however, was that initial public policies for sickle cell disease screening so intricately tied the disease to African origins that in some U.S. states only newborns identified (socially) as black were screened for the condition. This practice led to undetected cases and consequent harm for those with the diease who were not diagnosed early. Testing for cystic fibrosis provides another example. The condition is caused by any one of more than 1000 distinct mutations in a gene called CFTR. Mutation *patterns* vary by ancestry, meaning that commercial genetic tests are of greater or lesser efficacy depending on the geographical origin of the individual screened. The *frequency* of both the disease and mutation pattern varies by biogeographical ancestry, but few genetic conditions are specific to any human group. The racialization of disease is a *social* practice, a consequence of "doing race." Racialized diseases are created by linking genetic conditions to historically and socially constructed categories of group difference. The linkage of sickle cell disease to blackness is historically and socially contingent; it is not biological fact. Although genes control the expression of skin pigmentation, blackness cannot be found in biology.

Similarly, both Tay-Sachs disease and certain rare mutations in a gene that predispose to breast cancer risk were linked early on to

"Jewishness"—at least in part because many American Jews endorse scientific values and participate in research at high rates. The availability of blood specimens collected from Jewish volunteers enabled the early identification of several mutations found in higher frequency (but not exclusively) in those of Ashkenazi background, leading genetic testing companies to offer targeted testing for "Jewish mutations" (Parthasarathy 2007, 83). In the last decade, fundamental changes in the *practice* of genetic research—stimulated by the mapping of the full human genome—have further complicated our understanding of the links among genes, ancestry, and human disease.

A POST-GENOMIC MOMENT

One specific, unified message accompanied the official announcement of the completion of the Human Genome Project in 2000: human beings are essentially the same.[1] Once the full genome reference sequence was published, this central theme was widely proclaimed by scientists and politicians alike (Collins and Mansoura 2001; California Newsreel 2003). Human genetic sequences are 99.9 percent identical; of the 0.1 percent of the human genome that varies from person to person, only 3 to 10 percent of that variation is associated with geographic ancestry or "race" as classically understood (Koenig, Lee, and Richardson 2008). This message was nothing new. For decades, the finding that there is greater genetic variability "within groups" than "between groups" had generally been accepted as evidence that the human species is not divided into discrete races. Rather, genetic variation is continuous, or "clinal," the technical term used by population genetics researchers (Lewontin 1991; Serre and Pääbo 2004). Geneticists publicly interpreted these results as disproving a biological concept of race and voiced their hopes that such scientific findings might help counter racism. This unified message has been conveyed by professional associations (AAA 1998), major travelling exhibits mounted by science museums (AAA 2007), and popular television documentaries such as *The Human Family Tree*, aired by the National Geographic Society in 2009. Voice-overs in that program announce authoritatively, "We are all related. . . . We are basically identical." The notion that modern humans—despite widespread geographic

---

1 On June 26, 2000, President Clinton noted, "I believe one of the great truths to emerge from this triumphant expedition inside the human genome is that in genetic terms, all human beings, regardless of race, are more than 99.9 percent the same" (NHGRI 2000).

migrations following their departure "out of Africa"—are 99.9 percent similar, is invoked throughout the program as the camera pans to an extraordinarily diverse-looking group of people attending a street fair in Queens, New York. With the completion of the Human Genome Project, many imagined a future in which "race would become obsolete as attention shifted from the body politics of skin color, hair texture, and eye shape to the molecular-level biopolitics of the gene" (Koenig, Lee, and Richardson 2008, 1).

In actuality, since the mapping of the human genome, research has focused on human genetic *variation* and *differences* among groups (Jakobsson et al. 2008). This focus has rekindled debates about the connection between genetic traits (at the level of DNA) and human "racial" difference (Wilson 2001). "Scholars are divided on the question of whether racial categorization is an appropriate means of organizing potentially useful genetic data or a pernicious reification of historically destructive typologies" (Lee et al. 2008, 404).

In the nineteenth century, ideas of human difference were deeply linked with the biological theories of the day (see this volume's introduction); most aspects of human behavior, including intelligence, were ranked according to a social Darwinist evolutionary schema. That approach changed profoundly at the turn of the twentieth century with Franz Boas, the creator of American anthropology. The work of Boas and his students uncoupled biological race from theories of human culture, according diverse populations equal status and setting the stage for an anti-racist cultural relativism that became dominant following the atrocities of World War II (Pierpont 2004).

Thus, in the second half of the twentieth century, prior to the Human Genome Project's completion, most historians, social scientists, and race theorists afforded biology little status in theories of human difference (Fredrickson 2002). Contrary to these expectations and hopes, postgenomic science has *focused* on difference, reviving the idea of racial categories as proxies for true biological differences (Lee, Mountain, and Koenig 2001). Population genetics research and work by anthropological geneticists has focused on that small 0.1 percent margin of difference among human groups, using the tools of genetic difference to investigate human origins and ancient movements of populations (Li et al. 2008). Although highly contested and disputed, these minute differences are used in forensic investigations to solve crimes or even to adjudicate claims about national origins (Travis 2009). In addition, human geneticists argue that the genome holds the key to medically significant biological differences among human racial and ethnic populations. Increasingly, genetic variation among human populations—races, ethnicities, nationalities—is an object of keen biomedical interest (Bamshad et al. 2004). And ironically, this work—which reinstates the link between biology and lay concepts of race—is justified by the claim that it will lead to the elimination of racial and ethnic health disparities (Krieger 2005; Montoya 2007; Sankar 2006).

CAN GENETICS "PROVE" THE EXISTENCE OF RACE AND ITS LINK TO DISEASE?

"Race Is Seen as a Real Guide to Track Disease," announced a 2002 *New York Times* article, reporting on a new paper by Neil Risch et al. in *Genome Biology* (Wade 2002a). In that paper, Risch and colleagues argued that genetic differences among populations cluster into five major groups corresponding to "classical definition of races based on continental ancestry," and they boldly made the case for the "validity of racial/ethnic self-categorization" in genetic epidemiology research (Risch, Burchard, and Tang 2002). In challenging the seemingly unified chorus among scholars and scientists that race is a set of historically created and reinforced social ideas and practices, not rooted in human genes, the paper was a pivotal event in redirecting the emerging discourse on race and genetics. It was followed eight months later by a *New England Journal of Medicine* paper (Burchard et al. 2003) that not only advocated the use of race in human genetics research but framed its necessity in terms of the public policy goal of mitigating health disparities among racially identified populations. At the same time, other voices disputed the claim that genetic science had demonstrated the validity of traditional racial categories in studies of common illness, such as heart disease or diabetes (Cooper 2003).

The vigorous reassertion of the coupling of race and genes, once seen as antiquated, accompanies the shift of human genetic variation research into the genomic age. The new research revives old debates over the existence of a biological basis for race. But the new genetic race concept differs in important ways from its predecessors, as does the context of the debate.

THE DEVELOPMENT OF TOOLS TO INTERROGATE THE GENOME

Technologically, the genomic age institutes a shift from relatively limited gene-hunting research possible in Mendelian genetics to an era of whole-genome analysis. Confronted with a vast pool of largely undif-ferentiated genomic data, researchers must find ways to make sense of it. Much of the new genomics is not hypothesis-driven. Instead, researchers query the human genome, seeking distinctions and patterns as leads for further research. The data derived from the human genome, like any large, multidimensional database, can be probed and organized in vari-ous ways. Because it is an important and highly salient social category, race (as understood and lived in the social world) has rapidly become a prominent "search tool" in scientific efforts to make sense of human genetic variation.

Intensive work of this sort has resulted in large-scale studies seeking patterns in human genetic variation across the world. Most prominently, a paper published in 2002 by Noah Rosenberg became the most cited ar-ticle that year in the prestigious journal *Science* (Rosenberg et al. 2002). The study used a set of 377 genetic markers (microsatellites) that were as-sessed in 1,056 people. The 1,056 individual DNA samples were collected from 52 ethnically and linguistically diverse populations drawn from Africa, Asia, Europe, and the Americas. The paper graphically displayed the differences among human populations distributed across the world (also see Chapter 3). The team concluded that without using prior infor-mation about the origins of individuals, using a computer program called Structure, they were able to identify six genetic clusters. Five of these cor-respond to major geographic regions. Although the authors did not use the word "race" in the paper, their findings were widely reported in the popular media as demonstrating genetic *proof* of racial differences. In the *New York Times*, the science writer Nicholas Wade observed, "The issue of race and ethnicity has forced itself to biomedical researchers' attention because human populations have different patterns of disease" (Wade 2002b). Wade acknowledged that the authors themselves disavowed a racial interpretation of their findings, but he nonetheless invoked the term "race," linking it tightly to the needs of health research.

Slates of "neutral" genetic markers like those Rosenberg used are em-ployed widely by researchers seeking associations between genes and dis-ease occurrence. (These are variants that occur by chance, as discussed above.) If a disease is known to occur at different frequencies in groups of patients with varied biogeographical ancestry, then it is critical to correct for what is called "population stratification." Specifically, when searching for new associations between genetic mutations and disease, it is necessary to make sure that your genetic sample does not include DNA provided by different population groups that have different underlying frequency rates of the disease under study. If the sample is stratified in this way, the results will be incorrect. This is a legitimate and scientifically important use of ancestry information and of panels of genetic "ancestry-informative" genetic markers. Unfortunately, the population clusters created by using these markers are often assumed to map directly onto lay categories of race, even though this is not technically accurate (Bamshad et al. 2004).

The technology continues to change and develop. Once a single reference human genome was available, researchers' next step was to create tools to account for the full spectrum of human diversity. One such tool was the human "haplotype map," which sought to determine the patterns in the distribution of genetic polymorphisms across the globe (International HapMap Consortium 2005). Although the haplotype map project focused on seeking human genetic diversity, its sampling methods (perhaps unsurprising, but very important) reflected conventional understandings of race. Sampling was not driven by a "bottom-up" examination of genetic variation around the world but by a "top-down" approach that employed specific, socially and historically contingent, racial categories. DNA samples were not collected at random from throughout the globe (a strategy called "grid sampling" that involves drawing a grid on a world map and sampling from all the boxes) but in three identified human "populations." The populations selected, Northern Europeans, Nigerians from a single African tribe, and Asians (Han Chinese and residents of Tokyo), correspond to conventional racial thinking. Almost as if working from the same script, the most recent effort to categorize human genetic variation, the 1000 Genomes project, uses similar categories of European, Asian, and African (1000 Genomes 2008). This massive research effort seeks to collect and make available the *full* sequence data of 1,000 humans, essentially repeating the Human Genome Project 1,000 times.

These databases have lay conceptions of race literally *built into them*. Once instituted, these data become a reference point for further research, as the information is analyzed and transformed for use by specialists in other fields, ranging from the "recreational" genetic testing pursued by amateur genealogists via the Internet to mainstream biomedical research. When these race-inscribed categories are used uncritically and outside the context in which they were derived, they may become naturalized, reified, institutionalized ways of conceptualizing the human genome. These practices carry serious implications for all subsequent human genome research and for our shared social understanding of the category of race itself.

GENETIC ANCESTRY TESTING

Market forces further link genetic technologies with categories of human difference, specifically race. Claims about racial background can allegedly be documented through the services provided by online genetic genealogy companies, which provide public access to inexpensive genetic testing via the Internet (Koenig, Lee, and Richardson 2008). Companies offer to provide evidence of Native American or African ancestry, links to certain tribes, or claims to Jewish priestly status. These services use ancestry-informative markers, the technology developed to study the scientific concept of population stratification (discussed previously) to provide customers with recreational estimates of the percentages of their ancestry that are European, African, or Asian.

Recreational genetics introduces new and challenging frontiers in racial identity formation, fostering the notion of a tight linkage between genes and race. These testing services, like any commercial venture, sell both a product and a desire for the product. Marketing literature is laced with the discourse of racial purity and racial mixture, as well as constructs such as blood, kinship, ancestry, and homeland. The implications are as yet unclear; genetic testing could either complicate notions of racial purity or build them up. As ancestry testing becomes cheaper and more widespread, new configurations of racial and national identity may emerge. At the policy level, genetic race verification services have potentially serious implications for community concepts of kinship and nationhood. In the case of entitlements that are tied to race, such as affirmative action or tribal membership, genetic ancestry testing may inflame long-standing debates about eligibility and the social recognition of race as a class. The technology of biological race verification will change the terms of debate and analysis.

BIOMEDICAL APPLICATIONS OF HUMAN GENETIC VARIATION: RESEARCH, RACE, AND PHARMACOGENOMICS

As noted, genetic research on race increasingly takes place in a medical context. Throughout the twentieth century, human population genetics was most closely associated with anthropological efforts to reconstruct the history of human migration. This research succeeded in offering impressive corroboration for the "out of Africa" hypothesis of human colonization of the globe and demonstrated the associations among time, geographical distance, and genetic variation. In a departure from this anthropological context, current investment in genetic research on human population variation is increasingly driven by the goal of "personalized medicine," as well as that of alleviating "health disparities." Research on genetic variation among populations stratified by race is widely pursued as a step toward therapies tailored to individual genetic signatures, or personalized medicine (Wilson et al. 2001; Lee 2007).

Pharmacogenomics, or the search for genomic markers that may help physicians determine safe and effective drug dosage, is the first likely application of personalized medicine. Individually targeted therapies have long been promised as the hallmark of a future "molecular medicine." The same drug, at the same dose, works well in some people, has no effect in others, and may lead to serious adverse outcomes in some who take it. Speed of metabolism, like skin color, is under partial genetic control. Variation in individual response to the ingestion of substances—whether naturally occurring substances or manufactured drugs—varies across the globe. The classic example is the occurrence of a "flush response" after drinking alcohol, which occurs more commonly, but not exclusively, among those with Asian biogeographical ancestry. As the pharmaceutical industry seeks marketable technologies to remain profitable during an unexpected drought in medical breakthroughs, pharmacogenomics has become a particularly attractive investment. Converging with this trend, increased government interest in alleviating health disparities, which often fall along racial lines, has also directed resources toward research on genetic differences among races. The discourse of "health disparities" once focused primarily on differences in health outcomes and access to quality health care. Now a concern with health disparities fuels investment in research on, for instance, possible genetic causes of asthma in Hispanics. The pharmaceutical industry has also used the promise of remedying health disparities to lend a politically correct image to its efforts to market drugs or genetic tests to racial subgroups. The twin emphases on redressing health disparities and individualizing health care effectively shield race and genetics research from appearing as fringe or retrogressive as it once might have.

In their search for genetic signatures associated with differences in drug response, pharmacogenomics researchers focused first on differences between racial and ethnic populations (Genes, drugs, and race 2001). However, claims that such differences exist are often anecdotal, rarely validated, and lie beyond the scope of U.S. Food and Drug Administration (FDA) scrutiny (Tate and Goldstein 2008). Nonetheless, clinical practice reflects these trends of pharmacogenomics and has also begun to incorporate assumptions about racial ancestry and genetics. When attempting to individualize drug therapy, a clinician ideally should directly assess the genes controlling expression of a drug metabolizing enzyme rather than relying on either their impression of the patient's biogeographical ancestry or the patient's self-reported race. Since such tests are not yet available, doctors are likely to be moved by the new paradigm of research on racial variation in drug response to rely increasingly on hunches about an individual's likely ancestry, assessments that are particularly complex in plural societies like the United States. This reveals yet another way in which the scientific practices of "doing race" can have consequences in the social world.

In Chapter 3, Marcus Feldman argues forcefully that classic racial categories are not biologically useful for medical purposes. In a detailed review of recent human population genetics findings, he demonstrates why these findings yield insufficient information about the genetic signature of an individual. Feldman notes that the hope that race translates into useful clinical information remains premature. However, as both the hope of racially targeted drug therapy and the case of BiDil, discussed below, illustrate, prior assumptions about race and health frequently trump evidence.

RACE-TARGETED RESEARCH AND THERAPEUTICS: THE CASE OF BIDIL

Genetic research utilizes racially coded genomic data with the goals of understanding the distribution of disease in the human population and developing population-specific drugs. In 2005, BiDil became the first drug approved by the U.S. FDA for a racialized population (African Americans). The story of BiDil is complex and multifaceted (Sankar and Kahn 2005). On the surface, the approval of a drug for a specific population seems justified by claims of significant racial differences in the rate of heart failure between blacks and whites and by the results of a clinical trial of a combination drug product conducted exclusively in African Americans (Taylor et al. 2004; Temple and Stockbridge 2007).

As noted above, the Institute of Medicine has documented poor cardiovascular disease outcomes in blacks; that fact is not in dispute. However, through detailed historical and ethnographic analysis, Kahn (2004) has demonstrated that market forces—not improvements in care—actually motivated the creation of the first racially targeted drug.

BiDil was about to lose the patent protection initially awarded in 1987 for treatment of heart disease in the general population. The new race-based patent claim extended protection by 13 years, thereby enhancing the drug's profitability. In addition, in a previous clinical trial it had failed to outperform other products. The company that owned the drug rights was able to extend its patent protection by making a claim of racial specificity, even though the chemicals included in BiDil are known to work in all patients.

Kahn shows how the U.S. patent system—a previously unexamined venue for studies of "doing race"—forms part of a complex of institutional arrangements and practices that create incentives for drug companies to pursue race-specific applications of their products. Looking closely at the case of BiDil, Kahn reveals that once race is conceptualized as having value for pharmaceutical products, the patent system provides incentives for using race to maximize patent scope, duration, and robustness. He argues that classification rules in patent law that implicitly recognize race as a genetic category function as bureaucratic practices that have implications for our shared social understanding of race. Furthermore, the potential harms of these practices extend to the realms of drug development and drug therapy, leading to higher costs and less effective drugs. In the same way that cases of sickle cell anemia were "missed" in states that failed to include whites in newborn screening programs, those deemed black may not be offered drugs shown to be effective in broad-based clinical trials studying patients from diverse backgrounds, including European Americans. They may instead be offered only racially targeted medicines. Furthermore, the notion that racially targeted drugs may "solve" health disparities might undermine research efforts that seek the root cause of differential health outcomes by interrogating existing social inequalities. The patent system is one of several federal bureaucracies that have played a central role in linking race and genetics.

THE SYMBOLIC VALENCE OF CLASSIFICATION: THE SEGREGATION OF "BLACK" BLOOD

The intersection of genomic technologies, race, and biomedicine is only the latest example of the way novel scientific findings play out in a racialized society. The history of classification systems used for the storage of human blood for transfusion offers another useful example of "doing race." Once human blood groups were recognized early in the twentieth century, research quickly documented that the frequency of certain blood types varied across the world. In fact, in an era before the development of modern molecular genetics, blood group analyses were among the first techniques used to study human genetic variation and the history of migration across the globe. To some extent, individuals' biogeographical ancestry relates to the likelihood that they will have a particular blood type. For example, those with ancestry from Asia are more likely than other biogeographical groups to carry blood type B. Note that, with some exceptions, all blood groups are found throughout the world; what varies is the *relative frequency* of blood types O, A, B, or AB. (The distribution of other blood types, such as the Rh or Rhesus factor, also varies by biogeographic ancestry.) Karl Landsteiner's discovery of human blood groups was recognized with the Nobel Prize in 1930. The implications of this important discovery for ideas about race was drawn by the chairman of the Nobel committee at the award ceremony, who noted,

> The varying frequency of the individual blood groups in different races *points to essential constitutional differences*. Here Landsteiner's discovery opened up new fields for research on the racial purity of a people. Blood group determinations have shown that if an alien race is present within a population this race retains its specific blood group characteristics, even if it has lived away from its main and original homeland for centuries. (Kenny 2006, 473, emphasis added)

New scientific findings are immediately linked into existing social concerns, in this case notions of racial purity.

Biological difference is, of course, meaningful and of great consequence. Making correct distinctions among blood types—variations caused by antigens on the surface of red blood cells—is critical in the safe transfusion of blood. Blood typing according to ABO and Rh classifications (as well as other, less well-known systems) is routinely carried out prior to transfusion. Nonetheless, long after the practice of transfusion medicine became safe and commonplace because all blood was carefully typed for specific compatibility prior to use, American hospitals maintained a strict segregation of blood from black and white donors. "Black" blood was reserved for black patients, and "white" blood was reserved for whites, reflecting social practices of segregation common in the Jim Crow South. The American Red Cross initially refused to send "black blood" overseas for U.S. troops during World War II, though the group eventually compromised by sending it and strictly labeling the race of the donor (Kenny 2006). Symbolic apartheid of human blood persisted in American hospitals into the 1950s and 1960s (Lederer 2008).

In 1959 a major public dispute arose in response to the proposal that racially segregating blood could help reduce adverse reactions to the blood transfusions required for major cardiac surgery (Kenny 2006). A newly identified antigen named "Kidd" was found to vary in frequency between blacks and whites, sometimes leading to sensitization, a condition making it extremely difficult to find compatible blood. The *New York Times* played a major role in reporting about the proposal, put forth by several leading blood bankers. They suggested that segregating donor pools was a cost-effective way to make transfusions safer. The proponents argued that markers of human population difference were simply neutral, noting, "this may sound wrong sociologically . . . but it is scientifically correct" (Kenny 2006, 462). Only with the origins of the civil rights movement did a revised reading of the science of human blood groups arise. In 1959, proposals to segregate human blood were reported as a symptom of widespread racial discrimination, not as a necessary procedure to protect racial purity, supported by scientific fact.

THE ROLE OF THE MEDIA

Scientific research concerned with race or racial categories is often misinterpreted or simplified when journalists translate complex findings for the public (Condit et al. 2004). The BiDil case, for example, was widely—and simplistically—reported. Yet the media plays an inevitably critical role in shaping public understanding of research findings about genetic population differences. Geneticists may use great care to avoid inaccuracies in their writing about human population genetic difference. But this care can be undone at the moment of translation to the public. Nicholas Wade's coverage of the Rosenberg findings, discussed above, provides a useful illustration. The scientists on the team had carefully avoided the use of lay conceptions of race in their reports, but journalists turned, nonetheless, to the cultural logic of race in their explanations.

In a valuable essay, the journalist and science writer Sally Lehrman (2008) characterizes the news environment that makes it difficult for reporters to decouple race, genetics, and biology. Conventions in story framing and source selection often result in reductionist thinking about race and genetics. Most important, stories must attract attention; they must convey "news." Thus universities' press officers and scientific journals often oversimplify, noting that "the gene for x, y, or z" has been "found," or a "new drug found to treat heart disease in blacks" has been discovered. The fact that reporters are assigned to specialized "beats," such as sports or crime, increases the possibility of mistranslation. The scientific proposal to segregate blood for transfusion, noted above, coincided with the beginning of the civil rights movement. This social context provided journalists with a new language for discussing the implications of a seemingly "neutral" set of scientific facts describing allele frequency differences among human groups. A new "beat" for reporters had emerged. Few journalists become experts in the intricacies (and limitations) of genetic science as it applies to complex topics like the behavioral genetics of addiction or human population genetic studies. But journalists serve as the connectors and mediators who convey and interpret findings linking race with genetics for the public. Thus their use of racial categories and language must be accounted for when considering the policy implications of advances in genomic science. Reporters reflect lay conceptions and interpretations of race, a discourse that is also influenced heavily by U.S. regulatory requirements.

RACE AND THE CONDUCT OF SCIENCE: MANDATED ETHNIC AND RACIAL CATEGORIES IN BIOMEDICAL RESEARCH

Federal guidelines, in particular those promulgated by the U.S. Office of Management and Budget (OMB), provide specific, targeted incentives to see and use race and ethnicity in a manner that promotes the reification of race as a genetic category (Lee, Mountain, and Koenig 2001; Kahn 2006). Beginning in 1994, researchers with funding from the NIH were required to categorize all human participants in their research by sex and also according to racial and ethnic background (Epstein 2007; Hunt and Megyesi 2008a, 2008b). The motivation for this bureaucratic change was a claim based on justice: Many large clinical studies had only included white men, and thus the findings could not be applied to women. Rates and age of onset of heart disease, for instance, differ significantly between men and women; conducting research exclusively in white male subjects, because they were easier to recruit into clinical studies, clearly limited the findings. Similar logics were applied in arguments requiring the inclusion of minorities in federally funded research (Epstein 2007).

The U.S. National Institutes of Health, the largest funder of genomic research related to human health, enforces these rules (NIH 2001), as does the U.S. Food and Drug Administration (FDA). Although these regulations were initially envisioned as applying to the conduct of large-scale clinical trials, they are now enforced in all human research. Every scientist and clinician requesting funding from NIH (or reporting study results to the FDA) must report data using standard categories of race and ethnicity that are regulated by the OMB. The OMB categories, developed (and refined each decade) to guide the collection of census data, are required for all government data reporting.

However, there is a problem with applying these categories unreflectively in biomedical research (Kahn 2006). Developed for nonhealth purposes, such as ensuring diverse voting districts or aiding the enforcement of antidiscrimination legislation in schools and workplaces, census categories are fundamentally political tools (see Chapter 1). They are an inadequate reflection of *actual genetic variation* in human populations. Thus the race and ethnicity reporting categories that scientists are required to use may, ironically, lead to bad science. Researchers following regulatory recipes may set up comparisons according to social and political categories of race or ethnicity, while missing true sources of biological difference. People who identify as Hispanic, for example, have biogeographical ancestry from around the globe and yet are combined in a single group (Montoya 2007). Similarly, those classified as "Asian" in the U.S. Census have diverse geographical origins, from South Asia to Japan. There are harms in the uncritical use of race as a proxy for biological relatedness. This practice not only makes the science less accurate, but research methods and reporting of results strongly convey the notion that race is "real," a biological fact, and that the human population can be easily divided into distinct races (Lee 2007).

Although regulations set standards for reporting of human data using racial and ethnic categories, empirical studies have documented that in practice these categories are inconsistently, if not haphazardly, applied (Shanawani et al. 2006; Ma et al. 2007; Hunt and Megyesi 2008a). Self-report by research subjects is complicated by identity politics; many participants do not understand how questions soliciting "ethnic" affiliation differ from questions about classic racial distinctions (black, white, Asian, Native American). True measures of biogeographical ancestry have not been developed and validated. As noted above, Lee (2005) and others have documented how lay conceptions of race and ethnicity are built into the DNA storage repositories that support genetic research on topics such as pharmacogenomics or studies of disease etiology. The outcomes of studies using samples collected using OMB categories recreate the flaws of classification built into the databases themselves.

RACIAL REALISM

Lee (2008) points out an additional ethical dimension of what she terms "racial realism." Racial realists leverage recent population genetics research to assert that racial difference is a "hard" biological reality, easily discernible in the human body (Satel 2002). And they have enthusiastically incorporated into their platform the endorsement of racially targeted therapeutics in the name of social justice. At the same time, racial realist discourse allies itself with health policies that deemphasize social solutions to problems, such as disparities in health outcomes among racially identified groups. This approach is, in turn, tethered to a moral discourse of "personal responsibility." Genetic research on race is mobilized as a response to liberal models of race that focus on environmental and historical conditions as the root causes for health disparities. From this perspective, for example, the comparatively higher rates of addiction in Native American populations are hypothesized to stem from genetic variations, not from the complex history of dislocation and alienation that characterize reservation life set apart from American society (Dingel and Koenig 2008). The ways that scientists frame and explain genetic differences filter into political discourse and influences the *range* of perceived solutions to questions of inequality and justice. In health disparities research, the result is that social views of race lose ground to biological interpretations of difference.

CONCLUSION: THE APPROPRIATE USE OF "RACE" IN GENETICS RESEARCH

Discussing race across disciplinary boundaries is challenging. There are long-standing distinctions in the ways that scholars in the humanities, social sciences, and genetics approach the concept of race (Koenig, Lee, and Richardson 2008). In the humanities and social sciences, the view that race reflects social hierarchies rather than biological or genetic difference is the starting point of analysis. Visible differences in skin color or hair texture, while linked to concepts of race and self-evidently "genetic," do not fully explain the meaning of race in social life—that is, the way race functions as an empirically measurable determinant of social status, and thus of health outcomes. For historians, the very concept of race is imbued with the notion of hierarchical ordering; in the West, modern understandings, often justified by the science of the time, arose with the need to justify colonial expansion and domination (Fredrikson 2002).

Among researchers studying human genetic variation at the molecular level, however, the story is different. Genetic scientists disagree on the utility of racial classification for studying common disease, but they generally accept new data showing the range of human genetic diversity and its global patterning (Rosenberg et al. 2002; Feldman, this volume). Many consider the *possibility* of biological determinants of a range of differences among human populations defined by racial labels to be an open scientific question. They enthusiastically embrace new genomic technologies to elucidate the etiology of common illness, making use of the categories of difference required within U.S. regulatory regimes— categories that correspond to differences in lived experience in societies historically divided and structured by race. Asthma, diabetes, hypertension, and heart failure all are examined through a genetic lens. Unlike historians or sociologists, geneticists may assume that categories of difference "found in nature" can be deployed in *neutral* ways, acting as simple classifiers of true genetic variability.

There is an irony associated with the day-to-day performance of race in health disparities research that uses genetic tools. On one hand, the attention to group difference, the increasing focus on genetic variability, provides powerful scientific explanations of variation in disease susceptibility and pathophysiology. On the other hand, the very conduct and practice of the new genomic medicine has the unintended consequence of molecularizing the concept of race and of racial difference (Fullwiley 2007). As in nineteenth-century racial science, when difference is located in biology, the social world is erased, even if unintentionally.

What is the answer? The category of race, fundamentally a social category (although long intertwined with ideas of biological difference), *must* be used in biomedical research in order to assure that health disparities based on injustices may be tracked and addressed. At the same time, researchers must track and account for actual genetic variation associated with biogeographical ancestry. Can we accomplish both objectives at once?

I believe that we can. A recent statement published by a Stanford University faculty working group proposes ten principles to guide the use of racial categories in human genetics research (Lee et al. 2008). The authors note that using racial categories appropriately is an ethical obligation of all researchers, particularly those whose work targets health disparities. Changed practices of "doing race" in science—in particular, careful attention to language when discussing actual genetic differences across human groups—may alleviate the harm of a newly geneticized or molecularized understanding of race. The signers warn, "The 'gene' remains a powerful icon in the public imagination and is often misunderstood as deterministic and immutable. . . . [H]istory reminds us that science may easily be used to justify racial stereotypes and racist policies" (Lee et al. 2008, 3). It is critical for researchers to recognize that racial and ethnic categories are created and maintained within particular social and political contexts, and that those contexts change over time. Since racial classifications in medicine have sometimes reflected racist ideologies or prejudice—as when blood banks separated black and white blood for transfusion—it is critical to use care in assigning labels to participants in research studies or when rendering clinical care. One recommendation, suggested by the editors of several major scientific journals, is that authors specify exactly how and why human subjects or specimens like DNA are assigned a specific racial or ethnic identifier (Sankar and Cho 2002). Specific classifications, and comparisons across groups, must be justified, not simply assumed (Schwartz 2001; Braun et al. 2007). This obligation applies in spite of U.S. regulatory requirements for inclusion of all populations when conducting clinical research.

The concept of polysemy—the capacity for a word (or sign) to have multiple meanings simultaneously—may be helpful. Scientists and clinicians attentive to the complex history of the race concept will be able to apply a polysemic racial vocabulary in their everyday work, a set of definitions that avoids confusion between social race and true biological difference. When they do race, when they classify human research participants into categories or seek the root causes of health disparities, scientists must maintain a conceptual distinction between two senses of "race": race linked to genetic variation deriving from biogeographical ancestry *and* race as a reflection of the lived experience of social difference. Both senses are needed to make progress in alleviating health disparities. We must not ask "whether" race should be used in genetic research; rather, we must ask, "under what conditions and for what purposes?"[2]

---

2 I wish to thank Sandra Soo-Jin Lee, Joanna Mountain, Sarah Richardson, and all the participants in the volume *Revisiting Race in a Genomic Age* for many stimulating discussions about the intersections of race, health research, and genetics. Troy Duster's thinking deeply informed the policy recommendation in the conclusion of this essay. I am extremely grateful to Hazel Markus and Paula Moya for inviting me to lecture in their Stanford course and for recognizing the critical importance of biomedical practices to our shared social understanding of "doing race" in the United States.

Works Cited

•

1000 Genomes. (2008). *1000 Genomes: A deep catalog of human genetic variation*. Retrieved October 13, 2009, from 1000 Genomes Web site: www.1000genomes.org/page.php

(AAA) American Anthropological Association. American Anthropological Association statement on race. (1998). *American Anthropologist, 100*, 712–713.

(AAA) American Anthropological Association. (2007). *Race: Are we so different?* www.understandingrace.org/home.html

Bamshad, M., Wooding, S., Salisbury, B.A. and Stephens, J. C. (2004). Deconstructing the relationship between genetics and race. *Nature Reviews Genetics 5*, 598–609.

Braun, L., Fausto-Sterling, A., Fullwiley, D., Hammonds, E. M., Nelson, A., Quivers, W., Reverby, S. M., and Shields, A. E. (2007). Racial categories in medical practice: How useful are they? *PLoS Medicine, 4* (9), e271. doi:10.1371/journal.pmed.0040271

Burchard, E. G., Ziv, E., Coyle, N., Gomez, S. L., Tang, H., Karter A. J., Mountain J. L., Pérez-Stable E. J., Sheppard D., and Risch N. (2003). The importance of race and ethnic background in biomedical research and clinical practice. *New England Journal Medicine, 348*(12), 1170–1175.

California Newsreel. (2003). *Race: The power of an illusion*. Retrieved October 13, 2009, from California Newsreel Web site www.newsreel.org/nav/title.asp?tc=CN0149

Collins, F. S., and Mansoura, M. K. (2001). The human genome project. Revealing the shared inheritance of all humankind. *Cancer, 91*(1 Suppl.), 221–225.

Condit, C. M., Parrott, R., Bates, B. R., Bevan, J., and Achter, P. J. (2004). Exploration of the impact of messages about genes and race on lay attitudes. *Clinical Genetics, 66*(5), 402–408.

Cooper, R. S. (2003). Race, genes, and health-new wine in old bottles? *International Journal of Epidemiology, 32*(1), 23–25.

Caron, L., Karkazis K., Swan G., Raffin T. A., Koenig B. A. (2005). Nicotine addiction through a neurogenomic prism: Ethics, public health, and smoking. *Nicotine and Tobacco Research, 7*(2), 181–197.

(CRGGH) Center for Research on Genomics and Global Health. (2009). Retrieved November 26, 2009 at http://crggh.nih.gov

Dingel, M., and Koenig, B. A. (2008). Tracking race in addiction research. In *Revisiting race in a genomic age*, Koenig B.A., Lee S. S. J., Richardson S. (eds.). Piscataway, NJ: Rutgers University Press, 223–270.

Epstein, S. (2007). *Inclusion: The politics of difference in medical research*. Chicago: University of Chicago Press.

Fredrickson, G. M. (2002). *Racism: A short history*. Princeton, NJ: Princeton University Press.

Fullwiley, D. (2007). The molecularization of race: Institutionalizing human difference in pharmacogenetics practice. *Science as Culture, 16*(1), 1–30.

Genes, drugs and race. (2001). *Nature Genetics, 29*(3), 239–240.

Hunt, L. M., and Megyesi, M. S. (2008a). The ambiguous meanings of the racial/ethnic categories routinely used in human genetics research. *Social Science and Medicine, 66*(2), 349–361.

Hunt, L. M., and Megyesi, M. S. (2008b). Genes, race and research ethics: Who's minding the store? *Journal of Medical Ethics, 34*(6), 495–500.

International HapMap Consortium. (2005). A haplotype map of the human genome. *Nature, 437,* 1229–1320.

(IOM) Institute of Medicine. (2003). *Unequal treatment: Confronting racial and ethnic disparities in health care.* Smedley, B. D., Stith, A. Y., and Nelson, A. R. (eds.). Washington, DC: National Academies Press.

Jakobsson, M., Scholz, S. W., Scheet, P., Gibbs, J. R., VanLiere, J. M., Fung, H. C., Szpiech, Z. A., Degnan, J. H., Wang, K., Guerreiro, R., Bras, J. M., Schymick, J. C., Hernandez, D. G., Traynor, B. J., Simon-Sanchez, J., Matarin, M., Britton, A., van de Leemput, J., Rafferty, I., Bucan, M., Cann, H. M., Hardy, J. A., Rosenberg, N. A., and Singleton, A. B. (2008). Genotype, haplotype and copy-number variation in worldwide human populations. *Nature, 451*(7181), 998–1003.

Kahn, J. (2004). How a drug becomes 'ethnic': Law, commerce, and the production of racial categories in medicine. *Yale Journal of Health Policy, Law and Ethics, 4*(1), 1–46.

Kahn, J. (2006). Genes, race, and population: Avoiding a collision of categories. *American Journal of Public Health, 96*(11), 1965–1970.

Kenny, M. G. (2006). A question of blood, race, and politics. *Journal of the History of Medicine and Allied Sciences, 61*(4), 456–491.

Koenig, B. A., Lee, S. S. J., and Richardson, S. S. (eds.). (2008). *Revisiting race in a genomic age.* Piscataway, NJ: Rutgers University Press.

Krieger, N. (2005). Stormy weather: Race, gene expression, and the science of health disparities. *American Journal of Public Health, 95*(12), 2155–2160.

Lederer, S. E. (2008). *Flesh and blood: Organ transplantation and blood transfusion in twentieth-century America.* New York: Oxford University Press.

Lee, S. S. J. (2005). Racializing drug design: Implications of pharmacogenomics for health disparities. *American Journal of Public Health, 95*(12), 2133–2138.

Lee, S. S. J. (2007). The ethical implications of stratifying by race in pharmacogenomics. *Clinical Pharmacology and Therapeutics, 81*(1), 122–125.

Lee, S. S. J. (2008). Racial realism and the discourse of responsibility for health disparities in a genomic age. IN Koenig, B. A., Lee, S. S. J., and Richardson, S. S. (eds.). *Revisiting race in a genomic age.* Piscataway, NJ: Rutgers University Press, 342–358.

Lee, S. S. J., Mountain, J., and Koenig, B. A. (2001). The meanings of race in the new genomics: Implications for health disparities research. *Yale Journal of Health Policy, Law, and Ethics, 1*(1), 33–75.

Lee, S. S. J., Mountain, J., Koenig, B. A., Altman, R., Brown, M., Camarillo, A., Cavalli-Sforza, L., Cho, M., Feldman, M., Greely, H., King, R., Snipp, M., and Underhill, P. (2008). The ethics of characterizing difference: Guiding principles on using racial categories in human genetics. *Genome Biology, 9,* 404.

Lehrman, S. (2008). Cops, sports, and schools: How the news media frames coverage of genetics and race. In Koenig, B. A., Lee, S. S. J., and Richardson, S. S. *Revisiting race in a genomic age.* Piscataway, NJ: Rutgers University Press.

Lewontin, R. C. (1991). *Biology as ideology: The doctrine of DNA*. New York: Harper Perennial.

Li, J. Z., Absher, D. M., Tang, H., Southwick, A. M., Casto, A. M., Ramachandran, S., Cann, H. M., Barsh, G. S., Feldman, M., Cavalli-Sforza, L. L., and Myers, R. M. (2008). Worldwide human relationships inferred from genome-wide patterns of variation. *Science, 319*(5866), 1100–1104.

Ma, I. W., Khan, N. A., Kang, A., Zalunardo, N., and Palepu, A. (2007). Systematic review identified suboptimal reporting and use of race/ethnicity in general medical journals. *Journal of Clinical Epidemiology, 60*(6), 572–578.

Montoya, M. J. (2007). Bioethnic conscription: Genes, race, and Mexicana/o ethnicity in diabetes research. *Cultural Anthropology 22,* 94–128.

(NCI) National Cancer Institute. (2009). Tobacco control monograph 20. Phenotypes and endophenotypes: Foundations for genetic studies of nicotine use and dependence. Retrieved November 26, 2009, from http://cancercontrol.cancer.gov/tcrb/monographs/20/index.html

(NHGRI) National Human Genome Research Institute. 2000. Remarks made by the President, Prime Minister Tony Blair of England, Dr. Francis Collins, and Dr. Craig Venter on the completion of the first survey of the entire Human Genome Project. June 26. www.genome.gov/10001356

(NIH) National Institutes of Health, National Human Genome Research Institute. (2008). *NIH launches center to study genomics and health disparities*. Retrieved October 13, 2009, from National Institutes of Health, National Human Genome Research Institute Web site: www.genome.gov/26525381

(NIH) National Institutes of Health, Office of Extramural Research. (2001). *NIH policy and guidelines on the inclusion of women and minorities as subjects in clinical research*. Retrieved October 13, 2009, from National Institutes of Health, Office of Extramural Research Web site: http://grants.nih.gov/grants/funding/women_min/guidelines_amended_10_2001.htm

Parthasarathy, S. (2007). *Building genomic medicine: Breast cancer, technology, and the comparative politics of health care*. Cambridge, MA: MIT University Press.

Pierpont, C. R. (2004). The measure of America: How a rebel anthropologist waged war on racism. *The New Yorker, 80*(3), 48-63.

Serre, D., and Pääbo, S. (2004). Evidence for gradients of human genetic diversity within and among continents. *Genome Research, 14*(9), 1679–1685.

Risch, N., Burchard, E., Ziv, E., and Tang, H. (2002). Categorization of humans in biomedical research: genes, race and disease. *Genome Biology, 3*(7).

Rosenberg, N. A., Pritchard, J. K., Weber, J. L., Cann, H. M., Kidd, K. K., Zhivotovsky, L. A., and Feldman, M. W. (2002). Genetic structure of human populations. *Science, 298*(5602), 2381–2385.

Sankar, P. (2006). Hasty generalizations and exaggerated certainties: Reporting genetic findings in health disparities research. *New Genetics and Society 25*(3), 249–254.

Sankar, P., and Cho, M. K. (2002). Genetics: Toward a new vocabulary of human genetic variation. *Science, 298*(5597), 1337–1338.

Sankar, P., Cho, M. K., Condit, C. M., Hunt, L. M., Koenig, B. A., Marshall, P., Lee, S. S. J., and Spicer, P. (2004). Genetic research and health disparities. *Journal of the American Medical Association, 291*(24), 2985–2989.

Sankar, P., and Kahn, J. (2005). BiDil: Race medicine or race marketing? *Health Affairs* (Suppl.) Web Exclusives, W5-455-463. doi:10.1377/hlthaff.W5.455

Satel, S. (2002, May 5). I am a racially profiling doctor. *New York Times.* Retrieved November 30, 2009, from www.sallysatelmd.com/html/a-nytimes3.html

Schwartz, R. S. (2001). Racial profiling in medical research. *New England Journal of Medicine; 344*(18), 1392–1393.

Serre, D., and Pääbo, S. (2004). Evidence for gradients of human genetic diversity within and among continents. *Genome Research, 14*, 1679–1685.

Shanawani, H., Dame, L., Schwartz, D. A., and Cook-Deegan, R. (2006). Non-reporting and inconsistent reporting of race and ethnicity in articles that claim association among genotype, outcome and race or ethnicity. *Journal of Medical Ethics, 32*(12), 724–728.

Tate, S. K., and Goldstein, D. B. (2008). Will tomorrow's medicine work for everyone? In B. A. Koenig, S. S.-J. Lee, and S. S. Richardson (eds.), *Revisiting race in a genomic age.* Piscataway, NJ: Rutgers University Press, 102–128.

Taylor, A. L., Ziesche, S., Yancy, C., Carson, P., D'Agostino, R. Jr., Ferdinand, K., Taylor, M., Adams, K., Sabolinski, M., Worcel, M., and Cohn, J. N. (2004). African-American heart failure trial investigators: Combination of isosorbide dinitrate and hydralazine in blacks with heart failure. *New England Journal of Medicine, 351*(20), 2049–2057.

Temple, R., and Stockbridge, N. L. (2007). BiDil for heart failure in black patients: The U.S. Food and Drug Administration perspective. *Annals of Internal Medicine, 146*(1), 57–62.

Travis, J. (2009). Scientists decry isotope, DNA testing of 'nationality.' *Science, 326,* 30–31.

Wade, N. (2002a, July 30). Race is seen as real guide to track roots of disease. *New York Times,* F1.

Wade, N. (2002b, December 20). Gene study identifies 5 main human populations, linking them to geography. *New York Times,* A37.

Wailoo, Keith (2001). *Dying in the city of the blues: Sickle Cell Anemia and the politics of race and health.* Chapel Hill: University of North Carolina Press.

Wilson, J. F., Weale, M. E., Smith, A. C., Gratrix, F., Fletcher, B., and Thomas, M. G. (2001). Population genetic structure of variable drug response. *Nature Genetics, 29*(3), 265–269.

PART TWO

Racing Difference

5

The Jew as the Original "Other"

Difference, Antisemitism, and Race

Aron Rodrigue

•

This essay argues that the modern racialization of Jew-hatred was built upon centuries of anti-Jewish tropes that were grounded on traditional Christian views of Judaism and the Jews. It begins by providing a brief review of the construction of the Jew as Christianity's original other. Following a discussion of the situation of Jews in medieval Europe, it reviews some of the tropes associated with the diabolization of the Jew that have survived into the present day. After charting a shift in status for European Jews resulting from Enlightenment ideas of equality and citizenship, the essay considers the impact that the idea of race has had on the construction of human difference. In fact, many of the issues associated with race in modern times reproduce elements of the construction of difference and of the other inherited from anti-Jewish tropes. The essay concludes by arguing that, over time, antisemitism has became infinitely elastic, denoting a bewildering array of anti-Jewish thought and action; this ranges from an inchoate general dislike of Jews to full-fledged ideologies that see the Jews as the source of all evil, with the ultimate expression of hatred actualized during the Holocaust aiming for the total annihilation of all Jews everywhere.

WHAT DOES RACE HAVE TO DO WITH JEWS? DOES THE TERM "JEWISH" refer to people who share a particular race, or to a community of people who profess adherence to one of the three major Abrahamic religions?

187

Answering this question requires attention to the history of Judeophobia and its gradual transformation over the centuries into racist
antisemitism. While Jews are clearly people who share a religion and
cannot be said to be a race of people, nevertheless, their history has been
deeply affected by the concept of race as it arose in response to Enlightenment ideas of individuality and equal rights.

Judeophobia, or anti-Jewish thought and action in religion and society,
has marked much of Western civilization from late Antiquity onward.
The many fundamental transformations of Judeophobia over the centuries led to the emergence of a new term in the modern period to denote
it: "antisemitism." Frequently spelled "Anti-Semitism," the term points
to the racialization of the Jew as a "Semite," as a race apart. And yet, the
word obscures as much as it reveals. There has never been an ideology
and movement against "Semites," nor is it certain that there is a group
of people who could be identified by that designation. This constructed
and dubious category of peoples is based on the classification of some languages in the late eighteenth and early nineteenth centuries as "Semitic."
The term "antisemitism" was coined in 1879 by Wilhelm Marr, a leading
anti-Jewish polemicist and agitator, and it has always referenced Jews.
Hence, it is important to realize that the provenance of the term is located firmly within the camp of those for whom the principal enemy was
perceived as the Jew, and for whom the Jew was considered to be a racial other. At the end of the nineteenth century the term came to be used
widely throughout Europe by individuals and movements that wanted to
exclude Jews from much of social, political, economic, and cultural life.

THE JEW AS CHRISTIANITY'S ORIGINAL OTHER

One of the most popular misconceptions about the history of Judaism
and Christianity is that Judaism, as the mother religion of Christianity, preceded and then was superseded by the Christian religion. This
account of the relationship between the two religions, while fairly widespread in Christian contexts, is not entirely accurate. In fact, rabbinical
Judaism and Christianity crystallized as different rival sibling religions,
emerging from the same Judaic matrix of Roman Palestine; they were
the two winners among a range of Judaic groups and sects in deep
effervescence before and after the first century CE (Common Era). After
the conversion of the Roman Emperor Constantine circa 312 CE, however, Christianity gradually gained the upper hand. Constantine's conversion had important consequences for the future of both religions.

Throwing the full weight of political imperial power behind Christianity, Constantine put a stop to the persecution of Christians. The triumph of the latter led eventually to the promulgation of a series of increasingly harsh restrictions on Jewish life.

Christian theology remained marked for centuries by its rivalry and struggle with rabbinical Judaism. For example, despite the fact that the authorities responsible for ordering the crucifixion of Christ were pagan Romans, Christians laid the responsibility for his sacrifice at the feet of the Jews. Jews were accused in traditional Christianity of deicide, of crucifying God. Moreover, Christians saw Jews as stubbornly clinging to a superseded book, the Hebrew Bible, which Christians called the "Old Testament." According to Christian theology, the Old Testament was transcended by the New Testament, which was taken to be the repository of the new and final revelation for all humankind.

As a way of demarcating itself from Judaism, traditional Christianity built into its theology a set of binary opposites whose echoes, in secularized form, traverse much of Western civilization to our own day. Because Christianity, unlike Judaism, was from the beginning a proselytizing religion, Christians saw themselves as being for all people, while Judaism was about only one people. From a Christian perspective, Christianity represented universalism, while Judaism represented particularism. Similarly, Christianity was associated with the spirit, while Judaism was associated with the flesh, and Christianity was about love, while Judaism was about the law. As Christianity's influence spread throughout the West, the conception of the Jew as the paradigmatic other of Western culture, the very emblem of difference, became widely accepted.

It is a historical irony that the place of the Jew in Christian theology resulted both in the Jews' survival as a religious community and in their persecution by an increasingly powerful Christian Church. While pagan sects were eventually obliterated, Jews were allowed to exist as a barely tolerated minority group; they were to be kept around until they saw the error of their ways. Jews were encouraged to transcend difference and become the same through conversion to Christianity. Those who refused to convert were put in the position of a pariah group in dominant Christian society. They were relegated to certain urban and financial professions seen by Christians as unclean, such as money-lending and leather-making.

Over time, Jewish difference came to assume a spatial dimension. By the end of the sixteenth century the Jews could live in many European cities only in physically separate quarters, frequently walled off. The first such Jewish quarter, called the "ghetto," was located by the iron foundry in Venice. The widespread usage of this word in the modern period to denote poverty-stricken urban areas where a minority group predominates is emblematic of the continuities with the spatial segregation of difference that began with the Jews of Europe.

At the inception of the West, built as an integral part of the deep structures of Christian Western cultures, the Jews became part of the narrative as the binary opposite other. Eventually, as the West expanded and met different others, this original template was reproduced over and over again with other groups.

EMANCIPATION, MONEY, AND MODERNITY: THE SITUATION OF THE JEWS

The association of Jews in the popular imagination with money, and especially with usurious money-lending, dates back to their medieval outcast position. This association would have long-term consequences for the way Jews were viewed and treated in Western culture. One needs only to think of the figure of Shylock in Shakespeare's *Merchant of Venice* (circa 1598) to capture the resonance of the stereotypes associated with Jews. The play is set in Venice, where the first and paradigmatic ghetto setting the Jews apart was located. Shylock is the Jewish moneylender par excellence. And he wants his "pound of flesh" in revenge for an insult. He lends money to Antonio, a man he hates for having insulted him for being a Jew, but only on the condition that, should Antonio default on the loan, Shylock be allowed to take from him a "pound of flesh." When Antonio is indeed unable to pay back the loan, Shylock wants his "pound of flesh" in revenge for the insult. Even when a friend of Antonio's offers to pay more than the borrowed amount, Shylock refuses, intent on obtaining what was due to him. Just as Shylock is about to cut out a pound of flesh from Antonio, a lawyer finds a loophole, forcing Shylock to agree to take the money. He is then denied the payment and upon accusations of attempting to take the life of Antonio, he loses his property and is forced to beg for his life and convert to Christianity. Flesh, in the play, thus represents the materialism associated with the Jew. In spite of other elements that humanize Shylock in the play, he is immediately recognizable as the quintessential other, the Jew.

As an internal and despised other, the Jew became the perfect scapegoat for all the ills of European society. The Jews' positioning as the paradigmatic other of Western culture—the representative of religious and cultural particularism—had devastating consequences for Jews in

Christian-controlled Europe. In addition to being spatially segregated in ghettos and restricted to certain professions, Jews and some other non-Christians were subject to medieval sumptuary laws requiring them to wear hats or distinctive patches (a practice later revived by the Nazis) to distinguish them from Christians when they left the ghettos. Although such laws were unevenly enforced, they had the effect of stigmatizing Jews and making them easier for Christian authorities to monitor.

In addition, the wide dissemination of anti-Jewish stereotypes led to the growth of new and irrational types of hatred against Jews. Charges against Jews—accusing them of killing Christian infants for the use of their blood for ritual purposes (known as the blood libel), of desecrating the host used at mass, of poisoning wells in order to spread the plague and other diseases—emerged in Europe frequently after the twelfth century. Although not condoned by the upper echelons of the medieval Christian Church, these accusations continued to resonate in the popular imagination with remarkable tenacity over the centuries. Such charges, together with the accusation of usurious money-lending, diabolized the image of the Jew. Much of modern racial antisemitism was built upon this legacy from the Middle Ages.

The result of the stigmatization, segregation, and marking of Jews in medieval Europe underpinned an uneasy co-existence between Christians and Jews that could end rapidly at times of crisis. Social and economic unrest led periodically to physical violence against Jews and was often followed by expulsions. At times of renewed religious fervor, massacres devastated many Jewish communities in Western and Central Europe. One powerful example can be seen in what happened to European Jews during the First Crusade in 1096. The Crusades were a series of military campaigns to conquer the Holy Land, undertaken with the blessing of the Church and lasting over several centuries. Although the stated goal of the First Crusade was recapturing the holy city of Jerusalem from the control of the Muslims, many Jews ended up as victims. The First Crusade attracted a large number of poorer knights and peasants with deep resentments who vented their religious fervor on everyone they considered to be an infidel, including the European Jews living along the route to the Holy Land. Although the Church did not condone this action and took some pains to prevent or alleviate the slaughter, nevertheless, hundreds of Jews—particularly those living in Germany—were massacred by overzealous Crusaders along the way.

In another defining period in Jewish and European history, attacks on Jews in the Iberian peninsula in 1391 led to the conversion of tens of thousands, followed by other similar episodes throughout the fifteenth century. Suspicions about the true nature of these conversions as well as the incidence of persistence of Jewish practice among some converts led to great social conflict and to the establishment of the Spanish Inquisition at the end of the century to extirpate what was seen as the "Judaizing" heresy. Jews who had not converted were given in 1492, at exactly the same time as the voyages to the Americas by Columbus, the choice to convert or to be expelled. Thousands left Spain while equally large numbers chose to convert and stay. The Inquisition continued its task as the guardian of Catholic orthodoxy in the Iberian peninsula and the Americas for the two centuries that followed, prosecuting and burning at the stake those whom it suspected, frequently without any firm evidence, of following Jewish practices. As a result the Inquisition has become a byword for intolerance and fanaticism.

The situation of the Jews in Western Europe finally began to change as Enlightenment ideas about equal rights and citizenship began to gain ground. The Enlightenment refers to a time in Western thought and culture centered on the eighteenth century, but having roots reaching back to the early seventeenth century and effects lasting until the present day. It was characterized by the questioning of traditional values, customs, and beliefs and accompanied by major changes in the economic, scientific, and political spheres. With the rise of bourgeois society and culture came the foregrounding of such ideas as liberty, individual rights, more democratic government, reason, and the scientific method. Traditional religious authority and the theocratic governmental systems that supported it were increasingly challenged by new conceptions of secular authority represented by republicanism and democracy. With the advent of liberal thought and its promised inclusion of all in the polity on the basis of equality and civic participation, it became more and more untenable to exclude Jews from society and refuse them the same rights as citizens.

The French Revolution saw an important shift in the situation of Western European Jews. The French National Assembly issued in 1791 what would be one of the first acts of emancipation that would radically change their status in society. In the following document, the links between constitutional law, civic participation, and the rights of citizenship are clear:

> The National Assembly, considering that the conditions requisite to be a French Citizen, and to become an active citizen, are fixed

by the constitution, and that every man who, being duly qualified, takes the civic oath, and engages to fulfill the duties prescribed by the constitution, has a right to all the advantages it insures; Annuls all adjournments, restrictions, and exceptions, contained in the preceding decrees, affecting individuals of the Jewish persuasion, who shall take the civic oath. (Mendes-Flohr and Reinharz 1995, 118)

Over the course of the nineteenth century, Jews throughout Europe were gradually emancipated.

It is important to realize that the term "emancipation," which in the U.S. context is associated with the end of black slavery, is the very term that is used for the granting of equality to Jews in Europe. Indeed, the change in the status of blacks and Jews began at the same time. The Jews of France were emancipated in 1790–91, while black slavery in the French colonies of the West Indies was abolished in 1794 (to be reimposed by Napoleon a few years later). It is important to note that the emancipation of both blacks and Jews occurred largely as a result of the action of liberal associations and public figures militating for universalist inclusion for both groups.

Emancipation ended the pariah status of the Jew in Western societies. Leaving the ghettos in droves, many Jews embraced the promise of equality and of citizenship. They integrated and acculturated with great rapidity, rising in the worlds of business and liberal professions. Ironically, the very relegation of the Jews in the premodern period to urban areas and to the financial and medical professions put them in a position to take full advantage of modernity as it unfolded and transformed society. The industrialization and urbanization of the modern world favored sectors of the economy, such as money-lending (reconceived under capitalism as modern banking), medicine (crucial to the emerging scientific worldview), and other urban professions to which Jews had been traditionally consigned. Not only were Jews no longer constrained by the ghettos, they had access to skills that were invaluable in the formation of new businesses. In this way, Jews were advantageously positioned to benefit from the emerging capitalist economy.

The nineteenth century saw the dizzying upward mobility of many Jews in most Western societies. Emancipation brought by the spread of liberal politics as well as industrialization transformed Jewish communities out of all recognition. Not only did Jews benefit from modernity, they became, in the eyes of many, synonymous with it.

THE PARADOXES OF UNIVERSALISM:
FROM RELIGIOUS TO RACIAL OTHER

Many historians argue that modern antisemitism is the continuation of traditional medieval Judeophobia. The difference, they say, is in the modern secular language that antisemites use to convey their message. Other historians, however, point to a rupture—to Judeophobia's transformation by modern trends in society and culture. Both perspectives have merit. It is true that much of modern racial antisemitism has been built upon the legacy from the Middle Ages. At the same time, however, the idea of race introduced a dramatically new element, one that did not exist in the Middle Ages.

To understand how the concept of race plays into the history of the Jewish people, it helps to remember that Jews were regarded as the original other to Christianity. As noted above, Christianity began in the premodern period as a proselytizing religion that figured itself as being "for all"—that is, as a universal religion. It figured Judaism, by contrast, as exclusive and particular. In the modern period, the Christian universalist message for humankind remained largely intact even while it was slowly transformed and secularized. Whereas before the message was that Christianity was for "all men," now it was that "all men" had inherent rights to equality.

Although Jews benefited from the secularization of the Christian universalist message, the changeover was not uniformly positive for Jewish life and culture. Note that the structure of modern universalism did not develop the means to find a place for difference, whether in the form of gender or group belonging. Those Jews who readily assimilated—who gave their loyalty to their country and who abandoned many of the habits, beliefs, and rituals that had made them seem so different in favor of becoming more French or German—were able, at first, to reap the benefits of modern citizenship. But religious and cultural affiliations were not so easily dispensed with. While in the past the Jew had to convert to Christianity to join the universal, now she or he had only to give up her or his primary identification with other Jews. After all, how could someone claiming to be a (universal) citizen of a modern nation-state simultaneously remain different (and particular) by continuing to be a Jew? The formulation of the question during the emancipation debates at the time of the French Revolution speaks volumes. As Clermont-Tonerre, a leading liberal and pro-Jewish emancipation activist put it in 1789:

> We must refuse everything to the Jews as a nation and accord everything to Jews as individuals. . . . They must be citizens

individually. But, some will say to me, they do not want to be citizens. Well then! If they do not want to be citizens, they should say so, and then, we should banish them. It is repugnant to have in the state an association of non-citizens, and a nation within the nation. . . . In short, Sirs, the presumed status of every man resident in a country is to be a citizen. (Hunt 1996, 88)

The focus on universal citizenship required that each individual's primary commitment be to the nation-state. She or he was expected to reject primary associations with any ethnic and religious community that were viewed by the majority of citizens as excessively different, and therefore particular. Universalism presupposed the disappearance of difference in the public sphere and its retreat into the realm of the private. Judaism could exist, but only as a private expression of faith. It is worthwhile to notice in Clermont-Tonerre's statement the threat of expulsion for those unprepared to accept the premises of this universalism imposed from above.

As Christian Europe began to meet large numbers of different others in the course of overseas expansion—first in the Americas and then throughout the globe—the same dynamic of universalism/particularism that had constructed the Jew as the paradigmatic other from Late Antiquity through the Middle Ages came to apply to the people living in other regions. Native American peoples and then Africans, encountered increasingly in contexts of colonial expansion from the late fifteenth through the nineteenth century, presented some thorny problems for the Europeans. At stake was the question of how these others could or should be treated. Were they part of the universal human? Were they rational beings capable of self-governance? Did they have souls, and did they worship the true God? Moreover, if they were human, if they could be shown to be capable of self-governance, and if they willingly converted to Christianity, then how could their continued domination and enslavement be justified?

Race, as an immutable essentialist characteristic of humankind, provided the escape clause needed by those who wanted to justify the continued domination and enslavement of non-European and Jewish peoples. The idea of race as a categorizing method for ranking the different groups that comprised humankind emerged within the scientific impulses for classification embedded in modern science and in Enlightenment thought. At the same time, it also became part of the backlash against the universalist message of the Enlightenment and modernity.

Conservative and reactionary movements rejected the very premises of universalist equality and envisioned hierarchical social and political structures as the ideal mode of civilization. They availed themselves readily of the idea of race to justify the exclusion of radically different others. Their reasoning went something like this: If the "other" was so different that she or he could never become the same because of an inherent inferiority, then universalist equality could only be applied to the "civilized" white man. Even liberal progressive thought and politics could use race as an excuse to limit the promise of equality inherent in universalism. Hence, countries such as Great Britain and France that became democracies did not apply the principles of their political systems beyond the metropole, to the colonies. They did not grant equality to colonized populations. Similarly, the United States subverted, through the concept of race, its very foundational principles of equality. Bypassing the opportunity to enshrine the principle of human equality in its founding document, the authors of the United States Constitution, for example, refused to abolish black slavery. This is one of the great paradoxes inherent in the category of race. It is a thoroughly modern concept at the same time that it is completely reactionary.

Since the Jews were perceived as the great beneficiaries of modernity, they became one of the principal targets for the hostility and conflict that this profound transformation engendered. The second half of the nineteenth century saw a dramatic increase in anti-Jewish polemics and movements. Anti-Judaism migrated from a theological Judeophobia and became racist antisemitism, bringing with it elements from the past but now reformulating them within the modern discourse of race. What is worse, the idea of race closed off the old path of religious conversion. Conversion had been the medieval route of exit for the Jew who wanted to escape his or her pariah status. Now, however, difference (via race) was figured as an essential and immutable characteristic of a person. Unlike a creed, race could not be transcended by changing religions. Now, the other was destined to remain forever different because of blood.

In an extreme period of crisis, the Jews—the eternal other of the West, now the internal racial other—could be not only excluded but also excised altogether, annihilated, as happened during the Holocaust. For extremists like Hitler, since the different could not be made into the same, then it had no right to exist. Following the Nazi seizure of power in Germany in 1933, Jews were again cast into the position of pariahs, stripped of all rights, thrown out of professions, persecuted, and forced to emigrate. Race now became the deciding category of social and human biological engineering, with the Jew seen as a parasite that had to be eliminated, initially through expulsions and emigration. Once World War II broke out in 1939 the path of emigration closed and the rapid conquest of new territories, especially in Eastern Europe and Russia, brought millions of Jews under Nazi rule. Then emerged the full murderous potential of racialist ideology that saw the world in binary terms, and world history as the struggle for survival between races. The enemy race, the Jew, had to be utterly exterminated so that the white Aryan race could emerge triumphant. Six million Jews were annihilated systematically with mass shootings and gassing in extermination camps that were veritable factories of death. This was the extreme logical conclusion of the centuries-old diabolization of the Jews, rendered possible by the ascendance of modern racialism.

CONCLUSION

For the historian of Jews, it is all but impossible not to see in the history of the category of race and its continuing paradoxes in our own days the reflection of the problems associated with the old construction of Western universalism itself with the Jew as the minority, the other par excellence. With many new others coming under Western domination in the modern period, race emerged as a new category by which to classify and treat difference. The Jew was no longer the only other. But race as an essentialist category also brought with it, at a time of extreme crisis in the middle of the twentieth century, a radical antisemitic "Final Solution," total eradication, to the first "other" of the West that had incarnated difference for so many centuries. Race, from the perspective of Jewish history, is not just a descriptive category but one that is intimately linked to modern antisemitism, and metonymic with tragedy and death.

Select Bibliography

•

Chazan, Robert. 1997. *Medieval Stereotypes and Modern Antisemitism.* Berkeley: University of California Press.

Fredrickson, George M. 2002. *Racism: A Short History.* Princeton: Princeton University Press.

Hunt, Lynn, ed. 1996. *The French Revolution and Human Rights: A Brief Documentary History.* Boston: Bedford/St. Martin's.

Katz, Jacob. 1980. *From Prejudice to Destruction: Anti-Semitism*. 1700–1933. Cambridge, MA: Harvard University Press.

Langmuir, Gavin I. 1990. *Toward a Definition of Antisemitism*. Berkeley: University of California Press.

Levy, Richard S., ed. 2005. *Antisemitism: Historical Encyclopedia of Prejudice and Persecution*. Santa Barbara, CA: ABC-Clio Press.

Mendes-Flohr, P., and Reinharz, Y., eds. 1995. *The Jew in the Modern World: A Documentary History*. New York: Oxford University Press.

Mosse, George. 1978. *Towards the Final Solution: A History of European Racism*. New York: Howard Fertig.

Wistrich, Robert S. 1991. *Antisemitism: The Longest Hatred*. London: Methuen.

6

Knowing the "Other"
Arabs, Islam, and the West

Joel Beinin

[handwritten: Racism against Muslim and Islam]

This essay argues that Islam and the Muslim world have been misrepresented and misunderstood throughout history in ways that have served the West's own political and economic purposes. Because Western understandings and representations of this region have only rarely been informed by a deep knowledge of the languages, religions, histories, and cultures, we must confront our own scholarly practices if we hope to develop a more accurate understanding and empathic relationship to the peoples of the Muslim world. The essay begins by examining the practices of historians who have contributed to the false construction of the Arab world as utterly different from the West. After looking at the early history of Orientalism, it shows how the world powers of the twentieth century—specifically, the United States—continue to shape and mold the image of the "Middle East" and of the people who live there. It concludes by noting that, as is often the case when "we" think about "others," the way the West understands Islam tells us more about the West than it tells us about Arabs or Muslims. In studying "others," it is always important to ask where, by whom, and for what purpose our knowledge of them is produced.

[handwritten: how does a foreign face depict terrorism.] *[handwritten: 9-11 negatively depicted Muslims as terrorists.]*

SINCE THE IRANIAN REVOLUTION OF 1978–79, AND EVEN MORE SO SINCE the "War on Terror" initiated by former President George W. Bush after September 11, 2001, many Americans have imagined that we are engaged with a Muslim or Arab enemy who is completely different—in cultural, religious, political, and economic terms—from ourselves. The common U.S. American understanding of Arabs or Muslims is based on very little information about the hundreds of millions of diverse peoples who live, work, and play in the region of the world that many of us imagine to be the source of terrorism. Often what "we" think we *do* know about "them" is conceptually continuous with ill-informed Christian thinking about Islam during the Crusades.

The prevailing U.S. American understanding of relations between the Muslim world and the West tends to imagine a unified "Western civilization" to which Islam is entirely external and antagonistic. This view has little historical basis and obscures the history of mutually advantageous economic and cultural exchange between Europe and the Arab and Muslim world. This ignored history is arguably at least as significant as the more commonly known history of hostility and warfare.

ORIENTALISM

During the Crusades, a few of the Europeans who sought to conquer a part of the Muslim world developed an empathic understanding of Islamic societies and cultures. However, much of Western knowledge about the Middle East and Islam has been dominated by an ethnocentric approach that is now commonly called Orientalism. The term "Orientalism" refers to images, practices, institutions, ideas, and values that predispose Westerners to understand Muslims, Arabs, and the Middle East in predictable ways that devalue them and that imagine Islamic and Middle Eastern cultures to be antithetical and inferior to "Western culture." In this sense, Orientalism is a form of racism. It is not due to any natural antagonism between "Islam" and "the West" but is rooted in historically formed, power-laden human practices.

Many Orientalist scholars were instrumental in creating a mistaken and racialized conception of the Muslim world. Orientalist scholars' "knowledge" of Islam and Muslim societies both justified and was shaped by the European conquest of important parts of the Muslim world from the eighteenth century on. Europe's colonial and imperial projects were legitimized and authorized by a politics of knowledge that imagined Muslims to be incapable of governing themselves because they lacked rationality or modernity or some other characteristic that the West had in good supply.

Orientalism, like racism more generally, does not have a clear and consistent referential relationship to a "real Orient." Its coherence as a set of ideas and practices does not depend on what actually exists. Rather,

Orientalism has a logic and a reality-shaping power of its own. Since it does not have a stable referent, it is readily available for interpreting current events and placing them into profoundly ahistorical frameworks. To understand the terrorist attacks of September 11, 2001, as the result of an eternal "clash of civilizations" between "Islam" and "the West" serves as an example of this kind of Orientalist thinking (Abrahamian 2003).

HISTORY AND RELIGIOUS CONTENTION

A historical account of interactions between residents of different geographic regions can help us to understand how concepts and practices of specific forms of race come into being.[1] The West's conception of the Oriental "other" emerged through military, commercial, scientific, philosophic, and religious encounters. But Muslims, Christians, and Jews have never comprised entirely distinct and homogeneous civilizations. What we commonly call "the West" today includes regions ruled for centuries by Arab Muslim empires (e.g., Spain and Sicily) or the Ottoman Empire (e.g., Greece, Hungary, Romania, Bulgaria, Serbia, Bosnia, Albania). There are now millions of Arab, Turkish, and West African Muslim citizens and permanent residents in several countries of Western Europe, including France, Germany, and Great Britain.

Muslims first engaged with Christians and Jews during the lifetime of Muhammad, the prophet of Islam (571–632 CE). At that time, Arab Jews were clients and allies of the pagan Arabs of Medina, who began to convert to Islam when Muhammad emigrated there from Mecca in 622 CE. Arab Christians were encountered by Muslims in the early years of Islam's expansion. Many of them soon willingly converted to Islam.

The Mediterranean Sea linked, rather than isolated, Muslim, Jewish, and Christian cultural zones. Much of what we now consider to be "Western" knowledge is the product of long-term exchanges among Muslims, Christians, and Jews in the Mediterranean basin and its borderlands. They inherited and developed ancient Greek philosophy and sciences. Most of the corpus of ancient Greek philosophical, medical, mathematical, and scientific learning was unknown in medieval Western Europe, although it continued to be studied in the original Greek or Aramaic translation in the Middle East. In the eighth and ninth centuries, the 'Abbasid caliphs

---

1 Much of the first part of this essay was inspired by Zachary Lockman, *Contending Visions of the Middle East: The History and Politics of Orientalism* (Cambridge: Cambridge University Press 2004).

of Baghdad encouraged Arab Christians and Jews who also knew Greek or Aramaic to translate these texts into Arabic. Muslim scholars studied and developed this body of knowledge, especially in the fields of medicine, mathematics, optics, astronomy, and philosophy. From the twelfth century on, long after the scholarly heritage of classical Greece had been lost to Western Europe, many of these texts were translated from Arabic into Latin (sometimes via Hebrew), making them available in Western Europe for the first time in hundreds of years.

Religion is the singular arena in which there is a long history of contention between Islam and Christianity. However, the intensity and historical development of this religious confrontation has never been constant. Islam was and is Christianity's most proximate other: they have similar religious missions, competing narratives about holy places (Jerusalem in particular), and a common prophetic tradition stretching from Adam to Abraham to Moses to Jesus. Unlike Judaism, they are proselytizing faiths with global aspirations. However, there were both Muslim and Christian rulers who adopted tolerant and expansive attitudes toward the opposing faith: for example, the ʿAbbasid caliphs, al-Maʾmun (813–833 CE) and al-Muʿtasim (833–846 CE), the Caliph of Cordoba, ʿAbd al-Rahman III (912–961 CE), King Roger II of Sicily (1130–1154 CE), and King Alfonso "the Wise" of Castile (1252–1284 CE). On the whole, however, from the time Pope Urban II preached the first Crusade in 1095, Latin Europe became more militantly antagonistic toward Islam and, except in Spain, this antagonism was buttressed by considerable ignorance of even the most fundamental beliefs of Islam.

A good example of this ignorance appears in *The Song of Roland*, a French epic poem of unknown authorship composed around the time of the first Crusade. The poem, which can be considered a form of war propaganda, begins:

> *Charles the king our mighty emperor,*
> *Has been in Spain for all of seven years,*
> *Has won that haughty land down to the sea.*
> *There is no castle still opposing him,*
> *Nor town or wall remaining to be crushed,*
> *Except the mountain city, Saragossa.*
> *Marsilla holds it; he does not love God,*
> *But serves Mohammed and invokes Apollo.*
> *No matter what he does, his ruin will come.*
> (HARRISON 1970, 51)

Further on, the author tells us that after having lost the battle, the Muslims desecrated their "pagan idols"—Mohammed and Termagent, the latter a figure many medieval Europeans considered the chief pagan deity of Islam. *The Song of Roland* portrays Muslims as pagans and/or heretics—not believers in the same God that Christians and Jews worship, albeit with a different version of God's message to humankind.

After the first Crusade, Latin Christian scholars gradually began to acquire more knowledge of Islam. Peter of Cluny (1094–1156 CE), the abbot of the monastery that became the core of the University of Paris, directed a group of scholars in Spain to translate Arabic texts into Latin. This resulted in the first Latin translation of the Qur'an, by Robert of Ketton in 1143 CE. However, the knowledge of Islam that became available as a result of these translations remained on the margin of Western European scholarly knowledge for at least another seventy-five years.

For example, in *The Inferno*, the third book of his *Divine Comedy*, Dante (1265–1321 CE) depicts Muslims (here, Mahomet, or Mohammed and the fourth Caliph Ali) as schismatics and heretics—similar to the representation in *The Song of Roland*:

> *See how Mahomet's mangled and split open!*
> *Ahead of me walks Ali in his tears,*
> *His head cleft from the top-knot to the chin.*
>
> *And all the other souls that bleed and mourn*
> *Along this ditch were sowers of scandal and schism:*
> *As they tore others apart, so they are torn.*
> (DANTE 1954, CANTO XXVIII 31–36)

At the same time, Dante has a much more positive attitude toward the Muslim philosophers, Avicenna (Ibn Sina, 980–1037 CE) and Averroes (Ibn Rushd, 1126–1198 CE). They, along with the noble warrior Saladin (Salah al-Din, 1171–1193 CE), are placed in the outermost circle of hell, where they are spared the most gruesome tortures. This generosity reflects the expanding cultural horizons that would soon become manifest in the Italian Renaissance. However, it was still not possible to imagine that Muslims might have anything to look forward to other than eternal misery.

Once the Renaissance broke the intellectual and economic isolation of medieval Latin Europe, the requirements of commerce and statecraft augmented intellectual curiosity in impelling Europeans to develop a more realistic and reliable understanding of Islam. The Ottoman

Empire emerged in the fourteenth century as a Mediterranean and European power of the first order. Although the Ottomans posed a substantial military threat to the Habsburg Empire, laying siege to Vienna in 1529 CE, they were simultaneously allies of France. Hence, even when the military power of a Muslim empire posed a great threat to one part of Europe, the Ottomans were an integral part of the European state system and balance of power. They remained so until the second siege of Vienna in 1683 CE.

For more than two centuries after the Renaissance, Europeans—with the possible exception of the Italian city-states—traded with Muslim regions from a position of relative weakness. Europeans who traded with the Ottoman Empire or the Mughal Empire in South Asia needed to learn something of their languages and cultures. As a consequence of their alliance with France, the Ottomans granted commercial privileges, known as the *Capitulations* (from the Latin *capitula*, or chapter of a treaty), to France in 1535 CE, to be followed by a similar agreement with England in 1580 CE. The latter agreement allowed the English Levant Company, a royal monopoly, to begin operations in the Silk Road terminus of Aleppo in 1581 CE. Another and much more important royal monopoly, the British East India Company, was established in 1600 CE to conduct commercial activities in areas control by the Muslim Mughal Empire.

COMMERCE, EMPIRE, MISSIONARY WORK, AND ORIENTALISM

The commercial expansion of England in the Middle East and South Asia, which eventually developed into imperial rule, was the immediate context for the institutionalization of the study of Islamic languages, literature, and law in European universities and the consolidation of the academic discipline of Orientalism. The original funding for academic positions in Oriental studies tended to come from commercial interests. Later, several European and finally the United States governments became involved.

For example, the first professorship of Arabic in England was established at the University of Cambridge in 1632, followed by one at the University of Oxford in 1636. The Cambridge professorship was endowed by Thomas Adams, a London cloth merchant. In the course of the discussions leading to the establishment of the professorship, the vice-chancellor of Cambridge wrote to Adams stating that the objectives of the proposed position were political and commercial advantage as well as religious conversion:

> The work itself we conceive to tend not only to the advancement of good literature by bringing to light much knowledge which as yet is locked up in that learned tongue, but also to the good service of the King and state in our commerce with the Eastern nations, and in God's good time to the enlargement of the borders of the Church and the propagation of them that now sit in darkness. (Arberry 1960, 12)

The first occupant of the Cambridge professorship of Arabic was Edward Pococke Jr. (1604–1691) who had served as chaplain to the Levant Company in Aleppo from 1630 to 1636. He had studied Arabic, Turkish, and Syriac (closely related to the language spoken in Palestine at the time of Jesus) and had translated tracts on Christianity in an attempt to convert Muslims. Another prominent early Orientalist connected to England's commercial enterprises in the Muslim world was William Jones (1746–1794). In 1784, he established the Asiatic Society of Bengal, the first scholarly society devoted to amassing and disseminating Orientalist knowledge. Jones is often considered the founder of Orientalism as an academic discipline in Europe.

Orientalist scholarship in the United States was not very significant until it became stimulated by and associated with nineteenth-century Protestant missionary activity in Lebanon and Palestine. After the Second World War, an important current of American Orientalism allied itself to the social sciences, especially modernization theory. Modernization theory shaped the emergence of Middle East, Latin American, African, Southeast Asian, and other regional studies in the 1950s. Such interdisciplinary area studies were a distinctly U.S. American intellectual project whose political agenda was unconcealed: to create the knowledge necessary to contest the Soviet Union's presumed expansionist ambitions in various regions of the globe. Hence, the original federal funding for university-based area studies centers, study of critical languages, and graduate student fellowships was authorized by the National Defense Education Act of 1958.

Area studies training typically involved extended residence in the region and mastery of relevant languages. This provided scholars with a cultural context and a local social network that sustained the main intellectual claim of area studies—that it would encourage collaboration of scholars across disciplinary boundaries to produce a holistic knowledge of a given region. It was intended that much of this knowledge be policy relevant, and it was.

The collapse of the Soviet Union led to efforts to reshape, if not altogether dismantle, U.S. American area studies during the 1990s. The entire concept of area studies was dismissed as lacking disciplinary coherence and an intellectual project of the Cold War (Heginbotham 1994; Khalidi 1995). Federal funding had been declining since the late 1960s; foundations reduced or eliminated funding altogether. Social science disciplines, under the influence of rational choice theory, minimized the significance of area-specific knowledge.

POWER AND KNOWLEDGE

Is there a problem with the activity of men like Pococke and Jones and the many others who succeeded them? What could be the objection to attaining knowledge of Islamic languages and law? Is this not better than the ignorance of medieval Europe? On one level, there is no problem; knowledge always trumps ignorance.

The study of other people and cultures is not inherently illegitimate. But studying something always means studying it in relation to something else. There is no necessary harm in this; it is one of the main ways individuals and societies make sense of things. But to avoid misunderstanding we must be aware of our own historical and cultural positions as well as those of the objects of our study, the positions of authors we read, and the relations among these elements.

One commonly proposed solution to the problem of our relationship to the subjects of our knowledge is that we should be "objective" or "balanced." While superficially attractive, this approach is deeply flawed. Who has the authority to determine what is "objective" or where the correct balance lies between contending viewpoints on a controversial subject? For many, objectivity consists of a point of view consistent with their previously held opinions. Is there any logical basis for assuming that the truth of any proposition lies between (much less midway between) two opposing claims? Typically, individuals or groups with some form of social power determine what constitutes conventional wisdom and the parameters of legitimate debate on any topic. Divergent viewpoints are labeled "biased" or "unbalanced." Therefore, studying other cultures under the banner of "science" or "objectivity" without accounting for social relations of power is either naïve or malicious.

Michel Foucault's conception of the inextricable link between power and knowledge is one of the points of departure for Edward Said's well-known book *Orientalism*—a scathing critique of the European imagination of the Arab and Muslim world. According to Foucault:

> Power produces knowledge ... power and knowledge directly imply one another ... there is no power relation without the correlative constitution of a field on knowledge, nor any knowledge that does not presuppose and constitute at the same time power relations. (Foucault 1995, 27)

Anytime we know something we are also engaged in a relationship of power. Knowledge of another group's culture can give an advantage in social interactions and scientific knowledge; in the hands of a dominant group, it also bestows coercive power over other people. At the most basic level this is evident in the development of military technology from the galleons of the sixteenth century to nuclear weapons of the twentieth century. As noted above in the case of the British Empire, knowledge of another people's language and culture is often a consequence of contact between two peoples in an asymmetrical power relationship.

The linguistic study and legal classification in which William Jones engaged was simultaneously made necessary and possible by the East India Company's desire to control India. Jones seems to have enjoyed his work and had a respectful attitude toward his subject. And he had enormous intellectual energy. "It is my ambition to know India better than any European ever knew it," he proclaimed (Said 1978, 78). But he participated, wittingly or unwittingly, in the racism that justified this project; he invented the "Aryan Theory" of the common origins of Indo-European languages, such as Greek, Latin, and Hindi. The now discredited notion that this linguistic commonality proved the existence of an "Aryan race" was a staple of European racism for generations.

While Orientalist scholars did compile important knowledge of Muslim languages, law, and literature, this was commonly framed by the exercise of classifying the ways in which "they" are essentially different from "us." The majority of Orientalists, with important and noteworthy exceptions like Ignác Goldziher (1981), S. D. Goitein (1967–93), and Maxime Rodinson (1980) were convinced that "Islam" and "the West" were categories designating distinct and fundamentally different cultures, and harbored no doubt as to the superiority of Western culture. This is perhaps most clearly expressed in the phrase "clash of civilizations" coined by Bernard Lewis, whom many regard as the leading Orientalist scholar in the United States over the last several decades. This notion was later appropriated and brought to a wide audience by the Harvard political scientist Samuel Huntington, who argued that in the post–Cold War world, civilizations, defined primarily by religious traditions, would be the principal fault lines of global conflict (Huntington 1996).

EMPIRES AND MAPS

The link between knowledge and power can be discerned even in practices that appear to be "scientific" and "objective," like mapping. Maps appear to be a neutral form of knowledge. But the location of lines on maps, even the capacity to draw a map, often depends on the color of people's skins, their religion, and their relations of power. How did the continents of Europe and Asia come to be divided? Is there any "scientific" basis on which to draw this line? Is it logical that half of the city of Istanbul should lie in Europe while the other half is in Asia?

The geographical borders determining which countries comprise the "Middle East" have been constructed and reconstructed based on who the "other" was at any one point in time. As late as the early twentieth century, Western Europeans commonly considered large parts of what is unequivocally considered "Europe" today to be non-European. Greece, which many imagine to be the most influential source of "Western culture," was thought to be a semi-barbaric part of the Near East (Todorova 1997).

In 1902 Alfred Thayer Mahan (1840–1914), a captain in the U.S. Navy and the founding commander of the Naval War College, coined the term "Middle East." For Mahan, this region was distinct from the "Near East," which comprised the Balkans, western Anatolia, and the Levant. The Near East, including the Holy Land, was then ruled by the Ottoman Empire but populated by large numbers of Christians. In contrast, the "Middle East" designated the region extending from the Arabian Peninsula to Afghanistan and the borders of what is today Pakistan. Over the next fifty years, Mahan's terminology spread quickly, although by the Second World War, the distinction Mahan made between the Near East and the Middle East fell out of use; both terms came to designate more or less the same region, with the latter carrying with it a more archaic connotation. Both terms are clearly Euro-centric. Mahan explicitly imagined the Near and Middle East as locations on the way from London to India. Southwest Asia (a term analogous to East Asia or South Asia) would be a more neutral designation for the region and is the term the United Nations employs. But Southwest Asia and North Africa, which encompasses the region commonly considered a unit in U.S. American area studies, is a clumsy term and rarely used.

The demise of the Ottoman Empire and the political reconfiguration of the Middle East created new maps of the region after the First World War. In 1923 there was a forced population exchange between Greece and the newly established republic of Turkey—what we might now call a mutual ethnic cleansing (Naimark 2001). Subsequently, Turkey had almost no Christian and few Jewish citizens left. To the consternation of its secular nationalists, Turkey became culturally closer to the Arab world in the eyes of the West and therefore became identified as part of the Middle East. The Balkans, with most of their Muslim populations eliminated, were incorporated into Europe, albeit with much ambivalence and anxiety (Todorova 1997). By the Second World War, or shortly thereafter, the Anglo-American notion of the Middle East comprised Turkey, Iran, Egypt, Syria, Lebanon, Iraq, Transjordan, Palestine (still overwhelmingly Arab), Saudi Arabia, and the British protectorates that eventually became independent Yemen, Oman, Bahrain, Qatar, and the United Arab Emirates. Unlike the other countries of this group, which are in Southwest Asia, Egypt, except for the Sinai Peninsula, is in Africa. This representation puts Sudan and Afghanistan on the margins of the Middle East; sometimes they are included, sometimes not.

The region outlined above is not ecologically, linguistically, ethnically, or politically unified, although large parts of it were once part of the Ottoman Empire. While the dominant religion of the region is Islam, there have historically been, and currently exist, significant Christian and Jewish populations, and the Muslims are divided between Sunnis and Shi'a. Moreover, the four countries with the largest Muslim populations today—Indonesia, India, Pakistan, and Bangladesh—are outside the Middle East by all definitions.

As a result of U.S. American–inspired regional alliances formed to contain the Soviet Union during the Cold War, a new geographical concept emerged known as "the Northern Tier." This geographical region comprised the non-Arab states of Turkey, Iran, and Pakistan. This concept was embodied in the Baghdad Pact formed in 1955 by the United Kingdom, Iraq, Turkey, Iran, and Pakistan. Although it was not a formal ally of the United States at this time, Israel was pleased with this conceptual map because it emphasized the prominence of non-Arab peoples in the Middle East and their alignment with the West.

Britain hoped that Syria and Jordan would join the Baghdad Pact to complete the encirclement of the Soviet Union on its southwestern flank. However, Egypt's president, Gamal Abdel Nasser, emphatically opposed Arab participation in the Baghdad Pact because it would have permitted European military bases on Arab soil. British forces had invaded and occupied Egypt in 1882. It was not until 1954 that Egypt achieved an agreement for their evacuation, although the last British units did not leave the banks of the Suez Canal until June 1956. In this historical context, Nasser refused to join either the Western or the Soviet bloc; instead, he called for Arab unity and mutual defense. Nasser's popularity among Arabs outside Egypt led Syria and Jordan to opt out of the Baghdad Pact. Iraq also withdrew from the Baghdad Pact in 1958 after the overthrow of the pro-British Hashemite monarchy.

Nasser's regional geography was based on the concept of an "Arab World." This notion was based on Arabist cultural and political ideas that gained currency shortly before and during the First World War. At the time, most Egyptian intellectuals and political leaders did not consider Egypt an Arab country. Arab nationalism gained force in Egypt only in the 1930s, partly due to sympathy with the Palestinian Arab revolt of 1936–39. By 1955, Arab nationalism became the theory guiding Nasser's anti-imperialist foreign policy and his aspiration to lead the Arab states as a united bloc affiliated with the nonaligned movement he founded with India's Jawaharlal Nehru and Yugoslavia's Josef Tito. Nasser invoked Arab unity to support the Algerian war of independence against France, the brief union of Egypt and Syria in the United Arab Republic (1958–61), and many other political initiatives that undermined the efforts of Britain, France, and the United States to maintain colonial or neocolonial rule in the Middle East and North Africa. Arabism had great popular rhetorical appeal in the 1950s and 1960s. However, the efficacy of popular pan-Arab sentiment was limited. No state, especially not Egypt, subordinated its sovereign interests in favor of Arab unity in any substantial way (Kerr 1971).

The Arab world seems to be an attractive geographical classification because it was indigenously generated and aspired to a progressive political agenda. However, the Arab World has no place for the Kurds, Turcomans, Assyrian Christians, and Yazidis of Iraq; the Nubians of Egypt; the Christians and animists of Sudan; the Berbers of North Africa; and the Jews who once resided throughout the region. Many Lebanese Maronites have also felt threatened by pan-Arab nationalism. The 1958 Lebanese Civil War was fought over whether the Nasserist or the U.S.

American conception of the region would prevail there; the same issues, in a somewhat different configuration, set off the 1975–90 Lebanese Civil War. They emerged once again in the aftermath of the assassination of Lebanese prime minister Rafiq Hariri in February 2005. The civic liberties, cultural expression, and physical existence of these minority communities have been threatened by postcolonial states, especially Iraq, which adopted an authoritarian and homogeneous conception of Arab national identity whose epitome is the racialism of the Ba'th Party.

In conscious opposition to the pan-Arab nationalism of Nasser and the Ba'th, Saudi Arabia, with encouragement from the United States, promoted an alternative Islamic regional geography, arguing that the bond of Islam was stronger than the bond of Arab ethnicity. In 1965, King Faysal of Saudi Arabia called for an Islamic Pact to combat radical pan-Arab nationalism. The pact included Tunisian president Habib Bourguiba and the shah of Iran, who were staunchly pro-Western but openly hostile to traditionalist interpretations of Islam and not known for their piety (Ajami 1981).

Yet a fourth geographical configuration was drawn when the Saudis, along with Venezuela, initiated the founding of the Organization of Petroleum Exporting Countries (OPEC) in 1960. The original membership of OPEC united three Arab countries—Saudi Arabia, Kuwait, and Iraq—with two non-Arab countries—Iran and Venezuela. For OPEC, neither ethnicity nor religion but oil wealth drew a boundary that excluded oil-poor "radical" Arab states like Egypt and Syria which opposed Western influence in the Middle East. Nonetheless, all the states that joined OPEC after its establishment were Arab states, and Venezuela remains the only non-Muslim-majority member.

GEOGRAPHIES OF CRISIS

This last geographical vision leads us to the current world political situation and the political determination of "geographies of crisis." The rather different geographical schemas described in the previous section have two common elements. First, the mapped region centers on or is close to the Persian Gulf—the source of two-thirds of the world's known petroleum reserves. The British Empire retreated from the Gulf in 1971 after serving as the regional policeman for 150 years. That task then fell to the United States, which has attempted to develop military and diplomatic policies to support this objective ever since. The second is the assumption that this region, however mapped, was especially unstable and therefore susceptible to the designs of the Soviet Union. From the mid-1970s on, U.S. concern about the security of the Persian Gulf was enhanced because the Soviet Union was perceived as having had a recent series of foreign policy successes in Vietnam, Laos, Cambodia, Nicaragua, Grenada, Angola, Mozambique, Guinea-Bissau, and Zimbabwe.

The biggest regional shock in shaping this sense of crisis was the Iranian revolution of 1978–79. The overthrow of the shah of Iran, a major U.S. ally designated by the Nixon administration as a "regional influential" with responsibility for securing the Persian Gulf, could not be attributed to the Cold War or the Soviet Union. And the establishment of an Islamic republic contradicted the predictions of modernization theory, which envisaged Islam receding as a factor in Middle Eastern public life as the region became "modernized."

Whereas the Soviet Union disappeared in 1991, the problem of securing access to the petroleum resources of the Persian Gulf did not. Consequently, the United States has repeatedly pursued military engagements in a region of the world about which most U.S. Americans know little. Developing a nuanced understanding of Middle Eastern "others" who happen to live on top of "our" oil has been hindered by the popularity of the concept of "globalization." In the 1990s the notion of globalization undermined the earlier view that area-specific knowledge, including language training and extended residence in a region, were necessary to understand areas like the Middle East. However, the events of September 11, 2001, closed the debate about the necessity of knowing Arabic and other regional languages of the Muslim world and of having precise and sophisticated knowledge about countries and regions previously off the map of "globalization"—places like Afghanistan, Waziristan, Kurdistan, Anbar, and south Lebanon.

Since the 2003 American invasion of Iraq, Americans have learned that there are Sunni and Shi'a Muslims. Some political commentators began to speak of a new regional geography—the "Shi'a arc of crisis," including south Lebanon, Iraq, Iran, and the Shi'a minorities of the Persian Gulf, especially those of the oil-rich Hasa region of Saudi Arabia. The American "discovery" of shi'ism has been accompanied by a new misunderstanding that Shi'a organizations like Hezbollah in Lebanon or the Shi'a parties in Iraq are simply puppets of Iran.

Although there is now a broad consensus in the United States about the renewed importance of Middle East area studies, debates continue about how the region should be defined and the purposes to which knowledge about it should be put. These debates have been shaped by the radically different interests of the parties engaging in them. Before, and especially after, the invasion of Iraq, one particularly sharp question has been whether military intervention can be an effective means of transforming the Middle East.

At the World Economic Forum in Davos, Switzerland, in February 2004, Vice President Dick Cheney announced a "Greater Middle East Initiative" in the region stretching from Morocco to Pakistan. The Bush administration formally unveiled the policy at the G-8 talks and the NATO and European Union summits in June 2004. The Initiative focused on enhancing women's empowerment and expanding access to education in the context of promoting democracy, human rights, and free trade. Behind these fine words, however, lies the conception that this swath of the Muslim world is dangerous and backward—the principal source of global terrorism as well as the home of the preponderance of the world's proven oil reserves. The Bush administration sought to make this region safe and stable for the world capitalist market and seemed to prefer to do so by using armed force rather than uncertain negotiations.

It should come as no surprise that even Washington's closest allies in this region—Morocco, Egypt, and Pakistan—raised loud objections to the Greater Middle East Initiative. Egyptian president Hosni Mubarak pointedly voiced his opposition during a March 2004 tour of Italy, France, and the UK. "Any initiative imposed from abroad will be rejected by the people," he told *Le Figaro*. "How can you impose one ready-made solution on an expansive area that stretches from Mauritania to Pakistan?" he asked a reporter for *La Repubblica*. Mubarak further warned *Le Figaro* that "the priority in the Middle East is resolving the Arab-Israeli conflict, which is at the heart of all the region's problems" (Khalil 2004). This contradicted Vice President Cheney's suggestion that democracy comes first and clearly differed from the Bush administration's preoccupation with Iraq. Of course, as a client of the United States, Mubarak later had to retreat from his vocal opposition to the Bush administration's policy.

Not only autocratic regimes allied to the United States opposed the Greater Middle East Initiative. One of Egypt's most respected political commentators, the late Mohamed Sid-Ahmed, eruditely summarized the problem with the ethnocentric, Orientalist outlook of the Bush administration when he wrote:

> The plan divides the world into two categories of states. One category, made up of Western democracies under the leadership of the United States, is responsible for and capable of reforming the

world system. . . . The other category is made up of states incapable of standing up to the forces of evil and at risk, even, of becoming tools in their hands. In other words, some political entities are qualified to make history while others can only remain passive onlookers watching helplessly as it unfolds. (Sid-Ahmed 2004)

What neither the Arab states nor the various movements of opposition have so far been able to produce is a satisfactory alternative map of the region, like the Arab world championed by Nasser and the Ba'th in the 1950s and 1960s. The Arab summit of March 29, 2004, disintegrated before it convened because the participants could not agree on a counterproposal to the Bush administration's Greater Middle East Initiative.

For many U.S. Americans today, the most relevant map is the "Muslim world." Like previous maps, this vision is the product of its time. Therefore, while it reflects a certain historical and current reality, it is likely to be superseded. Foreigners should not and cannot intervene and impose their own map on this region in the name of democracy or any other value, no matter how attractive it may sound. The history of European and U.S. interventions in the Middle East offers little evidence that such impositions will have a positive outcome. Whatever maps the inhabitants of the region devise will be shaped by their own sense of their identity and their future.

The historical progression of the American relationship with the Middle East raises the question: Is the anti-Islamic racism now widespread in the United States chronic or situational? Once the postulate of an essential difference between "Islam" and "the West" is established, many other differences are derived. "They" lack rationality, secularism, modern sensibilities, national identity, economic development, science and technology, and so forth. Ultimately, "they" are terrorists. No one embracing this view, which has been the dominant one in Anglo-American intellectual life and in the mass media since September 11, 2001, has been able to explain how cool, rational, unified "Western civilization" produced the Irish Republican Army, the Basque ETA, or the violent groups of the German, Italian, and American far left of the late 1960s and early 1970s.

If we want to know about "them"—Muslims, Arabs, the Middle East—we must move beyond such facile concepts, even if they appear to offer an explanation for a problem of the moment. A good alternative is to begin with a sound knowledge of the relevant languages, religions, histories, and cultures. We must consider seriously the imperial histories of the West in the region and its contemporary legacies. We need to ask why the Middle East and North Africa, a region so rich in petroleum resources, is nonetheless among the poorest in the world. Above all, it is necessary to appreciate the historical and contemporary diversity of Muslim-majority societies and to avoid the false comfort of imagining that "they" are fundamentally different from "us." If we ask the right questions, there is no insurmountable barrier to an empathic and usable understanding of the Arab and Muslim world.

Works Cited

•

Abrahamian, Ervand. 2003. The U.S. Media, Huntington and September 11. *Third World Quarterly* 24 (3):529–44.

Ajami, Fouad. 1981. *The Arab Predicament: Arab Political Thought and Practice since 1967*. Cambridge: Cambridge University Press.

Arberry, A. J. 1960. *Oriental Essays: Portrait of Seven Scholars*. New York: Macmillan.

Dante Alighieri. 1954. *The Inferno*. Translated by John Ciardi. New York: New American Library.

Foucault, Michel. 1995. *Discipline and Punish: The Birth of the Prison*. New York: Vintage Books.

Goitein, S. D. 1967–93. *A Mediterranean Society: The Jewish Communities of the Arab World as Portrayed in the Documents of the Cairo Geniza*. Berkeley: University of California Press.

Goldziher, Ignác. 1981. *Introduction to Islamic Theology and Law*. Princeton: Princeton University Press.

Harrison, Robert, trans. 1970. *The Song of Roland*. New York: New American Library.

Heginbotham, Stanley J. 1994. Rethinking International Scholarship: The Challenge of the Transition from the Cold War. *Items* 48 (2–3): 33–40.

Huntington, Samuel. 1996. *The Clash of Civilizations and the Remaking of World Order*. New York: Simon & Schuster.

Kerr, Malcolm. 1971. *The Arab Cold War: Gamal 'Abd al-Nasir and His Rivals, 1958–1970*. London: Oxford University Press.

Khalidi, Rashid. 1995. Is There a Future for Middle East Studies? *MESA Bulletin*, July. fp.arizona.edu/mesassoc/Bulletin/Pres%20Addresses/khalidi.htm.

Khalil, Nevine. 2004. Peace Key to Democracy. *Al-Ahram Weekly* 681 (March 11–17).

Naimark, Norman. 2001. *Fires of Hatred: Ethnic Cleansing in Twentieth Century Europe*. Cambridge: Harvard University Press.

Rodinson, Maxime. 1980. *Muhammad*. New York: Pantheon Books.

Said, Edward. 1978. *Orientalism*. New York: Vintage Books.

Sid-Ahmed, Mohamed. 2004. A New Berlin Wall? *Al-Ahram Weekly* 681 (March 11–17).

Todorova, Maria. 1997. *Imagining the Balkans*. New York: Oxford University Press.

7

Eternally Foreign
Asian Americans, History, and Race

Gordon H. Chang

•

The history of the Asian presence in the United States highlights the interconnections between the "foreign" and "domestic" in the country's racial thinking. Indeed, dominant attitudes toward Asians, from the earliest days of their arrival in the United States, emphasized their racial "foreignness" and the impossibility of their becoming genuine U.S. citizens. Through much of Asian American history, it mattered little whether a person of Asian descent was a foreign-born immigrant or a U.S.-born citizen. In the eyes of many non-Asians, people of Asian descent have been seen as "eternally foreign" and as inseparable from their lands of ancestry. In this essay, I focus on three episodes from the history of Asians in the United States to illustrate the ways that Asian Americans have been viewed as perpetually linked to the foreign. These episodes include (1) the fear of the "yellow peril" in the late nineteenth century, (2) domestic policy and the internment of Japanese Americans in World War II, and (3) race and politics in the 1996 presidential campaign. These episodes reveal some, but certainly not all, of the different ways that race and the international context are important to consider in any discussion about race in the United States. Although there are, at present, many different Asian ethnic groups in the United States, this essay will draw principally from the experiences of Chinese and Japanese throughout U.S. history.

> *The Number of purely white People in the World is proportionally very small. All Africa is black or tawny. Asia chiefly tawny. America (exclusive of the new Comers) wholly so. And in Europe, the Spaniards, Italians, French, Russians and Swedes,*

are generally of what we call a swarthy Complexion; as are the
Germans also, the Saxons only excepted, who with the English
make the principal Body of White People on the Face of the
Earth. I could wish their Numbers were increased. . . . Perhaps
I am partial to the Complexion of my Country, for such Kind of
Partiality is natural to Mankind.
BENJAMIN FRANKLIN (1751, 234)

DISCUSSIONS ABOUT THE HISTORY OF RACE IN THE UNITED STATES
commonly focus on social and historical interactions that have occurred
on our country's soil as if it were removed from the rest of the world. But
ideas and practices about race—so deeply implicated in the United States
past and continuing present—are not just about what is called the domestic experience; they have always also had an international dimension. U.S.
citizens like Ben Franklin inherited from Europe notions about what we
today call race, but U.S. racial thought also developed out of experiences
with racial others in different regional and even global contexts. Slavery
in the United States was part of a system that embraced the entire Atlantic world—Europe, Africa, and beyond; attitudes about and treatment of
native peoples in North America were part and parcel of the expansion
of Europe and its encounter with indigenous peoples around the globe;
and attitudes toward Latinos are inseparable from U.S. expansionist
impulses into the Caribbean, Mexico, and South America. Similarly, to
facilitate its march to obtain what it wanted in Asia, the United States
had repeated encounters with Pacific island peoples. Attitudes toward
Asian Americans, then, have been inseparably linked to the country's
long and tumultuous relationship with Asia; they have been shaped by
that relationship at least as much as by the interactions that have taken
place between peoples of Asian and European descent on U.S. soil.

When we think about the ideological and cultural foundations of our
country, Franklin's ideas about race are as important to consider as are
his more commonly revered pronouncements about politics and science.
Race occupied a prominent place in mind, as it did for the country's other
early leaders, and, as he reveals, he thought about race in global ways.
His mid-eighteenth-century notion of "white" may surprise us today—
Swedes and Germans as "swarthy" and not white! But over time the category of "white" expanded to embrace other immigrant ethnic groups
from Europe while relegating other peoples to different color categories.
From Franklin's time on, the evolution of racial categorization has been

a central historical process in the construction of the United States itself and has inextricably linked the peopling of this country to the rest of the world. Indeed, as it has developed over time, the idea of race in the United States has come to imply the global, as it suggests not the oneness of the "human race" but the division of humanity into "races" with innate and indelible qualities that transcend actual social and cultural experience. The persistence of the idea of "race" has consistently and stubbornly challenged the cherished notion of the universality of the promise of the United States.

FEARS OF THE "YELLOW PERIL"

In the latter part of the nineteenth and early twentieth centuries, a deep anxiety swept the European and North American homelands, as the nations of these areas of the world spread their military, political, cultural, and economic control over ever greater areas of the rest of the world. The era of "high imperialism" witnessed the systematization of ideas about race (or what is called "scientific racism") that accompanied the expansion of colonial projects over nonwhite peoples in Asia, the Middle East, and Africa. Simultaneously, however, many people in Europe and the United States feared that the imperial homeland was itself insecure—that is, that the empire could strike back. One of the greatest anxieties that emerged was about a racial enemy that threatened the white dominion: it was called the "yellow peril." Even as many political and intellectual leaders believed that the future lay in the "white" domination of the world—in other words, that domination by the "white race" was destiny in a social Darwinist competition of the "survival of the fittest"—they worried about the "yellow race" as a potential rival (see Grant 1921; Stoddard 1920; London 1910, 277–289). Indeed, fears of the "yellow peril" had wide currency in U.S. culture in the early twentieth century.

The idea of "white" and "yellow" races emerged at the same time that the proposition of biologically based races became established. The belief was that race—generally defined as a large human group that shared fundamental features of mental abilities, personality, and character—decided everything. Physical appearances, such as skin color, were understood to be important markers of racial difference. Under this view, race—not culture, environment, individual choice, nations, or events—determined the past and even predicted the future. David Starr Jordan, a widely respected scientist and the first president of Stanford

University, expressed this idea about the centrality and permanence of racial difference (even as he used the term in ways somewhat different from our use today) when he wrote:

> The old word [blood] well serves our purposes. The blood which is "thicker than water" is the symbol of race unity. In this sense the blood of the people concerned is at once the cause and the result of the deeds recorded in their history. For example, wherever an Englishman goes, he carries with him the elements of English history. It is a British deed which he does, British history that he makes. Thus, too, a Jew is a Jew in all ages and climes, and his deeds everywhere bear the stamp of Jewish individuality. A Greek is a Greek; a Chinaman remains a Chinaman. In like fashion race traits color all history made by Tartars, or negroes, or Malays. (Jordan 1910, 9–10)

Jordan's were the words of an eminent intellectual, but the ideas he expressed were so common that they also ran through the broader, public imagination.

Beginning in the 1840s, Chinese immigration to the United States—even though minuscule compared to European immigration—provoked a violent reaction on the part of European Americans. Opponents of Chinese immigration saw Chinese people as genetically or culturally unfit and as undesirable residents of the United States. Anti-Chinese sentiment was expressed in numerous political speeches, tracts, and popular literature, as Chinese people became the targets of violence and political persecution. By the 1870s there were calls for their complete expulsion and exclusion from the country. Anti-Asian sentiment expressed itself not only in terms of a racial hierarchy but also in terms of racial threat. One the one hand, Asians were seen as racial inferiors who would somehow weaken the moral or social fabric of the country; on the other, there was widespread fear that Asians were real threats to white hegemony. One prominent expression of this thinking can be found in an 1880 novel by Pierton W. Dooner titled *The Last Days of the Republic*. In an attempt to alert the country to the Chinese danger, Dooner crafted an emotional story about what would happen to the United States in the event that it did *not* exclude the Chinese. In Dooner's tale, Chinese enter the country quietly as immigrants and, although they appear to be inoffensive, they harbor a master plan to conquer the country. One day, the Chinese collectively rise up and assume control through nefarious means over increasingly large parts of the country. They take over the South and become the new "race problem" (Dooner 1880, 173–174). The Negro, Dooner writes, "faded before this invasion, and gradually but rapidly and noiselessly disappeared" and the labor of those "cheerful, indolent people, [was] quickly and effectually supplied by the sober, industrious Coolie" (173–174). Eventually, "race war" ensues as the Chinese organize a huge army from their immense population and attack the unprepared and naïve whites. The Chinese seize Washington, D.C., raise their flag over the Capitol building, and incorporate the country into their empire. As a result, the "very name of the United States of America" was forever "blotted from the record of nations" (Dooner 1880, 256). Just two years after the publication of Dooner's novel, Congress passed the first of what would be many immigration exclusion acts that restricted Chinese entry into the country and denied the Chinese naturalization privileges.

Japanese immigrants in the early twentieth century found themselves similarly feared as the advanced detachment of a racial threat to the United States. Believed by many European Americans to be depraved, devious, and sinister, they, like the Chinese, were viewed as imperiling the United States. An article in the *San Francisco Chronicle*, February 23, 1907, titled "The Yellow Peril: How the Japanese Crowd Out the White Race," alerted its readers to the impending threat posed by a race of people whose genes made them forever alien and dangerous. The article claimed, "the Asiatic can never be other than an Asiatic, however much he may imitate the dress of the white man, learn his language and spend his wages for him. . . . The Japanese in California is just as intensely, eternally and essentially Japanese as though he had never left Yokoyama or the rice fields of his native country." And, like Dooner in his portrayal of the Chinese, writers warned of an impending Japanese invasion if the country did not wake and take action against Japanese immigrants. One of these fictions was a 1909 book called *The Coming Conflict of Nations: Or, The Japanese-American War: A Narrative*, by Hugh Fitzpatrick. Like Dooner's book, *The Coming Conflict* presents as "history" some possible political and economic developments. The book's narrator looks back from a future vantage point and recounts what supposedly has happened to the country. The book describes the way Japanese immigrants in the United States organize a vast, secret army. It depicts them as allying with the masses in India who revolt against British colonial rule, Filipinos angry at U.S. colonization of their homeland, and Mexicans who help them seize the Southwest and then turn against the United States. The plot goes on to have white U.S. citizens and their white British cousins eventually find common racial cause against the nonwhites and destroy their enemies in a global, brutal war. "Never before in modern history had such stupendous forces gathered for mortal combat. Was this the great battle of Armageddon, long since prophesied?" The book ends with an Anglo-American dominion over the world, hailed, by the author, as the condition "for Christ's transcendent Second Reign" (Fitzpatrick 1909, 220–260, 306).

Though Dooner and Fitzgerald may seem extreme to us today, there were hundreds of similar pieces of writing. This "yellow peril literature," as it is known today, reflected popular sentiment at the time and shared much in common with it. With explicit political messages, this literature portrayed Asians—whether they were of Chinese or Japanese ancestry—as so deeply foreign as to be inassimilable into the U.S. polity. Asians were biologically too distant and different from European Americans or irrevocably alien and undesirable in culture. They were inferiors and yet they also possessed certain features that made them threats to the country: they were ambitious, unknowable, cruel, violent, and thoroughly mendacious. And last, they would be forever loyal to their lands of ancestry, which meant they would be forever suspect. Violence, even war, was always close at hand.

The yellow peril literature was not the expression of a fringe element in society. Rather, it formed part of a broad political movement that resulted in actual federal legislation that limited, and then outlawed, immigration from Asia for much of the late nineteenth century and into the mid-twentieth century. The first major legislation was the Chinese Exclusion Act of 1882. Many other laws followed and were expanded to include other Asians, including those from Japan, Korea, Southeast Asia, the Philippines, and South Asia, as well as individuals from the Pacific islands. These immigration restriction and exclusion laws also prohibited Asian immigrants already in the country from becoming naturalized citizens. Asian immigrants became, in the language of the state, "aliens ineligible to citizenship." Thus was created a race-based category that thoroughly and comprehensively shaped the lives of Asians living in the United States. The category denied them the franchise and participation in the political process, it excluded them from a variety of occupations, it prohibited them in many states from owning property, and it created a social stigma of being legally unwanted in the United States. Denial of naturalization privileges only began to be overturned in 1943 when Chinese were finally given naturalization privileges (until then only whites and persons of African ancestry could become naturalized), and it was not until 1965 that the race-based categories and national origin quotas in U.S. immigration law were completely eliminated. Though the crude, extreme racism of the yellow peril literature has faded in time, many of the underlying prejudices continue as a subcurrent in U.S. culture, as we will see later in this essay.

Yellow peril fears produced much discriminatory federal and local legislation. It also contributed to the most dramatic—and traumatic—policy expression of the belief that Asians were a dangerous racial threat to the country: the internment of Japanese Americans during World War II.

DOMESTIC POLICY AND THE INTERNMENT OF JAPANESE AMERICANS

In its coverage of the Japanese attack on Pearl Harbor on December 7, 1941, *Time* magazine rhetorically asked: what would U.S. citizens "say in the face of the mightiest event of their time?" It then gave the answer: "What they said . . . was: 'Why, the yellow bastards!'" Other commentaries and political cartoons similarly referenced the "yellow peril." In the days following the attack, scores of people of Asian ancestry were physically assaulted throughout the country. A Japanese American farmer and his wife were shot and murdered in their home in the Imperial Valley of California and a Japanese American veteran of World War I was stabbed to death on a Los Angeles street on Christmas Eve. A Chinese American schoolteacher in Seattle's Chinatown was abducted and killed: he was found bound, bludgeoned, and almost beheaded. Authorities speculated that he had been mistakenly believed to be of Japanese ancestry (Dower 1986, 37, 80–81).

The war between the United States and Japan was especially emotional for many in the United States. It was conducted cruelly and brutally and in ways that distinguished it from the hostilities with Germany and Italy, the other enemies of the United States in World War II. From the highest reaches of power in Washington to the GIs fighting on the ground, U.S. citizens harbored the deepest hatred for the Japanese enemy, which was viewed not just as a political/military adversary but also as an especially savage, racial one. The way the war between the United States and Japan started also affected views in the United States of the Japanese government and its people. After years of growing conflict between the two powers over the control of East Asia and the Pacific, Japan launched the attack on the U.S. base in Hawaii in the hopes of disabling U.S. naval power in the Pacific. Though the Japanese government did not intend the attack to be a "surprise"—its declaration of war against the United States was to precede the assault, but problems in communications delayed the delivery—the devastating attack shocked the country and confirmed the long-standing belief in the innate treachery of the Japanese.

At home, Japanese immigrants and their offspring quickly came to be seen by European Americans as extensions of the hated Japanese enemy. As mentioned above, federal law had prevented the immigrant generation from obtaining U.S. citizenship. Even so, their children, born on U.S. soil, did possess citizenship. By the time the war started, two-thirds of Japanese Americans were citizens. To many in the U.S., however, this made no difference. They and their parents were seen as part of the enemy and their loyalty to the country was suspect. They were seen as a danger by virtue of their "blood." For example, U.S. Congressman John Rankin of Mississippi publicly announced, "Once a Jap, always a Jap. You can't any more regenerate a Jap than you can reverse the laws of nature" (Girnder and Loftis 1969, 101), while a prominent journalist wrote in the *Los Angeles Times*, "A viper is a viper wherever the egg is hatched." The deputy district attorney for Los Angeles County even declared that it was not the immigrants from Japan who worried him but rather their more acculturated children who could fool the unsuspecting: "the American-born Japs, not the alien Jap, but the American born. He is the danger" (Grodzins 1949, 120).

Though no evidence supported any suspicion of Japanese Americans collectively as threats to domestic security, U.S. federal policy called for drastic measures against all of them. These focused on a plan to move them en masse from their residences to federally operated internment camps, an idea that even the FBI opposed. In the early spring of 1942, President Franklin Roosevelt authorized the army to round up and move over 110,000 West Coast Japanese Americans, noncitizen and citizen alike, and incarcerate them in facilities in desolate locations far removed from their homes. The justification for such a mass action—unprecedented in U.S. history—was a vaguely defined "military necessity," as federal authorities concluded that the Japanese community in the country could not be trusted. General John L. DeWitt, the military official most responsible for the removal, stated his recommendation for the action this way: "The Japanese race is an enemy race and while many second and third generation Japanese born on United States soil, possessed of United States citizenship, have become "Americanized," the racial strains are undiluted. . . . It, therefore, follows that along the vital Pacific Coast over 112,000 potential enemies, of Japanese extraction, are at large today" (United States Department of War 1943, 34; see also Chang 1995). According to an article in the *San Francisco Chronicle* on March 3, 1942, the Washington state attorney general meanwhile declared that the presence of Japanese Americans placed the West Coast under a condition of "partial invasion." Japanese Americans suffered not just because some people thought they "looked like" the enemy. Rather, in the minds of many European Americans, people of Japanese descent—because of their race—*were* the enemy. The slander was even propagated by Dr. Seuss, a U.S. writer and cartoonist, and the author of the tolerance-promoting children's book *Horton Hears a Who,* in which he writes "A person's a person, no matter how small." In a cartoon Dr. Seuss did during the war, he portrayed a mass of Japanese Americans, indistinguishable from each other, assembling in preparation for doing harm to the United States. The banner under which he depicts them as marching, the "fifth column," referred to the enemy from within in time of war.

No other racial or ethnic group was treated in such a way during the war. Authorities did arrest and detain hundreds of suspect individuals of various other ancestries and backgrounds, but these were all individual cases and due process was strictly followed. Despite the fact that the United States was at war with both Germany and Italy during World War II, the collective loyalties of German Americans and Italian Americans, regardless of citizenship status, were never impugned or suspected. Unlike the Japanese, they were never considered an "enemy race." It was precisely the "racial" difference of the Japanese that made them a target of hatred and discrimination.

But who exactly counted as "Japanese"? The answer seemed simple enough to many in the U.S., but a brief look at the history of internment reveals the fundamental ambiguities, even illogic, of race-based thinking and policy. Federal authorities, for example, required that all persons with even one drop of "Japanese blood" in the western region of the United States submit themselves to what was euphemistically called "evacuation" (Weglyn 1976, 76–77). Persons with as little as one-eighth Japanese ancestry were considered "Japanese." A junior army officer involved in implementing the policy complained about the policy to his superior. In a letter to Captain Astrup dated July 16, 1942 (Japanese American Evacuation and Resettlement Records), H. P. Goebel told of a Mrs. Starr in San Francisco who was "half Japanese, born in Australia.

She married to a non-Japanese. Her son married to non-Japanese. She, her son and her grandchildren all had to be evacuated!" In implementing the order, no exemptions were made for age, gender, health, occupation, marriage partner, or even former honorable service in the U.S. military. For two years into the war, the army refused to accept Japanese Americans who tried to volunteer for service.

People of Japanese ancestry in the western United States were required to turn themselves in at designated "assembly centers" in the early spring of 1942. They could take only what they could carry. Some of the largest of these assembly points were race tracks, such as Santa Anita in Pasadena, which were converted into makeshift detention centers. Horse stalls served as residences for humans for months. Meals were taken at mess halls. By the early summer of 1942, special trains transported the "evacuees," as they were called, to ten long-term internment camps, which were composed of tar-paper barracks, enclosed by barbed wire, and controlled by armed soldiers in watchtowers. These camps became the homes of the Japanese Americans for an undetermined length of time. No one knew how long they would be required to stay and how, or whether, they would get out. Federal officials and employees, who were collectively called the "Caucasians," ran the camps. Curiously, authorities saw the term "Caucasian" as preferable to impersonal administrative titles and believed that it masked their power over the incarcerated population. The term, however, only emphasized the racial chasm.

This internment was an ordeal that tens of thousands of Japanese Americans endured for the entire war. Many elderly and weak of health died during what turned out to be four years of adversity. Guards shot those who strayed too close to the barbed wire. But not everyone lived in the camps for the entire war. As it progressed, federal policy shifted and allowed release for those who could "prove" their loyalty and to those who would serve in the U.S. army. By war's end 30,000 young Japanese Americans entered the army, voluntarily or through the draft, which was resumed for Japanese Americans in 1944. Two thousand served in the Military Intelligence Service and were stationed in the Pacific to help the U.S. military interrogate prisoners and gain information on the enemy. Most, however, served in Europe in the racially segregated 442nd Regimental Combat Team. Commanders believed it would be less confusing to white soldiers if the Japanese American combat troops fought in Europe rather than in the Pacific with its "yellow enemy." White officers commanded the all-Japanese American fighting unit, which distinguished itself for its bravery and sacrifice and became the most highly decorated army unit of its size in U.S. history. Hundreds of Japanese Americans were killed, and thousands were wounded in combat; twenty-one received Congressional Medals of Honor.

Many of the Japanese American soldiers who fought in World War II believed that the racial stigma they faced and that was used to rationalize the internment of their parents and relatives at home could best be challenged through their military service. They, like many others from marginalized communities of color in the country, believed that they had to prove their loyalty and worthiness for full citizenship and social acceptance through martial sacrifice.

Other Japanese Americans, however, responded differently to the choice they were given of military service or internment. Several hundred believed that internment was fundamentally unjust and declared they would not serve in the military or respond to the draft as long as the internment order remained. They did not understand how they could be expected to serve the United States while their families were incarcerated. These resisters tried to make their point through demonstrations and the courts. The authorities responded by convicting them and putting them into military prisons. Yet others believed that internment expressed such deep hatred toward them that they were better off leaving the country altogether. They figured that if the U.S. government was going to treat them as an enemy race, then they would, in turn, reject the United States. By war's end, almost 5,000 immigrants declared their desire to repatriate to Japan. More controversially, some 5,500 U.S.-born renounced their U.S. citizenship. They did so for a variety of reasons: bitterness, desire to avoid the draft, pressure, confusion. One of the citizen renunciants said he did so because it was "the one last thing I could do to express my fury toward the government of the United States" (Kiyota and Keenan 1997, 111–112). With the end of the internment order and the surrender of Japan, though, many of the renunciants asked to void their declaration. Over the next fifteen years, they would struggle to regain their citizenship, which most did by 1959.

The shadow of internment hung over Japanese Americans long after the internment camps finally closed in late 1945. The experience of having been considered an "enemy race" continued to shape their lives, whether they had gone to Japan, protested the unjustness of internment, or just tried to resume a normal life in the postwar United States. By the 1960s, public attitudes toward Japanese Americans had so dramatically shifted that journalists now started to call them a "model minority." Contributing to this change of heart was the transformation of Japan from enemy to Cold War ally. Japan, and by extension, Japanese Americans, were now in favor. The devotion of many Japanese Americans to hard work, sobriety, and political moderation that resulted from their wartime adversity were now all celebrated. Their desire to overcome suspicion and racial stigma had encouraged a patriotism that social commentators praised and used against the social activism of other minorities deemed more threatening to the established order. But Japanese Americans never forgot their wartime experience. Even though for thirty-five years many refused to discuss the war years and appeared to have put the experience of internment behind them, in the 1980s a widely popular movement to demand redress and reparations for internment swept the community. Thousands came forward at government hearings sponsored by a presidential commission that reviewed the wartime experience. After careful study and deliberation, the commission concluded that internment had been a "grave injustice" and that the rationale of "military necessity" was unfounded. Internment, the commission concluded, was itself a product of "race prejudice, war hysteria, and a failure of political leadership." It called on Congress to take steps to redress the past injustice. Eventually, Congress formally apologized to Japanese Americans and authorized monetary restitution to those interned. The legislation has become a benchmark for other continuing efforts to win forms of recompense for grave, historical injustice (Commission on Wartime Relocation 1982).

RACE AND POLITICS IN THE 1996 PRESIDENTIAL CAMPAIGN

One of the most tragic hate murders of an Asian American occurred in 1982 when two white, unemployed Detroit auto workers bludgeoned Vincent Chin to death after their encounter with him at a nightclub where he had held his bachelor's party. They were upset over the growing presence of Japan-made cars in the country and blamed Japanese for "stealing" their jobs. Chin was a young Chinese American, but it made no difference to the killers. Before repeatedly smashing Chin's head with a baseball bat, one of them said, "It is because of you motherfuckers that we're out of work." Instead of witnessing Chin's wedding, the invited guests attended his funeral. Adding further to the outrage of murder, the killers received only probation and a fine of less than $4,000.

Chin's death immediately assumed highly symbolic meaning. It highlighted in a terrible way the smoldering prejudices in the United States that identified Asian Americans as an extension of perceived foreign "enemies." Moreover, it was Chin's racial appearance—not his ancestry (he had been adopted by his parents from China as a baby), nor his citizenship (his father was a veteran of World War II)—that his murderers found objectionable. His was just one of a number of racial hate murders of Asian Americans that has occurred in recent decades; the perception of being foreign and a racial adversary continues to stigmatize those of Asian ancestry (National Asian Pacific American Legal Consortium 2002). Moreover, while Chin's individual murder dramatically highlighted the existence of this form of social prejudice, an incendiary political controversy that erupted during the 1996 presidential campaign revealed the existence of similar attitudes at the highest levels of politics in the country.

In the years after Chin's killing, Asian Americans who wanted to overturn the stigma of being viewed as "perpetually alien" encouraged active involvement in U.S. politics. What could better confirm one's U.S. identity than visible participation in the democratic process? In the 1980s and 1990s, increasing numbers of Asian Americans ran for office, served in political campaigns, and raised funds for candidates at local and national levels. However, the results of their efforts to overturn suspicion and the perception of aloofness were the reverse of their hopes.

In 1995–96, the national Democratic Party had identified Asian Americans as an important source of fund-raising and began to target Asian American donors specifically. President Bill Clinton's reelection team even included several Asian Americans to help with the effort, which succeeded in bringing in several million dollars. A scandal about unethical and illegal donations broke out, however, that focused on Asian American donations and on allegations that Chinese nationals were trying to influence the presidential election. At one point, the Justice Department had 120 attorneys and investigators looking into the allegations. In addition, both the Senate and the House held public hearings—the more extensive one being conducted by the Senate Committee on Governmental Affairs chaired by Senator Fred Thompson of Tennessee. The hearings opened with much fanfare about "hard evidence" regarding Chinese influence peddling, but despite four hundred subpoenas, two hundred interviews, thirty-three days of hearings, and seventy witnesses, the final report failed to substantiate the initial incendiary claims. The Democratic National Committee (DNC) itself conducted a special audit of its funds and scrutinized donors with

Asian-sounding surnames. The DNC later apologized for insensitivity in its aggressive review. In the end, several low-level Asian American fund-raisers connected to the DNC were convicted of violating campaign finance laws and several million dollars of donations were returned (Wu and Lim Youngberg 2001, 311–353).

The handling of the scandal again revealed the persistence of popular assumptions about Asian American foreignness and racial connections to a threatening power. Here are a few examples from the popular discourse on the controversy and, though many of these were offhand remarks, they point to the existence of sentiments that the guarded, formal language of everyday politics usually mask:

- Candidate Ross Perot in a campaign speech at the University of Pennsylvania told his audience, "Now then, Mr. Huang [one of the DNC fund-raisers under suspicion] is still out there hard at work for the Democrats. Wouldn't you like to have someone out there named O'Reilly? Out there hard at work. You know, so far we haven't found an American name."

- During the congressional hearings, politicians peppered their comments with pidgin that mocked Asian names and expressions. One senator, for example, said that Huang's salary depended on his efforts, saying "no raise money, no get bonus" and "two Huangs don't make a right." "Illegal donations are apparently only the tip of the eggroll," another politician declared. Representative Tom DeLay from Texas stated that a political candidate should probably be able to tell if contributions were coming from a foreign source, which was illegal, if one scrutinized donor names. "If you have a friend by the name of Arief and Soraya," for example, "and I cannot even pronounce the last name, Wiriadinata or something like that, who donated . . . and was friends with a guy named Johnny Huang . . . then there's a high probability that it's money from foreign nationals. . . . I could go on with John Lee and Cheon Am, Yogesh Ghandi, Ng Lap Seng, Supreme Master Suma China Hai and George Psaltis."

- The March 24, 1997, cover of the conservative magazine *National Review* featured a picture of what it referred to as "The Manchurian Candidates." It depicted President and Mrs. Clinton and Vice President Gore with caricatured Asian facial features, including buck teeth, slanted eyes, and a queue, dressed in stereotypical Chinese garb.

- An article in the *New York Times Magazine* stated satirically, "This fear of Asians isn't all bad. If riding a few Asians out of Washington on a rail helps generate support for campaign finance reform, well then, hitch up the ponies, giddyap!"
- Matt Fong, a Republican who ran for the Senate from California and was the state's treasurer, was asked by reporters for a major news magazine which side he would fight on in the event of war with China. Fong is a fourth-generation Chinese American, a graduate of the United States Air Force Academy, and a retired lieutenant colonel in the Air Force. Fong, shocked by the question, refused to respond to the insult.

The investigation into Asian American donations to the Clinton campaign had a chilling effect on Asian political involvement. Journalists reported that the White House backed away from appointing Asian Americans to White House positions because of the scandal. Chang Lin Tien, chancellor of the University of California, Berkeley, at the time, who had been a front-runner for a cabinet post before the scandal, was passed over for the appointment. Tien would have been the first Asian American in a presidential cabinet. Even the Japanese American former congressman Norman Mineta reportedly was dropped from consideration for a cabinet post because of the racial connection (Wu and Lim Youngberg 2001, 324). The campaign finance episode continues to haunt Asian Americans, many of whom wonder if the shadow of "foreignness" will ever be lifted.

LOOKING TOWARD THE FUTURE

The episodes discussed above have passed, but we have not completely left them behind. History is always with us, for what is the present if not the expression of what has come before? Put another way, we can illuminate the present by understanding what we have inherited.

To be sure, the episodes discussed above do not capture the entirety of Asian American experiences or how they have been perceived; the problem of race relationships and racial thinking in the United States is complex and multifaceted. Even so, the purpose of this essay has been to expand the way we might think about race by encouraging consideration of how international relations affect domestic policies. The yellow peril literature of the late nineteenth and early twentieth centuries was created in response to immigration and helped shape the United States' relationship with the nations of China and Japan. The internment of Japanese Americans in World War II highlights a domestic consequence of this international conflict. (Given more space, this essay might include consideration of the involvement of the United States in many other long and brutal wars in Asia, including in the Philippines, China, Korea, and Vietnam. Certainly, race was inextricably involved in all these conflicts—from the decision to engage in hostilities to the ways the wars were conducted, the perceptions of the enemy, and the consequences of these wars on Asians and others in the United States.) Moreover, the campaign finance scandal reveals how events can trigger the release of a racially tinged political discourse about foreignness and citizenship that may lie just beneath the surface of social pleasantries.

The United States' political discourse has come a long way from the time when leading citizens like Benjamin Franklin could muse about racial preferences in ways that would clearly be unacceptable today. Nevertheless, Asian Americans have reason to be concerned that they remain "strangers from a different shore" (to evoke the title of Ronald Takaki's popular history of Asian Americans) in the hearts of many in the country. We do not often hear expressions of the biological racism of the pre–World War II years now, but the more current "cultural racism," with its assumptions about deep, indelible, and incompatible cultural differences that separate people, is in full evidence. Witness much of the current furor about Asian (and of course Latino) immigration and the growing presence of Asian Americans in many spheres of U.S. life. To what extent, many Asian Americans wonder, is full acceptance in the United States based on race? How can the stigma of foreignness be left behind? Is there a continuing underlying suspicion of Asians that can explode in the event of international crisis?

The current fascination on the part of U.S. business with China's economic development has encouraged an unprecedented interest in Chinese language and culture. On the one hand, this has opened opportunities in the business world for many Chinese Americans, On the other, it has also stimulated anxiety among Chinese Americans about increasing condemnation by some in the United States of China's growing influence in the world. Commentators warn of the economic and military rivalry between China and the United States, while periodic reports from national security officials in Washington suggest that Washington sees China as its main geopolitical competitor in the world. Even respected journals such as the *Atlantic Monthly* talk openly about a "coming conflict" with China; its June 2005 cover story shows ominous

Chinese military personnel beneath the title, "How We Would Fight China" (Kaplan 2005; see also "America's Fear of China" 2007).[1]

In recent years there has been much attention to "globalization" and the spread of cosmopolitanism around the world. Simultaneously, forms of racism, ethnic and national chauvinism, xenophobia, and other extremist ideologies and practices closely associated with racism, have arisen for a variety of reasons: in reaction to the challenges and ambiguities of the increased interconnectedness of us all; as efforts to retain hierarchies and inequalities of power; to impose hegemony over an unruly world. Unfortunately, as regards "race," the future seems to hold peril as well as promise.

Works Cited

•

America's Fear of China. 2007. *The Economist,* 19 May.

Babbin, Jed, and Edward Timperlake. 2006. *Showdown: Why China Wants War with the United States.* Washington: Regnery.

Bernstein, Richard, and Ross H. Munro. 1998. *The Coming Conflict with China.* New York: Vintage.

Chang, Gordon H. 1995. *Morning Glory, Evening Shadow: The Wartime Writings of Yamato Ichihashi, 1942–1945.* Palo Alto, CA: Stanford University Press.

Commission on Wartime Relocation and Internment of Civilians. 1982. *Personal Justice Denied: Report of the Commission on Wartime Relocation and Internment of Civilians.* Washington, D.C.: U.S. Government Printing Office. December.

Dooner, Pierton W. 1880. *The Last Days of the Republic.* San Francisco: Alta California Publishing House.

Dower, John W. 1986. *War without Mercy: Race and Power in the Pacific War.* New York: Pantheon Books.

Fitzpatrick, Ernest Hugh. 1909. *The Coming Conflict of Nations or the Japanese-American War: A Narrative.* Springfield, IL.: H. W. Rokker.

Franklin, Benjamin. [1751] 1961. Observations Concerning the Increase of Mankind, Peopling of Countries, etc. In *Papers of Benjamin (Vol. 4): July 1, 1750–June 30, 1753*, edited by Leonard W. Labaree. New Haven: Yale University Press.

Girnder, Audrie, and Anne Loftis. 1969. *The Great Betrayal: The Evacuation of the Japanese-Americans during World War II.* New York: Macmillan.

---

1 In recent years, a flood of books has predicted war with China, much of it similar in tone to the yellow peril literature, as seen in some of the following titles: *The Coming Conflict with China* (Bernstein and Munro 1998), *Red Dragon Rising: Communist China's Military Threat to America* (Timperlake and Triplett 2002), *Showdown: Why China Wants War with the United States* (Babbin and Timperlake 2006), and *Unrestricted Warfare: China's Master Plan to Destroy America* (Liang et al. 2002).

Grant, Madison. 1921. *Passing of the Great Race: or, The Racial Basis of European History*. New York: Scribner.

Grodzins, Morton. 1949. *Americans Betrayed: Politics and the Japanese Evacuation*. Chicago: University of Chicago Press.

Japanese American Evacuation and Resettlement Records, 1930–1974. Bancroft Library, University of California, Berkeley.

Jordan, David Starr. 1910. *The Blood of the Nation: A Study of the Decay of Races through the Survival of the Unfit*. Boston: American Unitarian Association.

Kaplan, Robert D. 2005. How We Would Fight China. *Atlantic Monthly*, June.

Kiyota, Minoru, and Linda K. Keenan. 1997. *Beyond Loyalty: The Story of a Kibei*. Honolulu: University of Hawaii Press. Quoted in Mae Ngai. 2004. *Impossible Subjects: Illegal Aliens and the Making of America*. Princeton, NJ: Princeton University Press.

Liang, Qiao, Wang Xiangsui, and Al Santoli. 2002. *Unrestricted Warfare: China's Master Plan to Destroy America*. West Palm Beach: NewsMax Media.

London, Jack. 1910. The Yellow Peril. In *Revolution and Other Essays*. New York: Macmillan.

National Asian Pacific American Legal Consortium. 2002. *Audit of Violence against Asian Pacific Americans, 2002: Remembering: A Ten-Year Retrospective*. Los Angeles: National Asian Pacific American Legal Consortium.

Stoddard, Lathrop. 1920. *The Rising Tide of Color against White World-Supremacy*. New York: Charles Scribner's Sons.

Takaki, Ronald. 1989. *Strangers from a Different Shore: A History of Asian Americans*. New York: Little, Brown.

Timperlake, Edward, and William C. Triplett. 2002. *Red Dragon Rising: Communist China's Military Threat to America*. Washington: Regnery Publishing.

United States Department of War. 1943. Final Recommendation of the Commanding General, Western Defense Command and Fourth Army, submitted to the Secretary of War, February 14, 1942, in United States Department of War. *Final Report: Japanese Evacuation from the West Coast*. Washington, DC: U.S. Government Printing Office.

Weglyn, Michi. 1976. *Years of Infamy: The Untold Story of America's Concentration Camps*. New York: William Morrow.

Wu, Frank H., and Francey Lim Youngberg. 2001. People from China Crossing the River: Asian American Political Empowerment and Foreign Influence. In *Asian Americans and Politics: Perspectives, Experiences, Prospects*. Washington, DC: Woodrow Wilson Center Press.

8

A Thoroughly Modern Concept
Ethnic Cleansing, Genocide, and the State

Norman M. Naimark

•

Although inter-ethnic group violence has been a persistent aspect of social life across time, the twentieth century was unique in its perpetration of mass killings. Using examples from East Central Europe, Bosnia, Germany, and Armenia, this essay defines ethnic cleansing and differentiates it from genocide: ethnic cleansing is undertaken to drive people off their land, while genocide is the intentional killing of all or part of a people. After discussing the origins of ethnic cleansing in Europe during the twentieth century, the essay provides some prominent examples and develops a taxonomy of ethnic cleansing. It concludes with the observation that the traces of ethnic cleansing can be seen in every society, and its potentiality is part of all of us.

SINCE 2003, IN THE NORTH AFRICAN COUNTRY OF SUDAN, HUNDREDS of thousands of black African Muslims in the Darfur region have been subjected to rape, murder, and torture. Many more have had their livestock and household goods stolen and their lands seized. Meanwhile, in refugee camps in Chad and western Darfur, members of the Fur and other native peoples of the region have suffered and died in the tens of thousands from disease, exposure, and malnutrition, as some two million people have been displaced from their homes. The perpetrators of these crimes are armed Arab militias, known as Janjaweed ("devils on horseback"), who are widely believed to have the secret backing of the Sudanese government. The Janjaweed, who refer to their victims as "slaves," have committed these horrendous crimes both to punish their victims and to terrorize them into fleeing their native lands. Some label the conflict an instance of ethnic cleansing, by which they mean an attack on people for the purpose of driving them out of their native homes. Others, however, consider it genocide or intentional mass murder. Whatever one calls the conflict, international intervention is desperately needed but has been complicated both by the opposition of the Sudanese government and its allies and by the frustrating context of interconnected civil wars.

WHAT IS ETHNIC CLEANSING?

"Ethnic cleansing" came into the common lexicon of terms for social violence during the war in Bosnia in the spring and summer of 1992 (Gutman 1993). This complex war involved several ethnically defined groups of belligerents within Bosnia and Herzegovina: Bosnian Muslims/Bosniaks, Serbs, and Croats. Journalists, human rights activists, and Western politicians used the term to characterize attacks on Bosnian Muslims by Serbs. The idea was to drive the Muslims out of targeted Bosnian territory claimed by the Serbs. Eventually, the term was also applied to similar attacks by Croats against Bosnian Muslims. In the winter and spring of 1999–2000, the term "ethnic cleansing" was even more commonly applied to the attacks of Serbs against Kosovar Albanians. What Serbs defended as a counterinsurgency campaign against the KLA (Kosovo Liberation Army) was characterized by the international community as ethnic cleansing (Power 2002).

Is Ethnic Cleansing the Same as Genocide?

From the outset of the war in former Yugoslavia, commentators challenged the validity of the term "ethnic cleansing"; some viewed it as a euphemism for genocide. But a separate term is useful because it indicates a fundamentally different kind of criminal action against a group of "others." Genocide is the intentional mass murder of part of or all of an ethnic religious or national group; the elimination of a distinct people is the objective. Ethnic cleansing, by contrast, is the intentional removal of a people and, in most cases, of all traces of them from a concrete piece of territory. The goal is to get rid of the "alien" group and seize control of the territory they inhabit. Genocide and ethnic cleansing occupy adjacent positions on a spectrum of attacks on national, religious, and ethnic groups (Semelin 2005).

The definition of genocide was initially developed by the Polish-Jewish scholar Raphael Lemkin during World War II. Due in good part to his phenomenal efforts, the crime of genocide was recognized by the UN Convention on the Prevention and Punishment of the Crime of Genocide of December 9, 1948. The Convention's definition of genocide, which underlined the intentionality of the mass murder of part or all of a particular ethnic, religious, or national group, was later upheld in and refined by the International Courts formed for the purpose of trying criminals from the wars in former Yugoslavia and Rwanda (Schabas 2000). A new term was needed to describe an activity that has as its primary intention getting people to move off their land—forced deportation or "population transfer." The means by which this is accomplished occupy an arc of the legal to the semi-legal. As in the case of determining first-degree murder, intentionality is the critical distinction in deciding whether a conflict should be identified as ethnic cleansing or genocide.

Complicating the distinction between the two, forced deportation often takes place in the violent context of war, civil war, or aggression. In only the rarest cases do people peacefully leave their homes. Their families have deep roots in the locales, and their ancestors are buried in local graveyards. Their cultures are tied to the land that they and their forbears cultivated. The result is that forced deportation, even in times of peace, can quickly turn into campaigns of violence, as native inhabitants are ripped from their home villages and towns, terrorized into going, and killed when they try to stay. In this way, ethnic cleansing can easily turn genocidal. Michael Mann, in fact, thinks of genocide as a subcategory of "murderous ethnic cleansing" (2005).

Origins of the Term

The term "ethnic cleansing" has different meanings within different linguistic traditions. In its Slavic forms, "cleansing" (*chishchenie* in Russian, and *ciscenja* in Serbian and Croatian) often refers to political elimination or the purging of enemies. The purges or *chistki* of the Soviet Union provide a poignant example. The German word for cleansing, *Säuberung*, is also often used in the history of communism to indicate the purging of party ranks. *Säuberung* is also tied to the development of racial "science" in Germany at the turn of the twentieth century. Eugenics itself, as it came to maturity at the beginning of the twentieth century, was about racial cleansing, *Säuberung*, though its implications were not necessarily genocidal (Weitz 2003). In both Slavic and German usages, "cleansing" has a dual meaning: one purges the social community of foreign bodies, and one purges one's own people of alien elements. This latter association, which emphasizes self-purging, accounts in some measure for the fearsome up-close killing and barbarous mutilation of neighbors and acquaintances that characterizes a number of cases of ethnic cleansing.

The term "ethnic" derives from the Greek word for nation, "ethnos," but in its current usage, the word now refers to a specific group of people—what we call today an "ethnic group." Some uses of the term, especially in Europe and Russia, tend to be pejorative, meaning that the group involved is something less than a nation or nationality. There are ethnic studies programs and ethnic theme houses on American campuses without any sense of this negative connotation. In any case, no pejorative meaning is intended here. It is also important to point out that an "ethnic group" or "ethnicity" is extremely hard to define. Often the contours of an ethnicity are delineated by a dominant group that wishes to create or identify a clear "other" that does not exist. The borders of ethnicity are constantly shifting. Who is included and excluded has little to do with "objective" categories, since any categories we might use—race, religion, skin color, and so on—are themselves socially constructed and reified by their repeated application. The way these categories come to be defined is usually through history itself (Eley and Suny 1996). Moreover, ethnic cleansing and genocide often end up creating categories of ethnicity and nationality while, at the same time, perpetrators solidify these categories by expelling and murdering those they identify as belonging to these groups.

Is Ethnic Cleansing a "Modern" Phenomenon?

Scholars argue about the "modernity" of ethnic cleansing. Can it be traced back to the origins of human history or does it have a primarily twentieth-century character (Weitz 2003)? There are abundant examples from the ancient world, documented in both Homer and the Bible, where ancient nations attack "others" for the purposes of expulsion (Bell-Fialkoff 1996). The medieval and early modern world saw countless examples of sometimes murderous expulsions: the Jews in Spain (1492), the Albigensians in France (1209 and following), the Incas and Aztecs in the Americas (sixteenth century), and the Herrero and Nama peoples in Southwest Africa by German colonial forces (1904–05). Later, the settler and government attacks on North American Indians, Australian aborigines, and African peoples by their colonial oppressors could also be classified as ethnic cleansing. The "Trail of Tears" indicates the heavy losses to the Cherokee Nation on the long and treacherous road they were forced to traverse in the winter of 1838–39 from their homes in northwest Georgia to the Indian Territory, which is now the eastern part of the state of Oklahoma.

Certainly the twentieth century brought with it aspects of modernity that made ethnic cleansing more virulent, more complete, more pervasive, and more full of hate. The development of the nation-state and the end of empires gave the state unprecedented power and means for attacking and transferring large minority populations. The drive of modern states to categorize and homogenize their populations contributed to this phenomenon, as did the intolerance for political, social, and economic anomalies within their societies (Scott 1998). The development of integral nationalism at the end of the nineteenth century emphasized the racial content of national groups. Civic or political ideas of nationalism weakened; questions of ethnic essentialism became dominant. No longer was it enough to live, act, and speak like the dominant nationality to be a member of that group. Importance was now placed on "blood ties" and identifiable racial characteristics. Modern "ethnic entrepreneurs," politicians ready to exploit ethnic and national distinctions for the purposes of gaining and consolidating power, played an important role (Valentino 2004). The modern media made possible the fast and widespread dissemination of nationalist images and racial stereotypes. "Industrial murder" during World War I served as the backdrop for a century of ethnic cleansing and genocide (Bartov 1996).

ETHNIC CLEANSING IN THE TWENTIETH CENTURY

Prominent cases of ethnic cleansing in the twentieth century underline its modern character. In 1915, the Western-educated and modernizing young Turk government, concerned about the disintegration of the formerly great Ottoman Empire during World War I, attempted to bolster the idea and reality of a unified Turkish realm. This eventuated in a horrendous attack on the Armenian population (a generally financially strong Christian minority group). Many Armenian men were placed under arrest or killed right off; the rest of the population was forced to trek through the Anatolian highlands across the Euphrates river to Mesopotamia. These death marches ended in the first widely recognized case of genocide in the twentieth century. Questions remain about the causes of the genocide. Scholars disagree about the extent to which the deportations were instigated as a result of long-term planning on the part of the Turks or short-term reactions to military defeats, threats of partition, and Armenian uprisings during World War I (Bloxham 2005). The Turkish government continues to deny that there was genocide, which deeply offends Armenians who, like all people who have suffered the massive loss of land, life, and dignity, feel a need for their suffering to be acknowledged and recorded.

In 1921–22, Mustapha Kemal (Ataturk) responded to a Greek invasion from the Peloponnese by driving close to a million native Ottoman Greeks out of Anatolia. In this case, the Greeks were clearly subjected by the government of the infant Turkish Republic to ethnic cleansing and not to genocide. Although several hundred thousand Greeks died in the process of expulsion and resettling, the Turks aimed to forcibly deport the Greeks, not to kill them. In fact, the Lausanne Treaty of 1923 completed the process of removal by insisting on a population transfer of the remaining Greeks in Anatolia and the Turks in Greece. To this day, Lausanne remains an important precedent for the supposedly beneficial process of population exchange under international supervision.

Hitler's assault on the Jews began as a campaign of forced deportation and ethnic cleansing of the Jews from Germany and Europe. There was even a serious plan before the war to remove all the European Jews to Madagascar. Of course, this was meant as no favor to the Jews. The Nazis calculated that most would perish of disease and hunger (Jansen 1997). Given Hitler's murderous anti-Semitic ideology and the outbreak of World War II, the Nazi rhetoric of a "final solution" quickly mutated into a program of systematic mass murder and genocide, which we know today as the Holocaust. Especially when the Third Reich invaded the Soviet Union on June 22, 1941, most of the remaining restraints were removed from engaging in the large-scale massacres of Jews. Starting primarily with the execution of Jewish men in July and August 1941, SS units (the *Einsatzgruppen*) began massacring Jews of all ages and sexes by the early fall. At the Wannsee Conference in January 1942, the Nazis' bureaucracy focused its genocidal efforts on the construction of death camps and the elimination of the Jews in gas chambers. The result was concentration camps like Auschwitz and the mass murder of the European Jews.

Ethnic cleansing was characteristic of Stalinist policies toward a number of peoples within the Soviet Union. The case of the Chechens is the most notable, since the violent reverberations of that struggle continue to plague the Russian state and the Chechen people today. In February 1944, Stalin and his deputy, Lavrentii Beria, asserted that the Chechens and the Ingush, closely related nations of the Northern Caucasus, had collaborated with the Nazis and therefore should be removed from their homelands to the reaches of Central Asia. During the war, this fate befell other small nations of the Soviet Union also accused of collaboration, including the Crimean Tatars, the Balkars, the Karachaevtsy, and Kalmyks. These forced deportations are difficult to classify as genocide according to the 1948 UN definition since there was no demonstrable intent on the part of Stalin and Beria to kill large numbers of the deportees. Nevertheless, the brutal processes of the forced deportation of an entire people—in the case of the Chechens and Ingush, some 480,000 men, women, and children; their harsh transfer in closed, unsanitary freight cars; and their involuntary resettlement to barren and hostile lands in Kazakhstan—served as the source of substantial mortality. Close to 40 percent of the Chechen and Ingush peoples died in the course of this deportation and resettlement. The other "punished peoples" of the Northern Caucasus and Crimea fared little better. (Nekrich 1978).

At the end of World War II, the Polish and Czechoslovak governments decided to forcibly deport their respective German populations, together over 11.5 million people. This constituted the largest single case of ethnic cleansing in modern European history. No sooner were the Jews and other Nazi victims liberated from German camps than Germans themselves were detained in the same barracks. In the process of being forced from their domiciles, detained, and expelled from their homelands, as many as two million Germans may have died, mostly from disease, exposure, and malnutrition. There is considerable controversy in Germany, not to mention Poland and the Czech Republic, over whether to build a museum in Berlin to memorialize these victims of ethnic cleansing. The "Germans," after all, were ultimately responsible for the circumstances that prompted the deportation of their co-nationals. This also complicates the moral calculus of ethnic cleansing more generally; the victims are sometimes perpetrators. Moreover, the Potsdam Treaty of July–August 1945 provided an international imprimatur, on the model of Lausanne, for the "transfer" of the Germans from Poland and Czechoslovakia to occupied Germany and Austria. Despite the apparent legality of the transfer, there can be no question that many innocent Germans suffered the brutal consequences of this ethnic cleansing.

It was, as noted above, the war in Bosnia from 1992 to 1995 that gave "ethnic cleansing" its currency as a term for mass expulsion and killing. The international community appeared helpless as Serb militias attacked Bosnian Muslim civilians and expelled them from their homes. Bosnian Croats also attacked the Muslims. In Bosnia, Serb militias engaged in rape and mass rape, both to punish their victims for their very existence and to terrorize them and their families into fleeing their native territories. Animals were slaughtered, crops destroyed, and houses burned to the ground to ensure that the Muslims would not return. Altogether in Bosnia, some 250,000 people were killed and nearly two million displaced. During the war of 1991–92 between Serbia and Croatia, both nationalities engaged in the ethnic cleansing of the other, with the Serbs committing the worst crimes (Silber and Little 1995). In 1995, the Croats attacked Serbs in Krajina and drove them out of their homelands in Croatia in a campaign of ethnic cleansing. Later, in 1998–99, the Serbs tried to ethnically cleanse Kosovo of its majority Albanian population. After the Serbs lost the war in Kosovo, Kosovar Albanians turned the tables on the Serbs and engaged in scattered campaigns of ethnic cleansing against their former persecutors.

The International Criminal Tribunal for the Former Yugoslavia (ICTY) has attempted to bring to justice the leading perpetrators of war crimes and crimes against humanity during the conflagration in the Balkans. Serbs, Croats, and even some Bosnian Muslims and Kosovar Albanians have stood trial and been convicted of war crimes, many of which were associated with ethnic cleansing. When in July 1995 Bosnian Serb army units took control of the UN "safe area" of Srebrenica from the Dutch troops who were responsible for its protection, they massacred some 7,500 to 8,000 Bosnian Muslim men and boys and buried them in mass graves scattered around the region. This outraged the international community and led directly to serious NATO intervention in late August and September 1995. The ICTY has ruled that the Srebrenica massacre was a case of genocide, as distinct from the ethnic cleansing that had taken place up to that point in Bosnia. The court upheld the prosecutor's case that the Srebrenica massacre was carried out with the intention not just of killing Bosnian Muslims but of killing off a part of the Bosnian nation. The former Serbian leader Slobodan Milosevic was in the process of being tried for genocide and for crimes associated with ethnic cleansing when he died in The Hague on March 12, 2006. In all likelihood, given the evidence presented, he would have been convicted of having been an accomplice in genocide and not of the crime of genocide itself.

TAXONOMY OF ETHNIC CLEANSING

Cases of ethnic cleansing share six fundamental characteristics: (1) they take place under the cover of war; (2) they involve extreme applications of violence; (3) they target, in particular, women and children; (4) they destroy the victims' cultural artifacts; (5) they involve crimes against property as well as people; and (6) they seek to expel all members of the ethnic, religious, or national group.

Ethnic cleansing often takes place during periods of war or during the transition from war to peace. War provides a cover for political leaders to eliminate groups they are less likely to attack in peacetime. During war there is military censorship of the civilian press and complete control of transportation and communications. The militaries themselves are often implicated in ethnic cleansing and genocide. Though few combatants really acclimate to death, soldiers are accustomed to following orders, killing, and seeing dead bodies around them. Semi-autonomous paramilitary formations frequently do much of the damage, as seen in the case of Bosnia, the Armenian genocide, and the expulsion of the Greeks. Some paramilitary groups, like the Nazi SS units and the Soviet NKVD troops, are more directly employed by the state to carry out ethnic cleansing operations. War provides a strategic argument (Melson 1992). For example, the Armenians were accused of collaborating with the Russians; the Greeks with the British; the Tatars and Chechens with the Nazis; the Bosnian Muslims with the Turks and mujahadin; and the Jews simultaneously with Wall Street capital and with Bolshevism! These accusations of collaboration sometimes had a basis in fact, though in no case was it sufficient to justify forced deportation and genocide.

Although taking place during war, the violence of ethnic cleansing has a different character from that of warfare. In classic combat, men in military formations are grouped against each other and fight with guns and machines in a more or less reciprocal exchange. In ethnic cleansing, armed perpetrators usually attack unarmed civilians. Those who are conducting the "cleansing" have complete power over the other, producing a variety of brutal and sadistic practices that have little relation to the normal rules of military engagement. The perpetrators burn down homes, rape women and girls, beat helpless victims, and steal indiscriminately. In the process of dislodging peoples from their homes and their homelands, every cruelty—maiming, branding, torture—has been used. The sad truth of ethnic cleansing is that violence perpetrated against unarmed civilians is usually more devastatingly inhumane than the violence perpetrated against military opponents.

The violence of ethnic cleansing is also usually directed against women, children, and the elderly. Men of military age are often absent from the towns and villages, having fled to fight in another place, having emigrated with the intention of bringing families later, or having been captured, interned, or executed. The gendered quality of ethnic cleansing is notable, as is the misogyny. Unarmed women and girls are attacked and brutalized in almost every case. The history of rape, mass rape, and rape-murder in Bosnia-Herzegovina, where some 50,000 rapes are said to have taken place, was typical of many similar cases of ethnic cleansing around the world (Naimark 2001, 169). Females are targeted both as the biological source of the future of ethnic groups and as the bearers and teachers of national cultural values. They tend to be the primary victims of ethnic cleansing, as men are the major victims of warfare between militaries.

It is never sufficient in ethnic cleansing simply to expel a people from the territory they inhabit. Their physical and cultural monuments and artifacts are also targeted for destruction. Serbs routinely blew up mosques and desecrated Muslim graveyards; in Banja Luka alone, fourteen mosques were destroyed, two of them from the seventeenth century. Turks tried to destroy the remnants of Armenian and Greek civilizations in Anatolia. The Nazis burned synagogues, destroyed holy books, and used Jewish gravestones to pave streets. The Soviets destroyed Chechen graveyards, using the gravestones for factory floors. They also eliminated the names of Chechen towns and villages as well as of the Chechen autonomous province itself, carving up the former Chechen territory among its geographical neighbors. In Poland and Czechoslovakia, not only were German place names changed and German cultural monuments destroyed, but engravings in German were chiseled off tombstones, public buildings, and private homes. The idea is that no traces should be left of the national groups that once lived in the designated area. The groups that are ethnically cleansed are also written out of history, or else histories are rewritten to denigrate their roles in the region they formally inhabited.

As we have seen, there is nothing "clean" about ethnic cleansing. It is shot through with violence and brutality of the most extreme sort. But ethnic cleansing is also associated with crimes against property as well as people—that is, stealing and theft, both on the part of the state and of individuals. Although the motivations for the expulsions are

primarily political and ideological, not economic, the victims nevertheless were generally rich—Greeks, Armenians, Jews, Chechens-Ingush,
Germans, Bosnians, and Kosovar Albanians—and indeed had become
rich by exploiting their dominant neighbors. The idea was that those
cleansed deserved to be robbed and to have their land and goods ex-
propriated. Armenian property was seized by local Ottoman officials
and placed in warehouses, ostensibly to be returned to the Armenians
after their exile had ended. But this property, often quite substantial,
was quickly divided among the state, local officials, and rapacious individuals. Under the Nazis, the Jews had to pay and keep paying, first to
avoid deportation, then to avoid the ghettos, and then to survive in the
ghettos. Jewish property had long been seized by the state, Aryanized, or
destroyed when guards and SS overseers continued to rob the Jews and
violently collect their valuables on the way to the camps. In both Poland
and Czechoslovakia, the Germans were stolen blind. Even on regular
transports organized by the Allies after the end of World War II, Polish
and Czech customs officials boarded the trains and stole the Germans'
property. In the former Yugoslavia, Bosnian Muslims were beaten and
robbed repeatedly on their way out of their villages and towns. The Serb
paramilitaries were particularly well known for their rapacious attempts
to extort money and jewelry from their Muslims victims before allowing
them to leave for safe territory.

Ethnic cleansing is a totalistic process that allows no exceptions to
those deported. The implication of the very word cleansing is the idea
of eliminating all alleged impurities. Everyone has to go. This is related
to the modern state and its ability to identify and track down members
of the targeted ethnic group. It also derives from the modern state's
definition of ethnicity that makes no provisions for the real ambiguity and indeterminacy of the concept of "ethnic group." In the Soviet
passport, for example, the state recorded citizenship, USSR, and the
nationality or ethnic group. Those with Chechen or Ingush in their
passports in 1944 were deported, whether they were rural mountain-
eers, party leaders, army fighters, or heroes of the Soviet Union. No one
of Jewish background, no matter how Germanized and thoroughly
Christian, could escape the fatal implications of the Nazi racial laws.
In Poland and Czechoslovakia after the war, courts were set up to determine who was a German and who was not (Frommer 2005). Birth
and baptismal certificates were the crucial documents involved. The
Silesians of Poland—most of whom identified neither as Poles nor as
Germans, but rather as Silesians—were forced to chose. If German, they

had to go; if Polish, they could stay, and, from the Polish point of view, be "re-Polonized" (Madajczyk 1994).

WHAT DOES THE FUTURE HOLD?

As the case of Darfur demonstrates, there is no reason to assume that the history of ethnic cleansing in the twentieth century will not recur in the twenty-first. There is the threat of the ethnic cleansing of Serbs by Kosovar Albanians, once the independence of Kosovo is achieved. Iraq could well be a prime location of ethnic cleansing if the country is partitioned, as advocated by some policy makers, into Sunni, Shiite, and Kurdish territories. In Georgia, Indonesia, and Afghanistan, among other trouble spots in Eurasia, ethnic cleansing remains a major threat to minority nations. Political elites continue to use nationalist platforms to mobilize their populations and maintain their power against potential rivals. The mass media are employed to create historical images of national humiliation and suffering of the dominant nation. Stories of just revenge and retribution are promoted as a way to keep nationalist goals in public view. Even in Western Europe, the proliferation of nationalist rhetoric against minority peoples in general, and Muslim immigrants in particular, means that ethnic cleansing is not removed from potential historical agendas.

The international community remains today incapable of preventing, interdicting, or ending ethnic cleansing, just as it was in the twentieth century. Newspapers around the world in 1915 were filled with stories about the horrors of the Armenian genocide. Yet nothing was done to stop the killing, except for the protests of individuals, like the American ambassador, Henry Morgenthau, who tried in vain to get the American government involved. Similarly, the Greek "Catastrophe" was well known to Western governments. The British and Americans even had troops and naval vessels in the vicinity of the most serious violence. But the best they could do was to evacuate some of the victims and provide relief efforts once they arrived in Greece. As the threat to the Jews became more serious at the end of the 1930s, very few governments, the United States included, were willing to take in the increasing flow of Jewish refugees. At the same time, World War II was not fought in order to stop the persecution and mass murder of the Jews. Efforts to get Allied governments to bomb railroad lines to the death camps fell on deaf ears. We should also be clear about the fact that the 1946 Nuremberg Trials were more about trying the perpetrators of Nazi aggression than they were about prosecuting German war criminals who had engaged in genocide and ethnic cleansing.

A few journalists and politicians complained publicly about the ethnic cleansing by the Poles and Czechs of the Germans after the war. But on the whole, save for the Germans themselves, international society was relatively indifferent to the plight of the cleansed Germans. The forced deportation of the Chechen and Ingush peoples was not known to the outside world. But even if it was, it is fairly certain nothing would have been done at the time to stop it, especially given Stalin's excellent wartime reputation. Even today, the desperate situation of the Chechens receives very little attention from the international community and meets with appalling silence even among human rights activists in the West. The 2006 murder of Anna Politkovskaia, who, more than any other single Russian journalist, insisted on telling the story of Chechen (and Russian) suffering as a consequence of Moscow's policies, was also met with barely a ripple of protest from Western governments.

Part of the problem is the international community's attachment to norms of sovereignty, which makes it difficult to intervene in the internal affairs of another country. In Rwanda in 1994, some 800,000 people were killed in a genocide that could easily have been interdicted by the United Nations, which dawdled and delayed action until it was too late (Barnett 2002). In the case of Bosnia, this reluctance to act was overcome by the claim that Bosnia was an independent and sovereign state attacked from the outside by the Serbs and Croats. Even then, ethnic cleansing went on for three and a half years before the United States and NATO decided to intervene against Milosevic and the Serbs. Clearly, evidence of genocide in Srebrenica in July 1995 played a major role in this decision. But also the Croat defeat of the Bosnian Serbs in the Krajina made it apparent that opposition on the ground would be minimal. The Western bombing of Serbia in 1999 to prevent further ethnic cleansing of Kosovar Albanians was a precedent for the international community to intervene within countries (in this case in what remained of Yugoslavia) to defend the fundamental human rights of a minority people. Until the traumatic events of September 11, 2001, disrupted the international system and sent it spinning off on a new trajectory, it looked as if international norms about intervening in sovereign states in the name of human rights were changing. At this point, however, the American "War against Terrorism" has sharply bifurcated world opinion and completely overshadows the need for protecting the rights of minority and subjugated peoples against genocide, ethnic cleansing, and other crimes against humanity.

CONCLUSIONS

Thinking about ethnic cleansing in a comparative historical framework helps to elucidate cross-cultural commonalities. Commentators on the Balkans have too often and too assuredly attributed ethnic cleansing to the historical and cultural peculiarities of the South Slav peoples, in particular the Serbs. The issue is not so much particular cultural ideas or practices—Western or Eastern, Orthodox or Muslim—as it is historical contingency, the confluence of events, political leadership, and intercommunal hostility within the modern state. Neither the Turkish genocidal attacks on the Armenians nor the German elimination of the Jews was inevitable; they were based on concrete circumstances that emerged from the two world wars of the twentieth century and they were instigated by the warped ambitions of modern nationalist politicians. This does not lessen in any way the responsibility of individual citizens for the atrocities perpetrated against minorities within their communities. Nor does it relieve international institutions of their responsibilities for not having intervened when they might have prevented ethnic cleansing or alleviated the suffering of its victims.

Comparative reflection on the problems of ethnic cleansing also leads to the conclusion that each case must be understood in its full complexity, in its own immediate context, rather than merely as part of a long-term historical conflict between nations, Turks and Armenians, Germans and Jews, Russians and Chechens, or Serbs and Muslims (Browning, 1996). Ethnic cleansing is also not part of the cultural peculiarities of particular peoples. Unfortunately, its traces can be seen in every society, and its potentiality is part of all of us. Only by looking at ethnic cleansing in this fashion can we understand how it happened elsewhere and how to prevent it from happening again, abroad or at home.

Works Cited

•

Barnett, Michael. 2002. *Eyewitness to Genocide: The United Nations and Rwanda.* Ithaca, NY: Cornell University Press.

Bartov, Omer. 1996. *Murder in Our Midst: The Holocaust, Industrial Killing, and Representation.* New York: Oxford University Press.

Bell-Fialkoff, Andrew. 1996. *Ethnic Cleansing.* New York: St. Martin's Press.

Bloxham, Donald. 2005. *The Great Game of Genocide: Imperialism, Nationalism, and the Destruction of the Ottoman Armenians.* Oxford, UK: Oxford University Press.

Browning, Christopher. 1996. Human Nature, Culture, and the Holocaust. *Chronicle of Higher Education*, October 18.

Eley, Geoff, and Ronald Grigor Suny. 1996. *Becoming National: A Reader*. New York: Oxford University Press.

Frommer, Benjamin. 2005. *National Cleansing: Retribution against Nazi Collaborators in Postwar Czechoslovakia*. Cambridge, UK: Cambridge University Press.

Gutman, Roy. 1993. *A Witness to Genocide*. New York: Macmillan.

Jansen, Hans. 1997. *Der Madagaskar Plan: Die Beabsichtigte Deportation der Europäischen Juden nach Madagaskar*. Munich: Langen/Müller

Madajczyk, Piotr. 1994. *Przylaczenie Slaska Opolskiego do Polski 1945–1948*. Warsaw: PAN.

Mann, Michael. 2005. *The Dark Side of Democracy: Explaining Ethnic Cleansing*. Cambridge, UK: Cambridge University Press.

Melson, Robert F. 1992. *Revolution and Genocide: On the Origins of the Armenian Genocide and the Holocaust*. Chicago: University of Chicago Press.

Naimark, Norman M. 2001. *Fires of Hatred: Ethnic Cleansing in Twentieth-Century Europe*. Cambridge, MA: Harvard University Press.

Nekrich, Alexander. 1978. *The Punished Peoples: The Deportation and Fate of Soviet Minorities at the End of the Second World War*. New York: Norton.

Power, Samantha. 2002. *"A Problem from Hell": America in the Age of Genocide*. New York: Basic Books.

Schabas, William A. 2000. *Genocide in International Law*. Cambridge, UK: Cambridge University Press.

Scott, James C. 1998. *Seeing Like a State: How Certain Schemes to Improve the Human Condition Have Failed*. New Haven, CT: Yale University Press.

Semelin, Jacques. 2005. *Purifier et détruire: Usages politiques des massacres et génocides*. Paris: Editions du Seuil.

Silber, Laura, and Alan Little. 1995. *Yugoslavia: Death of a Nation*. New York: TV Books.

Valentino, Benjamin A. 2004. *Final Solutions: Mass Killing and Genocide in the 20th Century*. Ithaca, NY: Cornell University Press.

Weitz, Eric D. 2003. *A Century of Genocide: Utopias of Race and Nation*. Princeton, NJ: Princeton University Press.

PART THREE

Institutionalizing Difference

9

Race in the News
Stereotypes, Political Campaigns, and Market-Based Journalism

Shanto Iyengar

•

This essay considers the role of the media in news coverage of racial issues. I begin by discussing American society's failure to require news programming in the public interest before describing changing patterns of news consumption and the gradual emergence of local television news as a major news source. Next, I show that local news programs are doing race by systematically overemphasizing the issue of violent crime and by associating crime with the actions of racial minorities. This pattern of news coverage has predictable consequences; there is evidence of a racial double standard in the public's views about both crime and poverty. Whites react more harshly to black than white criminal suspects and also respond more generously to white than black victims of natural disasters. Finally, I turn to the use of racially coded "wedge" appeals in American political campaigns. The effect of news coverage and campaign advertising featuring media messages that broadly caricature African and Hispanic American is to exacerbate long-standing racial divisions and discord. The lack of a strong public broadcaster, coupled with the absence of programming requirements applicable to commercial media outlets, means that most media consumers will inevitably encounter stereotypic treatment of racial minorities. Under these circumstances, the prospects for racial and cultural inclusiveness are less than promising.

ON AUGUST 29, 2005, HURRICANE KATRINA HIT NEW ORLEANS WITH devastating force. In the immediate aftermath of the disaster, news coverage focused exclusively on the unprecedented scope of destruction and the thousands of residents left stranded in the city. Within forty-eight hours, however, the media began to feature reports (mainly unsubstantiated) of violence, looting, and crime. In fact, between August 31 and September 2, 15 percent of all broadcast and print news reports on Katrina made some reference to crime.[1]

Why was crime a news story in the context of this overwhelming disaster? Did the fact that it was poor African Americans who experienced the worst of Katrina's devastation play a role in making crime a focus of the news? In an idealized sense, news is supposed to serve as a mirror of "reality"; in the case of Hurricane Katrina, the unmistakable reality was the suffering of local residents and the inability of government organizations to deliver relief. The fact that news reports of the event paid significant attention to crime suggests that "mediality" (media accounts of events) is often a distorted mirror of events. As the case of Hurricane Katrina illustrates, violent crime is often treated as especially newsworthy when minorities are involved. Understanding the media's preoccupation with crime and other divisive issues, and how this preoccupation affects our understanding of race, is complicated and requires careful unpacking. It can be broadly attributed to (1) the failure of American society to require news programming in the public interest, and (2) the essentially self-interested behavior of news organizations and public officials.

NEWS AS "PUBLIC SERVICE"

In the United States, the majority of news outlets are corporately owned rather than publicly funded. The concept of public service broadcasting, introduced in Britain and adopted by most other democracies before World War II, treats the broadcast media as a major pillar of the democratic process. Broadcasters are mandated to provide a vibrant public forum in which citizens encounter significant diversity of perspectives on political issues and voice for all groups, no matter their size or influence (Benton Foundation 1999). In return for the provision of costless access to the publicly owned airwaves, radio and television stations must provide "payback" in the form of regular public affairs programming that informs and educates citizens on the issues of the day.

---

[1]This figure is derived from a content analysis of forty-one major national newspapers and three television networks (ABC, CBS, and NBC).

In the United States, the Carnegie Commission recommended the creation of public broadcasting, emphasizing the value of providing citizens with media programming that would allow them "to see America whole, in all its diversity." A major impetus to congressional adoption of the Carnegie Commission recommendations was the perception that commercial broadcasters could not be relied on to deliver informative content representing the myriad of groups and perspectives making up contemporary America. This pessimism was well founded. Research demonstrates that two sets of factors significantly influence news media civic performance—regulatory policy and market forces (Bishop and Hakanen 2002; Iyengar and McGrady 2006). Regulatory policy consists of two key elements; first, the establishment and continued support of a government-funded broadcasting network, and second, the enforcement of regulations that require privately owned media to deliver minimum levels of public affairs programming. The United States lags behind the rest of the world on both these regulatory factors. The Public Broadcasting Service (PBS) receives trivial government funding and has never been able to reach a significant share of the national audience (see Figure 9.1). In Europe, on the other hand, public broadcasters receive significant government subsidies and attract 30 to 40 percent of

FIGURE 9.1 | **AUDIENCE SHARE BY PUBLIC BROADCASTER.**

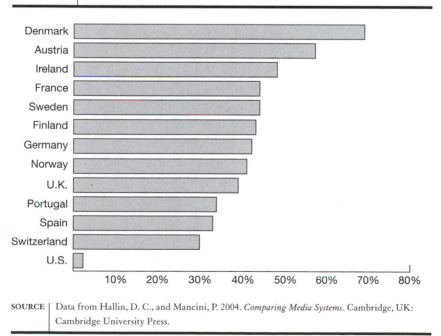

SOURCE | Data from Hallin, D. C., and Mancini, P. 2004. *Comparing Media Systems.* Cambridge, UK: Cambridge University Press.

the television audience. Public broadcasters in Europe attract large audiences despite the higher public affairs content and cultural diversity of their programs.

The great majority of Americans tune in to commercial television, and what they watch is entirely determined by corporate owners. The governmental agency charged with regulating the media is the Federal Communications Commission. This agency has adopted an increasingly laissez-faire approach, assuming that extensive free market competition will ensure the delivery of diverse perspectives on political and social issues. Most other democracies, while also moving in the general direction of deregulation, continue to maintain significant control over the content provided by both public and private broadcasters. Swedish public television, for example, "is obliged to carry cultural and quality programming, and 55 percent of its programming must be produced regionally outside Stockholm" (Williams 2003, 39). Canadian law requires Canadian broadcasters to provide media programming that is "predominantly and distinctly Canadian" and which reflects the multiracial and multilingual nature of Canadian society.

Market forces are the second factor influencing media performance. In societies where the media are predominantly privately owned (such as the United States), owners face strong incentives to minimize delivery of public affairs programming. To be profitable, news organizations must attract a substantial audience; programs that are watched by larger audiences attract more advertising revenue and ultimately drive out less sensationalist or dramatic, but more "substantive" or minority-oriented programming. In effect, the customer for private broadcasters is the advertiser and not the viewer; the broadcaster is motivated to attract the largest possible audience at the lowest possible cost. The end result is the delivery of programming with superficial content but wide appeal. In sum, weakened government regulation and competition between profit-seeking news organizations together ensure that the public service component of media delivery will be minimal. The entertainment value of programming consistently takes precedence over substantive content (Hamilton 2003).

The trend away from strict governmental regulation and toward infotainment is occurring worldwide. The impact of these forces, however, varies depending on other institutional factors, the most important of which is the strength of political parties. Countries with strong political parties are less dependent on the news media to provide an electoral forum and educate voters. In these countries, parties control the selection of candidates and can count on their supporters to cast "informed" (i.e., party-line) votes. In these countries, whether the media provide substantive or superficial coverage of public affairs is less consequential to the ability of citizens to participate. But a very different scenario applies to the United States. Over the past several decades American political parties have lost control over campaigns, and party leaders currently have little say in the selection of candidates (Polsby 1983). Autonomous and well-financed candidates hire professional consultants and strategists to run their campaigns and often take positions at odds with their party. The consultants are only interested in winning the particular race, even if it means using controversial, sometimes false, and divisive media messages. Since many Americans lack strong ties to a political party, these messages significantly influence how they cast their votes. In this world of entrepreneurial candidates and "floating voters," a candidate's media strategy can influence the eventual outcome.

WHERE AMERICANS GET THEIR NEWS

Two trends describe Americans' consumption of news over the past century. The first concerns the gradual replacement of print by broadcast news sources. With the development of radio in the 1920s and the immediate popularity of radio news, newspapers began to surrender their position as the market leader. The arrival of television in the 1950s only accelerated this shift, and the national newscasts aired by ABC, CBS, NBC soon emerged as the dominant source of daily news. In 1969, at the height of their dominance, the combined audience for network news accounted for three-fourths of all American households. More people (approximately twenty-five million) tuned in to any *one* of the network newscasts in the late 1960s than subscribed to the top twenty daily newspapers combined. As shown in Figure 9.2, the current audience for CBS News—the least popular of the three major network newscasts—easily surpasses the circulation of the newspaper *USA Today*.

The development of cable broadcasting in the early 1980s weakened the major networks' monopoly hold on the audience. CNN, the first "all news" cable network, was formed in 1980. It was soon to be followed by Fox News Channel, CNBC, and MSNBC. By 2002, 82 percent of American households had access to cable news channels.

The spread of cable television coincided with an even greater threat to network news—the increasing proliferation of local news programming. Responding to the low cost of producing local news and strong

FIGURE 9.2 | **BROADCAST VERSUS PRINT NEWS AUDIENCE.**

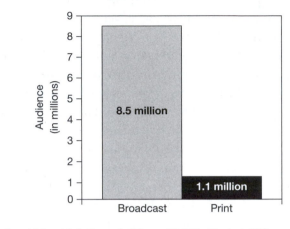

SOURCE | Data from Nielsen Media Research, *Editor and Publisher Yearbook*, 2003.

audience demand, station owners began to air multiple local newscasts and hybrid entertainment–news programs each day. In the 1960s most television stations broadcast a single local newscast; today, local news runs continuously. In the Los Angeles area, for instance, the three network-affiliated television stations air a total of 7.5 hours of local news each day between 4:00 P.M. and 7:00 P.M. The explosion in local news availability created a serious problem for network news; people began to watch local rather than national news. Between 1993 and 2003, the combined audience for the three evening newscasts dropped by nearly 30 percent—from forty-one million to twenty-nine million.

Recent breakthroughs in digital technology have transformed still further how Americans get their news. As the personal computer begins to rival television as the gateway to the outside world, competition for news audiences has intensified. The traffic to Internet news sites is already heavy; as of early 2005, nearly one in three Internet users reads a newspaper online. Today, virtually every major news organization reproduces its news offerings online, giving consumers instant, on-demand access to the news. The major Internet portals all provide access to news, but their content derives exclusively from conventional sources (newspaper, wire services, or television news). In some cases, such as MSNBC, media and technology companies have joined forces hoping to create synergy between established providers of news content (NBC) and technological giants (Microsoft).

THE ECONOMICS OF NEWS

Every day, major events and issues occur in the world at large with significant consequences for Americans. One expects these same events and issues to appear in the news. This "mirror image" definition stipulates close correspondence between the state of the real world and the content of news coverage. During times of rising joblessness, the news focuses on unemployment; when thousands of Sudanese civilians are massacred, the spotlight shifts to Sudan and to U.S. policy on Africa.

There are several challenges to the mirror image definition of news, but the most compelling is that news is simply what sells (Hamilton 2003). American consumers are free to choose from a wide array of news providers. Facing competition, rational owners inevitably choose to further their own interests rather than provide public service to the community. Thus, the content and form of news coverage are subject to the same logic that drives all other economic activity: minimize costs and maximize revenues.

Since all American news outlets (with the exception of National Public Radio and the Public Broadcasting Service) are privately owned, their survival depends on the size of their audience. Advertising is the principal source of revenue for publishers and broadcasters. The price of advertising depends on the size of the audience; the more popular the program, the greater the profit margin. Thus, "ratings" are the lifeblood of the broadcasting industry.

The A. C. Nielsen Company conducts quarterly ratings "sweeps" during the months of February, May, July, and November. The result of each sweeps period locks in advertising rates for individual programs and stations until the next period. Programs that suffer a decline in their ratings stand to lose significant revenue, so owners do their utmost to maintain or improve their ratings. In the case of news programs, the implications are obvious: entertainment value trumps substantive content. Thus, one-half of all network news reports broadcast in 2000 had no policy content; in 1980 the figure was approximately one-third (Patterson 2000). "Sensationalized" reports accounted for 25 percent of network news in the 1980s, but 40 percent in 2003. Clearly, news organizations have learned that fluff is more profitable than substance.

The expansion of local news programming in the 1980s and 1990s provides a compelling case study of the responsiveness of television station owners to economic constraints. First, local news is inexpensive to produce. The typical local newscast can be staffed by four or five all-purpose correspondents, an anchor or two, a weather forecaster, and a sports correspondent. Local news correspondents, in contrast with their network news counterparts, do not command extravagant salaries. Infrastructure costs for local news programming are similarly limited; for the typical news station, the single most expensive budget item is the monthly lease of a helicopter to provide immediate access to breaking news. All told, therefore, the cost of putting together a local newscast is modest.

Cost is only half of the programming equation. Local news is especially enticing to owners because it attracts large audiences. In many markets, more people tune in to local than network news. Not only is local news close to home and the source of both useful (the weather forecast and traffic reports) and personally engaging (the latest sports scores) information, but public affairs content can also be presented in ways that appeal to viewers. It is no accident that the signature "issue" of local news coverage is violent crime. From armed bank robberies to homicides, "home invasions," carjackings, police chases, and gang wars, violence occurs continually in local newscasts. Conversely, little time is devoted to nonviolent crimes such as embezzlement, insider trading, or tax evasion because they lack the "action" to command the attention of the viewing audience. Thus, "if it bleeds, it leads" is the motto of local news directors.

Stories about crime convey drama and emotion and provide attention-getting visuals. The allure of this combination for news directors is apparent across the country. In Los Angeles, for example, English-language commercial television stations aired a total of 3,014 news stories on crime during 1996 and 1997. As shown in Figure 9.3, the overwhelming majority of these reports focused on violent crime. The crime of murder, which accounted for less than 1 percent of all crime in Los Angeles County during this period, was the focus of 17 percent of crime stories. In fact, the number of murder stories equaled the number of stories focusing on all forms of nonviolent crime (Gilliam and Iyengar 2000). The results were identical across all six television stations whose offerings were examined.

Los Angeles television stations are not especially distinctive. A study of fifty-six different cities by Klite, Bardwell, and Salzman (1997) found that crime was the most prominently featured subject in the local news, accounting for more than 75 percent of all news coverage in some cities.

FIGURE 9.3 | **CONTENT OF TELEVISION CRIME COVERAGE, LOS ANGELES, 1996–1997.**

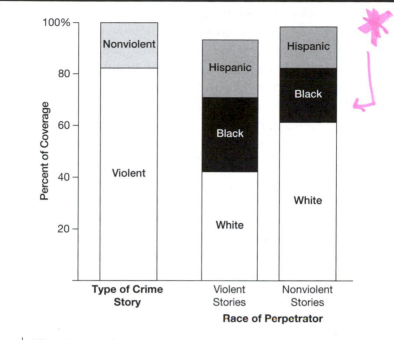

SOURCE | Gilliam, F. D., Jr, and S. Iyengar. 2000. Prime suspects: The influence of local television news on the viewing public. *American Journal of Political Science* 44:560–573.

Not only does broadcast news highlight violence, it links the issues of race and crime (Entman 1992; Entman and Rojecki 2000). Over 50 percent of the crime stories in the Los Angeles study provided information about a specific suspect. As shown in Figure 9.3, more often than not, the suspect was nonwhite. These findings parallel a detailed study of the three major weekly news magazines on the basis of which the author concluded that "criminals are conceptualized as black people, and crime as the violence they do to whites" (Elias 1994, 5).

Of course, the representation of different ethnic groups in crime news may reflect real-world trends. Research by Gilliam, Iyengar, Simon, and Wright (1996) compared television representation of minority suspects with actual arrest rates for different races in Los Angeles. The authors computed population-adjusted crime rates for whites, Hispanics, and African Americans, showing the degree to which these groups were either over- or underrepresented in both violent and nonviolent crime. Their data showed that although African Americans committed violent and nonviolent crime at about the same rate, television coverage of black crime focused more (by a factor of 22 percent) on violent crime. In the case of Hispanics, their actual participation in violent crime exceeded their participation in nonviolent crime by 7 percent, but as represented in the news, the disparity was 14 percent. Conversely, news coverage of white crime was distinctly more nonviolent than violent (by a factor of 31 percent), even though whites are only slightly more likely (by 7 percent) to engage in nonviolent rather than violent crime. Thus, this study concluded that local news overrepresented violent crime by African Americans and Hispanics, and underrepresented violent crime by whites.

EFFECTS OF CRIME NEWS ON AUDIENCE OPINION

Given the prominence of crime in news programming, an obvious question concerns the effects of racially "scripted" crime news on the viewing audience. One distinct possibility is that repeated exposure to news about crime makes the audience more aware and fearful of crime. In fact, communications scholars have documented a striking relationship between the level of news coverage and public concern for any given policy issue. An early statement of this "agenda-setting" hypothesis was formulated by Cohen (1963): the media, Cohen said, "may not be successful most of the time in telling people what to think, but it is stunningly successful in telling its readers what to think *about*" (Cohen 1963, 13). In other words, the media sets the public agenda.

There is ample evidence of media agenda-setting with respect to crime; over the past two decades Americans have regularly identified crime as among the three most important problems facing the country. This correspondence between the public and media agenda, in and of itself, does not establish the influence of the media. The media and the public may simultaneously respond to the same real-world events (Behr and Iyengar 1985). This is possible because unlike most issues, crime can be directly experienced. During periods of rising crime, for example, more people are victimized (or come in contact with crime victims), thus making them more concerned about the issue.

Examination of trends in actual crime rates, news coverage of crime, and public concern for crime does not lend support to the notion that real-world experiences shape both public concern and news coverage. In fact, over the past two decades the over-time trends in Americans' concern for crime and actual crime rates have moved in opposite directions! As shown in Figure 9.4, the FBI nationwide violent crime index

FIGURE 9.4 | **REAL-WORLD CUES AND PUBLIC CONCERN FOR CRIME, 1982–2001.**

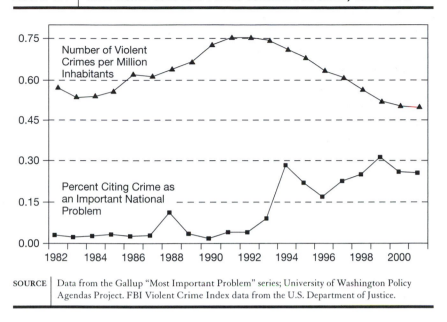

SOURCE | Data from the Gallup "Most Important Problem" series; University of Washington Policy Agendas Project. FBI Violent Crime Index data from the U.S. Department of Justice.

has declined significantly since the early 1990s. Despite the overall reduction in crime, the percentage of the public that cited crime as an important national problem increased substantially during this same period. Not coincidentally, the decade of the 1990s also witnessed a dramatic increase in the availability of local television news. Figure 9.4 suggests, at least in the case of crime, that public concern is more responsive to what appears on the television screen than to the state of the real world. \

* Repeated exposure to violent crime has made the American public fixate on crime as a political problem. (As we will note shortly, this fact has not gone unnoticed among those who seek elective office.) But is it sheer frequency of exposure or more subtle, qualitative aspects of crime news that drive public opinion on crime? Scholarly research suggests that the way in which the media frame the issue does matter. In an extensive content analysis of network news, Iyengar (1991) identified two distinct genres of news coverage for policy issues. "Thematic" framing encompasses news reports that place policy issues in some collective or societal context (e.g., rising crime rates in major urban areas or changes in the criminal justice system). "Episodic" framing, on the other hand, focuses on particular instances or exemplars of policy issues (e.g., the arrest of a suspect in the JonBenét Ramsey case). Not surprisingly, broadcast news tilts heavily in the direction of episodic reports; during the decade of the 1980s, for example, thematic stories accounted for only 10 percent of network news coverage of both crime and terrorism (Iyengar 1991).

How television news frames crime affects viewers' attributions of responsibility for the issue. When television news provides viewers with a collective or contextual frame of reference for crime (thematic framing), viewers are more likely to attribute responsibility (both in terms of responsibility for causing the problem and curing the problem) to societal factors. Thus, after watching a thematic report, people cited unemployment and racial discrimination as potential causes of crime and recommended improved educational opportunities for the poor as an appropriate remedy (Iyengar 1996). But when provided with the dominant episodic frame—news coverage focusing on a particular crime—they attributed responsibility not to societal or political forces but to the attributes of particular individuals or groups. For example, viewers cited amorality, laziness, and greed as relevant causes of crime. The predominance of episodic framing means that most Americans are drawn to dispositional rather than societal accounts of crime.

Recent work has extended the analysis of media frames to local news. Typically, local crime reports provide a physical description of the suspect in the form of a police sketch, security camera footage, or a mug shot. Race is a personal attribute that is evident in an episodic news report whereas poverty and other social factors are not. Episodic framing thus necessarily introduces racial stereotypes into the public's understanding of crime.[2] Viewers are compelled to evaluate their racial beliefs in light of what seem to be empirical realities. Lacking the focus on an individual suspect, thematic framing directs the viewers' attention to alternative and more contextual accounts of crime.

The regular coverage of crime by television news coupled with the dominance of episodic framing constitutes a strong implicit signal that members of minority groups are prone to engage in violent crime. Public opinion polls show that the news audience has accepted this message; that minorities are violence-prone is "deeply embedded in the collective consciousness of Americans" (Quillian and Pager 1999, 722; Hurwitz and Peffley 1997; Peffley and Hurwitz 1998).

Experimental research by Gilliam and Iyengar (2000) has confirmed the particular importance of racial cues in episodic crime reports. Using computer-based editing techniques, the researchers presented the *same* individual as either a white or an African American male suspect. Their

---

[2] For a similar argument, but applied to the issue of poverty, see Gilens 1996.

results showed that when the suspect was depicted as African American, the number of viewers who endorsed punitive criminal justice policies increased significantly. More tellingly, the researchers found that when the news story on crime made no reference to a criminal suspect, a significant number of viewers mistakenly recalled that the suspect was nonwhite.

The most recent example of crime news exacerbating racial bias comes from the previously cited study of news coverage of Hurricane Katrina. This study manipulated media framing of the disaster. The investigators presented one set of study participants with a news report that focused on looting and disorder in the aftermath of the disaster (the "crime frame"). Other participants read a news report that focused exclusively on the death and damage caused by the hurricane, with no reference to crime (the "disaster frame"). This report framed Katrina in either thematic (e.g., discussion of the scope of the disaster with no reference to individual victims) or episodic (e.g., the efforts of one family to relocate) terms. After reading the news report, participants were asked a series of questions concerning the appropriate level of government assistance for hurricane victims. As shown in Figure 9.5, participants exposed to the

FIGURE 9.5 | **FRAMING EFFECTS ON RECOMMENDED LEVEL OF DISASTER ASSISTANCE.**

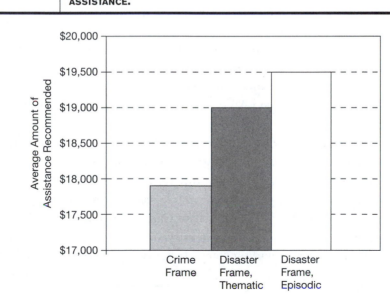

SOURCE | Online experiment conducted by Stanford University's Political Communications Lab in conjunction with the *Washington Post*, May 6–24, 2006.

report on crime and looting recommended significantly lower amounts of financial assistance for hurricane victims.[3] Thus, this study documents that when the news links natural disasters with crime, people see the victims of the disaster as less deserving.

In short, nonstop coverage of crime by television news encourages racial stereotyping. By associating crime with the actions of minorities, mere exposure to crime news is sufficient to prompt the expression of beliefs and opinions hostile to minorities.

WEDGE APPEALS IN POLITICAL CAMPAIGNS

Candidates for national and statewide office spend vast sums on television advertising hoping to attract votes by "selling" their candidacies. Since the 1960s, campaign ads have frequently cast racial minorities and policies that promote minority interests as threats to white voters. Typically, these ads are aired by Republican candidates who hope to persuade white Democrats to cross party lines. Consider the following scenario: as the 2008 election approaches, the economy is uncertain, Osama bin Laden remains at large, and American troops die every day in Iraq. A clear majority of the public thinks the country is on the wrong track. Under these conditions, voters direct their wrath at the party controlling the White House. Boxed in by an unpopular war and concerns over the economy, Republican candidates have a strong incentive to change the subject by campaigning on so-called wedge issues, such as the racial or gender identity of the Democratic nominee. Based on the idea of "divide and conquer," a wedge issue pits voters against each other not on the basis of their party affiliation but on their race or ethnicity.

Racial issues have divided Americans ever since the Civil War. In the most recent iteration of racial politics, white candidates present themselves as opponents of policies or programs that benefit minorities. Recently, the emergence of the immigration issue has injected a parallel division between Latinos and Anglos into campaigns. When California's Republican governor Pete Wilson ran a television ad in 1994 that began with the line "They keep coming," most Californians immediately understood what he meant. Cultural identity, or "family values," provides an alternative basis for dividing voters. Initially introduced by President

---

[3] The average amount of assistance awarded by participants in the crime frame condition was significantly lower than the averages in both other conditions.

Nixon in 1968 as an appeal to conservative southern Democrats, "family values" has since broadened into a code word for religious fervor and opposition to non mainstream lifestyles. A call for family values is generally interpreted as opposition to abortion, feminism, gay rights, and sex education in the public schools.

Wedge appeals based on race occurred in both the 1988 and 1996 presidential campaigns, with crime and illegal immigration, respectively, as the featured issues. Senator Robert Dole's attempts to run as a strong opponent of illegal immigration in 1996 made little difference in his overwhelming loss to President Bill Clinton. But in 1988, the election may well have turned on the notorious "Willie Horton" ad in which a Republican group attacked presidential candidate Michael Dukakis for his support of prison furlough programs. This ad featured an African American convict who had committed a violent crime while on a weekend furlough. The ad's controversial content generated extensive media attention across the country; the "Dukakis is soft on crime" message was recycled across the country, and Vice President George H. W. Bush overcame what was then a double-digit deficit in the polls.

Wedge issues are used more frequently in state and local races. In 1990, the conservative North Carolina Republican Jesse Helms was locked in a close Senate race with Harvey Gantt (the Democratic African American mayor of Charlotte). During the closing days of the race, Helms released an ad that condemned the use of affirmative action in employment decisions. This ad is credited with eliciting a significant increase in white turnout, leading to Helms's reelection.

In some races, wedge issues influence the eventual outcome indirectly by deterring one side from speaking out (for fear of offending white voters). In 1998, for instance, the groups opposing Proposition 209 (a measure that called for an end to affirmative action in California) tried repeatedly but unsuccessfully to persuade President Clinton to visit the state and speak out against the measure. At the time, Clinton's national popularity stood at nearly 60 percent, and Clinton led Dole by more than 20 points in California polls. Despite this thick security blanket, Clinton refused to get involved until the very last days of the campaign, when he made a speech in Oakland. His involvement proved too little, too late; on Election Day, Proposition 209 passed easily.

In more recent campaign cycles, immigration has overshadowed affirmative action as the wedge issue of choice. The country's preoccupation with terrorism following the attacks on the World Trade Center in

New York and the Pentagon on September 11, 2001, gives opponents of immigration a compelling rationale — "Let's not give potential terrorists easy entry into America." Given the size of California's immigrant population and the state's proximity to Mexico, it is not surprising that the Golden State finds itself in the forefront of the battle to limit immigration. To illustrate how the immigration issue has shaped California politics, I use two case studies: the 1994 race for governor between incumbent Republican Pete Wilson and the Democratic challenger, Kathleen Brown, and the 2003 special election to replace the Democratic governor, Gray Davis.

The 1994 Campaign: "They Keep Coming"

As the incumbent governor, Pete Wilson faced an especially challenging reelection in 1994. In his first term, he had presided over high unemployment and a net outflow of businesses. Wilson's Democratic opponent was the popular and well-known Kathleen Brown. The Brown campaign seized upon the recession as her signature issue; Brown's ads emphasized Wilson's inability to deliver economic relief and her own economic expertise (Brown was state treasurer). Using the economy as her theme, Brown established a substantial lead over Wilson.

Recognizing that he could not win a debate over the state of the economy, Wilson campaigned instead as a crime fighter and opponent of illegal immigration. He linked his candidacy to two well-known statewide propositions. Proposition 184 required the state to adopt a "three strikes" law and Proposition 187 limited or eliminated illegal immigrants' eligibility for a variety of government services. Both measures passed easily.

Wilson's efforts to change the subject were aided by Brown, who decided to engage Wilson on crime and immigration despite her well-known opposition to the death penalty and her support for immigrants' rights. The Brown campaign even released an ad attacking Wilson's decision to parole a violent offender. Predictably, this ad provoked a series of Wilson counterattacks on the subject of crime. Gradually, the California electorate was exposed to a genuine "dialogue" on the issues of crime and immigration, and voters' impressions of the candidates became increasingly colored by their opinions on these issues. On crime and immigration, most voters (including many Democrats) favored Wilson over Brown. As a result, Brown's support eroded over the course of the 1994 campaign (see Figure 9.6) and Wilson won reelection by a comfortable margin.

FIGURE 9.6 | **EROSION OF SUPPORT FOR BROWN IN 1994 CALIFORNIA GUBERNATIONAL CAMPAIGN.**

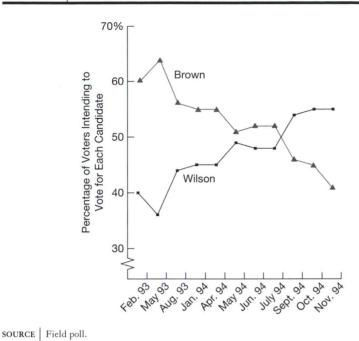

SOURCE | Field poll.

Drivers' Licenses and the Terminator

In 2003, less than one year after his reelection, Governor Gray Davis found himself the target of a recall campaign. Despite the substantial plurality of registered Democrats statewide, the measure passed, Davis was removed from office, and voters selected a Republican movie star (from a ballot that included more than 100 candidates), Arnold Schwarzenegger, as their new governor.

The conventional wisdom attributes these dramatic events to the state's continued economic woes, overcharging by energy companies, and the general sense that state government was "broken." Fed up with politics as usual, voters were willing to send the relatively colorless and unpopular incumbent home in favor of a celebrity figure uncontaminated by prior political experience.

This standard account of the recall of Davis and the election of Schwarzenegger misses one important ingredient of the recall campaign—Davis's much-publicized decision to sign into law a bill (SB 60) that provided drivers' licenses to people who had entered the state illegally. Under this bill, applicants without Social Security cards would be eligible for licenses if they provided a taxpayer identification number and one other form of personal documentation. Davis had initially vetoed the bill but reversed himself and signed it into law in September 2003, hoping to boost his standing with Hispanic voters and thus stave off the recall.

As far as public opinion was concerned, SB 60 was anathema (see Table 9.1). By overwhelming margins, Californians felt that the bill threatened national security. Among whites, opponents outnumbered proponents by a factor of 3:1. For voters concerned with immigration, then, Schwarzenegger—who had pledged to repeal the bill— was clearly the more desirable candidate.[4]

How did voter sentiment on the drivers' license issue play out in the recall election? A pre-election survey asked a representative sample of likely voters to evaluate Governor Davis's record in office (most thought he had performed very poorly), to indicate their feelings about Arnold Schwarzenegger, and, of course, to indicate their vote choice on the recall question and the replacement candidate ballot. Although evaluations of Davis and Schwarzenegger were influenced primarily by party identification (Democrats were less critical of Davis, Republicans more enthusiastic about Schwarzenegger), voters' positions on the drivers' license bill had almost as much impact on their candidate evaluations. Overall, immigration was a more powerful predictor of vote choice than the energy crisis, social issues such as abortion or gay rights, or generalized

---

[4] Governor Schwarzenegger's first legislative action, carried out on December 1, 2003, was to sign the repeal measure into law.

TABLE 9.1 | **IMMIGRATION IN THE 2003 RECALL CAMPAIGN**

Some people say that allowing illegal immigrants to get a driver's license will result in more insured drivers and safer roads. Others say that giving driving licenses to illegal immigrants will hurt national security. What do you think?

	All respondents	Whites	Nonwhites
More insured, safer roads	26	21	35
Hurt national security	56	64	44
Haven't thought about it	15	12	16
Hurt national security	32	25	44
Haven't thought about it	69	75	56

SOURCE | Knowledge Networks statewide survey of 1,124 CA residents.

cynicism over state government. The recall election was less about economic mismanagement or disaffection from state government and more about controlling immigration.[5]

The successful use of immigration as a wedge issue in the 1994 and 2003 campaigns suggests that the political environment in California has changed little over the past decade. This may seem paradoxical, given the substantial changes in the ethnic composition of the state population. Whites accounted for 60 percent of the adult population of the state in 1992, but only 47 percent in 2008 (Citrin and Highton 2002; Public Policy Institute of California 2008). The Latino share of the population, on the other hand, increased from 24 to 33 percent. However, the size of the two groups among the voting population has remained relatively stable. Whites accounted for 79 percent of California voters in 1992 and 70 percent in 2008, while the Hispanic share of the voting population increased from 10 to 15 percent over this same period. Thus, the increase in the Latino population has not translated into a corresponding increase in the Latino electorate (see Citrin and Highton 2002; Public Policy Institute of California 2008). Even allowing for considerable Latino skepticism over SB 60, one suspects that the outcome of the 2003 special election may have been different had the Latino share of voters matched their share of the adult population. Latinos remain significantly underrepresented in the electorate, while whites still account for the vast majority of voters. Interestingly, the 2008 California electorate is a virtual replica

---

[5] For a more detailed analysis, see Iyengar 2004.

of the 1980 population—70 percent white and only 14 percent Latino. In short, whites have retained their dominant political status, primarily because of low turnout among Latinos.

Given the distribution of ethnicity within the electorate, it should come as no surprise that candidates resort to appeals that capitalize on white racial identity. Were the situation reversed, and Latinos the majority electoral group, it is unlikely that issues of illegal immigration or eligibility for driver's licenses would gain significant political traction. An axiom of political campaigns is that candidates respond to the preferences of voters, not nonvoters; until the Latino vote begins to match the Latino population, the incentive to use wedge appeals remains strong. For those who seek less divisive campaigns, the answer lies in civic outreach and get-out-the-vote campaigns.

CONCLUSION

Candidates for elective office and owners of news outlets both behave as rational actors—the former seek to maximize their vote share, the latter their audience share. Neither has any compelling interest in the effects of their media presentations on race relations. As long as crime news attracts and holds a substantial audience, television stations will continue to highlight violence and mayhem; as long as wedge appeals entice voters to cross party lines, Willie Horton–type ads and grainy images of immigrants sprinting across freeways will continue to play a significant role in advertising campaigns.

The impact of racial cues in news programs and campaign advertising is especially influential in shaping white Americans' views about race for the simple reason that most whites have little personal contact with minorities. Despite the ever-increasing diversity of the American population and the passage of significant civil rights laws, most white people still live in racially homogeneous enclaves (Massey and Denton 1993; Charles 2003). The people they see and interact with on a daily basis are overwhelmingly white (Charles 2003). Unable to think of specific instances that might contradict the association between ethnicity and antisocial or dysfunctional behavior, they uncritically accept the implications of racially biased media messages. The vicious circle expands.[6]

---

[6] Whites' frequency of interpersonal contact with members of minority groups does not, in and of itself, contribute to weakening of racial prejudice and stereotyping. In fact, there is considerable evidence that whites living in areas characterized by a significant minority population are more threatened and hence more apt to buy into traditional stereotypes (Taylor 1998; Dixon and Rosenbaum 2004).

What might be done to break out of this circle? On the media side, we cannot expect any shift away from "infotainment" unless society imposes minimum "public service" obligations on broadcasters (Bishop and Hakanen 2002). In almost every other democratic society, broadcasters are treated as public trustees; in exchange for their free access to the publicly owned airwaves (worth billions of dollars), they are required to deliver some minimal degree of public service. In addition to providing more extensive and frequent coverage of public affairs, American broadcasters should also be required to air programs representing a wide array of cultural and political perspectives from the Black Muslims to the Christian Coalition.

An alternative means of increasing the public's potential exposure to substantive news programming is to strengthen the standing of the public broadcaster. As we noted at the outset, PBS has a tiny audience share when compared with most European public broadcasters. But PBS's ability to attract viewers has been compromised by the cutbacks in government financing. At present, PBS receives only a trivial portion of its operating budget from the federal government and is forced to devote significant amounts of broadcast time to fund-raising. In stark contrast, the BBC's annual revenues derive almost exclusively from government funds. Obviously, the BBC has much more freedom to develop programming initiatives that not only address important issues of the day but also attract a significant number of viewers.

Finally, it is difficult to imagine what might be done to discourage candidates from using divisive campaign rhetoric. As a form of political speech, campaign advertising is protected by the First Amendment, and as long as whites turn out to vote in greater number than nonwhites, playing the "race card" is rational candidate behavior. In recent years Congress has passed legislation designed to make candidates more accountable for the content of their advertising; the "in person" rule, for instance, requires candidates to appear in their ads and assure the viewer that they "approved" the content. This requirement may serve as a disincentive for candidates to campaign on the basis of race. A further deterrent is the tendency of the news media to "fact check" the content of candidate advertising. Since 1988, most major news outlets have taken to running "ad watches" in which they scrutinize and critique the accuracy of campaign ads. If each time a candidate produced an ad featuring an "us against them" appeal, he or she was cited by the press as a "race baiter," this would surely discourage campaign consultants from pursuing the strategy.

In the final analysis, however, the behavior of candidates and news organizations is dictated less by government strictures or efforts at monitoring and more by the behavior of consumers. The strongest disincentive to the use of racial appeals in campaigns is the possibility of a voter revolt: if the candidate who runs an ad featuring his support for the construction of a wall along the U.S. border suddenly finds that his support has dropped by ten points after the airing of this ad, he will surely advertise on some other issue. If television stations that feature the most gruesome footage of violent crime in their news programming discover that they are losing viewers to other sources, they will switch to some other formula. Ultimately, it is audience demand that is responsible for the supply of media programming. In that sense, consumers and voters get what they deserve. Whether that delivery is consistent with racial harmony in a functioning democratic society is another question.

Works Cited

•

Behr, R. L., and S. Iyengar. 1985. Television news, real-world cues, and changes in the public agenda. *Public Opinion Quarterly* 49:38–57.

Benton Foundation. 1999. *The public interest standard in television broadcasting*. Washington, DC: Advisory Committee on Public Interest Obligations of Digital Television Broadcasters.

Bishop, R., and E. A. Hakanen. 2002. In the public interest? The state of local television programming fifteen years after deregulation. *Journal of Communication Inquiry* 2:261–276.

Charles, C. Z. 2003. The dynamics of racial residential segregation. *Annual Review of Sociology* 29:167–207.

Citrin, J. and B. Highton. 2002. *How race, ethnicity, and immigration shape the California electorate*. San Francisco: Public Policy Institute of California.

Cohen, Bernard. 1963. *The press and foreign policy*. Princeton, NJ: Princeton University Press.

Dixon, Jeffrey C., and Michael S. Rosenbaum. 2004. Nice to know you? Testing contact, cultural, and group threat theories of anti-black and anti-Hispanic stereotypes. *Social Science Quarterly* 85:257–280.

Elias, R. (1994). Official stories: Media coverage of American crime policy. *Humanist*, 54, 3–8.

Entman, R. M. 1992. Blacks in the news: Television, modern racism, and cultural change. *Journalism Quarterly* 69:341–362.

Entman, R. M., and A. Rojecki. 2000. *The black image in the white mind: Media and race in America*. Chicago: University of Chicago Press.

Gilens, Martin. 1996. "Race coding" and white opposition to welfare. *American Political Science Review* 90:593–604.

Gilliam, F. D., Jr., S. Iyengar, A. Simon, and O. Wright. 1996. Crime in black and white: The violent, scary world of local news. *Harvard International Journal of Press/Politics* 1:6–23.

Gilliam, F. D., Jr., and S. Iyengar. 2000. Prime suspects: The influence of local television news on the viewing public. *American Journal of Political Science* 44:560–573.

Hamilton, J. T. 2003. *All the news that's fit to sell: How the market transforms information into news.* Princeton, NJ: Princeton University Press.

Hurwitz, Jon, and Mark Peffley. 1997. Public perceptions of race and crime: The role of racial stereotypes. *American Journal of Political Science* 41:374–401.

Iyengar, S. 1991. *Is anyone responsible? How television frames political issues.* Chicago: University of Chicago Press.

———. 1996. Framing responsibility for political issues. *Annals of the American Academy of Political and Social Science* 546:59–70.

———. 2004. Wedge issues in political campaigns: A voter guide. Unpublished Paper, Political Communication Lab, Stanford University.

Iyengar, S., and J. McGrady. 2006. *Media politics: A citizen's guide.* New York: W. W. Norton.

Klite, P., R. A. Bardwell, and J. Salzman. 1997. Local television news: Getting away with murder. *Harvard International Journal of Press/Politics* 2:102–112.

Massey, D. S., and N. A. Denton. 1993. *American apartheid: Segregation and the making of the underclass.* Cambridge, MA: Harvard University Press.

Patterson, T. E. 2000. *Doing well and doing good: How soft news and critical journalism are shrinking the news audience and weakening democracy—and what the news can do about it.* Prepared for the Joan Shorenstein Center on the Press, Politics, and Public Policy, John F. Kennedy School of Government, Harvard University.

Peffley, Mark, and Jon Hurwitz. 1998. Whites' stereotypes of blacks: Sources and political consequences. In *Perception and prejudice: Race and politics in the United States,* edited by J. Hurwitz and M. Peffley. New Haven: Yale University Press.

Polsby, N. *Consequences of party reform.* New York: Oxford University Press.

Public Policy Institute of California. 2008. Latino Voters in California. www.ppic.org/content/pubs/jtf/JTF_LatinoVotersJTF.pdf.

Quillian, Lincoln, and Devah Pager. 1999. Black neighbors, higher crime? The role of racial stereotypes in evaluations of neighborhood crime. Unpublished Paper, Department of Sociology, University of Wisconsin, Madison.

Taylor, Marylee C. 1998. How white attitudes vary with the racial composition of local populations: Numbers count. *American Sociological Review* 63: 512–535.

Williams, K. 2003. *Understanding media theory.* London: Hodder & Arnold.

10

Going Back to Compton
Real Estate, Racial Politics, and Black-Brown Relations

Albert M. Camarillo

•

In this essay, I examine the case of Compton, California, and draw on my memories of the city (I was born and raised there) and on the current research and public service work I have conducted there as an academic who returned "home" after thirty years, to trace out its transformation into a "city of color." Growing up in Compton and witnessing firsthand two decades of tremendous change provided me with a peculiar vantage point as a participant-observer of the first racial transformation of the city from white to black. When I returned three decades later as an academic, I gained an intimate and scholarly understanding of a second demographic transformation and its sociopolitical consequences for Compton as a Latino majority/African American minority city of color. Drawing on interviews and on other primary and secondary sources as well, I argue that current interactions between blacks and Latinos must be considered within a context of recent historical developments. In particular, ideas about group rights in the post–civil rights era, and ideas about multiculturalism—especially respect for ethnic/racial differences and visions of intergroup cooperation—have greatly influenced the relations in cities of color. Furthermore, below the radar screen of mass media there is evidence of grassroots organizing across traditional racial boundaries resulting in cooperation and collaboration between blacks and Latinos. These new dynamics between people of color are reshaping the nature of race and ethnic relations in the twenty-first century.

THE LONG, TORTUOUS HISTORY OF RACE RELATIONS IN THE UNITED
States has been shaped largely within a context of white/nonwhite
interactions. This history is a complex one affecting every region of the
nation, rural and urban areas alike. It is a history filled with innumerable
examples of conflict, bitterness, and tragedy, as well as one in which countless individuals and organizations have made strenuous efforts to overcome ethnic and racial divisions. Although relations between and among
various minority groups form an important part of the historical record,
the dominant paradigm for understanding race in America has revolved
around a framework of white and nonwhite. This framework, always
problematic when considering other racialized groups in the American
past, is particularly limiting when explaining race and ethnic relations in
the twenty-first century because of demographic changes that continue to
transform the nation's large cities and metropolitan suburbs.

"Minority-majority" cities, as some scholars have labeled them—or
"cities of color," as I refer to them—are the epicenters of a new frontier in American race relations. Understanding the nature of relations
between the minority groups that now form the majorities in city after
city, suburb after suburb, requires fresh perspectives. This is not to argue
that long-standing historical and sociological analyses of race relations
do not apply; they do. However, such analyses often do not go far enough
to explain current issues such as group competition over resources (e.g.,
city jobs, political power, public schools), conflict over space (public and
private), tensions arising from cultural differences (e.g., language use,
foods), and other factors that are critical for exploring many dynamics
that characterize intergroup relations in contemporary cities of color.

THE THREE FACES OF COMPTON
IN THE 1950S AND 1960S

I was a "baby boom" kid who grew up in the central Los Angeles metropolitan suburb of Compton in the post–World War II decades. I lived in
three different neighborhoods in the city during the 1950s and 1960s, but
I could scarcely appreciate in those years—as a young, naive boy coming
of age—what I now know about the dramatic changes that were reshaping the city that I called home. I experienced firsthand the three faces
of Compton: brown, black, and white. The Compton of my youth was
a place where European Americans, Mexican Americans, and African
Americans co-existed, sometimes in peace and other times at odds, but
mostly in separate neighborhoods of the city. As I matriculated through

the Compton public schools and moved to other neighborhoods with my family, I experienced these largely separate communities, which stamped my identity and influenced me in ways that I could only fully appreciate much later.

I came into this world as the sixth child of a Mexican immigrant father and a Mexican American mother. My father and his family and my maternal grandparents left revolution-torn Mexico in search of security and opportunity in Southern California. Both families were from Michoacán, a state in central Mexico, and both ended up living in Compton in the immediate post–World War I years. They were part of the small but growing community of Mexicans that migrated to Compton and the hundreds of thousands of others who settled in California and the Southwest during the early decades of the twentieth century. I was born in 1948 in the same little house where all my siblings were also born, a neighborhood we called simply *El Barrio*. Through age eight, the *barrio* was my social universe. Located on the north-central boundary of Compton and bordering the unincorporated areas of Los Angeles County known as Watts and Willowbrook, *El Barrio* is where Mexican Compton took root.

As a child, the *barrio* seemed to me thoroughly Mexican, a mixture of older Mexican immigrants who spoke only Spanish, and a first generation of Mexican Americans who, like my uncles and aunts, were fully bilingual. The younger kids, like me, were among the first in our families to speak mostly English by the time we entered kindergarten. The *barrio* was a relatively self-contained world where two local Mexican-owned markets, a *panadería-tortillería* (bakery-tortilla shop), a liquor store (owned by an Italian family), and a few other small, Mexican-owned shops were the center of the community. These small businesses were located alongside the Pacific Electric Railway tracks, the "Red Car" line that divided the *barrio*. To the north, the Mexican neighborhoods extended into the Willowbrook area but ended where the largely black neighborhoods of Watts began. Outside the few blocks of the *barrio* that housed the 200 to 300 Chicano (a term we often used to refer to one another) families in the neighborhood, working-class European American families lived in inexpensive homes scattered throughout the larger area of north-central Compton. Just to the east of the *barrio* lay the light industrial area along Alameda Street, places where many *barrio* residents found work and where we kids jumped fences to play games amid the toxic industrial sites in our backyards.

Our exposure to the world outside the *barrio* came when we attended the neighborhood elementary school or went along with our parents or sometimes with our older siblings to downtown Compton, the city's main retail area, a "Main Street USA" type of commercial strip along two blocks in the center of this city of about 72,000 people in 1960. Through most of the 1950s the face of Compton was mostly white, though Mexican Americans patronized the stores; blacks, however, did not frequent downtown stores and the one movie theater until the late 1950s and early 1960s. The elementary school I attended, located on the outskirts of the *barrio*, initiated my realization that we Mexican American kids were somehow "different," and that we were a minority in Compton. General Rosecrans School, the primary grade school I attended, was predominantly European American. This public elementary school brought my *barrio* friends and me into contact with the white children from the ethnically mixed nearby neighborhoods and with the more middle- and working-class children from the exclusively white neighborhoods across Rosecrans Avenue. Here is where we also encountered the first few black kids to enroll in school from the neighborhoods west of the *barrio*. Little did I know back in 1956, as a third grader, that I would reunite years later with some of my black and white classmates in other locations in the city.

I recall other experiences that exposed me to Compton outside the *barrio*. Unbeknownst to our parents, my older brother took me on Halloween nights across Rosecrans Avenue to go trick-or-treating at the homes of white folks, who gave us big candy bars. One of my uncles related to me recently in an interview how in his youth during the 1930s and early 1940s, Rosecrans Avenue, one of the main thoroughfares in Compton that bordered the *barrio*, was the "color line" boundary that Mexicans did not cross.

My life in the *barrio* came to an abrupt end in November 1956 when my parents sold the home they had lived in for twenty-six years (I was eight years old) to the Catholic Archdiocese. Our property was adjacent to the tiny ethnic parish church built for the growing number of Mexican parishioners sometime in the 1920s; a larger structure with buildings for the clergy and a parking lot was planned for the entire side of the block where our house was located. The Church asked my parents to sell their home; in the 1950s, a Catholic family like my own did not refuse a request by the Church in a Mexican community. My father found a vacant lot for sale in the southernmost section of Compton called Richland Farms. The name for this neighborhood was appropriate, for it bordered the largest undeveloped land base in South Los Angeles at the time (the Dominguez Hills–Carson area), a huge tract of land that many Mexican American and Japanese American tenant farmers cultivated but which was owned by whites. I went from living in the *barrio,* in an old, wood-exterior home my father had added on to after the arrival of new children, to a brand-new stucco home. My dad did all of the concrete–related work for the house; the only way he could afford this new home was by saving labor costs through the use of his skills as a cement finisher. Richland Farms, bordering what was then one of the last open, semi-rural areas in southern Los Angeles County, was the only area of Compton that allowed residents to keep horses and other animals on their property. The community consisted of white, mostly working-class and middle-class families, though some Mexican Americans and a few Filipino families were scattered throughout the neighborhoods. No African Americans lived in this part of Compton in 1956. But by the early 1960s, my neighborhood was rapidly changing.

The second elementary school I attended reflected the demographic transition in process in West Compton through the early 1960s. The school was located in the southwestern quadrant of Compton about a mile away from my new home, in the heart of a suburban tract of small, modest homes built in the immediate postwar years. The students at Longfellow Elementary were mostly white, with a few Mexican American kids, when I joined the third grade class in 1956. However, by the time I reached the sixth grade in 1960, the profile of the school had changed. A large number of African American kids were headed with me to Walton Junior High School, the newest of three middle schools serving West Compton neighborhoods.

When I began the seventh grade at Walton JHS my friends and classmates—white, Mexican, black, and a few Japanese—reflected a moment in time when this school and Westside neighborhoods were racially integrated. It was only a transitory moment. A barometer of racial change in West Compton in the 1960s, Walton Junior High School's population was about 20 to 30 percent African American when I arrived in 1960, but by the time I graduated in 1963, blacks composed about 90 percent of the students, and only a few white students remained. As a consequence, my social world turned completely black. My closest friends were black and my girlfriend was black. My favorite music was Motown, and as an athlete in three sports, I competed with and against African Americans (except when we played the two East Compton junior highs that were almost all white, and that we relished beating soundly in every sport!). It seemed at this stage in my life that my identity was as much black as it was Mexican, though there were times when I encountered blacks whom I did not know and was rudely reminded that I was not black.

My life among black friends in West Compton came crashing down on me unexpectedly in the summer of 1963 shortly after graduating from Walton JHS. The racial profile of my neighborhood, like so many in West Compton, was undergoing great change—whites were moving out en masse and blacks were moving in. My father, like so many others, believed property values would plummet as African Americans moved nearby. On the one hand, it might be considered odd that a Mexican immigrant would sell his home out of fear of depreciation because blacks had moved into the neighborhood, especially when seven years earlier he had faced housing discrimination himself. When he sold our home in the *barrio* and had inquired about property in the adjacent city of Lynwood, he was told by a realtor in this exclusively white suburb located just north of Compton that "We don't sell homes to Mexicans!" On the other hand, I can, in retrospect, understand why my father—a hardworking, mostly Spanish-speaking, labor-union advocate, and staunch Democratic Party voter—wanted to sell our home before his single greatest investment, at least in his mind, was jeopardized, for whatever reason.

My parents bought a home in the easternmost neighborhood of Compton that overlapped with the city of Paramount. I soon learned that I would have to attend the all-white high school in East Compton. I threatened to go live with black friends so I could attend Compton High instead of going to "that white school" on the Eastside. Of course, sixteen-year-olds usually lose these types of battles with their parents. In September 1963 I enrolled at Dominguez High School. My world went from black to white as I came to know the other face of Compton.

Dominguez High had a tiny Mexican American student population, approximately 5 percent of the student body. There was not one black kid in the entire school when I enrolled as a sophomore. I quickly adjusted to my new social reality, mostly, at first, through sports as I formed friendships with my football, basketball, and track squad teammates. The school's vice-principal knew that I had been involved in Walton JHS student government as a leader and encouraged me to run for president of the sophomore class. I did, and I won. As a result, I made more friends and was integrated into the student body. By the end of my first year at Dominguez I began to feel included. I no longer felt like the outsider, the new student from the Westside.

Dominguez High faced great challenges from 1964 to 1966. In 1965, my junior year, the first African American student enrolled in school and he became my football teammate. I remember vividly hearing another teammate say he was going to print "KKK" on his helmet and go after the "black bastard"—and he did. A few more African American students followed, and in my senior year dozens more were bused to Dominguez High from the black Westside, an effort by school district officials to desegregate. All hell broke loose as white boys fought with the blacks—someone scrawled "Niggers go home" on a building in the front of the school. Knowing about my roots on the Westside and the fact that many of the African American students now at Dominguez were my former classmates at Walton JHS, the school principal asked me as student body president to preside over a multiracial forum to help the school get past the worst days of racial tension. The fighting subsided, but most blacks and whites remained segregated in separate social worlds at Dominguez High.

I left Compton for UCLA in 1966, and by the time I graduated from college in 1970, Dominguez had become a predominantly black school; only a handful of white kids remained there. The transition from white to black that had occurred a few years earlier in West Compton was now repeated in East Compton. In the midst of these racial demographic changes, the *barrio*, by contrast, remained largely unchanged, at least until the late 1970s, when a new immigration from Mexico created yet another demographic transformation in the city.

Growing up in Compton during a period of enormous change gave me exposure to the lives of Mexican folks, African Americans, and European Americans that was unusual for anyone my age living in a still highly segregated America of the late 1950s and 1960s. I did not understand then what I now know about why these three communities were separate and unequal. When I was coming of age in Compton it was no coincidence that the city was divided residentially by race and ethnicity. Compton and the many emerging minority-majority cities like it during the second half of the twentieth century tell us a great deal about larger trends and processes of demographic change that are transforming metropolitan America. My young life was caught up in these changes, one person among millions of others who were part of the formative history of cities of color.

GOING BACK TO COMPTON, THIRTY YEARS LATER

Compton as a Minority-Majority City

With the exception of two cousins who still live in the city, all of my relatives had moved from Compton by the mid-1970s. My parents moved, in 1971, to the city of Stanton in Orange County; they were following three of my siblings who also relocated there. Although I did return to the *barrio* once, in the early 1990s, with my mother for a nostalgic visit in the waning years of her life, there was little else to bring me back to the Compton I once knew. I occasionally read articles in the *Los Angeles Times* about the troubles Compton encountered in the 1980s and 1990s and I was generally familiar with the notorious reputation the city had acquired—gang violence, black-Latino tensions, deteriorating schools, and the home of "gangsta rap" music. By the time I decided to return to Compton in 1999–2000, this time as an academic, I had been gone for three decades. Nevertheless, I wanted to understand from a scholarly perspective how and why the city had changed so drastically during my formative years and especially in the thirty years since I had left to pursue a career in higher education. What I discovered about Compton revived memories and opened my eyes to the tremendous changes the city had experienced since the time I had called it home. Reflecting a growing trend apparent among many suburbs throughout Los Angeles and California and even across metropolitan America, Compton had become a city of color (Camarillo 2007).

Compton's transformation in the second half of the twentieth century was part of broader societal changes that altered the character of Los Angeles and much of Southern California. Although the city was among the oldest American pioneer farming communities in Los Angeles County, established on a tract of land purchased from Juan José Dominguez's Rancho San Pedro in 1866, the town was not formally incorporated until 1888. A place with only a few thousand souls through the first two to three decades of the 1900s, Compton experienced substantial population growth during and after World War II, a development that reshaped communities across the region. War mobilization brought industry, people, and jobs to the booming Los Angeles metropolis, and Compton, like so many other suburbs, was caught up in a wave of growth. A city of about 16,000 people in 1940, Compton was home to nearly 48,000 by 1950 (Camarillo 2004).

The Role of Realtors in Residential Segregation

It was not happenstance that the vast majority of Compton's residents were white (approximately 93 percent) in 1950. As early as the 1920s, Compton realtors, like their counterparts throughout the state and nation at large, systematically excluded people of color from most city neighborhoods. Race-related restrictive real estate covenants forbade property owners to sell to anyone other than European Americans. These clauses in real estate deeds were ubiquitous and had enormous power in determining who could and who could not live in a neighborhood, a subdivision, or an entire city. The racially restrictive covenant was arguably the most important tool realtors and home owners had at their disposal to keep certain cities and neighborhoods white. Responding to a survey sent to realty boards up and down the state in 1927, the president of Compton's board frankly stated "all subdivisions in Compton since 1921 have restrictions against any but the white race. . . . we have only a few Mexicans and Japanese in the old part of the city" (Survey of Race Relations 1925–27). Up through the 1940s, Mexicans were restricted to one section of the city, north of downtown at the city's northern boundary— the neighborhood where all of the children in my family were born. In 1939, when officials with the federal Home Owners Loan Corporation (HOLC) surveyed the Los Angeles metropolitan area to determine the security ratings for federal financing of homes, the staff that visited Compton reported positively on most areas of the city with the exception of one: "The industrial section adjacent to the area on the east that contains many nondescript residential structures largely inhabited by Mexicans and other subversive racial elements." This report also noted that Compton's security rating was threatened by other "subversive racial elements from [the] north" (U.S. Home Owners Loan Corporation 1939). The north referred to here obviously included Watts, a community where blacks and Mexicans lived in large numbers, and still further north lay South Central Los Angeles, the district where the great majority of blacks in the City of Angels resided. The HOLC survey reports were critically important because the areas marked by officials within "red lines" were considered undesirable and, therefore, bad risks for federally funded home loans. "Red-lining" and restrictive covenants together created an invisible barrier that determined where people of color could live and where they could buy homes. However, forces at play near the northern borders of Compton sent this barrier crashing down beginning in the 1950s. In the decade after World War II, African Americans in Watts and in South Central were poised to spill over into the northwestern neighborhoods of Compton (Sides 2003).

Realtors, both black and white, played a key role in the demographic transition of Compton in the 1950s and 1960s. They did so by using "block busting" tactics to start what became a white exodus from Compton. For example, some of the first black families to buy homes in Compton were able to do so only because their white friends purchased homes from other whites only to turn immediately around and sell them to the African Americans. White realtors, realizing the profit to be made, urged white neighbors to sell quickly before prices plummeted. Black realtors also profited by enticing African Americans to purchase homes at high resale prices, thus encouraging more whites to flee. As more and more whites fled the Westside, realtors of both races fed the frenzy. The out-migration of white families occurred first in the northwest section of Compton bordering neighborhoods in South Central Los Angeles.

Middle-class and working-class African Americans seeking better housing and better schools for their children were drawn to Compton. For many black families from the South who had come to California in the postwar years and who previously had been excluded from predominantly white suburbs, Compton was perceived as a huge "move up." "This was the nicest, most beautiful little city [with] clean, tree-lined streets," recalled an African American resident who purchased a home in Compton in 1952. Another longtime citizen of the city similarly reminisced about how having a Compton address was a badge of status among African Americans in the 1950s and early 1960s: "If you said you lived in Compton, people thought you had money because it was predominantly Caucasian when we moved here" (Cropper 2005, 64). As the first black families moved into previously all-white neighborhoods in the 1950s, Compton's Westside became increasingly known as the "black side of town."

The Rise of Black Politicians and "Gangsta" Rap

My recollections of the changing demography of classmates at Walton Junior High are reflected in U. S. population figures for the 1960s. Between 1950 and 1960 the percentage of blacks in Compton, all of whom lived on the Westside, rose from 5 percent to 33 percent; whites composed 60 percent, and Mexican Americans made up 7 percent of the city's population. By the early 1960s, Compton's Realtors and residents had divided the city geographically, separating white/East Compton from black and brown/West Compton. The railroad tracks along Alameda Street were the literal line drawn in the sand to keep blacks out of the Eastside. However, the nearby Watts Riots in 1965 foiled any plan to keep minorities out of East Compton. The immediate cause of the unrest was the arrest of Marquette Frye, a twenty-one-year-old African American man detained by police for driving under the influence. Reflecting the urban violence plaguing many cities of color during that tumultuous time, and in response to reports of police brutality, the South Central neighborhood of Watts erupted into violence; many African Americans retaliated by rioting and attacking white businesses. Whites responded by fleeing en masse. By 1970, African Americans constituted the great majority in Compton, 71 percent, with Mexican Americans at 13 percent. Whites fell to 16 percent in 1970 and had nearly disappeared from the city's landscape by 1980 (U.S. Department of Commerce 1962, 1972a, 1972b, 1982; Franklin 1962).

African American leaders in Compton rejoiced as white flight gave them a chance to take over the reins of political power in the early 1970s. Having been shut out of city politics well into the 1960s, African Americans in Compton felt hopeful that a new day was dawning for them as federal dollars poured into the city to support a variety of programs. Compton was reportedly the first municipality west of the Mississippi River to be administered entirely by blacks. But hope turned to despair by the late 1970s and 1980s as problems facing the city mounted. The much-heralded white exodus of the 1960s created turmoil for Compton's infrastructure and tax base. The city's few banks closed, many medical facilities were boarded up, and the numerous auto dealerships that lined Long Beach Boulevard relocated. Small businesses followed suit, especially as the downtown business district spiraled downward into economic depression and physical deterioration. By the mid-1970s Compton's historic downtown was bulldozed and replaced with a commercial strip mall. The decreasing tax revenue hit the city hard, the schools in particular. Old school buildings began to crumble from neglect as the city's school system went into debt, one so great that by the late 1980s the California State Superintendent of Public Instruction threatened a takeover. In 1993 the bankrupt Compton Unified School District was the first such district to be handed over to a state-appointed administrator under receivership.

The reputation of Compton as a poor, black city with failing schools was made worse as rising gang activity and the introduction of crack cocaine led to spikes in violent crime and the city's dubious distinction as the "murder capital" of the nation by the late 1980s and early 1990s. The city was hurled into the regional and national consciousness as an African American ghetto where the Crips and Bloods and "gangsta rap" music were born (Camarillo 2001). Ironically, however, Compton was not entirely a black city by the 1980s and 1990s. In fact, the city was rapidly becoming Latino. A second racial transformation began to reshape Compton in the last quarter of the twentieth century, one as dramatic as the population change that catapulted the city from white to black during the 1950s and 1960s.

By the time I returned in 1999–2000, Compton clearly had become a Latino-majority city. The Mexican community where I was born and raised continued to be concentrated in the historic *barrio* of Compton, but the chief difference in 1999 was that Latinos—the vast majority were of Mexican origin and had immigrated since the 1970s—were now located in neighborhoods throughout the city. Compton's surging Mexican American and Mexican immigrant population was, and continues to be, part of a demographic shift that has recast the ethnic profile of the southern counties of California and the state in general. The so-called Latinoization of Los Angeles County since the 1970s has a Compton corollary. In 1970, for example, the percentage of Latinos of the total population in Los Angeles County was 15 percent (30 percent were foreign born). Between 1990 and 2005, the percentage of Latinos in the county had surged from 41 percent to 47 percent. In Compton, over the same years, the proportion of Latinos in the city went from 13 percent in 1970 to 36 percent in 1990; in 2005, Latinos comprised 58 percent of the total population. By contrast, the black population has declined during the same period. The African American population of the city peaked at 73 percent in 1980; it declined to 49 percent in 1990, and to 40 percent in 2005 (American Community Survey 2005). Immigration from Latin America and especially from Mexico (88 percent of Latinos in Compton have roots in Mexico) over the past three decades has been pivotal in turning Compton into a black-brown city.

BLACK-BROWN TENSIONS AND ATTITUDES

Compton is one of dozens of California cities of color where residents of different ethnic/racial backgrounds are grappling with tensions and, at the same time, making efforts to build unity from diversity. It is no surprise, however, that the public hears more about the black-brown tensions in Compton than they do about the black-brown struggles for conciliation. Standard sociological analyses and theories about ethnic group conflict and intergroup attitudes help us understand much about the hostility between Latinos and African Americans. Ideologies, stereotypes, prejudice, perceptions of group threat, and conflict and competition over community resources in an environment of structural inequality are all factors that characterize intergroup relations in the city (Bobo and Johnson 2000). But these and other sources of tension that help explain why mistrust, social distance, and conflict exist between blacks and Latinos can be understood only in the context of the legacies of the civil rights era, especially ideas about group rights and the politics of social justice. In many instances where conflict and tension have arisen between the two main groups in Compton, ideas about the rights accorded to particular groups surface to define the racial divide. From the arena of local politics, I draw on a few examples involving claims on institutional resources—in particular, those related to public education—to illustrate how issues of group rights and social justice often overlie contentious intergroup relations.

Since their rise to power following the European American exodus in the late 1960s, blacks in Compton have tightly controlled municipal politics. However, by the early 1990s, when population increases among Latinos pushed the group into majority status, several Mexican American leaders were voicing their discontent at the lack of representation by Latinos in elected or appointed positions in the city. Most African American elected officials in the city dismissed as unwarranted calls by certain Latino community leaders for political inclusion. Mexican Americans were viewed by blacks as newcomers to local politics who had not endured the struggles they had encountered in achieving civil rights and access to the political arena. For example, when Latino advocates tried in 2000 to convince Mayor Omar Bradley that their large community in Compton deserved some political representation in city hall, the mayor quipped: "Representation is not based on population. . . . [It] is based on participation. . . . And for the large part of the last three decades, Latino participation has not been extremely high" (Coile 2000). Earlier, in 1998, Bradley made clear his stance on Latino demands for political inclusion when he stated: "I see this as a well-constructed attempt to utilize the historical context of the African American civil rights movement for the benefit of a few people, who in fact probably don't even consider themselves non-white" (Fears 1998). From the perspective of African American leaders who had struggled to gain access to the right to vote and to representation in local government, Latinos were late arrivals—people who had not yet earned the right of political inclusion through voting and civil rights struggles.

Much to the chagrin of Latino leaders, these and other comments by black leaders exacerbated tensions and drove a wedge even further between the two groups. By the 1990s, voices of frustration and anger among Mexican Americans grew louder and more insistent. Complaints over political inclusion, representation, and fairness were aired publicly at city council meetings. With no Latino presence in city hall, a local Mexican American claimed, "there's no one to represent the Latino community . . . the mayor is black. . . . The city council is black. . . . There is not a single Latino representative on the council" (Coile 2000). An article in the *Los Angeles Times* in 1990 confirmed this observation, noting that "blacks control every public and quasi-public institution in Compton—the schools, City Hall, the Compton Chamber of Commerce, and the Democratic party machine—and show no sign they intend to share their power" (Fuetsch 1990). At a city council meeting in 1998, a Latino community member attempted to remind the all-black council of African Americans' exclusion from the city's political life a generation earlier and how they were perpetuating exclusion against Mexican Americans: "It was not that many years ago when black people were at this podium saying the same things of white folks. How could you forget?" (Fears 1998).

Some local Latino leaders became so exasperated with the slow pace of hiring Latinos for municipal jobs and in the school district that they proposed an affirmative action employment plan to the city council. Pedro Pallán, an advocate for the Mexican American community whose political aspirations were dashed by the mayor-elect in the early 1990s, stated: "Here we are, a truly minority community and the blacks are not giving us an affirmative action committee in either the city [government] or the school district." In response, a black school board trustee claimed that affirmative action was established as reparations for slavery and was "not based on going back and forth across the [U.S.-Mexico] border 10 to 15 times a year" (Fuetsch 1990). These two spokespersons, though at odds over the use of affirmative action, both invoked the language of group rights and referenced laws established to promote racial inclusion and opportunity. Other African American leaders, in response to Latino claims of underrepresentation in civic affairs, pointed to the lack of a civil rights history among Latinos as compared to blacks who struggled for generations to gain access to local institutions. A city councilman and former leader of the NAACP and noted in 1990 that "I have walked many picket lines in Compton [in the 1950s and 1960s]. . . . I have yet to have one Latino walk the picket line with me. . . . They crossed it many times" (Fuetsch 1990). Comments suggesting that Latinos had not yet paid their "political dues" only inflamed mistrust and animosity between the two groups. Refuting the claim that blacks gained political control of Compton through civil rights action, a Latino business leader in the city quipped: "Did they [blacks] really fight to get where they are now, or was it more or less that white people left and they were just here and took it [local politics] over? It was white flight, it was the Watts Riots . . . when they [whites] left" (Alatorre 2000).

Attitudes stemming from notions about group rights in the post–civil rights era not only affected how African Americans and Latinos often viewed one another regarding political matters, they reinforced other types of perceptions. Claims on the city, achieved by blacks who struggled against white intolerance and discrimination during the 1950s and into the 1960s, affect how some African Americans view their "sense of belonging," a view shattered by the transformation of the city into a majority Latino community. Language differences as well as different cultural and religious backgrounds surely help to explain social distance between members of the two groups, but among some older blacks who have resided in the city for decades, and some younger people who have grown up there, the decline of the once "good ol' days" in Compton, when the city was a beacon of opportunity for African Americans in Los Angeles, is entirely due to the increasing large Latino population. Among black residents who moved to the city in the 1960s and 1970s, before its reputation for crime and violence set in, many wax nostalgic about Compton as a haven for African Americans, a community where neighbors were like extended family: "When we came in we were literally embraced by the block club, by the community, which was predominantly black. This block had one of the most prolific block clubs in the city. . . . Our neighbors embraced us and loved us so much. It was great. We were at the right place at the right time" (Cropper 2005, 69). A woman who has resided in the city for more than half a century agreed: "Back then [the 1960s]," she said, "we were the only three blacks on the block and we stuck together. We had some friendly communities 'cause we were like family" (Cropper 2005, 69). Another woman who has lived in Compton for over forty years identified what she considered to be the "biggest problem in the city."

> We have a lot of problems because of the change in the demographics of people. We now have primarily Hispanics here or Latinos, whatever they call themselves. And unfortunately our buildings have [been] run down; the city looks dirty, it's not safe because of the drugs and the gangs. We didn't start having a graffiti problem until Latinos moved into Compton. It's really not the city you would want to live in as it was back in '63. (Cropper 2005, 70)

For yet other black residents of Compton, the dramatic growth of the Latino population, combined with other factors, contributed to the decline of the public schools and public services in general (Cropper 2005).

The anti-Latino sentiment among Compton's black residents has its reverse correlative among the Latino community of Compton. Negative perceptions of group threat and pejorative attitudes about African Americans also run deep among many Latinos. For example, a forty-year-old woman, an immigrant who came to the United States with her family in the early 1980s from Mexico and moved to Compton in the 1990s, recalled what she thought of Compton as she prepared to move there with her extended family.

> We heard there was a lot of vandalism and gangs. More than anything [I] thought about racism—racism between African Americans and Latinos. That was one of my biggest fears. More than vandalism, I was scared of racism. Initially it did seem like African Americans felt like they were the owners of the community. They felt like we were intruders. . . . It seemed they were angry with Latino people. (Avalos 2003)

A Mexican American woman in her forties, who had grown up in Compton during the 1970s and 1980s, remembered the constant warnings she received from friends and relatives about avoiding contact with blacks. Though she never experienced any personal conflict with African Americans, she was repeatedly told, "Oh, be careful when you go out because there's lots of blacks" (Quintana 2003). Perceptions such as these and others were real and often had the effect of creating social distance and distrust between African American and Latinos in Compton and throughout the region (Bobo et al. 2000).

The perceptions of both blacks and Latinos regarding the causes of the decline of the city must also be viewed within the broader context of the economic and institutional forces that set in motion the creation of cities of color such as Compton and that have thrust Latinos, blacks, and other poor groups into competition for an ever-decreasing piece of the pie. Contemporary cities of color are the products of generations of racism and structures of inequality that have turned many once-thriving suburban and urban neighborhoods into places with fragile infrastructures and municipalities struggling to provide basic services to residents. Schools often suffer from physical disrepair and lack of adequate resources. Pot-holed streets are commonplace and graffiti-marked buildings reveal the presence of youth gangs competing for neighborhood territory. High poverty and unemployment rates characterize a substantial proportion of the local populations that seem to be trapped at or near the bottom in the post-industrial economic order, a status from

which escape is difficult. Economic development and corporate investment in cities of color are rare in what is a recent history of a deepening
decline. These and other conditions in Compton and elsewhere aggra-
vate attitudes and perceptions held by Latinos and African Americans
that already tend to set them apart. Competition, real and perceived,
over scarce resources in the city often pits one group against others and
inflames negative sentiments simmering just below the surface. Mix in
problems of the language gap, cultural misunderstanding, and a mass
media that highlights these and other problems, and you have a recipe
for group contentiousness, conflict, and alienation. Yet, despite the factors that keep different groups of people apart in cities such as Compton,
there is evidence that some individuals and organizations are striving to
facilitate cooperation across ethnic, cultural, and racial lines.

FORGING A MULTIRACIAL, MULTICULTURAL
COMMUNITY

Amid the examples of distrust, disdain, fear, and social distance, there are
signs that African Americans and Latinos in Compton are attempting to
forge coalitions and to bridge historic divides. Examples of cooperation
and collaboration of the sort I discuss in this section are rarely reported in
the press because they are not deemed newsworthy by news media that
continue to focus on news that is dramatic and episodic—news of gang
violence, municipal corruption, and black-brown tensions (Wilson and
Gutiérrez 1985; Gandy 1998; Iyengar, this volume). Yet they exist. These
examples suggest that diverse people in cities of color such as Compton
may be able to build social and political ties that allow them to transcend
their differences and recognize their commonalities and mutual interests. And while the various efforts among blacks and Latinos to develop
bonds of mutual trust and cooperation might speak to pragmatic goals
that arise as a result of intergroup violence and tension, they must also be
viewed within the broader context of the ideas associated with multiculturalism. If defined partly by an intrinsic value placed on understanding
and appreciating differences among many types of human beings and
advocacy for collaboration among diverse ethno-racial, religious, and
cultural groups, then multiculturalism, as it manifests itself in Compton,
is a new development that has the potential to take this city of color in a
more positive future direction.

Religious and secular institutions and leaders are both contributing to
the establishment of a multicultural beachhead in Compton. For example,

responding to the growing discord in the 1990s among black and Latino advocates over political power and concerned about the increasing number of confrontations between African American and Mexican American gangs in the city, a group of church leaders formed Pastors for Compton (PFC). This group of Protestant and Catholic church leaders attempted to impress upon elected politicians the reality that equity between blacks and Latinos must be achieved in order to heal a divided community. Pastor of the Citizens of Zion Baptist Church and spokesman for PFC, the Reverend B. T. Newman, stated one of the practical objectives of the organization: "It's trying to preserve this transition [from majority black to majority Latino] to where it don't end up in war. I've learned if we have it right, we can share power" (Freer 2004, 33). Reflecting the sentiment of other religious leaders, the pastor of the Christian Methodist Episcopal Church, the Reverend William R. Johnson, invoked the need for political justice and inclusiveness when he claimed "We [African Americans] are today the entrenched group trying to keep out the intruders just as whites were once the entrenched group and we were the intruders." After attending a city council meeting where Latinos protested, an African American bystander voiced a similar refrain saying "Latinos should have a voice. . . . We went through the same thing when blacks came into the city and it was all white" (Freer 2004, 12).

Other groups and individuals in Compton have also promoted unity and integration among blacks and Latinos. In 1994, for example, two national civil rights advocacy organizations, the Mexican American Legal Defense and Education Fund (MALDEF) and the National Association for the Advancement of Colored People (NAACP), co-sponsored a "Unity Rally" with the intent of bringing Latinos and African Americans together to discuss mutual interests. The Reverend Reuben Anderson, one of the organizers, declared, "We recognize the ethnic diversity among us, yet we realize we have more in common that binds us together than issues that divide us" (Freer 2004, 33). A group calling itself Concerned Citizens of Compton, formed a few years ago, brought together African Americans and Latinos to deal with various problems facing residents. A member of the group, an immigrant who arrived from Mexico in 1974 who has lived in his Compton neighborhood since 1979, stated that because of the multiracial composition of the group that shares commons goals, they "talk about relations with other races . . . and that they [African Americans] are very happy with us [Latinos] and we really like working with them" (Gutiérrez 2003). A newly formed group in the city, Compton Community Partners, composed of black and Latino community-based, nonprofit organization leaders and educators, aims "to serve as a catalyst for change to help transform Compton into a city of civic-minded people who want to revitalize the community" (Compton Community Partners 2005). On various fronts, grassroots cooperation among African Americans and Latinos is taking shape.

Scattered evidence also exists suggesting that intergroup cooperation is occurring on a daily basis in the neighborhoods where Latinos and African Americans live together. A longtime black resident claims that he routinely sees young African American and Latina mothers watching out for each other's children playing on the streets and neighbors who extend cordial greetings, despite language barriers (Cleveland 2000). Another resident, a longtime Mexican American citizen of Compton, claimed that Latino and black neighbors banded together to rid their street of drugs and crime (Corral 2000). Every Sunday morning at Our Lady of Victory Catholic Church, the 9:00 A.M. English language mass brings together African American and Mexican American parishioners who pray together and greet one another after service. These and other examples of mutuality at a grassroots level may be missed by a sensationalist-oriented media, but they must be viewed alongside examples of mistrust and conflict that fill metropolitan newspapers and nightly news broadcasts in order to portray a more accurate representation of the complex realities of a multicultural city.

CITIES OF COLOR IN THE TWENTY-FIRST CENTURY

Compton is one of the hundreds of urban and suburban spaces across metropolitan America in the throes of population change. The beginning of the new century marked a milestone in the urban demographics of the nation: in 2001, more than half of America's largest cities had more blacks, Latinos, Asian Americans, and other racial minorities than whites. The number of these cities of color continues to rise. For example, between 1990 and 2000 the non-Hispanic white population in the 100 largest cities declined from 52 percent to 44 percent. In the fifty largest cities in 2006, whites were the minority population in thirty-five. In the twenty largest cities, nonwhite minorities, including Hispanics, increased their proportion of the total population from 38 percent in 1970 to 60 percent in 2000. Minorities now constitute the majority in nine of the ten largest cities in the nation, and together Latinos and African Americans form the majority in eight of these cities (Camarillo 2007; Berube 2003; Frey 2006).

The intergroup relations evolving in cities of color are reshaping the nature of race and ethnic relations in the twenty-first century. In Compton, as in other places, a complex process of change plays itself out every day with abundant examples of negative and positive intergroup relations. To be sure, the Compton of my youth is no longer, but the changing racial dynamics that I witnessed firsthand continue in different guises and under different circumstances. If the forces of multiculturalism can succeed in building a pluralistic, interactive community, then maybe the experiences of young people in Compton will be different from those I encountered in my youth.

Works Cited

•

Alatorre, Arnold. 2000. Interview with Albert M. Camarillo and Jeffrey B. Camarillo. Compton Oral History Project. Compton, CA, August 2, 2000.

Avalos, Martha. 2003. Interview with Prisilla Júarez. Compton Oral History Project. Compton, CA, August 20, 2003.

Berube, Alan. 2003. Racial and Ethnic Change in the Nation's Largest Cities. In *Redefining Urban and Suburban America: Evidence from Census 2000*, ed. by B. Katz and R. E. Lang. Washington, DC: Brookings Institution Press.

Bobo, Lawrence D., and Devon Johnson. 2000. Racial Attitudes in a Prismatic Metropolis: Mapping Identity, Stereotypes, Competition, and Views of Affirmative Action. In *Prismatic Metropolis: Inequality in Los Angeles*, ed. by L. D. Bobo, M. L. Oliver, J. H. Johnson and A. Valenzuela, Jr. New York: Russell Sage Foundation.

Camarillo, Albert M. 2007. Cities of Color: The New Racial Frontier in California's Minority-Majority Cities. *Pacific Historical Review* 76 (1):1–28.

———. 2004. Black and Brown in Compton: Demographic Change, Suburban Decline, and Intergroup Relations in a South Central Los Angeles Community, 1950 to 2000. In *Not Just Black and White: Historical and Contemporary Perspectives on Immigration, Race, and Ethnicity in the United States*, ed. by N. Foner and G. M. Fredrickson. New York: Russell Sage Foundation.

Camarillo, Jeffrey Benjamín. 2001. In and Out of Compton: The Impact of Demographic Change and Urban Decline in a Los Angeles Community, the Case of Compton. Senior Honors Thesis, Urban Studies Program, University of Pennsylvania.

Cleveland, Walter. 2000. Interview with Jeffrey B. Camarillo. Compton Oral History Project. Compton, CA, August 10, 2000.

Compton Community Partners. 2005. Focus Statement. Compton, CA

Coile, Zachary. 2000. "Growing Latino clout in Compton." *San Francisco Chronicle*, February 6.

Corral, Ramona. 2000. Interview with Jeffrey B. Camarillo. Compton Oral History Project. Compton, CA, August 4, 2000.

Cropper, Porsha Q. 2005. "Can We All Get Along?" Black Perceptions of Group Threat and the Challenge of New Racial Demographics in Los Angeles and Compton. Senior Honors Thesis, Comparative Studies in Race and Ethnicity, Stanford University.

Fears, Darryl. 1998. "Compton Latinos Still on Outside Looking In." *Los Angeles Times,* April 16, A-8.

Franklin, David. 1962. *Compton: A Community in Transition.* Los Angeles: Los Angeles Welfare Planning Council.

Freer, Regina. 2004. Black Brown City: Black Urban Regimes and the Challenge of Changing Demographics, a Case Study of Compton, California. Unpublished paper. Occidental College.

Frey, William H. 2006. Diversity Spreads Out: Metropolitan Shifts in Hispanic, Asian, and Black Populations since 2000. In *Brookings Institution Living Cities Census Series.* Washington, DC: Brookings Institution Press.

Fuetsch, Michele. 1990. "Latino Aspirations Rise in Compton." *Los Angeles Times,* May 7, B-1.

Gandy, Oscar H. Jr. 1998. *Communication and Race: A Structural Perspective.* London: Arnold.

Gutiérrez, Francisco. 2003. Interview with Paloma Rosenbaum. Compton Oral History Project. Compton, CA, July 21, 2003.

Quintana, Felisa. 2003. Interview with Crystal Garland. Compton Oral History Project. Compton, CA, August 1, 2003.

Sides, Josh. 2003. *L.A. City Limits: African American Los Angeles from the Great Depression to the Present.* Berkeley: University of California Press.

Stanford University. Survey of Race Relations. 1925–27. Box 2.

U.S. Department of Commerce. 1962. Characteristics of the Population—California 1960, ed. by Bureau of the Census. Washington, DC: Government Printing Office.

———. 1972a. Census of the Population, 1970: Characteristics of the Population—California. Washington, DC: Government Printing Office.

———. 1972b. Census of the Population and Housing, 1970: General Characteristics of the Population, ed. by Bureau of the Census. Washington DC: Government Printing Office.

———. 1981. Census of the Population, 1980: Age, Sex, Race and Spanish Origin of the Population, ed. by Bureau of the Census. Washington, DC: Government Printing Office.

———. 1982. Census of the Population, 1980: General Characteristics of the Population, California, PC 80-1-Bb, vol. 1, ed. by Bureau of the Census. Washington, DC: Government Printing Office.

———. 1993. Census of the Population, 1990. California 040, ed. by Bureau of the Census. Washington, DC: Government Printing Office.

———. *American FactFinder.* 2000. http://factfinder.census.gov.

———. *American Community Survey.* 2005. http://census.gov/acs/www/index.html.

U. S. Home Owners Loan Corporation. 1939. Security Map #1 Metropolitan Los Angeles, California. Washington, DC: National Archives.

Wilson, Clint C., and Felix Gutiérrez. 1985. *Minorities and Media: Diversity and the End of Mass Communication.* Thousand Oaks, CA: Sage.

11

Structured for Failure
Race, Resources, and Student Achievement

Linda Darling-Hammond

•

In this essay, I show that many students underperform, fail, and drop out of large urban high schools because they do not have access to well-prepared teachers or to a good-quality curriculum. I start from the perspective that academic underperformance is not primarily the result of deficiencies that reside in the students themselves but is instead substantially the consequence of inequality in educational resources. I begin with description of a successful high school and then discuss those factors that structure failure in schools serving primarily low-income racial/ethnic minority students. Those factors include school funding, teacher salaries, and teacher qualifications. The essay concludes with a discussion of the societal consequences of the achievement gap and describes the need for policies that can create more equal schools. The most important of these policies are equalizing access to school resources, creating a twenty-first-century curriculum, developing thoughtful methods of assessment, and supporting well-prepared teachers.

WHEN I WAS YOUNG, I SAW AND EXPERIENCED SOME OF THE RESULTS OF educational inequality, but it was only when I became a high school teacher in an urban school that I became conscious of how these disparities operate. My first teaching experience was in Camden, New Jersey, a community that was then virtually all black and where there was very little investment in the public schools. I quickly discovered that as a teacher you can work hard to create a little oasis in your classroom and make a small difference in the lives of your students, but you cannot, as an individual, truly transform schools that are structured to fail. Racism and unequal access to educational opportunity are systematized in this country's schools in ways that are invisible to most of us as students or even as teachers.

Many of the students at Camden High School, where I was learning to teach, were very bright, but they had access to few educational resources. The district spent only about half of what wealthy districts like Cherry Hill and Princeton could spend. I knew only that the book room was bare, there were few educational materials, classes were large, and just a handful of college preparatory classes were offered. Like many of my colleagues, I was underprepared for teaching, and there was a huge difference between my colleagues' access to learning opportunities in these high-poverty schools and that of teachers in wealthier districts. Although I didn't know it then, New Jersey had been repeatedly but unsuccessfully sued between the 1960s and the late 1990s for its unequal allocation of resources to Camden, Trenton, Newark, and other low-wealth districts serving students of color. When the state was finally forced by the courts to increase funding to these urban districts nearly thirty years later, many had become so dysfunctional that they were barely able to be repaired.

During my time in the classroom, I came to realize that schools themselves are often structured to produce high levels of failure, particularly big, comprehensive high schools in cities like Camden, Philadelphia, New York, Los Angeles, and many other places. It is easy for a student never to be well known or to feel he belongs if he attends school in a factory model warehouse with thousands of other students and where each student cycles through six or eight teachers in forty-five- or fifty-minute segments, and each teacher sees 150 to 200 students daily. When this student comes to school with challenges that require concern and attention, and he is only an anonymous cipher in an overcrowded classroom, the conditions for failure are established. It should be no surprise that more than half of students drop out of central city schools that are designed in this way.

CREATING SCHOOLS THAT WORK

In addition to working on teacher preparation issues, I have focused on the critical issue of redesigning schools. In the last decade, educators in a few cities throughout the country have seen what can happen when reformers reconceptualize schools and create small, personalized high schools for students who were previously underserved. In New York City, schools like the Urban Academy, International High School, and Vanguard High are among those that now routinely graduate at least 90 percent of their students and send 90 percent to college (Darling-Hammond, Ancess, and Ort 2002). A movement to redesign schools across the country is beginning to change the odds for students elsewhere as well.

Here in California at Stanford University, my colleagues and I used what was learned from these efforts to co-found the East Palo Alto High School. This is a charter high school and it is the first public school to exist in that community since 1975. At that time, East Palo Alto was an all-black community that lost its high school as a result of desegregation. Because communities were highly segregated as a function of discriminatory housing practices, the high school districts needed to find ways to integrate their schools. Rather than busing white students into East Palo Alto, the decision was made to close Ravenswood High School and bus students of color from that community to surrounding predominantly white communities. There, most were assigned to the bottom tracks of large comprehensive high schools, from which about two-thirds ultimately failed to graduate.

The East Palo Alto community is now predominantly Latino, with African Americans and Pacific Islanders making up about one-third of the community. The new high school serves about 300 students in a design in which all students take a college preparatory curriculum, with extra supports to ensure their success. Teachers are motivated to be there and are well prepared for the students they are teaching; they are engaged in continual learning to improve their practice during professional development time embedded in the school day. They work in teams that share students and plan together, and each teacher works closely with fifteen advisees and their families throughout the students' four years of school. With this design, of the first group of entering students who did not move away or transfer, the school graduated 93 percent and sent 90 percent on to higher education. It is possible to turn around the unequal educational outcomes to which we have become accustomed, but it is critical to understand how the system structures these outcomes before they can be changed.

UNDERSTANDING THE ACHIEVEMENT GAP

It is fashionable these days for policymakers to worry about the achievement gap—the large differential in measured achievement and school attainment of white students and students of color (predominantly African American and Latino students). The achievement gap has been widening in recent years. Indeed, according to many indicators of schooling success, educational access was more equitable in the mid-1970s than it is today.

During the years following *Brown v. Board of Education* when desegregation and early efforts at school finance reform were launched, and when the Great Society's War on Poverty increased investments in urban and poor rural schools, substantial gains were made in equalizing both educational inputs and outcomes. Gaps in school spending, in access to qualified teachers, and in access to higher education were smaller in the 1970s than they had been before and, in many states, than they have been since. In the mid-1970s college attendance rates were actually equivalent for a short period of time for white, black and Hispanic students (see Figure 11.1). The gains from the "Great Society" programs were later pushed back. Most federal programs supporting investments in college access and K–12 schools in urban and poor rural areas were reduced or eliminated in the 1980s. Meanwhile, childhood poverty rates,

FIGURE 11.1 | **COLLEGE ENROLLMENT RATES: ACTUAL AND TREND RATES OF IMMEDIATE ENROLLMENT IN POSTSECONDARY EDUCATION BY RACE/ETHNICITY, OCTOBER 1972–2003.**

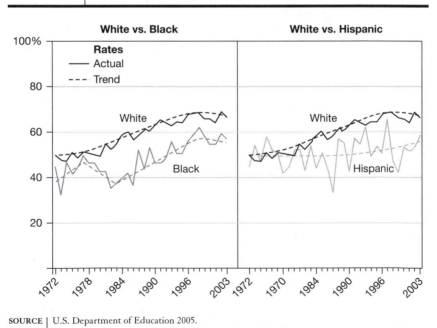

SOURCE | U.S. Department of Education 2005.

homelessness, and lack of access to health care also grew. Thus, it is no surprise that gaps in achievement began to widen again after the mid-1980s and have, in many areas, continued to grow in the decades since.

On national assessments in reading, writing, mathematics, and science, black students' performance continues to lag behind that of white students. In 2002, on the National Assessment of Educational Progress, the average black or Hispanic twelfth grader was reading at the level of the average white eighth grader. Scores in writing have also declined for eighth grade and eleventh grade black students since 1988. Although there have been some improvements in mathematics and science for fourth and eighth graders, the achievement gap has stayed constant or widened since 1990 (NCES 2005).

Progress in educational attainment, which was substantial after 1950, has also slowed. While graduation rates for black eighteen- to twenty-four-year-olds increased rapidly from under 50 percent to just over 75 percent between the 1950s and the early 1980s, these rates have been nearly stagnant for the last two decades. In recent years, dropout rates for African Americans have persisted near 13 percent (U.S. Census Bureau 2008). Meanwhile, graduation rates declined in such states as Florida, Georgia, New York, North Carolina, South Carolina, and Texas as policies that require passage of exit tests for graduation have been implemented, with the largest decreases for black and Latino students (NCES 2003).

The lack of progress in closing the gap during the 1990s is not entirely surprising, as the situation in many urban schools deteriorated in that decade. Drops in real per-pupil expenditures accompanied tax cuts and growing enrollments. Meanwhile, student needs grew with new waves of immigration, concentrated poverty and homelessness, and increased numbers of students requiring second-language instruction and special educational services.

EXPLANATIONS FOR INEQUALITY

Recurring explanations of educational inequality typically blame children and their families for lack of effort, poor child rearing, a "culture of poverty," or inadequate genes (e.g., Herrnstein and Murray 1994). The presumption that undergirds much of the usual conversation is that equal educational opportunity now exists; therefore, continued low levels of achievement on the part of students of color must be intrinsic to them, their families, or their communities.

What does not usually enter the conversation are the sources of inequality that actually exist in our schools. Educational outcomes for students of color are much more a function of their unequal access to key educational resources, including skilled teachers and a high-quality curriculum, than they are a function of race. These disparities reinforce the wide inequalities in income among families, with the most resources being spent on children from the wealthiest communities and the fewest on the children of the poor, especially in high-minority communities.

Whereas in most countries, schools are funded centrally and equally, in the United States the top 10 percent of districts spend ten times more than the bottom 10 percent. There are districts in this country that spend $40,000 per pupil, and there are others that spend $4,000 per pupil. Within a given state, the ratio of high- to low-spending districts is usually two or three to one. Nationwide, schools that serve students of color and low-income students have lower funding levels; larger class sizes; fewer well-qualified teachers; fewer college preparatory classes; and fewer books, computers, and other materials (Darling-Hammond 2004).

Here in California, funding has grown more inadequate and inequitable since the passage of Proposition 13, which limited property tax rates in 1979. As California's public schools became majority "minority," the state slipped to thirty-eighth in expenditures per student, forty-eighth in K–12 expenditures as a share of personal income, and fiftieth in the ratio of students per teacher by 2000 (EdSource 2001, 1). Meanwhile, inequality grew. As the California Postsecondary Education Commission (CPEC) noted:

> The gap in expenditures for education between the high-spending and low-spending school districts in our state in the 1991–92 school year was $1,392—a figure that placed our state at approximately the 30th percentile nationally. Today, that gap has risen to $4,480. . . . Perhaps the most disturbing part of this statewide picture is that many of the disparities noted above are consistently and pervasively related to the socioeconomic and racial-ethnic composition of the student bodies in school as well as the geographical location of schools. That is, schools in our low socioeconomic communities, as well as our neighborhoods with a predominance of Black and Latino families, often have dilapidated facilities, few or inadequate science laboratories, teachers in secondary schools providing instruction in classes for which they have no credential,

curriculum that is unimaginative and boring, and teachers who change schools yearly and lack the professional development to complement their teaching with new instructional strategies and materials. (CPEC 1998, 29)

Williams et al. v. California, a school finance equity lawsuit brought in 2000, documented the extraordinarily impoverished conditions in many schools, especially the growing number of "apartheid" schools serving almost exclusively low-income racial/ethnic minority students. This description of one San Francisco school serving African American and Latino students was typical of others in the California complaint:

> At Luther Burbank, students cannot take textbooks home for homework in any core subject because their teachers have enough textbooks for use in class only. . . . For homework, students must take home photocopied pages, with no accompanying text for guidance or reference, when and if their teachers have enough paper to use to make homework copies. . . . Luther Burbank is infested with vermin and roaches and students routinely see mice in their classrooms. One dead rodent has remained, decomposing, in a corner in the gymnasium since the beginning of the school year. The school library is rarely open, has no librarian, and has not recently been updated. The latest version of the encyclopedia in the library was published in approximately 1988. Luther Burbank classrooms do not have computers. Computer instruction and research skills are not, therefore, part of Luther Burbank students' regular instruction. The school no longer offers any art classes for budgetary reasons. . . . Two of the three bathrooms at Luther Burbank are locked all day, every day. . . . Students have urinated or defecated on themselves at school because they could not get into an unlocked bathroom. . . . When the bathrooms are not locked, they often lack toilet paper, soap, and paper towels, and the toilets frequently are clogged and overflowing. . . . Ceiling tiles are missing and cracked in the school gym, and school children are afraid to play basketball and other games in the gym because they worry that more ceiling tiles will fall on them during their games. . . . The school has no air conditioning. On hot days classroom temperatures climb into the 90s. The school heating system does not work well. In winter, children often wear coats, hats, and gloves during class to keep warm. . . . Eleven of the 35 teachers at Luther

Burbank have not yet obtained regular, nonemergency teaching credentials, and 17 of the 35 teachers only began teaching at Luther Burbank this school year. (*Williams et al. v. State of California* 2000)

Such profound inequalities in resource allocations are supported by the increasing resegregation of schools over the decades of the 1980s and '90s. In 2000, 72 percent of the nation's black students attended predominantly minority schools, up significantly from the low point of 63 percent in 1980. The proportion of students of color in intensely segregated schools also increased. More than a third of African American and Latino students (37 and 38 percent, respectively) attended schools with a minority enrollment of 90–100 percent. Furthermore, for all groups except whites, racially segregated schools are almost always schools with high concentrations of poverty (Orfield 2001). Nearly two-thirds of African American and Latino students attend schools where most students are eligible for free or reduced-price lunch.

One of the most important disparities resulting from inadequate spending in high-minority schools is a shortage of qualified teachers. For example, salaries for comparably educated and experienced teachers varied by a ratio of almost two to one in California in 2000, and the disparity grew to three to one when adjusted for local labor market differences (see Table 11.1). Cities like Oakland and San Francisco offer nearly $10,000 less for a beginning teacher than wealthy suburbs like Los Altos and San Mateo, and the disparities grow to as much as $30,000 for a teacher at the top of the scale. Furthermore, teachers in these urban districts often need to spend more of their own money for books and supplies, and they must contend with larger class sizes and fewer supports for themselves and for their students.

The primary result of these disparities is that the low-paying districts—again those that serve the least-advantaged students—have shortages of teachers. Indeed, in California a few years ago, there were 50,000 teachers who were teaching on emergency credentials, without training for their jobs. These teachers were almost entirely located in high-minority, high-poverty schools. In 2001, for example, students in California's most segregated minority schools were more than five times as likely to have uncertified teachers than those in predominantly white schools. In the 20 percent of schools serving almost exclusively students of color, more than 20 percent of teachers were uncertified (Shields et al. 2001; see Figure 11.2) Similar inequalities have been documented in lawsuits challenging school funding in Massachusetts, South Carolina, New York,

TABLE 11.1 | **RANGE OF CALIFORNIA SALARIES, 2000–2001**

Salary Schedule Level	Range of Regular Salaries (County, District)		Range of Adjusted Salaries Ratio to State Average (County, District)	
	From	**To**	**From**	**To**
Lowest	$23,194 (Lake County, Kelseyville Unified)	$45,709 (Alameda County, Pleasanton Unified)	0.502 (Santa Clara County, Alum Rock Union)	1.601 (Calaveras County, Vallecito Union)
BA+30, step 1	$27,639 (Tehama County, Reeds Creek Elementary)	$49,591 (Alameda County, Pleasanton Unified)	0.597 (Santa Clara County, Gilroy Unified)	1.601 (Calaveras County, Vallecito Union)
BA+60, step 10	$37,278 (Fresno County, Alvina Elementary)	$69,478 (Santa Clara County, Mountain View-Los Altos Union)	0.880 (Santa Clara County, Gilroy Unified)	2.205 (Riverside County, Corona–Norco Unified)

SOURCE | Data for lowest salary offered and BA+60, step 10, are from the California Department of Education School Fiscal Services Division, "Certificated Teacher Salary Schedule with Placement, 2000–2001" (form J-90). Data for the county salary adjustment (average earnings per job, 1999) are from California Department of Finance Economic Research, "California County Profiles," February, 2002.

and Texas, among other states. By every measure of qualifications—certification, subject matter background, pedagogical training, selectivity of college attended, test scores, or experience—less-qualified teachers are found in schools serving greater numbers of low-income and minority students (NCES 1997; Lankford, Loeb, and Wyckoff 2002). In Jeannie Oakes's (1990) nationwide study of the distribution of mathematics and science opportunities, students in high-minority schools had less than a 50 percent chance of being taught by math or science teachers who held degrees and licenses in the fields in which they were teaching.

These disparities are most troubling given recent evidence about the influence of teacher quality on student achievement. In an analysis of

FIGURE 11.2 | **DISTRIBUTION OF UNQUALIFIED TEACHERS IN CALIFORNIA, 2001.**

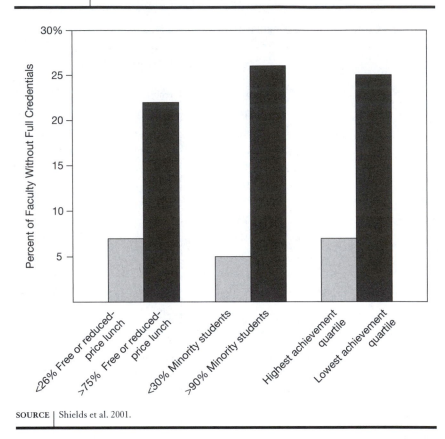

SOURCE | Shields et al. 2001.

900 Texas school districts, Ronald Ferguson (1991) found that the single most important measurable cause of increased student learning was teacher expertise, measured by teacher performance on a state certification exam, along with teacher experience and master's degrees. Together these variables accounted for about 40 percent of the measured variance in student test scores. Holding socioeconomic status constant, the wide variation in teachers' qualifications in Texas accounted for almost all of the variation in black and white students' test scores. That is, after controlling for socioecomic status, black students' achievement would have been closely comparable to that of whites if they had been assigned equally qualified teachers.

A number of other studies have found that teacher quality affects student achievement. Teachers who lack preparation in either subject matter or teaching methods are significantly less effective in producing student learning gains than those who are fully prepared and certified (Boyd et al. 2006; Darling-Hammond et al., 2005; Hawk, Coble, and Swanson 1985; Goldhaber and Brewer 2000; Monk 1994). The ways in which preparation matters, especially for students who rely primarily on school for opportunities to learn, were well expressed by this young recruit who entered teaching after a few weeks of summer training and left in his first year:

> I could maybe have done a bad job at a suburban high school. I stood to do an awful job at an [urban] school where you needed to have special skills. I just didn't ever know I needed them before I went in. I felt like, OK, I did the workshops; I know science; and I care about these kids. . . . You know, I had the motivation to help, but I didn't have the skill. It's sort of like wanting to fix someone's car and not having any idea how to fix a car. I wasn't equipped to deal with it, and I had no idea. (Darling-Hammond 1999, 21)

One of the outcomes of people coming into teaching without high levels of skill is that they are particularly unlikely to succeed in a setting where kids are not taught to read at home; where they may not speak English before they come to school; where the strategies that teachers need to be successful are much more demanding and sophisticated than they would need to be if these individuals were, for example, teaching in an affluent school where kids come already prepared to learn, with substantial prior knowledge, and with access to tutors and parents at home who have college educations.

Students' access to well-qualified teachers can be a critical determinant of whether they succeed on the state tests often required for promotion from grade to grade, for placement into academically challenging classes, and for graduation from high school. Researchers have found that the proportion of teachers in a school who are fully certified influences the likelihood that students will do well on required state tests, after controlling for student characteristics like poverty (Betts, Rueben, and Danenberg, 2000; Fetler 1999; Fuller 1998, 2000; Goe 2002).

This means that when students are denied access to teachers who are fully prepared, the society is also increasing the probability that they will not pass the tests that have been imposed in many states to determine grade promotion and graduation. This, then, greatly increases their odds of dropping out. The first time a student is retained in a grade, his or her odds of dropping out go up by 50 percent, and the second time, the odds increase by 90 percent. For those who do not graduate from high school, the odds that they will be employable go down substantially: Thus, one pathway to inequality leads to another.

When we look at the range of differences in schools fifty years after *Brown v. Board of Education*, discrimination is no longer de jure as a function of race; it is now built into school finance policy as a function of wealth and geographic location, but as segregation reasserts itself, the disparities play out substantially by race.

Ordinary Americans are often surprised when they learn about these disparities. They tend to believe that schools are equally funded and that everyone is starting with the same resources, and they don't realize that this is not the case. The contemporary discourse that poses the question "Why don't African American and Latino children achieve in school?" is typically fashioned around the assumption that all children have a level playing field in education and that some simply don't take advantage of it. Rectifying this is difficult because education is not understood by the courts as a federal civil right. So litigation to correct these inequalities must be brought state by state, at great expense and effort and with varying results. More than twenty-five states have experienced lawsuits arguing for equalization of resources over the last decade, but fewer than half of these cases have resulted in major changes in funding.

IMPLICATIONS OF EDUCATIONAL INEQUALITY

The consequences of inequality are more pronounced as education becomes increasingly important for success in society: Today, 70 percent of jobs are knowledge-work jobs requiring high levels of literacy and specialized skills beyond high school. By contrast, when our contemporary school system was organized a century ago, only about 5 percent of individuals were employed in highly skilled jobs, while most were employed in semi-skilled or unskilled roles in factories or on farms.

As the demands of the labor market have increased, the educational preparation of our youth has not: Only about 75 percent of students currently graduate from high school with a standard diploma—a proportion that has been flat for at least two decades—and only about 25 percent complete college. The proportion is much lower for students of color and has declined to less than 50 percent in some states, particularly those that have introduced exit exams. People who are undereducated can no longer access the labor market. With an economy that is demanding an increasingly better educated workforce, the effects on young people of dropping out of school are more negative than they have ever been, and are much worse for young people of color. In 1996, for example, a recent school dropout who was black had only a one in five chance of being employed, whereas the odds for his white counterpart were about 50 percent (NCES 1998, 100). Even recent high school graduates struggle to find jobs. Among African American high school graduates not enrolled in college, only 42 percent were employed in 1996, as compared to 69 percent of white graduates (NCES 1998, 100). Those who do not succeed in school are becoming part of a growing underclass, cut off from productive engagement in society.

Because the economy can no longer absorb many unskilled workers at decent wages, lack of education is increasingly linked to incarceration. More than half the adult prison population has literacy skills below those required by the labor market (Barton and Coley 1996), and nearly 40 percent of adjudicated juvenile delinquents have treatable learning disabilities that were undiagnosed and untreated in the schools (Gemignani 1994). This is substantially, then, an educational problem associated with inadequate access to the kinds of teachers and other resources that could enable young people to gain the skills that would enable them to become gainfully employed.

National investments in the last two decades have tipped heavily toward incarceration rather education. Nationwide, during the 1980s, federal, state, and local expenditures for corrections grew by over 900 percent (Miller 1997), while prison populations more than doubled (U.S. Census Bureau 1996, 219). During the same decade, per-pupil expenditures for schools grew by only about 26 percent in real dollar terms, and much less in cities (NCES 1994). Between 1980 and 2000, three times as many African American men were added to the nation's prison systems as were added to colleges. In 2000, an estimated 791,600 African American men were in prison or jail, and 603,000 were in higher education (Justice Policy Institute 2002).

Ironically, some educational reforms appear to be exacerbating this problem, as efforts to create new standards for students in the United States are, paradoxically, reducing educational access for many students of color. Many states and districts have put in place high-stakes testing systems that attach sanctions to students' scores on standardized tests. These include grade retention or promotion as well as graduation for students, merit pay awards or threats of dismissal for teachers and administrators, and extra funds or loss of registration, reconstitution, or loss of funds for schools. The federal No Child Left Behind Act of 2002 reinforces these systems, requiring all schools receiving funding to test students annually and enforcing penalties for those that do not meet specific test score targets.

However, these systems frequently result in students' dropping out in discouragement or being pushed out of school in order to boost schools' average test scores. Studies have linked school leaving rates in several states to the effects of grade retention, student discouragement, and school exclusion policies stimulated by high-stakes test. Researchers have found that systems that reward or sanction schools based on average student scores create incentives for retaining students in grade so that their grade-level scores will look better—a practice that increases later drop-out rates, excluding low-scoring students from admissions, and encouraging such students to transfer or drop out (Haney 2000; Heilig 2006; Jacob 2002; Orfield and Ashkinaze 1991; Smith 1986).

For example, when the Massachusetts exit exam took effect in 2003, and school ratings were tied to student pass rates in the tenth grade, greater proportions of students began disappearing from schools between ninth and tenth grades, most of them African American and Latino (see Figure 11.3.) In 2003, graduation rates for the group of ninth graders who had entered high school four years earlier decreased for all students, but most sharply for students of color. Whereas 71 percent of African American students graduated in the class of 2002, only 59.5 percent graduated among those who began ninth grade with the class of 2003, a proportion that dropped further in the following year (Bernstein 2004). Graduation rates for Latino students went from 54 percent in the class of 2002 to 45 percent in the class of 2003. Meanwhile, many of the steepest increases in test scores occurred in schools with the highest retention and dropout rates. For example, Wheelock (2003) found that in addition to increasing dropout rates, high schools receiving state awards for gains in tenth grade pass rates on the MCAS (the Massachusetts test) showed substantial increases in the prior year ninth grade retention rates and in the percentage of "missing" tenth graders. Thus, schools improved their test scores by keeping low-achieving students out of the testing pool, or out of school entirely.

Reform rhetoric notwithstanding, the key question for students, especially those of color, is whether investments in better teaching, curriculum, and schooling will follow the press for new standards, or whether standards built upon a foundation of continued inequality in education will simply certify student failure with greater certainty and reduce access to future education and employment. A related question, a half century

FIGURE 11.3 | **PERCENTAGE OF 9TH GRADE MASSACHUSETTS STUDENTS "LOST" BETWEEN 9TH AND 10TH GRADES.**

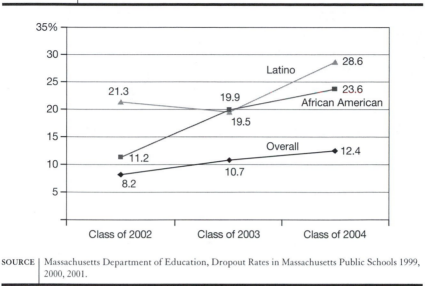

SOURCE | Massachusetts Department of Education, Dropout Rates in Massachusetts Public Schools 1999, 2000, 2001.

after *Brown v. Board of Education*, is what it will take to secure a constitutional right to equal educational opportunity for all children in the United States.

Data from the National Center for Education Statistics indicate that four-year graduation rates decreased between 1995 and 2001 in Florida, New York, North Carolina, and South Carolina where new high-stakes testing policies were introduced (see Figure 11.4). In all of these cases, four-year graduation rates for African American and Latino students have dropped even more precipitously than graduation rates for whites, standing at below 50 percent now. Although not all of those who fail to graduate in four years drop out—some graduate in five or six years or secure GED diplomas, and others move out of the state—federal statistics suggest that at least 30 percent of U.S. students in a given cohort are failing to graduate with a standard diploma, at a time when the society requires more education than ever (Barton 2005).

As a nation, we need to ask: How can we sustain an economy in the twenty-first century with these kinds of graduation rates from students in our schools? When high-achieving countries in Europe and Asia are graduating more than 95 percent of their students from high school and sending an increasing share to college, how can we imagine sustaining

FIGURE 11.4 | **STATE GRADUATION RATES, 1995–2001.**

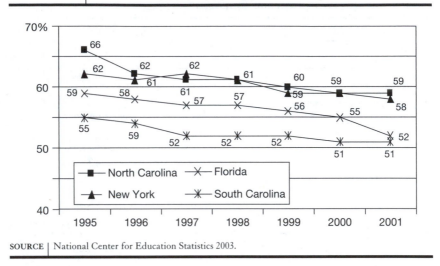

SOURCE | National Center for Education Statistics 2003.

a knowledge-based economy with a third of our young people unable to earn a living wage, and a large share placed on what has come to be known as the "school-to-prison pipeline"? This is really extraordinary, and it bodes ill for the nation as a whole. For example, for the people in my generation who expect to be receiving Social Security in ten years, there will only be three potential workers for every person on Social Security in 2020. If one of these three may not even be in the labor market producing wages and taxes to support our retirement—and may in fact be in prison costing taxpayers $30,000 a year or more—the social compact will completely collapse. This is an enormous elephant in the room that few policymakers are talking about—one with huge implications for what will happen to the future of our country.

HOW RESOURCES MAKE A DIFFERENCE

The advent of high-stakes testing reforms requiring students to achieve specific test score targets in order to advance in grade or graduate from school has occurred while educational experiences for "minority" students continue to be substantially separate and unequal. State efforts to set standards for all students for school progression and graduation while failing to offer equal opportunities to learn have stimulated a new spate of equity litigation in nearly twenty states across the country. These lawsuits—which may be said to constitute the next generation of efforts begun by *Brown v. Board of Education*—argue that if states require all students to meet the same educational standards, they must assume a responsibility to provide resources adequate to allow students a reasonable opportunity to achieve those standards, including well-qualified teachers; a curriculum that fully reflects the standards; and the materials, texts, supplies, and equipment needed to teach the curriculum.

Despite evidence of substantial inequality, opponents of school finance reform often argue that money doesn't make a difference (Hanushek 2003) and that unequal outcomes are simply an inevitable product of race and income. Starting from the perspective that student characteristics are the primary determinants of achievement, these analysts typically argue that after controlling for student background, school resources explain relatively little additional variance in achievement. Yet, if one starts from an alternative perspective—that deficiencies do not reside primarily in the students themselves and that school resources matter for learning—resources like teacher quality and class size are often found to explain about as much of the variation in achievement as race or poverty.

For example, in an analysis I conducted for the finance lawsuit in South Carolina, measures of teacher qualifications alone accounted for 64 percent of the total variance in student outcomes on the state tests (Darling-Hammond 2004). Adding the proportion of low-income and minority students in each district increased the variance explained to 84 percent. As found in other studies, the strongest predictors of student failure on the state tests were the proportion of uncertified teachers and a measure of teacher shortages.

In a similar analysis of Massachusetts data (Darling-Hammond 2004), we found that teachers' salaries, teacher certification, staff-to-student ratio, and district spending predicted 56 percent of the odds of students' failing the state test in mathematics, noticeably more than the influence of race. This suggests that if the state were to equalize funding and average teachers' salaries, and ensure that students had certified math teachers, it could eliminate more than half the differential in failure rates on the state mathematics test and begin to close the achievement gap.

Other research suggests that in addition to well-qualified teachers, what matters most for student learning includes small schools and classes as well as smaller schools that personalize the educational experience and create authentic, performance-based instruction (Darling-Hammond, Ross, and Milliken 2006). These schools create an utterly different experience from what young people would normally get in big urban high schools that have 4,000 to 5,000 students in an institution that runs almost like a prison, with more security guards and metal detectors than teachers in some cases. One of the things urban school reformers have demonstrated is that students succeed when we recreate schools of 300 to 500 students where teams of teachers work with the same students over multiple years in a supportive, personalized context and where there is a rich curriculum aimed at active learning, deep understanding, and real performance.

I learned early on as a teacher—and our teachers have learned in East Palo Alto—that many middle-class students may be willing to sit and do worksheets because somebody tells them that it is what they need to do in order to go to college or to get out of the classroom or to get a good grade, but our students are just not motivated by somebody telling them, "Do this because it is going to get you somewhere else." They have no experience of school having paid off for anyone in their lives or of what it might mean to go to college. If they are to do schoolwork, they actually have to engage with and enjoy the work and find it meaningful and important. So a lot of our work is around exhibitions and performances: students do community studies, research investigations, and authentic work that they exhibit to audiences beyond the teacher. For example, each year when tenth graders study South Africa, they reenact the South African Truth and Reconciliation Commission in a local courthouse in San Mateo where, as lawyers, witnesses, and jurors, they try the murderers of Amy Biehl and Steve Biko.

The curriculum is authentic to the learning tasks that are necessary. This is essential: our goal is not just getting young people through school; it is getting them through a kind of schooling process that is powerful and meaningful, that empowers them to use their knowledge for themselves, their families, and their community.

POLICY FOR EQUALITY: WHAT WE CAN DO

The common presumption that schools currently provide a level playing field paralyzes necessary efforts to invest in schools attended primarily by students of color. If academic outcomes for minority and low-income children are to change, reforms must alter the quality and quantity of learning opportunities our young people encounter. To improve achievement, school reforms must assure access to high-quality teaching within the context of a rich and challenging curriculum supported by personalized schools and classes. Accomplishing such a goal will require equalization of financial resources, changes in curriculum and testing policies, and improvements in the supply of highly qualified teachers to all students.

Resource Equalization

Progress in equalizing resources to students will require attention to inequalities at all levels—between states, among districts, among schools within districts, and among students differentially placed in classrooms, courses, and tracks that offer substantially disparate opportunities to learn. State funding should be allocated to students based on equal dollars per student adjusted (or weighted) for specific student needs, such as poverty, limited English proficiency, or special education status. Developing such an equitable, reliable base of funding is critically important so that districts can afford to hire competent teachers and provide reasonable class sizes and pupil loads, which are the foundational components of quality education.

Ferguson's (1991) findings about the importance of teacher expertise for student achievement led him to recommend that investments focus on districts' capacity to hire high-quality teachers. Several studies have documented how Connecticut eliminated teacher shortages, improved teacher quality, and raised student achievement by doing just that. When the state raised and equalized teacher salaries under its 1986 Education Enhancement Act, shortages of teachers evaporated, and within three years, most teaching fields showed surpluses, even in the urban areas. The state raised standards for teacher education and licensing, initiated scholarships and forgivable loans to recruit high-need teachers into the profession (including teachers in shortage fields, those who would teach in high-need locations, and minority teachers), created a mentoring and assessment program for all beginning teachers, and invested money in high-quality professional development, with special aid to low-achieving districts. By 1998, Connecticut had surpassed all other states in fourth grade reading and mathematics achievement on the NAEP and scored at or near the top of the rankings in eighth grade mathematics, science, and writing (Wilson, Darling-Hammond, and Berry 2001).

A systemic strategy like this one is essential if equity and quality are to go hand in hand. Such a strategy should incorporate, along with standards for student learning, standards for educational opportunity that create two-way accountability between the government and the schools. Such standards would ensure access to the resources needed for students to achieve the learning standards, including appropriate instructional materials and well-prepared teachers. Thus, for example, if a state's curriculum frameworks and assessments outline standards for science learning that require laboratory work and computers, certain kinds of coursework, and particular knowledge for teaching, states and districts would be responsible for allocating resources and designing policies to provide for these entitlements. Such a strategy would leverage both school improvement and school equity reform, providing a basis for state legislation or litigation where opportunities to learn were not adequately funded.

Curriculum and Assessment Reform

Today's learning standards require students to be able to engage in independent analysis and problem solving, extensive research and writing, use of new technologies, and various strategies for accessing and using resources in new situations. These are also the skills needed to succeed in today's modern economy and in college. Meanwhile, the curriculum offered to most African American and other students of color in U.S. schools is geared primarily toward lower-order "rote" skills—memorizing pieces of information and conducting simple operations based on formulas or rules. Students in schools that organize most of their efforts around the kinds of low-level learning represented by multiple-choice basic skills tests are profoundly disadvantaged when they encounter more rigorous expectations for performance, as the skills they have learned do not translate into these more advanced real-world skills (Darling-Hammond and Rustique-Forrester 2005). Major changes in curriculum and resources will be needed to ensure that these expectations are commonplace in the classrooms of students of color.

Initiatives to develop richer curriculum and more performance-oriented assessments that develop higher-order skills have sought to address this problem in states like Connecticut, Vermont, Nebraska, Maine, Oregon, and Kentucky. Their assessments, which use essays and oral exhibitions as well as samples of student work like research papers and science projects, resemble those used in most countries around the world, including the highest-scoring nations that outrank the United States. Unfortunately, the administration of the No Child Left Behind Act has tended to discourage the use of performance assessments and has reinforced the reliance on more narrow tests as well as their use for many purposes like grade retention and tracking—for which they were not designed and are not valid.

The issue of how tests are used is as important as the nature of the tests themselves. The standards for test use set by professional organizations—the American Psychological Association, American Educational Research Association, and National Council on Measurement in Education—indicate that high-stakes decisions should not be made only on the basis of a test score, and that other indicators of performance such as class work and teacher observations should be considered alongside test data. This is because no test is a foolproof predictor of ability or future performance. Most predict a small fraction of the variance in future performance in real-life settings. This has proven especially true for students of color whose background experiences often do not match those assumed by the test developers.

Thus, the outcomes of the current wave of curriculum and assessment reforms will depend in large measure on the extent to which developers and users of new standards and tests use them to improve teaching and learning rather than merely reinforcing our tendencies to sort and select those who will get high-quality education from those who will not. Policymakers will also need to pursue broader reforms to improve and equalize access to educational resources and support the professional development of teachers, so that new standards and tests are used to inform more skillful and adaptive teaching that enables more successful learning for all students.

These efforts to create a "thinking curriculum" for all students are important to individual futures and our national welfare. They are unlikely to pay off, however, unless other critical changes are made in curriculum, in the ways students are tracked for instruction, and the ways teachers are prepared and supported. Although mounting evidence indicates that low-tracked students are disadvantaged by current practice and that high-ability students do not necessarily benefit more from homogeneous classrooms than from heterogeneous grouping (Slavin 1990), the long-established American tracking system will be difficult to reform until there is an adequate supply of well-trained teachers—teachers who are both prepared to teach the more advanced curriculum that U.S. schools now fail to offer most students and to teach many kinds of students with diverse needs, interests, aptitudes, and learning styles in integrated classroom settings. This, in turn, requires reforms of teacher preparation to enable teachers to become effective in using a wide repertoire of strategies suited to different learning needs (Darling-Hammond and Bransford 2005).

Investments in Quality Teaching

A key corollary of this analysis is that improved educational outcomes will rest substantially on policies that boost attractions to teaching, especially in high-need areas, while increasing teachers' knowledge and skills as other high-achieving nations have done. Providing equity in the distribution of teacher quality requires changing policies and long-standing incentive structures in education so that shortages of trained teachers are overcome, and schools serving low-income and minority students are not disadvantaged by lower salaries and poorer working conditions in the bidding war for good teachers.

If we are serious about leaving no child behind, we need to go beyond mandates to ensure that *all* students have well-qualified teachers. Effective action can be modeled after federal investments in medicine. Since 1944, the federal government has subsidized medical training to fill shortages and build teaching hospitals and training programs in high-need areas—a commitment that has contributed significantly to America's world-renowned system of medical training and care. Intelligent, targeted incentives can ensure that all students have access to teachers who are indeed highly qualified. An aggressive national teacher quality and supply policy, on the order of the post–World War II Marshall Plan, could be accomplished for less than 1 percent of the more than $700 billion spent thus far [January 2007] in Iraq; and in a matter of only a few years, it would establish a world-class teaching force in all communities. Such a plan would have three essential components:

1. Recruit high-need teachers, through service scholarships and forgivable loans for those who agree to train in shortage fields and practice in high-need locations. As in North Carolina's successful Teaching Fellows model, scholarships for high-quality teacher education can be linked to minimum service requirements of four years or more—the point at which most teachers who have remained in the classroom have committed to remaining in the profession. Because fully prepared novices are twice as likely to stay in teaching as those who lack training, shortages could be reduced rapidly if districts could hire better prepared teachers. Virtually all of the vacancies currently filled with emergency teachers could be filled with well-prepared teachers if 40,000 service scholarships of up to $25,000 each were offered annually.

Recruitment incentives could also be used to attract and retain expert, experienced teachers in high-need schools. Federal matching grants could leverage additional compensation for teachers with demonstrated expertise who serve as mentors, master teachers, and coaches in such schools. For $500 million annually, stipends of $10,000 could be provided to 50,000 accomplished teachers who help improve practice in high-poverty schools. An additional $300 million in matching grants could be used to improve teaching conditions in these schools, including smaller pupil loads, adequate materials, and time for teacher planning and professional development—all of which keep teachers in schools.

2. Improve teachers' preparation through incentive grants to schools of education focused on strengthening teachers' abilities to teach a wide range of diverse learners successfully ($300 million). An additional $200 million should expand state-of-the-art teacher education programs in high-need communities that create "teaching schools" partnered with universities. As in teaching hospitals, candidates study teaching and learning while gaining hands-on experience in state-of-the-art classrooms. Effective models have already been created by universities sponsoring professional development schools and by school districts offering urban teacher residencies. These residencies place candidates as apprentices in the classrooms of expert urban teachers while they earn a stipend and complete their coursework, repaying the investment with at least four years of service. Such programs can create a pipeline of teachers prepared to engage in best practices in the schools where they are most needed while establishing demonstration sites for urban teaching. Funding for 200 programs serving an average of 150 candidates each at $1,000,000 per program per year would supply 30,000 exceptionally well-prepared recruits to high-need communities each year.

3. Support mentoring for all beginning teachers to stem attrition and increase competence. With one-third of new teachers leaving the profession within five years and higher rates for those who are underprepared, recruitment efforts are like pouring water into a leaky bucket. By investing in state and district induction programs, we could ensure mentoring support for every new teacher in the nation. Based on the funding model used in California's successful Beginning Teacher Support and Assessment (BTSA) Program, a federal allocation of $4,000 for each of 125,000 beginning teachers, matched by states or local districts, could ensure that a well-trained mentor coaches each novice.

In the long run, these proposals would save far more than they would cost. The savings would include the more than $2 billion dollars now wasted annually because of high teacher turnover, plus the even higher costs of grade retention, summer school, remedial programs, and lost wages and prison sentences for dropouts (another $50 billion increasingly tied to illiteracy and school failure).

CONCLUSION

As we move further into the twenty-first century, reducing inequality is essential to our nation's future. If "no child left behind" is to be anything more than empty rhetoric, we will need a policy strategy that equalizes access to school resources, creates a twenty-first-century curriculum for all students, and supports it with thoughtful assessments and access to knowledgeable, well-supported teachers. But this requires an ongoing struggle, one reminiscent of these words of Frederick Douglass:

> Power concedes nothing without a demand, it never has and it never will. If there is no struggle, there is no progress. Those who profess to favor freedom and yet deprecate agitation are men who want crops without plowing the ground, they want rain without thunder and lightning, they want the ocean without the awful roar of its waters. (Douglass 1991/1849)

This country's efforts to deal with the deeply institutionalized sources of inequality that are in place, especially in its school systems, will not occur through reforms that suggest we pursue the status quo. We will need to confront the realities of racism and disenfranchisement and remove their root sources if we are to move our system forward to one that will support us as a society in a century that is not going to be forgiving to societies that did not invest in the education of all their people. A democracy that will survive and thrive in a world that demands a well-educated citizenry must build a system that can ensure all students the right to learn.

Works Cited

•

Barton, P. E. 2005. *One-Third of a Nation: Rising Dropout Rates and Declining Opportunities*. Policy information report. Princeton, NJ: Educational Testing Service.

Barton, Paul E. and R. J. Coley. 1996. *Captive Students: Education and Training in America's Prisons*. Princeton, NJ: Educational Testing Service.

Bernstein, D. S. 2004. "Achievement Gap: This Is Improvement?" *Boston Phoenix*, June 11.

Betts, J. R., K. S. Rueben, and A. Danenberg. 2000. *Equal Resources, Equal Outcomes? The Distribution of School Resources and Student Achievement in California*. San Francisco: Public Policy Institute of California.

Boyd, D., P. Grossman, H. Lankford, S. Loeb, and J. Wyckoff. 2006. How changes in entry requirements alter the teacher workforce and affect student achievement. *Education Finance and Policy* 1 (2): 176–216.

California Postsecondary Education Commission (CPEC). 1998, December. *Toward a Greater Understanding of the State's Educational Equity Policies, Programs, and Practices*. Commission Report 98-5. Sacramento.

Darling-Hammond, L. 1999. The case for university-based teacher education. In *The Role of the University in the Preparation of Teachers*, ed. by R. Roth. Philadelphia, PA: Falmer Press, 13–30.

———. 2004. The color line in American education: Race, resources, and student achievement. *W. E. B. Du Bois Review: Social Science Research on Race* 1 (2): 213–246.

Darling-Hammond, L., J. Ancess and J. S. Ort. 2002. Reinventing high school: Outcomes of the Coalition Campus School Project. *American Educational Research Journal* 39 (3): 639–673.

Darling-Hammond, L. and J. Bransford. 2005. *Preparing Teachers for a Changing World: What Teachers Should Learn and Be Able to Do*. San Francisco: Jossey-Bass.

Darling-Hammond, L., et al. 2005. Does teacher preparation matter? Evidence about teacher certification, Teach for America, and teacher effectiveness. *Education Policy Analysis Archives* 13 (42): http://epaa.asu.edu/epaa/v13n42/.

Darling-Hammond, L., and E. Rustique-Forrester. 2005. The consequences of student testing for teaching and teacher quality. In *The Uses and Misuses of Data in Accountability Testing. The 104th Yearbook of the National Society for the Study of Education, Part II*, ed. by J. Herman and E. Haertel. Malden, MA: Blackwell, 289–319.

Darling-Hammond, L., P. Ross, and M. Milliken. 2006. High school size, organization, and content: What matters for student success? In *Brookings Papers on Education Policy*, ed. by Frederick Hess. Washington, DC: Brookings Institution Press, 1–42.

Douglass, F. 1991[1849]. Letter to an Abolitionist Associate. In *Organizing for Social Change: A Mandate for Activity in the 1990s*, ed. by K. Bobo, J. Kendall and S. Max. Washington, DC: Seven Locks Press.

EdSource. 2001, October. *How California Ranks: A Comparison of Education Expenditures*. Palo Alto, CA: EdSource.

Ferguson, R.F. 1991. Paying for public education: New evidence on how and why money matters. *Harvard Journal on Legislation* 28 (2): 465–498.

Fetler, M. 1999. High school staff characteristics and mathematics test results. *Education Policy Analysis Archives,* 7 (March 24): http://epaa.asu.edu.

Fuller, E. 1998, November. *Do Properly Certified Teachers Matter? A Comparison of Elementary School Performance on the TAAS in 1997 between Schools with High and Low Percentages of Properly Certified Regular Education Teachers*. Austin: Charles A. Dana Center, University of Texas at Austin.

Fuller, E. 2000, April. *Do Properly Certified Teachers Matter? Properly Certified Algebra Teachers and Algebra I Achievement in Texas*. Paper presented at the annual meeting of the American Educational Research Association, New Orleans, LA.

Gemignani, R. J. 1994, October. Juvenile correctional education: A time for change. Update on research. *Juvenile Justice Bulletin*. U.S. Department of Justice, Office of Juvenile Justice and Delinquency Prevention.

Goe, L. 2002. Legislating equity: The distribution of emergency permit teachers in California. *Educational Policy Analysis Archives* 10 (42): http://epaa.asu.edu/epaa/v10n42/.

Goldhaber, D. D. and D. J. Brewer. 2000. Does teacher certification matter? High school certification status and student achievement. *Educational Evaluation and Policy Analysis* 22: 129–145.

Haney, W. 2000. The myth of the Texas miracle in education. *Educational Policy Analysis Archives* 8 (41): http://epaa.asu.edu/epaa/v8n41/.

Hanushek, E. 2003. *The Structure of Analysis and Argument in Plaintiff Expert Reports for* Williams v. State of California. Available at www.mofo.com/decentschools/expert_reports/hanushek_report.pdf; accessed April 19, 2004.

Hawk, P., C. R. Coble, and M. Swanson. 1985. Certification: It does matter, *Journal of Teacher Education* 36 (3): 13–15.

Heilig, J. V. 2006. *Progress and learning of urban minority students in an environment of accountability.* Unpublished doctoral dissertation. Stanford University.

Herrnstein, R. J., and C. Murray. 1994. *The Bell Curve: Intelligence and Class Structure in American Life*. New York: Free Press.

Jacob, B. A. 2002. *The Impact of High-Stakes Testing on Student Achievement: Evidence from Chicago*. Working Paper. Harvard University.

Justice Policy Institute. 2002. *Cellblocks or Classrooms? The Funding of Higher Education and Corrections and Its Impact on African American Men*. www.justicepolicy.org/images/upload/02-09_REP_CellblocksClassrooms_BB-AC.pdf.

Lankford, H., S. Loeb, and J. Wyckoff. 2002. Teacher sorting and the plight of urban schools: A descriptive analysis. *Education Evaluation and Policy Analysis* 24 (1): 37–62.

Miller, J. G. 1997. African American males in the criminal justice system. *Phi Delta Kappan*, K1–K12, June.

Monk, D. H. 1994. Subject matter preparation of secondary mathematics and science teachers and student achievement. *Economics of Education Review* 13 (2): 125–145.

National Center for Education Statistics (NCES). 1994. *Digest of Education Statistics, 1994*. Washington, DC: U.S. Department of Education.

———. 1997. *America's Teachers: Profile of a Profession, 1993–94*. Washington, DC: U.S. Department of Education.

———. 1998. *The Condition of Education, 1998*. Washington, DC: U.S. Department of Education.

———. 2003. *The Condition of Education*. Washington, DC: U.S. Department of Education.

———. 2005. *National Assessment of Educational Progress Trends On-Line*. Washington, DC: U.S. Department of Education.

Oakes, J. 1990. *Multiplying Inequalities: The Effects of Race, Social Class, and Tracking on Opportunities to Learn Mathematics and Science*. Santa Monica, CA: The RAND Corporation.

Orfield, G. 2001. *Schools More Separate: Consequences of a Decade of Resegregation.* Cambridge, MA: Civil Rights Project, Harvard University.

Orfield, G., and C. Ashkinaze. 1991. *The Closing Door: Conservative Policy and Black Opportunity.* Chicago: University of Chicago Press.

Shields, P. M., et al. 2001. *The Status of the Teaching Profession 2001.* Santa Cruz, CA: Center for the Future of Teaching and Learning.

Slavin, R. E. 1990. Achievement effects of ability grouping in secondary schools: A best evidence synthesis. *Review of Educational Research* 60 (3): 471–500.

Smith, F. 1986. *High School Admission and the Improvement of Schooling.* New York: New York City Board of Education.

U.S. Census Bureau. 1996. *Statistical Abstract of the United States: 1996.* 116th edition. Washington, DC: U.S. Department of Commerce.

———. 2008. Table A-5a. The population 14 to 24 years old by high school graduate status, college enrollment, attainment, sex, race, and Hispanic origin: October 1967 to 2008. www.census.gov/population/socdemo/school/Table A-5a.xls

Wheelock, A. 2003. School Awards Programs and Accountability in Massachusetts: Misusing MCAS Scores to Assess School Quality. FairTest. www.eric.ed.gov/ERICDocs/data/ericdocs2sql/content_storage_01/0000019b/80/1b/15/2a.pdf

Williams et al. v. State of California. 2000. Superior Court of the State of California, Complaint 22–23. June.

Wilson, S. M., L. Darling-Hammond, and B. Berry. 2001. *Teaching Policy: Connecticut's Long-Term Efforts to Improve Teaching and Learning.* Seattle: Center for the Study of Teaching and Policy, University of Washington.

12

Racialized Mass Incarceration
Poverty, Prejudice, and Punishment

Lawrence D. Bobo and Victor Thompson

•

This essay maintains that the United States has developed a new, decidedly punitive law and order regime that at its core features racialized mass incarceration. We will show that over the past thirty years the United States has gone on an incarceration binge, a binge that has fallen with radically disproportionate severity on the African American community. The rise of the racialized mass incarceration society is attributable to the simultaneous processes of urban socioeconomic restructuring that produced intensified ghetto poverty and severe social disadvantage and dislocations through the 1980s to the present, on the one hand, and a series of social policy actions (and nonactions) that made jail or prison among the primary responses to urban social distress, on the other hand. During this time, social policy took this deeply punitive turn in substantial measure as a result of the effects of anti-black racism in American culture and public opinion. One result of these circumstances is a serious problem of legitimacy for the criminal justice system in the eyes of many Americans, especially but not exclusively African Americans.

ALTHOUGH A SMALL TOWN WITH A POPULATION OF LESS THAN 5,000, Tulia, Texas, is now a truly notorious place. In the summer of 1999, undercover police operative Tom Coleman, later named Texas Lawman of the Year, led a sting operation that resulted in forty-six arrests. Coleman testified in numerous trials in connection with these arrests though there were usually no corroborating witnesses, no tape-recorded or videotaped drug sales, no weapons confiscated, no piles of money seized, nor great supplies of drugs ever found. Indeed, the story ends badly for Coleman, once considered a symbol of a virtuous and aggressively pursued War on Drugs (so named by the federal government). He was recently convicted of perjury and placed on ten years' probation by the courts.[1]

Why such notoriety? Tulia and Officer Coleman are now the penultimate symbols of a drug war run amok and of deep-seated racial bias in the criminal justice system. Forty of the arrested townspeople were black and the remaining six were either Latinos or otherwise close to the black community (i.e., whites married to blacks). Most significantly, all of those incarcerated—more than twenty people spent time in jail, whereas many others were intimidated into taking plea deals—were ultimately pardoned by the then Republican governor, received significant cash settlements from the local government, and ultimately won $5 million in damages against the now disbanded Federal Drug Task force for which Coleman worked.[2]

Of course, from one vantage point, Tulia is a great aberration attributable to the overzealousness of one rogue cop. We reject this interpretation. This would be a more credible position if one or two rather than more than twenty people had not been wrongly imprisoned. Or, perhaps, if lower-level officials had intervened to prevent a travesty of justice rather than creating a context wherein the state legislature and governor were finally compelled to act as a result of legal and political pressure. From the very outset, indeed, aspects of the case itself cast doubt on such a generous interpretation (i.e., the lack of evidence Coleman provided, several early instances of dismissed charges when his allegations were easily proven to be complete fabrications, and the routine way in which all-white Tulia juries repeatedly convicted their arguably well-known black neighbors and sent them off to prison despite dubious charges). From another and more credible vantage point, however, Tulia is another example of the

---

[1] See the following news reports by Adam Liptak: "Texas Governor Pardons 35 Arrested in Tainted Sting," *New York Times*, August 23, 2003; and Steve Barnes, "National Briefing|Southwest: Texas: Ex-Narcotics Agent Gets 10 Years' Probation," *New York Times*, January 19, 2005.

[2] See Adam Liptak, "$5 Millions Settlement Ends Case of Tainted Texas Sting," *New York Times*, March 11, 2004; NAACP Legal Defense Fund, 2006, "Bad Times in Tulia: An African-American Community in Texas Is Victimized by the "War on Drugs,'" www.naacpldf.org/printable.aspx?article=64; and Jennifer Gonnerman: "Tulia Blues: How the Lingering Effects of a Massive Drug Bust Devastated One Family in a Small Texas Town," *The Village Voice*, July 31, 2001.

ways that profound racial bias is routinely mobilized into the operation of the modern criminal justice system.

RACIALIZED MASS INCARCERATION:
ROUNDING UP THE USUAL SUSPECTS

An enormous social change has steadily occurred in the arena of criminal justice. The United States is generally a far more punitive society today than it was just three decades ago. This change has been marked or designated with several different labels. These designations include the emergence of a "prison industrial complex," of a "carceral state," or the "mass incarceration society." All of these terms refer to a large-scale shift toward formal incarceration as our collective social response to crime.

The full reach of this change was captured in headlines from the *New York Times* in February 2008 that declared, "1 in 100 U.S. Adults behind Bars, New Study Says." The meaning of such a declaration is hard to judge without some more complete context for interpretation. As Figure 12.1 shows, since 1981 there has been a steady rise in the number of people in jail or prison, on parole, or on probation, with the numbers on probation or actually in prison undergoing the sharpest increase. In 1980, for instance, fewer than 300,000 people were in prison. By 2000, however, that number had risen to over 1 million. And by 2007 that

FIGURE 12.1 | **ADULT CORRECTIONAL POPULATION, 1980–2007.**

There were 7,328,200 adults under correctional supervision in 2007.

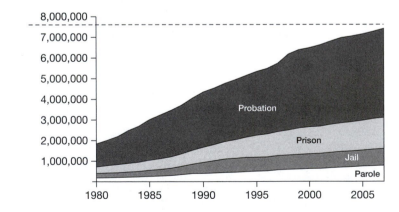

SOURCE | U.S. Bureau of Justice Statistics Correctional Surveys; totals for 1998–2007 exclude probation-ers in jail or prison.

number had reached above 1.5 million. If you include the number of people in jails, the total population behind bars in the United States was more than 2.3 million. All told, as the figure shows, by 2007 there were more than 7.3 million people under some form of "state supervision," a figure more than three times the rate observed in 1980. Recent reports by the Bureau of Justice Statistics suggest that trend for growth continues, though at a slightly slower rate of increase.

The trend in Figure 12.1 is striking but it also understates the magnitude of the change. Not evident in this figure is the fact that a prison population below 300,000 characterized most of the twentieth century in the United States. Starting as it does in 1980, this figure does not fully capture the extreme and abrupt character of the underlying social change, which can be traced mainly to post-1980 policy reforms. The sharp rise in reliance upon incarceration is more readily visualized in Figure 12.2, which traces just the number of male prison inmates in the United States from 1925 to 2006. A more than fifty-year period of relative stability in the rate of male incarceration in the United States is followed by a sharp and largely unabated climb in the post-1980 period.

The headline from the *New York Times* noted above ("1 in 100 U.S. Adults behind Bars") signals, first, the high absolute number of people now swept up by the criminal justice system and second, the dramatic break with a very long stretch of prior practice that the recent period

FIGURE 12.2 | **PRISON INMATES PER 100,000 MALES, 1925–2007.**

As of 2007, nearly 1 in 100 males were in prison (955 per 100,000).

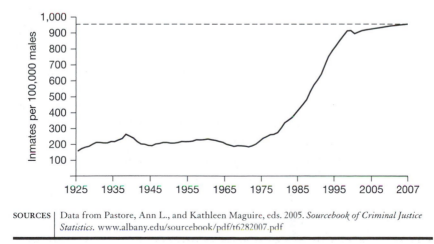

SOURCES | Data from Pastore, Ann L., and Kathleen Maguire, eds. 2005. *Sourcebook of Criminal Justice Statistics.* www.albany.edu/sourcebook/pdf/t6282007.pdf

represents. Crime policy scholars Henry Ruth and Kevin Reitz help put these trends in perspective in their recent book *The Challenge of Crime*.

> Over a one hundred year period, 1880 to 1980, the nation added a total of about 285,000 inmates to the prison systems. During just the ensuing twenty years, from 1980 to 2000, the nation added about 1.1 million inmates. From 1850 through 2000, the nation's prison system expanded about 206 times over, during a period of only about twelve-fold population growth. Total people on probation or parole status rose almost nine-fold between 1965 and 2000. (Ruth and Reitz 2003, 283)

Not captured by these numbers is also a lengthening of the average amount of time served. Mandatory minimum sentencing guidelines, three-strikes laws, various special enhancements (i.e., selling drugs near a school), and truth in sentencing provisions ensure that people convicted of crimes are not only more likely to end up in prison but are there for much longer periods of time. Likewise, the number of prisoners incarcerated under extremely harsh conditions, such as isolation and severely limited hours of physical mobility, has also risen while access to rehabilitative programs and educational opportunities has declined (Whitman 2003; Irwin 2007).

The U.S. rate of incarceration is now also arguably of historic proportions for a developed modern democracy. On an international scale, as Figure 12.3 shows, the rate of incarceration per 100,000 citizens in the United States far exceeds that of all other Western industrial nations. The ratio ranges from a low of roughly four to one when compared to our closest neighbor, Mexico, to very nearly twelve to one when compared to places like Sweden and Japan. Only Russia comes close, where the most recent data show an incarceration rate of 626 per 100,000 as compared to a U.S. rate of 762 per 100,000 in 2008. Even the Communist regime in Cuba, at 531 per 100,000, fails to reach the U.S. standard when it comes to incarcerating its population. As the *New York Times* editorial declared on March 10, 2008, "Nationwide, the prison population hovers at almost 1.6 million, which surpasses all other countries for which there are reliable figures. The 50 states last year spent about $44 billion in tax dollars on corrections, up from nearly $11 billion in 1987. Vermont, Connecticut, Delaware, Michigan, and Oregon devote as much money or more to corrections as they do to higher education. These statistics . . . point to a terrible waste of money and lives."

From one vantage point of observation this transformation can be accurately labeled "mass incarceration." Legal scholar and sociologist

FIGURE 12.3 | **INTERNATIONAL INCARCERATION RATES (PER 100,000), 2008.**

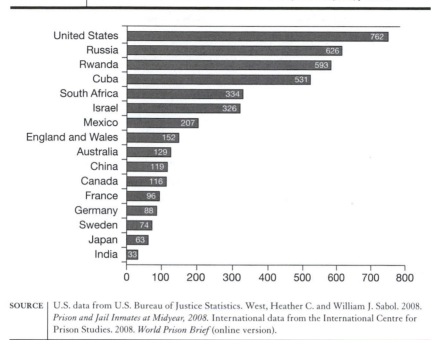

SOURCE | U.S. data from U.S. Bureau of Justice Statistics. West, Heather C. and William J. Sabol. 2008. *Prison and Jail Inmates at Midyear, 2008.* International data from the International Centre for Prison Studies. 2008. *World Prison Brief* (online version).

David Garland defined the mass imprisonment society as having two features: first, "a rate of imprisonment that is markedly above the historical and comparative norm for societies of this type," and second, "the social concentration of imprisonment effects," such that incarceration "ceases to be incarceration of individual offenders and becomes the systematic imprisonment of whole groups of the population" (Garland 2001, 5–6).

From a different vantage point, however, the label "mass incarceration" obscures the role of race in this social concentration of imprisonment. The "1 in 100" headline we quoted could just as easily, drawing figures from the same Pew Center Report (2008), have been "1 in 15 African Americans behind Bars," or even more distressing, "1 in 9 Black Men, age 20 to 34 behind Bars." That is, while the overall U.S. rate of incarceration is up very substantially, this shift has fallen with radically disproportionate severity on African Americans, particularly low-income and poorly educated blacks.

Indeed, the end result has been a sharp overrepresentation of blacks in jails and prisons. In 2007, as Figure 12.4 shows, black males constituted roughly 39 percent of incarcerated males in state, federal, and local prisons or jails, though representing only 12 percent of the total adult male

FIGURE 12.4 | **TOTAL POPULATION AND PRISON PERCENTAGES BY RACE FOR MALES, 2007.**

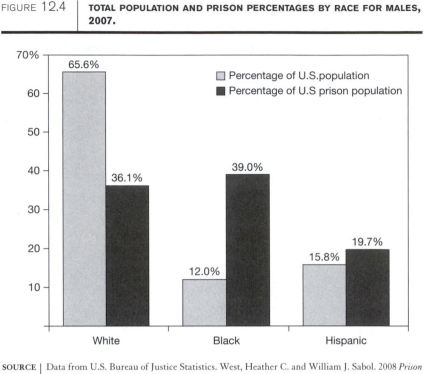

SOURCE | Data from U.S. Bureau of Justice Statistics. West, Heather C. and William J. Sabol. 2008 *Prison and Jail Inmates at midyear, 2007.*

population. White males, on the other hand, constituted just 36.1 percent of the male inmate population in 2007, well under their 65.6 percent of the total male population. The Hispanic population, which constitutes about 20 percent of the total inmate population, is also overrepresented but is much closer to its relative share of the total population of about 16 percent.

Again, these "one slice in time" numbers, even as extreme as they are, may fail to convey the enormity of the transformation that has taken place. In both absolute number and in terms of over-time change, the incarceration of African Americans has reached extraordinary levels. In 1954, there were only about 98,000 African Americans in prisons or jail (Mauer and King 2004). By 2002 the numbers had risen to 884,500, an increase of 900 percent. Today the number is nearly 1 million (913,800). In some states, such as California, blacks are incarcerated at a rate of 2,992 per 100,000 compared to 460 per 100,000 for non-Hispanic whites and 782 per 100,000 Hispanics.

To state the matter differently, current rates of incarceration are a recent phenomenon. As distinguished criminologist Alfred Blumstein (2001) has documented, the black incarceration rate nearly tripled between 1980 and 2000 and is now over eight times that for non-Hispanic whites. Indeed, fully 2 percent of the black population was incarcerated in 1999 and one in ten black males in their twenties were under some form of criminal justice supervision. This change has reached such a level that a black male born in the 1990s faced almost one in three lifetime odds of ending up in jail or prison as compared to well under one in ten lifetime chances for non-Hispanic white males (Blumstein 2001). This is not merely a story of mass incarceration: it is one of racialized mass incarceration.

STRUCTURAL CHANGE AND PUBLIC POLICY: RE-INSCRIBING RACE IN THE CRIMINAL JUSTICE SYSTEM

Distinguished legal scholar Randall Kennedy (1997) identifies unequal protection of the law and unequal enforcement of the law as the principal means whereby African Americans were discriminated against in the legal system. By unequal protection he means routinization of lesser protection by the legal system, particularly lesser protection of blacks when victimized by whites. By unequal enforcement Kennedy means the acceptance of arbitrary, capricious, and openly discriminatory treatment of those African Americans designated as crime suspects. Notorious cases in the unequal protection category would include condoning or ignoring physical violence by white slave owners against blacks, including sexual assaults and the rape of black slave women by their white male slave masters. The latter category of unequal enforcement includes mob rule and a rush to judgment in the face of a lynching mentality, tortured confessions, nonexistent or incompetent legal counsel, and direct government subversion of black social and political activism as occurred during Operation COINTELPRO. COINTELPRO was a Federal Bureau of Investigation program of surveillance and destabilization of domestic political activist groups. The Black Panthers became one of its principal targets, and in this case the FBI's activities reached far beyond monitoring to include sparking conflicts with rivial political groups and having agents penetrate groups in order to act as advocates or provocateurs for committing crimes (Kennedy 1997, 111–113).

Kennedy traces the historical development of legal rulings and legislation, suggesting that these most egregious, fairly overt, and at one time common expressions of racially discriminatory bias in the law have largely been resolved in favor of a more race-neutral or color-blind regime. He writes:

> the administration of criminal law has changed substantially for the better over the past half century and that there is reason to believe that, properly guided, it can be improved even more. Today there are more formal and informal protections against racial bias than ever before, both in terms of the protections accorded blacks against criminality and the treatment accorded to black suspects, defendants, and convicts. That deficiencies, large deficiencies, remain is clear. But comparing racial policies today to those that prevailed in 1940 or 1960 or even 1980 should expose the fallacy of asserting that nothing substantial has been changed for the better. (Kennedy 1997, 388–389)

To wit, the burden to make the case is on those who wish to charge that racial bias remains a significant factor in the criminal justice system.

Yet, if Kennedy is correct, this pushes to the forefront the question of why African Americans end up so disproportionately behind bars. Do blacks commit more crime and, therefore, deservedly find themselves more often behind bars? Or has the operation of racial bias in the criminal justice system taken on a new guise?

Black Poverty and Public Policy

It is beyond the scope of this essay to develop a full sociological account of what may be differential levels of black involvement in crime, but it is important to put this common perception in some perspective. At a minimum it is essential to recognize that any evidence of differential black involvement with crime reflects the interplay of key economic, political, and cultural factors. From our perspective, such outcomes stem from the joint effects of what the eminent sociologist William Julius Wilson (1987, 1996) has called the new or intensified ghetto poverty and the patterns of social adaptation it has spawned, on the one hand, and what social policy changes did to foster patterns of social disorganization, on the other hand. The latter includes sharp reductions in federal aid to cities and the panoply of policing and legal changes that made up the War on Drugs. That is, differential black involvement with criminal behavior is primarily traceable to differential black exposure to structural conditions of extreme poverty, extreme racial segregation, changed law enforcement priorities, and the modern legacy of racial oppression (Massey 1995; Wilson 1987; Sampson and Wilson 1995).

Wilson (1987) shows that massive economic restructuring, in the form of the de-industrialization of the American economy (i.e., shift from heavy goods manufacturing to a service-oriented and information processing economy) and the de-concentration of industry (i.e., a shift of goods manufacturing from cities to suburban or ex-urban rings), combined to create new, persistent, and intensely high rates of poverty and unemployment for inner-city African Americans, particularly those of low education and skill levels. As Massey (1995) has shown, when the class segregation of neighborhoods combines with extreme racial segregation of neighborhoods, the result is areas of intensive social disorganization and dislocation when severe economic contractions or downturns occur. In particular, the persistent weak attachment to the labor force among many prime working-age adults and a common experience of poverty and economic hardship in urban black communities create social spaces where bonds of family and community begin to fray and fall apart (Wilson 1996). Such an environment is ripe for higher levels of juvenile delinquency, drug use, and even violent crime (Massey 1995).

In short, macro-social transformations (i.e., major economic restructuring) usher into place differential meso-level or proximate social conditions and environments for blacks and whites (i.e., uniquely heightened rates of community levels of poverty and unemployment for blacks), which, in turn, transform micro-level experiences, processes, and outcomes (i.e., individual family disruption, welfare dependency, and greater susceptibility to involvement in crime). Critically, the depth of disadvantage experienced in many urban black environments should not be underestimated. As Sampson and Wilson explain:

> Although we knew that the average national rate of family disruption and poverty among blacks was two to four times higher than among whites, the number of distinct ecological contexts in which blacks achieve equality to whites is striking. *In not one city over 100,000 in the United States do blacks live in ecological equality with whites when it comes to these basic features of economic and family organization. Accordingly, racial differences in poverty and family disruption are so strong that the "worst" urban context in which whites reside is considerably better than the average context of black communities.* (1995, 42; italics added)

There is fundamentally a structural and ecological basis to the association between urban ghettoes and a problem of social disorganization and crime.

The War on Drugs

Intense urban black poverty and unemployment is not the whole story. Aggressive pursuit of the War on Drugs plays a large role in the disproportionate incarceration of African Americans. The process involves many different actors at different points in the system. In Figure 12.5 we attempt to capture elements of this process and explain why we believe it represents racial bias. The figure shows the percentage of the total U.S. population that is white at 66.8 percent, and the percent that is black at 11.9 percent. The next set of figures reports the percentage of white and black adults, respectively, who report some *illicit* drug consumption during the average month from the 2005 National Survey on Drug Use and

FIGURE 12.5 | **THE WAR ON DRUGS AND RACIAL DISPARITIES IN THE CRIMINAL JUSTICE SYSTEM.**

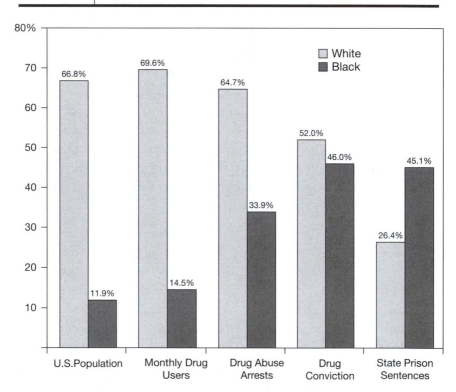

SOURCES | U.S. population data from the American Community Survey, 2006. Monthly drug users data from U.S. Department of Health and Human Services, National Survey on Drug Use and Health, 2005. Drug arrest data from Federal Bureau of Investigation, *Uniform Crime Reports, Crime in the United States, 2005.* Drug convictions data from U.S. Bureau of Justice Statistics, National Judicial Reporting Program, 2004. Prison sentences data from Harrison, Paige M., and Allen J. Beck for the U.S. Bureau of Justice Statistics, *Prisoners in 2005,* NCJ 215092.

Health. While reported usage rates of illicit drugs vary slightly between blacks and whites (9.2% for blacks compared to 8.1% for whites), it is important to note that the overall differences in the distribution of illicit drugs deviate very little from the overall white and black percentages in the population as a whole. That is, at least by this yardstick, there is no evidence of radically disproportionate representation of blacks among those Americans engaged in illegal drug consumption.

Once we shift our attention to drug-related arrests, however, we begin to discern one of the critical differences by race in how the War on Drugs is pursued. Blacks are almost 34 percent of those involved in drug-related arrests though only 14 percent of those among regular illegal drug users. The disparity grows even sharper as we switch attention to those who receive drug charge convictions—blacks constitute almost half of such cases. Likewise, blacks end up as nearly half of those serving state prison sentences for drug offenses compared to just 26 percent for the white population. Illegal drug consumption seems to know no race. Incarceration for drug-related charges, however, is something visited in a heavily biased manner on African Americans.

The Tulia, Texas, case is actually an illustrative if extreme instance of the type of biases at work to produce these sort of cumulative racial disadvantages and gaping disparities. First, local law enforcement aggressively pursued what, even in the most generous interpretation, were fairly low-level drug arrests and prosecutions (Provine 2007). Specifically, police, prosecutors, and judges repeatedly accepted the claims of a lone undercover operative, even when several cases of glaring falsehoods and lack of supporting evidence should have raised doubts about officer Coleman's claims. The three examples of glaring falsehoods are telling. Coleman brought charges against Tonya White. The prosecutor ultimately dropped the charges when it was established that she was at a bank in another state more than 300 miles away on the day and time Coleman had accused her of being involved in drug dealing. Billy Don Wafer produced employee time sheets establishing that he was at work when Coleman claimed he had sold him drugs. And charges against Yul Bryant were dismissed when Coleman's description of him as "a tall black man with bushy type hair" was contradicted by the fact that Bryant was only 5'6" and had been "bald for years."

Second, white public opinion supported the police and court actions. As the *New York Times* reported in one of its first major pieces on the Tulia case, "The reaction among most whites has been unflinching support of the operation and local officials. . . . The sheriff and the district attorney, who defend Mr. Coleman, also deny that the sting was racially motivated or that the town is biased" (Yardley 2000).

Third, the local media played a role in supporting the criminal justice official's claims and stigmatizing at least the individuals charged if not, in fact, the entire black community.[3] Again, as the *New York Times* reported, "The town's two newspapers had carried the story of the arrests on the front page, with the *Tulia Sentinel*, which is now defunct, describing the suspects as 'drug traffickers' and 'known dealers.' Television stations, tipped by the sheriff, had filmed the suspects as they were taken to jail after the sunrise arrests" (Yardley 2000). The racially charged character of this news coverage is difficult to deny. According to *The Village Voice*:

> Shortly after the arrests, *The Tulia Sentinel* ran a story on its front page with the headline "Tulia's Street Cleared of Garbage." A reader skimming the newspaper might have thought the article had something to do with local sanitation efforts. In fact, the first paragraph stated that the arrests of the town's "known" drug dealers "had cleared away some of the garbage off Tulia's streets." (Gonnerman 2001)

Perhaps what does make this case exceptional is that officer Coleman did ultimately confess that he "frequently used a racial epithet," namely, the N-word, though "he denied that he was a racist" (Liptak 2004).

Why regard the Tulia case as at all illustrative of a general set of processes?

As we have already discussed, the best credible evidence suggests that there is no gaping black-white difference in rates of illegal drug consumption, yet there are gaping differences in the rates at which blacks and whites end up behind bars. This strongly implies that something about law enforcement practices influences whether law-breaking behavior results in official actions and in particular whether it results in the most severe of available criminal sanctions. Those practices are clearly operating in a racially differential manner at least in effect if not in design and intent.

More than a decade ago Michael Tonry (1995) argued that it was completely foreseeable that the War on Drugs would be waged in a racially biased manner. This was so, he maintained, because much of the rhetoric and ambition of the drug war focused on cocaine and especially the trade

---

[3] Research has shown, in general, that local news media engage in a number of routine practices that at once play upon and reinforce anti-black stereotypes, particularly in the arena of crime news reporting. Entman and Rojecki (2000) show, for example, that black criminal defendants are more often shown in prison gear (e.g., orange jumpsuits) than white defendants, more often shown on a "perp-walk," less likely to be given a name, and so on.

in crack cocaine. This emphasis almost foreordained a heavy focus on urban, black environments as the front line of this new anti-crime crusade. Furthermore, it would be a much simpler task for police to pursue open-air, public space drug trafficking than the drug trade that took place behind closed doors, since the former is much more readily observable by police than the latter. Likewise, police would have a much easier task of inserting themselves into personal and community networks of interaction in disadvantaged black communities than in relatively stable and densely networked working- and middle-class white communities. And given political pressure to "show results," police could more and more rapidly show evidence of arrests by focusing on low-income black communities where the drug trade was more often done in more easily penetrated public spaces.

Carefully designed research by sociologist Katherine Beckett and her colleagues has yielded some of the most compelling evidence on just how substantial and institutionalized this racial bias is in actual practice (Beckett et al. 2005; Beckett, Nyrop, and Pfingst 2006). Specifically, they argue that the highly racialized discourse and politics that led to the War on Drugs has become institutionalized in street-level law enforcement practices. To wit, police selectively focus their attention on enforcement and arrests on the public space drug trade of crack among blacks and Latinos. Their own systematic observation of known drug-trading locations showed that police are more likely to pursue the black and Latino suspects in the area than the white ones. As Beckett and colleagues explain:

> Our findings indicate that the majority of those who deliver methamphetamine, ecstasy, powder cocaine, and heroin in Seattle are white; blacks are the majority of those who deliver only one drug: crack. Yet 64 percent of those arrested for delivering one of these five drugs is black. . . . Predominantly white outdoor drug markets received far less attention than racially diverse markets located downtown. . . . The overrepresentation of blacks and under-representation of whites among those arrested for delivering illegal narcotics does not appear to be explicable in race-neutral terms. (2006, 129)

Or, as criminologists Janet Lauritsen and Robert Sampson put it: "while 'crack' cocaine has generated an intense law enforcement campaign in our nation's black ghettos, 'powder' cocaine use among whites is quietly neglected (perhaps even portrayed as fashionable). These differences cannot be attributed to objective levels of criminal danger, but rather to the way in which minority behaviors are symbolically constructed and subjected to official social control" (1998, 79).

Some scholars suggest that anti-black racial bias is a key element in the emergence of the new law and order regime (Marable 2002; Soss, Fording, and Schram 2008). For example, David Jacobs and colleagues have shown that those states and jurisdictions with larger numbers of blacks—a condition that arguably fosters a greater sense among many white of competition and threat from minorities irrespective of the actual crime rate—adopt more punitive crime and social spending policies (Jacobs and Carmichael 2002; Jacobs and Tope 2007; see also Soss, Fording, and Schram 2008). Loic Wacquant (2001) has eloquently argued, in fact, that the emergence of the carceral state constitutes a fourth stage of racial oppression in the United States following on the legacy of first, slavery; second, Jim Crow racism; and third, the creation of the modern urban ghetto. He sees each institution as a distinctive way of controlling, regulating, and in a word, "oppressing" the black population.

Neither Soss and colleagues nor Jacobs nor Wacquant, however, provides a clear explication of the full sociocultural environment that makes racialized mass incarceration possible. To do that, one needs a more complete assessment of public opinion at the place where the problems of race and crime meet.

PUBLIC OPINION, PREJUDICE, AND PUNITIVENESS.

A troubled and troubling link between race, crime, and the functioning of the legal system is not a new condition for American society. Early statements of this troubled nexus can be found in the work of W. E. B. Du Bois ([1899] 2007) and of pioneering criminologist Thorstein Sellin (1928, 1935). Both argued that blacks are disproportionately swept into the criminal justice system but that this circumstance could not be understood apart from the systematic operation of a larger pattern of anti-black racial prejudice. Is anti-black racial prejudice a key component of the new law and order regime and of the emergence of racialized mass incarceration in the United States? We believe the answer is an unequivocal "yes."

Punitiveness and Racial Prejudice

One of the primary sociological foundations of the new law and order regime and of the racialized mass incarceration society is the decidedly

punitive tilt of U.S. public opinion. One indication of the degree of popular support for these policies is provided in Figure 12.6. It reports on the
percentages in a major national survey of white and black Americans
who support the death penalty, three strikes and you're out provisions,
and the trying of juveniles as adults if accused of a violent crime. Two
patterns stand out. First, for each of these policies—including the penultimate symbol and act of punitiveness, the death penalty—there is clear
majority support for the punitive policy among both blacks and whites.
Second, African Americans are uniformly less supportive of these harsh
criminal justice policies than are their white counterparts, even though
they too show a clear majority support for each. It is no mistake or exag-
geration to characterize U.S. public opinion on crime and crime policy
as decidedly punitive.

A punitive tilt in public opinion, especially one that largely includes
both white and black Americans, is scarcely a sign of anti-black racial
bias. We stress the logic of such bias, however, because these punitive
crime policy outlooks are strongly rooted in anti-black racial prejudice
(Bobo and Thompson 2006b). To prove this point, we examined the correlation between punitive crime policy outlooks (a measure that combines responses to the death penalty, three strikes, and juvenile offenders
questions shown in Figure 12.6) and a series of different indicators of
racial attitudes.[4] The racial attitude indicators included simple anti-
black stereotypes,[5] of intergroup affect or basic socioemotional feelings
toward blacks,[6] and of collective racial resentments of blacks.[7] Each of

---

[4] Respondents were asked if they "Strongly Oppose," "Somewhat Oppose," "Somewhat Favor," or
"Strongly Favor" the death penalty or three-strike laws. Similarly, respondents were asked if they
"Strongly Disagree," "Somewhat Disagree," "Somewhat Agree," or "Strongly Agree" that juveniles
should be tried as adults. A final "Punitiveness" scale was created based on the average scores of these
three items (Cronbach's alpha = .63).

[5] Respondents were asked to rate on a 10-point scale the degree to which they thought the following
words/phrases accurately described blacks: "law-abiding," "good neighbors," "lazy," "hard working,"
"violent," "intelligent," "welfare dependent," or "complain a lot." The final responses were combined
into a single "stereotype scale" (Cronbach's alpha = .87).

[6] Affect is the combination of two questions: "How often have you felt sympathy for blacks?" and "How
often have you admired blacks?" (Cronbach's alpha = .72).

[7] The "racial resentment scale" is the combined average of six questions that asked respondents to agree
or disagree with the following statements: "Irish, Italian, Jewish and many other minorities overcame
prejudice and worked their way up. Blacks should do the same without any special favors", "Over the
past few years, blacks have gotten less than they deserve", "Government officials usually pay less attention to a request or complaint from a black person than from a white person", "Most blacks who receive
money from welfare programs could get along without it if they tried", "If blacks would only try harder,
they could be just as well off as whites", "Generations of slavery and discrimination have created conditions that make it difficult for them to work their way out of the lower class" (Cronbach's alpha = .77).

FIGURE 12.6 | **PERCENT OF BLACKS AND WHITES WHO "STRONGLY FAVOR" THE DEATH PENALTY, LIFE IN PRISON FOR THREE VIOLENT FELONIES, OR TRYING JUVENILES AS ADULTS FOR VIOLENT CRIMES.**

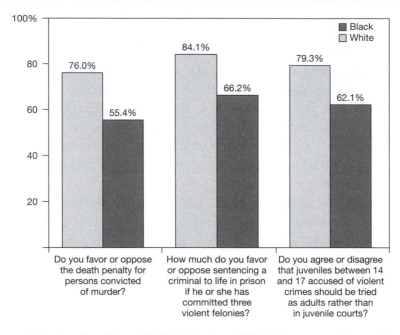

SOURCE | Data from *Race, Crime, and Public Opinion Survey*, 2001. Bobo, Lawrence, and Devon Johnson, Harvard University.

these measures has been used in a variety of previous studies and all have been shown to be reasonably reliable and valid measures of significant forms of racial prejudice.

Negative racial stereotypes, anti-black affect, and collective racial resentments all are positively correlated with criminal justice policy punitiveness. These correlations exist among both white and black Americans, though they are usually much stronger among whites. Our analyses, however, did not settle for merely examining correlations. We sought to determine whether demographic background characteristics—such as level of education, age, urbanicity, or region of the country—sometimes associated with levels of prejudice might account for these prejudice-to-punitiveness correlations. We also sought to determine whether alternative potential sources of punitive crime policy outlooks mattered. Among the competing hypotheses we considered were the possibility that conservative social values (indicated by conservative political ideology, Republican Party identification, and frequent church attendance), highly individualistic and dispositional views about the causes of crime, and other factors such as fear of crime, actual criminal victimization, actual levels of violent crime, or the number of blacks living in a respondents area, could better explain support for punitive crime policy preferences.

Our results consistently showed that collective racial resentment was an important predictor of support for punitive crime policies regardless of the control variables (e.g., demographic characteristics) or alternative explanations (e.g., social conservatism, crime causation beliefs, or other material social conditions) we also took into account. Indeed, no other variable aside from race itself mattered so consistently. The key relationship is shown graphically in Figures 12.7a and 12.7b. Figure 12.7a summarizes the effects of racial resentment on support for punitive crime policies. Even after controlling for every potential intervening variable in the relationship between racial resentment and support for punitive crime policies, we find overwhelming support for our thesis that when it comes to punishment, racial attitudes matter. Respondents

FIGURE 12.7a | **EFFECT OF RACIAL RESENTMENT ON PUNITIVENESS.**

Punitiveness and Racial Resentment were each measured on a scale from 1 to 5.

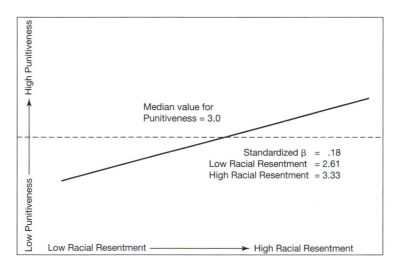

NOTE: Results from regression models that control for race, stereotypes, racial affect, age, sex, education, urbanicity, region, political ideology, church attendance, neighborhood context, fear of crime, and beliefs about why people commit crimes.

SOURCE | Data from *Race, Crime, and Public Opinion Survey*, 2001 and 2002. Bobo, Lawrence, and Devon Johnson, Harvard University.

FIGURE 12.7b | **DISTRIBUTION OF BLACKS AND WHITES BY RACIAL RESENTMENT.**

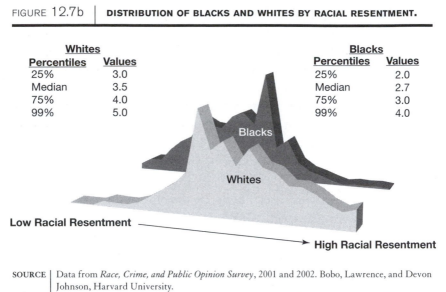

Whites				Blacks	
Percentiles	**Values**			**Percentiles**	**Values**
25%	3.0			25%	2.0
Median	3.5			Median	2.7
75%	4.0			75%	3.0
99%	5.0			99%	4.0

Blacks

Whites

Low Racial Resentment

→ High Racial Resentment

SOURCE | Data from *Race, Crime, and Public Opinion Survey*, 2001 and 2002. Bobo, Lawrence, and Devon Johnson, Harvard University.

with the lowest values of racial resentment were consistently below the median score of punitiveness (at 3.0 this roughly equates to "Somewhat Agree" with, or "Somewhat Favor" the policy). Comparatively, respondents who had high levels of racial resentment were much more likely to "Strongly Agree" with and "Strongly Favor" a more punitive course of action when it comes to dealing with criminal behavior.

We include Figure 12.7b to underscore an important set of ideas. Levels of collective racial resentment are much higher among white Americans than among black Americans. But we also want to point out that these are nonetheless culturally prominent ideas that are articulated through the media and from various both elite and lay sources. As a result, both whites and blacks have extensive exposure to such ideas, though these ideas encounter greater challenge, resistance, and alternative accounts among blacks than is likely to occur among whites.

This is an instance when it is of value to reflect carefully as much on what the findings did *not* show as on what they did show. Specifically, our results indicate that such factors as an individual's personal fear of crime, actual criminal victimization in the past, the actual rate of homicide in a respondent's larger community, and even the individual's own broad social values were not as important in predicting support for punitive crime policies as the degree to which she or he held strong collective resentments toward African Americans. To wit, a significant portion of the public appetite for harsh crime policies has its roots not in features of the crime problem itself or in the triumph of conservatism per se but rather in the prevailing and deeply troubling cultural legacy of anti-black racism in America. It seems unlikely to us, on the basis of these results, that the racialized mass incarceration society could or would have emerged, much less been sustained for as long as it has, absent a widespread cultural pattern and practice of contempt and derision toward African Americans.

A Crisis of Confidence

One feature of the new law and order regime is deep black-white polarization over the fairness and legitimacy of the legal system. This problem of legitimacy is not merely a vague sentiment that something is not quite as it should be. Whether we focus on police, prosecutors, or judges, we find that black and white Americans are very far apart in their assessments of whether agents of the criminal justice system treat people equally without regard to race. Figure 12.8 reports data on the degree of expressed confidence in judges, prosecutors, and police. In each instance two-thirds or more of white Americans expressed "some" or "a lot" of confidence that judges, prosecutors, and police, respectively, will treat blacks and whites equally. Just as consistently, fewer than one in three African Americans expressed such a viewpoint. Across the three items, the black-white difference averages a full fifty percentage points. Blacks and whites occupy profoundly different worlds when it comes to expectations for the performance of the criminal justice system.

We were particularly interested in determining whether this perception of race bias in the criminal justice system would have consequences. To examine this possibility we conducted two further experiments within the context of our national surveys both aimed at determining whether the perception of race bias would encourage blacks (or whites, for that matter) to engage in jury nullification. Jury nullification occurs when members of a jury panel, in effect, ignore the evidence and existing law in a case when they return a verdict in order to make a statement about what they see as a larger source of unfairness in the legal process. Indeed, some prominent legal scholars have called for just such behavior with regard to the incarceration binge and African Americans (Butler 1995).

In general, consistent with the expectation that perceived racial bias in the legal system predisposes individuals to act in ways that undermine the legal system, we find strong evidence of readiness to engage in jury

FIGURE 12.8 | **PERCENTAGE OF RESPONDENTS WHO HAVE "A LOT" OR "SOME" CONFIDENCE IN JUDGES, PROSECUTORS, AND POLICE.**

Respondents were asked how much confidence they had that judges, prosecutors, and police treat blacks and whites equally. There were four responses: "A lot of confidence," "Some confidence," "A little confidence," or "No confidence." This graph shows the combined responses for "A lot of confidence," and "Some confidence."

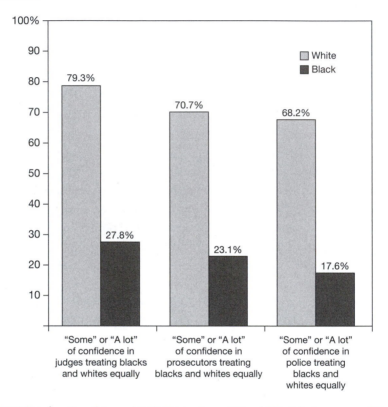

SOURCE | Data from *Race, Crime, and Public Opinion Survey*, 2001 and 2002. Bobo, Lawrence, and Devon Johnson, Harvard University.

nullification, particularly among African Americans but also among a nontrivial number of sympathetic whites. In one question we asked respondents to consider the hypothetical case of an African American male on trial for the first time for a nonviolent drug charge. We asked a randomly selected half of the respondents if they would be willing to let the individual go free even if the evidence presented tended to point toward his guilt. The other half of the respondents were asked if they would let the individual go free if his defense claimed that the arresting officer had been motivated by racial bias. A second experiment shifted

FIGURE 12.9 | **PERCENTAGE OF RESPONDENTS WHO WOULD BE WILLING TO ENGAGE IN JURY NULLIFICATION GIVEN THE FOLLOWING SCENARIOS.**

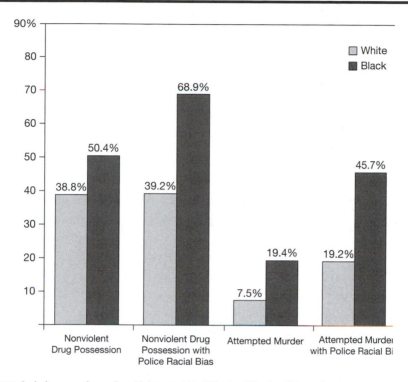

NOTE: Includes respondents who said they would be "Mostly willing," or "Very willing" to engage in jury nullification.

SOURCE | Data from *Race, Crime, and Public Opinion Survey*, 2001 and 2002. Bobo, Lawrence, and Devon Johnson, Harvard University.

to a case of an attempted murder charge, but otherwise paralleled the nonviolent drug possession experiment. Results for both are shown in Figure 12.9.

In both experiments these national sample survey data show, especially for the drug possession case, that large fractions of the African American population are ready to engage in jury nullification. Even when there is no mention of racial bias on the part of the arresting officer, fully 50 percent of blacks say they would consider voting to let the suspect go free if they were on a jury, as did nearly 20 percent of blacks in the case of an attempted murder charge. When the experimental manipulation explicitly raises the possibility of racial bias in the case readiness to engage in nullification rises in both cases. More than two-thirds support nullification in the drug charge case (up from 50 percent) and just under half (up from 20 percent) in the attempted murder charge report a higher level of readiness to engage in jury nullification. We found no experimental effect among whites in the drug charge case, though there was a high baseline level of support for nullification at approximately 39 percent.

We tested two more direct types of evidence to bear on the claim that it is the problem of perceived racial bias in the operation of the legal system that is responsible for these experimental results. We combined responses to the three questions on judges, prosecutors, and police treating blacks and whites equally to create a measure of perceived racial bias in the criminal justice system. This measure proves to be strongly related to a respondent's readiness to engage in jury nullification. Figure 12.10a maps the relationship between the perceived racial bias measure and willingness to engage in jury nullification regarding the drug charge case.

This perception of bias in the functioning of the criminal justice system takes on a special edge with regard to the war on drugs. We asked a separate series of questions specifically about the extent to which the conduct of the War on Drugs was carried out in a racially biased manner. Substantially more blacks than whites agreed with each of three statements concerning race bias in the war on drugs. For example, 66 percent of blacks but only 21 percent of whites agree with the statement that "drug laws are enforced unfairly against black communities" (Bobo

FIGURE 12.10a | **PERCENTAGE OF RESPONDENTS WHO WOULD BE "MOSTLY/ VERY WILLING" TO ENGAGE IN JURY NULLIFICATION FOR DRUG POSSESSION CHARGES BASED ON THEIR BELIEFS ABOUT RACIAL BIAS IN THE CRIMINAL JUSTICE SYSTEM, AFTER CONTROLLING FOR RELEVANT VARIABLES.**

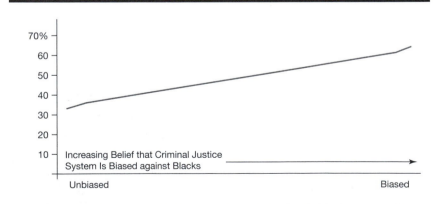

SOURCE | Data from *Race, Crime, and Public Opinion Survey*, 2001 and 2002. Bobo, Lawrence, and Devon Johnson, Harvard University.

FIGURE 12.10b | **PERCENTAGE OF RESPONDENTS WHO WOULD BE "MOSTLY/VERY WILLING" OR "MOSTLY/VERY UNWILLING" TO ENGAGE IN JURY NULLIFICATION BASED ON THEIR OPINIONS ABOUT DRUG LAWS.**

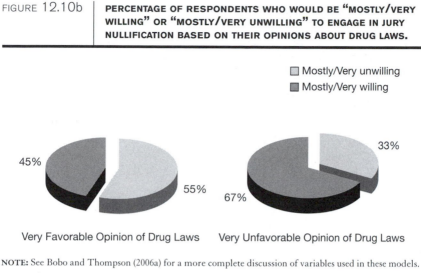

☐ Mostly/Very unwilling
■ Mostly/Very willing

Very Favorable Opinion of Drug Laws   Very Unfavorable Opinion of Drug Laws

NOTE: See Bobo and Thompson (2006a) for a more complete discussion of variables used in these models.

SOURCE | Data from *Race, Crime, and Public Opinion Survey*, 2001 and 2002. Bobo, Lawrence, and Devon Johnson, Harvard University.

and Thompson 2006a, 461). Figure 12.10b shows that this measure too is clearly related to readiness to engage in jury nullification in our hypothetical drug charge case. Sixty-seven percent of respondents with a low opinion of the War on Drugs (i.e., who believed it is racially biased) were "mostly" or "very willing" to vote to acquit someone they thought was probably guilty of a nonviolent drug charge as compared to only 45 percent of those with a high opinion of the War on Drugs.

In a democratic society the legitimacy of the legal system is of great importance (Blumstein 2001; Tyler and Huo 2002). People who see law enforcement and application of the law as fair are more likely to comply with the law and to be supportive of law enforcement efforts. It is also and perhaps more tellingly important because, according to basic democratic theory, individuals should stand equal before the law and the coercive powers of the state. Indeed, this is one of the fundamental expectations of any citizen in a democracy. The current punitive law and order regime and condition of racialized mass incarceration has created a real crisis of legitimacy for the legal system in the eyes of most African Americans and a nontrivial number of whites as well. These perceptions of serious racial bias are likely to have real consequences for how individuals engage and interact with agents of the criminal justice system.

A Durable Taste for Punishment?

Given our argument about the central sociological importance of public opinion as an underpinning of the racialized mass incarceration regime, it becomes urgently important to identify those strategies that might make it possible to move the mass public in less punitive, more preventative, and potentially more reintegrative directions with regard to criminal offenders. That is, we sought to determine whether criminal justice policy issues could be contextualized or "framed" in ways that would encourage less uniformly punitive reactions from the mass public. We conducted a series of four controlled "framing" experiments in national surveys to begin testing the limits of the taste for punitiveness. Our results, summarized in Table 12.1, have been only modestly reassuring about the potential to move public opinion.

Our initial experiment, which we labeled "The Death Row Demography" experiment, sought to determine whether drawing attention to the statistical fact of the mere overrepresentation of blacks on death row would be enough to weaken public support for the ultimate penalty. The experiment had three conditions that involved a standard

TABLE 12.1 | **PUNITIVENESS ISSUE FRAMING EXPERIMENTS**

Experiment	Manipulation	Effect
Death Row Demography	Blacks are about 12% of the U.S. population, but they [are almost half (43%) of those currently on death row] **OR** [were half of the homicide offenders last year.	None
Murder Victim Race Bias	At present, someone who murders a white person is much more likely to be sentenced to death than someone who murders a black person.	None
Innocent on Death Row	Since 1976, seventy-nine people convicted and sentenced to death were later found to be innocent and have now been released from prison.	None
Crack versus Powder Cocaine	Most of those convicted for crack cocaine use are blacks and most of those convicted for powder cocaine use are whites.	Approximately a 20 percentage point increase in disapproval for both blacks and whites

SOURCE | Bobo and Johnson 2004.

question on support for the death penalty, a second condition involving a pre-question declaration that almost half of the people on death row are black though blacks are only 12 percent of the population, or a third condition involving a pre-question declaration that blacks commit almost half of the nation's homicides though blacks are only 12 percent of the population. This experiment yielded no change across the three conditions in levels of support for the death penalty. This is a useful case to consider because in recent memory, the then-governors of Illinois and Maryland imposed brief moratoriums on application of the death penalty. They justified their actions at least partly on the basis of black overrepresentation and the potential appearance of bias that such over-representation created.

In the second experiment, which we labeled "The Murder Victim Race-Bias" experiment, we drew attention to the one way in which there is still clear evidence of race bias in the application of the death penalty. Compelling evidence has been amassed that in the United States someone who murders a white person, irrespective of all other features of the criminal suspect and of the crime itself, is a good deal more likely to receive a death sentence than someone who murders a black person, suggesting a clearly higher value placed on white lives than on black lives. This experiment, in the main, yielded negative results as well: drawing attention to bias on the basis of the murder victim's race did not substantially alter support for the death penalty.

In the third experiment, which we labeled "The Innocent on Death Row" experiment, we attempted to draw attention to the risk of executing an innocent person. That is, this experiment made no explicit reference to race but rather to the fact that a large number of people actually sentenced to death have been exonerated (79 such cases at the time the experiment was conducted and over 100 as of this writing). In this case we asked respondents if they would be more or less likely to vote for a gubernatorial candidate if that person called for a moratorium on the death penalty because of the risk of executing innocent people. A randomly selected half of the respondents got only this question whereas another randomly selected half were first told of the number of convicted death row inmates who had been exonerated. Strikingly, drawing attention to the risk of this irreversible and grave error did not significantly move public opinion.

In our fourth and final experiment, which we labeled "The Crack vs. Powder Cocaine" experiment, we drew attention to the differential sentencing penalties attached to these two forms of illegal drug consumption. In particular, we asked people whether they approved of substantially stiffer penalties attached to crack cocaine as compared to powder cocaine. One-half of the respondents, however, were informed that most of those arrested for powder cocaine use were white whereas most of those arrested for crack cocaine use were black. In this instance, we found a large 20 percentage point drop among both white and black respondents in support of the sentencing differential when the racial consequences were pointed out.

Taken as a whole, these results suggest both the strength of the punitive ethos in the mass public at present and the possibility of change with regard at least to some cases with drug-related charges. The latter result is particularly encouraging since the sort of violent crime to which the death penalty applies is not a major component of the racialized mass incarceration problem.

CONCLUSION: RACISM AND THE NEW LAW AND ORDER REGIME

Writing in 1899 in his magisterial work *The Philadephia Negro: A Social Study*, the great sociologist W. E. B. Du Bois declared:

> "Thus the class of Negroes which the prejudices of the city have distinctly encouraged is that of the criminal, the lazy, and the shiftless; for them the city teems with institutions and charities; for them there is succor and sympathy; for them Philadelphians are thinking and planning; but for the educated and industrious young colored man who wants work and not platitudes, wages and not alms, just rewards and not sermons—for such colored men Philadelphia apparently has no use." (Du Bois [1899] 2007, 243)

For Du Bois, Philadelphia at the dawn of the twentieth century was greatly concerned with how to respond to a problem of crime, particularly to what was regarded as "Negro crime." But at the same moment, little if anything was taking place to more fully include and make a place for the many blacks coming to the city merely hoping to lead decent lives. Had he lived to the present day, Du Bois might well sense a disturbing parallel between our times and this now century-old circumstance.

Beginning in a serious fashion in the 1980s, the United States embarked on a series of legal reforms that have made us a far more punitive society. Mandatory minimum sentences, three strikes and you're out laws, trying juveniles as adults, truth in sentencing practices, and a variety of other policies and practices contributed to an unprecedented rise in the reliance upon formal incarceration as our collective response to crime. In theory, these changes were neutral as to race. Moreover, they were largely implemented in the post–civil rights era when the most egregious forms of racial bias in the law and law enforcement had largely been wiped away. Nonetheless, the reach of an increasingly punitive state was not felt evenly across American society but instead fell with heavy disproportion on African Americans, particularly those of low income and education. We are thus prompted to modify the increasingly conventional social science wisdom that describes these changes as the emergence of the "mass incarceration" society to instead describe what has happened as the emergence of "racialized mass incarceration." As legal scholar Dorothy Roberts puts it: "African Americans experience a uniquely astronomical rate of imprisonment, and the social effects of imprisonment are concentrated in their communities. Thus, the transformation of prison policy at the turn of the twenty-first century is most accurately characterized as the mass incarceration of African Americans" (Roberts 2004, 1272–1273).

A critical element of our claim for racialized mass incarceration is the structure of and effects of public opinion. A necessary and constituent element of the development of the punitive law and order regime and of attendant patterns of racialized mass incarceration has been a set of anti-black attitudes and beliefs that are a significant element of the public appetite for punitive crime policy. Indeed, measures of anti-black racial prejudice are far more potent predictors of public support for the death penalty, three strikes and you're out provisions, and trying juveniles as adults than conservative social values, levels of violent crime, size of the black population, or beliefs about the fundamental causes of criminal behavior. The cultural legacy of anti-black racism is a major bulwark of the punitive law and order regime.

More than this, it is important to bear in mind how racialized mass incarceration has transformed life in many African American communities. Legal scholar Roberts summarizes it well: in "African American communities where it is concentrated, mass imprisonment damages social networks, distorts social norms, and destroys social citizenship" (2004, 1281). It damages networks by removing fathers, brothers, uncles from a web of mutually supportive family and community relationships. It damages broader social norms in two ways. First, it creates conditions wherein it becomes customary or ordinary for youth, especially young men, to expect to spend some time in jail or prison because they observe that a high fraction of the adult males in their lives and communities are incarcerated. Second, it creates a sense of contempt and illegitimacy toward law enforcement personnel who come to be regarded as an oppressive force in the community rather than partners in maintaining a high quality of life. And it undermines social citizenship by both profoundly stigmatizing those with criminal records and frequently expressly stripping even ex-felons of the right to vote.

The usual sociological inclination is to stress the class character of a form of social inequality, including the development of mass incarceration. And without doubt there is a critical sense in which levels of education and income play a crucial role in defining who is highly susceptible to incarceration and who is not, regardless of race. Yet, there is no sense in which the expansive reliance on incarceration has transformed the fabric of white communities, even working-class ones. For African Americans, however, the situation is quite a bit different. As sociologist Bruce Western puts it: "The criminal justice system has become so pervasive that we should count prisons and jails among the key institutions that shape the life course of recent birth cohorts of African American men" (Western 2006, 31).

The impact of racialized mass incarceration reaches across boundaries of class in black America. In our national surveys we asked respondents whether they had a close friend or relative who was "currently incarcerated." We found that only one out of ten whites responded affirmatively to this question in 2001–2002. In contrast, fully half of African Americans responded positively to the question, for a ratio of black to white of more than four to one. In Figure 12.11 we examine responses to this question by a combination of levels of education, income, and race. Even more striking is that among those whites with incomes below $25,000 a year and who had not completed high school, we still find just one in five responding "yes" to the friend or relative incarcerated question. However, that number is just below 60 percent (or more than five out of ten) among comparable blacks. If we shift attention to the high end of class hierarchy, we find among high-income whites ($60,000 or more) with a college education (or greater), less than 5 percent respond yes to the incarcerated friend or relative question. That is, virtually no high-status whites have such personal exposure to the carceral state. In sharp contrast, fully 31.7 percent of high-income high-education blacks responded yes to this question on personal exposure to the carceral state, for a black to white ratio of seven to one. Strikingly, the rate of such exposure for the very highest status African Americans exceeds that of the very lowest status whites, roughly one in three as compared to only one in five!

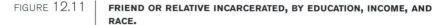

FIGURE 12.11 | **FRIEND OR RELATIVE INCARCERATED, BY EDUCATION, INCOME, AND RACE.**

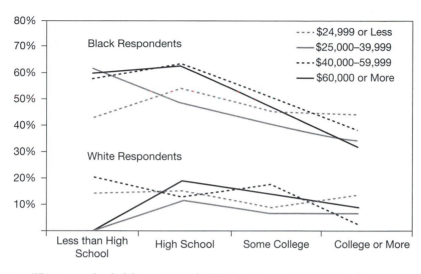

NOTE: Whites were only asked this question in the 2001 *Race, Crime, and Public Opinion Survey*.

SOURCE | Data from *Race, Crime, and Public Opinion Survey*, 2001 and 2002. Bobo, Lawrence, and Devon Johnson, Harvard University.

From our perspective on social policy choices and institutional practices, neither the nature of crime itself nor the distribution of who engages in law-breaking behavior produced the racialized mass incarceration society. Consequently, policy choices can also point us in a very different direction. Ruth and Reitz (2003) articulate a well-crafted set of high-level goals and more immediate reform considerations that should guide policymaking in this domain. In terms of high-level goals, they suggest that crime policy be formulated and routinely evaluated against five key ambitions: (1) the reduction of crime; (2) the reduction of public fear of crime; (3) justice for victims, offenders, and the larger community; (4) law and law enforcement practices that foster perceived legitimacy "within all relevant communities"; and (5) avoidance of the extension of law beyond those actions truly necessary to "address serious harm faced by society." Their analysis suggests that political entrepreneurs and short-term response to political- and media-manipulated "moral panics" have all too often been the impetus for major criminal justice reform (see Chambliss 1995; Beckett 1997), not careful research- and evidence-based criteria.

Ruth and Reitz also outline seven specific reforms to address the excesses of the current incarceration binge, all sensible recommendations from our perspective: (1) prioritize the use of incarceration primarily for a response to grave violence; (2) charter a permanent sentencing commission to reintroduce expert judgment and planning into law enforcement; (3) reverse policies of more and longer sentences for drug offenders; (4) conduct a national audit of the use of incarceration to determine whether the current massive level of intervention by the criminal justice system can withstand close scrutiny (against the standards outlined above); (5) promote effective helping programs for offenders to better assure their reintegration after a period of incarceration; (6) review policies dealing with those who are incarcerated since they are rarely involved in violent crimes, but their rates of incarceration are rising rapidly; and (7) *require that changes in punishment laws be preceded by a statement of the racial, ethnic, and financial changes that may result.* The latter point is of special concern to us. More serious and principled attention to the degree of extreme racial imbalance in the experience of incarceration should have taken place long ago. It is time to begin an honest discourse on the magnitude and fundamental source of racialized mass incarceration, perhaps the great social policy setback of the post–civil rights era.

We began by drawing attention to the Tulia, Texas, drug arrests that proved to be essentially fraudulent and racially motivated. We could just as easily have chosen any of several other prominent cases to highlight the problem of punitive excess in the legal system where African Americans pay a disproportionate price. Among the other high-profile cases to which we could have pointed are the "Jena 6" case in Louisiana; the police shootings of Abner Louima and Sean Bell in New York, or of Oscar Grant in northern California; or the general pattern of trying juvenile offenders as adults and sentencing them to life without the possibility of parole. Tulia is special because it represents such an extreme without being all that exceptional; because it involves the War on Drugs, which is such a crucial element of the problem of racialized mass incarceration; and because, in hindsight, we can fairly say that any justice system not already suffused with anti-black bias would have stopped such an outrage before routinely and methodically imprisoning more than a dozen people (more than 10 percent of Tulia's black population). As the NAACP Legal Defense Fund declares, "The Tulia 'sting' is representative of the failed 'War on Drugs,' which disproportionately targets minorities, and also often includes racially-biased police practices and secures convictions only after prosecutorial misconduct" (NAACP-LDF 2006, 1). Or, to quote Sammy Barrow, a black Tulia resident with four relatives swept up by the sting operation and who could just as well have been speaking about a national problem, "They declared war on this community" (Yardley 2000).

A long problematic connection between race and the functioning of the criminal justice system has been re-forged in the post–civil rights era. Instead of arriving at a circumstance of clear equal treatment before the law without regard to race, a set of social polices and institutional practices has emerged over the last three decades that has resulted in a new, deeply punitive law and order regime and a condition of racialized mass incarceration in the United States. These circumstances should trouble all those interested in racial justice and a fuller realization of the fundamental principles and promises of a democratic society.

Works Cited

●

Beckett, Katherine. 1997. *Making Crime Pay: Law and Order in Contemporary American Politics*. New York: Oxford University Press.

Beckett, Katherine, Kris Nyrop, and Lori Pfingst. 2006. Race, Drugs, and Policing: Understanding Disparities in Drug Delivery Arrests. *Criminology* 44: 105–138.

Beckett, Katherine, Kris Nyrop, Lori Pfingst, and Melissa Bowen. 2005. Drug Use, Drug Possession Arrests, and the Question of Race: Lessons from Seattle. *Social Problems* 52: 419–441.

Blumstein, Alfred. 2001. "Race and Criminal Justice." In *America Becoming: Racial Trends and Their Consequences*, vol. 2, eds. N. J. Smelser, W. J. Wilson, and F. Mitchell, 21–31. Washington, DC: National Academy Press.

Bobo, Lawrence D. 2004. Inequalities that Endure? Racial Ideology, American Politics, and the Peculiar Role of the Social Sciences. In *The Changing Terrain of Race and Ethnicity*, ed. M. Krysan and A. E. Lewis, 13–42. New York: Russell Sage Foundation.

Bobo, Lawrence D., and Devon Johnson. 2004. A Taste for Punishment: Black and White Americans' Views on the Death Penalty and the War on Drugs. *Du Bois Review* 1: 151–180.

Bobo, Lawrence D., and Victor Thompson. 2006a. Unfair by Design: The War on Drugs, Race, and the Legitimacy of the Criminal Justice System. *Social Research* 73: 445–472.

———. 2006b. Punitiveness and Prejudice:Racial Attitudes and Popular Support for Harsh Crime Policies. Paper presented at the annual meeting for the American Sociological Association, August 11–14, in Montreal, Canada.

Butler, Paul. 1995. Racially Based Jury Nullification: Black Power in the Criminal Justice System. *Yale Law Journal* 105: 677–725.

Chambliss, William J. 1995. Crime Control and Ethnic Minorities: Legitimizing Racial Oppression by Creating Moral Panics. In *Ethnicity, Race, and Crime:*

Perspectives across Time and Place, ed. D. F. Hawkins, 235–258. Albany: State University of New York Press.

Du Bois, W. E. B. [1899] 2007. *The Philadelphia Negro: A Social Study*, ed. Henry Louis Gates, Jr., with an introduction by Lawrence Bobo. New York: Oxford University Press.

Entman, Robert M., and Andrew Rojecki. 2000. *The Black Image in the White Mind: Media and Race in America*. Chicago: University of Chicago Press.

Garland, David. 2001. Introduction: The Meaning of Mass Imprisonment. In *Mass Imprisonment: Social Causes and Consequences*, ed. D. Garland, 1–3. Thousand Oaks, CA: Sage.

Gonnerman, Jennifer. 2001. Tulia Blues. *Village Voice*, July 31.

Irwin, John. 2007. *The Warehouse Prison: Disposal of the New Dangerous Class*. Los Angeles: Roxbury.

Jacobs, David, and Jason T. Carmichael. 2002. The Political Sociology of the Death Penalty: A Pooled Time-Series Analysis. *American Sociological Review* 67: 109–131.

Jacobs, David, and Daniel Tope. 2007. The Politics of Resentment in the Post–Civil Rights Era: Minority Threat, Homicide, and Ideological Voting in Congress. *American Journal of Sociology* 112: 1458–1494.

Kennedy, Randall. 1997. *Race, Crime, and the Law*. New York: Pantheon Books.

Lauritsen, Janet, and Robert J. Sampson 1998. Minorities, Crime, and Criminal Justice. In *The Handbook of Crime and Punishment*, ed. M. J. Tonry, 58–84. New York: Oxford University Press.

Liptak, Adam. 2004. $5 Million Settlement Ends Case of Tainted Texas Sting. *New York Times*, March 11, National Desk section, Late Edition — Final edition.
———. 2008. 1 in 100 U.S. Adults behind Bars, New Study Says. *New York Times*, February 28. www.nytimes/2008/02/28/us/28cnd-prison.html (accessed April 22, 2009).

Marable, Manning. 2002. *The Great Wells of Democracy: The Meaning of Race in American Life*. New York: Norton.

Massey, Douglas S. 1995. Getting Away with Murder: Segregation and Violent Crime in Urban America. *University of Pennsylvania Law Review* 143: 1203–1232.

Mauer, Marc, and Ryan Scott King. 2004. Schools and Prisons: Fifty Years after *Brown v. Board of Education*. The Sentencing Project. www.sentencingproject .org/pdfs/brownvboard.pdf.

New York Times. 2008. Prison Nation. March 10. http://www.nytimes .com/2008/03/10/opinion/10mon1.html (accessed April 22, 2009).

Pew Center on the States. 2008. *One in 100: Behind Bars in America 2008*. Washington, DC: Pew Charitable Trusts.

Provine, Doris Marie. 2007. *Unequal under Law: Race in the War on Drugs*. Chicago: University of Chicago Press.

Roberts, Dorothy E. 2004. The Social and Moral Cost of Mass Incarceration in African American Communities. *Stanford Law Review* 56: 1271–1305.

Ruth, Henry S., and Kevin R. Reitz. 2003. *The Challenge of Crime: Rethinking Our Response*. Cambridge: Harvard University Press.

Sampson, Robert J., and William Julius Wilson. 1995. Toward a Theory of Race, Crime, and Urban Inequality. In *Crime and Inequality*, ed. J. Hagan and R. D. Peterson, 37–54. Stanford, CA: Stanford University Press.

Sellin, Thorstein. 1928. The Negro Criminal: A Statistical Note. *Annals of the American Academy of Political and Social Science* 140: 52–64.

———. 1935. Race Prejudice in the Administration of Justice. *American Journal of Sociology* 41: 212–217.

Soss, Joe, Richard C. Fording, and Sanford F. Schram. 2008. The Color of Devolution: Race, Federalism, and the Politics of Social Control. *American Journal of Political Science* 52: 536–553.

Tonry, Michael. 1995. *Malign Neglect: Race, Crime, and Punishment.* New York: Oxford University Press.

Tyler, Tom R., and Yuen J. Huo. 2002. *Trust in the Law: Encouraging Public Cooperation with the Police and Courts.* New York: Russell Sage Foundation.

Wacquant, Loic. 2001. Deadly Symbiosis: When Ghetto and Prison Meet and Mesh. *Punishment and Society* 3:95–134.

Western, Bruce. 2006. *Punishment and Inequality in America.* New York: Russell Sage Foundation.

Whitman, James Q. 2003. *Harsh Justice: Criminal Punishment and the Widening Divide between America and Europe.* New York: Oxford University Press.

Wilson, William Julius. 1987. *The Truly Disadvantaged: The Inner City, the Underclass, and Public Policy.* Chicago: University of Chicago Press.

———. 1996. *When Work Disappears: The World of the New Urban Poor.* New York: Knopf.

Yardley, Jim. 2000. The Heat Is On a Texas Town after the Arrests of 40 Blacks. *New York Times,* October 7, National Desk section, Late Edition — Final Edition.

PART FOUR

Racing Identity

13

Who Am I?
Race, Ethnicity, and Identity

Hazel Rose Markus

•

Race and ethnicity shape history, politics, schools, neighborhoods, the media, and science. They also shape who we are—our identities. Our identities, in turn, influence how we think, feel, and act. I define identity as a social process and then describe identities as complex, dynamic, unique, individual as well as collective, projects that depend on the context. As with all identities, racial and ethnic identities are a blend of self-regard and how one perceives the regard of others. In the United States people often say "I don't see color"; they assume that race and ethnicity are irrelevant to their behavior and strive to "get beyond them." Yet if race and ethnicity are organizing dimensions of a nation, society, community, neighborhood, workplace, or classroom, they will necessarily be important for the identities of everyone who participates in these settings. This will be the case whether or not people are aware of their race or ethnicity and whether or not they claim a racial or ethnic association as an aspect of identity. Race and ethnicity influence identity and behavior in a wide range of ways, and this influence depends on the majority or minority status of the group with which one is associated, with how others see this group, and with the particulars of the context. Race and ethnicity are often a source of prejudice, discrimination, and inequality, but they are also a source of meaning, motivation, and belongingness. Finally, I provide some examples from social psychological research to illustrate the variety of ways that race and ethnicity answer the "Who am I?" question and influence behavior.

WHO AM I? AFTER YOU READ THIS FIRST PARAGRAPH — BUT BEFORE YOU read the rest of the essay—jot down some answers to this deceptively simple question. You may have been asking yourself this question since kindergarten and feel that you have a good idea of what the answers might be. Perhaps you have spent years making T-shirts and posters that display your answers to the world and now have no trouble filling in your profile information on social networking sites. Alternatively, you may find the question a relatively novel one and somewhat difficult to answer—at least without some more guidance about what kind of information is being requested. Yet, whether or not you have given much thought to this question, try to think about *what* you are thinking as you answer the question. Don't worry if your answers change as you read the chapter. This is not a test. There are no "right" answers—although some answers may make your life easier than others.

Every year, in a large introductory psychology class, I ask students to describe themselves. Stanford University has a very diverse undergraduate community; students come from throughout the United States and around the world. More than half of the students are non-white, and many Stanford students are not American. Consequently, when I do this exercise I get all sorts of answers to this question. Here is a sample of recent responses to the "Who am I?" question from some of the students who gave me permission to share them.

- *I am motivated, responsible, caring, serious, intelligent with many diverse interests, like to play Halo, tired from studying, Asian American.*
- *I am 21 years old, African American, a woman, a student, a teacher, a daughter, a sister, a granddaughter, a best friend and a girl friend. I am a poet, a dancer. I am an optimist/realist who seeks to find love. I am a child of God.*
- *I am unique, a student, a musician and a singer, a huge nut for pop-culture, a protector for my friends, a giving individual, can be brilliant when motivated, a son and brother, a person with "good toys," somewhat lazy, overly emotional, worried about exams.*
- *I am friendly, generally outgoing, talkative, a little lazy, determined, stubborn, self-righteous, a woman, agnostic Mexican American, proud of cultural roots, very sensitive, a little crazy, someone who likes to wear cute clothes.*
- *Tall, male, biracial, motivated when I need to be, but certainly not all the time, a leader when I want to be but it is fun to follow. I am nice, carefree, a huge slob, and most importantly rarely serious. I am going to apply to law school.*
- *I am a student, son, sociology major, Japanese.*

As you can see from these examples, the "Who am I?" question asks people to consider their selves, or their *identities*. Like these students, most people can quickly generate at least eight or ten characteristics with which to describe themselves, and, if given a bit more time, they can come up with another ten or so. This deceptively simple question opens a window into how people think about themselves—the stories they tell about themselves, who they would like to be, and who they are afraid of becoming. These answers, when combined with those of hundreds of other students in this class over many years, reveal some clear patterns. These patterns provide a set of interwoven insights into what identity is and why we have the ones we do. This essay is about why we answer the "Who am I?" question in the way we do and how this matters for behavior.

DEVELOPING AN IDENTITY

In 1673, René Descartes, while attempting to establish a set of true principles that could not be doubted, made a declaration that has become a mainstay of Western philosophy. He famously wrote: "I think, therefore I am." Descartes was not wrong, but his statement captures only half of the truth. It is also the case that "*you* think, therefore I am." For a long time my own field, social psychology, has been preoccupied with and fascinated by the unavoidably social process that gives rise to the self or identity. In describing what he called the "looking glass self," psychologist Charles Cooley (1922) suggested that other people are the mirror in which we see ourselves. And according to G. H. Mead (1934), without other people to respond to our actions, we would not be aware that we "are" or that we exist. Taking all this together leads to two central insights about identity: A person's identity depends on *her own view* of herself, but it also depends on *others' view* of her. In the paragraphs that follow, I elaborate these and other key features of the concept of identity. A good understanding of identity is fundamental to an accurate conception of the social categories of race and ethnicity.

Identities Are Where the Self Meets Society

If you look back at the answers of the six students above, you can see that identities are complex, multifaceted, and dependent upon people's self-descriptions. Any one person's identity is a mix of personal characteristics (outgoing, optimistic, carefree, motivated); social roles (sister, friend, teacher), activities (dancer, musician); preferences (likes to wear cute clothes); and descriptions of past and future states, particularly hopes (going to law school) and fears (worries about exams). Many people have considerable freedom to compose their identities as they like, choosing what to emphasize and what to downplay. Certainly, the way you describe yourself—as outgoing, an optimist, serious, giving, anxious, or with one of a hundred other attributes—is pretty much up to you. Even though many of the things you think about yourself come from the reflections of others, you can decide whether to think of yourself or to describe yourself in these ways. You are free to say "I like to dance," or "I am a dancer," or "moving my body to music makes me happy," or to make no mention of dancing whatsoever. Developing an identity requires selectivity and allows for considerable creativity, and to a large extent this depends on you. Clearly, then, your identity depends on how you identify yourself—that is, on how you think you are, or how you would like to be: motivated, nice, on your way to law school, and so on.

The second insight about identity is that our individual identities are, in part, given to us by *others*. A person's identity reflects her own list of who she is *but also* society's list of who she is, making it the meeting place between her and society. Many of the characteristics included in the students' responses above describe relationships and roles—I am a daughter, a brother, a student—and refer to many of the important categories that organize our communities and societies such as age, gender, race, and ethnicity. These aspects locate a person and give her a position in the world.

The realization that a person's identity necessarily involves others brings with it the realization that, with respect to her identity, she is not completely in control. Identities are only partly a matter of personal choice. The students in my examples can change their majors, their activities, and their preferences, but not all of their identity attributes are of this type. Unlike going to law school or being a dancer, most people have less freedom with respect to whether, when, and how to invoke or present identity characteristics involving our family relations or our ascribed race or ethnicity. To see what I mean, look back at the examples. Only one student gives her age. Five of the six say something that makes it evident that they are a male or a female. Five students mention either their ethnicity or race (Asian American, Mexican American, Japanese, African American, biracial), while one of the students mentions neither. In other words, some of the students mention their age, gender, race, or ethnicity and some do not—thus making it seem as though they have a choice regarding whether to identify themselves using these categories. Yet social psychological studies of identity reveal that whether people decide to emphasize age, gender, race or ethnicity in their own story of who they are, these characteristics will necessarily influence their identity and experiences in the world.

This is why identities are individual but also collective projects. A person cannot really answer the "Who am I?" question without thinking about what *other* people think of her. Her identity is not just her project alone; what her identity ends up being depends also on how other people identify her. Identities are, in fact, group projects, and as such, "you can't be a self by yourself." A person's identity depends on who she is in relation to others (a daughter, a girlfriend), as well as how others identify her (as a woman, as Mexican, as Japanese, or as African American).

Erik Erikson, one of the most important theorists of identity, described identity as what "the 'I' reflects on when contemplating the body, the personality, and the roles to which it is attached," and also as an implied constant conversation with the others with whom for better or for worse we are constantly comparing ourselves (1968, p. 217). Erikson's own life story demonstrates the power of others in determining one's identity. Erikson's parents, his Jewish mother and stepfather, had adopted him and raised him, giving him the last name of Homburger. Yet Erikson's biological father was Danish, and Erikson was tall, blond, and blue-eyed; he did not know the details of his birth until later in his life. What he did know was that during the weekend, at the Temple School where all the students were Jewish, he was teased for looking "Nordic." What he also knew was that during the week, at grammar school, where there were relatively few Jews, he was taunted for being Jewish. What identity is and how it is sensitive to the social context became a lifelong concern for Erikson.

Some of you may have had experiences that give you an insight into Erikson's identity predicament. Consider, for example, Sarah, an African American student in my class whose father identifies as black and whose mother identifies as white. In her junior year, Sarah enrolled in an overseas study program in South Africa. Arriving in Capetown, she identified herself as black just as she always had growing up in the Bay Area. The South African students, who have a very different set of historical and sociopolitical understandings of race, would have none of it. From their perspective, Sarah was obviously colored or maybe white, but certainly not black. Or consider Kenji, another student in the same class with Sarah. Growing up in Japan, Kenji never thought much about his ethnicity except on trips with his parents to Taiwan and Hong Kong. He knew at Stanford that his ethnicity would matter, yet when he arrived, he was surprised to realize that he was regarded as "Asian"—not Japanese, not East Asian, just "Asian." As Sarah and Kenji discovered, the answer to a question that seems so personal and private—"Who am I?"—was not completely up to them. Other people are always involved. Sometimes others affirm a person's identity and see her the way she would like to be seen, sometimes they ignore or deny the ways she would like to be seen, and at other times they impose on her a set of categories or labels that she dislikes, resists, or finds irrelevant. The fact that a person's identity comes in part from her relationships to others leads to a third significant feature of identity: because identities depend on the contexts from which they emerge, they are dynamic and evolving.

Identities Are Dynamic

As the examples of Sarah and Kenji show, the answers to the "Who am I?" question partly depend on the context—the "where" in the web of social relations a person is located at any particular time. There are, in other words, spatial as well as temporal dimensions to identity. As is the case with buying real estate, the three rules of understanding identity are "location, location, location." Who you are at any given moment depends on where you happen to be and who else is there in that place with you. Looking across the six self-descriptions quoted earlier, most include some mention of being a student. This is not accidental. The "Who am I?" question was posed in the classroom during exam week. Two students refer to exams and studying. Had we asked this question later in the day when the students were in the dorm or in their family homes, some different aspects of the students' identities would have surfaced.

To illustrate the effects of location on identity, consider a study my colleagues and I (Kanagawa, Cross, and Markus 2001) did in which we asked students in the United States and Japan the "Who am I?" question in one of four different locations—alone in the psychological laboratory, with a friend in the cafeteria, in their professor's office, or in a classroom with many other students. We found that their answers varied by location at the local as well as the national level. The students in the United States were most likely to describe themselves in terms of attributes (creative, athletic, friendly), while the Japanese students were most likely to describe themselves in terms of activities (working part-time, preparing for exams). This pattern reflects cultural differences between the two groups of students in the way they construct their identities, an issue to which I will return in more detail later on in this essay. For both sets of students, what they said and how much they said about themselves depended on the immediate situation. For example, when thinking about who they were while in the professor's office, the Japanese students seemed to become very aware of the high standards others might have for them and were more likely to make critical statements about themselves than were the students who described themselves while sitting alone in the laboratory.

It is important to note that the "Who am I?" question captures only the part of identity that a person is conscious of at a given moment in a given context, like a snapshot or a stop-action film clip of the whole identity. People move around from place to place, and even when they stay in one place, the context around them changes. Consequently, identities are always in flux. They are continually formed, expressed, changed, affirmed, and threatened in the course of everyday life. As a person moves from home, to the classroom, to the store, to the bank, to a university office, to the gym, or to the home of a friend, the different social worlds she is part of can all work to shuffle the various aspects of her identity.

Identities Are Unique

Finally, we come to our last insight about identity: every identity is unique. Because a person's identity is a joint project between her and the others around her, and because it changes over time and according to her environment(s), it is her personal signature. Although we all share many contexts with others (families, neighborhoods, schools, workplaces) and may develop some aspects of our identities that are similar to theirs, in the end, our identities derive from our particular experiences in the world, which are unlikely to overlap completely with those others. So, for example, when two people attend the same school, how the school context influences their separate identities will depend on many other aspects of their lives—whether they are female or male, Hispanic or white, whether they get good grades, and whether they are attending college in 1990 or 2008. Even twins who have grown up in the same family, experienced many of the same events, and formed relations with many of the same people are unlikely to have completely overlapping identities.

In sum, identities are complex, dynamic, and unique. In addition, and most notably for a volume on "doing race," they are social and depend on the context. In other words, they are both private and public property—others have a say in who a person becomes. This is the case even if the person says, for example, "I don't think of myself as black," or "I don't think of myself as white" or "I am Filipino but I don't think about it." If a social category matters in a given community, and if a person claims an association with this category, *or* if others associate her with this category, that category will have some impact on her behavior.

THE BEHAVIORAL SIGNIFICANCE OF IDENTITY

"We don't see things as they are, we see them as we are" is a claim widely attributed to Anaïs Nin, a French-Cuban writer known for her diaries and journals. This statement summarizes one powerful role of identity: how a person sees the world depends on her identity, and her identity depends on her experiences in the world. For the sake of illustration, consider two students who attend the same university. As students at the same school, they will probably have some overlapping experiences. Yet a white female student from San Francisco majoring in biology is likely to have had a somewhat different social history and to have gained a different repertoire of experiences from those of a Latino student from Atlanta who is getting a degree in electrical engineering. As a result of having different histories and experiences, they are likely to develop different understandings about and perspectives on the world. Through our particular individual experiences we all begin to develop frameworks of meaning and of value—what psychologists call schemas—to help us make sense of the world and organize our experiences. These interpretive schemas guide us; they tell us what is real, what is true, and what should matter. Moreover, because they reflect who we are and how we are positioned in the world, these schemas are deeply interwoven with our identities. Since different identities indicate different locations in the various social networks and contexts of our lives, they will be associated with different perspectives and understandings. This is why paying attention to people's identities is an important part of understanding the social world.

In addition to telling us what to pay attention to and what to *see*, our identities also tell us how to think, feel, and act—what to do and what not to do (Markus and Sentis 1982; Oyserman and Markus 1993). They help us determine what is good, what is bad, what should count, and what should not. Identities, then, are both frames of reference and sets of blueprints for action. Given this foundational role of identity, any situation or event that is relevant to an aspect of identity can have a powerful impact on your actions.

An easy way to see identities at work in organizing the world is to ask a number of people for directions to the same location and then track the reference points. The foodie/gourmet will tell you to go a block until the Left Bank restaurant, then go halfway down that street until you see Whole Foods Market, and slow down right before the driveway to Peet's Coffee store. The contractor will tell you to go a block and a half until Home Depot, turn right just past the big construction site, and look for the driveway by the office building with all the new solar panels. For the foodie/gourmet, food plays an important role for her identity, as construction does for the contractor. These important aspects of identity then become the point of orientation for the individual's behavior. In other words, "we see things as we are."

Figure 13.1 illustrates some elements of the dynamic and relational process through which our social experiences in the world have an influence on identity and behavior. Race and ethnicity, because they are the focus of this essay, are shown in bold. However, depending on the context and the details of our particular lives, many other social categories are also likely to be important in shaping our experiences. Moreover, the influences of these different social categories will intersect, depending on the particular social situation and which aspects of identity are salient. As the earlier student self-descriptions suggest, we see ourselves in terms of categories that blend race, gender, and age—"21-year-old African American woman." Specifically, however, in

FIGURE 13.1 | **THE SOCIETY-IDENTITY-BEHAVIOR-SOCIETY CYCLE.**

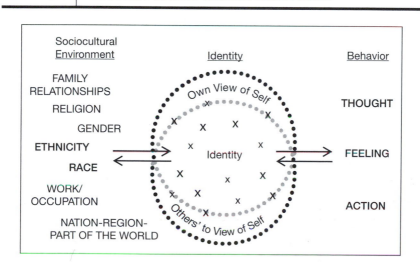

those spaces where race and ethnicity are salient, the social categories of race and ethnicity will influence identity. In Figure 13.1, identity is indicated as the meeting place described earlier—that is, as a combination of a our *own* view of *ourselves* with *others' views* of us. Sometimes, in some situations, these views converge; at other times or in other situations, they diverge. The Xs in the figure refer to those schemas about the self that derive from previous social experience and that provide the interpretive frameworks, the anchors, and the benchmarks for behavior. The role that race and ethnicity will play in identity depends on the details of our social experience both currently and as we were growing up. For some of us, the schemas related to race or ethnicity will be highly elaborated and chronically accessible for making sense of the world (indicated by the bold Xs); for others these schemas may be less dense and may become available only when something in a social situation makes them relevant. In general, however, our actions will reflect these schemas and will, in turn, reinforce them.

Nin's observation that "we see things as we are" suggests that identities can provide powerful clues for predicting behavior—our own and others. If we know something about a person's life experiences, we can make a reasonable guess about some features of her identity. From there, we can hypothesize about what her interpretive schemas are likely to be—that is, what she is likely to pay attention to, what she might care about, what might please her, what might make her sad, what might prepare her to fight, or even to die. Events that are consistent with a person's preferred identities (past, present, or future) or that affirm her in some way—put her in a good light, make her feel competent or proud—are likely to have consequences that she will regard as desirable. Events that are inconsistent with or that threaten a person's identity—make her feel anxious, incapable, humiliated, or ashamed—are likely to have undesirable consequences (see in this volume Steele, Chapter 14; Fryberg and Watts, Chapter 17). If the rule of thumb for understanding political events is to "follow the money," surely the rule for understanding behavior is to "follow the identity."

RACE AND ETHNICITY AS A SOURCE OF IDENTITY

Whenever someone participates in a group or community or society, the factors that are important in how the nation, states, cities, neighborhoods, families, and schools are organized will have some influence on who she is, whether she notices them, and whether she thinks a particular factor is important to her. If a category—whether it is race, gender, ethnicity, or religion—is associated with the distribution of power, resources, status, respect, knowledge, or other cultural capital in a particular context, that category will matter for identity. For example, in the United States, everyday life is powerfully shaped by the categories of race and ethnicity. A person's race and ethnicity influences where she is likely to live and who her friends are likely to be. They also predict her health and wealth as well as the quality of schools, neighborhoods, workplaces, medical care, and other life outcomes she is likely to have access to (Krysan and Lewis 2005; Massey and Denton 1992). Of course, there are many other factors that matter for these outcomes as well, but the extent to which race and ethnicity are important to a person's life chances often remains unseen or even deliberately ignored. After all, as Americans, we want to believe in the hope expressed by the American Dream—that all that matters for success is the willingness to work hard, and that who you are or where you have come from should not matter. Certainly, as the election of Barack Obama powerfully reveals, the American Dream can sometimes be realized. His election proves that an association with a non-mainstream racial and ethnic category does not, by itself, preclude inclusion and full success in our society.

Yet, in American society, the race or ethnicity you are associated with does still matter. It will continue to matter until the realities of American life—the policies, institutions, representations, and everyday social practices—reflect broadly the ideals of the American Dream. At present, race and ethnicity still afford some people a wide set of advantages and privileges that are systematically denied to others. However, not everyone is equally aware that this is the case; those in the minority ethnic or racial group are much more likely to understand this connection than those in the majority. Studies over several decades have documented the tendency of people in the majority not to be aware of their own race or ethnicity and so not to mention it as an answer to the "Who am I?" question (Tatum 2002; Oyserman 2008). This is the key to why some white people are perplexed about why people of color refer to or focus on their race or ethnicity. From the majority and/or dominant location, race and ethnicity are unremarkable and irrelevant. Like water to the fish, the racial or ethnic aspects of identity are invisible. In a now-classic piece on white privilege, Peggy McIntosh (1997) suggests that one of the hidden privileges of being white in the United States is that a white person can choose to ignore her racial identity and to imagine that she can be "beyond race." She can claim not to see race and to regard herself only as a human being.

Defining Race and Ethnicity

One significant misconception about race and ethnicity is that they are products of the body or the blood—inherent qualities that are present and unchangeable inside a person from birth. Yet race and ethnicity are anything but natural. Rather than permanent, immutable characteristics of a person, specific races and ethnicities are organizational categories that have been created by humans over time as a way of orienting themselves in the world. As Paula Moya and I define the concepts in the introduction to this book, race and ethnicity are dynamic sets of ideas (e.g., meanings, values, goals, images, associations) and practices (e.g., meaningful actions, both formal and routine) that people use to distinguish groups of people from other groups and to organize their own communities. Throughout history, differences in the physical characteristics of people such as skin color, eye color, and hair texture have become associated—deliberately as well as inadvertently—with different meaningful behavioral outcomes, both positive and negative. Specific racial and ethnic categories (i.e., Asian, Black, Latina/o) are, in this way, human-made, as are the identities based on them.

The circumstance of dividing up the world according to visible physical and behavioral characteristics, while understandable, is not inevitable. It is not necessary for people to be divided by skin color, or according to the continent on which some of their ancestors might have lived several generations ago. The world could be arranged so that the physical characteristics now used to assign race and ethnicity do not matter for life outcomes. Of course, some people will argue that humans will always make some type of distinction to note who is "our kind" and who is not. Importantly, however, the basis of these distinctions can vary and, in fact, have varied throughout history. For example, in ancient Greece, distinctions were not made on skin color—this came with modernity and science—but in terms of language and belief. Most likely language and belief had as much of an impact on a person's identity and his life chances in ancient Greece as race and ethnicity do now in the United States of America.

Up to this point, I have been using the terms *race* and *ethnicity* simultaneously in a way that might give the impression that these two concepts are interchangeable. While they do overlap in meaning, and though they are similar in the way they are formed by others and have been reinforced throughout history to the present day, there is a very important difference between the two that must be addressed.

First, the term *race* specifically indexes a history in which group characteristics have been used to establish a hierarchy and to accord one group a higher status and the other group a lower status (Fredrickson, 2002). Therefore, categorizing people as a racial group draws attention to the difference in the power relationships among this group and other groups. Race is important for identity because if a person is associated with a racial group, her race is likely to have affected the way she has been viewed and treated by others. Many of the ideas and practices associated with particular races have been constructed and imposed on the group by those not associated with the group and are unlikely to be claimed by those associated with the group. When people do claim association with a particular racial group, they are often acknowledging, as a part of their identities, the history of unequal relations between their group and a dominant group. Categorizing people as an *ethnicity*, on the other hand, focuses attention on differences in meanings, values, and ways of living (social practices) that are often regarded as equally viable and need not establish a status ranking among the groups. People in groups called ethnicities are often relatively willing to claim or elaborate these differences between the groups they are associated with and other groups.

When a person identifies with an ethnic group, her focus is usually on how people in the in-group—those who identify with her group—think about their group. By contrast, when a person thinks about her group as a racial group, her focus is likely to be on how people in the out-group—those who do not identify with her group—think about her group. She is, moreover, likely to be highly aware of the nature of the power relations between her group and other groups.

Using the definitions of race and ethnicity presented above, most groups can be classified as ethnic, racial, or both. In practice in the United States, African Americans typically think of themselves as a racial group, Asian Americans more commonly identify themselves as an ethnic group, and Latino/as sometimes classify themselves as one or the other or both. Yet groups typically conceptualized as races can also be analyzed as ethnic groups, and ethnic groups can be analyzed as racial groups, a process that will certainly have consequences for identity. The case of Muslims with Middle Eastern heritage living in the United States is a good example.

Before the attack on the World Trade Center and the Pentagon on September 11, 2001, in most instances, Muslims with Middle Eastern heritage were considered ethnic groups, and members of that group identified themselves as Muslim and Middle Eastern, because that was the way they saw themselves. New meanings and representations are now associated with being Muslim and Middle Eastern, and those identified with this group must now deal with these imposed representations as they negotiate their identities. To the extent that being Muslim is being broadly devalued and Muslims are facing increasing prejudice and discrimination, we can say that this ethnic group is being racialized.

When and How Race and Ethnicity Matter

I have suggested here that if race and ethnicity are important in society, they will always have an impact on identity, and if they have an impact on identity, they will influence some aspect of behavior. Currently, in American society, one finds a great deal of anxiety around racial and ethnic identities. Many imagine that these social distinctions can be only the basis of division and conflict, and that our individual and societal goal should be to get beyond these group boundaries. Yet while racial and ethnic identities can certainly be the basis of prejudice, discrimination, and inequality (as many essays in this volume reveal), they can also—and sometimes simultaneously—be the source of pride, meaning, motivation, and belongingness.

   Specifying the type of influence race and ethnicity will have for identity and action and whether it will be personally or collectively beneficial or detrimental for behavior is currently the focus of a great deal of exciting research and scholarship in the social sciences and humanities (see Alcoff 2006; Alcoff, Hames-García, Mohanty, and Moya 2006; Alcoff and Mendieta 2003; Fiske, Kitayama, Markus, and Nisbett 1998; Heine 2008; Moya 2002; Moya and Hames-García 2000; Prentice and Miller 1999; Steele, Spencer, and Aronson 2002). The evidence is now compelling. Race and ethnicity influence identity (1) whether or not people are aware of their race or ethnicity, and (2) whether or not they claim a racial or ethnic association (develop an elaborated self-schema) as an aspect of identity. When and how racial and ethnic associations and categorizations influence identity and behavior depends on a wide array of personal and social factors, including how others in a given context (e.g., nation, neighborhood, workplace, classroom) regard the ethnic or racial group with which a person is associated, and whether others regard that person as belonging to the group.

This research reveals that racial and ethnic associations can pattern behavior in ways that are surprising and not always immediately apparent. Very significantly, however, to say that race or ethnicity "influence" or "constitute" identity is not to say they *determine* identity. Race and ethnicity are among many influences that can shape identity. People are indeed intentional agents who, as I have noted, can be highly selective in what aspects of their experience they attend to and elaborate. Once a person becomes aware of her race and ethnicity and its potential role in shaping behavior, she can (1) *claim* this influence and emphasize its role in identity or (2) actively *resist* any influence of race and ethnicity. That said, given a society organized according to race and ethnicity, it would be impossible for her to escape *all* influence. Even if she actively tries to separate herself from these categories, the very fact of separating herself from them will affect her behavior and remind her that she has to contend with their effects.

Psychological Research on Race and Ethnicity

Because race and ethnicity are only an aspect of a person's overall identity, a person typically cannot parse her experience into its racial or ethnic components. Consequently, the question of how race and ethnicity influence identity and behavior requires a variety of approaches and some considerable research ingenuity. The "Who am I?" question that gave rise to the descriptions of identity at the beginning of the chapter is a quick and relatively easy way for a researcher to elicit some aspects of identity, but, of course, it advantages the preferred aspects of one's identities and those aspects of identity that are active at the moment. The "Who am I?" question does not tap those parts of our identities that we are not aware of or that are not under our personal control, and it does not reveal the ways in which our identities influence our behavior. For this reason, social psychologists employ a variety of other measures, including surveys and the observation of behavior in carefully controlled laboratory situations. In the next section, I describe a series of experiments done by researchers in social psychology that together illustrate three broad and surprising ways in which race and ethnicity shape behavior. These examples demonstrate how race and ethnicity can (1) provide frameworks of meaning, (2) provide motivation for behavior, and (3) be a source of belongingness.

HOW RACE AND ETHNICITY SHAPE
IDENTITY: A SAMPLER

Race and Ethnicity as Frameworks of Meaning

People do not make their lives from scratch. In the United States, for example, we receive many messages, sometimes explicit, sometimes tacit, about what Americans believe is valuable, moral, real, and true. These messages tell us who is good and who is bad, what is the right way to behave and what is not, what it means to be a mother, a father, a child, or even just a person. Typically, these answers are not verbalized or written out, and most often we are completely unaware that these questions have been asked and answered for us. Instead, we just go about our lives, unaware that we are living according to a particular set of norms and behaving in ways that seem to us to be the "natural" or "normal" or "human" way. These "natural," "normal," or "human" ways of interacting and being in the world are oftentimes shaped by race and ethnicity. It is in this way that race and ethnicity are powerful sources of designs for living and of schemas for making sense of the world.

The ethnic patterning of our thoughts, feelings, and actions typically comes into high relief only when we change contexts or meet someone who has been steeped in the idea and practices of another ethnic context and discover that the normal or obvious thing to think or feel or say now seems peculiar or inappropriate. To illustrate this point I start by describing some patterns of behavior in the United States.

In the United States it is important to be an *independent* person—an autonomous individual who knows what she thinks and believes and is in control of her actions (Fiske et al. 1998; Triandis 1991). This is not just a set of values; it is also a to-do list that organizes the flow of everyday life in many American contexts. To encourage independence and the development of personal preferences, goals, and perspectives, American lives are arranged to foster this independence. If they can afford it, American parents give infants their own bedrooms. Children choose their own breakfasts and their school activities from a wide array of options. Regardless of the circumstances, Americans explain their own actions and those of others as expressions of individual preferences and choices. The importance of independence, of standing up for convictions, and of going your own way and doing your own thing is manifest in practices of language, caretaking, schooling, work, and the media. Americans did not just dream up this model; it is written into the Declaration of Independence (the founding document of our country) and is the result of thousands of years of Western philosophical and religious thinking. Under this view, "goodness" or morality involves maintaining independence and protecting the "natural rights" of each individual. These ideas and practices are representative of one way of being that is typical of people in America, particularly European Americans. For example, if your ethnicity is European American, then this way of understanding yourself as an independent individual is probably thoroughly embedded in your identity—not just in *what* you say about yourself (e.g., independent, go-getter, stand up for what you believe in) but also in the *way* you talk about yourself.

Consider this: the American students who described themselves in the opening examples might be surprised to find that their answers to the "Who am I?" question reveal a style of describing themselves that is very common among people who have lived in middle-class North American contexts where the independent model of self is common. It is, moreover, quite different from the style of people who have inhabited other contexts where different models of how to be a self are common. Specifically, the American self-descriptions contain many extremely positive trait adjectives—caring, intelligent, brilliant, friendly, outgoing, motivated, and only a few negative descriptors. This style of description suggests an awareness of the self as a separate entity made up of various specific attributes. These students seem confident and certain in their descriptions; they do not qualify their statements.

The independent model of the self is so thoroughly inscribed in American society (particularly in mainstream or middle-class European American contexts) that often we do not realize that other models of the self exist and that our behavior has been shaped according to one particular model of how to be a self. For example, in many ethnic contexts outside North America and Northern Europe (as well as some within these contexts), being a good or appropriate person requires being, not an independent person, but an *interdependent* person. When a model of the self as interdependent organizes social life, people understand and experience themselves less as separate autonomous individuals and more as interconnected parts of a larger social whole. From this perspective, actions necessarily involve an explicit awareness of others and adjusting behavior to that of others. Rather than separation from others, it is fitting in, being part of, and contributing to one's family or one's work or other social group that explains behavior. The identities that result from participation in worlds structured according to these ideas and practices will resonate with and reflect these ideas.

Take, for example, the student who identifies as Japanese but does not include a list of adjectives, as do all the other students who are American. Consider also the following two descriptions given by Japanese students at Kyoto University. These descriptions are from a study that made a careful comparison of patterns of self-description of students from one ethnic group, European Americans, with students from another ethnic group, Japanese (Markus and Kitayama 1998).

- *I do what I want to do as much as possible, but I never do something which would bother other people. Although sometimes I make a decision all by myself, if it is related to a group or it involves a very important decision, I always talk to somebody in order to make a final decision.*
- *I am rather gentle and respect harmony with people. I express my own interests to a certain degree, but I avoid conflicts almost all the time. I behave in order for people to feel peaceful.*

Both of these Japanese students start by describing themselves, but within the first sentence they mention other people—specifically, adjusting to, harmonizing with, and not bothering other people. An analysis of hundreds of Japanese descriptions reveals that an awareness of interdependence, a sense of the self as in a network with others and in relationship with others, is a common characteristic (Cousins 1989; Kanagawa et al. 2001). Further, these students, like many Japanese students, describe themselves with actions rather than with trait adjectives. Moreover, although both students describe themselves positively, they emphasize being cooperative, gentle, and peaceful rather than as happy, motivated, or brilliant.

This sense of the self as an interdependent part of the family is common among East Asian ethnic groups, like the Chinese and other many East Asian–origin immigrants who have settled throughout the United States. This interdependence has its roots in a Confucian tradition, which includes cultivating the social order, knowing one's own place in the social order, meeting the expectations of others, and being sensitive to the demands of the social situation (Hwang 1999; Tsai 2005). Just as the United States began with ideas and practices promoting independence that were present and central to the very conception of the United States, so too are the ideas and practices promoting East Asian ethnicities present from its earliest history. This fact demonstrates the power of the context in forming identity. While we can choose how to construct ourselves in many respects, we are nonetheless powerfully influenced by shared understandings about the "right" way to be a self.

These differences in ways of understanding the self—as independent or as interdependent—have many implications for identity and behavior. For example, when researchers asked Chinese American and European Americans mothers in Los Angeles what was important for raising children (Chao 1993), they gave somewhat different answers. European American mothers stressed nurturing and building the child's self-esteem and individuality, dealing with emotions, developing confidence and independence, and creating an environment that the child would experience as fun or enjoyable. The Chinese American mothers, by contrast, stressed the cultivation of a good relationship with the child, education, respect for and getting along with others, self-reliance and the maintenance of Chinese culture. These mothers had been brought up in an environment that encouraged and valued interdependent ways of interacting with others, and their own child-rearing practices reflected that. Just as the foodie/gourmet in the earlier example used messages related to food to guide her behavior, Chinese American mothers will use their schemas of interdependence to guide the way they raise their children. Both sets of mothers build on their own ethnic-specific understandings of the right way to be to. Chinese American mothers are more likely to create and promote opportunities for their children that will foster within them an appreciation for interdependence and working with others, while European American mothers will do the same for their children with an emphasis on promoting independence.

This process does not just occur at home; it also takes place in the world outside the home. For example, beginning at the preschool level, European American teachers arrange their classrooms and their lessons to allow students to have a great deal of choice in their activities. Through their choices, students can manifest their individuality, express themselves, and become active agents in control of their own behavior. When interdependence is given greater weight, as in East Asian homes and schools, the focus is on activities that teach children their proper roles and on how to adjust to and cooperate with each other. In Japanese classrooms, children are encouraged to work in groups of five or six to create a group poster or storyboard. They are given only a few sets of scissors and crayons so that they have to share and coordinate their efforts (Tobin, Wu, and Davidson 1989). The emphasis is on how to fit in with others and on appreciating and understanding group life. The patterns of independence and interdependence characteristic of these different ethnicities are institutionalized in the lives that the children lead, and most often parents, children, and others are not aware that things could be otherwise. This speaks to the power of ethnicity as a set of ideas and practices that can shape identity, thoughts, feelings, and actions in multiple ways, many of them unseen.

Sociocultural psychologists are now examining models of the self in many ethnic contexts in the United States and around the world, revealing a variety of models for identity and how these differences shape thoughts, feelings, and actions. For example, they find that interdependence and the importance of relations is more central to behavior in many other ethnic contexts than it is in European American ones. In Mexican contexts, for example, knowing one's place in the social hierarchy is often emphasized; respect, deference, and obedience to elders are expected (Valdez 1996). Among peers, cooperation, solidarity, and similarity are more likely to be emphasized than difference or uniqueness. The family and not the individual is a foundational reality such that loyalty to and helping the family and extended family is often expected and required.

The European American notion that growing up means becoming independent and separating from expectations and constraints of family can be a peculiar idea for many Mexican and Mexican American students. Whenever I ask for a show of hands of those students who call home frequently, students with Latino backgrounds are decidedly more likely to raise their hands than are the European Americans students for whom independence and some separation from family is a desirable sign of maturity. A study comparing Mexican college students with European American college students asked students before solving a set of anagrams either to think of a good time they had had with their *family* or a time they felt good about *themselves* and then to write a paragraph about it. The European American students solved the most anagrams after they wrote about feeling good about themselves—in fact, most students wrote about a successful achievement. In contrast, the Mexican students solved the most anagrams after recalling a good time with their families (Savani, Alvarez, and Markus 2008). Affirming their identity as independent motivated the Americans, while affirming their identity as an interdependent family member motivated the Mexicans.

People who identify as Mexican American often take on aspects of both ways of being—the independence emphasized in European American contexts and the interdependence emphasized in Mexican contexts. For Mexican Americans, one recent study showed they were just as likely as European American students to describe themselves as independent, but they were decidedly more likely to also describe themselves as interdependent and connected to family. They were also more likely than European Americans to report that it would be difficult to be happy if someone in their family were sad (Mesquita, Savani, Albert, Fernandez de Ortega, and Karasawa 2006). For Mexicans and Mexican Americans, the emphasis on family and respect, as well as being independent, forms the foundation for their identities.

Interdependence in conjunction with independence seems to be a defining element of many African American ethnic identities as well. Although there are still very few comparative studies that examine the specific behavioral consequences of these identities, a growing literature reveals a moral imperative to help others (Burlew, Banks, McAdoo, and Azibo 1992; Hudley, Haight, and Miller 2003) and an emphasis on unity and equalitarianism, but also a strong focus on independence and self-expression (Jones 1999; Nobles 1991; Oyserman, Gant, and Ager 1995), For example, among the six self-descriptions at the beginning of the essay, the student who identified herself as African American was in fact the most explicitly interdependent in her self-description, characterizing herself in terms of her relationships as a "student, a teacher, a daughter, a sister, a granddaughter, a best friend and a girl friend." Notably, however, another student who identified as biracial did not use any relational or role terms in answer to the "Who am I?" question. Considering these two examples together underscores that ethnicity is a dynamic set of ideas and practices. How people engage with them and respond to them depends on how much exposure they have had to them, what other ideas and practices they have been exposed to, and very importantly, on other important social distinctions such as gender and social class.

These examples illustrate the ways in which race and ethnicity create frameworks for identity. A person's racial and ethnic contexts are the sources for something that is typically invisible to her; they do not provide the exact answer to the "Who am I?" question, but they specify for her what it means to be a person, and set up some general tasks that will guide her actions. Additionally, a person's ethnic and racial contexts can be the source of models of emotion, (i.e., how, when, and what to feel), and models of morality (i.e., what is good, what is bad, what is fair, what is just, what is well-being, satisfaction, or the good life, etc.). Research that reveals these various models and their behavioral consequences is important because it reveals that *everyone is ethnic*. Thus, everyone's way is a *particular* way, and no one person is truly just "standard issue." Thinking, feeling, and acting are not neutral acts, nor are they simply products of the brain and body. Instead, our actions have a deep structure that derives from who we are and how we are located in the world, and one important feature of how we are located is our race or ethnicity.

Race and Ethnicity as Motivators for Behavior

The studies discussed in the previous section explored the consequences of ethnicity by grouping people based on their ethnic background and examining differences in thought and formation of identity. Other social psychological studies have examined how ethnicity and race shape behavior by asking people directly about the racial and ethnic aspects of their identities or by observing actual behavior when race and ethnicity are made salient.

As discussed in the previous section, European American ethnicity is defined by ideas and practices that promote identities that value independence and separation from others, while East Asian ethnicity fosters identities that value interdependence and being in connection with others. To examine how identities form around independence or how interdependence influences behavior, one team of researchers examined the ways these two ethnic groups differed in their motivation as a function of their identity. They did this by giving eight-year-old Asian Americans and European Americans a choice of which category of five-letter anagram puzzles they wanted to solve (Iyengar and Lepper 1999). The goal was to unscramble the letters and make a word; then the researchers counted how many puzzles the children solved correctly. The puzzles were equally difficult in all categories and differed only in their labels. The performance of the eight-year-olds who chose for *themselves* which puzzle to solve was compared to the performance of a group of eight-years-olds who believed their *mothers* chose which category of puzzle they were to solve. As American educators would predict, the European American eight-year-olds solved the most puzzles correctly when they chose the puzzle category *themselves*. In contrast, the Asian American children solved the most anagrams correctly when they solved the anagrams their *mothers chose for them*.

For European American students—who are socialized with the ideas of individuality and independence—it is an imposition to have another person, particularly one's mother, pick the type of puzzle to solve. Even at the tender age of eight, these students experience their mother's choice as an act that threatens their individuality and freedom. They identify with being able to make their own choices; they want to be under no one else's power but their own. When the students in the study worked under this threat to their independence, they performed less well, solving few word puzzles. In contrast, the Asian American students are likely to have identities that value the ideas of fulfilling parental expectations and honoring their families. They are likely to have understood this same activity—their mother's choice of the puzzle—not as an imposition on their freedom but instead as an attempt to guide them or support them. What was important was to perform well. This study is a powerful example of how the ideas and practices associated with one's ethnicity can shape meaning, motivation, and behavior, even when there is no mention of race and ethnicity.

Yet, not everyone who is associated with a racial or ethnic group is going to be influenced by the ideas and practices of the group in the same way. In fact, maybe it is an important part of your identity to *not* be a part of your racial or ethnic group. This, too, will have consequences for behavior. For example, Oyserman and her colleagues (Oyserman, Kemmelmeier, Fryberg, Brosh, and Hart-Johnson 2003) wondered whether the way students think about their own racial or ethnic group would make a difference for their motivation and performance. To study this question they surveyed an integrated middle school where students were African American, Hispanic, or American Indian and asked the following question: "What does it mean to you to be a member of your race or ethnic group?" They found three types of answers to this question. Some students answered with what the researchers called in-group responses, or responses indicating the students embraced being a part of their race or ethnic group as part of their identity. For example, one student responded, "It means the world to me, I'm glad of my ethnicity. I wouldn't want to be anything else." Another student said it means "eating the foods, talking to my friends, and color of my complexion in the mirror." These two students clearly identified with their racial or ethnic group. They had a *racial* or *ethnic self-schema.*

Other students in the middle school ignored or resisted their racial or ethnic label; they attempted to reject, as significant for their identity, being a part of their racial or ethnic group. One said, "Really my race does not matter to me." One responded, "Nothing," and another said, "It means nothing to me. I think it does not matter how you feel about your ethnic group." These students were *aschematic* (or *without a schema*) for their race or ethnicity. A third group of students showed a concern for their in-group *and also* a concern for their connection to the larger or mainstream society. In other words, these students had a *dual schema*— they claimed for themselves their racial or ethnic identity *as well as* their membership or engagement with larger or majority society. For example, in response to what it means to be a member of your race or ethnicity, one student said, "Every time that I step out of my house I feel as though someone is waiting for me to screw up. So I feel that as a black male I have a responsibility to set a good example for me in the world and for the people of my race." Another said, "Being a member of this race helps me strive to be a successful person in the world [where] we African Americans are minorities but also members." A third student answered, "I am good at most things most people are good at and proud of what African Americans did for the world." When these three groups were compared for their end of quarter grades, the students who received highest last quarter grades were those who had a dual schema—an identity that included an awareness of their in-group and also an awareness of the role of their in-group in the larger mainstream society.

In a second study, the three groups of students—those with a racial self-schema, those without a racial schema, and those with a dual schema—were given a novel mathematical task and asked to solve the problem in as many ways as possible. Specifically they were asked to use the numbers 2, 3, or 7 to obtain the number 36 by adding, subtracting, multiplying, and using the number as many times as they wanted. Again in this study, those students who ignored their racial or ethnic identity or who claimed it did not matter to them performed less well, whereas those students with a dual schema had the most motivation and persisted the longest on the task, both in the laboratory and at school. In other words, an identity defined in terms of both the in-group and the mainstream group was linked to better performance, and this dual schema seems to have served as a buffer against the negative representations that are prevalent in the world. When an event in the environment makes one's race or ethnicity salient, identifying with both the in-group and the mainstream can be helpful. Because you see the world as you are, you are likely to think about positive representations of yourself as an in-group member *and* positive representations of yourself as a member of the larger society. When these positive representations come to mind, they can both be used to confront and contest the prevalent negative stereotypes.

Other researchers have examined the behavioral consequences of race and ethnicity not by observing the behavior of those associated with the group or by asking them about what their group means to them but by making the views *other* people hold about their group more salient. In a series of studies, Steele and his colleagues (Steele 1997; Steele et al. 2002; see Steele, Chapter 14 of this volume, for a full discussion) made the views that *other* people hold about one's group more or less relevant and examined how these views can threaten identity and have a detrimental effect on academic performance. In particular, they showed that those in the minority in society, like African Americans in the United States, can experience a threat to their identity because of the fear of being seen in a negative light from their racial group association. If there is some cue in a situation—as in a classroom—that students might be judged in terms of this pervasive stereotype or if there is a worry that they could do something that inadvertently confirms it, their academic performance can suffer.

To explore this idea, researchers set up an experiment in which a group of black college students and a group of white college students were matched for their ability level so that even before the study began the experimenters knew that these students' ability level was the same. Then the experimenters mentioned to half the students before taking the test (a difficult section of the GRE) that the test was a measure of verbal ability. This instruction made the common stereotype that black students do not perform well academically directly relevant to the student's performance on the test. For the other half of the students, nothing was said about the test being diagnostic of ability and instead they were told that the experimenters were trying to determine how problems are solved.

While there was no difference between black and white students in the "nondiagnostic" or problem-solving condition, when the black students thought that the test was diagnostic of their ability, they performed significantly less well than whites. Most important, these students did not need to *believe* the pervasive stereotype about their group and low ability or performance. When the identity threat was present, *simply being aware* of the stereotype was enough to depress these students' performance. When, on the other hand, the threat was lifted from the situation—that is, when they were told that the test was not diagnostic and so they did not have to worry about how their performance would reflect on their group—their performance improved. These studies suggest that a person does not have to personally identify with her racial group to be affected by the group. Simple knowing how others see the racial group she could be associated with is enough to have an effect on a person's performance.

Race and Ethnicity as a Source of Belongingness

Finally, our identities locate us in social spaces and tell us where we belong. Often people are unaware of this very important consequence of their race or ethnicity in defining who they are until something or someone questions their belongingness. Cheryan and Monin (2005) examined what happens when a person is not recognized as a member of an important group that they claim as self-defining, that is, when their belongingness is denied, again highlighting the importance of others in defining identity. Even when you claim race or ethnicity as part of your identity, other people can contest this claim. The focus of this study is the predicament of Asian Americans who report that others often ask them "Where are you *really* from" as if they are not fully American or do not belong in America to the same extent as other Americans.

In this study white Americans and Asian Americans were approached on campus and asked, "Do you speak English?" These students were compared with those in a control condition who were not asked this question. The researchers predicted that while this question would not bother white Americans, it would be subtly but powerfully threatening for Asian Americans because it would bring to mind a discrepancy between their own view of themselves as Americans and others' view of them as foreigners. The researchers also predicted that they would want to assert their American identity in some way, to show that they belonged to this country. Following the question, the participants were given a questionnaire that asked them to list as many American TV shows from the 1980s as they could remember. These students had grown up in the '80s and so knowledge of these shows would indicate a familiarity with American popular culture. In the control condition in which no question was asked, white Americans spent more time recalling shows than Asian Americans. Yet in the "Do you speak English" condition, it was the Asian Americans who spent more time remembering shows from the 1980s. So for the Asian Americans who claimed being American as part of their identity, this threat to their belongingness set up by the question about their language served as a motivation to expend more effort to recall the shows and prove and validate their identity as Americans.

This study is a striking reminder that people are very sensitive to whether they belong in a situation and will often seek out ways to show that they do belong. Cohen and his colleagues (Cohen, Garcia, Apfel, and Master 2006) reasoned that if the group with which you are associated is in the minority and regarded negatively by many in your community or society—an experience that is common for many who are Latino American or African American in the United States—you are very likely to feel unwelcome and as if you don't belong unless someone does something to explicitly suggest that you do. They reasoned that many racial or ethnic minority students may lack feelings of belongingness in society in general, particularly in schools, and so have more difficulty identifying as a student or as a learner. To test this idea they carried out a series of studies in which black and white middle school students were randomly assigned to an intervention group or a control group. Students in the intervention group were asked at the beginning of the school year to identify what mattered to them most—family, art, religion, athletics, and so on—and then to write a paragraph explaining why. The invitation to write about themselves was a simple indication that someone in the school was interested in them. Those in the control group were asked to select something that didn't matter to them and explain in a paragraph why it might matter to someone else. At the end of each semester Cohen and colleagues collected the students' grades.

The results point to the importance of identity. In each year of the two years of the experiment, the black students who wrote about what was important to them scored better (about one-third of a letter grade) than those in the control group. No such effect was observed for the majority white students who presumably felt relatively more at home at school and as if they belonged from the very beginning of the year. This very simple, one-time writing task seems to have had a positive effect on the performance of those students who might question whether they are welcome in the school. Writing gave them an opportunity in the school setting to present who they were and to foster a sense of identity with the school.

CONCLUSION

This brief survey of some recent empirical studies in psychology reveals that race and ethnicity can influence behavior in a wide variety of ways.

The studies sketched here are among hundreds that further reveal the powerful and diverse behavioral effects of racial and ethnic identities. They show that we can be aware of the influence of race and ethnicity on our behavior or that these effects can be completely outside our awareness. Sometimes these influences can be intentional as in the direct teaching of ethnic or racially specific ways of being, and sometimes their influence is indirect and unintentional and comes about as people absorb normative patterns of association (e.g., black = crime; American = white). The effects of race and ethnicity can be detrimental to individual behavior, impairing motivation, performance, or engagement; but they can also be beneficial, providing meaning and enhancing motivation, performance, and belongingness. The effects of race and ethnicity on identity and behavior are highly variable; they depend on the particular social context and the cues these contexts contain about the meaning of race and ethnicity. Moreover, many of the effects depend on other people—sometimes the actions of specific others and sometimes others in general. What is clear, however, is that race and ethnicity matter for identity and for answering the "Who am I?" question.

Although it is a popular and comforting idea that we might ignore or go beyond race and ethnicity and be color-blind or post-race, the psychological study of the consequences of race and ethnicity reveals that given the current patterning of the world, this is probably an impossibility. If race and ethnicity matter for the ways that communities, societies, and nations are organized and how life is lived in these spaces, they will necessarily matter for identities because identities are the meeting place of individuals and societies. Race and ethnicity then become sources of identity—sources of our selves and of who we are. And as we have shown here, we see (and react to) the world not as it is, but as we are. This is not a weakness or a moral failing or an expression of racism or ethnocentrism. In every context, significant social distinctions shape identity, which, in turn, shapes behavior and society. The operation of this cycle is a social psychological fact. While it is not possible to live outside the society-identity-behavior-society cycle, the cycle itself is a result of human activity over time. Ultimately the consequences of the cycle will depend on how people individually and collectively make sense of race and ethnicity and on whether and how they build it into their worlds. As I noted at the beginning of the essay, there are no right answers to the "Who am I?" question. The answers can and do change frequently, yet for better and for worse, the answers will always shape behavior, reflecting one's own—but also others'—thoughts, feelings and actions.

Works Cited

•

Alcoff, Linda Martín. 2006. *Visible Identities: Race, Gender, and the Self*. New York: Oxford University Press.

Alcoff, Linda Martín, Michael R. Hames-García, Satya P. Mohanty, and Paula M. L. Moya, eds. 2006. *Identity Politics Reconsidered*. New York: Palgrave Macmillan.

Alcoff, Linda Martín, and Eduardo Mendieta, eds. 2003. *Identities: Race, Class, Gender, and Nationality*. Malden, MA: Blackwell.

Burlew, Ann Kathleen, W. Curtis Banks, Hariette Pipes McAdoo, and Daudi Ajani Ya Azibo, eds. 1992. *African American Psychology*. Newbury Park, CA: Sage.

Chao, Ruth. 1993. *East and West Concepts of the Self Reflected in Mothers' Reports of Their Child Rearing*. Unpublished manuscript. Los Angeles: University of California, Los Angeles.

Cheryan, Sapna, and Monin Benoît. 2005. Where are you really from? Asian Americans and identity denial. *Journal of Personality and Social Psychology, 89*(5), 717–730.

Cohen, Geoffrey L., Julio Garcia, Nancy Apfel, and Allison Master. 2006. Reducing the racial achievement gap: A social-psychological intervention. *Science, 313*, 1307–1310.

Cooley, Charles Horton. 1922. *Human Nature and the Social Order* (rev. ed.). New York: Charles Scribner's Sons.

Cousins, Steven. 1989. Culture and self-perception in Japan and the United States. *Journal of Personality and Social Psychology, 56*, 124–131.

Erikson, Erik H. 1968. *Identity: Youth and Crisis*. New York: Norton.

Fiske, Alan P., Shinobu Kitayama, Hazel Rose Markus, and Richard E. Nisbett. 1998. The cultural matrix of social psychology. In *Handbook of Social Psychology* (4th ed.), ed. Daniel Todd Gilbert, Susan T. Fiske, and Gardner Lindzey, 915–981 San Francisco: McGraw-Hill.

Fredrickson, George. 2002. *Racism: A Short History*. Princeton, NJ: Princeton University Press.

Heine, Steven J. 2008. *Cultural Psychology*. New York: Norton.

Hudley, Edith V. P., Wendy L. Haight, and Peggy J. Miller. 2003. *"Raise Up a Child": Human Development in an African-American Family*. Chicago: Lyceum.

Hwang, Kwang-kuo. 1999. Filial piety and loyalty: Two types of social identification in Confusianism. *Asian Journal of Social Psychology, Special issue: Theoretical and Methodological Advances in Social Psychology, 2*, 163–183.

Iyengar, Sheena S., and Mark R. Lepper. 1999. Rethinking the value of choice: A cultural perspective on intrinsic motivation. *Journal of Personality and Social Psychology, 76*, 349–366.

Jones, James M. 1999. Cultural racism: The intersection of race and culture in intergroup conflict. In *Cultural Divides: Understanding and Overcoming Group Conflict*, ed. Deborah A. Prentice and Dale T. Miller, 465–490. New York: Russell Sage Foundation.

Kanagawa, Chie, Susan E. Cross, and Hazel Rose Markus. 2001. "Who am I?" The cultural psychology of the conceptual self. *Personality and Social Psychology Bulletin, 27*(1), 90–103.

Krysan, Maria, and Amanda E. Lewis. 2005. The United States today: Racial discrimination is alive and well. *Challenge, 48*, 34–49.

Markus, Hazel Rose, and Shinobu Kitayama. 1998. The cultural psychology of personality. *Journal of Cross-Cultural Psychology, 29*(1), 63–87.

Markus, H., and Sentis, K. 1982. The self in social information processing. In *Social Psychological Perspectives on the Self*, ed. Jerry Suls. Hillsdale, NJ: Erlbaum.

Massey, Douglas S., and Nancy A. Denton. 1992. Racial identity and the spatial assimilation of Mexicans in the United States. *Social Science Research, 21*, 235–260.

McIntosh, Peggy. 1997. White priviledge: Unpacking the invisible knapsack. In *Race: An Anthology in the First Person*, ed. B. Schneider, 120–126. New York: Three Rivers Press.

Mead, George Herbert. 1934. *Mind, Self and Society*. Chicago: University of Chicago Press.

Mesquita, Batja, Krishna Savani, David Albert, Hilda Fernandez de Ortega, and Mayumi Karasawa. 2006. Beyond the dichotomy of cultures: Emotions in Mexican, Japanese, and European American contexts. Unpublished manuscript.

Moya, Paula M. L. 2002. *Learning from Experience: Minority Identities, Multicultural Struggles*. Berkeley: University of California Press.

Moya, Paula M. L., and Michael R. Hames-García, eds. 2000. *Reclaiming Identity: Realist Theory and the Predicament of Postmodernism*. Berkeley: University of California Press.

Nobles, Wade W. 1991. African philosophy: Foundations of black psychology. In *Black Psychology* (3rd ed.), ed. Reginald L. Jones, 47–64. Hampton, VA: Cobb and Henry.

Oyserman, Daphna. 2008. Racial-ethnic self-schemas: Multidimensional identity-based motivation. *Journal of Research in Personality, 42*, 1186–1198.

Oyserman, Daphna, Larry Gant, and Joel Ager. 1995. A socially contextualized model of African American identity: Possible selves and school persistence. *Journal of Personality and Social Psychology, 69*, 1216–1232.

Oyserman, Daphna, Markus Kemmelmeier, Stephanie Fryberg, Hezi Brosh, and Tamera Hart-Johnson. 2003. Racial-ethnic self-schemas. *Social Psychology Quarterly, 66*, 333–347.

Oyserman, Daphna, and Hazel Rose Markus. 1993. The sociocultural self. In *Psychological perspectives on the self* (Vol. 4), ed. Jerry Suls, 187–220. Hillsdale, NJ: Erlbaum.

Prentice, Deborah, and Dale Miller. 1999. *Cultural Divides: Understanding and Overcoming Group Conflict*. New York: Russell Sage Foundation.

Savani, Krishna, Ayme Alvarez, and Hazel Rose Markus. 2008. Relations as a source of motivation. Unpublished manuscript, Stanford University

Steele, Claude M. 1997. A threat in the air: How stereotypes shape intellectual identity and performance. *American Psychologist, 52*, 613–629.

Steele, Claude M., Steven Spencer, and Joshua Aronson. 2002. Contending with group image: The psychology of stereotype and social identity threat.

In *Advances in Experimental Social Psychology* (Vol. 4), ed. Mark P. Zanna, 379–440. San Diego, CA: Academic Press.

Tatum, Beverly. 2002. The Complexity of Identity: "Who am I?" In *Why Are All the Black Kids Sitting Together in the Cafeteria?* (rev. ed.). New York: Basic Books.

Tobin, Joseph J., David Y. H. Wu, and Dana H. Davidson. 1989. *Preschool in Three Cultures*. New Haven, CT: Yale University Press.

Triandis, Harry C. 1991. Cross-cultural industrial and organizational psychology. In *Handbook of industrial and organizational psychology*, ed. Harry Triandis, Marvin D. Dunnette, and Leaetta M. Hough, 103–172. Palo Alto, CA: Consulting Psychologists Press.

Tsai, Annie Y. 2005. Equality or propriety: A cultural models approach to understanding social hierarchy. Unpublished doctoral dissertation, Stanford University.

Valdez, Guadalupe. 1996. *Con Respeto: Bridging the Distance between Culturally Diverse Families and Schools*. New York: Teachers College Press.

14

In the Air between Us
Stereotypes, Identity, and Achievement[†]

Claude M. Steele

•

Through an exploration of the phenomenon of stereotype threat, I examine the subtle but powerful ways in which the devaluing and marginalizing views of others can influence individual achievement and performance. Specifically, I describe how the pervasive negative stereotypes of African Americans in U.S. society create a condition of stereotype threat for African American college students. Because negative stereotypes about blacks influence how African American students are judged and treated in many different settings, and because the students are not always in a position to demonstrate the falseness or inapplicability of the stereotype to their own lives, they are always subject to the fear that they might inadvertently confirm a negative stereotype. This fear, in turn, creates stress that depresses individual students' performance. A series of experiments show that stereotype threat is powerful enough to depress performance on standardized tests like the SAT, and that it has an especially powerful effect on the most motivated, confident, and skilled students. For example, African American students performed significantly worse than white students on tests they believed were diagnostic of their intellectual ability. When they were told that the test was not diagnostic of their ability, however—a condition that effectively lifted the stereotype threat—African American students performed on par with their white peers. I conclude the essay with a discussion of ways educators can remedy the detrimental effects of stereotype threat by creating conditions of "identity safety."

[†]This essay originally appeared as "Stereotype Threat and African-American Student Achievement." 2003. In *Young, Gifted, and Black: Promoting High Achievement among African-American Students*. By Theresa Perry, Claude Steele, and Asa G. Hilliard III. Boston, MA: Beacon Press. Permission to reprint was granted by the Beacon Press.

THE BUILDINGS HAD HARDLY CHANGED IN THE THIRTY YEARS SINCE I'D been to the small liberal arts school quite near the college that I attended. In my student days I had visited it many times to see friends. This time I was there to give a speech about how racial and gender stereotypes, floating and abstract though they might seem, can affect concrete things like grades, test scores, and academic identity. My talk was received warmly, and the next morning I met with a small group of African-American students. I have done this on many campuses. But this time, perhaps cued by the familiarity of the place, I had an experience of déjà vu. The students expressed a litany of complaints that could have come straight from the mouths of the Black friends I had visited there thirty years earlier: the curriculum was too white, they heard too little Black music, they were ignored in class, and too often they felt slighted by faculty members and other students. Despite the school's recruitment efforts, they were a small minority. The core of their social life was their own group. To relieve the dysphoria, they went home a lot on weekends.

I found myself giving them the same advice my father gave me when I was in college: lighten up on the politics, get the best education you can, and move on. But then I surprised myself by saying, "To do this you have to learn from people who part of yourself tells you are difficult to trust."

Over the past four decades African-American college students have been more in the spotlight than any other American students. This is because they aren't just college students; they are cutting edge in America's effort to integrate itself in the nearly forty years since the passage of the Civil Rights Act. These students have borne much of the burden for our national experiment in racial integration. And to a significant degree the success of the experiment will be determined by their success.

Nonetheless, throughout the 1990s the national college dropout rate for African Americans has been 20 to 25 percent higher than that for whites. Among those who finish college, the grade point average of Black students is two-thirds of a grade below that of whites.

A recent study by William Bowen and Derek Bok, reported in their book *The Shape of the River* (1998), brings some happy news: despite this underachievement in college, Black students who attend the most selective schools in the country go on to do just as well in post-graduate programs and professional attainment as other students from those schools. This is a telling fact in support of affirmative action, since only these schools use affirmative action in admissions. Still, the underperformance of Black undergraduates is an unsettling problem, one that may alter or hamper career development, especially among Blacks not attending the most selective schools.

Attempts to explain the problem can sound like a debate about whether America is a good society, at least by the standard of racial fairness, and maybe even about whether racial integration is possible. It is an uncomfortably finger-pointing debate. Does the problem stem from something about Black students themselves, such as poor motivation, a distracting peer culture, lack of family values, or—the unsettling suggestion of *The Bell Curve*—genes? Or does it stem from the conditions of Blacks' lives: social and economic deprivation, a society that views Blacks through the lens of diminishing stereotypes and low expectations, too much coddling, or too much neglect?

In recent years this debate has acquired a finer focus: the fate of middle-class Black students. Americans have come to view the disadvantages associated with being Black as disadvantages primarily of social and economic resources and opportunity. This assumption is often taken to imply that if you are Black and come from a socioeconomically middle-class home, you no longer suffer a significant disadvantage of race. "Why should the son of a Black physician be given an advantage in college admission over the son of a white delivery-truck driver?" This is a standard question in the controversy over affirmative action. And the assumption behind it is that surely in today's society the disadvantages of race are overcome when lower socioeconomic status is overcome.

But virtually all aspects of underperformance—lower standardized test scores, lower college grades, lower graduation rates—persist among students from the African-American middle class. This situation forces on us an uncomfortable recognition: that beyond class, something racial is depressing the academic performance of these students.

Some time ago two of my colleagues, Joshua Aronson and Steven Spencer, and I tried to see the world from the standpoint of these students, concerning ourselves less with features of theirs that might explain their troubles than with features of the world they see. A story I was told recently depicts some of these. The storyteller was worried about his friend, a normally energetic Black student who had broken up with his longtime girlfriend and had since learned that she, a Hispanic, was now dating a white student. This hit him hard. Not long after hearing about his girlfriend, he sat through an hour's discussion of *The Bell Curve* in his psychology class, during which the possible genetic inferiority of his race was openly considered. Then he overheard students at lunch arguing that affirmative action allowed in too many underqualified Blacks. By his own account, this young man had experienced very little of what he thought of as racial discrimination on campus. Still, these were features of his world. Could they have a bearing on his academic life?

My colleagues and I have called such features "stereotype threat"—the threat of being viewed through the lens of a negative stereotype, or the fear of doing something that would inadvertently confirm that stereotype. Everyone experiences stereotype threat. We are all members of some group about which negative stereotypes exist, from white males and Methodists to women and the elderly. And in a situation where one of those stereotypes applies—a man talking to women about pay equity, for example, or an aging faculty member trying to remember a number sequence in the middle of a lecture—we know that we may be judged by it.

Like the young man in the story, we can feel mistrustful and apprehensive in such situations. For him, as for African-American students generally, negative stereotypes apply in many situations, even personal ones. Why was that old roommate unfriendly to him? Did that young white woman who has been so nice to him in class not return his phone call because she's afraid he'll ask her for a date? Is it because of his race or something else about him? He cannot know the answers, but neither can his rational self fully dismiss the questions. Together they raise a deeper question: Will his race be a boundary to his experience, to his emotions, to his relationships?

Consider the experience that Brent Staples, now an editorialist for the *New York Times,* recounted in his autobiography, *Parallel Time* (1994). When he arrived at the University of Chicago's Hyde Park campus to begin graduate school in psychology, he noticed that as an African-American male dressed like a student, he seemed to make people apprehensive; on the street people seemed to avoid him, in shops security people followed him, and so on. After a while he realized that he was being seen through the lens of a negative stereotype about his race. It wasn't that he had done anything to warrant this view of him—as in taking too much food, for example. It was simply that he was an identifiable member of a group about whom existed a broadly held negative view of their proneness to violence. Moreover, walking the streets of Hyde Park, he was in a situation where this negative view was applicable to him—every time he was in the setting. Thus this stereotype confronted him with an engulfing predicament. It was relevant to a broad range of behaviors in the setting—just walking down the street or entering a store, for example, could be seen by others through the lens of the stereotype as foreshadowing danger. Also, everyone in his environment knows the stereotype. Thus it could influence and coordinate how he was judged and treated by many people. And it would be difficult for him to prove to people, on the spot, that this view of his group was not applicable to him as a person. In these ways, then, the threat posed by this group stereotype becomes a formidable predicament, one that could make it difficult for him to trust that he would be seen objectively and treated with good will in the setting. Such, then, is the hypothesized nature of stereotype threat—not an abstract threat, not necessarily a belief or expectation about oneself, but the concrete, real-time threat of being judged and treated poorly in settings where a negative stereotype about one's group applies.

MEASURING STEREOTYPE THREAT

Can stereotype threat be shown to affect academic performance? And if so, who would be most affected—stronger or weaker students? Which has a greater influence on academic success among Black college students—the degree of threat or the level of preparation with which they enter college? Can the college or other educational experience be redesigned to lessen the threat? And if so, would that redesign help these students to succeed academically?

As we confronted these questions in the course of our research, we came in for some surprises. We began with what we took to be the hardest question: Could something as abstract as stereotype threat really affect something as irrepressible as intelligence? Ours is an individualistic culture; forward movement is seen to come from within. Against this cultural faith one needs evidence to argue that something as "sociological" as stereotype threat can repress something as "individualistic" as intelligence.

To acquire such evidence, Joshua Aronson and I (following a procedure developed with Steven Spencer) designed an experiment to test whether the stereotype threat that Black students might experience when taking a difficult standardized test could depress their performance on the test to a statistically reliable degree. We brought white and Black Stanford students into the laboratory and gave them, one at a time, a very difficult thirty-minute section of a Graduate Record Exam subject test in English literature. Most of these students were sophomores, which meant that the test—designed for graduating seniors—was particularly hard for them— precisely the feature, we reasoned, that would make this simple testing situation different for our Black participants than for our white participants, despite the fact that all the participants were of equal ability levels measured by all available criteria. (The difficulty of the test guaranteed that both Black and white students would find the test frustrating. And it is in these situations that members of ability-stereotyped groups are most likely to experience the extra burden of stereotype threat. First, the experience of frustration with the test gives credibility to the limitation alleged in the stereotype. For this reason, frustration can be especially stinging and disruptive for test-takers to whom the stereotype is relevant. Second, it is on a demanding test that one can least afford to be bothered by the thoughts that likely accompany stereotype threat.)

A significant part of the negative stereotype about African Americans concerns intellectual ability. Thus, in the stereotype threat conditions of the experiments in this series, we merely mentioned to participants that the test was a measure of verbal ability. This was enough, we felt, to make the negative stereotype about African Americans' abilities relevant to their performance on the test, and thus to put them at risk of confirming, or being seen to confirm, the negative stereotype about their abilities. If the pressure imposed by the relevance of a negative stereotype about one's group is enough to impair an important intellectual performance, then Black participants should perform worse than whites in the "diagnostic" condition of this experiment but not in the "nondiagnostic" condition. As Figure 14.1 depicts, this is precisely what happened: Blacks performed a full standard deviation lower than whites under the stereotype threat of the test being "diagnostic" of their intellectual ability, even though we had statistically matched the two groups in ability level. Something other than ability was involved; we believed it was stereotype threat.

But maybe the Black students performed less well than the white students because they were less motivated, or because their skills were somehow less applicable to the advanced material of this test. We needed some way to determine if it was indeed stereotype threat that depressed the Black students' scores. We reasoned that if stereotype threat had impaired their performance on the test, then reducing this threat would allow their performance to improve. We presented the same test as a laboratory task that was used to study how certain problems are generally solved. We stressed that the task did not measure a person's level of intellectual ability. A simple instruction, yes, but it profoundly changed the meaning of the situation. In one stroke "spotlight anxiety," as the psychologist William Cross once called it, was turned off—and

FIGURE 14.1 | **WHITE AND BLACK PARTICIPANTS' SCORES (CONTROLLED FOR SAT) ON A DIFFICULT ENGLISH TEST AS A FUNCTION OF CHARACTERIZA-TION OF THE TEST.**

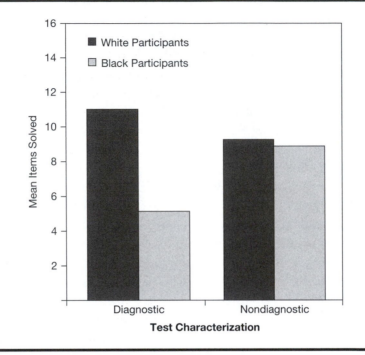

the Black students' performance on the test rose to match that of equally qualified whites (see Figure 14.1). In the non–stereotype threat conditions, we presented the same test as an instrument for studying problem solving that was "nondiagnostic" of individual differences in ability—thus making the racial stereotype irrelevant to their performance.

Aronson and I decided that what we needed next was direct evidence of the subjective state we call stereotype threat. To seek this, we looked into whether simply sitting down to take a difficult test of ability was enough to make Black students mindful of their race and stereotypes about it. This may seem unlikely. White students I have taught over the years have sometimes said that they have hardly any sense of even having a race. But Blacks have many experiences with the majority "other group" that make their race salient to them.

We again brought Black and white students in to take a difficult verbal test. But just before the test began, we gave them a long list of words, each of which had two letters missing. They were told to complete the words on this list as fast as they could. We knew from a preliminary survey that twelve of the eighty words we had selected could be completed in such a way as to relate to the stereotype about Blacks' intellectual ability. The fragment "—ce," for example, could become "race." If simply taking a difficult test of ability was enough to make Black students mindful of stereotypes about their race, these students should complete more fragments with stereotype-related words. That is just what happened. When Black students were told that the test would measure ability, they completed the fragments with significantly more stereotype-related words than when they were told that it was not a measure of ability. Whites made few stereotype-related completions in either case.

What kind of worry is signaled by this race consciousness? To find out, we used another probe. We asked participants on the brink of the difficult test to tell us their preferences in sports and music. Some of these, such as basketball, jazz, and hip-hop, are associated with African-American imagery, whereas others, such as tennis, swimming, and classical music, are not. Something striking emerged: when Black students expected to take a test of ability, they spurned things African-American, reporting less interest in, for instance, basketball, jazz, and hip-hop than whites did. When the test was presented as unrelated to ability, Black students strongly preferred things African-American. They eschewed these things only when preferring them would encourage a stereotypic view of themselves. It was the spotlight that they were trying to avoid.

Another question arises: Do the effects of stereotype threat come entirely from the fear of being stereotyped, or do they come from something internal to Black students—self-doubt, for example?

Beginning with George Herbert Mead's idea of the "looking-glass self," social psychology has assumed that one's self-image derives in large part from how one is viewed by others—family, school, and the broader society. When those views are negative, people may internalize them, resulting in lower self-esteem—or self-hatred, as it has been called. This theory was first applied to the experience of Jews, by Sigmund Freud and Bruno Bettelheim, but it was also soon applied to the experience of African Americans, by Gordon Allport, Frantz Fanon, Kenneth Clark, and others. According to the theory, Black students internalize negative stereotypes as performance anxiety and low expectations for achievement, which they then fulfill. The "self-fulfilling prophecy" has become a commonplace about these students. Stereotype threat, however, is something different, something external: the situational threat of being negatively stereotyped. Which of these two processes, then, caused the results of our experiments?

Joshua Aronson, Michael Lustina, Kelli Keough, Joseph Brown, Catherine Good, and I devised a way to find out. Suppose we told white male students who were strong in math that a difficult math test they were about to take was one on which Asians generally did better than whites. White males should not have a sense of group inferiority about math, since no societal stereotype alleges such an inferiority. Yet this comment would put them under a form of stereotype threat: any faltering on the test could cause them to be seen negatively from the standpoint of the positive stereotype about Asians and math ability. If stereotype threat alone—in the absence of any internalized self-doubt—was capable of disrupting test performance, then white males taking the test after this comment should perform less well than white males taking the test without hearing the comment. That is just what happened. Stereotype threat impaired intellectual functioning in a group unlikely to have any sense of group inferiority (Aronson et al. 1999).

In science, as in the rest of life, few things are definitive. But these results are pretty good evidence that stereotype threat's impairment of standardized-test performance does not depend on cueing a preexisting anxiety. Steven Spencer, Diane Quinn, and I have shown how stereotype threat depresses the performance of accomplished female math students on a difficult math test, and how that performance improves dramatically when the threat is lifted (Spencer, Steele, and Quinn 1999).

We recruited women and men students at the University of Michigan who were quite good at math—with entering math SAT scores in the top 15 percent of the Michigan student population—and who were identified with math in the sense of seeing it as very important to their personal and career goals. We brought them into the laboratory one at a time, and to mimic the condition that seemed to produce women's math underperformance in the real world, we gave all participants a very difficult math test—a twenty-five-minute section of the Graduate Record Exam in mathematics. The sheer difficulty of the test, we reasoned, would be enough to make the negative stereotype about women's math ability relevant to them personally, despite their confidence in their mathematical abilities, and thus to threaten them with the possibility that they would be confirming the stereotype, or be seen as confirming it. Following our real-world observations, we assumed that nothing more pointed than taking such a test would be required to evoke this threat, and in turn, this threat should depress women's performance relative to men's, even though we had selected men and women who were equally good at math and cared equally about it.

This is precisely what happened. In one early experiment, women underperformed in relation to men on a difficult math test but not on a difficult English test, and in another, women again underperformed in relation to men on a difficult math test but not on an easier math test that did not cause the same level of frustration.

With these findings we had produced the same gendered pattern of behavior that we had observed in the real world of difficult math classes. But these findings, again, did not establish that it was stereotype threat that was responsible for depressing women's performance on the difficult test. As was pointed out to us, they could reflect the fact that women have some lesser capacity specifically for math that reveals itself only when the math is very difficult. To distinguish between these explanations, we devised a condition in the next experiment, as we did in the experiment with Black and white Stanford students, that reduced stereotype threat by making the stereotype irrelevant to performance. The test was presented to all participants as one that did not show sex differences, as a test in which women always did as well as men—thus making the stereotype about women's math ability irrelevant to interpreting their experience while taking this particular test. The results in this condition were dramatic. As Figure 14.2 shows, women given this instruction performed just as well as equally skilled men and significantly better than women in the stereotype-still-relevant condition of this experiment in which participants were told that the test did show gender differences.

The mere relevance of the negative stereotype to their own math performance, presumably occasioned by their performance frustration, was enough to undermine the test performance of strong women math students who cared a lot about math. Jean-Claude Croizet, working in France with a stereotype that links poor verbal skills with lower-class status, found analogous results: lower-class college students performed less well than upper-class college students under the threat of a stereotype-based judgment, but performed as well when the threat was removed.

The stereotype threat's impairing effects also generalize to other performance domains. Stone and his colleagues (1999) have established an intriguing effect of stereotype threat on sports performance. They asked elite athletes at the University of Arizona, Black and white, to perform ten holes of golf in a miniature laboratory course. To invoke a stereotype that would put the performance of white athletes under threat, they introduced the task as a measure of "natural athletic ability." Under this representation, one that puts white athletes under the added risk of confirming or being seen to confirm a negative group stereotype, the white

FIGURE 14.2 | **MEN'S AND WOMEN'S MEAN SCORE (CONTROLLED FOR GUESSING) ON A DIFFICULT MATH TEST AS A FUNCTION OF CHARACTERIZATION OF THE TEST.**

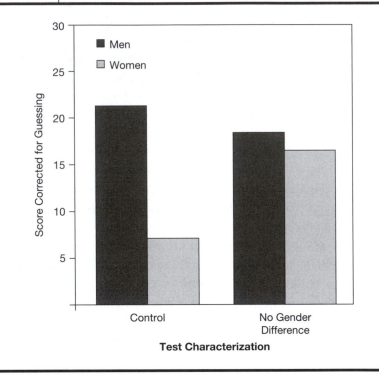

athletes significantly underperformed in comparison with the Black athletes. But Stone et al. were able to reverse this pattern of results—so that white athletes outperformed Black athletes on the same task—by representing the task as a measure of "sport strategic intelligence," a representation that now put the performance of Black athletes under the threat of confirming a negative group stereotype. These results show the group-by-situation variability of stereotype threat but also suggest its generalizability in real life across groups, settings, and types of behavior.

HOW STEREOTYPE THREAT AFFECTS PEOPLE DIFFERENTLY

Is everyone equally threatened and disrupted by a stereotype? One might expect, for example, that it would affect the weakest students most. But in all our research the most achievement-oriented students, who were also the most skilled, motivated, and confident, were the most impaired by stereotype threat. This fact had been under our noses all along—in our data and even in our theory. A person has to care about a domain in order to be disturbed by the prospect of being stereotyped in it. That is the whole idea of disidentification—protecting against stereotype threat by ceasing to care about the domain in which the stereotype applies. Our earlier experiments had selected Black students who identified with verbal skills and women who identified with math. But when we tested participants who identified less with these domains, what had been under our noses hit us in the face. None of them showed any effect of stereotype threat whatsoever.

These weakly identified students did not perform well on the test: once they discovered its difficulty, they stopped trying very hard and got a low score. But their performance did not differ depending on whether they felt they were at risk of being judged stereotypically.

This finding, I believe, tells us two important things. The first is that the poorer college performance of Black students may have another source in addition to the one—lack of good preparation and, perhaps, of identification with school achievement—that is commonly understood. This additional source—the threat of being negatively stereotyped in the environment—has not been well understood. The distinction has important policy implications: different kinds of students may require different pedagogies of improvement.

The second thing is poignant: what exposes students to the pressure of stereotype threat is not weaker academic identity and skills but stronger academic identity and skills. They may have long seen themselves as good students—better than most. But led into the domain by their strengths, they pay an extra tax on their investment—vigilant worry that their future will be compromised by society's perception and treatment of their group.

This tax has a long tradition in the Black community. The Jackie Robinson story is a central narrative of Black life, literature, and journalism. *Ebony* magazine has run a page for fifty years featuring people who have broken down one or another racial barrier. Surely the academic vanguard among Black college students today knows this tradition—and knows, therefore, that the thing to do, as my father told me, is to buckle down, pay whatever tax is required, and disprove the damn stereotype.

That, however, seems to be precisely what these students are trying to do. In some of our experiments we administered the test of ability by computer, so that we could see how long participants spent looking at different parts of the test questions. Black students taking the test under stereotype threat seemed to be trying too hard rather than not hard enough. They reread the questions, reread the multiple choices, rechecked their answers, more than when they were not under stereotype threat. The threat made them inefficient on a test that, like most standardized tests, is set up so that thinking long often means thinking wrong, especially on difficult items like the ones we used.

Philip Uri Treisman, an innovator in math workshops for minority students who is based at the University of Texas, saw something similar in his Black calculus students at the University of California at Berkeley: they worked long hours alone, but they worked inefficiently—for example, checking and rechecking their calculations against the correct answers at the back of the book, rather than focusing on the concepts involved. Of course, trying extra hard helps with some school tasks. But under stereotype threat this effort may be misdirected. Achievement at the frontier of one's skills may be furthered more by a relaxed, open concentration than by a strong desire to disprove a stereotype by not making mistakes.

Sadly, the effort that accompanies stereotype threat exacts an additional price. Led by James Blascovich, of the University of California at Santa Barbara, we found that the blood pressure of Black students performing a difficult cognitive task under stereotype threat was elevated compared with that of Black students not under stereotype threat or white students in either situation (Blascovich et al. 2001).

In the old song about the "steel-drivin' man," John Henry races the new steam-driven drill to see who can dig a hole faster. When the race is over, John Henry has prevailed by digging the deeper hole—only to drop dead. The social psychologist Sherman James uses the term "John Henryism" to describe a psychological syndrome that he found to be associated with hypertension in several samples of North Carolina Blacks: holding too rigidly to the faith that discrimination and disadvantage can be overcome with hard work and persistence. Certainly this is the right attitude. But taken to extremes, it can backfire. A deterioration of performance under stereotype threat by the skilled, confident Black students in our experiments may be rooted in John Henryism.

This last point can be disheartening. Our research, however, offers an interesting suggestion about what can be done to overcome stereotype threat and its detrimental effects. The success of Black students may depend less on expectations and motivation—things that are thought to drive academic performance—than on trust that stereotypes about their group will not have a limiting effect in their school world.

Putting this idea to the test, Joseph Brown and I asked, How can the usual detrimental effect of stereotype threat on the standardized-test performance of these students be reduced? By strengthening students' expectations and confidence, or by strengthening their trust that they are not at risk of being judged on the basis of stereotypes? In the ensuing experiment we strengthened or weakened participants' confidence in their verbal skills, by arranging for them to have either an impressive success or an impressive failure on a test of verbal skills, just before they took the same difficult verbal test we had used in our earlier research. When the second test was presented as a test of ability, the boosting or weakening of confidence in their verbal skills had no effect on performance: Black participants performed less well than equally skilled white participants. What does this say about the commonsense idea that black students' academic problems are rooted in lack of self-confidence?

What did raise the level of Black students' performance to that of equally qualified whites was reducing stereotype threat—in this case by explicitly presenting the test as racially fair. When this was done, Blacks performed at the same high level as whites even if their self-confidence had been weakened by a prior failure.

These results suggest something that I think has not been made clear elsewhere: when strong Black students sit down to take a difficult standardized test, the extra apprehension they feel in comparison with whites is less about their own ability than it is about having to perform on a test and in a situation that may be primed to treat them stereotypically. We discovered the extent of this apprehension when we tried to develop procedures that would make our Black participants see the test as "race-fair." It wasn't easy. African-Americans have endured so much bad press about test scores for so long that, in our experience, they are instinctively wary about the tests' fairness. We were able to convince them that our test was race-fair only when we implied that the research generating the test had been done by Blacks. When they felt trust, they performed well regardless of whether we had weakened their self-confidence beforehand. And when they didn't feel trust, no amount of bolstering of self-confidence helped.

ACUTE REACTIONS AND CHRONIC ADAPTATIONS TO STEREOTYPE THREAT

A brief word about the reactions—short- and long-term—that stereotype threat elicits. Early on in our research program (Aronson, Quinn, and

Spencer 1998; Steele 1992, 1997), we emphasized how stereotype threat can lead people to disidentify with the domains in which they experience the threat. Pain is lessened by ceasing to identify with the part of life in which the pain occurs. This withdrawal of psychic investment may be supported by other members of the stereotype-threatened group—even to the point of its becoming a group norm. But not caring can mean not being motivated. And this can have real costs. When stereotype threat affects school life, disidentification is a high price to pay for psychic comfort. Still, it is a price that groups contending with powerful negative stereotypes about their abilities—women in advanced math, African Americans in all academic areas—may too often pay.

As research on this question has progressed, two things have become clear: First, people's reactions to stereotype threat include both acute protective reactions and chronic identity adaptations, and second, these reactions are remarkably nuanced, in the sense of taking many concrete forms, so that the picture painted in the previous paragraph is only part of the story. The range of reactions—from avoidance, to counter-stereotypic behavior, to disengagement, to full disidentification—form a continuum of psychological responses, just now being studied in a rigorous way with controlled experiments. I address these complex issues in much greater depth elsewhere (Steele, Spencer, and Aronson 2002). But one thing one can say is that some of these strategies—however useful psychologically—do have the effect of lowering performance.

Having a social identity that can elicit devaluation in a setting that one wants to belong to causes conflicting motivations of the sort that W. E. B. Du Bois may have had in mind when he described the "double consciousness" inherent in the African-American experience. One is motivated to detect cues signaling identity-based devaluation, and yet one is motivated not to detect them. One becomes sensitive to the very things one least wants to see. The resulting ruminative conflict coupled with the threat of devaluation in the setting stand as ongoing pressures against, at the very least, a full engagement in the setting, and at the most, the ability to endure it at all.

REMEDYING THE DETRIMENTAL EFFECTS OF STEREOTYPE THREATS

What are some of the remedies that schools and colleges can use to reduce the negative effects of stereotype threat on minority students, and African-American students in particular?

Policies for helping Black students rest in significant part on assumptions about their psychology. Often they are assumed to lack confidence, which spawns a policy of confidence-building. This may be useful for some students. But the psychology of many others, including the best prepared and most committed students, appears different—underperformance appears to be rooted less in self-doubt than in social mistrust.

We have seen that underachievement problems are caused, in some part, by threat, by persistent patterns of stereotype threat that, as something tied to a person's social identity in school and workplace settings, can become a chronic feature of his or her experience in those settings. Despite the many cues in a setting that can evoke a sense of threat, therefore, a remedial strategy has to somehow refute that threat or its relevance to the target. My colleagues and I have recently called this goal "identity safety" (Markus, Steele, and Steele 2000; Plaut 2002; Purdie et al. 2001). To the extent that it is achieved in an academic setting, it should weaken the sequelae of identity vigilance, mistrust, disidentification, and underperformance. So it follows that education policy relevant to non-Asian minorities might fruitfully shift its focus toward fostering identity safety—and its correlate, racial trust—in the schooling situation, at least among students who come to school with good skills and high expectations. But how should this be done?

Identity safety may be easier to achieve than it might seem at first glance. A couple of school-based examples will suggest some fruitful directions. Again, research on how to create identity safety is complex and expanding, and I explore it in much greater depth elsewhere (Steele, Spencer, and Aronson 2002).

Research shows that solutions include strategies at the level of (1) pedagogy and relationships between individual teachers and students; (2) institutional and contextual changes; and (3) individual personal responses.

To explore the relational component, Geoffrey Cohen, Lee Ross, and I took up the question of how a teacher or a mentor could give critical feedback across the "racial divide" and have that feedback be trusted. We reasoned that an answer to this question might yield insights about how to instill trust more broadly in the schooling environment. Cohen's hunch was that niceness alone wouldn't be enough. But the first question had to be whether there was in fact a racial divide between teachers and students, especially in the elite college environment in which we worked.

We set up a simple experiment. Cohen asked Black and white Stanford students one at a time to write essays about their favorite teachers, for possible publication in a journal on teaching. They were asked to return several days later for feedback on their essays. Before each student left the first writing session, Cohen put a Polaroid snapshot of the student on top of his or her essay. His ostensible purpose was to publish the picture if the essay was published. His real purpose was to let the essay writers know that the evaluator of their writing would be aware of their race. When they returned days later, they were given constructive but critical feedback. We looked at whether different ways of giving this feedback engendered different degrees of trust in it.

We found that neither straight feedback nor feedback preceded by the "niceness" of a cushioning statement ("There were many good things about your essay") was trusted by Black students. They saw these criticisms as probably biased, and they were less motivated than white students to improve their essays. White students took the criticism at face value—even as an indication of interest in them. Black students, however, faced a different meaning: the "ambiguating" possibility that the criticism was motivated by negative stereotypes about their group as much as by the work itself. Herein lies the power of race to make one's world insecure—quite apart from whatever actual discrimination one may experience.

But this experiment also revealed a way to be critical across the racial divide: tell the students that you are using high standards (this signals that the criticism reflects standards rather than race), and that your reading of their essays leads you to believe that they can meet those standards (this signals that you do not view them stereotypically). This shouldn't be faked. High standards, at least in a relative sense, should be an inherent part of teaching, and critical feedback should be given in the belief that the recipient can reach those standards. These things go without saying for many students. But they have to be made explicit for students under stereotype threat. The good news of this study is that when they are made explicit, the students trust and respond to criticism. Black students who got this kind of feedback saw it as unbiased and were motivated to take their essays home and work on them even though this was not a class for credit. They were more motivated than any other group of students in the study—as if this combination of high standards and assurance was like water on parched land, a much-needed but seldom-received balm. In a situation that would otherwise cause a trust-breaking social identity threat among Black students—as evidenced by the results in the other feedback conditions—this simple relational strategy of using high standards and ability affirmation was sufficient to completely overcome the mistrust. The entire context did not have to change for trust to be achieved; one stereotype-refuting relational act was enough.

Contextual solutions are themselves possible, and just being explored rigorously in studies. They include direct interventions designed to refute the possibility of the stereotype threat, representing a philosophy and reality of diversity, and demanding fair, procedural justice for all groups. The findings here are complex and evolving (Steele, Spencer, and Aronson 2002). As this research progresses, it will, I believe, be very important for educational policy makers.

Almost invariably when my colleagues and I give talks about stereotype threat and how to reduce it in school or organizational settings, a question arises: "You have a lot to say about how situations and relationships can be changed to preempt or reduce this threat. But what can individuals, the potential targets, do to cope with this threat, to reduce its effect on them?" The answer to this question, from the standpoint of our theory, begins with the same assumption as the other strategies of remedy: to reduce this threat, individuals have to do something that disarms the appraisal hypothesis that they are under threat, or that, if they are, it will significantly affect them.

Influenced by the research of Carol Dweck and her colleagues (c.f. Dweck, Chiu, and Hong 1995), Joshua Aronson, Carrie Fried, and Catherine Good (2002) tested the hypothesis that a personal theory of intelligence as incremental—the view that one's intelligence is expandable through effort and experience—could reduce the impact of stereotype threat on people whose intellectual abilities are negatively stereotyped. Dweck has distinguished two personal theories about the nature of intelligence, one that assumes intelligence is essentially a fixed entity and the other that assumes it is expandable. Aronson, Fried, and Good reasoned that if the characteristic impugned in a negative stereotype is seen as improvable rather than fixed, then the threat of the stereotype is not as great. Thus, holding the theory that one's intelligence is malleable could be an effective strategy to cope with the threat posed by negative ability stereotypes.

Aronson, Fried, and Good examined whether this strategy could reduce the effect on academic performance of the negative ability stereotypes that African-American students face. To do this, they developed a clever way of manipulating the theory of intelligence held in a sample of Black and white college students. They cast study participants in the role of "long-distance" mentors to individual elementary school students who were ostensibly from disadvantaged backgrounds. The job of the college-aged mentors—done in a single session—was to write letters to the younger mentees urging them to apply themselves to their schoolwork and, in the critical condition, to think of their intelligence as something that was expandable. Ostensibly to make these letters convincing, the college mentors were supplied compelling descriptions of how intelligence, even the brain itself, could be modified and expanded by effort and learning, something, of course, obviously borne out by contemporary psychology and neuroscience.

Of course the focus of this study was not on the young mentees, but on how the experience of having advocated a malleable theory of intelligence affected the mentors themselves. For the Black college-aged mentors, the group whose abilities are presumably under the threat of negative stereotypes about their group, the effect of this manipulation was dramatic. Compared with Black students who did not write a letter, or who wrote a letter without the "malleability" content, Black students who wrote the "malleable" letter believed that intelligence was more malleable, reported enjoying academics more, saw academics as more important, and most dramatically, at the end of the academic quarter, got significantly higher grades.

Here, then, is clear evidence of something an individual can do to reduce the threat posed by negative ability stereotypes: adopt a self theory of intelligence as expandable. Such a theory may foster achievement through multiple effects. But over the long run, we suggest that one of its ingredients is its ability to dampen the threatening meaning of negative stereotypes about intellectual ability. Again, this is one example of an individual strategy. For an exploration of many others, see Steele, Spencer, and Aronson 2002.

A final example set in situ, in the buzz of everyday life, shows that relatively modest interventions to create identity safety in real-world settings can have a dramatic effect.

Steven Spencer, P. G. Davies, Kent Harber, Richard Nisbett, and I undertook a program aimed at incoming first-year students at the University of Michigan. Like virtually all other institutions of higher learning, Michigan had evidence of Black students' underachievement. Our mission was clear: to see if we could improve their achievement by focusing on their transition into college life.

We also wanted to see how little we could get away with—that is, to develop a program that would succeed broadly without special efforts. The program (which started in 1991 and is ongoing) created a racially integrated "living and learning" community in a 250-student wing of a large dormitory. It focused students on academic work (through weekly "challenge" workshops), provided an outlet for discussing the personal side of college life (through weekly rap sessions), and affirmed the students' abilities (through, for example, reminding them that their admission was a vote of confidence). The program lasted just one semester, although most students remained in the dormitory wing for the rest of their first year.

Still, it worked: it gave Black students a significant academic jump start. Those in the program (about 15 percent of the entering class) got better first-year grades than Black students outside the program, even after controlling for differences between these groups in the skills with which they entered college. Equally important, the program greatly reduced underperformance: Black students in the program got first-year grades almost as high as those of white students in the general Michigan population who entered with comparable test scores. This result signaled the achievement of an academic climate nearly as favorable to Black students as to white students. And it was achieved through a concert of simple things that enabled Black students to feel racially secure.

One tactic that worked surprisingly well was the weekly rap sessions—Black and white students talking to one another in an informal dormitory setting, over pizza, about the personal side of their new lives in college. Participation in these sessions reduced students' feelings of stereotype threat and improved grades. Why? Perhaps when members of one racial group hear members of another racial group express the same concerns they have, the concerns seem less racial. Students may also learn that racial and gender stereotypes are either less at play than they might have feared or don't reflect the worst-feared prejudicial intent. Talking at a personal level across group lines can thus build trust in the larger campus community. The racial segregation besetting most college campuses can block this experience, allowing mistrust to build where cross-group communication would discourage it.

Our research bears a practical message: even though the stereotypes held by the larger society may be difficult to change, it is possible to create niches in which negative stereotypes are not felt to apply. In specific classrooms, within specific programs, even in the climate of entire schools, it is possible to weaken a group's sense of being threatened by negative stereotypes, to allow its members a trust that would otherwise be difficult to sustain. Thus when schools try to decide how important Black-white test-score gaps are in determining the fate of Black students on their campuses and in their schools, they should keep something in mind: for a great portion of Black students the degree of racial trust they feel in their campus life, rather than a few ticks on a standardized test, may be the key to their success.

Bibliography

•

Abrams, D., and M. A. Hogg. 1999. *Social Identity and Social Cognition*. Malden, MA: Blackwell.

Allport, G. 1954. *The Nature of Prejudice*. New York: Addison-Wesley.

Ambady, N., M. Shih, A. Kim, and T. L Pittinsky. 2001. Stereotype Susceptibility in Children: Effects of Identity Activation on Quantitative Performance. *Psychological Science* 12: 385–90.

Aronson, J. 1997. *The Effects of Conceptions of Ability on Task Valuation*. Unpublished manuscript, New York University.

————. 1999. *The Effects of Conceiving Ability as Fixed or Improvable on Responses to Stereotype Threat*. Unpublished manuscript, New York University.

Aronson, J., C. Fried, and C. Good. 2002. Reducing the Effects of Stereotype Threat on African American College Students by Shaping Theories of Intelligence. *Journal of Experimental Social Psychology* 38: 113–25.

Aronson, J., and C. Good. 2001. *Personal versus Situational Stakes and Stereotype Threat: A Test of the Vanguard Hypothesis*. Unpublished manuscript, New York University.

Aronson, J., M. Lustina, C. Good, K. Keough, D. Steele, and J. Brown. 1999. When White Men Can't Do Math: Necessary and Sufficient Factors in Stereotype Threat. *Journal of Experimental Social Psychology* 35: 29–46.

Aronson, J., D. M. Quinn, and S. J. Spencer. 1998. Stereotype Threat and the Academic Performance of Women and Minorities. In *Prejudice: The Target's Perspective*, ed. J. K. Swim and C. Stangor. San Diego, CA: Academic Press, 83–103.

Aronson, J., and M. F. Salinas. 2001. *Stereotype Threat, Attributional Ambiguity, and Latino Underperformance*. Unpublished manuscript, New York University.

Ashe, A. 1993. *Days of Grace*. New York: Knopf.

Bargh, J. A., M. Chen, and L. Burrows. 1996. Automaticity of Social Behavior: Direct Effects of Trait Construct and Stereotype Activation on Action. *Journal of Personality and Social Psychology* 71: 230–44.

Benbow, C. P., and J. C. Stanley. 1983. Sex Differences in Mathematical Reasoning Ability: More Facts. *Science* 222: 1029–31.

Blascovich, J., S. J. Spencer, D. M. Quinn, and C. M. Steele. 2001. Stereotype Threat and the Cardiovascular Reactivity of African-Americans. *Psychological Science* 12: 225–29.

Bowen, W. G., and D. C. Bok. 1998. *The Shape of the River: Long-Term Consequences of Considering Race in College and University Admissions*. Princeton, NJ: Princeton University Press.

Branscombe, N. R., and N. Ellemers. 1998. Coping with Group-Based Discrimination: Individualistic versus Group-Level Strategies. *In Prejudice: The Target's Perspective*, ed. J. K. Swim and C. Stangor. San Diego, CA: Academic Press, 243–66.

Brewer, M. B., and R. B. Brown. 1998. Intergroup Relations. In *The Handbook of Social Psychology*, 4th ed. Vol. 2, ed. D. T. Gilbert, S. T. Fiske, and G. Lindzey. Boston: McGraw-Hill, 554–94.

Brown, J. L., and C. M. Steele. 2001. *Performance Expectations Are Not a Necessary Mediator of Stereotype Threat in African American Verbal Test Performance.* Unpublished manuscript, Stanford University.

Brown, R. P., and R. A. Josephs. 1999. A Burden of Proof: Stereotype Relevance and Gender Differences in Math Performance. *Journal of Personality and Social Psychology* 76: 246–57.

Brown, R. P., E. C. Pinel, P. Renfrow, and M. Lee. 2001. *Stigma on My Mind: Individual Differences in the Experience of Stereotype Threat.* Unpublished manuscript, University of Oklahoma.

Cohen, G. L., C. M. Steele, and L. D. Ross. 1999. The Mentors' Dilemma: Providing Critical Feedback across the Racial Time. *Personality and Social Psychology Bulletin* 25: 1302–18.

Cole, S., and E. Barber. 2000. *Increasing Faculty Diversity: The Occupational Choices of High Achieving Minority Students.* Report prepared for the Council of Ivy Group Presidents.

Crocker, J., and B. Major. 1989. Social Stigma and Self-Esteem: The Self-Protective Properties of Stigma. *Psychological Review* 96: 608–30.

Crocker, J., B. Major, and C. Steele. 1998. Social Stigma. In *The Handbook of Social Psychology*, 4th ed. Vol. 2, ed. D. T. Gilbert, S. T. Fiske, and G. Lindzey. Boston: McGraw-Hill, 504–53.

Crocker, J., K. Voelkl, M. Testa, and B. Major. 1991. Social Stigma: The Affective Consequences of Attributional Ambiguity. *Journal of Personality and Social Psychology* 60: 218–28.

Croizet, J. C., and T. Claire. 1998. Extending the Concept of Stereotype Threat to Social Class: The Intellectual Underperformance of Students from Low Socioeconomic Backgrounds. *Personality and Social Psychology Bulletin* 24: 588–94.

Crosby, F. J. 1984. The Denial of Personal Discrimination. *American Behavioral Scientist* 27: 371–86.

Crosby, F. J., D. I. Cordova, and K. Jaskar. 1993. On the Failure to See Oneself as Disadvantaged: Cognitive and Emotional Components. In *Group Motivation: Social Psychological Perspectives*, ed. M.A. Hogg, and D. Abrams. Hertfordshire, UK: Harvester Wheatsheaf, 87–104.

Cross, W. E., Jr. 1991. *Shades of Black: Diversity in African-American Identity.* Philadelphia: Temple University Press.

Davies, P. G., and S. J. Spencer. 1999. *Selling Stereotypes: How Viewing Commercials Can Undermine Women's Math Performance.* Presented at the annual meeting of the American Psychological Association. Boston, August.

Davies, P. G., and S. J. Spencer. 2001. *Stereotype Threat and Taking Charge: The Effect of Demeaning Commercials on Women's Leadership Aspirations.* Unpublished manuscript, Stanford University.

Deaux, K., and B. Major. 1987. Putting Gender into Context: An Interactive Model of Gender-Related Behavior. *Psychological Review* 94: 369–89.

Devine, P. G. 1989. Stereotypes and Prejudice: Their Automatic and Controlled Components. *Journal of Personality and Social Psychology* 56: 5–18.

Dweck, C. S., C. Chiu, and Y. Hong. 1995. Implicit Theories and Their Role in Judgments and Reactions: A World from Two Perspectives. *Psychological Inquiry* 6: 267–85.

Folkman, S., R. S. Lazarus, R. J. Gruen, and A. DeLongis. 1986. Appraisal, Coping, Health Status, and Psychological Symptoms. *Journal of Personality and Social Psychology* 50: 571–79.

Goffman, E. 1963. *Stigma*. New York: Simon & Schuster.

Good, C., and J. Aronson. 2002. The Development and Consequences of Stereotype Vulnerability in Adolescents. In *Adolescence and Education*. Vol. 2, *Academic Motivation of Adolescents*, ed. F. Pajares, and T. Urdan. Greenwich, CT: Information Age Publishing.

Good, C., J. Aronson, and J. A. Harder. 2001. *Stereotype Threat in the Absence of a Kernel of Truth: Unfounded Stereotypes Can Depress Women's Calculus Performance*. Unpublished manuscript, Columbia University.

Graham, C., R. W. Baker, and S. Wapner. 1984. Prior Interracial Experience and Black Student Transition into Predominantly White Colleges. *Journal of Personality and Social Psychology* 47: 1146–54.

Inzlicht, M., and T. Ben-Zeev. 2000. A Threatening Intellectual Environment: Why Females Are Susceptible to Experiencing Problem-Solving Deficits in the Presence of Males. *Psychological Science* 11: 365–71.

Jensen, A. R. 1980. *Bias in Mental Testing*. New York: Free Press.

Jonides, J., W. von Hippel, J. S. Lerner, and B. Nagda. 1992. *Evaluation of Minority Retention Programs: The Undergraduate Research Opportunities Program at the University of Michigan*. Presented at the annual meeting of the American Psychological Association. Washington, DC, August.

Josephs, R. A., M. L. Newman, R. P. Brown, and J. M. Beer. 2001. *Using the Relationship between Status and Testosterone to Explain Stereotype-Based Sex Differences in Cognitive Performance*. Unpublished manuscript, University of Texas.

Jost, J. T., and M. R. Banaji. 1994. The Role of Stereotyping in System-Justification and the Production of False Consciousness. *British Journal of Social Psychology Special Issue: Stereotypes: Structure, Function, and Process* 33: 1–27.

Kleck, R. E., and A. Strenta. 1980. Perceptions of the Impact of Negatively Valued Physical Characteristics on Social Interaction. *Journal of Personality and Social Psychology* 39: 861–73.

Lazarus, R. S. 1986. Emotions and Adaption: Conceptual and Empirical Relations. *Nebraska Symposium on Motivation* 16: 175–266.

Lepper, M. R., M. Woolverton, D. L. Mumme, and J. L. Gurtner. 1993. Motivational Techniques of Expert Human Tutors: Lessons for the Design of Computer-Based Tutors. In *Computers as Cognitive Tools: Technology in Education*, ed. S. P. Lajoie, and S. J. Derry. Hillsdale, NJ: Lawrence Erlbaum.

Leyens, J. P., M. Desert, J. C. Croizet, and C. Darcis. 2000. Stereotype Threat: Are Lower Status and History of Stigmatization Preconditions of Stereotype Threat? *Personality and Social Psychology Bulletin* 26: 1189–99.

Macrae, C. N., G. V. Bodenhausen, A. B. Milne, and J. Jetten. 1994. Out of Mind but Back in Sight: Stereotypes on the Rebound. *Journal of Personality and Social Psychology* 67: 808–17.

Major, B. 1995. *Academic Performance, Self-Esteem, and Race: The Role of Disidentification*. Presented at the annual meeting of the American Psychological Association. New York, August.

Major, B., and T. Schmader. 1998. Coping With Stigma through Psychological Disengagement. In *Prejudice: The Target's Perspective*, ed. J. K. Swim, and C. Stangor. San Diego, CA: Academic Press, 219–41.

Major, B., S. J. Spencer, T. Schmader, C. T. Wolfe, and J. Crocker. 1998. Coping with Negative Stereotypes about Intellectual Performance: The Role of Psychological Disengagement. *Personality and Social Psychology Bulletin* 24: 35–50.

Markus, H. R., C. M. Steele, and D. M. Steele. 2000. Colorblindness as a Barrier to Inclusion: Assimilation and Nonimmigrant Minorities. *Daedalus* 129: 233–59.

McGuire, W., C. McGuire, P. Child, and T. Fujoko. 1987. Salience of Ethnicity in the Spontaneous Self-Concept as a Function of One's Ethnic Distinctiveness in the Social Environment. *Journal of Personality and Social Psychology* 36: 511–20.

Osborne, J. W. 1997. Race and Academic Disidentification. *Journal of Educational Psychology* 89: 728–35.

Osborne, J. W. 2001. Testing Stereotype Threat: Does Anxiety Explain Race and Sex Differences in Achievement? *Contemporary Educational Psychology* 26: 291–310.

Oyserman, D., K. Harrison, and D. Bybee. 2001. Can Racial Identity Be Promotive of Academic Efficacy? *International Journal of Behavioral Development* 25: 379–85.

Pinel, E. C. 1999. Stigma Consciousness: The Psychological Legacy of Social Stereotypes. *Journal of Personality and Social Psychology* 79: 114–28.

Plaut, V. C. 2002. Cultural Models of Diversity: The Psychology of Difference and Inclusion. In *Engaging Cultural Differences: The Multicultural Challenge in Liberal Democracies*. ed. R. Shweder, M. Minow, and H. R. Markus. New York: Russell Sage Foundation.

Pronin, E., D. M. Steele, and L. Ross. 2001. *Stereotype Threat and the Feminine Identities of Women in Math*. Unpublished manuscript, Harvard University.

Purdie, V. J., C. M. Steele, P. G. Davies, and J. R. Crosby. 2001. *The Business of Diversity: Minority Trust within Organizational Cultures*. Presented at the annual meeting of the American Psychological Association. San Francisco, August.

Ramist, L., C. Lewis, and L. McCammley-Jenkins. 1994. *Student Group Differences in Predicting College Grades: Sex, Language, and Ethnic Groups*. College Board report no. 93-1, ETS no. 94.27. New York: College Entrance Examination Board.

Sartre, J. P. 1948. *Anti-Semite and Jew*. Trans. J. G. Becker. New York: Schocken Books.

Sekaquaptewa, D., and M. Thompson. 2002. The Differential Effects of Solo Status on Members of High and Low Status Groups. *Personality and Social Psychology Bulletin* 28: 694–707.

Shih, M., T. L. Pittinsky, and N. Ambady. 1999. Stereotype Susceptibility: Identity Salience and Shifts in Quantitative Performance. *Psychological Science* 10: 80–83.

Spencer, S. J., E. Iserman, P. G. Davies, and D. M. Quinn. 2001. *Suppression of Doubts, Anxiety, and Stereotypes as a Mediator of Effect of Stereotype Threat on Women's Math Performance*. Unpublished manuscript, University of Waterloo.

Spencer, S. J., C. M. Steele, and D. M. Quinn. 1999. Stereotype Threat and Women's Math Performance. *Journal of Experimental Social Psychology* 35: 4–28.

Stangor, C., C. Carr, and L. Kiang. 1998. Activating Stereotypes Undermines Task Performance Expectations. *Journal of Personality and Social Psychology* 75: 1191–97.

Staples, B. 1994. *Parallel Time: Growing Up in Black and White*. New York: Pantheon Books.

Steele, C. M. 1975. Name-Calling and Compliance. *Journal of Personality and Social Psychology* 31: 361–69.

————. 1992. Race and the Schooling of Black Americans. *Atlantic Monthly* 269: 68–78.

————. 1997. A Threat in the Air: How Stereotypes Shape Intellectual Identity and Performance. *American Psychologist* 52: 613–29.

————. 1999. Thin Ice: Stereotype Threat and Black College Students. *Atlantic Monthly* 248: 44–54.

Steele, C. M., and J. Aronson. 1995. Stereotype Threat and the Intellectual Test Performance of African Americans. *Journal of Personality and Social Psychology* 69: 797–811.

Steele, C. M., S. J. Spencer, and J. Aronson. 2002. Contending with Group Image: The Psychology of Stereotype and Social Identity Threat. In *Advances in Experimental Social Psychology*, Vol. 34, ed. M. Zanna. Academic Press.

Steele, C. M., S. J. Spencer, P. G. Davies, K. Harber, and R. E. Nisbett. 2001. *African American College Achievement: A "Wise" Intervention*. Unpublished manuscript, Stanford University.

Steele, S. 1990. *The Content of Our Character: A New Vision of Race in America*. New York: St. Martin's.

Stone, J., C. I. Lynch, M. Sjomeling, and J. M. Darley. 1999. Stereotype Threat Effects on Black and White Athletic Performance. *Journal of Personality and Social Psychology* 77: 1213–27.

Stricker, L. J. 1998. *Inquiring about Examinees' Ethnicity and Sex: Effects on AP Calculus AB Examination performance*. College Board report no. 98-1, ETS research report no. 98-5. New York: College Entrance Examination Board.

Taylor, D. M., S. C. Wright, F. M. Moghaddam, and R. Lalonde. 1990. The Personal/Group Discrimination Discrepancy: Perceiving My Group, but Not Myself, to Be a Target for Discrimination. *Personality and Social Psychology Bulletin* 16: 254–62.

Tyler, T., P. Degoey, and H. Smith. 1996. Understanding Why the Injustice of Group Procedures Matters: A Test of the Psychological Dynamics of the Group-Value Model. *Journal of Personality and Social Psychology* 70: 913–30.

Tyler, T., H. Smith, and Y. J. Huo. 1996. Member Diversity and Leadership Effectiveness: Procedural Justice, Social Identity, and Group Dynamics. *Advances in Group Processes* 13: 33–66.

von Hippel, W., C. Hawkins, and J. W. Schooler. 2001. Stereotype Distinctiveness: How Counterstereotypic Behavior Shapes the Self-Concept. *Journal of Personality and Social Psychology* 81: 193–205.

Wegner, D. M. 1994. Ironic Processes of Mental Control. *Psychological Review* 101: 34–52.

Wenzlaff, R. M., and D. M. Wegner. 2000. Thought Suppression. *Annual Review of Psychology* 51: 59–91.

Wheeler, S. C., W. B. Jarvis, and R. E. Petty. 2001. Think unto Others: The Self-Destructive Impact of Negative Racial Stereotypes. *Journal of Experimental Social Psychology* 37: 173–80.

Wheeler, S. C., and R. E. Petty. 2001. The Effects of Stereotype Activation on Behavior: A Review of Possible Mechanisms. *Psychological Bulletin* 127: 797–826.

Wolsko, C., B. Park, C. M. Judd., and B. Wittenbrink. 2000. Framing Interethnic Ideology: Effects of Multicultural and Color-Blind Perspectives on Judgments of Groups and Individuals. *Journal of Personality and Social Psychology* 78: 635–54.

15

Ways of Being White
Privilege, Perceived Stigma, and Transcendence

Monica McDermott

•

In this chapter, I argue that white racial identity is more complex and more various than most people think. From months of participant observation research in two urban communities, as well as a series of interviews with residents of southern Appalachia, I have observed the powerful effects that local understandings of race, class, and history have on whites' experience of white racial identity. To understand the ways that white racial identity is a product of local circumstances, I analyze three case studies, two involving participant observation research in Atlanta and Boston and a third based on interviews conducted in rural Kentucky, Tennessee, and Virginia. I show that white identity can be experienced in at least one of three ways: as a privilege to defend, as a perceived stigma, or as an identity to be transcended. Many factors influence how being white is experienced by a given individual, but four factors are especially important for how whiteness will be experienced: (1) The size of the local nonwhite (in the case of my research, black) population; (2) the availability of other plausible racial identities from which to choose to affiliate; (3) the social class of most whites in the local area; (4) and the strength of white ethnic identities in the local area.

SEVERAL YEARS AGO, WHILE I WAS DOING ETHNOGRAPHIC RESEARCH ON the different ways to be white in America, I had a startling encounter

I would like to thank Mario Small and Rebecca Sandefur for their detailed comments on earlier drafts. I have also received helpful feedback on presentations of this material from Mary Waters, Chris Winship, Larry Bobo, Paula Moya, Gwen Dordick, and Irene Bloemraad.

that beautifully illustrated how complex white racial identity really is (McDermott 2006). The experience drove home the point that how race works depends heavily on the local context. This is what happened. I was employed as a convenience store clerk in a working-class neighborhood in Atlanta when two black prostitutes who worked a corner near the store came in to buy some drinks and snack food. The store was busy, and I left my job stocking the cooler to help out the other cashier. The first customer I served was one of the prostitutes. When I told her the bill came to $3 and some change, she told me that she had already given me a $10 bill. When I told her that I had not received any money from her, she raised her voice, insisting that she had just laid it on the counter in front of me. The other four customers, all white men who were not regular customers (they did not seem to be from the neighborhood), looked around nervously. The other two cashiers, both black, stopped what they were doing and watched the drama unfold.

I restated that I had not taken the money. The prostitute yelled, "I saw you take it! I saw you take it and put it in your pocket!" I angrily denied taking the money, and told her she could come back when the manager was around and watch the store videotape. She yelled again that I took her money; I yelled back, "Pay your bill and get out of here or I'm going to call cops!" She screamed, "Why you gonna call the cops? Did I curse at you? Did I?" as she leaned in through the window of the bulletproof glass enclosure near my register. At this point, the other customers were getting even more nervous. One of the white men in line said, "I really think you should call the cops now."

Perhaps I should have called the cops. But I was too insulted by the idea that she was accusing me of pocketing her money to stop and consider that option. What I did instead surprised even myself: I leaned in toward the woman and shouted, "Get out of my face!" Clearly, she wasn't expecting me to respond like this. She backed away, cursing, as her partner paid her bill. As she was leaving, she shouted back, "You're not even worth it. A white person working in a place like this!" As a clerk, I was relieved to have the potentially explosive incident end; as a sociologist, I was fascinated by her parting shot.

The encounter reflects local attitudes toward working-class whites in a working-class white neighborhood that is surrounded by predominantly black neighborhoods—if you are "a white person working in a place like this," there must be something wrong with you. Being white, and the privileges that often go with it, should have provided for a better job or employment in a better neighborhood. Instead, in the context in which I was working, my white skin served to mark my presumed inferiority, at least in the absence of any other information about me.

METHODS

One of the greatest obstacles to understanding the ways that white Americans understand their racial identity is the politically charged, highly salient nature of race in the United States. The meanings attached to racial identity are difficult for many people to articulate, but the way racial identities play out in everyday interactions between people of different races can have powerful implications for racial relations. For many working-class or poor whites who live in an area with a large black population, the lack of a strong ethnic identification or other available racial identities will facilitate the kind of experience I had working as a clerk in that store—that is, white racial identity as perceived stigma. On the other hand, working-class and poor whites with a strong ethnic identification will be more likely to experience whiteness as a privilege in need of defense. For this reason, the discovery of these meanings depends upon observations in a natural setting over a substantial period of time. Survey studies can help us to understand how people explicitly think about their own and others' whiteness (e.g., Bobo and Massagli 2001). But I am more interested in how whiteness is experienced on an everyday and local level and it is hard to get this kind of information through direct questioning. This is why I chose the method of participant observation in which I worked and lived in various locales, observing the many and varied interactions between people of different races, but without drawing attention to myself as an observer of racial dynamics.

To have maximal observations of white interactions with blacks, I selected as research sites two neighborhoods in Atlanta and Boston that are primarily white but surrounded by largely black areas. The two sites were matched as closely as possible on characteristics such as income, education, occupation, and race but were located in two cities with very different racial compositions and histories of European immigration. Table 15.1 presents the general demographic characteristics of each area, approximated to shield the identification of specific neighborhoods. These three case studies are not presented here as an empirical test of hypotheses; rather, they are used to illustrate general processes influencing the varied experiences of white racial identity that are also evident in the larger literature on the subject.

TABLE 15.1 | **GENERAL DEMOGRAPHIC CHARACTERISTICS**

	White	Black	Median Family Income	Poverty Rate
Holton	80%	10%	$28,000	12%
The Crescent	35%	60%	$18,000	19%
Atlanta	31.1%	67.1%	$25,173	27.3%
Greenfield	85%	10%	$40,000	8%
Greenfield+Surrounding Area	45%	50%	$34,000	12%
Boston	63.0%	25.5%	$34,377	18.7%
Central Appalachia	96.8%	2.2%	$21,982	22.2%
Appalachian Region	90.4%	7.7%	$29,728	11.9%
United States	73.1%	12.0%	$35,225	13.7%

SOURCE | Figures for Boston, Atlanta, and the United States from 1990 U.S. Census; figures for Appalachia from McLaughlin et al. (1999).

While my two research sites shared some important similarities, they also differed in important ways. Atlanta, like much of the South, has not been a major receiving city for European immigrants, and consequently white ethnicities have little visibility. Atlanta is also a majority black city, and blacks have prominent leadership roles in politics and business. It is sharply divided into an affluent, primarily white residential area in the northern half of the city and a low-income, primarily black residential area in the southern half of the city. Boston, on the other hand, is residentially segregated by race but is less clearly divided into racially distinct halves than Atlanta. White ethnicity is also highly visible in Boston, which has historically received large numbers of Irish, Italian, and other European-origin immigrants. Perhaps most significant, blacks are a minority of Boston's population, where politics and business are both white-dominated. Boston has witnessed notorious instances of racial violence, such as the anti-busing riots of the 1970s, while Atlanta is known as "the city too busy to hate" in a region of the country with a long history of racial violence.

In addition to "hanging out" with neighborhood residents in both communities, I also took a job as a convenience store clerk. In this kind of job, I could unobtrusively watch interactions between a large number of whites and blacks going about their daily business. I had the chance to get to know fellow cashiers and regular customers while my apparent status as working class made it easier for local working-class residents to accept me as a peer. Since my co-workers, customers, and neighbors believed I was a cashier rather than a researcher, few whites felt the need to sanction their speech or reactions as they might have if they had known a researcher was observing them. Since most of the people in these two communities were not aware that I was studying them, I have made every effort to protect their confidentiality. None of the actual names of people or places are used, and some minor details are changed. In reporting others' racial identities, I identify a person as "white" or "black" only if she has been unambiguously so designated by herself or other people. In both communities, others always identified me as a "white" person and directed their comments to me as such.

I based the third case study, of the Melungeons in Central Appalachia, on in-depth interviews rather than participant observation. Since the Melungeons illustrate the transcendent experience of racial identity, the self-identified members of this group had already given considered reflection to the issue of race and were often eager to talk about their racial identity; in fact, they had traveled to conventions throughout Central Appalachia to do precisely that. Hence asking Melungeons directly about their experiences with white racial identity was much less problematic than it would have been in Atlanta and Boston.

WHITENESS AS PERCEIVED STIGMA:
THE CRESCENT, GEORGIA

The area in which I lived and worked for five months in Atlanta is a part of the area called "the Crescent"; it consists of three neighborhoods: Holton, Hillcrest, and Spotsville. All of the neighborhoods are predominantly working class with a significant minority of poor and middle-class residents. Holton is almost three-quarters white, while the majority of Spotsville's residents are black; Hillcrest's population is about evenly split between blacks and whites, with a tiny minority of Hispanics (Table 15.1). Interracial contact in the Crescent is frequent, although only a few residential areas are racially mixed. While doing my fieldwork, I lived in Holton and worked in a convenience store near the border between Holton and Spotsville.

Shortly after my arrival in Atlanta, I obtained a job as a clerk in a neighborhood convenience store and in an area department store. This work brought me into contact with a wide variety of people, many of

whom were from the immediate area. As the work was neither ter-
ribly strenuous nor time-consuming, there was plenty of time to talk
with customers, who would often linger in the store. I also formed close
relationships with my co-workers, most of whom were black, and developed friendships with a couple of regular customers (both whites), one
of whom introduced me to a large number of neighborhood residents.
I spoke regularly with my neighbors and was involved in a community
organization, but the vast majority of my data came from my work in
the convenience store.

The store was extremely busy, and a wide range of people would come
through on any given day; while many of the customers were from the
surrounding area, there were also lots of people who frequented the
store because it was near a major highway. These customers tended to
be whites dressed in professional attire and were easily distinguishable
from neighborhood residents. Most of the cashiers were black, although
there was one other white cashier who worked on my shift. In addition,
most of the cashiers were women, although there were three black men
who worked as cashiers, and a white man who did light maintenance
at the store. Vendors who regularly visited the store were mainly white
men, although there was one black woman who worked as a vendor.
Hence there were numerous interracial interactions within the store itself as well as interactions between different social classes.

The experience of whiteness in the Crescent provides an intriguing
example of the ways in which racial cues are bound up with class and the
local context. "White" is typically conceived in terms of economic and
social advantage and residence in predominantly white, affluent areas.
What, then, becomes of the white racial identity of those whites who
are poor or working class and live in an area with a substantial black,
working-class population? I found that being a white person in this type
of neighborhood is a very different experience from being a white person
in a predominantly white area. Whiteness becomes a badge of inferiority—
one that is contingent upon a global view of whites as more deserving of
nice neighborhoods and good jobs than blacks. Both blacks and whites
of various class backgrounds tended to assume that the whites who lived
and worked in the Crescent were somehow defective; that whites living
among large numbers of poor and working-class blacks were somehow
less capable than whites who live in majority white neighborhoods.

The encounter with the prostitute described earlier gave me insight into
the phenomenon of whiteness as a perceived stigma even as it helped solidify my relationship with the other two cashiers, Madge and Telika,

who were working with me that day. Madge is a black woman in her late twenties who has worked at General Fuel for more than a year; Telika is a black woman in her early twenties who has worked at the store since she relocated from the Northeast a year ago. At first, they muttered, "Girl, I can't believe you just did that." Then Telika said, "You can hang with me in my neighborhood anytime." The story was told to the next shift of cashiers (all black) who reacted with surprise to the tale. One of the black women, Jamila (married and in her twenties), stared at me with her jaw dropped when she heard the story; she asked incredulously, "Did you really do that?" When I answered in the affirmative, she and the other cashiers laughed, shaking their heads in disbelief. My co-workers were not surprised by the scam run by the prostitute but rather by my reaction to it—the expected behavior from a white person is to quietly accept the abuse. As I was later to learn, a dominant stereotype of whites in this area, held by blacks as well as many whites themselves, is that whites are weak and submissive.

Because the area has few readily available low-skill jobs and many whites in the area feel that they receive negative treatment, many local whites have come to believe that whites are discriminated against in the hiring process while blacks are favored. Different from the oft-repeated refrains against affirmative action in public discourse, which involve claims about preferential treatment, this perception of anti-white discrimination includes the sense that an unspoken "No Whites Need Apply" policy is in effect for low-skill jobs in the area.

Paradoxically, negative stereotypes of poor and working-class whites who live among blacks has everything to do with the overarching racist paradigm governing urban America. Dead-end jobs, substandard housing, and high crime are associated with black neighborhoods and black people. While most Americans acknowledge the historical existence of blocked opportunities for blacks (especially in the Jim Crow South), an individualist worldview places much of the onus of success and failure upon individual efforts. This, in turn, often leads to cultural explanations of group disadvantage, such as inner-city blacks exhibit a culture of poverty, black men are violent, black women prefer to live off welfare, and so on. Structural explanations of disadvantage for whites or blacks are not a part of the standard American discourse (Bettie 2003). Because whites are not typically thought to exhibit a culture of poverty, cultural explanations based on ideas about groups' differing values fall apart. When cultural explanations are not available, the harshest of judgments about an individual's life circumstance ensue. Working-class white racial identity in the Crescent presents an ironic case of positive group stereotypes serving as a hindrance to disadvantaged members of the dominant racial group.

I discovered that simply having light skin guaranteed few of the privileges I had assumed it would as I attempted to secure employment in the neighborhood I had carefully chosen based on census tract data. Finding a low-paying, low-skill job in the Crescent is difficult regardless of one's race; hiring queues often consist of several dozen people for jobs such as cashier or salesperson. Many of the stores with "Help Wanted" signs in the window are not currently hiring but like to have a set of applications on file due to the high turnover rate in low-skill jobs. My hopes of quickly finding a low-wage retail position began to dwindle after a week of avid searching. I tried different strategies—playing up my previous retail experience and playing down my educational background, for example, yet the results were the same. Then, I responded to an ad for a cashier at a gas station that was a mere five-minute drive from my house; I rushed over early in the morning on the day that the ad appeared and filled out an application. The store was small but clean, with a large enclosure of bulletproof glass surrounding two cash registers. A middle-aged black woman with large scars across her face cheerfully handed me the application form. This time I decided to be honest about my years of schooling, and I wrote a short essay about my academic interest in race relations and my desire to work in a racially diverse environment. I submitted the application to the usual refrain of "We'll call you if we need you," and left disappointed. However, the (white) owner of the store did call two hours later, quizzing me about my desire to work in a racially diverse location. Was I serious about the job? Did I know what kind of neighborhood this was? I managed to convince him of my willingness to work at General Fuel, and he told me to report for work at 6 A.M. the next day. He also mentioned that despite my being "overqualified" for the position, he would have to start me out at "$5.75 . . . just like everybody else. Then we can raise it up. But you have to start the same."

I got this job by means that few residents of the Crescent would be able to match: an unsolicited writing sample led to my being hired. Few applicants for this kind of position would likely attempt such a strategy, given their probable educational background and cultural experience. Even after getting the interview with the owner, I still needed to assure him that I knew what I would be getting into—that the racial composition of the store's workers and customers would not be a problem for me. The fact that the owner was concerned about whether I could adapt to the racial composition of the workplace rather than its class composition, the hazardous nature of the job, or the repetitive and physically demanding qualities that some of the tasks required suggests the salience of race in the local labor market. Employers' suspicions that white job applicants will not work well with black co-workers or customers may make it difficult for low-skilled whites to obtain jobs in predominantly black areas. Only after I explicitly stated that I desired a "racially diverse" workplace did I obtain an interview for such a position.

After I had been working as a cashier at General Fuel for several days, a large, middle-aged white man in work clothes approached me. I was stocking sugar packets near the coffee machine and was out of earshot of the other (black) cashiers who were in the booth with the cash registers. The man leaned over toward me and said, "It sure is good to see you working here." I thanked him and asked him if he came into the store a lot. He told me that he had just moved here and that he worked for "a wrecking company just up the street." I told him that I had also recently moved to Holton (the predominantly white part of the Crescent). He responded, "You know, a lot of white people have applied to work here, and they haven't hired any of them." His positive response to my working at General Fuel had less to do with my ability to efficiently stock sugar packets and more to do with the group I represented: the stigmatized whites of Holton.

Not only did community members perceive anti-white employment discrimination, but also white management explicitly stated their preferences for black employees. Hank, the white owner of the convenience store, and Stephanie, the white manager, both of whom lived outside the city of Atlanta, later told me that they were leery of hiring whites from the neighborhood because they suspected most of them of drug abuse. On one occasion, when Stephanie and I were the only cashiers on duty, she commented after a white male customer had left that "they're not used to seeing only white people in here." She told me that there used to be white men who worked in the store, but they had been fired for one reason or another. I asked if there had ever been white women working in the store. "Sure," she responded, and went on to talk about a white woman who had been employed about a year ago. She was "funny" and "well liked," but turned out to be a crack addict, "but she hid it really well." She and Hank did not find out about her crack habit until she started taking money from the register. Despite her addiction, her bottom teeth were not rotted away, which Stephanie claims is the telltale sign of "being on the pipe." Stephanie related this to a general problem that whites in the area have with drugs.

In contrast, black employees with drug problems were not viewed as representatives of a widespread drug problem among neighborhood blacks. During the course of my employment at the store, two black employees (one male and one female, both in their early twenties) were fired for smoking marijuana while on the job; two more black employees were fired for theft. Hank's only comment about the drug incident involved bemoaning the fact that Max had been such a reliable worker and he hated to lose him over something so stupid. There were no recriminations over the hiring of black employees, no claims that he and Stephanie "should've known better" than to hire a black worker.

In these cases, the negative behavior of one or two members of the local white population can be seen as representative of the group as a whole, while the negative behavior of black workers is seen as reflective of individual failings rather than of behavior that is characteristic of an entire group. Neighborhood residence and social class limit this projection of individual behavior upon the behavior of the group; it is not the case that the entire white population of the United States, Georgia, or even Atlanta is seen as beset by drug problems. Rather, whites living in this specific section of Atlanta are viewed in this way.

Of course, it is possible that whites in this area really are damaged and defective in some way; certainly there are numerous whites in the Crescent who are beset by drug and alcohol problems, mental illness, or substandard living conditions. But that is not the entirety of what I observed. A number of my neighbors in Holton did not fit the image of dysfunction projected upon them. One writes poetry, another does not touch alcohol or drugs for religious reasons, and a third had retired after thirty years with the same company; they are all painfully aware of the stereotypes about residents of Holton, but their lifestyles do not fit these stereotypes. They have stayed in Holton out of a desire to be close to family members, friends, and churches, or because housing is too expensive in other parts of the city. In the words of one middle-aged white woman living in Holton: "It is one of the few places a person without a lot of money could live that wasn't either Section 8 or the projects."

In the Crescent, whites living and/or working in the area are seen as damaged in some way; if they were "real" white people, they would have moved up and out by now. Racial segregation, class inequality, and racial stereotypes create an atmosphere in which whiteness can signify individual failure. In an ironic flip side of the stereotype that blacks belong in service jobs or doing manual labor, the stereotype that stigmatizes whites in the Crescent is the one that dictates that whites should be at least middle class and living in safe neighborhoods. In this way, the overarching racial paradigm in the United States facilitates the function of whiteness as a mark of inferiority in this neighborhood; it is because white skin is associated with privilege and dark skin is not that whites who are not successful are given an especially low status.

Whiteness as a perceived mark of inferiority is generated by the functioning of whiteness as a concomitant of privilege and benefit in the larger society. Americans' lack of a vocabulary for articulating inequality in anything other than race-based terms is the backdrop for white racial identity as perceived stigma. To the extent that low social status, blocked opportunity, decrepit housing, and failing schools are understood in terms of racial configurations and stereotypes rather than class-based, structured inequality, one can expect "whiteness" to be the touchstone for the articulation of the working-class white experience in neighborhoods like "the Crescent" in Atlanta.

WHITENESS AND PRIVILEGE: GREENFIELD, MASSACHUSETTS

I also worked as a convenience store clerk in "Greenfield," a largely white and mainly working-class neighborhood located in a corridor of Boston that is predominantly black. Unlike similar areas in Atlanta, most of the whites in Greenfield identify with a traditional ethnic group, mainly Irish. While most blacks in Atlanta are native-born, a high percentage of blacks in Greenfield identify as West Indian. Over half of the workers in Greenfield are employed in white-collar jobs. Most of these are clerical positions; fewer than 20 percent of adults aged twenty-five or older have received a bachelor's degree. Most adults are employed as clerical or service workers, and the median family income is slightly below the median family income for the city of Boston.

The "Quickie Mart" where I worked as a cashier is located in the middle of a major commercial district in the neighborhood and is more commonly accessed by foot than by car. Consequently, most of the customers I observed and interacted with were local residents. The presence of a lottery machine in the store ensured a steady stream of regular customers, most of whom would stay in the store to scratch their tickets and fill out their bet slips. Both blacks and whites worked as vendors who would visit the store regularly, although all of the other cashiers in the store were white. In contrast to the store in Atlanta, my co-workers were all men when I first started work; a woman was hired about a month after I was.

To the residents of Greenfield, white racial identity means something very different from the burden perceived by the residents of the Crescent. The behaviors and attitudes of the white working-class residents of Greenfield are more in line with those presented in much of the existing literature on whiteness: there is often a sense of superiority and an air of entitlement expressed by whites relative to blacks. At the same time, however, there is also a perception that the community is filled with whites who are "damaged goods." For example, I was told by two of my white male co-workers that I would never find a "stable" man in Greenfield, that everyone is "messed up" in some way.

While there were numerous confrontations between cashiers and customers, none that I either participated in or witnessed involved derision of race or status, although there were plenty of interactions that involved racial stereotyping and accusations of prejudicial treatment. For example, a female Haitian immigrant and a white male clerk had a screaming match about the price of a gallon of milk; after the woman stormed out of the store, the clerk remarked that "it's a cultural thing, they're used to haggling over everything." Unlike at General Fuel, no one at the Quickie Mart derided the clerks for being white and "working in place like this." This is the case despite the objectively worse working conditions of the Quickie Mart; it was frequently dirty, disorganized, and permeated by a foul odor. It paid the same hourly wage as the comparatively sparkling General Fuel, and working there could hardly be considered an elevation in status relative to the Atlanta store. While some conflicts at the Quickie Mart did involve accusations of racism, such as the young black man who accused me of being a racist for not offering him a bag for his milk—bags were never offered for the gallon-sized milk containers—contact never involved asserting someone's worthlessness because he or she is white.

The low-wage labor market in the Boston area is quite different from the job market in Atlanta. While high-wage jobs are difficult to obtain for those without college educations—as they are throughout the country—low-wage jobs are relatively plentiful in the Greenfield neighborhood. The Quickie Mart position was the first job that I applied for, and I was given the job on the spot after being grilled about my background. The manager, "Gus," was a white man in his fifties of Italian and Irish Catholic descent. One of the first questions he asked me after he received my job application was if I had any "street smarts"; I replied that I did and assured him that I wasn't a "pinhead." He said that he didn't want me to "turn Harvard," meaning to become fed up and quit after a couple of weeks. I laughingly assured him that I would not.

When I told him that "the money would be nice, but I'm mainly doing it for the experience," he asked me if my "mommy was rich"; I replied in the negative, and said, "It isn't like that." Gus noted approvingly that I graduated from a Roman Catholic university that has a large Irish and Italian Catholic student body, and mentioned that he had gone to junior high in a predominantly Irish Catholic neighborhood and had taken courses at a Catholic college. Immediately after this he commented that "we [the store employees] are like one family." He then said he'd "give me a shot," finally admonishing me "not to be ashamed of my education." In Atlanta my challenge in getting hired was to prove that I was a researcher unlike the other whites in the neighborhood; in Boston I had to prove that I was like the other "family" members with whom I would be working in the store. When I left the Quickie Mart five months later, my position had yet to be filled despite the posting of a "Help Wanted" sign several weeks earlier.

At the bar across the street from the Quickie Mart, affirmative action was a common topic of conversation. Racial hiring quotas, especially for the fire department and police force, were singled out for special approbation. In their criticisms of affirmative action, the white patrons of the bar voiced familiar arguments: for example, that hiring should be based only on "merit," that affirmative action was inherently unfair, and that such policies did nothing to help relations between the races. In Atlanta, by contrast, I heard only two remarks about affirmative action: one white man was critical of the awarding of construction contracts to a black contractor, while a white police officer praised affirmative action policies and said they were "long overdue."

In comparison with the Atlanta store, whites in the Greenfield store desired more social distance in their interactions with strangers who were black. For example, a black woman who appeared to be in her fifties or sixties was waiting behind a white woman in her thirties who frequently came in to the store with her young son. On this particular day, the boy had been playing with a toy while his mother waited, and after a couple of minutes had dropped the toy near the black woman's feet. This woman apparently did not realize that the toy belonged to the boy and asked me if I would like her to put the toy back where it belonged. As I replied that I could take care of it, the white woman angrily snapped, "That's his toy!" The black woman began apologizing profusely; the white woman merely stared straight ahead with a stony expression on her face. Moments later, the white woman rolled her eyes at me and gestured in the direction of the black woman. The gesture was both disapproving and dismissive, and was directed to me under the assumption that I shared her perspective. The white woman was a regular customer and was typically polite and deferential toward my white co-workers and me.

Several local whites expressed concern about the increasing black presence in the neighborhood. One morning, three older white women came into the otherwise empty store to buy lottery tickets. They had been harassed by several teenagers, some black and some white, who were hanging out in front of the store. One of the women, who was a regular customer, described to me how the young men had treated her and her friends. We chatted a bit about how troublesome the young people were, and she then leaned in toward me, putting her elbows on the counter, and said, "You know, um, Greenfield's getting to be just as bad as Maxwell [a predominantly black neighborhood in Boston that had been predominantly white thirty years ago] and Maxwell Avenue is awful." I nodded without saying anything. She went on, "You know, Greenfield used to not let blacks in at all and now it's turning into Maxwell. It's awful." I made no response, and she quickly added that she lived on Central Avenue [in Greenfield] and that three families, whom she implied were black, had moved in on her street and that they were good people: "You know, one of them was a teacher, another one was a lawn doctor [he worked in landscaping] and they took care of their property." She continued: "You know, I think it's when they own their own property they're good but when they're renters forget about it. They just don't care. They mess the place up, they wreck the places."

In Greenfield, white racial identity confers certain perceived rights and privileges: rights to white schools, white neighborhoods, and white jobs. While these expectations are largely invisible to middle- and upper-class whites, working-class whites in Greenfield are constantly confronted with threats to their accustomed level of segregation and privilege. Day-to-day interactions with blacks highlight the importance of certain privileges to this group of working-class whites, much as affirmative action programs adopted by colleges and universities have laid bare the privileged expectations of more affluent whites.

THE TRANSCENDENCE OF WHITENESS IN SOUTHERN APPALACHIA

Southern Appalachia has long been one of the poorest regions of the United States (Precourt 1983). Unlike those who live in many other areas of the country that have endured long-term struggles with poverty, most of the residents of Appalachia are white. In images ranging from news footage of Lyndon Johnson's visit to the region to promote the War on Poverty to films such as *Deliverance*, the connection between affluence and whiteness is sharply challenged (Jarosz and Lawson 2002). Consequently, residents of Appalachia are aware of the stereotypes that depict them as poor and backward "hillbillies." In the last several years, a curious phenomenon has emerged in southern Appalachia that is gradually transforming the boundaries of "whiteness" in the region. A fascinating counterpart to the relationship between class and whiteness in Atlanta emerges, as stigma and disadvantage are used not as touchstones for negative racial attitudes but instead act as motivating forces behind claims of a nonwhite identity. The stigma of whiteness is managed by displacing whiteness itself rather than by displacing the stigma.

"Melungeons" are a mixed-race group historically thought to have lived in the hills and hollow of eastern Tennessee, southwest Virginia, and eastern Kentucky; the name has been resurrected as an active identity for thousands of Appalachian residents who previously considered themselves white. Melungeons have been a part of Appalachian folklore for centuries. In the 1960s, anthropologist Brewton Berry was unable to locate a single Melungeon for his book *Almost White*, although he was continually assured that he would find them "in the next hollow" (Berry 1969, 16). By the end of the nineteenth century, Melungeons had lost their property and other legal rights after being classified as "free persons of color" by census takers, and over time many tried to pass as white or intermarried with local white and mulatto populations (Elder 1999). Although they are widely considered to be a mix of European, African, and American Indian ancestry, the precise racial background of the group remains unclear.

After the 1994 publication of N. Brent Kennedy's *The Melungeons: The Resurrection of a Proud People*, a regional spotlight was turned on the Melungeons. Kennedy received considerable local press in support of the book, and suddenly thousands of white Appalachians became convinced that they have Melungeon heritage. The Internet became the primary medium for the distribution of information about Melungeons, with several popular Web sites and an e-mail list. The Melungeon Heritage Association, formed in 1998, has sponsored three annual conferences, or "unions," each of which has attracted hundreds of people interested in exploring their Melungeon roots. The Melungeon Heritage Association commissioned a DNA analysis of "Melungeon" hair samples to determine the racial makeup of the group; the results were ambiguous (McGowan 2003).

I attended two of these unions, one held in Wise, Virginia, in May 2000, and the other held in Kingsport, Tennessee, in June 2002. At these gatherings, I interviewed twenty-five attendees about their Melungeon ancestry. I also analyzed Web sites, Internet postings, and newspaper articles involving the explosion of interest in Melungeons. I found that the people who told me the stories of how they had discovered their Melungeon heritage were angry about stereotypes of Appalachia as a backward, impoverished area. An experience of being white yet disadvantaged underlies their embrace of the Melungeon identity. For example, Darlene Wilson, a frequent speaker at Melungeon Unions, claims that "Appalachia is that one place that ain't never gonna get white enough." This phrase, which I heard echoed by other Union attendees, equates "white" with "acceptable" or "privileged." Forsaking one's whiteness for a localized multiracial identity is a means of making sense of a history of victimization. There is little to be proud of in the moniker "white trash" (Hartigan 1997a, 1997b); the Melungeon Pride movement embraces a history of oppression centered on race rather than class.

Among the men I interviewed at the Melungeon Union was the apparently white Aaron, who had light skin, light brown hair, and a light brown beard. He proudly declared his Melungeon identity and discussed his journey from "white" to "Melungeon" in considerable detail. He said that after discovering his Melungeon roots, "I don't know who I'm going to be prejudiced against. All that they were is a part of me." He asserts that everyone has some experience of persecution, implying that none of us should be prejudiced as a result. Like many who embrace a Melungeon identity, Aaron takes special exception to the characterization of Appalachians as poor. Aaron says that most families in Appalachia were Scots-Irish immigrants who wanted to "live in peace" and "get away from folks who wanted to prevent them from doing so." Melungeons, he suggests, have had an even more difficult time in the world than have the descendents of Scots-Irish immigrants, who are stigmatized as poor whites, because the Melungeons were considered "trash people," who experienced prejudice and social exclusion. They fled this persecution by "poor Appalachian folks" by going away from the mainstream to the hills and hollows of Northeast Tennessee, Kentucky, and Virginia. Like many of those involved in the Melungeon Pride movement, Aaron has ambiguous feelings about "poor Appalachian folks." Poor whites in Appalachia have rarely been portrayed as noble suffering victims but are instead often objects of derision, "hillbillies." Aaron identifies poor whites as Melungeons' primary oppressors. In this way, Aaron can express his sense of victimization while distancing himself from a polluted identity. Melungeons are portrayed as the victims of prejudice, driven into isolation by ignorant "whites."

Geneva, now in her early seventies, remembered being teased by other children for having darker skin when she was younger but was never considered to be any race other than white. She recounts a history of discrimination because of her poverty and her Appalachian origins. Her father was a farmer and miner in eastern Kentucky. In 1925 he moved the family to a much poorer area, because, she claims, her father was "trying to get white enough." Geneva describes their new community, also in eastern Kentucky, as a "poor, ignorant place." Like Aaron, Geneva believes that poor whites in the area, whom she remembers as teasing and taunting her, are extremely racist.

Geneva is also angry about stereotypes of Appalachian residents held by people in other parts of the country. When she moved to Ohio, realtors showed her only "dumps" because, she believes, they thought people from Appalachia should expect no better. Her nephew Lonnie, who is in his mid-forties, remembers encountering similar treatment when he moved to Ohio about ten years ago. He was about to sign a lease for a home when the landlord discovered, in conversation, that he was from eastern Kentucky. The landlord quickly decided to pull out of the rental agreement. In response to Lonnie's puzzled queries, the landlord insisted that he did not want any "bird dogs" running around the place, tearing up the yard. Lonnie claims that this is a common stereotype of people from Appalachia—that they own "bird dogs" and do not take care of their homes and yards.

Both Lonnie and Geneva beam with pride when discussing their Melungeon roots. When I asked Lonnie whether discovering his mixed-race background bothered him at all, he promptly responded, "Being bald bothers me more than being dark." Proudly claiming to have black ancestry is not usual behavior for whites anywhere, especially poor and working-class whites in the South. However, because others treat Lonnie as if he is white, his Melungeon identity poses little risk to him in his day-to-day life, having more of the character of the "optional" ethnic identity that Waters (1990) describes among middle-class suburbanites.

Rhonda expresses some of the trepidation a person socially considered to be "white" might experience when she believes she has discovered nonwhite ancestry. She described her first reaction to the discovery of her Melungeon roots as "fear." She lived in Norton, Virginia, which had a nearby Melungeon community on Stony Mountain; members of the community were "set apart and persecuted" and were referred to by other whites as "Stony Mountain Ramps." There was a "stigma" attached to them. However, as Rhonda learned the history of Melungeons (primarily from N. Brent Kennedy, a childhood friend and leader of the Melungeon revival), she "gained enlightenment," and felt that there was no shame in being Melungeon.

Rhonda's biography had elements in common with most of the stories of the people I interviewed at the Melungeon Union. Other whites discriminated against her because of her "Appalachian" residence, leading her to feel not white enough. As a musician who often played at "rough" bars in the mountains, she expressed admiration for the music of blacks ("they've got soul") as well as for the strong, silent Melungeons who would protect her and her bandmates as they left the bars. She said she felt very honored to be a member of the group. Less honorable, however, is being simply a white Appalachian. Rhonda described attending a job-related conference in Atlanta where she claims that she was "constantly teased for being from the mountains." For example, an executive running a large meeting jokingly prefaced information with comments such as, "This applies to everyone but Rhonda from southeastern Virginia" (implying she would not understand detailed information), which was met with raucous laughter by the other attendees.

Two middle-aged sisters from central Virginia illustrate an exception to the whole-hearted embracement of mixed-race identity. They view researching their Melungeon heritage as a "fun" activity and base their Melungeon connection upon their mother's maiden name rather than upon their own physical appearance or that of relatives. When I asked if they consider themselves to be anything other than "white," they were taken aback. They nervously laughed, and both replied that they were still white. As they were the first to have responded to my question this way—the other self-identified Melungeons I talked with no longer consider themselves to be white—I asked about their experience growing up in Appalachia. The older sister stated that they did not, in fact, originate from Appalachia; rather, their mother's family hailed from southwestern Virginia. They "enjoy the foods and music" of Appalachia but do not consider themselves to be Appalachian; consequently, they have no instances of discrimination to report.

These sisters provide an exception that supports the connection I have identified between people's personal histories as stigmatized (white)

Appalachians and their desire to abandon whiteness in exchange for a nonwhite identity. In the words of Bill Fields, a speaker at the Melungeon Union in Wise, Virginia, "We're all part of something much larger than any one particular background. People who were raised white can look at their background and see some African there. They are redefining white, making it a large continuum."

True transcendence of white identity is likely quite uncommon. Because there are very few blacks in southern Appalachia to take notice, the Melungeons' attempts at transcendence elicit little criticism from blacks who might be offended at blithe associations with their own historical oppression. While the popularity of Melungeon identity in some respects reflects the process of "ethnic renewal" among adults claiming American Indian ancestry (Nagel 1995), it differs because most Melungeons seek no material rewards as a result of their racial status. The Melungeons are not, nor are they likely to be, a federally recognized tribe, and many of those claiming Melungeon ancestry are older adults already well established in their occupations and unlikely to obtain any resources for claiming to be partly black.

CONCLUSION

White identity is dominant in the American racial paradigm, as the benefits of whiteness are evident in a number of socioeconomic and health measures (Hayward et al. 2000; Hughes and Thomas 1998). Thus, white racial identity—or "whiteness"—has been defined and discussed largely in terms of its privilege and invisibility (Frankenberg 1993, 2001). While variations in the experience, meanings, and content of white racial identity are often acknowledged (Delgado and Stefancic 1997), there has been little systematic analysis of the causes or forms of these variations.

The three examples discussed in this chapter of Melungeons, whites in Boston, and whites in Atlanta serve to illustrate that white racial identity is not an individual attribute but instead is experienced in one of three primary ways: as stigma, privilege, or an identity to be transcended. These three categories of experience reflect different spatial arrangements— white racial identity experienced as stigma in one setting could be experienced as privilege in a different time and place. Moreover, the same person can experience all three types of white racial identity, depending on the context. For example, an individual might experience white racial identity as a stigmatized identity at the local level but as a privileged identity when the nation is the frame of reference (Delaney 2002). Each of these ways of experiencing white racial identity is more or less likely to occur given the existence of a constellation of social structural factors (Table 15.2).

White racial identity as an experience of privilege clearly corresponds with whites' status as the dominant group in the American racial landscape. Nonetheless, the privilege of whiteness can take several different forms, each emphasized by different literatures on the white racial experience. The defensive expression of white privilege is the form that has been the primary focus of past research, as with the working-class whites in Boston, who experience whiteness as a tenuous privilege that must be defended in neighborhoods, schools, and jobs. On the other hand, white racial identity is almost invisible to many whites. This unremarked experience of white privilege is a dominant theme in the whiteness studies literature. White nationalism or separatism, while sharing some characteristics with defensive white privilege, is much more aggressive and overtly hostile in its policing of the boundaries of white racial identity. Those who have been mobilized by such movements are, one might argue, offensively white. Regardless of the experience of whiteness, each understanding of white racial identity presented in Table 15.2 reflects an overarching racial hierarchy in which whites are dominant and nonwhites are subordinate. It is important to note that white racial identity is a stigma for some whites a portion of the time only because the expectations for whites—that they be materially advantaged and live apart from blacks—are not met. White racial identity is transcended when the status threat of identifying with nonwhiteness is diminished or nonexistent.

Despite similar socioeconomic backgrounds, whites in Appalachia, whites in the Crescent in Atlanta, and whites in Greenfield in Boston

TABLE 15.2 | **FACTORS INFLUENCING EXPERIENCE OF WHITE RACIAL IDENTITY**

	Large Black Population	Other Available Racial Identities	High Socioeconomic Status	Strong Ethnic Identification
Perceived Stigma	Yes	No	No	No
Defensive Privilege	N/A	No	No	Yes
Colorblind Privilege	N/A	No	Yes	N/A
Offensive Privilege	No	No	No	No
Transcendence	No	Yes	No	No

have very different understandings of their own racial identities. These different perceptions reflect the combination of racial composition and the history of class and race relations. In Appalachia, blacks are less than 10 percent of the population; they comprise only 2 percent of the population in central Appalachia (McLaughlin et al. 1999). Appalachia has long been represented to the nation as a whole as a region of white poverty and ignorance, while Atlanta, like many urban centers, has been portrayed as home to affluent whites and poor blacks. For Atlanta whites, adopting a nonwhite identity would imply an acceptance of inferior social status, but doing so enables residents of Appalachia to think of themselves as victims of racial oppression rather than as ignorant poor people.

The attitudes of many working-class whites in both Boston and Atlanta can be characterized as "racist" in some respects, but the character and manifestations of these attitudes is quite different in the two areas. White ethnic consciousness and conflict has played a much larger role in Boston than in Atlanta. In Boston, blacks are a small percentage of the overall metropolitan population; their presence in the government and business elite of the city has paled in comparison to their numerical, political, and economic strength in the Atlanta metropolitan area. Ethnic self-identification was also much more frequent and fervent in Boston. There were only two occasions on which whites in Atlanta referred to themselves as belonging to any ethnic group other than white; these both involved discussions of Cherokee heritage.

Additionally, working-class movements, especially labor unions, have had a dramatically larger presence in Boston. While racial conflicts have been a significant problem for both cities, class-consciousness has been a prominent feature of Boston rather than Atlanta. Whites in Greenfield described with pride their childhoods in housing projects, the long and hard working days of their fathers, and the discrimination against their parents by the "Yankee" business owners. Conversely, whites in the Crescent typically avoided discussions of humble origins. "White trash" was a commonly heard epithet in Greenfield but rarely used in the Crescent. Paradoxically, the success of working-class (often racially exclusive) movements coupled with the overwhelming white majority in the Boston area may have lent an air of superiority to the whites in Greenfield relative to blacks. In the Boston area, there are material gains to protect; in Atlanta, poor and working-class whites see less of the payoff of having white skin.

Most whites in the Crescent and in Appalachia believe that they have not reaped the benefits of whiteness and that white skin can actually be a liability. While the whites in the Crescent are certainly not free of racist attitudes, the expressions of racial animosity in the Crescent tend more commonly to be motivated by defensiveness rather than an assertion of rights or superiority. Conversely, whites in Appalachia reject whiteness in favor of a nonwhite identity. They reinterpret their history of negative experiences as generated by their racial origins rather than their class origins. The notion that they "could never be white enough" succinctly addresses this point.

As increasing class polarization occurs in both the white and black communities, the paradoxical negative effects of being white in a poor neighborhood in a predominantly black city may be more frequently observed. Hartigan (1999), for example, finds that many Detroit residents, both white and black, hold poor inner-city whites in low esteem. The dramatic growth of the Melungeon Pride movement in Appalachia signals a different reaction to the perceived stigma of whiteness, one that has the potential to change the boundaries and meanings of white racial identity.

Types of white identity have different implications for race relations. For example, when whiteness is experienced as privilege, conflict between white and nonwhite groups is most likely to occur (Shanahan and Olzak 1999). Consequently, it is important to identify different experiences of white racial identity as a means of creating social and political interventions that appeal to the circumstances and understandings of different groups of whites. While historical narratives of the unique struggles (and successes) of African Americans might appeal to the sensibilities of whites who experience their racial identity as a privileged one, whites who experience their identity as a stigma are more likely to respond positively to an articulation of the similarities between class inequality and racial inequality.

Considering white racial identity as neither a fixed construct nor as a constantly changing state of mind but rather as a set of dynamic yet patterned social experiences and interactions can help in understanding the connections between identity and context. The three experiences of white racial identity explored here can be thought to exist as "dynamic equilibria" (White 1992) resulting from processes of interaction and racial awareness that occur repeatedly in similar ways. Considering white racial identity as stigma, privilege, or a transcendent status can be a first step in clarifying predictors of prejudice and racial conflict.

Bibliography

•

Berry, Brewton. 1969. *Almost White*. London: Collier-Macmillan.

Bettie, Julie. 2003. *Women without Class: Girls, Race and Identity*. Berkeley: University of California Press.

Billings, Dwight B., Gurney Norman, and Katherine Ledford, eds. 1999. *Confronting Appalachian Stereotypes: Back Talk from an American Region*. Lexington: University Press of Kentucky.

Bobo, Lawrence D. and Michael P. Massagli. 2001. Stereotyping and Urban Inequality. In *Urban Inequality: Evidence from Four Cities*, ed. Alice O'Connor, Chris Tilly, and Lawrence D. Bobo, 89–162. New York: Russell Sage Foundation.

Brodkin, Karen. 1998. *How Jews Became White Folks and What That Says about Race in America*. New Brunswick, NJ: Rutgers University Press.

Delaney, D. 2002. The Space that Race Makes. *Professional Geographer* 54:6–14.

Delgado, Richard and Jean Stefancic, eds. 1997. *Critical White Studies: Looking behind the Mirror*. Philadelphia: Temple University Press.

Elder, Pat Spurlock. 1999. *Melungeons: Examining an Appalachian Legend*. Blountville, TN: Continuity Press.

Finlay, Nikki McIntyre. 2000. Finding Work in Atlanta: Is There an Optimal Strategy for Disadvantaged Job Seekers? In *The Atlanta Paradox*, ed. David Sjoquist, 217–243. New York: Russell Sage Foundation.

Frankenberg, Ruth. 1993. *White Women, Race Matters: The Social Construction of Whiteness*. Minneapolis: University of Minnesota Press.

———. 2001. "Mirage of an Unmarked Whiteness." In *The Making and Unmaking of Whiteness*, ed. Birgit Brander Rasmussen, Eric Klinenberg, Irene J. Nexica, and Matt Wray, 72–96. Durham, NC: Duke University Press.

Hartigan, John, Jr. 1997a. Establishing the Fact of Whiteness. *American Anthropologist* 99:495–505.

———. 1997b. Unpopular Culture: The Case of "White Trash." *Cultural Studies* 11:316–343.

———. 1999. *Racial Situations: Class Predicaments of Whiteness in Detroit*. Princeton, NJ: Princeton University Press.

Hayward, Mark D., Eileen M. Crimmins, Toni P. Miles, and Yu Yang. 2000. The Significance of Socioeconomic Status in Explaining the Racial Gap in Chronic Health Conditions. *American Sociological Review* 65:910–930.

Hughes, Michael and Melvin E. Thomas. 1998. The Continuing Significance of Race Revisited: A Study of Race, Class, and Quality of Life in America, 1972 to 1996. *American Sociological Review* 63:785–795.

Ignatiev, Noel, and John Garvey, eds. 1996. *Race Traitor*. New York: Routledge.

Jarosz, L., and V. Lawson. 2002. "Sophisticated People versus Rednecks": Economic Restructuring and Class Difference in America's West. *Antipode* 34:8–27.

Kennedy, N. Brent. 1994. *The Melungeons: The Resurrection of a Proud People: An Untold Story of Ethnic Cleansing in America*. Mercer, GA: Mercer University Press.

McDermott, Monica. 2006. *Working-Class White: The Making and Unmaking of Race Relations*. Berkeley: University of California Press.

McGowan, Kathleen. 2003. Where Do We Come From? The Melungeons, Who Count Elvis Presley and Abraham Lincoln among Their Kin, Turn to DNA Genealogy to Resolve a Longstanding Identity Crisis. *Discover* 24 (May): 58–63.

McLaughlin, Diane K., Daniel T. Lichter, and Stephen A. Matthews with Glynis Daniels and James Cameron. 1999. Demographic Diversity and Economic Change in Appalachia. Prepared for the Appalachian Regional Commission.

Merrick, Margaret. 2000. The Melungeon Heritage. *The Berea Alumnus*. Spring.

Nagel, Joane. 1995. American Indian Ethnic Renewal: Politics and the Resurgence of Identity. *American Sociological Review* 60:947–965.

O'Brien, Eileen. 2001. *Whites Confront Racism: Antiracists and Their Paths to Action*. Lanham, MD: Rowman and Littlefield.

Precourt, Walter. 1983. The Image of Appalachian Poverty. In *Appalachia and America: Autonomy and Regional Dependence*, ed. Allen Batteau, 86–110. Lexington: University Press of Kentucky.

Schuman, Howard, Charlotte Steeh, Lawrence Bobo, and Maria Krysan. 1997. *Racial Attitudes in America*. Cambridge, MA: Harvard University Press.

Shanahan S., and S. Olzak. 1999. The Effects of Immigrant Diversity and Ethnic Competition on Collective Conflict in Urban America: An Assessment of Two Moments of Mass Migration, 1869–1924 and 1965–1993. *Journal of American Ethnic History* 18(3):30–64.

Waters, Mary C. 1990. *Ethnic Options: Choosing Identities in America*. Berkeley: University of California Press.

White, Harrison. 1992. *Identity and Control*. Princeton, NJ: Princeton University Press.

Wildman, Stephanie M., and Adrienne D. Davis. 1996. *Making Systems of Privilege Visible: How Invisible Preference Undermines America*. New York: New York University Press.

Winant, Howard. 2001. White Racial Projects. In *The Making and Unmaking of Whiteness*, ed. Birgit Brander Rasmussen, Eric Klinenberg, Irene J. Nexica, and Matt Wray, 97–112. Durham, NC: Duke University Press.

16

Enduring Racial Associations
African Americans, Crime, and Animal Imagery

Jennifer L. Eberhardt

•

This essay examines two common racial associations in contemporary U.S. society: the association of blacks with crime and the association of blacks with animals. A series of social psychological studies are presented that document the pervasiveness of such associations and that demonstrate their power to influence basic psychological functions—perception, attention, memory, and judgment. I emphasize the potentially powerful negative consequences of these associations for criminal justice as well as for everyday social interactions.

I HAVE HAD THE OPPORTUNITY TO LISTEN TO MY THREE GREAT AUNTS TELL the story of how we acquired the Eberhardt family name. Their grandfather and his two brothers were slaves in Hartwell, Georgia. At some point, each of them was sold off to a different slaveowner. Each of them had a first name only and when slavery ended, they all took on the family name of their previous slaveowner. One took the name Fitten. One took the name Herd. And my great-great-grandfather took the name Eberhardt. We lost contact with the Fittens and Herds soon after slavery. The Eberhardts remained in Hartwell as sharecroppers. And in the early 1920s, York Eberhardt, my great-grandfather, decided to head north to Cleveland—to escape the daily reminders of a slave past.

My husband's family left Georgia at about the same time for the same city, but for a different reason. His father's older brother, then a teenager, made the mistake of wearing a new suit into the southern town near where they lived. A white boy said to him, "Who is the nigger in the new suit?" as he smashed an ice cream onto his lapel. The chain of events after that is sketchy, but my husband's father remembered running behind his big brother, carrying the shells that his brother loaded into and emptied from his shotgun to ward off the white boys who had pursued him back to their house. Fearful of a mob, and of a sheriff more likely to treat him as criminal than as victim, my husband's uncle that night boarded a train north, and the entire family soon followed. Whatever they couldn't carry, they left behind. The uncle's youthful desire to show off his new suit violated the etiquette of the southern racial hierarchy and demanded the defection of his entire family from the only home they had ever known.

My children are the descendents of these African Americans. They are just a few generations removed from people who were enslaved, dehumanized, criminalized. Yet, they will mature in a society that has been profoundly transformed, socially and legally. They may take for granted events that my great-aunts never thought they would live to see—a black man becoming president of the United States and a black woman, herself a lawyer as well as a descendent of slaves, becoming the nation's first lady. Such events have led some to believe that we are now living in post-race America, free from subjugation and racial bias.

In this essay, however, I focus on powerful racial associations involving African Americans that continue to subjugate. First, I discuss social psychological research designed to examine the association of blacks with crime. Next, I examine an association with deep historical roots but which many assume dissipated generations ago—the association of blacks with animals. Well into the twenty-first century, my colleagues and I are finding that African Americans continue to be dehumanized. They continue to be perceived as apelike. And such associations can lead to terrible consequences in the context of criminal justice.

My purpose in this essay is not to document the history of these cultural associations across time but to understand the impact of that history on our psyches. I am a social psychologist. I study how social and cultural factors influence human perception and behavior. In a series of tightly controlled laboratory studies, I provide here examples of how racial associations can alter basic psychological functioning and can do so in ways that are beyond our immediate awareness and in spite of our egalitarian desires.

THE CRIMINAL

Let us begin with the association of blacks with crime. Of course, there are many factors that influence this association. For instance, the stereotype of blacks as hostile, dangerous, or criminal is one of the strongest stereotypes of blacks in American society (Devine and Elliot 1995). It shows up in study after study. And although not everyone endorses the stereotype, nearly everyone knows of its existence in our society. Other factors are sociostructural. Crime statistics, for instance, certainly contribute to an association of race and crime. Black males, in particular, are grossly overrepresented in prisons and in jails relative to their numbers in the population (Western 2006). And such disparities have not escaped the popular press; they appear repeatedly in news reports throughout the nation. So we have stereotypic beliefs and we have intense racial stratification working together to support and strengthen the association between blacks and crime.

In the first part of this essay, I introduce studies designed to explore how the black-crime association influences cognitive processes. I highlight various points in the criminal justice system—from the very first encounter police officers have with a suspect to the sentences that jurors deliver—and I suggest that at each point, the black-crime association influences how we think, how we reason, and how we literally "see."

Weapon Detection

How might the black-crime association influence how we see, and why might this be important? One might imagine that this association could be quite important in the context of policing. In many officer-involved shootings, for example, officers must determine whether they believe a weapon is present, and based on this assessment, decide whether to shoot. The association of blacks with crime might lead laypeople and police officers alike to more quickly detect a gun in the hands of a black person than a white person, even when the image of that gun appears blurry to them. Moreover, the speed and ease with which they recognize the gun might further strengthen the association of blacks with crime. In the first study I introduce, my colleagues and I asked the question: Can simple exposure to black faces lead people to see weapons better? Is the association between blacks and crime so strong that it can literally guide our vision? To investigate this question, my colleagues and I (Eberhardt, Goff, Purdie, and Davies 2004) brought white male college students into the laboratory to participate in a study that involved performing two, supposedly unrelated, tasks. For the first task, study participants were seated at a computer screen and they saw a focus dot appear at the center. They then saw flashes of light appear around that focus dot. Their goal was to indicate, by pushing a button, on which side of the computer screen each flash of light appeared, and to do this as quickly as possible. Now, these flashes were actually the faces of young men that were appearing on the screen at such a rapid rate that the participants could not consciously detect them. Exposing people to images that are beneath their conscious awareness is called subliminal priming. It is a standard technique that has been used in both social and cognitive psychology for decades. We used this subliminal priming procedure to expose participants to an entire series of black male faces, to an entire series of white male faces, or to no faces at all (i.e., to blurred images that looked like abstract art).

After this priming procedure, we asked participants to perform an object recognition task—a task that participants were told was unrelated to the priming task. For this task, all of the participants were presented with a series of objects that were severely degraded (see Figure 16.1). These objects appeared on the computer screen one at a time, and each object was slowly brought into focus (in a series of forty-one steps or frames). The participants' goal was to indicate by pushing a button the point at which they could recognize what each object was. Some of these

FIGURE 16.1 | **EXAMPLES OF DEGRADED IMAGES USED IN STUDY.**

The 41-frame continuum began with the most degraded image (frame 1) and ended with the least degraded image (frame 41).

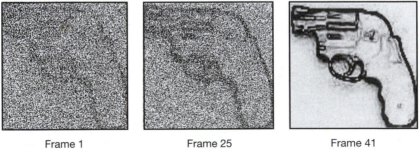

Frame 1   Frame 25   Frame 41

SOURCE | Eberhardt et al. 2004.

objects were related to crime (e.g., guns and knives) and some were not (e.g., staplers and cameras).

As predicted, we found that exposing participants to the faces beforehand did not influence the number of frames they needed to accurately identify the crime-irrelevant objects. However, initial exposure to black faces beforehand drastically reduced the perceptual threshold at which the participants could accurately recognize the crime objects (see Figure 16.2). All of a sudden, they needed less information (i.e., fewer frames) to recognize that they were being shown a gun or a knife. In contrast, those participants who had been initially exposed to the white faces beforehand needed more information (i.e., more frames) to recognize that they were being shown guns and knives. In sum, exposure to black faces facilitated the detection of crime objects whereas exposure to white faces inhibited the detection of those very same objects. These findings reveal that when people see black faces or think "black people," they are also immediately thinking "crime." The argument is that this explains why the participants in our study who had been primed with black faces were able to quickly determine that the blurry image was a gun.

Racial Profiling

My collaborators and I extended this research by examining the same association with different questions mind: When people think about crime,

FIGURE 16.2 | **WEAPON DETECTION RESULTS.**

Weapon detection differs for those previously exposed to white faces, no faces, or black faces.

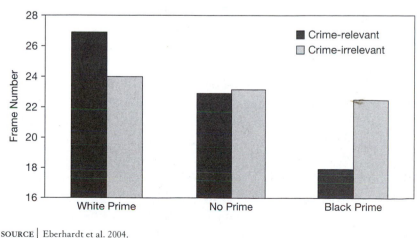

SOURCE | Eberhardt et al. 2004.

do they think about black people? Does thinking about crime draw attention to black Americans? Perhaps under these conditions, blacks are more likely than whites to be placed under surveillance. In a study intended to investigate this issue, my collaborators and I invited white male undergraduates into the laboratory. This time, half of these student participants were subliminally primed with crime-relevant images on a computer screen. (We exposed these students to crime images to get them to think about crime.) Next, the students were asked to complete a dot probe task. For the dot probe task, the students saw a black face and a white face appear on the computer screen simultaneously. These faces disappeared. A dot then appeared where one of the faces used to be. The study participants were then asked to locate the dot as quickly as possible on the computer screen. When the dot was in a location near the black face, we expected participants who had been initially exposed to the crime images to be faster at finding the dot than participants who had not been exposed to these crime images. The idea is that once we get people to think about crime, they will begin to look at the black face. The speed with which they found the dot was used as a proxy for where they were looking. If they found the dot faster when it was placed near the black face, for example, then it is likely that they were focusing their attention on the black face.

Here is what we found. When the dot was placed near the black face, the student participants found that dot much faster when they were primed to think of crime than when they were not primed. That is, when the students were primed to think of crime they were much more likely to look at the black face. So simply exposing participants to guns and knives did indeed place black male faces under surveillance (see Figure 16.3a). As suspected, this pattern did not emerge for those primed with white faces.

We then repeated this study with police officers (Eberhardt et al. 2004) to shed light on a basic question: When police officers are on the lookout for criminal activity—when they are thinking about violent crime—are they more inclined to focus on a black face than a white face? Indeed, this question is at the heart of the debate on racial profiling. To investigate this, we chose a method that was quite similar to the one in the study we conducted with students. But in this case we primed half of the police officers with words associated with violent crime rather than crime images. On a computer screen, we subliminally exposed these officers to words like "arrest," "apprehend," "capture," "shoot." And, as suspected, the pattern of results is identical to what we observed with students (see Figure 16.3b). When police officers are thinking of capturing, arresting, or shooting, they are drawn to the black face.

FIGURE 16.3a | **COLLEGE STUDENT RESULTS.**

Those previously exposed to crime objects are more likely to look at the black faces (i.e., they are faster to locate the dot near the black face) than those not exposed to crime objects.

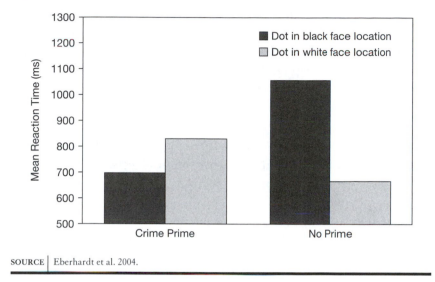

SOURCE | Eberhardt et al. 2004.

FIGURE 16.3b | **POLICE OFFICER RESULTS.**

Police officers were also more likely to look at black faces after being exposed to crime objects than when they were not exposed to crime objects.

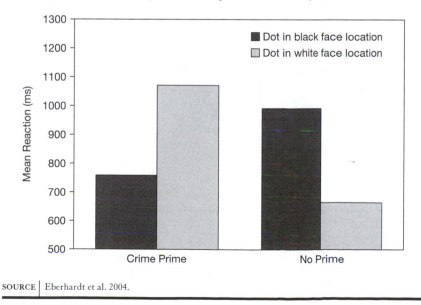

SOURCE | Eberhardt et al. 2004.

False Identification

At the very end of the police officer study, we took the officers through a surprise face identification task. We presented them with a black lineup and a white lineup and we asked them to pick out the faces they were shown earlier in the study. A picture of the black lineup is shown in Figure 16.4. The fourth person in this lineup was actually the target face they were shown earlier in the study. Two of the faces were placed in the lineup because they were judged (by a separate group of study participants) to be more stereotypically black than the target. These are Faces 2 and 3. Faces 1 and 5 were placed in the lineup because they were judged to be less stereotypically black than the target face.[1]

We found that officers made about the same number of errors on this task, regardless of their initial exposure to crime objects. However, when officers who were exposed to the crime-relevant words made an error on this task, they were likely to recall seeing a more stereotypically black face than they actually did. That is, when they were prompted to think about capturing, arresting, and shooting, and they made an error—they thought they saw Face 3 or they thought they saw Face 2. These results

---

FIGURE 16.4 | **A LINEUP OF BLACK FACES RANGING IN THEIR PERCEIVED STEREOTYPICALITY.**

These faces vary on how stereotypically black they are perceived to be—e.g., Face 3 is considered most stereotypical, while Face 5 is seen as least stereotypical.

| 1 | 2 | 3 | 4 | 5 |

SOURCE | Eberhardt et al. 2004.

---

1 We allowed this separate group of participants to make judgments of stereotypicality using any physical features they wished (e.g., skin color, lip thickness, nose width, hair texture). Despite these liberal instructions, study participants were in high agreement about which faces were more or less stereotypical.

could have implications for the choice of whom police officers approach and stop on the street—even when they are acting on the basis of suspect descriptions. Black people who appear most stereotypically black may be most vulnerable to stops and searches. These results could have implications for eyewitness testimony as well. Black people who appear most stereotypically black may be the most vulnerable to false identifications in real lineups—even when the actual suspect is present in the lineup.

Death Sentencing

Results like these could even have implications for sentencing decisions. When jurors are deciding whether to sentence someone to death, they are deciding, in part, about what punishment is sufficient to "right the wrong" that has been committed. They are deciding on what type of payback would be just. This "just deserts" perspective on punishment has been with us for centuries. In fact it is well represented in the work of the eighteenth-century philosopher Immanuel Kant (1797/2002). In his writing, Kant tells us that "punishment should be pronounced over all criminals, proportionate to their internal wickedness." In our research, we asked the question: Could the physical features that mark race be a proxy for internal wickedness? And if so, are black defendants who look more stereotypically black more likely to be perceived as wicked and punished accordingly? An overlooked factor in understanding how the death penalty is decided upon may have to do with Kant's notion of internal wickedness. Perhaps still today, American citizens look upon a black face, use the blackness of his physical features as a proxy for internal wickedness, and decide to punish accordingly.

I examined this issue in a study with Paul Davies, Valerie Purdie-Vaughns, and Sheri Johnson (Eberhardt, Davies, Purdie-Vaughns, and Johnson 2006). We used a large dataset of defendants that was constructed by David Baldus and colleagues (Baldus, Woodworth, Zuckerman, Weiner, and Broffitt 1998). This dataset contained over 600 defendants who were charged with crimes that occurred in Philadelphia, Pennsylvania, between 1979 and 1999. We examined the cases only involving black defendants who were convicted of crimes for which they were eligible for a death sentence. We gave the photographs of these black defendants to naïve study participants, who rated each defendant's face on how stereotypically black it appeared to them. The study participants had no idea that these were the faces of convicted criminals. They did not know how we located the faces. They simply looked at each face and rated it on stereotypicality. We were interested in whether these stereotypicality ratings, nevertheless, would be related to the actual decisions jurors made in sentencing defendants to life or death.

We found that for black defendants who were convicted of killing black victims, how stereotypically black the defendant appeared was not related to sentencing decisions (Figure 16.5a). Black defendants who were high in stereotypicality were sentenced to death at exactly the same rate as black defendants who were low in stereotypicality. However, we found that for black defendants who were convicted of killing white victims, there was a huge stereotypicality effect (Figure 16.5b). Looking "more black" more than doubled their chances of receiving a death sentence. This effect was significant even though my collaborators and I controlled for factors like aggravators (e.g., the defendant's prior convictions), mitigators (e.g., the defendant's impaired ability to appreciate the criminality of his conduct), the severity of the crime, the victim's socioeconomic status, the defendant's socioeconomic status, and the defendant's attractiveness. Despite taking into account all of these variables, black defendants appeared to be punished in proportion to the blackness of their physical features. Black defendants who were perceived to be more stereotypically black were perceived to be more deathworthy than black defendants who were perceived to be less stereotypically black.

FIGURE 16.5a | **DEATH SENTENCING RATES FOR DEFENDANTS PERCEIVED AS HIGH OR LOW ON STEREOTYPICALITY WHO WERE CONVICTED OF KILLING BLACKS.**

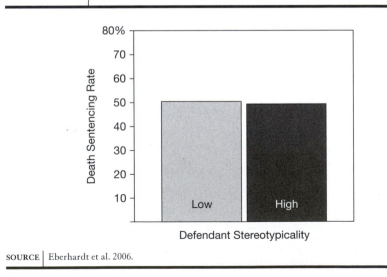

SOURCE | Eberhardt et al. 2006.

FIGURE 16.5b | **DEATH SENTENCING RATES FOR DEFENDANTS PERCEIVED AS HIGH OR LOW ON STEREOTYPICALITY WHO WERE CONVICTED OF KILLING WHITES.**

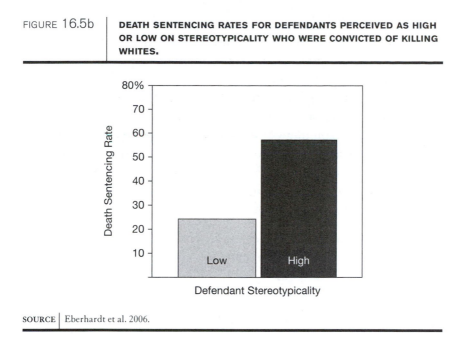

Defendant Stereotypicality

SOURCE | Eberhardt et al. 2006.

Our results resonate with decades of research demonstrating that convicted criminals are more likely to be sentenced to death when their victims are white than when their victims are black. Might the internal wickedness of the defendants matter most when the victims are most worthy of saving? Perhaps these results underscore how people continue to value the lives of whites more than the lives of blacks. In the second part of this essay, I present studies designed to look at the most extreme form of black devaluation. I argue that black people are not only viewed as more criminal but as somehow less human than whites.

THE APE

For centuries, blacks have fought to be recognized as fully human. This is a battle that has occupied the minds of some of the most influential black scholars of all time. In fact, W. E. B. Du Bois writes about this very issue in the foreword to his classic book *Black Reconstruction*:

> It would be only fair to the reader to say frankly in advance that the attitude of any person toward this story will be distinctly influenced by his theories of the Negro race. If he believes the Negro in America and in general is an average and ordinary human being, who under given environment develops like other human beings,

then he will read this story and judge it by the facts adduced. If, however, he regards the Negro as a distinctly inferior creation, who can never successfully take part in modern civilization and whose emancipation and enfranchisement were gestures against nature, then he will need something more than the sort of facts I have set down. But this latter person, I am not trying to convince. I am simply pointing out these two points of view, so obvious to Americans, and then without further ado, I am assuming the truth of the first. In fine, I am going to tell this story as though Negroes were ordinary human beings, realizing that this attitude will from the first seriously curtail my audience. (1935)

From slavery through emancipation, blacks have fought to be regarded, not in that in-between status—somewhere between ape and human—but to be fully human. This is an old battle, one of which people claim little knowledge, let alone discuss openly. In fact, in one study, Phillip Goff, Melissa Williams, Matthew Jackson, and I (Goff, Eberhardt, Williams, and Jackson 2008) asked college students to tell us what social group has been associated with apes. Most claimed no knowledge that blacks have been associated with apes. When we asked them to tell us what animals have been associated with African Americans, again, most claimed no knowledge of an association between blacks and apes. In fact, in none of our initial studies did people express knowledge of a stereotypic association between African Americans and apes. Yet in study after study, my colleagues and I were finding that people still today make this association. And this association alters how blacks are seen and treated in the modern world.

Ape Detection

We began to test for the presence of the association by using some of the same paradigms I discussed in part one of this essay. In one study, for example, we subliminally primed participants with faces. Immediately following this subliminal priming procedure, we presented participants with a series of images that were severely degraded. This time, all of the images were animals. Some were apes, and some were non-apes (e.g., alligators, squirrels, and elephants).

What did we find? Exposing people to black faces or white faces did not influence their ability to detect the non-ape images (see Figure 16.6). In contrast, brief exposure to the black faces had a huge effect on participants' ability to detect the ape images. Participants who were exposed

FIGURE 16.6 | **ANIMAL DETECTION RESULTS.**

Animal detection differs for those previously exposed to white faces, no faces, or black faces.

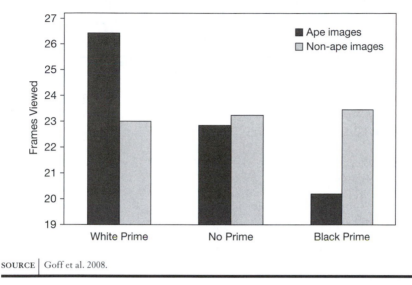

SOURCE | Goff et al. 2008.

to the black faces beforehand needed a lot less information (i.e., fewer frames) to determine that the ape images were indeed apes. Exposure to black faces facilitated the detection of these ape images, whereas exposure to white faces inhibited the detection of these very same ape images. For the first time, we documented the association of blacks with apes, not in old movie clips, not in nineteenth-century American literature, not in the newspapers of the Jim Crow South, but in the minds of ordinary Americans in the twenty-first century.

Reviewing these findings brought to mind words that I heard growing up in Cleveland: "Have Mercy." "Have Mercy" were the words I heard African Americans utter to recognize something as too much or too little, or too big to fit into words, but mostly, too significant to let go by without comment. "Have Mercy" came to mind when I looked at these study results for the first time. Could these results be true? And what does it mean about who we are and what we believe?

Understandably, my collaborators and I kept repeating studies of this type to make sure the results were reliable. The results were always the same. For example, we extensively examined what emerged as the primary alternative explanation for our findings: color matching. That is, because blacks are dark and apes are dark, the black-ape association could be driven, not by a conceptual link between blacks and apes, but by a visual link that is based upon color similarity. To examine this alternative explanation, we tested the black-ape association with line drawings of apes rather than color images. We wanted to see if the association would still be present, even when the apes shown to participants had their dark color removed. We also tested the association with ape names rather than ape pictures. We tested this association with line drawings of black and white faces. We tested the association with stereotypically black and white names rather than with the faces of blacks and whites. We tested the black-ape association forward and backward—in every way we could think of. The results were always the same.

Visual Attention

Just as we did with the black-crime association, we documented the power of the black-ape association to direct visual attention. In one study, for example, we subliminally primed half of our student participants with line drawings of ape images. We then asked them to complete the dot probe task I described in the first part of this essay. What did we find? When people are prompted to think of apes, they are visually drawn to the black face (see Figure 16.7). So associated are blacks with apes that participants are well over 2,000 milliseconds faster to locate the dot when it is placed near the black face if they have been prompted to think of apes than if they have not been prompted to think of apes. My collaborators and I measured this effect in milliseconds, yet we speculate that decades are packed in those milliseconds. Centuries are reflected in those milliseconds. Our nation's history with slavery, with Reconstruction, with eugenics, with racial subjugation and segregation can be detected in our psyches and in a matter of milliseconds. Moreover, we suspect that when this centuries-old black-ape association is recruited in the context of crime, it can lead to negative consequences. Not just in terms of how black suspects are seen but in how much violence is okay to direct at them.

Violence Justification

To examine this tolerance for violence, we invited white college students to participate in another study (Goff et al. 2008). In this study, we subliminally exposed participants to words associated with great apes

FIGURE 16.7 | **DOT PROBE RESULTS.**

Those previously exposed to line drawings of ape images are more likely to look at the black faces—i.e., they are faster to locate the dot near the black face—than those not exposed to ape images.

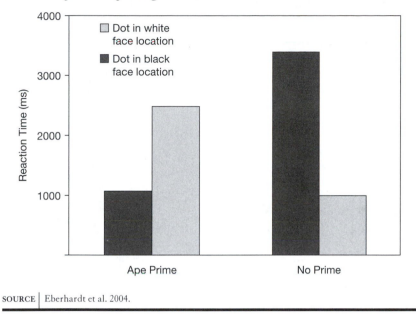

SOURCE | Eberhardt et al. 2004.

or not. Next we had them watch an actual video clip of police officers attempting to detain a suspect using extreme physical force. Participants saw either the mug shot of a black suspect or a white suspect at the very beginning of the video. Just after watching the video, the participants answered questions about how justified and necessary the use of force was.

We found that when participants were led to believe that the suspect was white, exposing them to the ape words did not make them think the beating was any more justified. When the participants were led to believe the suspect was black, however, the ape words made a huge difference (see Figure 16.8). When participants were exposed to words like "gorilla," "chimp," and "orangutan," they thought the black suspect was much more deserving of the treatment he got. They were significantly more likely to believe that the black suspect's behavior made an extreme level of physical force necessary. They were more likely to believe that the police were justified in the amount of force they used.

FIGURE 16.8 | **JUSTIFICATION OF POLICE VIOLENCE RESULTS.**

Justification of police violence is highest for those who are exposed to words associated with apes and led to believe suspect is black.

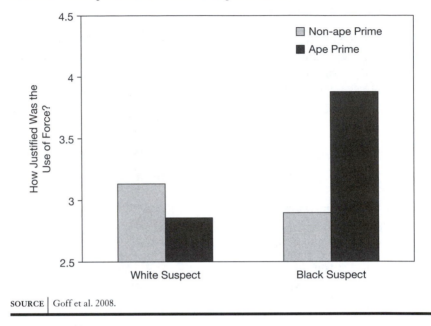

SOURCE | Goff et al. 2008.

Death Sentencing

Finally, we conducted a study to examine the extent to which animal imagery is related to death sentencing decisions. For this study, my collaborators and I (Goff et al. 2008) took a dataset that contained defendants who were convicted of crimes that were committed in Philadelphia and who became eligible for death somewhere between 1979 and 1999. This was the same dataset used in the death sentencing study I discussed in the first part of this essay. This time, we attempted to locate articles written about these defendants in the *Philadelphia Inquirer*. We then asked naïve raters to code these news articles on animal imagery. They coded the articles for words like "brute," "savage," and "predator."

What did we find? We found significantly more animal-related words in the news articles describing black defendants (an average of 8.5 words) than white defendants (an average of 2.2 words). And finally, the news articles about those black defendants who received death sentences contained significantly more animal-related words (an average of 12.7

words) than the articles about those who received life sentences (an average of 6.2 words).

THE ROLE OF ANIMUS

Surprisingly, antipathy toward blacks does not play a significant role in maintaining the black-ape association or the black-crime association. In fact, in every study where we measured people's racial attitudes, those attitudes did not matter. Anti-black prejudice does not appear to dictate how strongly people associate blacks and apes. Anti-black prejudice does not appear to dictate how strongly people associate blacks and crime. Moreover, in the studies where we have employed ethnic minorities as study participants, the ethnicity of the participant makes no difference. Whites and ethnic minorities display the same pattern of associations.

My collaborators and I believe that this association is held in place, instead, through implicit knowledge. For example, throughout U.S. history, black people have been represented as less than human, and people, still today, learn to associate blacks with apes because of those representations. When people read about criminal cases, for example, they not only pick up on the details of each case, they pick up on the words used to describe defendants. And slowly and perhaps unintentionally, they begin to form associations between blacks and apes. Slowly, unintentionally, they begin to form associations between blacks and crime.

There is evidence for race-based associations all around us, not only in the data from tightly controlled studies or in the news articles written about convicted criminals, but also in our daily lives and our interactions with others—even those closest to us. To underscore the close proximity of these associations, allow me to tell a personal story before closing this essay. A couple of years ago, I was flying back to California with my son, who was just five years old at the time. We had been in Boston. My husband is a law professor at Stanford and he was teaching at the Harvard Law School for a short time as a visiting scholar. He stayed behind to teach for a couple of weeks, and I was bringing my son back home to California. So we were on the plane. My son looks up and sees the only black man on the plane and he says to me, "Hey, that guy looks like Daddy." Clearly he is seeing something I am not. I struggle to see the resemblance. I look at this man's long dreadlocks, and I think to myself, "Now, my husband is bald." I look at his height. He is a good six inches shorter than my husband. I look at his facial structure. No, there is no resemblance there. I look at his skin color, his eye color, his hands, his clothing—and I cannot come up with a match. Just as I am about to probe my son on the issue, he looks up at the man again and says in a slow, reflective voice, "I hope he doesn't rob the plane." Perhaps I misunderstood him, so I asked, "What did you say?" He says again, "I hope he doesn't rob the plane." And I asked, "Why? Why would you say that? You know Daddy would not rob a plane." And he says to me, "I don't know why. I don't know why I said that. I don't know why I was *thinking* that." Even with no evildoer—even with no explicit hatred— the black-crime association remains. The black-ape association remains. Sadly, despite the attempts of black families throughout the nation to escape the reminders of a slave past and the real threat of violence— despite the election of the first black president—some associations still haunt us.

CONCLUDING REMARKS

Through a series of social psychological studies, I have shown you the power of racial associations to influence our perception, our attention, our judgments, and our actions. I have shown you the power of stereotypic associations to act forward and backward. You have seen how these associations can act upon the psyches of students, of police officers, of jury members, of whites, and of racial minorities. And it is egregious. These associations might operate through implicit mechanisms. They might be based on implicit knowledge. However, when we take a moment to think about the consequences of that knowledge, two words come to mind: Have Mercy.

Works Cited

•

Baldus, D. C., G. Woodworth, D. Zuckerman, N. A. Weiner, and B. Broffitt. 1998. Racial discrimination and the death penalty in the post-Furman era: An empirical and legal overview, with recent findings from Philadelphia. *Cornell Law Review, 83*, 1638–1770.

Devine, P. G., and A. J. Elliot. 1995. Are racial stereotypes really fading? The Princeton trilogy revisited. *Personality and Social Psychology Bulletin, 21*, 1139–1150.

Du Bois, W. E. B. 1935. *Black Reconstruction in America 1860–1880*. New York: Free Press.

Eberhardt, J. L., P. G. Davies, V. J. Purdie-Vaughns, and S. L. Johnson. 2006. Looking deathworthy: Perceived stereotypicality of black defendants predicts capital-sentencing outcomes. *Psychological Science, 17,* 383–386.

Eberhardt, J. L., P. A. Goff, V. Purdie, and P. G. Davies. 2004. Seeing black: Race, crime, and visual processing. *Journal of Personality and Social Psychology, 87,* 876–893.

Goff, P. A., J. L. Eberhardt, M. J. Williams, and M. N. Jackson. 2008. Not yet human: Implicit knowledge, historical dehumanization, and contemporary consequences. *Journal of Personality and Social Psychology, 94,* 292–306.

Kant, I. 2002. *The Philosophy of Law: An Exposition of the Fundamental Principles of Jurisprudence as the Science of Right.* Translated by W. Hastie. Clark, NJ: Lawbook Exchange. (Original work published in 1797.)

Western, B. 2006. *Punishment and Inequality in America.* New York: Russell Sage Foundation.

17

We're Honoring You, Dude

Myths, Mascots, and American Indians

**Stephanie A. Fryberg and
Alisha Watts**

•

American Indian mascots are still common throughout the United States even though their use has been widely contested. This essay examines the psychological impact that social representations, like American Indian mascots, can have on the members of the groups that are associated with these representations. To explain this impact we use recent research findings to debunk a set of popular myths that fuel the American Indian mascot controversy. First, we explain how social representations, such as mascots, can shape how individuals understand themselves. Second, we discuss how stereotypic social representations negatively influence psychological well-being for American Indians. Third, we demonstrate that seemingly positive stereotypical social representations, such as Disney's Pocahontas and the Cleveland Indians' Major League Baseball team mascot, can have negative psychological consequences for American Indians, and that this holds even for those who support the use of mascots. Fourth, we explore how social representations of American Indians influence European Americans. Finally, we discuss the implications of debunking popular myths for the American Indian mascot controversy and for other underrepresented groups (e.g., African Americans and Mexican Americans).

IMAGES OF AMERICAN INDIANS ARE PREVALENT IN AMERICAN culture—on television, in films, at sporting events, and even in schools. For example, you may encounter an American Indian mascot image when you attend a Washington Redskins football game, watch a University of North Dakota Fighting Sioux sporting event on television, or simply pass a T-shirt-clad sports fan on the street. Despite a long-standing national debate, many American high schools (e.g., Osceola High School Chieftains in Wisconsin, Napa High School Indians in California), universities (e.g., University of North Dakota Fighting Sioux, Florida State University Seminoles), and professional sports teams (e.g., Cleveland Indians, Atlanta Braves, Washington Redskins) continue to use American Indian team names and mascots.

The mascot imagery ranges from the Cleveland Indians Chief Wahoo mascot, which is a red-faced, big-nosed, grinning, cartoonlike character adorned with a headband and a feather, to the former University of Illinois Chief Illiniwek mascot, who is a European American male attired in traditional chief regalia (i.e., buckskin dress and leggings, moccasins, and a chief's headdress) who performs quasi-traditional dances. Across the country, many other sports teams use American Indian names and symbols. For example, the logo of the Atlanta Braves major league baseball team is a red tomahawk. To music identified as the Tomahawk War Chant, the Braves fans perform "The Chop," which is a repetitive bend of the arm at the elbow and is intended to evoke a swinging tomahawk.

Proponents of American Indian mascots argue that these images do not offend American Indians and that they stimulate interest in American Indian culture and history. For example, the Honor the Chief Society, a group that was set up to defend the use of the Illinois mascot, claims that mascots elicit positive feelings for the team and for American Indians in general (2002). By contrast, opponents of using American Indian mascots argue that these images harm and offend, rather than honor, American Indians. They suggest that American Indian mascots are dehumanizing and restrict the full membership of American Indians in American society. Specifically, mascot opponents question the claim that American Indians feel honored when a European American man dresses up in traditional Indian regalia and dances around a football field or basketball court, or when the opposing teams chant "Scalp the Indians" or "Kill the Indians." These opposing views fuel an ongoing passionate national debate about the use of American Indian mascots.

BACKGROUND OF THE CONTROVERSY

While a wide range of both Native and non-Native organizations have taken strong positions against the use of American Indian mascots, a few organizations advocate keeping them. As noted above, the University of Illinois Honor the Chief Society contends that American Indian mascots honor and benefit American Indians, stating that "when people take the time to learn about the First Nation People for whom the State of Illinois was named, and reflect upon how Chief Illiniwek is portrayed by her flagship University, they are better able to recognize the difference between an athletic mascot and a time-honored symbol of tradition and respect" (2007). Additionally, Washington Redskins vice president Karl Swanson asserts that his team name "symbolizes courage, dignity and leadership" and that since the team does not use the name and image with negative intent, then it cannot be offensive (Price 2002).

Several predominantly American Indian organizations disagree with this perspective. The Society of Indian Psychologists, the National Congress of American Indians, the National Indian Education Association, and the Native American Journalists Association officially oppose the use of American Indian mascots. Moreover, a wide range of predominantly non-Native organizations, including the United States Commission on Civil Rights, the National Collegiate Athletic Association, the American Psychological Association, the American Anthropological Association, the American Sociological Association, the National Coalition for Racism in Sports and Media, and the North American Society for Sociology of Sport also officially oppose and recommend bans on the use of these mascots. For example, in 2001, the United States Commission on Civil Rights argued that mascots and related names, performances, and images are "disrespectful and offensive to American Indians and others who are offended by such stereotyping." Similarly, in 2005, the American Psychological Association declared that the use of American Indian mascots "undermines the ability of American Indian Nations to portray accurate and respectful images of their culture, spirituality, and traditions" and "is a detrimental manner of illustrating the cultural identity of American Indian people through negative displays and/or interpretations of spiritual and traditional practices."

Despite the increasing number of national organizations that officially oppose the use of American Indian mascots, the debate continues. Many people fail to grasp the significance of the American Indian mascot controversy. On the surface, American Indian mascots are simply mascots; importantly, however, they are not the same as animal mascots, such as the Chicago Bears, the Philadelphia Eagles, the Oregon State University Beavers, the University of California at Santa Cruz Banana Slugs, the University of Connecticut Huskies, or the University of Arizona Wildcats, or even other ethnic group mascots, such as the University of Notre Dame Fighting Irish or the Minnesota Vikings. American Indian mascots represent a group of people who historically have been, and in many instances continue to be, mistreated in American society. Historically, Irish Americans were also mistreated in American society, but contemporary Irish Americans fare quite well as a group and do not typically report much discrimination. Mascot proponents often overlook the unique dual status of American Indian mascots as both team representations and group representations.

The dual status of American Indian mascots is brought into high relief by asking, for example, whether African Americans would feel honored if a European American man painted his face black and ran around a field imitating a "tribesman" from West Africa or whether Christians would feel honored by someone running around wearing the liturgical vestments used by clergy during services. While many people might immediately feel outrage at the thought of such acts, these same people often feel no comparable outrage over the use of American Indian mascots. Why is this? One possible reason is that despite an abundance of research demonstrating the negative effects of stereotypical group representations on group members, many people continue to believe that mascots are just mascots. This myth takes a number of forms including "It's just a mascot," "If you don't believe the stereotypes, they can't hurt you," "But we're honoring American Indians" and "If American Indians aren't offended, then mascots must be okay."

MYTH 1: "IT'S JUST A MASCOT!"

American Indian mascots may seem relatively unimportant compared to other pressing national issues. In fact, those who support the use of American Indian mascots often argue that they are "just mascots" and that the entire mascot controversy is blown out of proportion. Those against the use of American Indian mascots argue that they are more than "just mascots"—that they are, in fact, powerful social representations that affect how American Indians are viewed and how American Indians view themselves.

The power of American Indian mascots is that they are widely circulated public or *social representations* of American Indians in American society. The psychologist Serge Moscovici defines social representations as widely distributed images, beliefs, and assumptions that help individuals know how to think and behave in their social worlds (1988). Social representations are everywhere—in institutions (e.g., schools, churches), in social structures and practices (e.g., the law, pedagogy, families, teams), and in everyday artifacts (e.g., television programs, films, posters, textbooks). They constitute the meaning systems that individuals use to orient themselves in social environments and provide a shared language for individuals to communicate with one another (Moscovici 1973/1988, 1984).

Social representations also provide answers to the questions "Who am I?" and "Who are we?" (i.e., Who is my group?). To answer these questions, people look to the available social representations of their group. They use these representations to help define themselves and to understand how they are defined by others. This is the social nature of being a person. Consider the cartoon below.

When the young man in the cartoon learns that the young woman is an American Indian, he brings to mind all the social representations (e.g., Chief Wahoo, Pocahontas, and the cigar store Indian) he has learned about American Indians. He concludes that she does not fit these representations, and says, "Really? You don't look like an Indian." At first glance, the young man's response may seem ill intentioned (e.g., insensitive, discriminatory, or even racist). A social representation approach suggests an alternative explanation. Namely, the young man associates

American Indians with the limited set of social representations (i.e., mascots, caricatures, and stereotypes) available in American society. These representations then define the group "American Indians" in his mind. To conclude that the young woman is American Indian, he first needed to "match" her to one of his available social representations. When she did not match any of these representations, he concluded that she must not be American Indian. The young man's social representations of American Indians not only influence his thoughts about and behavior toward the young American Indian woman, they influence the young woman's thoughts about herself and the actions she takes. Regardless of the young man's intentions, his comment challenges her identity as an American Indian. Even though the young woman may resist or contest this challenge, to answer the question "Who am I?" she has to contend with the available popular representations of American Indians.

Unfortunately for the young woman, American Indians are not widely represented in the public eye. One reason this is true is that American Indians are a numerically small group. According to the 2000 census, American Indians constitute less than 1 percent (.9) of the U.S. population. In addition, American Indians are fairly invisible in and segregated from mainstream society. Approximately 40 percent of American Indians reside on Indian reservations (Family Education Network 2002), many of which are in fairly remote parts of the country, and roughly one-fourth of American Indians live in poverty, more than twice the national average (U.S. Census Bureau 2000). All of these factors contribute to decreased opportunities for American Indians and to their decreased visibility.

The American media also reflects this decreased visibility. In a two-week composite of prime time television programming in 2002, only six characters (.4 percent) were identified as American Indian (Mastro and Behm-Morawitz 2005), and in a composite week of television commercials, only nine characters (.4 percent) were identified as American Indian (Mastro and Stern 2003). Similar results were found with a content analysis of newspapers and films, revealing that approximately .2 percent of newspaper articles and popular films featured American Indians (Fryberg 2003).

One consequence of the decreased visibility of American Indians is that most Americans have no direct or personal experience with contemporary American Indians. As a result, most mainstream views of American Indians are formed and fostered by indirectly acquired information. For example, one of the authors of this essay (Stephanie

Fryberg) has conducted several studies showing that like the young man in the cartoon, individuals unfamiliar with American Indians characterize American Indians as they are portrayed in the media—as spiritual, in tune with nature, warriorlike, and as people with social problems. The majority of these representations are tied to sports teams (e.g., Major League Baseball's Cleveland Indians and Atlanta Braves; the National Football League's Washington Redskins; and college sports teams such as the University of Illinois Fighting Illini) and to Hollywood movies (e.g., Disney's *Pocahontas, The Last of the Mohicans,* and *Dances with Wolves*), and portray American Indians as figures from the eighteenth and nineteenth centuries. These representations have a powerful influence on how non-Natives think about American Indians: "For many non-Indians, an Indian must resemble a historical image, one frozen in the past and in historical archives—the noble, proud warrior dancing about and worshipping nature's mysteries" (Trimble 1987, 214).

The decreased visibility of American Indians, when combined with limited social representations, creates a situation in which the few prevalent representations of American Indians emerge as particularly strong communicators of how American Indians should appear and behave. Take the performances of Chief Illiniwek, the former University of Illinois mascot, as an example (Figure 17.1). When Chief Illiniwek[1] dances around the gym at halftime or in a homecoming parade, he is not simply generating enthusiasm for the team and intensifying hopes for future victory. His performance also shapes how onlookers define American Indians. It communicates to the audience, including those who identify as American Indian, that this is one of a few publicly agreed-upon ways for American Indians to look and act.

The number of available representations of any given group determines the power of each social representation to define the group. If one group is represented in a wide variety of ways, while another group is represented in a limited number of ways, then the narrowly defined group will be more influenced by the public or social representation. For

---

1 In February 2007, the University of Illinois announced that Chief Illiniwek would "no longer perform at athletic events on the Urbana-Champaign campus" (University of Illinois Office for University Relations 2007). Chief Illiniwek made his final appearance at a University of Illinois men's basketball game on February 21, 2007, and on March 13, 2007, the University of Illinois Board of Trustees voted to retire Illiniwek's name, image, and regalia (University of Illinois Office for University Relations 2007). A few months later, in October 2007, Chief Illiniwek was brought out of retirement for a special appearance at the University of Illinois homecoming parade (Saulny 2007), and in April 2008, the "Council of Chiefs," a group of previous Chief Illinewek performers, named a student to portray the chief for the next academic year (Monson 2008).

FIGURE 17.1 | **CHIEF ILLINIWEK, FORMER UNIVERSITY OF ILLINOIS MASCOT.**

example, whereas one can always find a wide variety of representations of European Americans on television, it is difficult to locate any notable representations of Asian Americans, Mexican Americans, and, in particular, American Indians. The limited social representations of these groups affect the collection of identity resources (i.e., information about "Who am I?" or "Who are we?") that are available for self-definition. For example, it may be difficult for a young woman to imagine herself simultaneously as an American Indian *and* as a lawyer, surgeon, or college professor because there are few, if any, social representations of American Indians in these professions. Just as a limited wardrobe means that one has restricted access to clothing combinations or outfits, a limited number of social representations for the group(s) with which one associates can mean that one has limited access to various possible identities. American Indians can try to ignore the common representations of American Indians but they cannot live completely outside of them. Even opposing these representations means engaging them. In this way, mascots are more than "just mascots"; they convey what it means to be an American Indian in contemporary society.

MYTH 2: "STICKS AND STONES MAY BREAK MY BONES, BUT [STEREOTYPES] WILL NEVER HURT ME."

When social representations characterize a group in a rigid or static manner, they are referred to as stereotypes. *Stereotypes* are powerful, hard-to-break mental links between a social group and a limited set of behaviors or traits. When people repeatedly see American Indians portrayed as mascots, they form automatic associations, or stereotypes, between American Indians and the common characteristics of American Indian mascots (e.g., aggressive, noble, violent, stoic, savagelike, spiritual). One popular myth about stereotypes is that if group members do not believe a stereotype or choose to ignore the stereotype, then it will not influence them. The implication is that if American Indians do not believe that American Indian mascot stereotypes are harmful, they will not be affected by exposure to the mascot stereotype. Some mascot advocates even suggest that American Indians who "allow" American Indian mascots to impact their well-being are mentally "weak" or at least overly sensitive. At issue, then, is whether negative stereotypes detrimentally affect the individuals who are the target of the stereotype even when individuals resist or contest the stereotype.

Social psychologists Claude Steele and Joshua Aronson (1995) have shown conclusively that negative stereotypes adversely impact the performance of individual group members. Their studies demonstrate that in a performance situation (e.g., taking a test), the concern that one's performance might confirm a stereotype about one's group, what is referred to as *stereotype threat*, can impair performance (see also Steele 1997, Steele et al. 2002). For example, to test the impact of the stereotype of intellectual inferiority on performance, Steele and Aronson gave European American and African American students a difficult verbal test from the Graduate Record Examination (GRE). They told half of the students that the test measured intelligence and the other half of the students that the test was a problem-solving exercise and was not indicative of ability. European American students performed equally well regardless of how the test was described. African American students, however, performed worse when the test was described as an intelligence test than when the test was described as a problem-solving exercise. In addition, when African American students were asked to indicate their race on a pre-test questionnaire, they also underperformed, even if the test was not described as a measure of intelligence. Steele and Aronson suggest that concern with confirming the stereotype that African Americans are less intelligent than European Americans interfered with the performance of African American students.

Since the initial stereotype threat studies described above, over 100 journal articles have confirmed that negative stereotypes have negative consequences for members of stereotyped groups, including Latinos, women in math, students from low socioeconomic status backgrounds, and European Americans in interracial interactions. Stereotype threat works by disrupting concentration. Toni Schmader and Michael Johns (2003), for example, found that women who took a math test described as a math intelligence test—the stereotype threat condition—did not perform as well as women who took the same test not described this way. Stereotype threat reduced women's working memory capacity, their ability to hold many thoughts simultaneously. In other words, when a member of a stereotyped group is placed in a situation in which he or she could be stereotyped, the pressure of trying to avoid confirming the stereotype disrupts thinking so much that performance is impaired and thus, the stereotype is inadvertently confirmed.

Stereotype threat research also demonstrates that negative stereotypes detrimentally affect the stereotyped individuals, *even when the individuals do not consciously believe the stereotypes.* Amy Kiefer and Denise Sekaquaptewa (2007a, 2007b), for example, found that women who did not consciously endorse the stereotype about women in math still underperformed in the stereotype threat condition. Finally, stereotypes do not, as some suggest, just impact the mentally "weak." Notably, they impact the highly devoted. Several other studies have shown that students who are very identified with school or who have a particular appreciation for stereotype-relevant domains, such as women who love math or minority students who aspire to get good grades, are more vulnerable to stereotype threat than students who are less invested. In fact, women who do not care about math, and minorities who do not care about school, are the only ones who are protected from stereotype threat effects. In other words, despite the widespread popular belief that only sticks and stones can do harm, the research evidence now reveals conclusively that negative group stereotypes can have dire consequences for individuals who are the targets of those stereotypes (see, e.g., Aronson et al. 1999; Spencer et al. 1999; Keller 2007; Major and Schmader 1998; Major et al. 1998; Crocker et al. 1998).

MYTH 3: "BUT I'M HONORING AMERICAN INDIANS!"

If American Indian mascots are negative stereotypes, then believing that they could have a negative effect on American Indians is simple.

In fact, as noted above, stereotype threat theory argues that negative stereotypical representations harm members of the stereotyped groups. But what if American Indian mascots are perceived as positive stereotypical representations of American Indians? Proponents of American Indian mascots often argue that American Indian mascots positively portray, and thus honor, American Indians. Are these mascots positive, harmless representations in the way the mascot proponents suggest, or is it possible they are positive, yet harmful to American Indians? Given the lack of public consensus on the issue, we begin by asking whether a positive representation can harm the group members.

Previous social psychological research suggests that some positive stereotypes can harm group members. Sapna Cheryan and Galen Bodenhausen (2000), for example, found that the "Asians have superior mathematical ability" stereotype leads to "choking" (i.e., underperformance on a math test). Specifically, when ethnicity is made overtly salient for Asian American university students who are about to take a math test, the pressure to conform to the positive stereotype (i.e., superior mathematical ability) interferes with the student's ability to concentrate on the math test and, thus, decreases their performance. Similarly, Fiske and colleagues (2002) found that when attributes like warm and affectionate are directed toward women, they simultaneously elicit associations about not being competent. Rarely are women viewed as both affectionate and competent. American Indian mascots may similarly elicit both positive and negative associations for American Indians.

Imagine an American Indian woman who has just started school at a predominately European American university. The young woman wants to be taken seriously as a student and an intellectual. To accomplish this, however, she must confront the social representations of American Indians held by professors and peers. Initially, they seem to hold generally positive views of American Indians, but in time, she realizes that while they embrace the idea of her as an American Indian, they do not acknowledge her ideas or her experiences as an American Indian. Her professors and peers are likely to know more about Hollywood representations of American Indians than they do about contemporary American Indians. They may ask her whether her family lives in a teepee or whether she had to buy new clothes (i.e., trade in her buckskin for jeans and T-shirts) when she came to the university. They ask her for information about Indian gaming (i.e., casinos) and about the use of American Indian mascots, but not about national or international issues. They may ask about tribal and family ceremonies but will not ask for help with calculus or invite her to join their research lab. The problem is that the idea of "good student" simply does not come to mind when they think of her. For the young American Indian woman to be taken seriously as a student and an intellectual, she must both prove her academic ability *and* help those around her to build the association between "American Indian" and "good student." While many students are asked to demonstrate their ability, very few have the additional burden of teaching others how to think about their group.

In a series of research studies, Fryberg and her colleagues (2008) asked whether seemingly positive representations of American Indians negatively influence how American Indians see themselves. To explore this possibility, they went to schools with relatively large American Indian populations. The first three studies were conducted at high schools on American Indian reservations in Arizona and the fourth study was conducted at a predominantly American Indian university in Kansas. The researchers exposed American Indian students to an American Indian social representation and then assessed a variety of outcomes. The American Indian students in the study saw one of three social representations: an American Indian mascot image (Chief Wahoo, the Cleveland Indians Major League Baseball team mascot), a list of stereotypes about American Indians (e.g., three statistics about high rates of school dropout, depression, and suicide in the American Indian community), or a non-mascot social representation (a picture of the Pocahontas character from Disney's *Pocahontas* film).

To assess whether the three social representations bring to mind positive or negative associations, students saw one of the three American Indian representations and then wrote down the first five thoughts that came to mind. Analyses of these thoughts showed that American Indian high school students noted largely positive associations with Chief Wahoo and Pocahontas (i.e., approximately 80 percent of their listed thoughts were positive) and largely negative associations with the negative stereotypes (i.e., 91 percent of the thoughts they listed were negative).

Next, Fryberg and her colleagues explored whether the three American Indian social representations influenced American Indian students' everyday well-being. The researchers found that American Indian students who saw an image of Chief Wahoo or Pocahontas, the two American Indian social representations that brought to mind positive associations in the first study, reported lower self-esteem and lower community worth than students in the control group. Students who read the negative stereotypes also reported lower self-esteem and community

FIGURE 17.2 | **EFFECT OF STEREOTYPES ON THE SELF-ESTEEM OF AMERICAN INDIAN STUDENTS.**

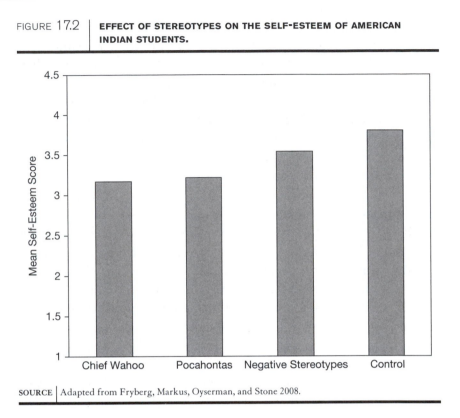

SOURCE | Adapted from Fryberg, Markus, Oyserman, and Stone 2008.

worth than students in the control group, but students who saw Chief Wahoo and Pocahontas reported even lower self-esteem than students who saw the negative stereotypes (Figure 17.2).

One possible explanation for the negative consequences is that American Indians were depicted as caricatures (i.e., as cartoonlike). Given the range of American Indian mascot images, the authors next asked whether mascots that portray American Indians as more humanlike would yield similar results. To assess this question, the researchers carried out another study and included two new American Indian mascot representations in addition to Chief Wahoo: Chief Illiniwek, the University of Illinois mascot, and the Haskell Indian mascot (the Haskell Indian Nation's University mascot, a predominantly American Indian university). A picture of the actual Chief Illiniwek mascot, a European American male dressed in "traditional" chief regalia, was taken from the Internet, and a picture of the Haskell Indian, a purple and gold (school colors) drawing of an American Indian man wearing a chief's head-dress, was taken from the university Web page. Chief Wahoo represents a predominantly non-Native organization and the Haskell Indian represents a predominantly American Indian university. In addition, the researchers added a social representation from the American Indian College Fund, which depicted an attractive young American Indian woman standing in front of shelves of microscopes. The caption on the advertisement read, "Have you ever seen a real Indian?"

Following exposure to the representations, students completed a *possible selves* measure. (In this line of research, "possible selves" are defined as the future goals or aspirations people hope to achieve or fear not achieving.) Specifically, participants were asked, *"Think a minute about next year and what you will be like this time next year. What do you expect you will be like? Write down at least four ways of describing yourself that will probably be true of you next year. You can write down ways you are now or ways you expect to become."* After the study was complete, research assistants coded the number of achievement-related possible selves reported by students (e.g., getting good grades, graduating from college, getting a good job). They found that American Indian students exposed to any one of the three American Indian mascot representations (i.e., Chief Wahoo, Chief Illinewek, or the Haskell Indian) reported fewer future goals or aspirations related to achievement compared to students not exposed to a representation (control group) and to students exposed to the American Indian College Fund advertisement.

The research described here debunks the myth that positive representations must elicit positive or at least neutral outcomes. Chief Wahoo and Pocahontas, both seemingly positive representations of American Indians, depressed how American Indian students felt about themselves and their communities. The authors suggest that both of these representations portray American Indians as "frozen" in the past, that is, as historical figures rather than contemporary people. When American Indians see these representations, they are reminded of the limited ways in which they are seen by mainstream society. Hence, mascots may be intended to honor American Indians, but by reminding them of the limited ways in which they are seen by mainstream society, they harm American Indians.

MYTH 4: "IF AMERICAN INDIANS AREN'T OFFENDED, THEN MASCOTS MUST BE OKAY."

Just as some mascot proponents argue that positive representations do not harm, other mascot proponents argue that if American Indians like or agree with the use of American Indian mascots, then they cannot have harmful consequences. The underlying assumption is that harm requires an offended party, and that "allowing" representations to influence us is a choice.

Over the past decade, a few large national organizations have played major roles in the mascot controversy. The National Annenberg Election Survey, conducted by the Annenberg Public Policy Center (2004), for example, claimed that 91 percent of the 768 self-identified American Indians polled reported that the NFL Washington Redskins team mascot does not bother them. The Peter Harris Research Group for CNN/ *Sports Illustrated* found that 36 percent of the 351 self-identified American Indians who lived on Indian reservations said the word "Redskin" offended them. Moreover, 58 percent of the American Indians polled said they objected to mascots dressing up in "Indian" headdresses, wearing war paint, and dancing around with a tomahawk (Price 2002). In contrast, *Indian Country Today* (2001), a national American Indian newspaper, conducted a poll of its readers and found that 81 percent of American Indians felt American Indian mascots are "predominantly offensive to natives." These findings were widely circulated in the media without sufficient attention paid to the limitations of the data collection or to the background and history of the mascot controversy. Of all the poll results, the Peter Harris Research Group poll received the most attention because it was published in *Sports Illustrated*. The end result is a bias, on the part of the American public, toward believing that American Indians enjoy being represented as mascots and therefore, that mascots must be acceptable for public use.

Finally, in a study conducted in 2003, Fryberg asked American Indian participants whether they agreed or disagreed with the use of American Indians as mascots and whether they thought it was "respectful" for European Americans to dress up as American Indians (e.g., the University of Illinois' Chief Illiniwek). She examined the differences between students who agreed with the use of American Indian mascots and students who disagreed with their use. Among students in the control group (those who did not see a representation), those who agreed with the use of American Indian mascots and those who disagreed with the use of these mascots showed no difference in community worth. However, among students who saw the Chief Wahoo image, those who *agreed* with the use of American Indians as mascots reported *less* community worth than those who disagreed with the use of American Indian mascots. The results of these studies run contrary to the expected finding that if American Indians like or agree with the use of American Indian mascots, then they will also do no harm. To the contrary, students who

FIGURE 17.3 | **STUDENTS' COMMUNITY WORTH AND THEIR OPINIONS ON USING AMERICAN INDIAN MASCOTS.**

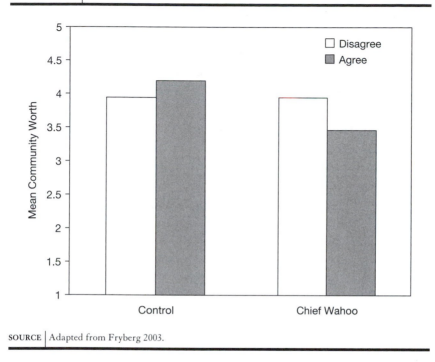

SOURCE | Adapted from Fryberg 2003.

disagreed with the use of the mascots fared better than students who agreed with their use (Figure 17.3).

MYTH 5: "THE MASCOT CONTROVERSY IS AN AMERICAN INDIAN ISSUE; MASCOTS DON'T AFFECT ME."

If American Indians do not benefit from the use of American Indian mascots, then why do they remain such a prominent figure in schools, universities, and athletic domains? One possibility is that non-Natives reap the benefits of using American Indian mascots. As mentioned above, many people do not understand the importance of the mascot controversy, but it is also the case that many people believe the mascot issue is solely an "American Indian" issue. This suggests that European Americans are influenced neither positively nor negatively by the use of American Indian mascots. While that may be true, a social representational approach suggests otherwise. American Indian mascots are, by nature, social products that require some amount of social agreement and social engagement. In this sense, both Natives and non-Natives engage with American Indian mascot representations. The question being addressed here is whether American Indian social representations also influence how European Americans think about themselves (i.e., self-esteem).

To examine this question, Fryberg and her fellow social psychologist Daphna Oyserman conducted a study in which European American students were shown one of three social representations of American Indians (2008). Fryberg and Oyserman used the same American Indian social representations (i.e., Chief Wahoo, Pocahontas, and negative stereotypes) as were used in the studies with American Indian students. After being exposed to one of the three representations, the participants then completed a self-esteem measure. While American Indian students reported lower self-esteem after viewing Chief Wahoo and Pocahontas, Fryberg and Oyserman found the *opposite* effect for European American students. That is, compared to students in the control group (those who saw no representations), European American students reported *higher* self-esteem when exposed to one of the three American Indian social representations (i.e., Chief Wahoo, Pocahontas, and negative stereotypes; Figure 17.4).

FIGURE 17.4 | **EFFECT OF AMERICAN INDIAN STEREOTYPES ON THE SELF-ESTEEM OF EUROPEAN AMERICAN STUDENTS.**

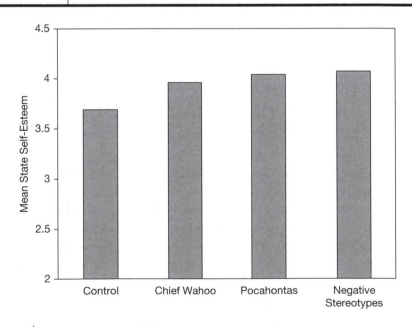

SOURCE | Adapted from Fryberg and Oyserman 2008.

Fryberg and Oyserman provide two explanations for these findings. The first involves downward social comparison, which is the act of comparing one's self with a person or group who is worse off. In previous studies, downward comparisons have been shown to provide a positive boost to the self-esteem of members of the dominant group because they offer a pleasing reminder of one's own relative success. This argument is particularly relevant to the Negative Stereotypes condition. European American students report higher self-esteem because the negative stereotypes of American Indians remind them that their group is doing quite well. But why would European Americans feel better after viewing seemingly positive, albeit stereotypical, American Indian representations (i.e., Chief Wahoo and Pocahontas)?

To explain these results, Fryberg and Oyserman use the concept of *basking in reflected glory*—or what Robert Cialdini has called "BIRGing" (1976). BIRGing involves associating one's self with the positive attributes or successes of another. Like downward social comparison, BIRGing also offers opportunities for enhancing self-esteem. Fryberg and Oyserman suggest that America's obsession with American Indian mascots is another form of BIRGing. Specifically, they argue that American Indian mascots remind Americans of a romanticized past in which pioneers were "claiming the American frontier." This past is reflected in American "westerns" (e.g., *The Lone Ranger*), films (e.g., *Dances with Wolves*), games (e.g., "cowboys and Indians"), and legends (e.g., the Thanksgiving story), and ultimately in the social representations individuals have about American Indians. In these representations, American Indians are "frozen in the past"; they are portrayed as characters from the eighteenth and nineteenth centuries (Trimble 1987). By making the association between American Indians and the American frontier past, Americans can collectively BIRG American Indians with little risk of negative repercussions. They are, in effect, taking ownership of the desirable parts of American Indian history and merging the positive attributes associated with this history into their own self-evaluations; hence the reason mascot proponents claim that American Indian mascots are not about American Indians, but rather, are about *American* history and *American* traditions. If Americans associate American Indian images with a romanticized, ideal, frontier past, then these images are really for the benefit of mainstream Americans, not American Indians. In fact, American Indian concerns may not even come into play.

This research debunks the myth that American Indian mascots are an "American Indian issue" and have no bearing on non-Natives. To the contrary, it supports Richard King's suggestion that European Americans have much to gain from retaining American Indian mascots and may explain the tenacity with which many Americans cling to American Indian mascots (2004).

SUMMARY OF FINDINGS: IMPLICATIONS FOR THE AMERICAN INDIAN MASCOT CONTROVERSY

The current controversy over the use of American Indian mascots is about more than "just mascots." From the point of view of the target—American Indians—Indian mascots do not honor their target. Instead they perpetuate stereotypes that negatively impact American Indians regardless of whether the representations are seen as positive or negative, and regardless of whether American Indians agree or disagree with being used as mascots. American Indian mascots and other related stereotypical representations of American Indians reinforce ideas of American Indians as "tee-pee-dwelling," spiritual beings who "commune with nature" or as aggressive, uncivilized, noble "savages" who existed in the eighteenth and nineteenth centuries (United States Commission on Civil Rights 2001). In this way, American Indian mascots prevent non-Natives from gaining an accurate understanding of both the historical and the contemporary experiences of American Indians. Mascots thus limit the way people view American Indians and restrict the variety of ways in which American Indians can view themselves.

BEYOND THE MASCOT CONTROVERSY: SOCIAL REPRESENTATIONS OF MINORITIES IN AMERICAN SOCIETY

This chapter illustrates the critical role that social representations play in providing people with a code for understanding "who they are" and "how they are seen by others." All individuals look to the available social representations of their group(s) to determine what is possible and what is not possible for them. For many groups (e.g., African Americans, Mexican Americans, women), however, the prevalent social representations of their group are often more narrow in scope than the social representations of majority group members (e.g., middle-class, male European Americans). When minority group members enter a domain in which no representation of the group with which they are associated exists (i.e., they are invisible in the domain) or only negative representations exist (i.e., they are viewed as struggling or as not having sufficient ability), they may experience additional barriers (e.g., difficulties identifying with the domain and low expectations on the part of peers, teachers, or co-workers) and difficulties (e.g., not being admitted to the school, not receiving the job) in their effort to belong and to be successful in the domain.

One way to reduce the effects of such representations is to eliminate the negative and limiting representations from performance-related contexts (e.g., schools, athletic domains, and work places). Another option is to create, distribute, and institutionalize a wider variety of social representations. When individuals see themselves positively and inclusively represented in a particular domain, they are more likely to perceive themselves as belonging in the domain and as able to succeed in the domain. Finally, increasing the number of prevalent representations also reduces the power that any one representation has to define individual group members. In essence, increasing the number of representations provides individuals with more choice about who and what defines them.

The impact of social representations on individuals and the struggle to change negative and limiting representations has a long and important history. Take, for example, the "Sambo" stereotype of African Americans. For much of the early 1900s, "Sambo" portrayed black males as dancing, dim-witted, laughing, bug-eyed, and big-lipped characters. In the entertainment domain (i.e., shows, books, cartoons), "Sambo" was featured as the butt of every joke (Boskin 1988). During the civil rights era, however, as African Americans fought for equal treatment, Sambo-like characters and *Amos 'n' Andy* type shows[2] slowly disappeared from popular American media. The civil rights era raised awareness about the unequal treatment of African Americans and, as such, brought into high relief the power of these blatantly derogatory and stereotypic representations to define them. As a result, the struggle over social representations gave way to a new view of African Americans.

Today, a wider array of positive representations of African Americans exists. When young African Americans examine what is possible for them, they can see themselves represented in public figures, such as President Barack Obama; former Secretary of State Colin Powell and former

---

2 *Amos 'n' Andy* began as a radio show performed by several European Americans that ran until November 1960. The characters in this show embodied several of the common stereotypes of African Americans at the time. The radio show was later adapted to television and ran seventy-eight episodes between 1951 and 1953. It was canceled amid protests by the NAACP, but ran in syndication until 1966 (Ely 1991; MacDonald 1993).

Secretary of State Condoleezza Rice; the sixteenth Surgeon General, Dr. David Satcher; and acclaimed attorney Johnnie Cochran. Certainly negative and limiting stereotypical representations of African Americans exist, but considerable progress has been made. Prevalent social representations influence how people think and act and how they treat members of other groups. Continuing the struggle over social representations is essential if America is to become a more equal and just society.

One group that has played an important role in the struggle over the role of social representations is social scientists. By examining both the prevalence and the positive and negative effects of social representations, their research can provide critical information that will allow people to make informed decisions about the appropriateness of social representations in various domains. By analyzing the power of social representations, social scientists provide policy makers, teachers, administrators, and employers the opportunity to create environments in which all people have an equal opportunity to succeed.

Works Cited

•

American Psychological Association. 2005. APA resolution recommending the immediate retirement of American Indian mascots, symbols, images, and personalities by schools, colleges, universities, athletic teams, and organizations. www.apa.org/releases (accessed June 11, 2006).

Annenberg Public Policy Center. September 24, 2004. Most Indians say name of Washington "Redskins" is acceptable while 9 percent call it offensive, Annenberg data show. Press release. www.annenbergpublicpolicycenter.org/Downloads/Political_Communication/naes/2004_03_redskins_09-24_pr.pdf (accessed May 30, 2008).

Aronson, Joshua, Michael Lustina, Catherine Good, Kellie Keough, Claude M. Steele, and Joseph Brown. 1999. When White men can't do math: Necessary and sufficient factors in stereotype threat. *Journal of Experimental Social Psychology, 35* 29–46.

Boskin, Joseph. 1988. *Sambo: The Rise and Demise of an American Jester.* New York: Oxford University Press.

Cheryan, Sapna, and Galen V. Bodenhausen. 2000. When positive stereotypes threaten intellectual performance: The psychological hazards of "model minority" status. *Psychological Science 11,* 399–402.

Crocker, Jennifer, Brenda Major, and Claude M. Steele. 1998. Social stigma. In *The Handbook of Social Psychology*, 4th ed., D. T. Gilbert and S. T. Fiske, 504–553. Boston: McGraw-Hill.

Ely, Melvin Patrick. 1991. *The Adventures of Amos 'n' Andy: A Social History of an American Phenomenon.* New York: Free Press

Family Education Network. 2002. American Indians: Census facts. www .factmonster.com/spot/aihmcensus1.html (accessed October 10, 2005).

Fiske, Susan T., Amy J. Cuddy, Peter Glick, and Jun Xu. 2002. A model of (often mixed) stereotype content: Competence and warmth respectively follow from perceived status and competition. *Journal of Personality and Social Psychology 82*, 878–902.

Fryberg, Stephanie A. 2003. Really? You don't look like an American Indian: Social representations and social group identities. PhD diss., Stanford University. *Dissertation Abstracts International 64*(1549), 3B.

Fryberg, Stephanie A., Hazel Rose Markus, Daphna Oyserman, and Joseph M. Stone. 2008. Of warrior chiefs and Indian princesses: The psychological consequences of American Indian mascots. *Basic and Applied Social Psychology 30*(3), 208–218.

Honor the Chief Society. 2002. Evidence demands a verdict. www.honorthechief .org/news_demand-verdict.html (accessed December 20, 2006).

———. 2007. History. www.honorthechief.org/history.html (accessed November 2, 2007).

Indian Country Today. 2001. American Indian opinion leaders: American Indian mascots. Editors report, August 7. www.indiancountrytoday.com/ archive/28190854.html.

Keller, Johannes. 2007. Stereotype threat in classroom settings: The interactive effect of domain identification, task difficulty and stereotype threat on female students' math performance. *British Journal of Educational Psychology 77*, 323–338.

Kiefer, Amy K., and Denise Sekaquaptewa. 2007a. Implicit stereotypes and women's math performance: How implicit gender-math stereotypes influence women's susceptibility to stereotype threat. *Journal of Experimental Social Psychology 43*, 825–832.

———. 2007b. Implicit stereotypes, gender identification, and math-related outcomes: A prospective study of female college students. *Psychological Science 18*, 13–18.

King, C. Richard. 2004. This is not an Indian. *Journal of Sport and Social Issues 28*, 3–10.

MacDonald, J. Fred. 1993. *Blacks and White TV: Afro-Americans in Television since 1948.* Chicago: Nelson-Hall.

Major, Brenda, and Toni Schmader. 1998. Coping with stigma through psychological disengagement. In *Prejudice: The Target's Perspective*, ed. Janet K. Swim and Charles Stangor, 219–241. San Diego: Academic Press.

Major, Brenda, Steven J. Spencer, Toni Schmader, Connie T. Wolfe, and Jennifer Crocker. 1998. Coping with negative stereotypes about intellectual performance: The role of psychological disengagement. *Personality and Social Psychology Bulletin 24*, 34–50.

Mastro, Dana E., and Elizabeth Behm-Morawitz. 2005. Latino representation on primetime television. *Journalism and Mass Communication Quarterly 82*, 110–130.

Mastro, Dana E., and Susannah R. Stern. 2003. Representations of race in television commercials: A content analysis of prime-time advertising. *Journal of Broadcasting and Electronic Media 47*, 638–647.

Monson, Mike. 2008. New Chief Illiniwek portrayers announced. *News-Gazette,* April 29.

Moscovici, Serge. 1988. Notes toward a description of social representations. *European Journal of Social Psychology 18*, 211–250.

————. 1984. The phenomena of social representations. In *Social Representations,* ed. Robert M. Farr and Serge Moscovici, 18–77. Cambridge, England: Cambridge University Press.

————. 1973/1988. Preface to *Health and Illness: A Social Psychological Analysis,* by Claudine Herzlich. London: Academic Press.

Oyserman, Daphna, and Hazel R. Markus. 1990. Possible selves in balance. *Journal of Social Issues 42,* 141–157.

Oyserman, Daphna, and Hazel R. Markus. 1993. The sociocultural self. In *The Self in Social Perspective,* ed. Jerry M. Suls, 187–220. Hillsdale, NJ: Lawrence Erlbaum.

Price, S. L. 2002. The Indian wars. *Sports Illustrated*, March 4, 66–72.

Rollins, Peter C., and John E. O'Connor, eds. 1998. *Hollywood's Indian: The Portrayal of the Native American in Film.* Lexington: University Press of Kentucky.

Saulny, Susan. 2007. University reverses policy to allow mascot's return. *New York Times,* October 28.

Schmader, Toni, and Michael Johns. 2003. Convergent evidence that stereotype threat reduces working memory capacity. *Journal of Personality and Social Psychology 85*, 440–452.

Spencer, Steven J., Claude M. Steele, and Diane M Quinn. 1999. Stereotype threat and women's math performance. *Journal of Experimental Social Psychology 35*, 4–28.

Steele, Claude M. 1997. A threat in the air: How stereotypes shape intellectual identity and performance. *American Psychologist 52*, 613–629.

Steele, Claude M., and Joshua Aronson. 1995. Stereotype and the intellectual performance of African Americans. *Journal of Personality and Social Psychology, 69*, 797–811.

Steele, Claude M., Steven J. Spencer, and Joshua Aronson. 2002. Contending with group image: The psychology of stereotype and social identity threat. In *Advances in Experimental Social Psychology*, Vol. 34, ed. Mark. P. Zanna, 379–440. San Diego, CA: Academic Press.

Trimble, Joseph E. 1987. American Indians and interethnic conflict: A theoretical and historical overview. In *Ethnic Conflict: International Perspectives*, ed. Jerry Boucher, Dan Landis, and Karen Arnold Clark, 208–229. Beverly Hills: Sage.

University of Illinois Office for University Relations. February 16, 2007. Chief Illiniwek will no longer perform. Press release. www.uillinois.edu/chief/ChiefRelease2-16-07.pdf (accessed May 30, 2008).

U.S. Census Bureau. 2000. Census 2000 Gateway. http://www.census.gov/main/www/cen2000.html (accessed October 10, 2005).

U.S. Commission on Civil Rights. 2001. Statement of the U.S. Commission on Civil Rights on the use of Native American images and nicknames as sports symbols. April 13, 2001. www.usccr.gov/press/archives/2001/041601st.htm (accessed December 20, 2006).

PART FIVE

Re-presenting Reality

18

Another Way to Be
Women of Color, Literature, and Myth

Paula M. L. Moya

•

How can literature help in studying the way race and ethnicity work? In this essay, I address this question by considering the role that literature, as an aesthetic artifact, can play in confirming and shaping, as well as challenging, the pervasive sociocultural ideas of our society. I start by recounting the knowledge-generating potential of literature before examining closely the formal features of Helena Maria Viramontes's short story "The Moths." I then discuss the historical and cultural context relevant to both the setting and the writing of this short story in Chicana/o Los Angeles before turning to an account of the ancient Aztec goddess Coyolxauhqui as a way of highlighting the story's imaginative potential. My goals in this essay are dual: (1) to demonstrate the role of the literary critic in analyzing the minute, day-to-day interpersonal interactions as well as the larger cultural and institutional structures that reinforce a racially and gender-stratified society; and (2) to highlight the way some works of literature, especially literature written by marginalized peoples, can both critically explore as well as attempt to revise an unjust social world. Literature, I argue, is an important arena within which scholars can explore the workings of human identity—of which race, ethnicity, and gender are crucially important aspects.

OVER THE PAST TWELVE YEARS, I HAVE HAD EXTENSIVE EXPERIENCE working and teaching in two interdisciplinary programs at Stanford University: Comparative Studies in Race and Ethnicity, and Feminist

Studies. Because of this, I have been challenged to think of how literary studies distinguishes my work on race, ethnicity, and gender from that of a sociologist or historian or social psychologist. I have found that while many people can imagine how history, sociology, or social psychology can contribute to an understanding of race, ethnicity, and gender, often they are less certain about the role literary studies might play in understanding these important social formations. I argue in this essay that literature can provide us with an important source of knowledge about the pervasive cultural ideas (or ideologies) through which individuals apprehend their world(s) (Jameson 1981; Saldívar 1990). Moreover, because the meaning of any given work of literature is only fully realized in the interaction between the text and its reader, *how we read* a literary work can tell us a great deal about *who we are* in relation the world(s) we live in, the world(s) represented in the text, and the world(s) from which the work of literature emerged (Booth 1988; Mohanty 1993; Moya 2002, 2006). As a literary critic who is interested in the study of race, ethnicity, and gender in the twentieth and twenty-first centuries, I turn to works of literature, rather than to surveys or social psychological experiments or historical archives, to garner my "evidence," and to present my findings about the way these important social processes matter to people's lives.

EXPLORING IDENTITIES IN LITERATURE

In the introduction to this volume, Hazel Markus and I define race and ethnicity as dynamic sets of historically derived and institutionalized ideas and practices that arise under particular circumstances and have significant and measurable effects. Under our definitions, a racial or ethnic identity is not an essential, fixed, and stable "thing" unto itself; it is not something that we *have,* or that we *are.* Rather, racial and ethnic (and, for that matter, gender) identities are actions that people—as members of social groups vying for power and privilege in a complex social world—*do,* to themselves and to each other. Identities embody social relations; they are the momentary concretizations of ongoing interactions between individuals-as-members-of-social-groups. Defining identities in this historically and socially specific yet dynamic way enables us to understand why identities serve as crucial indices of power and privilege in the social worlds from which they emerge.

In my previous work, I argued that some identities are better than others for providing us with a critical perspective from which we can disclose the complicated workings of ideology and oppression. Identities that question, or exist in opposition to, the status quo have the potential to discover and then to limn the contours of existing structures of power. In other words, people who either claim or are seen to have "outsider" identities often are ideally placed to learn how federal, state, municipal, tribal, or familial power structures work, because they are the ones who are likely to have that power directly enforced on their bodies or through their lives. Imagine, for example, that a young Mexican American girl is expected by her mother to iron her brother's clothes, clean her brother's room, and wait on her brother's friends. Now imagine that she is gay—that even while she is performing these chores for her brother and his friends, she wants not to be loved *by* people like them, but rather to love (women) *as* her brother and his friends are allowed to do. This is the exact situation the Chicana lesbian writer Cherríe Moraga found herself in as a young girl. It was being expected to cater to her brother while having a Chicana lesbian identity that positioned Moraga to learn the way patriarchal and heterosexist family structures systematically advantage heterosexual males by catering to their comfort and desires, even as those same structures systemically deny her own (Moraga 1983). For this reason, the study of outsider or minority identities can be especially valuable for scholars interested in how structures of power shape individual people's experiences. Examining minority identities is thus central to the project of discovering new—or reviving old—forms of knowledge that might help chart a way out of an oppressive society or social formation (Mignolo 2000; Moya 2002; Mohanty 2003; Hames-García 2004; Teuton 2008; Siebers 2008).

In this essay, I extend my previous work on the concept of identity to suggest that literature can be especially valuable for exploring the dynamics of gender, racial, and ethnic identities. The knowledge-generating potential of literature derives, I argue, from its constitutive features. Accordingly, I begin with a definition of what literature is before showing what a thorough literary critical interpretation of a good work of literature can do.

In my view, literature is most productively understood as *a creative and formal linguistic engagement—in the form of an oral or written artifact—with the historically situated cultural and political tensions that express themselves at the level of individual subjective experience* (Moya in preparation). Like other aesthetic artifacts such as film, painting, music, and drama, literature is a formal representation that mediates an author's (and subsequently a reader's) apprehension of his or her own world. Every act of representation is, at its core, also an act of interpretation. This is because to create the aesthetic object, an artist must choose and organize, into a more or less coherent whole, a set of images, metaphors, character types, and other formal devices. Accordingly, a work of literature never represents the world "as it really is" but rather filters through a literary form the hopes, dreams, illusions, and (sometimes faulty or partial) knowledge of the author of the work. And because authors are cultural beings, their hopes, dreams, illusions, and knowledge are not unique to themselves (Markus and Nurius 1986; Markus, Mullally, and Kitayama 1997; Markus, this volume). Instead, those hopes and dreams engage—sometimes positively, sometimes negatively—the pervasive sociocultural ideas of the society within which the author lives.

An important feature of some works of literature is that they allow for a kind of time travel that is most effectively captured in storytelling media such as literature or film. Stories, by definition, have a sequence of events that unfold successively through time (story time as well the real time of the reader) even when the narration (the telling) of the story is not linear. A story might begin generations in the past and then carry the reader up through the present and into the future. The significance of this feature reveals itself when we consider that the effects of time on the development of a self, or the effects of past historical events on the shape of present-day institutions, are difficult for most people wo are living in the "now" to understand. Such knowledge can only be revealed over time—whether that time is measured by the span of a person's lifetime or by centuries of record keeping. The time-traveling features of some works of literature enable a reader to understand how a character's "now" self might have been shaped by a "past" self, as well as how that character will evolve into a "future" self. And because the operations of gender, race, and ethnicity are dynamic and extend through time, the time-traveling features of literature make it a particularly effective way of exploring and representing the complex manner by which these social processes affect individuals' experiences and shape their identities. As with the example of novelist Octavia Butler's *Kindred*—which tells the story of a black woman from the twentieth century who is pulled back in time into chattel slavery and then returns to the present, only to find that she has lost an arm—literature can also show how past oppressive racial structures do damage to possible future selves.

A second important feature of some works of literature is their potential to introduce a reader to other, and possibly better, ways of being in the world. Whenever a person reads a literary work of substantial complexity, the possibility exists for her to engage in a kind of "'world'-traveling" whereby she enters into another, and (depending on who she is and what the book is about) possibly quite alien, world.[1] The world depicted in the book might be set in the future, or in the past; it might be a completely imaginary world, or a society that is geographically and culturally distant from the reader. A reader who takes up a story or book about a world that is far from her own will be exposed to situations, feelings, attitudes, and characters (implied people) that she does not encounter in her everyday life. Moreover, because of their transportability through space and time, some stories and books allow readers who live in racially segregated and economically stratified societies like our own to be exposed to a variety of alternative perspectives that they might not otherwise be exposed to. Although some people do have friends from a wide variety of racial, cultural, and economic backgrounds, many more people associate only with those who are very similar to them. In the case of some works of literature written by racial, ethnic, or gendered "others," the effect can be (although it is not always the case) that readers are pulled in and given a kind of access to a way of conceptualizing the world that they might otherwise never be exposed to, even if they live and work side by side with people associated with other races. The activity of reading good literature thus has the potential to expand the reader's horizon of possibility for experiential encounters.

There is one other feature of some good works of literature that makes them especially valuable for exploring gender, racial, and ethnic identities. I am referring to the focus of most literature on human experience. In general, political scientists focus on a society, while sociologists focus on a demographic group. Historians usually focus on the changes that take place over time in a society or a demographic group, while social psychologists typically take a snapshot of an individual's mental state at a given moment in time within a controlled situation. Many works of literature, by contrast, take as their customary focus the lives over time of a range of characters—especially the characters' experiences, feelings, and identities. By representing the interconnected lives of different characters—all of whom are negotiating multiple and overlapping structures of power and privilege—a good work of literature can reveal how gender, race, and ethnicity constrain and enable characters' bodies, behaviors, and ideas. In this way, some works of literature can help readers understand how gender, race, and ethnicity actually *matter*— both in the sense of being important and in the sense of how the social

---

1 I am borrowing Maria Lugones's suggestive phrase " 'world'-traveling," to indicate the different subjective worlds we humans occupy. See Lugones, "Playfulness, 'World'-Traveling, and Loving Perception."

processes of gender, race, and ethnicity become materialized in individual lives.

Through a reading (interpretation) of the much-anthologized short story "The Moths," by the Chicana author Helena Maria Viramontes, I demonstrate the latent potential of good multicultural literature to travel backward and forward in time and to expand a reader's horizon of possibility for experiential encounters. I further show that when a story such as "The Moths" is interpreted well, it can be an important contributor to our knowledge about race, ethnicity, and gender. Not only does it provide a critical analysis of the social world(s) from which it emerged, it demonstrates the mutual constitution of racial, class, and gender identities and points toward different, less oppressive, identities and ways of interacting with others.

READING "THE MOTHS"

According to the literary critic Rust Hills in *Writing in General and the Short Story in Particular*, the characteristic focus of a short story is "something that happened to someone" (1977, 1). A short story, like a novel, is a narrative form, and as such, it has a beginning, middle, and end as well as a plot, with buildup, climax, and denouement. But an important feature of the short story form is an internal coherence and a narrative compression that is less characteristic of the novel form. Typically, a short story is more tightly organized than a novel; for this reason, the narrative energy of a short story usually goes toward giving the context for and setting up the situation in which something happens to someone.

At the most basic level, what "happens" to the unnamed narrator in "The Moths" is that her grandmother's death prompts her transition from girlhood to womanhood. She makes the transition by agreeing to care for her dying grandmother, by attending to the body immediately after her grandmother's death, and by realizing (through her emotions and actions) the importance of certain values and practices normally associated with the activity of mothering.

Of course, much more takes place in the story than simply what "happens" at the level of the plot. Narrative perspective, theme, temporal structure, and the symbolism of "The Moths" all work together to set up the plot situation in which the transition will occur. Taking as my point of entry the opening paragraph, I look at each of these in turn:

> I was fourteen years old when Abuelita requested my help. And it seemed only fair. Abuelita had pulled me through the rages of

scarlet fever by placing, removing and replacing potato slices on the temples of my forehead; she had seen me through several whippings, an arm broken by a dare-jump off Tío Enrique's toolshed, puberty, and my first lie. Really, I told Amá, it was only fair (27).[2]

A wealth of information is contained in this short paragraph. With the very first word, "I," we notice that the story is told in the first person, from the perspective of this one young woman. With the second word, we notice that the story is told in the past tense. These two simple words, "I was," coming at the very beginning of the story set up for us a series of expectations—they cue us to the fact that time has passed, and that something important has happened between the time in which the story is set and the time of the telling of the story. In other words, the very fact that the story is told in the past tense clues the reader to expect that some sort of transition will occur during the course of the story.

The next thing we find out is that the narrator of the story was fourteen years old when the story takes place. She is on the brink of adulthood, standing on the border between girlhood and womanhood. This sense of being on the boundary is reinforced by the narrator's reference to puberty, and to a loss of innocence implied by a "first lie." Additionally, we note the use of Spanish names—Abuelita, Tío Enrique, Amá—in a story that is written in English. The linguistic code-switching in this paragraph points to a border line between Spanish and English—the transgression of which is an intimate part of the everyday life of this young Mexican American female character.

Other significant aspects of the first paragraph are the theme of reciprocity and an emphasis on female interdependence that is contrasted, over the course of the story, with nonreciprocal male authoritarianism. The narrator tells us that "it seemed only fair" and then again "it was only fair" that she be asked to care for her grandmother. The repeated use of the phrase "only fair" emphasizes the justice of being expected to respond in kind; the narrator's grandmother had cared for her, and now it is time for her to repay the favor. Moreover, the repeated use of the phrase "only fair" indicates that reciprocity is—for the narrator, at least—an important value; it constitutes for her what is good, right, beautiful, and just (all traditional connotations of the word "fair"). It is important for us as readers to note this emphasis on reciprocity, because it sensitizes us to see in the narrated events of the story the reality that the

---

2 This and subsequent page numbers refer to Helena Maria Viramontes, 1985, "The Moths," in *The Moths and Other Stories*, Houston, TX: Arte Publico Press.

society in which the narrator lives is *not* a fair one; it does not treat this young girl kindly, nor does it operate according to an ethic of reciprocity.

The Use of Time in "The Moths"

Throughout the story, Viramontes makes effective use of flashbacks to provide the context for the transition that is about to happen. These flashbacks occur at the point when the narrator switches to the "would always" verb tense. The "would always" verb tense refers to an old habit that stopped sometime in the undifferentiated past; it denotes something often repeated in the past but no longer done. We see this verb tense for the first time in the third paragraph of the story just after the narrator tells us about the incident in which her abuelita shaped her hands back to size using a balm of moth's wings and Vicks. After that, she tells us, her Amá "would always" send her over to her grandmother's house. The "would always" verb tense is used frequently in the next two paragraphs, although the "always" is more often implied than present in the text.

There are, in fact, several different past verb tenses used in the story. In addition to "would always," there is the past continuous verb tense: "was dying." The past continuous indicates that a longer action in the past has been interrupted—usually by a completed action set in the simple past: "Abuelita snapped," "she died." There is also the past perfect, a verb tense that refers to an action completed before something else that happened in the past: "had pulled," "has seen," "had forgotten." These verb tenses correspond to distinct temporal modes in the story, each of which refers to a distinct phase in the narrator's emergence into womanhood.

The final verb tense in the story is one that is not set in the past but that transforms the present into a temporality that is timeless, mythic, and universal—what we might call "prophetic" time. This tense appears in only one paragraph—the paragraph that signals the beginning of the event (the grandmother's death) that "happens" to the story's narrator:

> There comes a time when the sun is defiant. Just about the time when moods change, inevitable seasons of a day, transitions from one color to another, that hour or minute or second when the sun is finally defeated, finally sinks into the realization that it cannot with all its power to heal or burn, exist forever, there comes an illumination where the sun and earth meet, a final burst of burning red orange fury reminding us that although endings are inevitable, they

are necessary for rebirths, and when that time came, just when I switched on the light in the kitchen to open Abuelita's can of soup, it was probably then that she died (31).

My point is that verb tenses in "The Moths" create what I see as the story's three distinct temporalities. These are the *situational past*, the *time of the past self*, and the *time of the possible self* (see Table 18.1).

As Table 18.1 illustrates, the *situational past* in "The Moths" refers to the temporal mode in which the story is situated. It is set in the verb tense of "past continuous." The *situational past*, as I define it here, embeds within it events in the "simple past" verb tense, such as the actual event of Mama Luna's death. In turn, the *time of the past self* refers to the way the narrator used to be, before that way of being was interrupted by the events in the story that will lead to the transition we are led to expect. This temporal mode is set in the "would always" verb tense, and it is the one in which the protagonist has the most significant interaction with her grandmother. And finally, the *time of the possible self* is the temporal mode in which the dreams, hopes, and illusions of the narrator—dreams, hopes, and illusions that the reader comes to understand as contesting the dominant values and practices of the society she lives in—are expressed. This temporal mode corresponds to what I have called "prophetic time" and it is timeless, mythic, and universal.

The temporality corresponding to the *time of the possible self* is the one to which we need to pay the most attention in interpreting this story. Why? Because the paragraph in which it occurs prepares the way for the transition that is at the heart of this beautifully crafted work. At the level of discourse, the paragraph accumulates images of transition: from

TABLE 18.1 | **TEMPORAL MODES IN VIRAMONTES'S "THE MOTHS"**

Verb Tense	Temporal Mode
Past Continuous	**Situational Past**
• Simple Past	• The temporality in which the story is set
• Past Perfect	
Would Always	**Time of the Past Self**
	• The temporality in which the narrator has the most significant interaction with her abuelita
Prophetic or Mythic Time	**Time of the Possible Self**
	• The temporality in which the dreams, hopes, and illusions of the narrator are expressed

one mood to another, one season to another, one color to another, day to night, life to death, light to dark, death to rebirth, defiance to resignation, natural to artificial light, closed to open. These multiple transitions signal the move into the realm of possibility; we enter a temporal imaginary in which it might be possible for the young girl to leave behind her past self and become a different kind of woman—a self with agency, a woman who nurtures and is nurtured in turn, a person not at the mercy of an unkind society that treats her with casual, or concentrated, disdain.

At the level of symbolism, the move to prophetic time in this paragraph opens up the story even further, as it prompts us to consider the historical and cultural contexts within which this story must be interpreted.

Historical and Cultural Contexts for "The Moths"

For the purpose of understanding why it is important to consider a story's cultural and historical contexts, it is useful to think of the short story as the literary equivalent of a social psychological experiment. The author creates a character and puts that character into a hypothetical situation and makes something happen that will test or challenge the character in some fundamental way. But just as the social psychological researcher cannot adequately interpret a particular behavior or reaction in an experiment unless she has a nuanced understanding of the larger cultural context, so, in interpreting a short story, the literary critic must be able to understand and explain the events of the story in terms of the cultural and historical context from which it emerges.

I begin, then, with some brief biographical facts. Helena Maria Viramontes was born in 1954 and raised in the Mexican barrios of Los Angeles. She did her undergraduate work at Immaculate Heart College in Los Angeles before entering the M.F.A. program at the University of California, Irvine, in 1981. In a talk she gave in my class on February 4, 2002, Viramontes explained that she left the M.F.A. program after one of her teachers (a white man) complained about her tendency to write about Chicana/os. She should, he explained, write about "people" instead. Only after the publication of her collection *The Moths and Other Stories* by Arte Publico Press in 1985 did she return to the program; she received her M.F.A. in 1995. Currently, Viramontes is a professor of English and creative writing at Cornell University and the author of several books, including two novels: *Under the Feet of Jesus* (1995) and *Their Dogs Came with Them* (2007).

Viramontes's former teacher's insensitive remark points to one important context within which this story must be understood—that of Mexican-origin people as a racialized minority group within the United States. The point is not just that Mexican Americans were a numerical minority, but rather that they faced pervasive discrimination as a result of being identified with that group—to the point, apparently, where Viramontes's teacher was unable to see them as worthy subjects for a work of literature. Especially during the time in which this story is set, limited employment opportunities, residential segregation, underfunded schools, inadequate services, and unmerited disrespect were all "identity contingencies" (Steele 2004; Steele et al. 2002) Mexican Americans faced as a result of their racial and ethnic identities (Camarillo 1979; Montejano 1987; Gutiérrez 1995; Sánchez 1993; Foley 1997; Ruiz 1998). As people who were associated with a group with little power and less privilege, they were seen by Viramontes's professor as marginal beings and thus unworthy to be protagonists (that is, main characters) of the human experience.

We see allusions to the material conditions and disrespect faced by Mexican Americans in Los Angeles in the young girl's interaction with "Jay," the proprietor of the grocery store she visits to buy supplies. The narrator tells us, "Most of the time Jay didn't have much of anything. The tomatoes were always soft and the cans of Campbell soups had rusted spots on them. There was dust on the tops of cereal boxes" (30). We see, moreover, that the narrator is subject to a kind of irrational disrespect from Jay resulting from a momentary confusion on her part: "At first Jay got mad because I thought I had forgotten the money" (30). But, we might ask ourselves, why should he be mad? If, in the story, the narrator-character *had* forgotten the money, then *she* would have been the one inconvenienced by having to go home to get it. The most the Jay character would have had to do is hold the groceries aside for her. It is hard for us to know whether the narrator is subject to this unmerited disrespect because of her age, her race, or her gender—or a combination of all three. Nonetheless, it is clear that Jay feels entitled to treat her poorly; he feels no compunction about taking out his aggression, resentment, and frustration—whatever their true source—on her.

A second important context for this story is Mexican Catholicism. The great majority of Mexican-origin people are Catholic for the historical reason that Spain made the conversion of indigenous people a central aspect of its colonial project. In fact, Catholicism is such an integral part of Mexican life that it is sometimes hard to separate the culture from the religion. In "The Moths," Mexican Catholicism appears most obviously in her father's insistence that the narrator attend mass every Sunday: "He would pound his hands on the table, rocking the sugar dish or spilling a cup of coffee and scream that if I didn't go to mass every Sunday to save my goddamn sinning soul, then I had no reason to go out of the house, period. Punto final" (29). Moreover, her father's insistence that she go to mass dovetails nicely with a third context—that of the patriarchy of both Mexican and American culture.

The *Oxford English Dictionary* defines patriarchy both as "a form of social organization in which the father or oldest male is the head of the family, and where descent and relationship are reckoned through the male line," and as "a social system in which men predominate in positions of power and influence in society, with cultural values and norms being seen as favoring men." A feature of patriarchy as it operates in both Mexican and American cultures is that women are assigned the role of "culture bearer." Thus, we see that the narrator's mother is held responsible by her father for her "lousy ways of bringing up daughters, being disrespectful and unbelieving" (29). Additionally, the narrator's older sisters are drawn into the drama, as they are socialized to participate in the disciplining of the young girl (29). This example provides further evidence of how someone with an "outsider" identity can be ideally situated—as a result of having that identity and so having an oppressive power directly enforced on her body—to learn about the ordinary and day-to-day workings of the specific system of power that oppresses her.

In fact, the story shows us, through the narrator's inability to accept or conform to them, the pervasive gender values of the society in which the story is set. From the very first paragraph, we see that the narrator is having difficulty embodying the culturally prescribed ideal of Chicana womanhood. She isn't "even pretty or nice like [her] older sisters"; she couldn't do the "girl things" they could do (27). Instead, she is a "tomboy" with "bull hands" that are "too big to handle the fineries of crocheting or embroidery" (27). She isn't "respectful" because she questions authority, and she reacts (inappropriately according to the standards of her society) with anger and violence to being made fun of for being outside this ideal feminine type (27). The consequences for her nonconformity are painful: she is subjected to her sisters' ridicule as well as to her father's physical abuse.

Thus far, I have focused on the historical and cultural contexts that are most relevant to the *setting* of the story. These contexts are most important for revealing how race and ethnicity shape the identities of the characters. Now I want to mention additional contexts relevant to the *writing* of the story. These contexts are much more significant with respect to the identity of the author.

As a young woman growing up in East Los Angeles in the 1960s, Viramontes was an active participant in the left social movements that were sweeping the country. One of the most important was the Chicano movement, an ethnic civil rights movement that emerged in the 1960s alongside other ethnic civil rights and left liberation movements (Muñoz 1989; Garcia 1997). Mexican Americans throughout the country, but especially in the West and Southwest, asserted a newfound pride in their previously denigrated racial and linguistic heritage and created for themselves an oppositional identity that they called "Chicano." An integral part of the Chicano movement was the reclamation of Mexican cultural icons such as Pancho Villa or Emiliano Zapata and the use of indigenous (primarily Aztec) mythology and symbolism. The turn toward the indigenous that was apparent in Chicano movement art and literature should be understood as an explicit rejection of the ideas and practices associated with Eurocentric notions of European racial or cultural supremacy. Indeed, it is no accident that the first literary prize awarded by Chicanos for Chicano literature was called the Premio Quinto Sol. El Quinto Sol, or the Fifth Sun, is a reference to the present age in the Aztec cosmology (Calderón 2005).

Yet another important context for the formation of Viramontes's identity, and the work she subsequently produced, was the ideological coming together of feminist activists and artists who were developing their identities as radical nonwhite women just as she began her writing career. In the late 1970s, Chicana, black, American Indian, and Asian American women began to organize together around a new and historically specific activist identity that they called "women of color" (Lorde 1984; Moraga and Anzaldúa 1981; Anzaldúa 1990, 1987).[3] Feminists of color created this new social movement in response both to ethnic nationalist (and sexist) civil rights movements run primarily by minority men, as well as gender-universalist (and race-blind) feminist organizations run primarily by middle-class white women. Women-of-color activists, including many artists and writers such as Toni Cade Bambara, Barbara Smith, Cherríe Moraga, Gloria Anzaldúa, Mitsuye Yamada, and

---

[3] "U.S. Third World Feminism" was an analogous term employed by some women of color in the 1980s and 1990s. It was used primarily to signal an experiential connection with nonwhite or "Third World" women living in countries other than the United States, particularly in what is now called the Global South.

Audre Lorde, began to share ideas about what it meant to be nonwhite women living, loving, and working in late twentieth-century America. In the process, they developed a political identity as "women of color" as well as a distinct "woman-of-color consciousness." A woman-of-color consciousness has been central to the interpretive perspectives and representational practices that authors such as Helena Maria Viramontes employ in their writings.

At the heart of a woman-of-color feminist consciousness is a conviction regarding the knowledge-generating significance of identity—a conviction on which I base my own interpretive practices as a literary critic. Drawing on the writings of Cherríe Moraga (1983), I have argued elsewhere that knowledge can be linked to "our skin color, the land or concrete we grew up on, our sexual longings" without being uniformly determined by them. In other words, the "physical realities of our lives" will profoundly *inform without necessarily limiting* the contours and the contexts of both our theories and our knowledge (Moya 1996, 2002). For this reason, the effects that the "physical realities of our lives" have on us—on our values, our practices, and our knowledges—are what need to be addressed by scholars who are concerned with understanding the complex relationship between identity, the creation of knowledge, and the legitimate or illegitimate use of power (Collins 1990; Mohanty 1997; Moya and Hames-García 2000; Moya 1996, 2002; Alcoff 2006; Alcoff et al. 2006).

The Role of the Literary Critic

Let me pause to discuss the role of the literary critic before introducing another element to my reading. As I indicated earlier, a literary critic's evidence is the text she is interpreting. Her role in analyzing a short story like "The Moths" is thus to unpack the narrative compression of the story and to interpret its events, symbols, themes, and structure in terms of the ideas and practices that reflect, promote, and contest the pervasive sociocultural ideals of the world(s) with which the story engages. As a part of her practice, the literary critic bears in mind that the aesthetic artifact she is examining most likely has been carefully and thoughtfully crafted by one or more authors. She reasonably assumes, then, that seemingly inconsequential details might have been put there to serve some specific purpose. This is why when a literary critic notices something odd in the plot of the story, or in the way the story is being told, she will take it as a signal to stop and pay close attention. It is her job to figure out what meaning-making purpose such anomalies might be serving. By way of illustrating, I provide below an example of one such an anomaly in "The Moths" and explain what it might mean.

Earlier, I noted that the shift in verb tense (from past tense to mythic time) was a signal to the reader that something is about to happen. This, together with the anomalous naming of Mama Luna, made me wonder about what the narrative move into a mythic temporality might be accomplishing in this story. Consider for a moment the way naming works in this story. We never learn the name of the narrator, and with the exception of brief references to Tío Enrique and Teresa, all the characters are identified by their social roles: Amá, Apá, granddaughter, older sisters. This indicates that the characters in the story do not represent individuals as much as they represent subject positions within a prevailing social order. So, it is notable that the narrator's grandmother is named, and that her name is Mama Luna. Her name, when set in the context of the tendency among movement-era Chicanos and Chicanas to draw upon indigenous (primarily Aztec) mythology for inspiration suggests a link to the story of Coyolxauhqui, an ancient Mesoamerican goddess who is associated with the moon. The Coyolxauhqui story comes from a powerful Mexica legend that has survived in various (weakened) forms for over 500 years. Most Mexicans and Mexican Americans know aspects of this legend—such as the belief that the full moon is a malevolent force that can harm unborn children—even if they are unfamiliar with the goddess, or unaware of how their beliefs connect with her story.

My purpose in excavating the legend of Coyolxauhqui in this essay is to show how gender and ethnicity matter for the formation of identities over time—even when individuals are unaware of the specific myths that have helped to shape their cultural contexts. The Coyolxauhqui story is a formative myth that operates for many Mexican Americans in a way that people who are unfamiliar with Mexico's history may need help—in the form of additional information—to understand. As a result of their hybrid cultural history, Mexican Americans are heir to a Mesoamerican mythic system, just as they are heir to the several mythic systems that have come down to them through Western culture. Most Americans easily recognize how Greek and Judeo-Christian myths have informed the images and narratives of much of Western literature. The difference in this case is that "The Moths" is drawing in an oblique way on a myth that most Americans (including many Mexican Americans) are not consciously aware of. The significance of the Coyolxauqui myth for my reading of "The Moths" becomes apparent when we notice the critique of religion expressed as the substitution of a patriarchal male God with a matriarchal alternative, the prominent symbolism involving the sun and the moon, and the thematic emphasis on mother-daughter relationships. I turn to the legend, before explaining each of these points in turn.

Coyolxauhqui: An Aztec Story of Dismemberment and Mother-Daughter Betrayal

The story of Coyolxauhqui's military defeat and bodily dismemberment at the hands of her brother Uitzilopochtli was collected and recorded by Fray Bernardino de Sahagún as one among a number of legends, tales, and histories related to him by indigenous scribes in the years after the fall of the Mexica (or Aztec) empire. Fray Bernardino collected the material into twelve books, referred to today as *The Florentine Codex*, that are the major source of information we have about the indigenous cultures of Mesoamerica prior to Spanish conquest.

Like that of other societies in other places and other times, the religious worldview of the Aztecs at the time of the Spanish conquest was a syncretic one. In the older Otomi tradition, Coyolxauhqui was the moon goddess. In the relatively more recent Mexica tradition, she was the daughter of Coatlicue and sister of the Centzonuitznaua, or four hundred stars, and of Uitzilopochtli, the god of war and a manifestation of the sun god. Uitzilopochtli was the principal god of the Mexica, who, prior to their ascendance to power over the various tribes living in the valley of Mexico, were a "ragtag" tribe of warriors (Gordon Brotherston conversation with author, January 17, 2006).

The story begins with Coyolxauhqui's mother, Coatlicue, doing penance at Coatepec. As Coatlicue sweeps the temple, a ball of feathers appears and falls on or touches her. Coatlicue tucks it into her bosom for safekeeping and goes on with her task. When she is finished, she looks for the ball of feathers. But it has disappeared, and she is pregnant. When Coatlicue's daughter, Coyolxauhqui, and her four hundred sons, the Centzonuitznaua, find out about this unexpected and shameful pregnancy, they become infuriated and decide to kill their mother. The infant in her womb, who is Uitzilopochtli, hears the commotion and calls out to his mother that he will protect her. At this point, everyone stops and girds for battle. Then, at the decisive moment, Uitzilopochtli is born and appears fully armed with the fire serpent xiuhcoatl, with which he strikes his sister:

Then he pierced Coyolxauhqui, and then quickly struck off her head. It stopped there at the edge of Coatepetl. And her body came falling below; it fell breaking to pieces; in various places her arms, her legs, her body each fell. (Fray Bernardino de Sahagún [1540–1585])

After Coyolxauhqui's murder and dismemberment, Uitzilopochtli pursues the Centzonuitznaua, making them flee into the southern sky while he remains victorious.

At an allegorical level, the Coyolxauhqui myth represents the daily struggle between the moon and stars and the sun, in which every morning the sun once again wins the battle, banishing the moon and the stars to the southern sky. It also provides an explanation for why the moon appears and disappears in fragments, waxing and waning in phases every month (Museo del Templo Mayor 2006, 2008). But the story is a story of parthenogenesis as well as a story of kinship relations. Apart from its obvious importance as the origin story of the sun and war god, Uitzilopochtli, we can interpret it as a story of a mother who betrays her daughter by giving birth to her murderer, or of a daughter who betrays her mother by attempting to control, through matricide, her mother's fecundity and/or unsanctioned sexuality. Either way, the rift between the mother and the daughter in this story symbolized the inauguration of Aztec warrior society (represented by the birth of Uitzilopochtli) and affirmed an ideology of male dominance (represented by Uitzilopochtli's decisive defeat of the powerful daughter Coyolxauhqui and the collective of sons, the four hundred stars, who were allied with her). And, in fact, the story of Coyolxauhqui's defeat was very important to the Mexica. According to the Mesoamerican specialist Gordon Brotherston (conversation with author January 17, 2006), the story of Coyolxauhqui's dismemberment by Uitzilopochtli was an origin story for the Mexica, serving both to explain and to justify their ascendance to power over the other tribes residing in pre-Columbian Mesoamerica.

Coyolxauhqui's defeat and dismemberment is represented and memorialized in the huge and imposing Coyolxauhqui stone, a round disc that weighs eight tons and is 10.66 feet in diameter (see Figure 18.1). The stone was discovered in 1978 by electric grid workers who were doing maintenance work in the center of present-day Mexico City (Museo del Templo Mayor 2006, 2008). The unearthing of the stone sparked a major archeological project at the site of what turned out to have been the ceremonial center of the ancient Mexica city of Tenochtitlán. Archeologists have since

FIGURE 18.1 | THE COYOLXAUHQUI STONE.

determined that the stone was discovered in the original location where the Mexica had placed it, at the foot of the south stair of the fourth rebuilding (ca. 1469–81) of the major Aztec temple, known today as El Templo Mayor (see Fig. 18.2).

The significance for the Mexica of the Coyolxauhqui stone and of where they placed it becomes evident when we consider that a representation of Uitzilopochtli (in the form of the stone of the Fifth Sun) would most likely have been housed *inside and at the top* of the same temple (see Fig. 18.3).[3] The Coyolxauhqui stone was thus prominently displayed by the Mexica so as to be a graphic and highly visible reminder of Uitzilopochtli's birth and most important victory.

So, while Coyolxauhqui herself may not have been an important deity for the Mexica, the story of her defeat and dismemberment appears to

[3] The stone of the Fifth Sun, more commonly known to us as the Aztec Calendar stone, is similar to the Coyolxauhqui stone in that it is a circular carving. However, it differs significantly in that it represents the sun god as both all-powerful (his tongue is in the form of a sacrificial knife) and at the center of the cosmos. The stone of the Fifth Sun was carved around the same time as the Coyolxauqui stone (est. 1479) and is somewhat larger; it weighs twenty-four tons and is twelve feet in diameter.

FIGURE 18.2 | SCALE MODEL OF EL TEMPLO MAYOR, ARROW POINTING TO LOCATION OF THE COYOLXAUHQUI STONE.

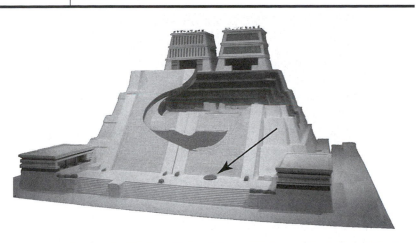

FIGURE 18.3 | THE STONE OF THE FIFTH SUN.

have been at the very core of Mexica cultural and political identity. It is not surprising, then, that aspects of the Coyolxauhqui legend have survived into the present day within the (not always conscious) cultural memories of Mexican and Mexican American people. While there is no explicit allusion to the Coyolxauhqui legend in the story, an understanding of the symbolism behind this formative origin myth thus shows how a Chicana/o ethnic context influences the identities that are represented in the story.

The Symbolic Re-membering of Coyolxauhqui: The Rebirth of the Daughter as Mother

I suggested earlier that "The Moths" presents a critique of the Catholic religion through a substitution of a patriarchal male God with a ma-triarchal alternative. Let me explain how this works. Remember that it is the father who insists that the young girl go to mass, and who digs his nails into her arm to make sure she understands "the importance of catechism" (29). Even though the young girl puts on her best shoes and grabs her missal and veil before heading out the door, she does not go to mass. Instead, she turns left and goes to her grandmother's house. The grandmother, with her gray eye that makes the narrator feel "safe and guarded and not alone," takes the place of God, who is "supposed" to do this, but does not (28). Organized religion, represented by the chapel with the "frozen statues" with "blank eyes," is not represented in the story as a sacred place for the young girl. She leaves the chapel without blessing herself.

The grandmother's house, in marked contrast to the chapel, is a woman-centered sanctuary where the young girl participates in the making of an alternative female sociality. In the grandmother's house, women's everyday chores are transformed into sacred practices full of meaning. The young girl nurtures her grandmother's plants, and is nurtured in return by gaining a sense of worth, efficacy, and power (28). The grand-mother's house is a place of refuge where the young girl's "bull hands" can be put to productive use. It is there that we see her working through her pain and anger as she uses her hands in a healing ritual to crush the tomatoes and chiles in a molcajete for her own and her grandmoth-er's nourishment (30). She and her abuelita communicate not through words (or the Word)—textual or oral—but through touch, household chores, and everyday actions. And finally, although displaying affection in a conventional way is difficult for the narrator—she does not kiss her grandmother—she finds a way to care for her grandmother by rubbing her body with alcohol and marijuana and by ministering to her when she is ill. These scenes with the grandmother involving the narrator's hands offer a noticeable contrast to the scene where she stands in front of her mother with her "hands just hanging helplessly by [her] side" (30).

Those helplessly hanging hands capture beautifully the young girl's discomfort with the gendered, racial, and ethnic identity scripts that have
been thrust upon her by the people she lives among. Thus, by representing the grandmother's house as a sacred refuge, and the young girl's interactions with her grandmother as the means by which she participates
in an alternative female sociality, the story anticipates the possibility that
the narrator may yet find another way to be in the world.

The prominent symbolism involving the sun and the moon further
link the Coyolxauhqui legend to the story's critique of a patriarchal
Catholic worldview. Recall from my earlier discussion that the story
moves into the *time of the possible self* just as the sun goes down and the
grandmother passes away. In a nod to a Mesoamerican cyclical cosmology, the story prompts the reader to remember that endings are both inevitable and necessary for rebirths (31). The fact that this temporal shift
occurs at the moment of the sun's setting serves to remind the reader
that just as the sun is victorious every morning against the moon and
the stars, so do these same antagonists defeat him every evening. The
climax of the story comes right after the young girl uses her hands for
the tender undressing and sacramental bathing of her abuelita following
Mama Luna's death of stomach cancer. In her reconstructed religion, the
young girl plays the role of priest. She goes to the linen closet, takes out
bleached white towels, and "[w]ith the sacredness of a priest preparing
his vestments, [she] unfolded the towels one by one on [her] shoulders"
(31). The story thus opens up the possibility that the young girl may be
able to create for herself a new, more affirming, identity through her
participation in an alternative matriarchal spirituality.

The end of story enacts a rebirth in which the young girl plays the
part of both mother and child. Stepping into the bathtub with her dead
grandmother, she symbolically reenters the waters of the womb and begins to heal herself in communion with her mother and grandmother.
Part of this process involves learning to mother as well as to be mothered.
As she holds her grandmother in the water, the young girl smoothes
her grandmother's hair, and consoles her—much in the way a mother
soothes a small child. Amid multiple images of boundary confusion—
the bathwater overflows the tub onto the tile; the grandmother's soul is
released in the form of hundreds of small gray moths; and the narrator
imagines accompanying her grandmother on her journey toward death
with chayote vines that "crawl up [the grandmother's] fingers and into
the clouds"—the narrator is finally able to enact a rebirth that will lead
to a reconciliation (32). Using a grammatical formulation that mimics

the hiccup that is part of a sob, she is finally free to express her great desire for her mother: "I wanted. I wanted my Amá." Once the narrator is able to acknowledge this need, once she is able to acknowledge the hurt and the love she feels—for herself, for her grandmother, and for her mother—only then is she able to cry. She becomes simultaneously the woman who is being born and, in a sense, the mother of the newborn woman that she is. She is born anew as a woman in a context that affirms interdependence, reciprocity, and physical as well as emotional care (32). In the process, the story symbolically repairs the mother-daughter bond and enacts a re-membering of that long ago daughter, Coyolxauhqui. The symbolic rebirth and her new way of interacting with the women in her life opens up for the young girl the possibility that she might be able to forge a new kind of identity. Thus, "The Moths" takes us back to the moment of birth to rewrite the origin story. Instead of the son, it is the daughter who is (re)birthed, and instead of dismemberment, separation, and violence, what comes out of *this* birth is forgiveness, reunion, remembrance, and love figured as interdependence and care.

CONCLUSION

Because the behaviors and practices depicted in any work of literature encode underlying values and ideas, examining our own as well as fictional characters' behaviors and practices in and through literature can help us to see the dominant ideas and values of any given society and to understand how the social processes of gender, race, and ethnicity affect individual experience and identity. This is one significant function of good works of literature. But a second function of some important works of literature is helping us to imagine what certain alternative values, ideas, and identities to the dominant ones might be. Indeed, part of what is involved in changing the world we have in common, in figuring out how to get from our world to a better one, is imagining as well as actively bringing about other ways of being in that world. As artifacts of the imagination, literary works are *by their very nature* engaged in imagining other ways of being. Sometimes they do it by depicting worlds that look very similar to our own, with characters that are similar to people we know; sometimes they do it by depicting worlds and characters that are wholly alien to us. Whether a work of literature is "realistic" or "fantastical," despairing or hopeful, it is almost always an ethical engagement with some past, future, familiar, or foreign world.

In my reading of Helena Maria Viramontes's tightly woven and beautifully written short story "The Moths," I show that the different verb tenses in the story correspond to different temporalities, and that shifts among the verb tenses set the reader up to expect shifts in perspective. I further show that the shift into prophetic time, what I call the *time of the possible self*, cues the reader (not necessarily at a conscious level) to interpret the events in terms of what might be, rather than what is. The use of prophetic time moves the story into a temporal imaginary in which it might be possible for the young girl to reconcile with her mother, leave behind her split self, and become a different kind of woman—a woman with a transformed identity; a woman with agency who can construct for herself a more life-affirming world than the one she lives in.

The possibility of positive change suggested by the story's use of different temporalities is reinforced at both the story and symbolic level. At the level of the story, Viramontes depicts the grandmother's house as a woman-centered sanctuary in which the young girl participates in the making of an alternative female sociality that valorizes interdependence, reciprocity, and physical as well as emotional care. At a symbolic level, Viramontes's evocation of the Coyolxauhqui story—through references to (1) the ongoing battle between the sun and the moon, (2) the cycle of death and rebirth, and (3) the importance of repairing the shattered relationship between a mother and her daughter—reinforces the idea that life-affirming change is possible for women who are willing to turn away from a violently patriarchal order and create new identities by finding different and better ways of interacting with others.

By situating "The Moths" in relation to its social and political contexts, and by attending to the story's theme, symbolism, and narrative structure, I demonstrate how the story works as a creative and formal linguistic engagement with historically situated cultural and political tensions that express themselves at the level of individual or subjective experience. The story represents the minute day-to-day interpersonal interactions that give rise to gender, racial, and ethnic identities, even as it represents (and so makes possible for us as readers) more interdependent, reciprocal, caring, and forgiving ways of interacting with others. This, then, is how some works of literature—both as aesthetic artifacts and through literary critics' interpretation of those artifacts—provide us with an important source of knowledge about the pervasive cultural ideas (or ideologies) through which we apprehend our several, as well as our shared, social world(s). This is why reading and analyzing a story like

"The Moths" is a crucial part of helping anti-racist activists and scholars to imagine what some viable alternative (i.e., more just and humane) ideas, values, practices, behaviors, and identities might possibly be.

Works Cited

•

Alcoff, Linda Martín. 2006. *Visible Identities: Race, Gender, and the Self*. New York: Oxford University Press.

Alcoff, Linda Martín, et al. 2006. *Identity Politics Reconsidered*. New York: Palgrave.

Anzaldúa, Gloria, ed. 1990. *Making Face, Making Soul/Haciendo Caras: Creative and Critical Perspectives by Feminists of Color*. San Francisco: Aunt Lute Books.

Anzaldúa, Gloria. 1987. *Borderlands/La Frontera: The New Mestiza*. Midway: Spinsters Ink Books.

Booth, Wayne. 1988. *The Company We Keep: An Ethics of Fiction*. Berkeley: University of California Press.

Brotherston, Gordon. 2006. Conversation with author. Stanford, CA, 17 January.

Calderón, Héctor. 2005. *Narratives of Greater Mexico: Essays on Chicano Literary History, Genre, and Borders*. Austin. University of Texas Press.

Camarillo, Albert. [1979] 1996. *Chicanos in a Changing Society: From Mexican Pueblos to American Barrios in Santa Barbara and Southern California, 1848–1930*. Cambridge, MA: Harvard University Press.

Collins, Patricia Hill. 1991. *Black Feminist Thought: Knowledge, Consciousness, and the Politics of Empowerment*. New York: Routledge.

Foley, Neil. 1997. *The White Scourge: Mexicans, Blacks, and Poor Whites in Texas Cotton Culture*. Berkeley: University of California Press.

Fray Bernardino de Sahagún, Arthur J. Anderson, and Charles E. Dibble. [1540–1585] 1982. *Florentine Codex, A General History of the Things of New Spain. Book 3—The Origin of the Gods*. Salt Lake City: University of Utah Press.

Garcia, Alma M. ed. 1997. *Chicana Feminist Thought: The Basic Historical Writings*. New York: Routledge.

Gutiérrez, David G. 1995. *Walls and Mirrors: Mexican Americans, Mexican Immigrants, and the Politics of Ethnicity*. Berkeley: University of California Press.

Hames-García, Michael. 2004. *Fugitive Thought: Prison Movements, Race, and the Meaning of Justice*. Minneapolis: University of Minnesota Press.

Jameson, Fredric. 1981. *The Political Unconscious: Narrative as a Socially Symbolic Act*. Ithaca, NY: Cornell University Press.

Lorde, Audre. 1984. *Sister Outsider: Essays and Speeches*. Berkeley: Crossing Press.

Markus, Hazel Rose, and Paula Nurius. 1986. Possible Selves. *American Psychologist*. 41:954–969.

Markus, Hazel Rose, Patricia R. Mullaly, and Shinobu Kitayama. 1997. Selfways: Diversity in Models of Cultural Participation. In *The Conceptual Self in Context: Culture, Experience, Self-Understanding* eds. U. Neisser and D. S. Jopling. Cambridge, UK: Cambridge University Press.

Mignolo, Walter. 2000. *Local Histories/Global Designs: Coloniality, Subaltern Knowledges, and Border Thinking*. Princeton, NJ: Princeton University Press.

Mohanty, Chandra Talpade. 2003. *Feminism without Borders: Decolonizing Theory, Practicing Solidarity*. Durham, NC: Duke University Press.

Mohanty, Satya P. 1993. The Epistemic Status of Cultural Identity: On *Beloved* and the Postcolonial Condition. *Cultural Critique* (Spring):41–80.

Mohanty, Satya. 1997. *Literary Theory and the Claims of History: Postmodernism, Objectivity, Multicultural Politics*. Ithaca, NY: Cornell University Press.

Montejano, David. 1987. *Anglos and Mexicans in the Making of Texas, 1836–1986*. Austin: University of Texas Press.

Moraga, Cherríe. 1983. *Loving in the War Years: Lo Que Nunca Pasó por Sus Labios*. Cambridge, MA: South End Press.

Moraga, Cherríe and Gloria Anzaldúa. [1981] 1983. *This Bridge Called My Back: Writings by Radical Women of Color*. Latham, NY: Kitchen Table: Women of Color Press. Originally published by Persephone Press, Watertown, MA, in 1981.

Moya, Paula M. L. 2006. What's Identity Got to Do With It? Mobilizing Identity in the Multicultural Classroom. In *Identity Politics Reconsidered*, eds. L. M. Alcoff, M. R. Hames-García, S. P. Mohanty and P. M. L. Moya. New York: Palgrave Macmillan.

Moya, Paula. 1996. Postmodernism, "Realism," and the Politics of Identity. In *Feminist Genealogies, Colonial Legacies, Democratic Futures*, eds. M. Jacqui Alexander and Chandra Talpade Mohanty. New York: Routledge.

———. 2002. *Learning from Experience: Minority Identities, Multicultural Struggles*. Berkeley: University of California Press.

———. In preparation. *Another Way to Be: Writings by Women of Color*.

Moya, Paula, and Michael Hames-García. 2000. *Reclaiming Identity: Realist Theory and the Predicament of Postmodernism*. Berkeley: University of California Press.

Muñoz, Carlos, Jr. 1989. *Youth, Identity, Power: The Chicano Movement*. New York: Verso.

Museo del Templo Mayor. 2008. Sala 4: Huitzilopotchli. [Cited 5 July 2008] Available at www.templomayor.inah.gob.mx/sala4.htm.

———. 2006. Hall 4: Huitzilopochtli and Coyolxauhqui. [Cited 5 February 2006] Available at archaeology.la.asu.edu/TM/pages2/sala4.htm

Oxford English Dictionary. March 2000. Draft Revision, s.v. "patriarchy."

Roth, Benita. 2004. *Separate Roads to Feminism: Black, Chicana, and White Feminist Movements in America's Second Wave*. New York: Cambridge University Press.

Ruiz, Vicki L. 1998. *From Out of the Shadows: Mexican Women in Twentieth-Century America*. New York: Oxford University Press.

Saldívar, Ramón. 1990. *Chicano Narrative: The Dialectics of Difference*. Madison: University of Wisconsin Press.

Sánchez, George J. 1993. *Becoming Mexican American: Ethnicity, Culture, and Identity in Chicano Los Angeles, 1900–1945*. New York: Oxford University Press.

Siebers, Tobin. 2008. *Disability Theory*. Ann Arbor: University of Michigan Press.

Steele, Claude. 2004. Not just a test. *The Nation* 287.17: 38–40.

Steele, Claude, Steven J. Spencer, and Joshua Aronson. 2002. Contending with group image: The psychology of stereotype and social identity threat. *Advances in Experimental Social Psychology.* 34: 379–440.

Teuton, Sean Kicummah. 2008. *Red Land, Red Power: Grounding Knowledge in the American Indian Novel.* Durham, NC: Duke University Press.

Viramontes, Helena Maria. 2007. *Their Dogs Came with Them.* New York: Atria Books.

———. 1995. *Under the Feet of Jesus.* New York: Dutton Press.

———. 1985. "The Moths." *In The Moths and Other Stories.* Houston, TX: Arte Publico Press.

19

Hiphop and Race
Blackness, Language, and Creativity

**Marcyliena Morgan and
Dawn-Elissa Fischer**

•

This essay examines the complexity inherent in the representation of race and racism in Hiphop. In particular, it focuses on how devotees employ tropes of blackness to carry out critical analyses of racism, class privilege, ethnic and national conflicts, and other social, political, and cultural issues in the United States and around the world. This complexity is examined in two ways. First, we discuss blackness in Hiphop as it refers to the art of representing social, political, spatial, and artistic contexts that are critical of and confront mainstream American practices of exclusion, indifference, and supremacy toward the black community. This is followed by an analysis of how African American language and language ideology are used in Hiphop to represent racism and injustice.

FIGHTING POWER: IN-DIFFERENCE AND RACE

*So when the rain comes down on you
My question is "What you gonna do?"
From where I stand you can fold your hand and let your world
 crumble
Or fight back and keep it on the humble
I know my choice.*
(AKROBATIK 2008)

RACE, AND IN PARTICULAR BLACKNESS, HAS PLAYED A CRUCIAL ROLE in the creation, mythology, and meanings of Hiphop from the start. Though Hiphop's originators and innovators comprised a diverse group of creative youth, in the 1970s the media and society at large mainly described Hiphop as created by poor young blacks in the inner city who did not—and would not—fit into society at large. Discarded and demonized by the dominant culture, which saw them as living in squalor and in need of support,[1] the black and brown urban youth who created Hiphop did more than create a new musical style. As they danced in the streets, dressed in clothes designed for style, comfort, and the "bizness" of Hiphop; constructed and repurposed sound systems, synthesizers, and mixers; spoke witty and sometimes profound rhymes to beats; and spray-painted their reality, legends, and neighborhoods onto anything with a flat surface, they left an imprint on the spaces and places of their lives. Hiphop reintroduced new generations of Americans and the world to the modern and daily realities of living where circumstances are often unjust and always complex. Hiphop became the heir to the fights of the civil rights and Black Power movements for inclusion, respect, and an equal and fair chance in society—whether the leaders of those movements liked it or not. Fighting back against the messages they got from mainstream American society, which seemed to consider them both dangerous and disposable, Hiphop wanted "the whole wide world to know they are here!"

Blackness was important to the birth of Hiphop in yet another way. The youth who birthed Hiphop had grown up within the ideology of African American communities and culture with established and well-known social and political activities and discourse that critique and work to change the American system of justice (Dawson 2003). This ideology includes a direct and indirect critique of the American political and judicial system that victimized blacks; active resistance against racist practices; and the recognition that observing and living with racist practices affects African American and non-African American values and beliefs as well. In African American communities, resistance against oppression and movements for equality has included physical protests as well as critical narratives, political movements, creative art movements, verbal genres, and more. Because the creators of Hiphop were part of a generation of youth who had been attacked and marginalized through

---

1 Indeed, the bulk of scholarship at the time not only bordered on cultural voyeurism, it treated young black men, and Hiphop culture in particular, as simultaneously "socially pathological," an "endangered species," and "at risk" (Males 1996).

governmental and educational policies supported by both black and white adults, Hiphop's notion of building and representing did not rely on black nationalist ideology (cf. Shelby 2005). The struggle for freedom and equality assumes that it is mandatory that all groups receive equal treatment in order to guarantee the rights of any group. The fight has been for a deep commitment to the American Dream with a relentless and critical eye toward its promise of freedom and equality for all.

The role of blackness in Hiphop shows up as well in its deployment of African American culture and language, in particular African American English (AAE). Theories of vernacular language demonstrate that African American youth respond to society's attempt to stigmatize and marginalize AAE usage by their continued use of it and innovations within the norms of both dialects. Consequently, discourse styles, verbal genres, and dialect and language contrasts became tools to not only represent African American culture but also youth alienation, defiance, and injustice in general.

Finally, Hiphop is often associated with blackness because of its oft-recited origin narratives, which situate its cultural genesis in neighborhoods with primarily black and brown residents.[2] Since the East Coast (or East Side) was the birthplace of Hiphop, its urban terrain became synonymous with Hiphop's very existence. Through Hiphop artistry, the local descriptions of East Coast areas set the standards for reclaiming urban spaces that were black and brown kids' neighborhoods to be the foundation and heart of the city. In sum, the history of the African American community's interaction and attitude toward race, racism, and power—domination and subjugation—meant that Hiphop's beginning was an overall critique of both social class and racial categorizing and stereotyping and racism in general.

REPRESENT, RESPECT, AND COME CORRECT: RACE NOT, WANT NOT

Although Hiphop is now a global phenomenon with obvious political and cultural influence, during its early days of party deejays (DJs) and emcees (MCs), little attention was paid to the growing cultural and creative representation of urban life and power politics of Hiphop. The societal reaction was basically "Whatever they are crying about is their fault in this land of plenty." Moreover, for many immersed in their

---

2 The term "origin narrative" in this essay is akin to what is also called Hiphop "history" (Chang 2005; Fricke and Ahearn 2002; Kitwana 2005).

middle-class suburbs and outside urban and poor communities, the sight of urban youth rhyming and performing acrobatic movements in the streets may have reassured them that poor youth and people of color were content. Yet this oversight is surprising because African Americans have sung and danced their way through every protest, civil rights, Black Power, and revolutionary movement in which they have participated. Song, dance, art, and rhyme are not peripheral to African American culture but part and parcel to it. It is real life, both serious and play, and it is through these arts that Hiphop MCs burst into the forefront. And it was because many had underestimated the significance of art in the African American community that those outside of Hiphop did not have an inkling of what might happen and how it could affect racial politics and understanding in the United States and the world.

There are at least three reasons that the social, cultural, and political power of Hiphop was not immediately apparent in the art form. First, it was because of *who* did it. Hiphop was founded by black and brown youth who typically received underfunded formal education, enjoyed few social class privileges, and were routinely demonized and dismissed by society. Second, it was *where* they did it. The Bronx had long been declared a war zone, uninhabitable, resourceless, and suffocating from a culture of poverty and hopelessness. In the late 1970s and early 1980s, the popular media characterized life in the Bronx as a lawless wasteland, making it the "poster child" of urban decay. Journalists reporting on President Jimmy Carter's 1977 visit highlighted the devastation and government neglect of the Bronx; the same year, the *New York Times* considered it to be "as crucial to an understanding of American urban life as Auschwitz is crucial to an understanding of Nazism" (Worth 1999). The 1981 movie *Fort Apache, The Bronx* further sensationalized the area as overrun with nihilism and desolation. To add insult to injury, in 1981, the *Los Angeles Times* declared that the Bronx is "both a place and a scare-word." Last, it was *what* they did: without formal training, urban youth transformed public space and influenced society and the world at the highest level of thinking and artistic creativity. Hiphop raised philosophical questions, introduced new technologies, and reinterpreted old ones. It incorporated the artistic traditions of dance, verbal art, visual art, musical and sound production, and traditions and cultural practices that previously coexisted and only occasionally bonded together in African American culture, and decisively united them into a powerful "workforce" of art.

For the young people who lived there, The Bronx in the late 1970s and early 1980s was a resource and the center of energy and American culture.

Taking what had been used to demonize them in the eyes of mainstream America, they *"brushed the dirt off their shoulder"*[3] and turned the negative words and circumstances into sources of creativity and resistance, writing their existence into the urban space of The Bronx, New York, and eventually the world. Not only did youth throughout the world learn about The Bronx, Bedford Stuyvesant (BedStuy), and Harlem, but also Brooklyn (BK), Hollis (in Queens), Jamaica (in New York), Queens (The Bridge), Staten Island (Shaolin), and New York housing projects like the Marcy Projects and city avenues and streets like Houston in New York City and Hollis Avenue in Queens. In the process of creating a new visual, poetic, and dance aesthetic, Hiphoppers literally mapped onto the consciousness of the world a place (and an identity) for themselves as the originators of an exciting new art form. They thus created value out of races and places that had seemed to offer only devastation.

NO BAITING AND NO HATING: HIPHOP 101

Devotees refer to Hiphop's four artistic areas of emceeing, deejaying, dance (b-boy and b-girl), and graffiti writing/aerosol art as elements. Just as the earth and human beings comprise elements that bind them and make them whole, so does Hiphop. While DJs provided the foundation for Hiphop, MCs became the focus of Hiphop culture as it grew beyond the confines of New York. MCs not only had a lot to say, they consistently worked to find many ways to tell their story. They introduced tales of Hiphop's beginnings, struggles, personalities, spaces, and places. They highlighted local associations by describing and naming neighborhoods, public transportation systems, schools, and highways. The focus on race and place resulted in narratives that transformed urban landscapes like The Bronx into shared-scapes based on the desire to represent particular communities and connect them to each other (Lefebvre 1991).

As the influence of Hiphop spread and more and more youth became involved in its creation, territorial wars soon developed over what neighborhood had the right to different aspects of the Hiphop origin narrative. Anything valuable is worth fighting over, and the foundation of Hiphop was no exception. The Bronx won the rights to the DJ history through

---

3 This is a reference to Hiphop artist's Jay-Z's 2003 song "Dirt Off Your Shoulder" that was referenced by Barack Obama during his presidential campaign.

constant repetition of the first time DJ Kool Herc connected his sound system and mixed records. Yet it was quickly clear that battles over local rights to the first time for Hiphop's other elements would never settle a claim. Instead, battles over who first created b-boy moves, graffiti styles, DJ techniques, and lyrical and production styles fuel excitement, purpose, an audience, and sense of local community.[4]

Whether these narratives reflect specific factual details is less significant than that they reflect the spirit of the moment, central figures, sacred spaces and places, and the sense that an amazing and significant artistic and social movement was created because its originators believed in themselves and the potential of their community in spite of their current conditions. The Hiphop origin narrative is even more impressive considering that these stories have been reproduced in manifold ways in popular literature (e.g., *The Source Magazine*, Viacom's music video industries such as MTV, BET, and VH1), and consumed by youth as well as followers who identify with Hiphop all over the world. The consumption of these narratives has facilitated the emergence of an imagined community of "Hiphoppers" through a common literacy and common struggle against controlling mechanisms of the state as well as those who either intentionally deceive or fall prey to the complicated workings of the state (Anderson 1991; Beebe et al. 2002; Dyson 2001; Heath 2006; hooks 1992).[5] This common origin can be demonstrated by the fact that any youth (from Italy to Japan) identified with this global culture can usually recount a narrative that generally begins with Kool Herc's technological innovation and climaxes with the global popularity of Run DMC.[6]

---

4 This is not to suggest that original innovators cannot be identified for some things. Rather, except for a few cases, especially those concerning technology and DJs, it is difficult to claim to be the first and only when so many youth were involved in the same movement.

5 In the past, this belief was represented by terms such as "the man," "uncle tom," "the establishment," "hegemony," "white power," and "white supremacy." These terms are reminiscent of particular political rhetoric utilized for social movement building with "anti-establishment" efforts such as the Black Panther Party. Early Hiphop artists came of age and began the production of their art in this atmosphere, so it is common to see remnants of this rhetoric in the lyricism of Hiphop. It should be no surprise that they incorporated the oppositional political rhetoric (e.g., "black is beautiful" and "power to the people") of the time to voice their predicament and cope with harsh realities (cf. *Wild Style* and *Style Wars*). Here, the term "the state" refers to governments or nation-states that determine legislation that affects the peoples discussed.

6 For instance, most Hiphop-identified participants' history and origin narratives concerning Hiphop will begin as follows with the overproduced and overpublished story of artist Kool Herc (aka Clive Campbell): "In 1967, Kool Herc emigrated from Jamaica to [the] West Bronx. . . . He extended break beats as a deejay . . . and Hiphop was born" (see Fujita 1996; Gilroy 1993; Hebdige 1987; Kitwana 2005; Morgan 2009; Pipitone 2006; Spady, Alim, and Meghelli 2006).

As important to Hiphop as representing the landscape from which one came, is the need to transform it into something bigger and better. Hiphop did not begin as an oppositional genre. Its originators were participating in something that was creative and productive that represented them. Because they created Hiphop in spite of society's critique, it emerged as oppositional and in discourse with the prevailing stereotype of "the hood." Through Hiphop, impoverished neighborhoods were re-imagined as utopian and ideal spaces in that they are ruled by honorable women and men, many with superhuman abilities, who see through deception and, in the words of Public Enemy, "fight the powers that be" and represent her and his neighborhood and the Hiphop world in general. Similarly, artists often insist that where they were born is also where God and the gods roamed.

The transformation of the land of the ghetto into the land of myth and where the future of humankind will be decided is comparable to the epoch battle of good and evil in Tolkien's Middle-earth and has resulted in what Murray Forman calls "the extreme local" (2002, xvii). It is constructed in relation to local culture and history that is seen as particular, but through which other neighborhoods and the world are also evaluated. Never accepting defeat, and armed with one's own strength, insight, and the righteousness of the black culture and struggle, anything is possible—including an upending of the racial hierarchy. Unlike Tolkien's world that does not include people of color as heroic, in Hiphop it is the One who is considered the most threatening and despised in American public culture that is the most ethical and heroic—the Black Man. As Eric B & Rakim (1988) explain:

> *From century to century you'll remember me*
> *In history—not a mystery or a memory*
> *God by nature, mind raised in Asia*
> *Since you was tricked, I have to raise ya*
> *From the cradle to the grave, but remember*
> *You're not a slave*
> *[...]*
> *But I'm here to break away the chains, take away the pains,*
> *remake the brains, reveal my name*

Whether one calls this space the counterpublic or underground, it threatens dominant discourse about black and urban youth and forces recognition from society. Through MC rhymes like Rakim's above, Hiphop intentionally attacks and redesigns how urban spaces occupied by youth are conceived, lived, and perceived (Lefebvre 1991; McCann 1999).

Whether from The Bronx, the Caribbean, Puerto Rico, Atlanta, Chicago, South Carolina, New York, New Jersey, or Los Angeles—the youth who fashioned the art, culture, and politics of Hiphop were reared on endless tales of the American Dream versus black experiences of what is often called the American Nightmare. These tales serve as examples of how one must develop a sense of self-worth, overcome obstacles, and continue to fight for freedom and equality. They took lessons from stories like the one about Malcolm X, the black Muslim leader, who was told by his high school counselor that he should not aim too high "for his own good." They reminded themselves of the way police seem to serve and protect others and that as the comedian Richard Pryor once observed, American justice is directed at "just us."

Narratives of coping and perseverance traveled alongside cultural documentaries like *Wild Style* (1982) in which the filmmaker Charlie Ahearn communicates this through juxtaposed images of a dilapidated Bronx in the late 1970s, as seen through a window by a depressed and alienated graffiti writer riding on a train. This setting is accompanied by the uplifting sounds of Grandmaster Flash's eclectic, electronic musical production. In the song, Flash's lyricist, Melle Mel, rhymes:

> Look past the garbage, over the trains, under the ruins, through the remains, around the crime, and pollution, and tell me, where I fit in? South Bronx, New York, that's where I dwell. To a lot of people, it's a living hell—full of frustration and poverty. But wait— that's not how it looks to me. It's a challenge, an opportunity, to rise above the stink debris. You got to start with nothing, and then you build. Follow your dream until it's fulfilled. (Ahearn 1982)

Thus it is not surprising that as the Hiphop group dead prez (2000) proclaimed, through the resolve of those involved in Hiphop culture, they created something "bigger than Hiphop."

BLACK IN BUSINESS: CALLING OUT RACE AND CLASS

As noted above, an important element of Hiphop is the language. The language of African American youth residing in urban areas has been a subject of interest to linguistics and sociology since the 1970s, when the work of William Labov (1972) focused on urban youth as dialect innovators. AAE's persistence as a social dialect also suggests that youth operate with a highly structured language ideology and anti-language and counterlanguage (Halliday 1976, 1978; Morgan 2002).[7] Counterlanguages are often found in situations of inequality where one group has power over another and where speaking one's mind may result in punishment of some sort (e.g., slavery, Jim Crow). The group that has little power and whose behavior is controlled may develop a secret and often embedded system of communication that is not easily understood by those in power. In contrast, Hiphop discourse is not concerned with sustaining a system hidden from dominant culture as such. Rather, Hiphop constantly uses the tools of counterlanguage through local references and the creation of new words, pronunciations, spellings, and meanings that may be unknown within the dominant culture. But its purpose is to produce an in-your-face anti-language. Hiphop wants you to know that they use a counterlanguage and that the dominant culture can never really know what they mean.

Hiphop relies on the African American ideology of the WORD by exposing and expanding on those language elements that are marked as black, working class, and regional and by focusing on them through the following tenets: (1) Sounds, objects, and concepts embody and index memory, community, and social world. (2) Choices of language and dialect can signify status, beliefs, values, and specific speakers. (3) All meaning is co-constructed (co-authored).

The first tenet refers to the importance of signifiers or indices and emblems of black urban life. These may include use of and references to AAE, General English (GE) proverbs, popular and children's television, movies, neighborhoods, streets, public transportation systems, prisons, police stations, and the things youth must deal with. However, these items' value may change quickly. Thus it is not only the popular items that have exchange value for youth culture but also how they function within a system of markedness where the notion of normal, expected, and stable are disrupted by forms, references, expressions, and so on that question what is considered normal and accepted. Moreover, a system of markedness functions within popular and local trademarks and brands (cf. Coombe 1996; Bucholtz and Hall 2004) and youth may use the system to mark the same symbol as both positive and negative in any given moment.

The second position is concerned with identity, ideology, power, and knowledge of and attitudes toward language use. It directly refers to the possibility of altering symbols and trademarks as a means to exploit

---

7 The theory of counterlanguage is an adaptation of Halliday's (1976, 1978) theory of anti-languages.

and subvert them. As Stuart Hall says, "Identities are . . . constituted within, not outside of representation . . . within, not outside, discourse, and constructed through, not outside, difference (1996,4)." This concept of dialect choice appears in Big L's (2000) song "Ebonics" when he proclaims: "I talk with slang and I'ma never stop speakin' it." Nas dialogues with him in the chorus: "Speak with criminal slang/ That's just the way that I talk, yo/ Vocabulary spills, I'm ill."

The third and final point makes obvious that neither youth nor the artist stands alone as an independent individual. Rather, the ties to the audience/generation, speech community, and urban youth bring him or her into existence. In this sense, an artist is a composite of his or her audience—representing experiences that are shared—and the audience determines whether the artist can assume that role. Thus, in this respect, any person anywhere in the world who claims to be Hiphop reinforces these ties and the shared values of the Hiphop Nation.

Through these tenets, in Hiphop, the *WORD* is the bible and the law on how one represents. It is the core of the Hiphop nation, the power, trope, message, and market all in one. But it goes even further. Hiphop language ideology is based on black resistance and representation. Within this tradition it recognizes that black voices are routinely marginalized within wider society, and thus this language ideology is one that assumes that agency and power reside in the ability to produce this discourse. The discourse itself is proof of Hiphop's existence and its ability to infiltrate and interfere with dominant culture. Thus references to public individuals, events, objects, and so on are indexical and can stand for, point to, and connect and target particular groups and contexts (Peirce 1960; Silverstein 1998). As a consequence, Hiphop is always concerned with context and reifies local and in-group knowledge as it points and "shouts out" to its members. It relies on the secret handshake, knowing look, and coded message. It signals the existence of an alter-entity—black youth as thinkers, critics, and creators of language, culture, art, and ideas.

Because referents in Hiphop are often unspoken, what might seem to be a simple narrative of one's experience in life is usually a commentary on shared knowledge of how social structures impact individual lives in similar ways and create collective identities among those affected. For example, Mia X's "Mommie's Angels" (1997) is not just a personal reflection on her plight as a single mother and struggling rap artist, it shares insight about a common situation of single mothers worldwide and particularly black women in America who are marked as "welfare queens," "whores," and other derogatory identifications that degrade their humanity and ignore their struggles to provide for their families. Mia X relates:

> *Mommie, pulled some rabbits out some hats to pay the bills*
> *And fix ya meals, cause you both gave me the will power*
> *To tower over obstacles in our path*
> *And when I'm sad, ya innocence makes me laugh*
> *[. . .]*
> *And I'ma keep doing all I can*
> *To make a strong black woman and man, out my angels.*
> (MIA X 1997)

Similarly, Mos Def's "Mr. Nigga" (1999) is not just about his own experiences with racial profiling in the United States and abroad, as well as everyday racist encounters; he also connects his experiences to people in the public sphere (e.g., Michael Jackson) as well as unknown individuals. Mos Def observes:

> *Some folks get on a plane go as they please*
> *But I go over seas and I get over-seized*
> *London, Heathrow, me and my people*
> *They think that illegal's a synonym for Negro*
> *[. . .]*
> *Even for the big American rap star*
> *For us especially, us most especially*
> *A "Mr Nigga" VIP jail cell just for me*
> (MOS DEF 1999)

Jean Grae utilizes this narrative strategy within the realm of fiction when she performs a white teenage personality, Rebecca Gates Scott, to break silence about childhood sexual abuse, high school bullying, teasing, rape and other forms of gender-based, domestic, and structural violence in her song "Taco Day" (2001). Grae utilizes AAE linguistic forms of directness as well as truth-telling and signifying to recount the narrative of an abused adolescent that was all too familiar to the public in the post-Columbine atmosphere in which her song debuted. Invoking the youth's mental state, Grae annunciates the /r/ sound in teachers, bleachers, cheering, and whispering as part of her storytelling strategy: "I hear them talking about me . . . /All my friends /even the teachers/even when I'm cheering/I can hear them whispering way up in the bleachers."

Following this narrative tradition of both Hiphop and AAE language ideology, the Japanese MC K Dub Shine flexes his cultural critique through storytelling in a 2003 recording of "Save the Children" (Fischer 2007). He adopts the trope of MC as savior described earlier and builds from knowledge he collected growing up, observing in communities, to "call out" issues of rampant domestic abuse and child abuse in Japanese society. K Dub Shine asserts:

> *I don't want to see any more tears from children*
> *child abuse is something that cannot be forgiven*
> *people abuse kids like it's a daily / usual / conventional practice thing*
> *language and violence, watch how you use them*
> *[. . .]*
> [chorus]
> *if there is a kid that looks like he / she was beaten, let me know*
> *if there is a house that seems suspicious, let me know*
> *if there is someone who needs help, let me know*
> *if you hear someone crying, let me know*

This narrative strategy reflects theory building among MCs and is similar to African American narratives collected by John Gwaltney (1980), who notes:

> From these narratives—these analyses of the heavens, nature and humanity—it is evident that black people are building theory on every conceivable level. . . . These people not only know the troubles they've seen, but have profound insight into the meaning of those vicissitudes.
>
> (1980, XXVI)

These narrative traditions that are incorporated in Hiphop and AAE language ideologies and comprise a powerful discourse strategy that, as the discussion in the next section about the global reach of Hiphop will show, has now traveled far from the landscape in which it was created.

HIPHOP NATION'S GLOBAL REACH

In 1992, when the group Public Enemy toured Europe with the rock group U2, their charge to Hiphop's nation of millions was "Fight the Power!" This slogan began to appear on walls in England, Poland, Italy, and more. In fact, not only did a worldwide audience quickly gravitate to Hiphop's unrelenting critique of society as well as its notion of community, recognition, and representation, Hiphop fit within already established international local and national movements for justice, education, rights, and independence (e.g., Sansone 2003; Skelton and Valentine 1998).

When Hiphop discourse strategies are utilized by artists and peoples outside of African diasporic communities, we see how understanding "the black experience" can scaffold information concerning basic human equality and liberty. Hiphop's political utility comes largely from its association with a black body politic, and its popular cultural presence allows it to be accessed and appropriated through performative measures. As St. Clair Drake (1980) observed in his analysis of anthropology and the black experience, "beyond the black experience lies the human experience." In the words of one Japanese national Hiphop artist, "I use black power to fight white power" (Fischer 2007).

African Americans have long been conceptualized as trailblazers fighting against state regulation of identity that is intrinsic in colonial and, as we are witnessing, postcolonial processes. Through the production of a Hiphop origins narrative that situates the cultural genesis in specific, struggling African American (and immigrant African Caribbean) communities, the culture of Hiphop lends its political capital to *anyone* seeking redress for the transnational character of political and economic injustice (Harrison 2000). Consequently, as U.S.-based racial politics are exported abroad, the culture and politics of African Americans are also exported. This includes African American resistance narratives and strategies, especially ones that have historically been transmitted through popular cultural genres that then become of particular interest as an oppositional strategy for local populations.[8] There are many international and global instances where African American symbols of blackness are incorporated within cultural and national politics and art. In Japan since World War II, jazz, blues, reggae, dancehall, and now Hiphop have occupied an oppositional utility to state-regulated identificatory practice—whether that practice comes from the U.S. military, multinational corporations, or Japanese state policies (Davis 2000; Lie 2001; Sterling 2006).

Likewise, there are many examples of African-descent community-based organizations (CBOs) in Kenya and even Norway that have also operationalized (U.S.-based) black popular culture in post-independence

---

[8] Scholars have documented this role of African American popular culture within African diasporic communities (Gilroy 1993, 2000; Hall 1996; Harrison 2002; Mercer 2000) as well as within non-African diasporic communities (Atkins 2001; Chaney 2002, 115; Ramsey 2003; Rose 1994, Sterling 2003, 2006) outside of the United States.

eras to resist state-sanctioned oppression and policies (e.g., *Hip Hop Colony*, Afrikan Youth in Norway, RIZE Mzani). In Spain, the Negu Gorriak embedded black nationalist rhetoric in rap lyrics from groups like Public Enemy to give voice to the group's speech community as well as the Basque political agenda (Urla 2001). Similarly, the Web site "Hiphop Reader" from Milan, Italy, uses symbols and expressions from the Black Panther Party to utilize the transnational conversation between Italian Hiphop and (black) American Hiphop to build on the youth social movement. Members of the Universal Zulu Nation featured in B+ and Eric Coleman's film *Brasilintime* also speak to the utility of black identity in American Hiphop as an example of "fighting the power" and agitating for social justice and equality across class in Brazil. Afrikan Youth in Norway feature Hiphop artists from the United States as well as Norway and various African countries to mark their annual commemoration of Afrikan History Week, which was of course inspired by the educational work of Carter G. Woodson. Rushay Booysen in Port Elizabeth utilizes Hiphop and its technological savvy and focus to build programs that seek to bridge digital divides in his South African community. During the 2005 youth riots outside of Paris, France, youth blared Hiphop to fuel their battle cries.

The widespread influence of Hiphop in youth culture throughout the world is the result of both the knowledge of African American citizenship struggles and artists and organizations that support global Hiphop. One of the most significant influences in the international spread of Hiphop as grounded in the African American and black experience is the Universal Zulu Nation. Afrika Bambaataa founded the Universal Zulu Nation as a community-based organization in the Bronx that sought peace, unity, and harmony among battling gangs and peoples. Bambaataa, who had been involved in gangs and was a well-respected DJ, successfully unified gang members and worked with youth to create community-grounded social programs and political agendas (Chang 2005; Perkins 1996). Beginning as the Bronx River Organization and later The Organization (in 1973), it was renamed Zulu Nation a year later, and as its influence spread around the world, it became known as the Universal Zulu Nation (UZN).

Even twenty-five years later, its leadership (as well as its many members spread throughout the world) continues to meet and plan and create programs that seek social justice and the eradication of human inequality. Zulu Nation utilizes black liberation ideologies of the 1970s to bring its many global followers to a mantra of interplanetary humanism. The new belief systems all have tenets that pronounce basic human equality and explicitly denounce constructions of race as well as other racist activities to separate and hierarchically situate human beings. Indeed, Bambaataa comments:

> [M]y thing is to always try to bring people together in unification and to see ourselves as humans on this planet so-called Earth, and what can we do to change the betterment of life for all people on the planet Earth and to respect what so-called black, brown, yellow, red and white people have done to better civilization for people to live on this planet so-called Earth, and recognize that we are not alone. (Stewart 2007)

Hiphop could have been reduced to a culturally insular community, but it consistently escapes from the slippery ties of regionalism, commercialism, race baiting, and hating. The struggle to include race as a fact of American life and power and as a cultural experience as well as injustice in the form of racism and class privilege has required contortionist moves on the part of the Hiphop community. Hence, Hiphop is being utilized for global movement building and as a strategy for redressing injustice. Race is evoked as a criticism to racism and other similarly constructed injustices through narratives of diaspora and related discursive practice.

CONCLUSION

Though Hiphop's influence on youth is often overstated, in some respects it has done more to challenge U.S. racism and racial stereotypes among young people than traditional civic resistance strategies. Moreover, it has managed to do this while highlighting unique and culturally valued aspects of different societies and communities. Hiphop's familiar slogan "Get in where you fit in" claims inclusion as the foundation of Hiphop ideology, but within parameters. While in African American culture the focus is on justice, freedom, and equal representation inclusion in the wider society, Hiphop's argument is for inclusion of everyone who respects Hiphop, irrespective of race, class, gender, sexual orientation, religion, nation, or any other characteristic.

The notion that everyone has the right to be represented affects every aspect of Hiphop culture. However, this notion does not necessarily protect previous generations' ideas of cultural and societal norms and values. In particular, Hiphop's notion of black identity is often criticized as a disruption in black political and social history that does not acknowledge previous and relevant social, cultural, and artistic movements that preceded Hiphop (e.g., Reed 1992). Yet, while the civil rights and Black Power struggles of the 1950s, 1960s, and 1970s may have introduced the myth of a united, politically, and socially homogeneous African American community, Hiphop members boldly and brazenly argue for the "real" in relation to national as well as regional and local identities and loyalties. Hiphop is not about erasing race but acknowledging it in all of its aspects; it wants to talk about how racism affects us all.

Youth are socialized into Hiphop through elaborate ritualized practices and activities that ensure the constant attention to skill and reinvigoration of Hiphop.[9] Part of these practices is recognizing and studying Hiphop's origins and major moments in its development. Examples of the former could include UZN's "Infinity Lessons," which is a code of conduct and educational guide for members, or performing groups like Dilated Peoples referencing key players in Hiphop's evolution, such as Afrika Bambaataa or DJ Premier, at concerts. This creates recognition of the race and class of its founders and innovators as well as tensions regarding race.

Although race is viewed by the media and in dominant society as largely negative, Hiphop views it as multirepresentational and symbolic. It is this tension that revitalizes the "level playing field" of Hiphop and constructs it as a nonracist genre designed to confront power. Through both commercial and underground media, the art, dance, music, and words of Hiphop transcend language, neighborhoods, cities, and national boundaries, resulting in international varieties where marginalized groups and political parties appropriate Hiphop as a symbol of resistance and where ethnic, religious, and regional disputes are renegotiated.[10] Hiphop fights for local and national identity and against marginalization of any group that comes together around Hiphop's edicts.

Works Cited

•

Ahearn, Charlie. 1982. *Wild Style*. DVD. Los Angeles: Rhino Home Video.
Akrobatik [Jared Bridgeman]. 2008. Rain. *Absolute Value*. New York: Fat Beats Records.
Anderson, Benedict. 1991. *Imagined Communities: Reflections on the Origin and Spread of Nationalism*. New York: Verso.

---

9 See Morgan's (2009) explanation concerning concepts of "the battle" and "the critic" as well as standards in Hiphop culture.

10 See James Spady et al. (2006), Sunaina Maira (1999), Tony Mitchell (2001).

Atkins, E. Taylor. 2001. *Blue Nippon: Authenticating Jazz in Japan*. Durham: Duke University Press.

Beebe, Roger, Denise Fulbrook, and Ben Saunders, eds. 2002. *Rock over the Edge: Transformation in Popular Music Culture*. Durham: Duke University Press.

Big L. 2000. Ebonics (Criminal Slang). *The Big Picture*. New York: Rawkus Records.

Bucholtz, Mary, and Kira Hall. 2004. Theorizing Identity in Language and Sexuality Research. *Language in Society* 33: 469–515.

Chaney, David. 2002. *Cultural Change and Everday Life*. New York: Palgrave.

Chang, Jeff. 2005. *Can't Stop, Won't Stop: A History of the Hip Hop Generation*. New York: St. Martin's Press.

Coombe, Rosemary. 1996. Embodies Trademarks Mimesis and Alterity on American Commercial Frontiers. *Cultural Anthropology* 11: 202–224.

Davis, John H. 2000. Blurring the Boundaries of the Buraku(min). In *Globalization and Social Change in Contemporary Japan*, edited by J. S. Eades, Tom Gill, and Harumi Befu, 110–122. Melbourne: Trans Pacific Press.

Dawson, Michael C. 2003. *Black Visions: The Roots of Contemporary African-American Political Ideologies*. Chicago: University of Chicago Press.

dead prez. 2000. *Let's Get Free*. New York: Loud Records.

Drake, St. Clair. 1980. Anthropology and the Black Experience. *The Black Scholar* 11(7):29.

Dyson, Michael Eric. 2001. *Holler If You Hear Me: Searching for Tupac Shakur*. New York: Basic Civitas Books.

Eric B & Rakim. 1988. Follow the Leader. *Follow the Leader*. Germany: MCA.

Fischer, Dawn Elisa. 2007. "Kobushi Ageroo! (Pump Ya Fist!)": Blackness, "Race," and Politics in Japanese Hip-Hop. PhD diss, University of Florida, Gainesville.

Forman, Murray. 2002. *The 'Hood Comes First: Race, Space, and Place in Rap and Hip-Hop (Music/Culture)*. Wesleyan: Wesleyan University Press

Fricke, Jim, and Charlie Ahearn. 2002. *Yes Yes Y'all: The Experience Music Project: Oral History of Hip-Hop's First Decade*. Cambridge, MA: Da Capo Press.

Fujita, Tadashi. 1996. *Tokyo Hip Hop Guide*. Tokyo: Ohta Publishing.

Gilroy, Paul. 1993. *Small Acts: Thoughts on the Politics of Black Cultures*. London: Serpent's Tail.

———. 2000. *Against Race: Imagining Political Culture beyond the Color Line*. Cambridge, MA: Belknap Press of Harvard University Press.

Grae, Jean. 2001. Taco Day. *Pity the Fool*, prod. by Mr. Len. Matador Records.

Gwaltney, John. 1980. *Drylongso*. New York: Random House.

Hall, Stuart. 1996. What Is This "Black" Black Popular Culture? In *Stuart Hall: Critical Dialogues in Cultural Studies*, edited by David Morley and Kuan-Hsing Chen, 465-475. New York: Routledge.

Halliday, M. A. K. 1976. Anti-Languages. *American Anthropologist* 78(3): 570–584.

———. 1978. *Language as Social Semiotic: The Social Interpretation of Language and Meaning*. London: Edward Arnold.

Harrison, Faye V. 2000. Facing Racism and the Moral Responsibility of Human Rights Knowledge. *Annals of the New York Academy of Sciences* 925: 45–69.

———. 2002. Global Apartheid, Foreign Policy and Human Rights. *Souls* 4(3): 48–68.

Heath, R. Scott. 2006. True Heads: Historicizing the Hip-Hop "Nation" in Context. *Callaloo* 29(3): 846–866.

Hebdige, Dick. 1987. *Cut 'n' Mix: Culture, Identity and Caribbean Music*. London: Methuen.

hooks, bell. 1992. *Black Looks: Race and Representation*. Boston: South End Press.

Jay-Z. 2003. Dirt Off Your Shoulders. *The Black Album*. New York: Roc-A-Fella/Island Def Jam.

Kitwana, Bakari. 2005. *Why White Kids Love Hip Hop: Wangtas, Wiggers, Wannabes and the New Reality of Race in America*. New York: Basic Books.

Labov, William. 1972. The Logic of Nonstandard English. In *Language in the Inner City*, 201–240. Philadelphia: University of Pennsylvania Press.

Lefebvre, Henri. 1991. *The Production of Space*. Trans. D. Nicholson-Smith. Oxford: Blackwell.

Lie, John. 2001. *Multi-Ethnic Japan*. Cambridge, MA: Harvard University Press.

Maira, Sunaima. 1999. Identity Dub: The Paradoxes of an Indian American Youth Subculture. *Cultural Anthropology* 14(1): 29–60.

Males, Michael. A. 1996. *The Scapegoat Generation: America's War on Adolescents*. Monroe, ME: Common Courage Press.

McCann, Eugene J. 1999. Race, Protest, and Public Space: Contextualizing Lefebvre in the U.S. City. *Antipode* 31(2) 163–184.

Mercer, Kobena. 2000. A Sociography of Diaspora. In *Without Guarantees: In Honour of Stuart Hall*, 233–244. New York: Verso.

Mia X. 1997. Mommie's Angels. *Unlady Like*. Los Angeles: Priority Records.

Mitchell, Tony, ed. 2001. *Global Noise: Rap and Hip-Hop Outside the USA*. Middletown, CT: Wesleyan University Press.

Morgan, Marcyliena. 2002. *Language, Discourse and Power in African American Culture*. Cambridge, MA: Cambridge University Press.

———. 2009. *The Real HipHop: Battling for Knowledge, Power, and Respect in the LA Underground*. Durham: Duke University Press.

Mos Def. 1999. Mr. Nigga. *Black on Both Sides*. New York: Rawkus Records.

Peirce, Charles Sanders. 1960. *Principles of Philosophy and Elements of Logic*. Vols I and II of *Collected Papers of Charles Sanders Peirce*. Cambridge, MA: Harvard University Press.

Perkins, William Eric, ed. 1996. *Droppin' Science: Critical Essays on Rap Music and Hip Hop Culture*. Philadelphia: Temple University Press.

Pipitone, Giuseppe. 2006. *Bigger than Hip Hop: Storie della Nuova Resistenza Afro-americana*. Milan: Agenzia X.

Ramsey, Guthrie P., Jr. 2003. *Race Music: Black Cultures from Bebop to Hip-Hop*. Berkeley: University of California Press.

Reed, Adolph. 1992. Posing as Politics. *Village Voice* 5 (December 1995): 187.

Rose, Tricia. 1994. *Black Noise: Rap Music and Black Culture in Contemporary America*. Middletown, CT: Wesleyan University Press.

Sansone, Livio. 2003. *Blackness without Ethnicity: Constructing Race in Brazil*. New York: Palgrave Macmillan.

Shelby, Tommie. 2005. *We Who Are Dark: The Philosophical Foundations of Black Solidarity*. Cambridge, MA: Harvard University Press.

Silverstein, Michael. 1998. The Uses and Utility of Ideology: A Commentary. In *Language Ideologies: Practice and Theory*, edited by B. Schieffelin, K. Woolard, and P. Kroskrity, 123–145. Oxford: Oxford University Press.

Skelton, Tracey, and Gill Valentine. 1998. *Cool Places: Geographies of Youth Culture*. London: Routledge.

Spady, James G., H. Samy Alim, and Samir Meghelli. 2006. *Tha Global Cipha: Hip Hop Culture and Consciousness*. Philadelphia, PA: Black History Museum.

Sterling, Marvin. 2003. Performing Gender, Race and Ethnicity in the Afro-Asiatic Transnational: Dancehall Reggae Culture in Japan. Paper presented at the *Boston University Blacks and Asians in the Making of the Modern World Conference*. Boston, MA. April 13.

————. 2006. The Symbolic Constitution of Japanese Dancehall. *Social and Economic Studies: Special Issue on Popular Culture* 55 (1&2): 1–24.

Stewart, Adhimu. 2007. Afrika Bambaataa Can't Stop the Planet Rock. *Earwacks Online Magazine* http://earwaks.com/hiphop/179/afrika-bambaataa.html (accessed March 31, 2008).

Urla, Jacqueline. 2001. We Are All Malcolm X!: Negu Gorriak, Hip-Hop, and the Basque Political Imaginary. In *Global Noise: Rap and Hip-Hop Outside the USA*, edited by Tony Mitchell, 171–193. Middletown, CT: Wesleyan University Press.

Worth, Robert. 1999. Guess Who Saved the South Bronx? The Silent Partner in Community Development. *Washington Monthly Online* 31: 4.

20

The "Ethno-Ambiguo Hostility Syndrome"

Mixed Race, Identity, and Popular Culture

Michele Elam

•

In this essay, I examine the way Aaron McGruder's nationally syndicated comic strip The Boondocks *uses both the form and content of the comic genre (considered by many as merely low-brow entertainment) to enter into some of today's fiercest, most important public discussions about the salience of race and "mixed race."* The Boondocks *challenges both the idea that race is—or should be—primarily a matter of personal choice and privacy, and the belief that mixed race "rights" mean documenting family genealogy rather than social justice advocacy. I argue that by questioning the current vogue for racial hybridity over monoracialism,* The Boondocks *illustrates the necessity of resisting the temptation to "get over" or "go beyond" race. The strip offers a call for a new kind of racial education, one attentive to a wider spectrum of racial identities and experiences, and more keenly informed about the social and political implications of race. Part of McGruder's twenty-first-century education involves an appreciation of popular culture's potent role in generating and shaping those identities, experiences, and histories.*

> *Laughter and its forms represent . . . the least scrutinized sphere of the people's creation.*
> M. M. BAHKTIN, *RABELAIS AND HIS WORLD*

528

Let The Boondocks *go on its merry, subversive way ("Hey, it's just a cartoon") and hope that, somewhere down the road when we all live in a more just America, we will look back and say that in the beginning, the revolution wasn't televised, it was on the comics page.*

MICHAEL MOORE, FOREWORD, *A RIGHT TO BE HOSTILE*

THE BOONDOCKS IS RENOWNED FOR ITS ACUTE, AND OFTEN controversial, cultural commentary on racial politics in America. Not surprisingly, the phenomenon of "mixed race" identification has not escaped McGruder's eye—nor his ire. Through his "mixed race" character, Jazmine, McGruder makes visible some of the most pressing cultural fears and hopes about what exactly "mixed race" is—as well as what its political implications might be in what the novelist Danzy Senna has famously nicknamed the "Mulatto Millennium" (1998, 12). As Senna wryly notes, "mixed race"–identified people have been increasingly fêted as the poster children of modernity, ambassadors to a new raceless world:

> Strange to wake up and realize you're in style. . . . It was the first day of the new millennium and I woke to find that mulattos had taken over. . . . According to the racial zodiac, 2000 is the official Year of the Mulatto. Pure breeds (at least the blacks ones) are out and hybridity is in. America loves us in all our half-caste glory. (12)

Mulatto glam, after all, pays not only cultural but political dividends. The *New York Times* has announced that old-school "ethno-racial identity" has come and gone, replaced by the A-list hotshots of "G.A.: Generation Ambiguous." And galvanized by the 2000 Census—which allowed for an unprecedented "mark all that apply" (MATA) option—advocates for "mixed race" "official" identification have gained tremendous legal leverage and national recognition. *The Boondocks*, which McGruder calls a "space for a kind of playful black intelligentsia" (McGrath 2004), can thus be usefully seen as a form of pop-cultural intervention in contemporary debates over multiracial identity.

Although sociology and philosophy have begun disciplinary examinations of the cultural and demographic phenomenon of "mixed race" in the so-called post–civil rights era, I show that noninstitutional and unofficial mediums—in this case, comics—can also provide insightful, and sometimes even more astute, commentary on the subject. The cultural critic Scott McCloud has argued that comics—also called sequential art, graphic storytelling, or visual narrative—have the same status as literature and art (2000, 10–11). I would add that comics, like other arts, have claims on social reality. The peculiar claims of fiction on the world are not mimetic but constitutive—that is, art's power does not come so much from mirroring the world as in reimagining it. Art has the unique ability to represent social anxieties and fantasies without necessarily legislating action, to offer a place where sometimes latent or unspoken public concerns can be addressed, a place to experiment with various responses or alternative resolutions. In this way, art provides an imaginative space for the gestation of ideas that both respond to and shape public perceptions and political consensus.

THE "MIXED RACE MOVEMENT"

Dozens of organizations, Web sites, affinity and advocacy groups, magazines, media watches, and journals—all focused on the "mixed race experience"—have emerged in the last few years.[1] The representations generated by the "mixed race movement" (a provisional term, since the "movement" is an uneasy and evolving coalition of interracial couples, transracial adoptees, and mixed-race-identified young people) are transforming both the language and the landscape of race politics. Their varied agendas have at times collaborated with, and at times been co-opted by, conservatives such as the arch Republican whip Newt Gingrich and the former University of California regent Ward Connerly. Gingrich advanced the lobby in Congress for a multiracial option on the 2000 Census; Connerly has made clear his desire to do away with both affirmative action programs and racial categorization itself (2000). Most recently,

---

1 A short list of some of these Web sites and advocacy groups includes the Association of MultiEthnic Americans (www.ameasite.org); Famlee (www.scc.swarthmore.edu/-thompson/famless/home.html); Hapa Issues Forum (www.hapaissuesforum.org); Interracial Individuals Discussion List (www.geocities.com/Wellesley/6426/ii.html) Project RACE—Reclassify All Children Equally, Inc (projectrace.home.mindspring.com); *Interrace* (members.aol.com/intrace/index.html); *Interracial Voice* (www.webcom.com/-intvoice); *MAVIN: The Articulate Journal of the Mixed-Race Experience* www.mavin.org; Swirl (www.swirl.com); Eurasian Nation (www.eurasiannation.com); the Fusion Series (www.fusionseries.com); Mixed Media Watch (www.mixedmediawatch.com); the Loving Day Project www.lovingday.org; the Hapa Project/Kip Fulbeck (www.thehapaproject.com); the Multiracial Activist (www.multiracial.com). Additionally, the last five years have seen a surge in college course offerings in the humanities and social sciences on this subject at Harvard, Yale, New York University, Vassar, Stanford, most University of California schools, and many other colleges. The popular organization EurasianNation even offers a link on its Web site to "The Top 19 Mixed Race Studies Courses" in the United States and Canada.

Connerly's proposed "racial privacy act" attempted to enlist multiracial advocates for his cause. The "Privacy Act," known also as California Proposition 54: Classification by Race, Ethnicity, Color, or National Origin, was placed on the October 7, 2003, California State Election ballot as an Initiative Constitutional Amendment. Both Gingrich and Connerly have publicly aligned themselves with many of the mixed-race advocates' stated goals, especially those that might disable race-based policies in the name of traditional American ideals of ahistorical self-invention and libertarian "privacy rights."

It is, therefore, important to examine the political nature, versus taxonomic neutrality, of "mixed race." Sociologists have suggested that mixed race constituencies are, in part, political invention (Williams 2006; DaCosta 2007). I, too, take as a given that the rise of "mixed race" people is not simply a disinterested statistical phenomenon related to immigration, or a demographic inevitability following the 1967 *Loving v. Virginia* U.S. Supreme Court decision legalizing interracial marriages in the United States. McGruder's *The Boondocks* moves beyond what pose as politically innocent questions of demographics (e.g., "Why do there seem to be more 'mixed race' people now?") to ask what leads us to ask that question in the first place. We might ask instead: "Why now and with what effect are more people identifying and being identified as 'mixed race' in the United States?" The very idea of "mixed race" has been naturalized; a generation ago, almost no one understood this as a legal, political, or experiential category. Very specific ideas about what it means and what it looks like to be "mixed race" have been normalized in the media, in marketing, on anthology covers, and in K–12 educational literature (M. Elam forthcoming), so that "mixed race" people have come to stand as beautiful, bodily testaments to the success of the American democratic experiment and the archaism of the color line.

Enter Aaron McGruder. His internationally acclaimed comics are a thorn in the side of both the political Right and the Left. He offered searing send-ups of nearly everyone in the George W. Bush administration, calling the president a "moron," and offering Condoleezza Rice a personal ad for a "Female Darth Vader type seeks loving mate to torture": "High-ranking government employee with sturdy build seeks single black man for intimate relationship. Must enjoy football, Chopin, and carpet bombing" (McGrath 2004). One of his favorite targets is the black megamillionaire Bob Johnson of B.E.T—or as the main character in the strip, Huey, calls the Black Entertainment Today network, "Black Exploitation Television" or "Butts Every Time."

My focus here is several episodes of *The Boondocks* in which McGruder features a twenty-first-century "mixed race" character, one prepubescent, ten-year-oldish Jazmine DuBois, whose black father, Tom, and his white wife, Sarah, are both lawyers. Jazmine has just arrived in the largely white "upscale neighborhood of Woodcrest" (McGruder 2000, 10), where the black protagonist Huey and his younger brother Riley have also recently located. Woodcrest, significantly, is based loosely on the middle-class suburb of Columbia, Maryland, where McGruder was raised, an intentional community, an interracial social experiment that was "envisioned as a sort of integrationist, post–civil rights utopia—developed by the Rouse Company in the mid-nineteen sixties . . . featuring an official "Tree of Life," and streets and neighborhoods with names like Hobbitt's Glen and Morning Walk and Elfstone Way. (Huey and Riley live on Timid Deer Lane, one block over from Bashful Beaver)" (McGrath 2000, 17). Jazmine is light-skinned with what she calls "frizzy hair" that she defensively and repeatedly insists is not an Afro. This new millennial mulatta, is, according to Huey, a "textbook case" of "Afro-Denial" and "Ethno-Ambiguo Hostility Syndrome" (McGruder 2000, 23). And, as he tells her parents, he knows the cure: "an immediate intervention of positive Nubian reinforcement" to lead her down the "long hard road to afrocentric wellness" (23). Huey's and Jazmine's exchanges are amusing, of course, but they also cogently explore the political implications of post-race identity in the United States and by extension, vet competing narratives about the epistemic significance of racial experience itself.

RACE AS FREE CHOICE AND "COMPULSORY BLACKNESS"

> *I have the right*
> *To identify myself differently than strangers expect me to identify*
> *To identify myself differently than how my parents identify me*
> *To identify myself differently than my brothers and sisters*
> *To identify myself differently in different situations.*
> MARIA P. P. ROOT, "A BILL OF RIGHTS FOR RACIALLY MIXED PEOPLE"

Because the issue of race is often cast among mixed race advocates as an issue of free will, arguments for and against mixed race identification are often pitched as battles between self-definition and group attribution. Maria Root, for instance, a psychologist and early "guru" of the mixed race movement, authored the 1996 "A Bill of Rights for Racially Mixed

People," which emphasizes the battle for autonomy in self-definition. McGruder's comic directly challenges the frequent assertion among mixed race advocates that they cannot identify as they please because black people, in particular, coerce them into a stifling monoracialism. For Jazmine, this translates into her complaint (emphasized with childish foot-stamping): "I resent racial categories!" (McGruder 2000, 13).

Despite these high-minded assertions of independence, Jazmine's white mother is, ultimately, the architect of her daughter's position. In one series of *The Boondocks'* panels, for instance, her mother adamantly tells Jazmine's school principal on the phone that her daughter is neither white nor black, that "it's up to Jazmine to construct her own identity. We don't want anyone doing that for her. Is that clear? . . . If she must be called anything, use the term 'multiracial.' Never 'white.' Never 'black.' Ok?" To which the principal responds, "Never 'black.' Got it." Then he turns to a teacher who is listening in, puts his hand over the phone, and whispers confirmation of the teacher's suspicions: "She's black" (McGruder 2000, 71). According to Jazmine's mother, the choices she makes on her daughter's behalf should be immune to unseemly school, state, government, and political interests (that is, should be legally protected by the likes of Ward Connerly's "racial privacy" act). But the principal's quick cut to the chase makes clear that what he hears through the multiculti talk is the buried claim and ultimate point: "never black" (71).

In effect, Mrs. DuBois grants herself proxy to represent her child's interests, but in doing so, she inadvertently flags the limits of the autonomy she touts. Autonomy is always limited, McGruder reminds us, whether by legal guardianship and age restriction or, more generally, by historical circumscriptions of free will and choice. The principal *is* annoyingly dismissive of the parent's direction and *does* officiously challenge her authority to dictate her daughter's race; but the exchange also dramatizes the cultural fact that Jazmine alone does not get to declare her race (or racelessness) by *fiat*, and neither can Mrs. DuBois be the sole and self-ordained arbiter of race. The mother thinks family determines racial identification; the principal thinks that race affiliation trumps filial kinship.

The white mother is McGruder's special target, and she is culturally significant in this scenario because white middle-class mothers were among the first to exert pressure on the legislature to change racial categorization. Susan Graham, co-founder of Project Race, who urged adoption of a multiracial classification on forms requiring racial data, was among the white mothers who successfully lobbied the Office of Management and

Budget (OMB) in the late 1990s to change the 2000 Census category options. Jon Michael Spencer, in *The New Colored People: The Mixed Race Movement in America* (1997), scathingly indicts Graham's crusade, not only because she trotted out her biracial child before the OMB in what he felt was an exploitative appeal to sentiment, but also because Graham insists that everyone from Halle Berry to Langston Hughes should (or in Hughes's case, she says would have if he could have) identified as multiracial rather than black. The irony of mandating, in the name of free choice, that people of mixed race descent must identify as such is lost on Graham. This is a common irony: mixed race advocates tend to proscribe and prescribe multiracial identification as dogmatically as the monoracialism they "vilify" for *its* dogmatism (Childs 2004, 143). So it is particularly salient that in *The Boondocks'* battle—framed as maternal rights versus states' rights—Jazmine's mother thinks that calling her daughter black is an institutional act of racial conscription. The claim that black people are twisting the arms of their lighter-skinned brethren, basically bullying them into enlistment, is the refrain one hears frequently in the reader criticisms of the comic series (Powell 1999). In fact, Maria Root provocatively argues that mixed people are "oppressed" by black-identified people for this reason, saying that "multiracial people experience a 'squeeze' of oppression *as* people of color and *by* people of color" (Root 2004, 144), mostly through racial coercion (insisting they are inescapably black) but also as often, though contradictorily, by racial gatekeeping (saying they're not "black enough"). Riffing on Adrienne Rich's notion of "compulsory heterosexuality," Jayne Ifekwunigwe calls this "compulsory Blackness" (2004, 189). This reimagining of blackness as a tyrannical rather than a liberatory force in the mobilization of civil rights has become a representative move in "mixed race" discourses. Monoracialism is increasingly cast as an antiquated and reactionary holdover from Black Nationalism, ill-fitted for today's demographic and political realities.

The recasting of the players in the political scene (such that the oppressed are billed as oppressors) is precisely what gets challenged in *The Boondocks*. Huey, for instance, thinks that calling Jazmine black simply amounts to the historical recognition of the ongoing effects of the "one-drop" rule and of the heterogeneity within blackness itself. Because most African Americans have mixed heritage, calling oneself black *and* mixed is, arguably, a kind of redundancy. Thus, both the principal's and Huey's eye-rolling at the DuBois family's (multi)racial equivocation make clear that they understand race as something neither Jazmine nor her mother can simply waive or command away. Furthermore, both Huey and the principal suspect that the DuBois's refusal of racial categories is less about "accurately" accounting for genealogical diversity than it is an opting out of blackness in particular.

Thus when Huey tells Jazmine that it's "good to have more black people around," she replies with racial goose-stepping: "Um . . . gee, um why . . . why would you think I was . . . um . . . black. . . . I just want to be human" (McGruder 2000, 10–11). Rather than admit a racial connection, she waxes at length about her status as, she says, "special" and "lonely," offering up a maudlin soliloquy to the heavens about being "different from everyone else" like "a yellow flower right in the middle of a bunch of red roses" (27). Huey already takes as a given Jazmine's inclusion in the "black race," so her pleas of alienation ring hollow. Through such scenes, Jazmine's histrionic hand-wringing is portrayed as not merely self-indulgent but moot. Huey's retort that "You're black. Get over it" sounds the same as the principal's assertion of Jazmine's blackness, but it is very different (27). The principal reduces race to expedient administrative categories. In contrast, Huey's reality check of Jazmine rejects the notion of racial identity as individual private property and reframes racial identity as a matter of public negotiation, social location, cultural affirmation, political commitment, and historical homage. For Huey, race is not an arbitrary imposition but an occasion for social insight and historical sensibility. McGruder's comic strip provides a unique opportunity for the exploration of these complex social issues and suggests the subtle ways that art, and the humanities more generally, participate in and shape contemporary dialogues about race in the twenty-first century.

FRIZZY HAIR AND FAMILY TREES

> *Black women artists have stolen a march on both visual theory and criticism. Having emerged in record numbers and gained unprecedented visibility in the past two decades, they have frequently engaged aspects of current body/gaze discourses. But in doing so, they often push these preoccupations into unfamiliar territory—invoking the intricate, aesthetic and social histories of black "hair" politics.*
> JUDITH WILSON, "ONE WAY OR ANOTHER: BLACK FEMINIST VISUAL THEORY"

Nowhere is Huey's perspective on race so clear as in his frequent insistence that Jazmine's hair is an Afro. Although it may seem that Huey is engaging in racial tagging, he does not equate race with Jazmine's locks or any other physical or physiognomic marker. Indeed, Huey's harassment actually challenges visual ascription as a legitimate process by which to assign race. Does Jazmine's blackness, or her racial ambiguity, lie in her body or in the cultural training that teaches us how and what to see? What constitutes an "ambiguous" body in one time and place is not a transhistorical given. Rather, it varies with the interpretive frameworks available in the particular context. At any given historical moment, the common sense of who gets read as black changes: who "looks" black in 1830s New Orleans may be very different from who "looks" black in 1990s Jackson Hole.

On my reading, Huey is not trying to shoehorn Jazmine into blackness; she already appears to him as one familiar type on the historical and visual spectrum of black people. With his insistence that Jazmine's hair is not just "frizzy," as she insists, but akin to Angela Davis's famous 'fro, he visually locates Jazmine in a political history in which black women appear in all shapes and colors—those with straight hair, blonde hair, light skin, light eyes, and so on—including the novelists Frances E. W. Harper and Nella Larsen, the civil rights activists Diane Nash and Angela Davis, and the philosopher and performance artist Adrian Piper, to name a few. To Huey, Jazmine is never beyond the pale of blackness: she is black, front and center. Jazmine, however, admits she has no idea who Angela Davis is. The fact that she knows nothing of the radical black feminism that Davis stands for, or how Davis's Afro signified black resistance to an entire generation of women—*this* is what Huey criticizes. And when Huey calls Jazmine "Mariah"—as in Carey—he sees her ambivalence about being black as smacking of celebrity angst, a petty complaint that could only be made by a privileged few—rich and famous or just very light-skinned (McGruder 2000, 10). Huey, then, is not simply a slave to the biological sophistry and legal fiction of the one-drop rule; his commitment to monoracialism stems from an awareness of race and its cogency as fully historical and political. In that sense, the new "race problem" is that, as a latter-day Du Bois (as in W. E. B.), Jazmine represents a new and disturbing twist on double consciousness, one that amounts to an *un*consciousness of the processes and politics of race altogether.

For similar reasons, *The Boondocks* uses parody to criticize one of the mainstays of the mixed race representation: the obligatory rehearsal of one's multiracial family tree. Replacing calls for social justice or racial equity, the most often-repeated goal of "mixed race rights" is merely to "name all the parts of myself." The emphasis on exercising this "right" can suggest that identity is just a matter of documentation and thus obscure the way identity works as a social index and interpretive framework. The rhetorical or graphic display of the family tree (almost de rigueur in the growing genre of mixed race narratives) participates in a racial gaze that can interrupt political reflection. So, when Huey asks Jazmine, "Ok . . . if you're not black, then what are you, hmmm?" she responds dutifully with a list documenting down to the fraction her ethnic racial portfolio: "My mother is one-quarter Irish, one-quarter Swedish, and one-half German, and on my father's side is part Cherokee, and my grandfather is mostly French, I think, because he's originally from Louisiana, and his father was from Haiti I believe, which makes me . . ." To this, Huey responds, "Which makes you as black as Richard Roundtree in *Shaft in Africa*" (McGruder 2003, 15). For Jazmine and her family, description substitutes for politics, genealogy for political discussions of the body politic. The family tree has come to stand *in* for social change; that is, being able to represent one's family tree has become a political end in itself.

In this exchange, Huey disparages not so much Jazmine's mixed genealogy as he does the idea that a recapitulation of ethnic and national descent really says anything meaningful about racial identity. At the very least, his retort suggests, her genealogy is neither progressive nor does it have sufficient explanatory force. Rather, Jazmine's accounting retroactively ratifies the idea of racially homogeneous categories and national identities by suggesting that each parent's race or ethnicity is unitary. Her laundry list also collapses blood and nation and then fractionalizes both—how else can the notion of "one-quarter Swedish" make sense? Huey interrupts her, and the discourse itself, by insisting on the political nature of racial identity; he teases her by saying "I understand, Jazmine. I'm mixed too." The next frame shows an up-close shot of Jazmine's face, which lights up pathetically as she says hopefully, "You are?" Huey responds by claiming to be "part Black, part African, part Negro, and part colored"—designations that do not pretend to be descriptive, that all carry heavy historical and political implication. He then walks off wailing "Poor me. I just don't know where I fit in" as she cries after him (again): "You're making fun of me!" (McGruder 2003, 16).

Of course, Huey *is* making fun of Jazmine in this exchange. However, his send-up is social critique to the degree that it does not concede the reduction of racial identity to the sum of one's parts; he does not think of race in terms of blood but in relation to representation. *Shaft in Africa*, after all, is late in the series of 1970s campy sex-and-adventure Blaxploitation films.

Huey's invocation of the hyper-blackness represented in the Blaxpoitation genre of film is a spoof *of* them—he is not concerned with black authenticity but with cultural figurations of blackness. Race, for McGruder, is always cast as a matter of historical consciousness, social play, and political engagement. In such scenes, *The Boondocks* replaces mere optic confirmation of race with black cultural performance and historical citation as more useful markers of racial identity.

COMIC FORM AND SOCIAL COMMENTARY

It is striking how *The Boondocks* both invokes and refuses the graphic narrative's conventions of form in the service of social commentary. According to the comic artist and critic, Will Eisner, "the artist must work from a 'dictionary' of human gestures" that are both drawn from "personal observations and an inventory of gestures, common and comprehensible to the reader" (2005, 101). McGruder's distinctive use of Japanese anime-based manga, a Japanese pop-comic style that has its origins as a low-class protest form, has a characteristic typology—high brow, large eyes—that is often described as flat, two-dimensional, static. Anime tends toward the hyperbolic; it suggests a "type," a timeless or fixed quality to ethnic character.

The use of the cartoon form in representing race is risky when one considers the nineteenth-century history of racial caricature in which black people's permanent immaturity, their putative atavism, is encoded through exaggerated features. According to Henry Wonham, one formal and political response to caricature is realism. He points out that the link between a "realist aesthetics and the politics of emancipation" has become something "approaching a literary-critical doctrine" (2004, 5). This commitment to the high moral earnestness of the Real is especially true when dealing with certain kinds of subjects. So, for instance, when Art Spiegelman's *Maus I* (1986) was first published, there was much disquiet among many who felt that representation of the Holocaust demands the strictest forms of realism; requires first-person testimony, authenticated facts, photo documentary; and a posture of reverence, needless to say, and, therefore, the comic genre was deemed a wholly inappropriate, even sacrilegious, form for these purposes. Similarly, the race problem is seen by many as no laughing matter—as sacrosanct; social protest, some argue, is better waged on the streets, through the ballot box, or in sober editorials. Furthermore, because the comic medium has been used *against* racial advances, such people see it as a particularly unfit mechanism to be reappropriated for racial justice—a kind of taking up with the devil. It seemed to point to McGruder's hubris in trying to use the "master's tools to dismantle the house," to paraphrase Audre Lorde, or as McGruder puts it, to put a "foot in the ass of The Man" (McGruder 2003). Aesthetic form and political effect cannot be conflated, however, and ethnic caricature and realism are *not* opposite poles on a spectrum: "these two aesthetic programs, one committed to the representation of the fully humanized individual, the other invested in broad ethnic abstractions, operate less as antithetical choices than as complementary impulses" (Wonham 2004, 8). Both, Wonham argues, try to "'lay bare' the essence of the human subject, whether through type or character"; and in fact, in myriad ways "ethnic caricature performs an integral function *within* the political and aesthetic program of American realism" (2004, 10, 8).

In fact, McGruder actively manipulates the conventions of racial caricature in order to reveal social reality (and potentially effect social change). He plays with physiognomic taxonomies through anime's distinctive focus on the face. Eisner notes that the face, in particular, "has an essential role in communicating emotion through codified gestures that are culturally recognizable" and as such the face is "expected to act as an adverb to the posture or gesture of the body . . . [and] the head (or face) is often used by artists to convey the entire message of bodily movement" (Eisner 2005, 111). McGruder's characters are nearly all head and face, and through them he invokes and revokes traditional stereotyping: he features, for instance, disproportionately large eyes but *no* lips, the corresponding requisite in black minstrelsy. His main black characters are children, calling up the equation of black people as infantile, but McGruder's young people have anime's extremely high brows, which in this context clearly suggest intellect and intense social conscience rather than childish ignorance and civic incapacity. Furthermore, there is nearly no attention to the body *below* the head, decoupling the association of black people with the flesh and body rather than spirit and mind. In this way we have black people in view but not on display. His images do not trigger the visual conventions historically associated with black people and thus do not whet further the appetite for black spectacularity.

Finally, McGruder does an end run around the supposed racial limitations of black-white technology in graphics, the idea that visual contrast through pixel density limits print medium's ability to represent color variation and distinction. His characters are all shades of black; moreover, they appear dark or light only in relation to other characters, emphasizing the provisional, situational perception of color.

THE MIS-EDUCATION OF JAZMINE

It is true that a sense of mixed-race identity could be a power-
ful factor in raising the awareness of all mixed-race people;
but it is also true that . . . that which is well intentioned could
become a tragedy.

RICHARD E. VAN DER ROSS, *THE NEW COLORED PEOPLE*

Although, in one sense, *The Boondocks* freezes time through typology, McGruder keeps race and history in motion. His characters never grow up, but they do learn; their bodies are static, but they mature politically. This is one of the many paradoxes of time in the comic strip. For instance, most people self-identifying as mixed race are under the age of twenty-five, so in that sense—*even though Huey and Jazmine are the same age*—Jazmine represents a generational break with Huey's mode of seeing blackness. It is true that Huey indicts the basis for Jazmine's racial ambivalence, but the strip suggests that Huey must accommodate or at least better account for Jazmine's unique racial experiences. The rapprochement between them occurs through mutual education.

Jazmine's education is akin to that chronicled in Carter G. Woodson's famous treatise *The Mis-Education of the Negro* ([1933] 2006) in the sense that she learns to leverage her own particularly racialized experience to counter the white social "mis-education" she has received. But even more so, and despite Huey's taunts, her mixed racial anxieties are not entirely dismissed within McGruder's graphic narrative. For instance, her several complaints of Huey "making fun" of her sound both like a whine *and* a legitimate refusal to give up the possibility that she might have a different racialized experience from his.

Some of the most powerful moments in the strip occur when Jazmine begins to develop a more theoretically sophisticated identity, one in which she moves from understanding herself in terms of solitary existential angst (a misunderstood girl with bad hair) to seeing herself in relation to history and political imperatives. She comes to understand black critiques of American history not through Huey's lectures but in dealing with a little white neighbor, Cindy. Cindy thinks black people are only hip-hoppers and gangstas, understands "color-blindness" as a "disease," and does not know that "there were slaves in America during independence day" (McGruder 2000, 16, 38). After these exchanges with Cindy, Jazmine concludes that "maybe Huey was right" when he refuses to celebrate the July 4 holiday and spends it "writing some letters to some of the countless black men in America's prisons" and meditating "on the meaning of liberty" (38). She wants simply to be a "peaceful citizen of earth" and desperately to be "friends again," but he suggests that cannot happen until she accepts her Afro and what it represents (25, 23).

Huey critiques her naïveté and Eurocentrism, but it is actually through Jazmine's exchanges with Cindy that she begins to assess her own experience, drop her claims to "racelessness," and move toward not so much a recognition of her "mixed" experience as sui generis but as a sense of it as distinctive on a continuum with black experience as represented by Huey and his brother (McGruder 2000, 95). Her education points to one of the more promising directions emerging in progressive mixed race politics, in which, as Ronald Sundstrom suggests, there must be a "conscious effort to uphold moral obligations to parent communities . . . a commitment to fight racial hierarchy and racism . . . a rejection of white privilege" and a sense of "irony" (2001).

But if Jazmine is educated into a capacious blackness, Huey's education requires a complementary hybridization on his part. As he puts it in one of the editorial inserts in which Huey is trying to write a book about black neoconservatives, Huey is poised between academe, which to him seems removed from the world, and a globalized hip-hop culture that risks giving it up to bling-bling (McGruder 2000, 69). His incendiary book title, *Ward Connerly Is a Boot-Licking Uncle Tom*, is supposedly an effort to "transcend cultural barriers"—since, Huey philosophizes, everyone knows what an "uncle tom" is—without losing his political edginess (69). A possible crossover model, Huey suggests, is represented by Raekwon the Chef (the hip-hop group Wu Tang Clan's primary lyricist). Like McGruder's blend of hip-hop savvy and Japanese pop cultural forms in anime, the Wu Tang Clan musical group fuses black vernacular culture with Japanese camp. Both go beyond what Anthony Appiah (2006) calls "cultural contamination," but the Clan (with its anti-Klan outlook) is also known for its self-reflective politics, its social critiques of corporate consumerism, and its resistance to gratuitous booty. Raekwon illustrates Huey's own dilemma as someone trying to bridge a cultural divide: the performer is someone who is both famous and obscure. He is an icon in the hip-hop community but, he notes, an unknown to most academics. Huey's striving to merge two views of the world makes him more, not less, like Jazmine with her racial bi-focalism.

CONCLUSION

The Boondocks encourages us to analyze the way that a comic strip, like some other literary and dramatic forms, can help us understand that the mixed race category is not a solution to the "race question" but is an index of national anxieties and ambitions involving race. Stanley Crouch was among the first to proclaim that "race is over" (1996). Since then, others also have rung race's death knell: Holland Cotter claims that the time for "ethno-racial identity" is past, that we are now witnessing the coming of "postblack or postethnic art" (2001, 2004); Debra Dickerson demands the "end of blackness" (2005); and Anthony Appiah advances a "new cosmopolitanism" that celebrates cultural contamination over what he sees as antiquated tribalism (2006). We are told that ethnic hybridity—and "mixed race" in particular—heralds "racelessness" (Zack 1995), a step "beyond race" (Cose 1998), the "end of racism" (D'Souza 1996), a gesture "against race" (Gilroy 2001), the "new racial order" (Daniel 2001), and a "new frontier" free of identity politics and its supposedly irresistible essentialism (Michaels 1998; Root 2004). But *The Boondocks* suggests both that "mixed race" is no panacea and that the obituaries on race are premature and politically suspect. McGruder's representations of Jazmine prompt us to consider how, for example, the cultural cachet of being mixed is occurring in concert with the dismantling of affirmation action and the weakening of traditional civil rights lobbies. By mining the social potency of the comic genre itself, McGruder criticizes the attack on all identity projects as merely "identity politics" and uses the graphic narrative form to flush out and flesh out many of the complicated issues related to "mixed race" identification. It is true that any one political platform or clear party agenda is hard to harness from the pages of this comic series—both the political Right and the political Left are targeted by McGruder's biting social critique. But perhaps it is his ability to use comics to unsettle everyone—of whatever political or racial persuasion—that may explain McGruder's impact on the current and vigorous debates about the continuing significance of race.

Works Cited

•

Appiah, Kwame Anthony. 2006. The Case for Contamination. *New York Times Magazine*, 1 January, Section 6, 30–37.

Bahktin, M. M. 1984. *Rabelais and His World*. Trans. Helene Iswolsky. Bloomington: Indiana University Press.

Childs, Erica Chito. 2004. Multirace.com: Multiracial Cyberspace. In *The Politics of Multiracialism*, ed. Heather Dalmage. Albany: SUNY Press.

Connerly, Ward. 2000. *Creating Equal: My Fight against Racial Preferences*. New York: Encounter Books.

Cose, Ellis. 1998. *Color-Blind: Seeing beyond Race in a Race-Obsessed World*. New York: Harper Perennial.

Cotter, Holland. 2001. Beyond Multiculturalism, Freedom? *New York Times*, 29 July, Section E, 1.

———. 2004. "Black" Comes in Many Shadings. *New York Times*, 13 August, Section E, 29.

Crouch, Stanley. 1996. Race Is Over. *New York Times*, 26 September, Section 6, 170.

DaCosta, Kimberly McClain. 2007. *Making Multiracials*. Palo Alto, CA: Stanford University Press.

Daniel, G. Reginald. 2001. *More Than Black? Multiracial Identity and the New Racial Order*. Philadelphia: Temple University Press.

Dickerson, Debra. 2005. *The End of Blackness: Returning the Souls of Black Folk to Their Rightful Owners*. New York: Anchor.

D'Souza, Dinesh. 1996. *The End of Racism: Principles for a Multiracial Society*. New York: Free Press.

Elam, Michele. Forthcoming. *The Souls of Mixed Folks*. Palo Alto, CA: Stanford University Press.

Eisner, Will. 2005. *Comics and Sequential Art: Principles and Practices of the World's Most Popular Art Form*. Tamara, FL: Poorhouse Press.

Ifekwunigwe, Jayne O. 2004. Let Blackness and Whiteness Wash Through: Competing Discourses on Bi-Racialization and the Compulsion of Genealogical Erasures. In *Mixed Race Studies: A Reader*, ed. Jayne O. Ifekwunigwe. New York: Routledge.

Gilroy, Paul. 2001. *Against Race: Imagining Political Culture beyond the Color Line*. Cambridge: Harvard University Press.

McCloud, Scott. 2000. *Reinventing Comics: How Imagination and Technology Are Revolutionizing an Art Form*. New York: HarperCollins.

McGrath, Ben. 2004. The Radical: Why do editors keep throwing "The Boondocks" off the funnies page? *The New Yorker*, 19 April. Available at www.newyorker.com/archive/2004/04/19/040419fa_fact2

McGruder, Aaron. 2000. *The Boondocks Collections: Because I Know You Don't Read the Newspaper*. New York: Andrew McMeel.

———. 2003. Introduction. *A Right to Be Hostile: A* Boondocks *Treasury*. New York: Three Rivers Press.

Michaels, Walter Benn. 1998. Autobiography of an Ex-White Man: Why Race Is Not a Social Construction. *Transition* 73 (1998): 122–143.

Moore, Michael. 2003. Foreword. *A Right to Be Hostile: A* Boondocks *Treasury*. New York: Three Rivers Press.

Powell, A. D. 1999. The Multiracial Activist [an online blog]. Entry on 6 June 1999 [cited 19 September 2005]. Available at www.multiracial.com/readers/responses-boondocks.html

Root, Maria P. P. 1996. A Bill of Rights for Racially Mixed People. In *The Multiracial Experience: Racial Borders as the New Frontier*, ed. Maria P. P. Root. Thousand Oaks, CA: Sage.

————. 2004. Within, Between, Beyond Race. In *'Mixed Race' Studies: A Reader*, ed. Jayne O. Ifekwunigwe. New York: Routledge.

Van Der Ross, Richard. 1997. Foreword. *The New Colored People: The Mixed Race Movement in America,* by Jon Michael Spencer. New York: New York University Press.

Senna, Danzy. 1998. The Mulatto Millennium. In *Half and Half: Writers Growing Up Biracial and Bicultural*, ed. Claudine Chiawei O'Hearn. New York: Pantheon.

Spencer, Jon Michael. 1997. *The New Colored People: The Mixed Race Movement in America*. New York: New York University Press.

Spiegelman, Art. 1986. *Maus I: A Survivor's Tale: My Father Bleeds History*. New York: Pantheon.

Williams, Kim. 2006. *Mark One or More: Civil Rights in Multiracial America*. Ann Arbor: University of Michigan Press.

Wilson, Judith. 2003. One Way or Another: Black Feminist Visual Theory. In *The Feminism and Visual Culture Reader*, ed. Amelia Jones. New York: Routledge.

Wonham, Henry. 2004. *Playing the Races: Ethnic Caricature and American Literary Realism.* New York: Oxford University Press.

Woodson, Carter G. First published in 1933. Reprint 2006. *The Mis-Education of the Negro.* New York: Dover Press.

Zack, Naomi. 1995. *Race and Mixed Race*. Lanham, MD: Rowman and Littlefield.

21

We Wear the Mask
Performance, Social Dramas, and Race

Harry J. Elam Jr.

•

In this essay, I explore how, when, and where race generally, and blackness specifically, is performed. Identifying and analyzing race as a type of performance, I argue, can prove enormously productive in determining the social politics and cultural dynamics of this most powerful and controversial concept. To demonstrate the interrelation of racial performances in everyday life to those on stage and in film, my examples are far-ranging, going from the horrible spectacle of slavery to the plays of Lorraine Hansberry to the trial of O. J. Simpson to hip-hop performance and, finally, to the film Bamboozled. *These examples provide evidence for performance as both a mode of analysis and a subject of study. I analyze both historical events and representations from contemporary films and music as types of performances that can inform our understanding of race, its constitution, its operation, and its significance.*

> *We wear the mask that grins and lies,*
> *It hides our cheeks and shades our eyes, —*
> *This debt we pay to human guile;*
> *With torn and bleeding hearts we smile,*
> *And mouth with myriad subtleties.*
> PAUL LAURENCE DUNBAR, "WE WEAR THE MASK," 1896

WHAT IS THE RELATIONSHIP BETWEEN RACE AND PERFORMANCE? What does it mean to understand or to imagine race as performed? As revealed in the poem quoted above, race and performance have often been historically linked. Performing a role or wearing a mask of servitude became a critical mode of survival for African American people in the time of slavery. Through the analysis of such performances, we can understand not only how certain racial performances can serve as masks but how we can *un*mask race. Race is not a static thing but a fluid concept with very real effects whose meanings can change depending on the context. The meanings of race, and of blackness, in the United States have changed considerably from the time of slavery to the twenty-first century. Racial performances have evolved accordingly.

THE REALITY OF RACE

Definitions of race, like the processes of theater and performance, fundamentally depend on the relationship between the seen and the unseen, between the visibly marked and the unmarked, between the "real" and the illusionary. Historically, the dominant discourse on race has asserted that visible differences among peoples signify that "real," unquestionable, biologically based racial differences exist. In the past, Western science, philosophy, and literature repeatedly associated black skin and the "Negroid" race with intellectual inferiority and cultural primitivism while whiteness has been associated with beauty, intelligence, and privilege. Contrary to such popular understanding, however, recent studies in the natural and social sciences have established that visible bodily variations in hair color and skin texture do not correspond to a fixed unchanging biological category we can call race. Rather, through time, race has operated not as a biological certainty but as a social script and culturally constructed category employed to separate peoples and to maintain hierarchies of power. I am not suggesting that race is unreal or an illusion, but rather that the meanings and definitions of race are not stable and are far from fixed.

While there are no essential or biological bases for race, the visual markings that we associate with race continue to have real meanings and effects. People have suffered and continue to suffer because they look a certain way. For example, after the attack on the World Trade Center and the Pentagon on September 11, 2001, the outward expressions of hate and violence in the United States against people who appear to be Arab have grown exponentially. The play *Les Blancs*, written in 1969 by Lorraine Hansberry,[1] offers one of the clearest and most powerful

---

1 While Hansberry wrote the play *Les Blancs*, her former husband Robert Nemiroff completed it for the stage in 1969. Hansberry was extremely ill with cancer at the time. See Wilkerson's discussion (2001) of the play's completion.

meditations on the constructed "reality" and situational meanings of race. Throughout the play, an African intellectual character, Tshembe Matoseh, and a white American liberal, Charlie Morris, engage in a series of polemical debates on race. Charlie, an American reporter, has come to the fictive Zatembe to write a book on the Medical Mission that is there. Tshembe has returned home to Zatembe from London to attend his father's funeral. What they both find is a Mission in crisis and a country on the verge of an explosion in racial bloodshed that will overturn decades of colonial rule. Charlie and Tshembe face off against each other in attempt to make sense of the chaos, the racial madness, and the political upheaval that surrounds them. During one such encounter, the following discussion unfolds:

> **TSHEMBE:** Race—racism—is a device. No more. No less. It explains nothing at all.
> **CHARLIE:** Now what in the hell is that supposed to mean?
> **TSHEMBE:** I said racism is a device that, of itself, explains nothing. It is simply a means. An invention to justify the rule of some men over others. . . . I am simply saying that a device is a device, but that it also has consequences; once invented it takes on a life, a reality of its own. So, in one century, men invoke the device of religion to cloak their conquests. In another, race. Now in both cases you and I may recognize the fraudulence of the device, but the fact remains that a man who has a sword run through him because he is a Moslem or a Christian—or who is shot in Zatembe or Mississippi because he is black—is suffering the utter reality of the device. And it is pointless to pretend that it doesn't exist—merely because it is a lie! (Hansberry 1969, 92)

In this passage from *Les Blancs*, Hansberry suggests that the meanings of race are conditional, that the illusion of race becomes reality through its application. This passage, despite being written forty years ago, has a particular contemporary relevance. It locates the current debates over the definitions of race in decidedly and purposefully theatrical terms: "Race is a device." Theater is built upon such devices. During the time that we sit and watch a theatrical event we accept certain devices as real—a diaphanous piece of fabric can represent an ocean, or an actor wearing simple makeup can become a giant bird. Such devices and their employment convey meaning and have real power in the theater.

Because race works as a device, it has very real consequences. A person can suffer from the "utter reality of the device," as Tshembe says. Accordingly, race functions on a continuum that navigates between its social and historical constructions and the particulars of lived experience. For many people of color negotiating this dynamic spectrum, legally mandated fictions of race have often structured their reality. For example, in 1882 the Chinese Exclusion Act barred reentry of resident alien Chinese to the United States, and the U.S. Supreme Court backed this law as constitutional. In the court case, *Chae Chan Ping v. United States*, the U.S. Supreme Court concluded that Chinese immigrants had an unfair advantage in the labor market because of their industriousness and frugal nature. In addition, the court in their findings argued that the Chinese people inherently remained strangers in the land because they were unable and unwilling to assimilate into U.S. society. Thus, the Chinese fell victim to the device of race and accompanying assumptions about "Chineseness" that became law. According to the Supreme Court, the belief that the Chinese could not possibly conform to cultural norms of white America justified their exclusion.

Similarly, to acknowledge the presence of slaves within the Southern census and the awarding of congressional boundaries while also justifying the system of slavery, the Constitution at its inception proclaimed that a black person constituted only three-fifths of a human. Later, with the growth of the slave economy as well as Northern abolition efforts, the Mason-Dixon line came to demarcate the separation between an African American's status as slave or free individual. At the same time, the one-drop rule—despite any visual clues to the contrary—determined that any person containing one drop of black blood was "black" and therefore should be denied the rights of citizenship. These types of figurative ideas—symbolic representations such as an imaginary line across the country or words on a piece of paper that made a black person either a slave or free—became powerful because they were backed up by the law. Historically, the particular collisions of the real and the figurative have proved consequential for African Americans, and it is within this context that performances of race have been enacted.

PERFORMANCE AND RACE

To understand how race might be performed, I employ three definitions of performance. Richard Schechner in *Between Theater and Anthropology*

(1985, 35) defines performance as "restored behavior" or "twice-behaved behavior." If performance is restored behavior, then it is inherently connected to social and cultural interactions. Expanding Schechner's definition, Elin Diamond (1996, 2) perceives performances as cultural practices that "conservatively re-inscribe or passionately reinvent the ideas, symbols, and gestures that shape social life." Inevitably, then, performances must negotiate systems of power, cultural and social mores, values, and beliefs. Adding to these definitions of performance, Joseph Roach (1996, 218) argues that "performance is a particular class or subset of restored behavior in which one or more persons assume responsibility to an audience and to a tradition as they understand it." The consideration of audience awareness and responsibility brings a degree of self-awareness to the concept of performance. Also explicit in this conception is the power of the audience within performance to interpret and determine meaning. Here, I am talking about the performances not simply onstage but in everyday life, where the people one interacts with can constitute an audience.

Combining and transferring these definitions of performance to the terrain of race enables us to consider whether there are moments when we "do" race or when race is "a thing done." At these moments, the performer repeats, reinscribes, or even reconfigures established gestures, behaviors, linguistic patterns, cultural attitudes, and social expectations associated with race. Accordingly, performances of blackness, historically as well as in our contemporary age, often act as reaffirmations and renegotiations of cultural identity or as methods of cultural or personal survival.

In slavery times, Negro spirituals such as "Swing Low, Sweet Chariot" contained coded, rather than explicit, messages about real plans for escape to the North within the figurative tale of a chariot coming to carry them to the afterlife in Heaven. Such "masking" enabled black performances to function on a variety of levels. Even as they performed for the entertainment of the white master, slaves could simultaneously ridicule or potentially undermine his control through the mechanism of performance. Everyday survival on the plantation also necessitated the employment of certain coded performances, playing deferential subservience or feigned ignorance. Slaves would knowingly perform the role of the ignorant, happy darky in front of the master or overseer in order to avoid physical abuse or unwanted labor. The Dunbar poem quoted at the start of this essay powerfully expresses the historic employment of the mask of racial performance as a strategy of black survival.

RACIAL PERFORMANCES ON TRIAL:
THE CASE OF O. J. SIMPSON

Performing Blackness

The O. J. Simpson criminal trial in 1995 represents a potent site in which to observe strategies of black performance in operation. At the time, O. J. Simpson, known during his playing days as "The Juice," was one of the most — possibly the most — recognizable former athletes in the country. After his retirement from professional football in 1979, O. J.—with his dashing good looks and charming smile—had become a well-known pitchman for a wide variety of commercial products, including Hertz cars and, of course, orange juice. He also became a minor actor in low-brow comedy films such as *The Naked Gun* (1988). It was a shock to the nation, then, when the Heisman Trophy–winning running back from the University of Southern California and a Hall of Fame National Football League player for the Buffalo Bills was accused of brutally murdering his estranged wife Nicole Brown Simpson and her friend Ron Goldman with a knife in the front courtyard of her condominium in Brentwood, California, on the night of June 12, 1994. Because of O. J.'s fame and football glory as well as the provocative racial dynamics of the case that recalled historically rooted racial stereotypes— the beautiful and "innocent" white woman and the purportedly "brutish" black man—the case drew national and even international media attention. Live television broadcasts every day in the summer and fall of 1995—the precursor of "Reality TV" in the twenty-first century—made the O. J. Simpson criminal trial the so-called trial of the century.

Through his wealth and celebrity, O. J. was able to assemble a "Dream Team" of legal counsel featuring an African American lead attorney—the dynamic Johnnie Cochran, whose list of former clients ranges from Black Panther activist Geronimo Pratt to pop singer Michael Jackson. From the outset, Johnnie Cochran and the other defense lawyers on O. J.'s defense team decided not to play up his status as a celebrity icon but rather to reposition their client within the historical context of black survival against police abuse and other forms of social oppression. They did this by characterizing him as a black man wronged. However, Cochran was not the only one to use the device of race. Both sides prominently and purposely featured black attorneys in an attempt to use blackness to serve its own ends. Accordingly, clashes over constructed racial boundaries and definitions of blackness played out repeatedly in the Simpson criminal trial.

Events during the course of the trial repeatedly revealed race as not simply a product of visual markings but also of action and behaviors. At one critical juncture early in the trial, the defense and prosecution argued over the admissibility of evidence relating to the racism of Mark Fuhrman, a white detective. Since Fuhrman was one of the primary investigating officers with damning evidence, challenging his testimony was crucial to the defense team's strategy. Eventually the so-called Fuhrman tapes would prove a judicial juggernaut, damning the case of the prosecution and solidifying the conspiratorial theories of the defense. Prior to the discovery and release of these records, defense attorney Johnnie Cochran pressed for the right to include testimony confirming Fuhrman's use, several years earlier, of the infamous "N" word. Christopher Darden, the black lead attorney for the prosecution, challenged the inclusion of this evidence on the grounds that the presentation of the "N" word by a white officer before a majority black jury was simply too volatile. He further argued that Fuhrman's racism had little bearing on the case because of his limited involvement. Cochran seized the opportunity to stand before the court and the televisions of the nation and remark:

> I would be remiss were I not at this time to take the opportunity to respond to my good friend, Mr. Chris Darden. His remarks this morning are perhaps the most incredible remarks I've heard in a court of law in the thirty-two years I've been practicing law. His remarks are demeaning to African Americans as a group. . . . And so I want to apologize to African Americans across this country. It is demeaning to our jurors to say that African Americans who have lived under oppression for two hundred plus years cannot work within the mainstream, cannot hear these offensive words. (Darden 1996, 204)

Through this moment of apology as performance, Cochran strategically drew a circle around his own construction of blackness that excluded Darden. Cochran—who in previous years had been the lawyer for the former Black Panther and noted political prisoner Geronimo Pratt—effectively positioned himself as a "race man" and a defender of the people. He contrasted his self-image with that of Darden, the enemy who insulted and offended African Americans. Cochran's words acted to negate Darden's visible markings of blackness and attempted to undermine the prosecution's desire to gain racial favor through the prominent placement of this black prosecutor. Cochran performed race to his advantage and set forth the idea that race is not simply something that is marked on the body. Darden, as a result, became construed by many as a "traitor to his race."

Immediately following Cochran's televised performance of this moment, Darden received a myriad of angry phone calls with messages such as "Don't ever refer to yourself as black, 'cause you ain'" (Darden 1996, 206). This response from an incensed, presumably black observer, as well as the exchange between the black lawyers over the "Fuhrman tapes," demonstrates the effect that the reiteration of certain cultural practices, social attitudes, and codes of behavior can have on the construction of race. In this instance, these factors, highlighted by the racial performance of Cochran, served to determine racial belonging more than skin color did.

It is worth noting that Darden, in a conscious or perhaps unconscious effort to reclaim his blackness, opens his memoir of the trial, *In Contempt*, with a quote from Martin Luther King Jr. By invoking Dr. King at the beginning of his book, Darden aligns his own struggle for justice in the Simpson trial with the efforts led by Dr. King for African Americans to achieve racial justice and equality. In this way, Darden sought to reverse the effect of Cochran's memorable performative racial exclusion of him in the Simpson trial.

Trading Races

The defendant, O. J. Simpson, has had his own difficulties negotiating racial boundaries. Long before his legal troubles, O. J. consciously sought to differentiate himself—with his white wife and wealthy lifestyle—from the black masses. At the pinnacle of his commercial success as a national spokesman for Hertz, O. J. proclaimed that he had become "colorless." A well-known series of Hertz ads in the 1980s featured the former footballer running through airports and deftly leaping over counters on his way to his Hertz automobile. In this commercial enactment, O. J. represented not just black men or superior athletes, but everyone: "Let Hertz put you in the driver's seat" was the company's early slogan. In their O. J. airport ads, Hertz asserted that "you" could be, like O. J, just as "effortlessly" renting their automobile. Perhaps he bought into the hyperbole of this ad or became caught up in his own amazing American success story. In any case, O. J.'s claim of colorlessness implied that he had somehow transcended race—or at least had overcome blackness.

One distinct problem with O. J.'s perception of himself as colorless was that it ignored the implicit and explicit racializations of power, privilege, behavior, and values always and already active in the United States. As a consequence, whiteness and its associated accoutrements have become unconsciously and consciously understood as the norm. Normative whiteness in American social, cultural, and legal practices operates as a virtually invisible but seductive agent. An ever-present white/black dichotomy figures achievement, success, wealth, and rationality as properties of whiteness, while blackness comes to represent criminality, lawlessness, and failure. Accordingly, O. J. Simpson's previous career as a Hertz pitchman provided him with advantages traditionally connected to whiteness, while his hyperpublicized trials for the murders of his white estranged wife and Ron Goldman plunged him back into blackness together with its negative associations.

A classic send-up of O. J.'s plunge back into blackness was dramatized in a now famous skit entitled "The Racial Draft" from the second season of the comedian Dave Chappelle's show on the Comedy Central network. The skit took the form of a mock draft in the style of the National Football League in which various racial groups competed for the racial allegiance of various celebrities whose racial identities are in some way ambiguous. In the skit, the white and black delegations bicker over whether the black delegation can claim the white rapper Eminem (who performs in a "black" hip-hop style), while the white delegation retains the racial rights to both Colin Powell (the first African American to serve as secretary of state) and Condoleezza Rice (the second African American to serve as secretary of state). The argument is squelched when the white delegation offers to give O. J. Simpson back to the black people if the whites are allowed to keep Eminem. The black delegation gladly agrees. Cheerfully, the white announcer intones, "O. J. Simpson, black again."[2]

Performing Whiteness

The white announcer's glee on Dave Chappelle's show recalls the highly charged responses of many whites to the 1995 "Not Guilty" verdict in the Simpson trial. In fact, the outrage and disgust of some white viewers to this verdict can be construed as a performance of whiteness. In this case, their doing of whiteness was constituted primarily in direct relation to blackness and in contrast to the joy of many black respondents to the announcement of the verdict. According to the way many

---

2 I am indebted to Michele Elam for this observation. See M. Elam's discussion (forthcoming) of "The Racial Draft."

whites interpreted the aftermath of the verdict, the intelligent, rational, logical response of whites was separated from the uneducated and emotional black response. With the assistance of the media, angry whites interpreted the verdict as a gross miscarriage of justice perpetrated by irresponsible, and mostly black, jurors. For example, the conservative television commentator Ben Stein cynically asserted that, "the whites will riot the way we whites do: leave the cities, go to Idaho or Oregon or Arizona, vote for Gingrich . . . and punish the blacks by closing their day care programs and cutting off their Medicaid" (Crenshaw 1997, 141–142).

With these words, Stein performs race by explicitly invoking white privilege and black difference. His vituperation reflects and reaffirms the value of whiteness on and through his association of blacks with poverty and welfare. Republican Representative Bob Dornan from California indignantly proclaimed: "O. J. is guilty 15 times. . . . John Cochran is guilty of murder." And then went on to say, "He [Simpson] won't do any movies; any producer that employs him, I'll be sure, is painted with a big 'S' for 'Shame'" (CNN 1995). In his comments, Dornan performs race by convicting not only O. J. but also the black lead defense counsel. He then calls for "white racial solidarity" on the part of white Hollywood producers in an attempt to bar O. J. from ever working in the industry again.

Reiterating historical misconceptions of white superiority, some whites decried the inability of inferior blacks to judge the evidence truthfully. A cry came out from many corners of white America to reform the criminal justice system, to change the construction and selection of juries, and to end an insistence on unanimous jury decisions in criminal cases. Some white commentators even argued that blacks would never convict a black man for murder, despite the overwhelming evidence of African American conservatism on crime and the fact that jails and prisons around this country have been filled to the brim with black prisoners who have been convicted by juries of their black peers. Evident and implicit in all these pronouncements was a desire to restore white hegemony and to terminate the threat posed to it by this verdict.

These performative reiterations of whiteness after the announcement of the "Not Guilty" verdict reaffirmed white racial attitudes that have solidified throughout American history. Moreover, the resulting perceptions of the black threat to white institutions and power directly correlate with the backlash against affirmative action policies, political correctness, and diversity programs in the late 1990s. Conservative critics such as Dinesh D'Souza, George Will, and William Bennett branded the "Not Guilty" verdict by a predominantly black jury as another example of pernicious race consciousness and as further evidence of the need to do away with "racial-thinking" and preference programs that mandated such racial awareness.

Race as a Doing

My examination of the way race—both blackness and whiteness—was performed in response to the "Not Guilty" verdict in the O. J. Simpson case is not meant to deny the diversity and complexity of reactions of individuals. Not all whites responded like the dominant media portrayal of their response; similarly, not all members of the black community supported O. J. and rejoiced at his acquittal. In fact, the concept of one singular "black community" that defies geographic, economic, and ideological boundaries is simply a construction. It, too, contains performative dynamics—its invocation creates barriers of inclusion and exclusion that solidify racial differences and fuel racial antagonisms. The media's representation of a happy black community thus reinvoked normative whiteness even as it enabled angry whites to cry racism and to dismiss the verdict delivered by the predominantly black jury as a travesty, a misguided form of racial revenge for previous injustices. The repeatedly displayed, contrasting images of blacks exalting and whites in tears failed to examine the level of meanings present in these seemingly diametric reactions. They served only to reinforce the dichotomies associated with whiteness and blackness in American social, cultural, and economic interactions.

Staged on live television and transmitted across the country and the world, O. J.'s trial and its aftermath constitute sites where race becomes spectacle. Examining the broadcast spectacle of the O. J. trial dramatically demonstrates how certain social scripts enacted in everyday life can determine the import and meanings of race. Within this example, we can see race as an active doing.

Rap and Racial Performance

But what do performances on an actual stage tell us about the doing of race? How can critical analysis of this genre that we conventionally know as performance inform us about these social scripts and the situational significance of race offstage? To answer these questions, I turn first to the performance of rap and hip-hop and then to a brief discussion of two contemporary films.

Implicitly and explicitly the production of rap music and the transmission of hip-hop culture foreground questions of racial performance and highlight the problematic nature of racial authenticity. The rap performer, perhaps more than any other kind of musical artist, is concerned with self-fashioning and masking. Here, I mean masking not in the sense of hiding one's "true" identity but in the sense of putting on or performing a social identity and a public persona. Take, for example, the imaginative and creative names of rappers such as Snoop Dogg, Queen Latifah, Nas, Jay-Z, or GURU. Through the process of naming, the rapper constructs himself or herself for public consumption. A rap moniker often informs us about the performer's history while also giving a signal as to his or her musical style. While Fresh Prince serves up commercial "flava," C-Murder intones hard-core "gangsta" rhythms. In addition to the self-creation expressed in naming, the interruption of conventional musical presentation in rap performance allows for a different understanding of the body and voice as musical instruments. Instead of singers singing and musicians playing wind, percussion, or string instruments, rap features the lyrical skills of the rapper, the sampling of beats, and often even the presentation a "human beat box"—the body, mouth, and microphone serving as a drum machine.

Yet even as rap in performance may exalt in the flash and splash of self-conscious self-presentation, it simultaneously celebrates the seeming authenticity of "realness." "Realness" suggests being true to one's roots and one's cultural foundation. It is a political and cultural stance that gives voice to the conditions and experiences of urban blackness. Thus, "keeping it real" potentially ties the black performer to the black collective while drawing borders around his or her practice and how that practice relates to, or is true to, his or her community. Most particularly, the vernacular, the black folk, the huddled masses are what is "real." Thus, rap music is perhaps the one contemporary social and political arena that inverts the traditional hierarchy of white privilege and challenges normative whiteness. While elsewhere white equals good and black equals bad, in rap music the raw, black city cool is decidedly good and "real."

Realness thus correlates to certain attitudes, behaviors, historical experiences, and paradigms of black authenticity. Black youth perform realness and affirm their cultural identity and their street credibility, through dress, attitude, and style. Paradoxically, rap performances serve as the embodiments of black authenticity or realness but also work as tactics through which black authenticity is achieved. In performance,

cultural identity. Realness in rap depends on the careful articulation of these factors. While the form and its celebration of self-fashioning rely on the "doing" of certain codes of racial performance, it also reinforces a particular hierarchy of class. Class functions as a vital determinant of realness. And it is on and through hip-hop performance that the meanings of class, as well as race, can be advanced and understood.

So, although Eminem has black friends in *8 Mile* and associates with black hip-hop luminaries in real life, his interaction with black bodies does not necessarily represent the possibility of new cross-racial politics but perhaps a new, complex form of black cultural traffic. In his performance, blackness is both embraced and resisted. For Eminem is not a wigger—his transaction with black bodies is not about miscegenation nor racial mimesis. Rather, Eminem uses his verbal dexterity to make rap his own; his success grants license for white working-class entrance and participation in hip-hop. After Eminem, rap is far from just a "black thing."

Race and the Realm of the Visual

But what of racial visibility—what of bodily markers like skin color and hair type—if performance is so critical to understanding racial meanings? A troubling negotiation of race, identity, and visibility in performance plays out in Spike Lee's 2001 film *Bamboozled* and helps us to see how intimately connected these factors are. At the violent resolution to the film, the fictitious revolutionary rap group, the Mau Maus, gun down Mantan, the star of the New Millennium Minstrel Show, killing him on a live Internet broadcast across the globe. They murder him, they claim, for performing and perpetuating negative images of the black race. As the self-satisfied Mau Maus exit the building where the murder took place, all but one are gunned down in hail of bullets by New York's finest—who, of course, arrive at the scene too late to save Mantan. The one Mau Mau not killed appears to be white—that is, he has light skin and "white" features, while the others are easily identifiable as black because of their darker skin. Earlier in the film, this seemingly white rapper had extolled the power of blackness and his relation to it while surrounded by the other Mau Maus. Through his dress and in his verbal dexterity with black urban vernacular he had pointedly performed blackness. Moreover, he identified himself as black and the others accepted this identification.

After his compatriots are killed and as the police handcuff him, the "white" Mau Mau professes his blackness and begs to be treated like his friends. He shouts: "I'm black: one-sixteenth, one drop of black blood is all that's required. Why didn't you kill me?" His rap name with the Mau Maus is in fact "1/16th Black," so his callout to the police is at once a reciting of his name, an outing of his unmarked racial history, and a calling for the recognition of his identity. Yet, his is a performance of blackness that—in this context—goes unacknowledged. The police do not bother to recognize his clothing, his gestures, his language, and his reiteration of black behavioral codes. Instead, they shoot only those Mau Maus with visible and stereotypically "black" skin and features.

Still, 1/16th Black's invocation of the one-drop rule takes us back to an earlier time of racial performances and a history of passing. In the early twentieth century, blacks passing as white could be understood to be performing race in the service of economic and social survival. Clearly, such performances were enabled by the person's color and proximity to whiteness. The character 1/16th in *Bamboozled*, however, eschews the privilege of his hue and performs race not for the purpose of surviving but in a call for death. His claim thus seems to be an insane or unreal claim to blackness; he actually weeps because he is not martyred with the others. For this Mau Mau, execution by the police would mean the success of his performance as black. Through this disturbing action, the film differentiates performance from lived experience and suggests that the lived world of "blackness" is often simply defined by how one looks; it's straightforwardly a matter of how one looks in the moment the cops decide whom to shoot. This suggests that even as the meaning of blackness is constructed, it is not infinitely negotiable in all places and at all times. As Ralph Ellison so eloquently noted in *Invisible Man* (1952), "Now black is . . . an' black ain't."

CONCLUSION

The racial performances in *Bamboozled* as well as in *8 Mile* and the other works discussed here point to the situational significance of race and the role that performance can play in determining its meanings. Understanding race as performance, as a "doing" and as a "thing done," enables us to serve as audience members, witnessing and responding to these enactments, and at the same time as to operate as performance critics, analyzing the social, cultural, and historical frames in which racial performances occur. With the ever-increasing intrusion of technology into all aspects of daily life, the performances of race will evolve even further—how should we understand, for example, the performance of race in the purportedly color-blind world of cyberspace? The role that performances of race play within our culture must be more significantly interrogated. Through an attention to race as performance we can analyze how race operates, how it is invoked and abused, and how it is invented (and reinvented) with each use.

Works Cited

●

CNN. 1995. Politicians Speak Out on Simpson Verdict. CNN.com, October 3. www.cnn.com/US/OJ/verdict/political/index.html.

Crenshaw, Kimberley Williams. 1997. Colorblind Dreams and Racial Nightmares: Reconfiguring Racism in the Post–Civil Rights Era. In *Birth of a Nation'hood: Gaze, Script, and Spectacle in the O.J. Simpson Case*, ed. Toni Morrison and Claudia Brodsky Lacour. New York: Random House.

Darden, Christopher. 1996. *In Contempt*. New York: Regan Books.

Diamond, Elin. 1996. Introduction to *Performance and Cultural Politics*, ed. E. Diamond. New York: Routledge.

Elam, Harry J., Jr. 2001. The Device of Race: An Introduction. In *African American Performance and Theater History*, ed. H. J. Elam Jr. and D. Krasner, 3–16. New York: Oxford University Press.

———. 2005. Change Clothes and Go: A Postscript to Postblackness. In *Black Cultural Traffic: Crossroads in Performances and Popular Culture*, ed. H. J. Elam Jr. and K. Jackson., 379–388. Ann Arbor: University of Michigan Press.

Elam, Michele. Forthcoming. *Mixtries: Mixed Race and the New Millennium*. Palo Alto, CA: Stanford University Press.

Ellison, Ralph. 1952. *Invisible Man*. New York: Modern Library Edition, 1994.

Hansberry, Lorraine. 1969. *Les Blancs*. In *Collected Last Plays of Lorraine Hansberry*, ed. R. Nemiroff. New York: New American Library, 1983.

Roach, Joseph. 1996. Kinship, Intelligence and Memory as Improvisation: Culture and Performance in New Orleans. In *Performance and Cultural Politics*, ed. E. Diamond. New York: Routledge.

Schechner, Richard. 1985. *Between Theater and Anthropology*. Philadelphia: University of Pennsylvania Press.

Wilkerson, Margaret. 2001. Political Radicalism and Artistic Innovation in the Works of Lorraine Hansberry. In *African American Performance and Theater History*, ed. H. J. Elam Jr. and D. Krasner, 40–56. New York: Oxford University Press.

CREDITS

———

Copyright Acknowledgments

"Hiphop and Race: Blackness, Language, and Creativity" copyright © 2010 by Marcyliena Morgan and Dawn-Elissa Fischer.

"The 'Ethno-Ambiguo Hostility Syndrome': Mixed-Race, Identity, and Popular Culture" copyright © 2010 by Michele Elam.

"We Wear the Mask: Performance, Social Dramas, and Race" copyright © 2010 by Harry J. Elam Jr.

Text and Figures

George M. Fredrickson: "Models of American Ethnic Relations: A Historical Perspective." In *Cultural Divides: Understanding and Overcoming Group Conflict.* © 1999 Russell Sage Foundation, 112 East 64th Street, New York, NY 10021. Reprinted with permission.

Maria P. P. Root: Excerpt from "A Bill of Rights for Racially Mixed People," *Multiracial Experience: Racial Borders as the New Frontier* by Maria P. P. Root. Copyright © 1996 by Sage Publications, Inc. Reproduced with permission of Sage Publications in the format Textbook via Copyright Clearance Center.

Claude M. Steele: "Stereotype Threat and African-American Student Achievement" from *Young, Gifted, and Black* by Theresa Perry, Claude Steele, and Asa G. Hilliard III. Copyright © 2003 by Theresa Perry, Claude Steele, and Asa G. Hilliard III. Reprinted by permission of Beacon Press, Boston.

Figure 3.1, p. 146: Reprinted by permission from Macmillan Publishers Ltd: L. Luca Cavalli-Sforza, Marcus W. Feldman, Figure 3 from "The Application of Genetic Molecular Approaches to the Study of Human Evolution," *Nature Genetics*, Vol. 33 (2003). Copyright © 2003, Nature Publishing Group.

Figure 3.2a, p. 148: N. A. Rosenberg, et al., Figure 2 from "Clines, Clusters, and the Effect of Study Design on the Inference of Human Population Structure," *PLoS Genetics*, Vol. 1, No. 6 (2005). © 2005 Rosenberg, et al.

Figure 3.2b, p. 149: Jun Z. Li, et al., Figure 1A from "Worldwide Human Relationships Inferred from Genome-Wide Patterns of Variation," *Science*, Vol. 319, No. 5866 (Feb. 2008). Copyright © 2008, The American Association for the Advancement of Science. Reprinted with permission from AAAS.

Figure 17.2, p. 470: Stephanie A. Fryberg, Hazel Rose Markus, Daphna Oyserman et al., Figure 1 from "Of Warrior Chiefs and Indian Princesses: The Psychological Consequences of American Indian Mascots," *Basic & Applied Social Psychology*, Vol. 20, No. 3 (2008). Copyright © 2008 Psychology Press. Reprinted by permission of the publisher (Taylor & Francis Group, http://www.informaworld.com).

Photographs

Page 118: U.S. Census Bureau, Public Information Office (PIO); **p. 120:** U.S. Census Bureau, Public Information Office (PIO); **p. 268:** Mark Thornhill, *North County Times;* **p. 442:** Copyright © 2004 by the American Psychological Association.

INDEX